Dictionary of Jewish Terms

A Guide to the Language of Judaism

Ronald L. Eisenberg

Schreiber Publishing
Rockville, Maryland

Dictionary of Jewish Terms
Ronald L. Eisenberg

Published by:

Schreiber Publishing
Rockville, MD 20849 USA
www.schreiberpublishing.com

Library of Congress Cataloging-in-Publication Data

Eisenberg, Ronald L.
Dictionary of Jewish terms : a guide to the language of Judaism / Ronald L. Eisenberg.
p. cm.
ISBN 978-0-88400-334-2 (hardcover)
1. Judaism—Terminology. 2. Hebrew language—Terms and phrases. I. Title.

BM50.E485 2008
296.03 22

2008000572

Printed in the United States of America

For Zina Schiff,

Avlana Kinneret, and Cherina Carmel,

my beautiful wife and daughters whose support and love
constitute my definition of mishpachah

Introduction

Have you ever encountered a Hebrew or Yiddish word and wanted to know what it meant in English? Have you ever wanted a succinct description of a Jewish holiday, prayer, or life-cycle event? Would you like to have at your fingertips a concise summary of the weekly Torah readings and the major issues addressed in each tractate of the Talmud? And have you ever wondered about the "Jewish view" of a variety of issues? The *Dictionary of Jewish Terms: A Guide to the Language of Judaism* is the result of my own search for answers to such questions.

Judaism is a unique language. In the Ashkenazic tradition, this is expressed in the Hebrew and Aramaic of its sacred texts and prayers, as well as in the colorful Yiddish of Eastern European Jewry which spread to America with the massive immigration in the early 20th century. This dictionary also encompasses the Sabbath and festivals, which form the basis of the Jewish year, and the *mitzvot*, which detail the prescribed daily activities and the ethical value system that are the essence of traditional Jewish behavior. In addition, it describes the distinctive symbols and customs of Judaism, as well as some terms associated with modern Israel. All of this and much more can be found among the more than 2,500 entries in *Dictionary of Jewish Terms: A Guide to the Language of Judaism*.

When deciding how to present this wealth of information, my major goal was to make it easily accessible to the reader. Multivolume encyclopedias and scholarly texts are ideal for in-depth study, but not for ease in rapidly finding a concise, easy-to-understand explanation of words or concepts. Conversely, short one-line definitions of a limited number of words leave the reader hungry for more. *Dictionary of Jewish Terms: A Guide to the Language of Judaism* takes a middle approach – broad in expanse of the terms discussed but with explanations that provide a clear summary of the topic. Rather than cluttering up the entries with endless cross-references, the reader can quickly discover any unfamiliar words by looking them up in the alphabetically arranged text.

Dictionary of Jewish Terms: A Guide to the Language of Judaism is designed to be a valuable resource for all Jews who want to be more knowledgeable about the vocabulary of their traditions, as well as for non-Jews who want to gain an understanding of the terminology of Judaism.

I want to gratefully acknowledge the invaluable assistance of Dr. Elliot Lefkovitz, Professor of Jewish History and Holocaust Studies at the Spertus Institute of Jewish Studies in Chicago, who critiqued the manuscript and offered many superb suggestions for improving it.

Language

No knowledge of Hebrew, Aramaic, or Yiddish is required to use this book, since all words in these languages are transliterated into English. Transliteration is a difficult task, because the sounds of one language often cannot be reproduced precisely in another. The basic guidelines used in this book are as follows:

- a — as in father (shalom, *baruch*)
- e — as in men (*lechem, berachot*)
- ei — as in say (*Aleinu, Kol Nidrei*)
- i — as in key (*mitzvot, rimonim*)
- o — as in go (Torah, shofar)
- u — as in tune (Yom Kippur, *tikun olam*)
- ch — as in Bach (guttural "h" sound in *rachum, berachot*) (in Yiddish words such as *cholent*, it may also be pronounced as "ch" as in chip)
- ' — indicates the sound of the "i" in "vim" at the beginning of a word to mean "and" (*v'ahavta*), or indicates a pause between two adjacent sounds (Tu b'Shevat)

A major question is how to transliterate Hebrew words that end with the letter "*hei*." Although there is a recent trend in Israeli periodicals to drop the "h," most readers are comfortable with ending such words with "ah," which is the general spelling used in this book. Exceptions are the words yeshiva, shiva, halacha, and aggada.

A

Abba. Familiar form of the Hebrew word for "father," equivalent to "daddy."

Abbreviations (*rashei teivot*). Shorthand forms for common words and phrases that are extensively used in the Talmud and later rabbinic literature. A double quote is usually inserted in place of the eliminated letters or words. A common abbreviation after the name of a deceased person is *z"l* (*zichrono livracha*; of blessed memory).

Ablution (ritual washing). During rabbinic times, ritual washing was prescribed for a number of conditions of "impurity" to enable a person to engage in cultic observances, such as bringing sacrifices to the Temple. Today, women after menstruation or childbirth, and converts at the end of the conversion process, immerse themselves in a ritual bath (*mikveh*). Individuals wash their hands before eating or praying, as well as after rising from sleep, urinating or defecating, and touching a corpse. Some Orthodox men immerse themselves in the *mikveh* on Fridays and before Jewish holidays, and a scribe (*sofer*) immerses himself before embarking on the sacred task of writing a Torah scroll. There is also the ancient custom (based on Num. 31:22-23) of immersing in a *mikveh* all new cooking pots and dishes purchased from non-Jews.

Abomination. Although the English term means "exceptionally loathsome, wicked, vile, or hateful," the Hebrew equivalent (*to'evah*) in the Bible denotes something that is forbidden or ritually unclean ("taboo") according to the Israelite religion. Among the activities labeled as *to'evah* are idolatry, sacrificing blemished animals, dedicating children to Molech, resorting to mediums and magic, and a broad range of sexual activities such as incest, bestiality, adultery, homosexuality, and having sex with a woman during her menstrual period (see individual entries). The term *to'evah* is also applied to cursing parents, using false weights and measures, and the shedding of blood.

Acacia (*shittah*). The only wood used in the building of the Tabernacle and its accessories (Ark, Altar, Table, staves) (Exod. 25-27). A hard but light and water-resistant wood, acacia was used extensively for construction and shipbuilding during biblical times.

Academies - see Talmudic academies.

Accidents. The Bible describes four basic types of unintentional damage to people and property (Exod. 21:18-36; 22:4-6) – injury occurring (a) during the course of normal activity (a goring ox not previously known to be savage); (b) due to a stationary source of potential danger (open pit in a public street); (c) on private property rather than a public place (livestock let loose to graze in a neighbor's field or vineyard); and (d) as the result of consequential damage (sparks from a fire kindled by a person in his own field that are carried by the wind, setting set fire to a neighboring field). The general principle in Jewish law is that each person is responsible for all damage caused by his property or his actions if he fails to take appropriate care to prevent it. This is equivalent to the modern concept of negligence as a failure to meet the duty of "reasonable care."

Accommodationism. The conviction that Jews and Judaism can adopt ideas from the general culture and still remain loyal to their essential tenets and beliefs. As Solomon Schechter argued, Jews and Judaism have always incorporated outside ideas. However, these have the potential either to be integrated and strengthen the community, or to be alienating, dangerous, and rejected. The father of medieval Jewish philosophy and the founder of accommodationist thinking was Saadia Gaon (9th-10th century), who maintained that it was possible to reach the same truths through philosophy as from faith (Revelation) by the proper application of rational deduction and analysis. In the 19th century, the early German Reform adopted an extreme accommodationist view, defining Judaism as "ethical monotheism" and arguing that it was essentially the same as Christianity, so that Jews should be granted the same rights as their gentile neighbors. Until the Holocaust, accommodationists championed the idea of continuous revelation, which posits that everything becomes "progressively" better. This led to Mordecai Kaplan's conception of Judaism as an "evolving Jewish civilization." (See also *particularism*.)

Acharei Mot.[1] The 6th *parashah* in the Book of Leviticus (16:1-18:30), it describes the rituals for Yom Kippur and lists the prohibited sexual relationships (see marriages, prohibited), a passage that is read in synagogue during the afternoon service on the Day of Atonement.

Acharit ha-yamim (end of days) - see Eschatology.

Acharonim. Later rabbinic authorities, as distinguished from the early authorities (see *rishonim*). The dividing line between these two groups of scholars is generally placed between the 14th and 15th centuries, although a precise date has not been clearly established.

Acronym. Use of the initial letter(s) of words in a sequence, or parts of a proper name, as an abbreviation that can be more easily pronounced and remembered. "Rambam" is an acronym for **Ra**bbi **M**oses **b**en **M**aimon (Maimonides), and "Rashi" is an acronym for **Ra**bbi **Sh**lomo ben **Y**itzchak.

Acrostic. Poetic technique in which each verse begins with the next letter of the Hebrew alphabet (e.g., *Ashrei*), or their initial letters spell out the name of the author (e.g., *Lecha Dodi*). On Yom Kippur, the two confessionals are acrostics. *Al Chet* is a double Hebrew alphabetical acrostic of 44 transgressions with two sins allotted to each letter; *Ashamnu* consists of 24 transgression in alphabetical order in Hebrew, with the last letter used three times. Acrostics used in Jewish liturgy facilitate memorization of the prayers.

Ad lo yada (until he does not know). Parade of costumed revelers, which is a prominent feature of Purim observance in Tel Aviv. The term derives from the statement of Rav (Meg. 7b), the renowned Babylonian talmudic scholar, mandating that a person become so "mellowed with wine" on Purim that "he cannot tell the difference (*ad lo yada*) between 'Cursed is Haman' (*arur Haman*) and 'Blessed is Mordecai' (*baruch Mordecai*)" – the Hebrew letters in both phrases having an identical numerical value (502).

Ad me'ah v'esrim shanah. Literally "until 120 years," a popular expression of good wishes on a birthday, because this was the life span of Moses (see 120).

Adam. First human being and a collective term for humankind.

Adam Kadmon. The kabbalistic concept of "Primordial Man," which links God, Man, and the World. In Lurianic Kabbalah, *Adam Kadmon* is the first being to emerge from *Ein Sof*, the infinite Godhead. In this way, the same cosmic elements of the *sefirot* are found in the "body" of *Adam Kadmon*, so that Man can truly be described as having been created in the Divine image. The *sefirot* and the four worlds are described as having emanated from the ear, nose, eyes, and mouth of *Adam Kadmon*.

Adar. The 12th and final month of the Jewish calendar (February/March). To ensure that the festivals fall during their appointed seasons in the solar year (in the Northern Hemisphere), an extra month is added to the Jewish lunar calendar 7 times in 19 years. This is called *Adar Sheni* (Second Adar), which immediately precedes the month of Nisan, the first month in the Jewish religious year. Because the festival of Purim is celebrated during this month, the Rabbis exclaimed, "with the start of the month of Adar our joy greatly increases" (Taan. 29a).

Adir Hu (Mighty is He). One of the songs following the formal recitation of the Haggadah at the Passover seder. An alphabetical acrostic, *Adir Hu* contains a refrain pleading for the rebuilding of the Temple, symbol of Israel's restoration, and the inauguration of the Messianic Age, "speedily, in our days."**Admor**. Title of Hasidic rabbis. It is an abbreviation of the Hebrew words ***Ad**onenu*, ***Mor**enu*, *ve-**R**abenu* (our lord, teacher, and master). (See also *tzadik*.)

Adon Olam (Lord of the World/Eternal Lord). An inspiring song of praise attributed to Solomon ibn Gabirol, an 11th-century Spanish philosopher who was one of the most renowned of the liturgical poets (see *paytanim*). One of the most popular hymns, *Adon Olam* is generally sung at the conclusion of the Sabbath and festival *Musaf* (additional) services, in a variety of musical settings. *Adon Olam* concludes the bedtime prayers, based on its final verses: "Into God's hand I entrust my spirit when I sleep – and I shall awaken! With my spirit shall my body remain, God is with me. I shall not fear." It also is traditionally recited on one's deathbed.

Adonai (lit., "my Lords"). Current pronunciation of the holiest and most distinctly Jewish name of God, written in the Hebrew Bible with the four consonants *YHVH*. Referred to as the "Tetragrammaton," it was regularly pronounced with the proper vowels by all Israelites until the destruction of the First Temple in 586 B.C.E. However, its use was eventually restricted to the *Kohen Gadol* (High Priest) in the Holy of Holies on Yom Kippur, and to other *kohanim* when reciting the Priestly Blessing during the daily services in the Temple. When the Second Temple was destroyed, the word lost its vocalization. By the time of the Talmud, the term "*Adonai*" was generally used as a substitute for *YHVH*, as in the standard prayer formula, "*Baruch Ata Adonai.*"

Adonai imachem (may the Lord be with you). Among Sephardim, the words spoken by a person called for an *aliyah* before reciting the preliminary *Barchu*. The congregational response is *Yevarechecha Adonai* (may the Lord bless you).

Adoption. Although not a precisely defined institution in Jewish law, the rabbinical court has the authority to appoint a guardian who has essentially the same responsibilities as a biological parent – to provide for the upbringing, education, and shelter of a child and to administer his/her property. It is considered a mitzvah to raise an orphan in one's home. According to Jewish law, the religious status of adopted children is based on that of their parents. Although adopted children may assume the name of their new family, the privileges and obligations of being a *kohen* or a *levi* depend solely upon birth. Conversely, children born to a *kohen* or *levi* retain this classification regardless of the status of their adopted family. Once adopted, children are treated as if they were natural members of the family. Therefore, they should love, respect, and honor their adoptive parents and observe all the laws of mourning, including the saying of *Kaddish*. An adopted child who is not definitely known to be Jewish must undergo formal conversion to be considered a Jew.

Adoshem. Derived from a combination of two names of God – *Adonai* and *ha-Shem* (the Name) – it is a substitute for speaking either of these names or, in writing, to avoid risking the erasure or defacement of God's name.

Adultery. The Seventh Commandment (Exod. 20:13; Deut. 5:18) that prohibits a married woman from having sexual intercourse with a man other than her husband. In biblical times, both parties were subject to the death penalty. Along with idolatry and murder, adultery (and incest) is one of the three cardinal sins that are forbidden even if it means sacrificing one's life. The prohibition against adultery was extended to include most contact with the opposite sex, which the Rabbis feared could lead to a level of lust that was virtually equivalent to adultery itself. When polygamy was permissible, as during biblical times, a married man was not forbidden from having sexual relations with an unmarried woman as long as he could theoretically marry her. A woman suspected by her jealous husband of adultery (see *sotah*) could prove her innocence by successfully surviving the complicated ordeal of drinking the "water of bitterness." Adultery by a husband became grounds for a wife to obtain a divorce.

Aelia Capitolina. Latin name for the Roman city built on the site of Jerusalem by Emperor Aelius Hadrian. It was dedicated to the Roman god, Jupiter Capitolinus, to whom a temple was built on the site where the Second Temple once stood. Some scholars believe that this pagan construction resulted in the disastrous Bar Kochba revolt of 132-135 C.E., though archeological finds suggest that the major building activities occurred only after the rebels were defeated. Jews were forbidden to live in the city, a ban that continued through the 4th century.

Afikoman. From a Greek word meaning "dessert," it is the larger portion of the middle *matzah*, divided early during the Passover seder, which is ceremonially eaten after dinner. Indeed, the seder cannot conclude until all guests share a piece of this "dessert." It is customary for the seder leader to hide the *afikoman* and, after the children have "stolen" it, to "ransom" the *afikoman* after the meal for presents or money. According to the Talmud, this practice encourages the children to remain awake during the seder (Pes. 109a).

Afterlife. Judaism has always maintained a belief in an afterlife, though there has been a broad spectrum of views in different historical eras concerning such core issues as the immortality of the soul, the resurrection of the dead, and the nature of the World to Come (see *olam ha-ba*) after the messianic redemption. Though firmly convinced of the reality of a World to Come, Maimonides wisely stated that we mortals can have no real knowledge about its nature. Even if we did have some information concerning the afterlife, we would be incapable of comprehending it, since the World to Come would have a different dimension of existence beyond time or space and thus it would be beyond our ability to describe it or even conceive of it. Nevertheless, the Jewish tradition assures us that, even in this life, one can experience a sample of the World to Come. As the Talmud states, "three things give us a foretaste of the World to Come – the Sabbath, a sunny day, and sexual intercourse" (Ber. 57b). Some modern thinkers have interpreted the concept of immortality metaphorically, as living on in the memory of loved ones.

Afterlife, who merits an. The Talmud states that "all members of the people of Israel have a portion in the World to Come" (Sanh. 90a), while Maimonides asserted that this also applied to "the pious of the nations." The Talmud describes a scenario in which a person goes before the heavenly tribunal for a final day of judgment and is asked five questions (Shab. 31a). Rather than the questions one might expect – Did you keep the Sabbath? Did you maintain a kosher home? Did you give to charity? – they are (a) Were you honest in your business dealings? (b) Did you set aside time to study Torah? (c) Did you have children? (d) Did you hope for redemption? and (e) Did you search for wisdom?

Afternoon service - see *Mincha*.

Aggada. Non-legal rabbinic writings in the Talmud and Midrash that include statements of major moral and ethical principles (often elucidated by the use of parables and anecdotes), stories about biblical heroes and the great Rabbis, and Jewish folklore. Unlike *halacha*, *aggada* is not legally binding. It serves to explain and clarify Jewish laws and customs and accentuate the ethical ideas of the Torah.

Agudat Yisrael. Worldwide organization of Orthodox Jews, which was founded in 1912 in Poland to defend the traditional Jewish way of life and counter the influence of secular ideas. It is led by a rabbinic council of prominent talmudic scholars, which hands down decisions on Jewish law.

Agunah (chained woman). One whose marriage has in fact ended, but who legally remains a married woman (bound to a husband who no longer lives with her) and thus is unable to remarry. The *halacha* prescribes that a marriage can only be dissolved by divorce or by the death of either spouse. According to Jewish law, divorce requires that the husband deliver a divorce document (see *get*) to his wife. (This is not required by the Reform and Reconstructionist movements.) If the husband either willfully refuses to deliver a *get* (despite the threats and punitive measures of a Jewish court) or is legally incompetent to grant it (usually because of insanity), divorce is not possible and the wife becomes an *agunah*. Similarly, if the husband deserts his wife and disappears, or if he dies but there is no valid testimony to that fact, the woman remains legally married and cannot wed another. One recent approach to the *agunah* problem is a prenuptial agreement whereby the husband commits himself to appear before a rabbinical court to deliver a bill of divorce to his wife.

Ahavah Rabbah ([With] great love). Second of the two blessings preceding the recitation of the *Shema* that is recited in the morning in the Ashkenazic tradition. It extols the Divine love that underlies the relationship between God and the Jewish people, which is solidified by the Revelation of the Torah. Committing the worshiper to study the Torah and obey its laws, *Ahavah Rabbah* is an appropriate introduction to the *Shema*, which contains biblical selections. It also is an appeal that God will redeem the Jewish people from exile, returning them from dispersion in the Diaspora to the Land of Israel. When saying the phrase "Bring us in peace from the four corners of the world," the worshiper draws the four corners of the *tallit* together and continues to hold them throughout the recitation of the *Shema*, kissing the fringes each time the word *tzitzit* is mentioned.[2]

Ahavat Olam ([With] everlasting love). Second of the two blessings preceding the recitation of the *Shema* that is recited in the evening in the Ashkenazic tradition and in both the morning and evening by Sephardic and Italian Jews. Like the longer and more complex *Ahavah Rabbah*, it is a paean to the Divine love that forms the basis for the relationship between God and the Jewish people and commits the worshiper to study the Torah and obey its laws.

Ahavat Yisrael. Literally meaning "love of [the people of] Israel," this Hebrew phrase is generally used in reference to the special relationship existing among Jews. Nevertheless, Jews are also commanded to love the stranger.

Akdamut. Medieval Aramaic *piyyut*, literally meaning "prelude," that is chanted responsively in Ashkenazic synagogues just before the Torah reading on Shavuot. Composed in the 11th century by Meir ben Isaac Nehorai of Worms (Germany), it describes the angelic praise of God in the heavens and the earthly partnership between God and the Jewish people, who remain faithful despite their suffering.

Akedah (binding of Isaac). The Hebrew term for the biblical account of the Divine command to Abraham to offer his son Isaac as a sacrifice to test the Patriarch's loyalty and faith (Gen. 22). It was stopped at the last moment by an angel of God, who promised that Abraham's descendants would be "as numerous as the stars of heaven and the sands on the seashore." This biblical section is the Torah reading for the second day of Rosh Hashanah.

Al Chet (For the sin [which we have committed before You]). First words and name of the major confession of sins recited on Yom Kippur during the *Amidah*. A litany of 44 transgressions arranged as a double Hebrew alphabetical acrostic with two sins allotted to each letter (only one letter per sin among Sephardim), it is divided into three parts that are each followed by the formula: "And for all these, O God of forgiveness, forgive us, pardon us, grant us atonement." *Al Chet* is recited in the first person plural as a congregational confessional.

Akkad. City-state of Semitic people who settled among the Sumerians in northern Mesopotamia. The Akkadian Empire, sometimes viewed as the first in human history, was established by Sargon and reached its height between the 24th-22nd centuries B.C.E., before the rise of Babylonia.

Al ha-Nissim (For the miracles). Opening words and name of a prayer of thanksgiving to God that is recited in the *Amidah* and the Grace after Meals during Chanukah and Purim. It is followed by a summary of the event that is celebrated on the festival.

Al Naharot Bavel (by the rivers of Babylon; Psalm 137). On weekdays, it is customary to recite this psalm before the Grace after Meals, in memory of the destruction of the First Temple in 586 B.C.E. On Sabbaths and festivals, and at the meals celebrating a wedding, circumcision, or *pidyon ha-ben* (see *se'udat mitzvah*), when joy should not be constrained by remembering catastrophic events, the Grace after Meals is preceded by the singing of *Shir ha-Ma'alot* (Psalm 126).

Alav (fem. **Aleha) ha-shalom**. Literally meaning "peace be upon him/her," this Hebrew expression is equivalent to "May he/she rest in peace" and is customarily said after mentioning the name of a person who has died.

Aleinu (It is our duty). Literally meaning "it is upon us," the opening word and name for a prayer proclaiming the sovereignty and unity of God. Originally used as the introduction to the *Malchuyot* (Kingship) section of the *Musaf Amidah* on Rosh Hashanah, since the 13th century it has been recited at the conclusion of every prayer service. The *Aleinu* combines the idea of Israel as a Chosen People with the challenge that Jews exert every effort to perfect humanity under the kingdom of God. It concludes with the fervent hope for a time when idolatry will vanish and the entire world will recognize the one true God.

Aleph (1). The 1st letter of the Hebrew alphabet, with a numerical value of 1.

ALEPH (2). Umbrella organization of the Alliance for Jewish Renewal.

Aleph-Bet. The names of the first two letters, this term is used to denote the entire Hebrew alphabet, which consists of 22 letters. Five of these (*kaf, mem, nun, pei, tzadi*) have special final forms. The letters of the Hebrew alphabet play an important symbolic role in Jewish mysticism.

Aleppo Codex. The oldest and most famous manuscript of the Bible. Written in Tiberias in 920 and annotated by Aaron ben Asher, it became the most authoritative Jewish biblical text. It was used by Maimonides in his exposition of the laws governing the writing of Torah scrolls in his codification of Jewish law (see

Mishneh Torah). Initially brought to Jerusalem, the Codex was stolen and taken to Egypt, where it was redeemed by the Jewish community of Cairo. At the end of the 14th century, the Codex was brought to Aleppo (Syria), for which it is now named. For the next five centuries it was kept closely guarded in the basement of the main synagogue in Aleppo and considered the community's greatest treasure. During the anti-Jewish riots of December 1947, the ancient synagogue where it was kept was broken into and burned, and the Codex itself disappeared. A decade later, it was smuggled into Israel and presented to the President of the State, though most of the section containing the Five Books of Moses had been lost.

Aliyah (1). Literally meaning "ascent," this Hebrew word is used to describe the honor of being called up to the *bimah* to read a portion from the Torah. Originally, each person called up actually read a portion from the scroll. Later, a special reader (see *baal korei*) was appointed for this purpose, and those who are called up for an *aliyah* only recite the blessings before and after the Torah reading.Traditionally, the privilege of the first *aliyah* is given to a *kohen*, and the second *aliyah* is allocated to a *levi*. The remaining *aliyot* are distributed among the rest of the congregation, who are classified as "Israelites." Reform and some liberal Conservative synagogues have abolished the distinction between *kohen*, *levi*, and Israelite, both because it is difficult to verify the lineage of any Jew and because of a belief in equality for all their members. The number of *aliyot* varies widely. Three people are called to the Torah on Monday and Thursday mornings, on Sabbath afternoons and the *Mincha* service on Yom Kippur, on the festivals of Chanukah and Purim, and on all fast days. There are four *aliyot* on Rosh Hodesh and on the intermediate days (see *chol ha-mo'ed*) of Passover and Sukkot; five on Rosh Hashanah and on the festival days of Passover, Shavuot, and Sukkot; six on the morning of Yom Kippur; and seven on Sabbath morning.

Aliyah (2). Although generally translated as "immigration," in this context *aliyah* represents the fundamental ideal of Zionism – moving from the Diaspora to settle in the Land of Israel and personally participate in the rebuilding of the Jewish homeland, thus raising the Jew to a higher plane of self-fulfillment as a member of the renascent nation.

Aliyah Bet. Hebrew term for the "illegal" immigration into the Land of Israel during the Mandatory period to circumvent the British restrictions severely limiting the number of Jews permitted to legally come from Europe to Palestine. In the 1930's, *Aliyah Bet* played a significant role in bringing to Palestine Jews seeking to escape Nazi persecution. The activities of *Aliyah Bet* continued during and after World War II. At the time of the establishment of the State of Israel in 1948, some one quarter of its Jewish inhabitants had arrived through the activities of *Aliyah Bet.*

Aliyah, Fifth. Immigration in the decade before World War II (1929-1939) of more than 250,000 Jews, many of whom were fleeing Germany and Austria following Hitler's rise to power, which transformed the character of the *yishuv*. Constituting the first large-scale influx from Western and Central Europe, they transferred large amounts of capital and contributed valuable skills and business experience. A relatively high proportion of them practiced medicine or one of the other professions, and they provided a majority of the musicians who formed the new Philharmonic Orchestra (see Israel Philharmonic Orchestra) as well as a considerable part of its audiences. The flood tide of immigration was halted in 1936 with the onset of the Arab revolt and almost eliminated by the infamous White Paper of 1939, which prevented tens of thousands of Jews from escaping the impending catastrophe in Europe.

Aliyah, First. Spanning the years 1882-1903, it consisted of individuals and small groups, about 25,000 in all and mostly from Eastern Europe, who fled pogroms, czarist repression, and grinding poverty to establish settlements in the Land of Israel. The first permanent Jewish settlements in Palestine (Rishon le-Zion, Petah Tikvah, Rosh Pinna, Zichron Ya'akov) faced severe financial crises that threatened their very existence. They probably would have been abandoned if financial resources had not been provided by Baron Edmond de Rothschild (1845-1934). In addition to supporting agricultural settlements, Rothschild played a major role in the development of the wine industry in the Land of Israel and was a co-sponsor of the Palestine Electric Corporation. (See also *BILU*.)

Aliyah, Fourth. From 1924–1928, about 67,000 immigrants came to the Land of Israel, more than half escaping the economic crisis and anti-Jewish policies in Poland. Some 80% of these newcomers were middle class and had some capital of their own, which they invested in small workshops and factories as well as the construction of housing in the towns and main cities, considerably increasing the urban population.

Aliyah, Second. Immigration from 1904-1914 of about 40,000 pioneers, primarily from Eastern Europe, who generally worked as hired laborers in settlements or the cities and laid the foundation for the labor movement. Imbued with socialist ideals and severely disappointed by the failure of the 1905 revolution (as well as shocked by the 1903 Kishinev pogroms), they decided to create their own revolutionary movement on the basis of national revival and socialist ideals. More self-reliant than their predecessors, the members of the Second Aliyah were determined to develop a workers' commonwealth in the Land of Israel. They established the first Jewish labor parties (see *Po'alei Zion*) and self-help institutions, associations for self-defense (see Hashomer), and the first collective settlements (see *kevuzot*), and laid the foundations for a new Hebrew press and literature. The Second Aliyah, which included such prominent future leaders of the State of Israel as David Ben Gurion and Itzhak Ben Zvi, was interrupted by the outbreak of World War I.

Aliyah, Third. Beginning immediately after World War I and lasting until 1923, it brought more than 35,000 young pioneers (see *chalutzim*) belonging to the *He-Chalutz, Hashomer ha-Tza'ir, Betar*, and *Mizrachi* movements. These groups set up a network of training centers in the Diaspora, in which members studied the ideals of their Zionist movement, learned Hebrew and its literature, and gained experience in manual labor and farming. This ensured that the young men and women arrived in Palestine not as complete novices, but equipped with a consistent social philosophy, experience living in communes, and at least some rudimentary skills. Together with the veterans of the Second Aliyah, they paved the way for a future state by establishing the Histadrut; playing a leading role in the creation of the Haganah; providing workers for the construction of housing and roads and the beginnings of industry; strengthening the foundations of Jewish agriculture; and expanding the map of Jewish settlement by founding many *kibbutzim* and *moshavim*.

Aliyot, priority in distributing. In traditional synagogues, the privilege of the first *aliyah* is given to a *kohen* and the second *aliyah* is allocated to a *levi*. The remaining *aliyot* are distributed among the rest of the congregation, who are classified as "Israelites."[3] From the third onward, the general custom for prioritizing *aliyot* is: (1) a bridegroom on the Sabbath *before* his wedding; (2) a boy who has turned 13 years of age (bar mitzvah); (3) the father of a newborn infant, male or female, on the first Sabbath that the mother appears in the synagogue; (4) a bridegroom on the Sabbath *after* his wedding; (5) the father of a baby girl who is to be named; (6) one observing *yahrzeit* for a parent on that day; (7) the father of a baby to be circumcised on that day or during the coming week; (8) one observing *yahrzeit* for a parent during the coming week; (9) one required to recite the thanksgiving blessing of *gomel*; (10) one who is about to leave on a long journey or has just returned from one; and (11) a distinguished guest in the community. When two or more people at services are observing the same occasion, priority is generally given to a regular worshiper over one who comes infrequently and to a member of the congregation over a non-member.[4]

Allegory – see *Remez*.

Alliance Israélite Universelle. International Jewish organization, founded in Paris in 1860 to protect Jewish civil and religious rights and to promote education and professional development among Jews around the world so that they would become productive citizens and bring honor to their religion.**Alma d'shikra**. Literally meaning "world of falsehood" and an Aramaic term from the mystical *Zohar*, it is the concept that truth is elusive and dwelling behind a whirl of veils, so that what we see is an unreal illusion. In our material world, the realm of total spirituality and absolute truth is unknowable and unattainable. Consequently, the mystic tries to pierce through the veils of illusion to the reality that exists beyond it. As Franz Rosenzweig stated, "truth is a noun only for God; for human beings it is an adjective." According to this view, a person can never know "the truth," but only reflections or shadows of that truth.

Almond. With its Hebrew name (*shaked*) coming from a root meaning "wakeful" or "to hasten," the almond is the first tree to flower in Israel – blooming as early as January or early February, while other fruit trees are still bare. Accordingly, the Rabbis selected the period when almond trees flower as the time for the festival of Tu b'Shevat, the New Year of the Trees.[5] At the time of the Korach rebellion in the wilderness, it was Aaron's rod that miraculously sprouted almond blossoms, unequivocally indicating that God had chosen him to lead the people as the High Priest (Num. 17).

Alphabet – see *Aleph-Bet*.

Al-pi heter iskah. Hebrew words added to a legal document to make an interest-bearing business transaction comply with Jewish law, thus avoiding the biblical prohibition against lending at interest. (See also *heter iskah*.)

Altalena. Cargo ship carrying munitions and fighters for the paramilitary Irgun, which anchored off the coast of Israel in June 1948, just after the beginning of the War of Independence. The Haganah, by then the official army of the State of Israel, refused to allow the Altalena to land and unload because of the fear that the Irgun would start a revolt to topple the provisional government. After fruitless negotiations, David Ben Gurion ordered the Haganah to sink the ship. For decades, the Altalena affair remained a major source of bitter controversy in Israeli political discourse. Proponents of Ben Gurion's actions praised them as essential in establishing the government's authority and discouraging factionalism and the formation of a rival army. Opponents, led by Menachem Begin, condemned the unnecessary violence and claimed that opportunities for a peaceful resolution were intentionally frustrated by Ben Gurion and top Haganah officers.

Altar (*Mizbeach*). Raised surface or platform on which sacrifices were performed in the Sanctuary. There was a Bronze Altar for burnt offerings and a Golden Altar for incense. Originally, an altar could be anywhere and sacrifices performed by anyone. Eventually, a sacrificial cult became more institutionalized and limited to special practitioners and specific places. Altars were permanent fixtures in the Jerusalem Temple, which became the only permitted site of sacrificial worship. Over time, the term "altar" came to designate the central location for liturgical functions in the synagogue, such as reading the Torah (see *bimah*). The Rabbis considered the dinner table to be symbolic of the Altar in the Temple (Ber. 55a).

Because salt was brought with all offerings, the custom developed of sprinkling salt on the Sabbath *challah* to commemorate the sacrificial system

Alter-kocker. Yiddish term used disparagingly to describe a crotchety, fussy, ineffectual old man. The term is often abbreviated as "a.k."

Am ha'aretz. Literally "people of the land," a Hebrew phrase used in the Bible to refer to the Jewish masses. In talmudic times, this term was applied to the common people who did not observe rabbinic ordinances. Eventually, it became a derogatory term to denote an ignoramus, one lacking knowledge of Jewish tradition and laws; a vulgar, boorish, ill-mannered person; or a country bumpkin.

Am Yisrael (people of Israel). This general Hebrew term denotes the worldwide Jewish community, as in the popular song, **"***Am Yisrael Chai*" (the People of Israel live). It is estimated that there are now 13-14 million Jews, most of whom live in the United States or Israel.

Amalek. Nomadic tribe living in the Sinai desert and southern Negev that perpetrated a cowardly and unprovoked attack upon weary stragglers at the rear of the Israelite column as they wandered in the wilderness soon after the Exodus from Egypt (Exod. 17:8-16). They were only repelled after a difficult struggle. Amalek became regarded as the epitome of evil, leading to the Divine command to "blot out the remembrance of Amalek from under heaven; do not forget!" (Deut. 25:19). This passage is read as the *maftir* portion in synagogue on the Sabbath immediately preceding Purim. It is most appropriate at this time since, according to the Book of Esther, the arch-villain Haman was a direct descendant of Agag, the king of the Amalekites.

Amen. Ancient response of affirmation that what another has stated is the truth. When said after a petitionary prayer, it is the equivalent of "so may it be." Originating in the Torah, "amen" has now become a word in almost every language and is used by Christians and, to some degree, by Muslims. According to the Talmud (Shab. 119b), "amen" is an acronym for *El melech ne'eman* (God, the faithful King).

American Israel Public Affairs Committee (AIPAC). Washington-based advocacy organization for Israel, established in 1954, which works aggressively on legislation affecting the State of Israel and encourages political activism on its behalf.

American Jewish Committee. National Jewish organization, founded in 1906, that seeks to prevent the violation of civil and religious rights of Jews worldwide and to relieve the plight of Jews suffering from persecution and disasters. The

American Jewish Committee also promotes constructive relations among the various religious, ethnic, and racial communities in the United States. It has issued the American Jewish Yearbook each year since 1909.

American Jewish Congress. Devoted to the Zionist support of a Jewish homeland since its founding in 1918, the American Jewish Congress has also championed the First Amendment issue of separation of church and state as well as civil rights and civil liberties for both Jews and non-Jews throughout the world.

American Jewish Joint Distribution Committee. Known popularly as the "Joint," it was founded in 1914 to serve as the overall distribution agency for funds collected by various American Jewish groups for overseas relief. During World War II, it provided significant aid to European Jewry. After the establishment of Israel, the "Joint" has been active in sponsoring programs of relief, rescue, and renewal. It has helped the State address its most urgent social challenges, based on the traditional principles that all Jews are responsible for one another and that "to save one person is to save the world."

Amidah (standing [prayer]). Known popularly as the *Shemoneh Esrei* (18 [blessings], though there actually are 19) and referred to in the Talmud as simply *Ha-Tefillah* (The Prayer), the *Amidah* has been the core of the prayer service since the destruction of the Second Temple. It contains the primary elements of prayer – praise, petition, and thanksgiving. The *Amidah* consists of three introductory and three concluding blessings that are unchanging. On weekdays there are 13 intermediary blessings; the number and content vary among the different services on Sabbaths and festivals. Traditionally, the *Amidah* is said silently and then repeated (with some additions) by the prayer leader if there is a *minyan*. The *Amidah* uses the first person plural, and private petitions are inserted at its conclusion. The blessings were composed during the first centuries B.C.E. and C.E. and edited into a final form by Rabban Gamaliel II.

Amidah, concluding benedictions. These three unchanging blessings are *avodah* (service), *modim* of the Rabbis (thanksgiving), and the prayer for peace.

Amidah, intermediary benedictions. The weekday *Amidah* contains 13 intermediate blessings, which are essentially requests related to the needs of both the individual and the Jewish nation. The six petitions for personal needs are further subdivided into those of a spiritual nature – wisdom and understanding (see *binah*), repentance (see *teshuvah*), and forgiveness of sins (see *selichah*); and those of a physical, material or emotional character – redemption and security (see *ge'ulah*), health (see *refu'ah*), and economic prosperity (see *birkat hashanim*). The six petitions for specific Jewish national aspirations that are related to various aspects of messianic redemption include: ingathering of the dispersed exiles (see *kibbutz galuyot*); restoration of justice (see *mishpat*); destruction of Israel's enemies (see *minim*); prayer for the righteous (see *tzadikim*); restoration of Jerusalem (see *Yerushalayim*); and the coming of the Messiah (see *birkat David*). The final intermediate blessing requests that God hear the prayers of all Israel (see *tefillah*).

Amidah, introductory blessings. These three unchanging blessings are *avot* (fathers), *gevurot* (powers), and *kedushat ha-Shem* (holiness of the Name [of God]).

Amora (explainer). Name for a teacher of Jewish law in the Land of Israel and Babylonia after the redaction of Mishnah by Judah the Prince (c. 200 C.E.). The discussions of the *amora'im* (200-500 C.E.), who interpreted the Mishnah and applied it to case law, form the Gemara, which together with the Mishnah constitute the Babylonian Talmud and the Palestinian Talmud. The sources mention several thousand *amora'im*.

Amos. Earliest of the literary prophets and 3rd of the minor prophets (mid-8th century B.C.E.). A shepherd from Tekoa in the hills of Judah, Amos went to sell his animals in nearby Beit El, the principal religious center of the Northern Kingdom of Israel. There he cried out against the injustice and poverty of the masses under King Jeroboam II, attacking the wealthy minority who feasted while disregarding the poor, hungry, and landless. Advocating for the primacy of ethical behavior over the sacrificial cult, Amos called for justice for all humanity and was the first to see God as the universal Lord of all the nations. Although he sorrowfully predicted that the punishment of Israel would be its destruction by Assyria, Amos dreamed of a future golden age of peace, when the exiles of Israel would return home, rebuild their wasted cities, replant vineyards, and "nevermore be uprooted from the soil I have given them" (9:14-15).

Amulets. Charms or talismans that Jews have worn to magically protect themselves from the "Evil Eye." Generally either attached to clothing or hung as a necklace or bracelet, amulets may contain parchment inscribed with biblical or other quotations, the names of angels, or permutations and combinations of the letters of the different names of God. Some believe that the efficacy of an amulet depends not only on the inscription, but also on the piety of the person who wrote it. The Talmud states that it is forbidden to recite verses of the Torah for the purpose of curing an existing illness, but it is permitted "to guard" against possible future sickness (Shev. 15b) – and this distinction was equally applied to amulets. Although belief in the protective power of amulets greatly decreased in the West after the Emancipation of European Jewry, they remained in common use in Eastern Europe until the Holocaust. Amulets are still popular among Jews of Middle Eastern and North African descent, especially in Israel, where they have aroused controversy during political campaigns when distributed by certain ultra-Orthodox parties under the auspices of prominent rabbis.

Angel (*malach*). Spiritual being who ministers to God and appears to human beings when on a special mission. From a Greek word meaning "messenger," angels are distinguished by their obedience to the Divine will.

Angel of Death (*Malach ha-Mavet*). Allegorical figure who takes the soul from the body. Because in Jewish tradition the Angel of Death is merely a messenger carrying out Divine decrees, its powers are severely limited. Legends relate how it can be overcome, such as by the study of Torah or some exceptional act of piety or goodness. According to legend, the three Patriarchs, as well as Moses, Aaron, and Miriam, were said to have died by a kiss from God, rather than from the sword of the Angel of Death. Many Jewish customs associated with death and burial developed from the belief that the soul of the deceased needs protection from the Angel of Death or his agents.

Ani le-dodi ve-dodi li (I am my beloved's and my beloved is mine). This verse from Song of Songs (6:3) is often used in connection with the wedding ceremony. Elul, the month preceding Rosh Hashanah (with its themes of renewal and return) is a Hebrew acronym of this phrase. With the "beloved" traditionally referring to God, the Rabbis took this verse to describe the particularly loving and close relationship between God and Israel. Separated from each other during the Three Weeks, Israel and God meet again on Tu b'Av and their love slowly intensifies. The climax of their relationship occurs on Yom Kippur, when Israel is forgiven for the shameful incident of the Golden Calf, which had initially precipitated the process of mourning, repentance, and renewal.[6]

Ani Ma'amin (I believe [with complete faith]). First words of each of Maimonides' Thirteen Principles of Faith. The 12th of these – "I believe with complete faith in the coming of the Messiah. Even though he may tarry, nevertheless I anticipate every day that he will come" – has been set to music in a powerful hymn of faith that was sung by victims of the Holocaust as they went to their deaths.

An'im Zemirot (Let me chant sweet hymns). Also known as *Shir ha-Kavod* (Song of Glory), it exalts the power and magnificence of God using a series of striking anthropomorphic metaphors that draw on biblical and midrashic sources. It was written by Judah the Pious, a 12th-century German mystic who was the central figure of the Hasidei Ashkenaz. In traditional Ashkenazic synagogues, *An'im Zemirot* is recited in front of the open ark at the conclusion of the *Musaf* (additional) service on the Sabbath and festivals, with a child often leading the congregational singing.

Animals, cruelty to – see *Tza'ar ba'alei chaim*.

Aninut (mourning). Status of a bereaved person (*onen*) during the period between the death and burial of a close relative, when the official mourning period begins. The *onen* may not eat in the presence of the body; consume meat or wine; recite the Grace after Meals; partake in a festive meal or celebration; bathe for pleasure; get a haircut; engage in conjugal relations; conduct business; or study Torah (which is considered a source of enjoyment). If death occurred on the Sabbath, or if the Sabbath is part of the *aninut* period, the *onen* is obligated to discharge all religious obligations and is permitted to eat meat and drink wine on that day (MK 23b). However, the *onen* may not study Torah or accept an *aliyah*.

Anointing. In ancient Israel, aromatic oil was used to consecrate priests, prophets, and kings, as well as holy places and sacred vessels. Eventually, the Hebrew word "*mashiach*" (anointed one) became synonymous with the descendant of the royal house of David who would usher in the Messianic Age. After the destruction of the Second Temple, anointing ceased to have a role in Jewish ritual.

Anthropomorphism. Greek term referring to the attribution of human behavior or characteristics to inanimate objects, animals, natural phenomena, or divine beings. According to traditional Jewish belief, God is non-corporeal. All statements in the Bible ascribing physical attributes to God are mere metaphors attempting to describe an otherwise incomprehensible Deity, thus enabling human beings to address and pray to a transcendent Being.

Anti-Defamation League (ADL). Founded in 1913 by the B'nai B'rith to combat anti-Semitism, the ADL has fought bigotry and discrimination, counteracted anti-Israel propaganda, and worked generally on behalf of Jewish interests and concerns.

Anti-Semitism. Hatred of, or opposition to, Jews. The term "anti-Semitism" was coined in Germany in 1879 in a pamphlet by William Marr, who preached a "racial scientific" rather than religious anti-Semitism. In its most virulent form in Nazi Germany, anti-Semitism began with degrading the Jews by removing their civil, political, social, economic, and religious rights, before eventually murdering them. However, the concept of hatred of the Jews has existed for more than 2,000 years, as exemplified by Haman in the Book of Esther and then by the Catholic Church ever since it rose to power in the Roman Empire during the reign of Constantine (early 4th century). Church doctrine taught that the Jews had committed deicide and consequently were rejected by God. In the Middle Ages, anti-Semitism led to discrimination, persecution, forced conversion, and expulsion.

Anusim. Literally meaning "compelled ones," this Hebrew word has been applied to Jews who were forced to convert to another religion on pain of death, most notably in late 15th-century Spain. Many continued to secretly preserve their Jewish customs and teach them to their children. The most famous *anusim* were the Jews of Spain and Portugal who were compelled to convert to Christianity but remained secret Jews (see *Conversos*).

Apikoros. Literally meaning "an adherent of Epicurean philosophy," this term is used disparagingly to refer to a Jewish unbeliever and skeptic who disobeys the commandments, ridicules the Torah, and rejects the rulings of the rabbis.

Apocalypse. From a Greek word meaning "revelation," the term "apocalyptic" is generally applied to a literary genre in which vivid symbolic images and visions are used to describe future events at the "end of time," prophesying an ultimate Day of Judgment and the coming of the Messianic Age. Typically written during times of danger and stress, in Jewish tradition these works were primarily composed during the final centuries of the Second Temple era and shortly after its destruction (200 B.C.E.–100 C.E.). Parts of the Bible, especially Ezekiel and Daniel, contain apocalyptic references, as do numerous pseudoepigraphical books of the Apocrypha.

Apocrypha. Literally meaning "hidden books," the collective name for Jewish books written in the Hellenistic and Roman periods that were included in the Septuagint but not accepted into the normative Hebrew canon. Largely comprised of historical and ethical works, they include 1-2 Esdras (Ezra), Wisdom of Solomon, Wisdom of Ben Sira, Judith, Tobit, Baruch, the Letter of Jeremiah, 1-4 Maccabees, and the Psalms of Solomon.

Apodictic. Unlike most Near Eastern law, which was expressed in a conditional form (see casuistic), much of biblical legislation consists of terse statements of prohibition or command. The best-known examples of such apodictic laws are the second, third, and last five of the Ten Commandments,[7] prohibiting sculptured images, swearing falsely, murder, adultery, stealing, bearing false witness, and coveting, all of which begin with "You shall not" and represent unconditional commands. However, not all apodictic laws are negative. The fourth ("Remember the Sabbath day") and fifth ("Honor your father and your mother") are unequivocal positive commandments, as is the famed "Love your neighbor as yourself" (Lev. 19:18). Apodictic laws represent general principles and were not designed to be applied in court.

Apostate. A Jew who has rejected Judaism and converted to another religion. The most famous apostate mentioned by name in the Talmud was Elisha ben Abuya. Judaism differentiates between a person who voluntarily abandoned the faith and one who was forced to convert. Whether the former still remains a Jew has been the subject of intense controversy. The standard precedent for almost a millennium has been the ruling of Rashi, who concluded that, even if a "bad Jew," the person remained a Jew according to *halacha*. Nevertheless, many authorities totally rejected this view, convinced that a person who has left Judaism and joined another religious faith can no longer be considered a Jew. (See also *mumar*.)

Apple (*tapuach*). In the Bible, the apple is known for its sweet aroma and taste. The fruit figures prominently in several Jewish customs. On Rosh Hashanah, the eating of apples dipped in honey symbolizes the wish for a prosperous and sweet new year. Ashkenazic Jews also eat apples at the Passover seder as part of the *charoset*.

Arachin (**Ar**.). The 5th tractate of Kodashim (holy things) in the Mishnah, it deals with the laws of valuations of people, houses, fields, and objects vowed to the Sanctuary (Lev. 27:2-29).

Aramaic. Ancient Semitic tongue that was the official language of the Persian Empire and became the vernacular of the Israelites who were exiled to Babylonia after the destruction of Jerusalem in 586 B.C.E. During the Second Temple period, Aramaic replaced Hebrew as the medium of everyday speech. Aramaic is the primary language of both the Palestinian and Babylonian Talmuds (except for the Mishnah, which is in Hebrew), the Midrash, and an authorized translation of the Bible known as Targum Onkelos. Aramaic became the key language of Jewish mysticism. It also is the language of such prayers as *Kol Nidrei* and the *Kaddish*, as well as parts of the Passover Haggadah (the section beginning with the words "*Ha lachma anya*" [This is the bread of affliction] and the concluding *Chad Gadya*).

Arami oveid avi. Opening Hebrew words of the declaration made by a farmer bringing the first fruits (see *bikurim*) to the Temple in Jerusalem (Deut. 26:5-8). Translated either as "a wandering Aramean [Jacob] was my father" or "an Aramean [the deceitful Laban] tried to destroy my forefather [Jacob]," these verses became an important part of the Passover Haggadah.

Ararat. Mountain range where Noah's ark came to rest after the Flood (Gen. 8:4). It is located in eastern Turkey near the point where the borders of Turkey, Iran, and Armenia meet.

Aravah – see Willow.

Arba kanfot (four corners) – see *Tallit kattan*.

Arba kosot – see Four cups.

Arba minim – see Four species.

Arba Turim (Four Rows). Code of Jewish law written by Jacob ben Asher in the 13th century and a precursor of the *Shulchan Aruch*.

Arbitration. Method of settling disputes, in which both parties voluntarily agree to submit the issue to the judgment of one or more independent parties. Under Jewish law, the arbitration panel is generally composed of three people. In most cases, each party to the dispute selects one arbitrator, and the two arbitrators then choose a third. As in a regular court, the decision of the majority prevails and is final.

Arbor Day – see Tu b'Shevat.

Archeology. Derived from two Greek words, *archaios* (ancient) and *logos* (knowledge), archeology is the scientific study of the material remains of the past, such as human artifacts and monuments. In the Land of Israel, archeology has supplemented the written record of the Bible to provide insight into the lifestyles of the Jewish people in antiquity. The principal method of archeology is excavation, the systematic removal of accumulated earth and debris covering ancient remains. Whole cities and settlements have been discovered arranged one atop the other, forming artificial mounds (see *tel*). The dating of various strata is sometimes based on absolute criteria, by demonstrating levels of destruction associated with known events, inscriptions, and coins. Relative dating can be accomplished by the discovery of artifacts such as pottery shards, which are practically indestructible and contain valuable information. As pottery styles changed and developed through the ages, these shards are the best indication of the chronology of a settlement. Famous archeological sites in Israel include Masada, Hatzor, Lachish, Gezer, Megiddo, Herodian, and Caesarea (see individual entries). After the Six Day War of 1967, extensive excavations were begun in the vicinity of the Western Wall and the Old City of Jerusalem.

Architecture. In Israel, from the beginning of the modern Zionist movement to the present, building design in Jewish towns and settlements has been primarily conditioned by the urgent housing requirements of the various waves of immigration. During the Ottoman period, there were two broad categories of structures – Arab village buildings, constructed on the traditional pattern without architects, using building materials found nearby and in distinctive harmony with the terrain; and town architecture, which was typically Mediterranean, based on southern Italian mixed with traditional Arab styles. In addition, there were buildings erected by the Turkish government, which employed German architects and were of a high standard and restrained style. Large-scale Jewish immigration after World War I brought in its wake an acute housing shortage, leading to a rush of building unprecedented in Middle Eastern countries. However, many of the buildings of the period were badly designed by self-taught technicians in the field. Exceptions were the Bauhaus style buildings in Tel Aviv, now recognized as historical landmarks. During the same period, there also was an attempt by creative architects to achieve a modern Middle Eastern style. However, some European architects who immigrated to Palestine made no attempt to adapt the styles of their former homes to local topography or climate or to translate them into local terms. In the early 1950's, thousands of new immigrants were living in tin huts, wooden prefabricated structures, and tents. Permanent accommodations had to be built quickly and cheaply (see *shikun*). Quantity was the sole criterion and the qualitative side was neglected; the materials as well as the architectural and aesthetic aspects were downplayed in favor of efficiency and execution. However, Israel now boasts a host of striking and noteworthy buildings, many of them situated on the campuses of major educational institutions throughout the country.

Aristeas, Letter of. Pseudoepigraphical work, ascribed to the historian Aristeas, which describes the origin of the Septuagint, the Greek translation of the Bible.

Ark (1). *Aron Kodesh* in Hebrew (lit., "holy chest"), the repository in the synagogue in which the Torah scrolls are kept. Hearkening back to the biblical Ark of the Covenant, the ark in a modern synagogue is usually set into or against a wall that faces toward Jerusalem (east, in the United States). In Jerusalem, the ark is placed on the wall of the synagogue that faces the Temple Mount. In most synagogues, the ark is the most significant architectural feature.

Ark (2). Floating structure in which Noah and his family survived the great Flood that God sent to destroy the entire human race because of their sinfulness. The ark was also the home of a male and female of every "unclean" species of living creature (to allow for their regeneration; Gen. 6:20), and seven pairs of each type of "clean" animal (needed for sacrifices after the Deluge; Gen. 7:2)

Ark of the Covenant. Oblong portable cabinet of acacia word, inlaid with pure gold both inside and outside, which contained both the shattered First Tablets and the intact Second Tablets of the Ten Commandments, as well as an *omer* of manna and the rod of Aaron. It was also said to contain the Book of Deuteronomy written by Moses. The Ark of the Covenant was carried by the Levites during the Israelites' trek through the wilderness as a visible reminder of the covenant between God and the people, providing assurance that the Divine Presence was always with them on their journey. Originally housed in the Tabernacle (see *Mishkan*), in the First Temple the Ark of the Covenant was kept in the Holy of Holies. Sometime before the destruction of the First Temple, the Ark of the Covenant disappeared and no trace of it has ever been found.

Armageddon. Apocalyptic battle prior to the Messianic Age at the end of days, when the forces of evil will be utterly destroyed by the forces of good. The term is also used in popular parlance to refer to any great loss of life in battle or even to the use of weapons of mass destruction. The word "Armageddon" may derive from the Hebrew phrase *Har Megiddo* (Mountain of Megiddo), which is situated in the southern Jezreel Valley and overlooks the site of many decisive battles in ancient times.

Aron Kodesh – see Ark.

Artificial insemination. In discussing the biblical law requiring a High Priest to marry a virgin (Lev. 21:13), the Talmud stated that he would be permitted to wed a virgin who became pregnant accidentally after bathing in water containing human semen (Chag. 15a). Consequently, virtually all rabbinic rulings on artificial insemination by a donor have refused to brand the act as adultery or regard the resulting child as illegitimate (see *mamzer*). Nevertheless, most Orthodox Jewish authorities condemn the practice on various legal grounds (e.g., placing into doubt the paternity of the child; the possible risk of an incestuous marriage between blood-relations conceived by a common donor; and mutual rights and duties [maintenance, honor, inheritance] of child and parents). In contrast, artificial insemination using sperm from the husband is generally accepted as a way to fulfill the duty of procreation, if for some reason normal conception is impossible.

Arusah. Affianced bride who, for all practical purposes, is regarded as a married woman (*eshet ish*). She is thus prohibited to any other man, since any such relationship would be considered adultery. (See *kiddushin*.)

Asceticism. A regimen of denying physical or psychological desires to avoid the temptations and distractions that hinder spiritual development. This might include frequent fasting, not drinking wine, wearing rough clothing, and distancing oneself from contact with other people. Although not a strong force in normative Judaism, which respects the human body and emphasizes moderation, Jewish groups utilizing ascetic practices included the Nazirites and Rechabites of the Bible; the Essenes during late Second Temple times; the Avelei Zion and the Hasidei Ashkenaz in the Middle Ages; and the devotees of some forms of kabbalistic thought.

Aseret ha-Dibrot. Hebrew term for the Ten Commandments.

Asham – see Guilt offering.

Ashamnu (We have transgressed). Initial word and name of the shorter confession of sins recited on Yom Kippur during the *Amidah*. It consists of 24 moral transgressions in alphabetical order in the Hebrew, with the last letter used three times. As each sin is recited, it is customary to lightly touch one's heart as a sign of contrition and spiritual awakening.

Asherah. Hebrew term that is translated as "idolatrous tree" or "sacred post." It was the symbol of Astarte, the Canaanite goddess of fertility and consort of El. Upon entering the Land of Canaan, the Israelites were commanded to "tear down their altars, smash their pillars, and cut down their sacred posts" (Exod. 34:13; Deut. 7:5, 12:3).

Ashkenazim. Designation first used in the Middle Ages for the Jews living in northwest Europe (northern France and western Germany) and the religious and cultural traditions they followed. Today, it refers to Jews of Northern and Eastern European (including Russian) background, with distinctive liturgical practices and religious and social customs that are contrasted with the Sephardim, Jews whose roots trace back to Spain and the Mediterranean region. Today, some 80% of world Jewry is of Ashkenazic origin.

Ashrei (Happy are they). Consisting of Psalm 145 plus two introductory verses (Ps. 84:5, 144:15) and one concluding verse (Ps. 115:18), it is read twice in the morning service (in the *Pesukei de-Zimra* and toward the end), and at the beginning of the afternoon service. The *Ashrei* might have been recited as early as the Second Temple period. Predominantly a Hebrew alphabetical acrostic, with the exception of the letter *nun*,[8] it contains the verse, "You open Your hand and satisfy the desire of every living thing," providing the comforting assurance that God's mercy is the ultimate source sustaining life.

Asiyah (action). In kabbalistic lore, the lowest of the four worlds or levels of creation. Because it is the realm of physical reality that requires full protection, at a Tu b'Shevat seder this world is represented by fruits and nuts that have tough outer shells, which must be discarded, and an inside that can be eaten – pomegranates, walnuts, almonds, pine nuts, chestnuts, hazelnuts, coconuts, Brazil nuts, pistachios, pecans, bananas, and melons.

Asmachta. From an Aramaic root meaning "support" or "reliance," a talmudic term denoting that a biblical text is used to support a *halacha*. It also is applied in civil law to a contract in which one of the parties binds himself to an unreasonable penalty, which presumes that there was a lack of deliberate intention on the part of the person entering into it. The general rule is that "an *asmachta* does not give title" (BB 168a), meaning that there must be other proof that the parties regarded the contract as binding.

Assimilation. The process of becoming incorporated into mainstream society by adopting the language, manners, and customs of the place in which one lives. For centuries, strict observance of Jewish laws and customs pertaining to dress, food, and religious holidays kept Jews separate and distinct from the culture of the country within which they were living. However, with the dawn of the Enlightenment (*Haskalah*), the opportunity arose for Jews to adapt to European culture while remaining Jewish. A key proponent of this concept in Germany was Moses Mendelssohn. However, Jews soon learned that merely adapting their culture and way of life to those of the majority was not sufficient to become fully accepted by their neighbors. Full citizenship and social and economic advancement required conversion to Christianity, so that baptism became the "ticket of admission to European civilization." The majority of Jews, however, refused to abandon Judaism.

Assyria. Ancient region on the upper Tigris River in western Asia Minor, named for its original capital, Assur. After being conquered first by the Akkadians and then by the Amorites and Babylonians, in the 12th century B.C.E. Assyria became an empire under Tiglath-Pileser, controlling the northern half of Mesopotamia from its capital, Nineveh. After almost two centuries of decline, Assyria was revitalized in the 9th century B.C.E. and established a powerful empire. In 722, it conquered the Northern Kingdom of Israel, dispersing its inhabitants (see Ten Lost Tribes) throughout the realm. The Assyrian advance was halted in 701, just before it reached the gates of Jerusalem. Less than a century later (612), the Babylonians destroyed Nineveh and the Assyrian Empire collapsed.

Astrology. The ancient study of the connection between the cycles of heavenly bodies and human behavior and the development of a systematic attempt to track this knowledge. Although indirectly condemned in the Bible and rejected by Maimonides, several medieval scholars (Saadia Gaon, Abraham ibn Ezra) and the kabbalists were great students of astrology. Some vestiges of astrology remain in Jewish folklore. *Mazel tov* (good luck; lit., "good constellation") has become the most common expression of congratulations among Jews. A person who succeeds in all his endeavors is know as a *bar mazel* (son of luck), while one who fails at everything is scorned by the Yiddish term "*shlimazel*."

Asur (prohibited). One of the three basic categories of Jewish law, it refers to a strictly forbidden activity.

Asylum – see Cities of refuge.

Ata hareitah (You have been shown). Opening Hebrew words introducing the series of biblical verses praising the wonders and glory of God that are recited by the prayer leader and repeated by the congregation before removing the Torah scrolls from the ark to begin the seven *hakafot* on Simchat Torah.

Atarah (crown). Reinforced band of cloth sewn to the top of the *tallit*. It is usually decoratively embroidered or inscribed with the Hebrew blessing for putting on the garment. When a man is buried in his *tallit*, the *atarah* is removed.

Atonement, Day of. English term for Yom Kippur, a time devoted to individual and communal repentance in which each Jew and the entire Jewish people strive to literally become "at one" with God through acts of atonement that will result in a change of conduct.

Atzei chaim. Literally "trees of life," the Hebrew term for the wooden rollers to which the Torah scroll is attached. The ends of the rollers, which protrude beyond the parchment, serve as handles for lifting and carrying the Torah and rolling it to the appropriate section to be read. The term is based on the verse, "It [the Torah] is a Tree of Life (*etz chaim*) to those grasp it" (Prov. 3:18). Some raise the base of the *atzei chaim* when they pronounce any form of the word "Torah" in the blessings recited before and after reading it, indicating that it is the identical Torah that Moses received on Mount Sinai.

Atzilut (emanation). In kabbalistic lore, the highest of the four worlds or levels of creation. As purely spiritual, the world of *atzilut* cannot be symbolized in any material way. Thus, it is the only one of the four worlds that is not represented by any fruit at the Tu b'Shevat seder.

Aufruf. Literally "calling up," this Yiddish term refers to the Ashkenazic custom of honoring a bridegroom by calling him up to the Torah on the Sabbath before his wedding. On this day, the bridegroom has precedence over all others, including a bar mitzvah, in being called for an *aliyah*. (Both the bridegroom and the bride-to-be are called to the Torah in liberal synagogues.) In the synagogues of medieval Europe, the *aufruf* was an opportunity to publicly announce the forthcoming wedding and to make certain that no congregant was aware of anything that would invalidate the marriage.

Auschwitz. Polish town (Oswiecim) near Cracow, which was the site of the largest concentration/death camp built by the Nazis. The original concentration camp was Auschwitz I, which remained the main camp that housed, among other elements, Gestapo torture cells and the barracks where gruesome pseudo-scientific medical experiments were performed. Auschwitz II, also known as Auschwitz-Birkenau, contained gas chambers and crematoria that could incinerate almost 5,000 human beings each day. Auschwitz III, also known as Monowitz, and its some 40 sub-camps used an endless supply of cruelly exploited slave labor for industrial production. Its chief facility was the I.G. Farben Buna plant for synthetic fuel production. Dagesch, a Farben subsidiary, produced the Zyklon B gas used in the gas chambers of Auschwitz-Birkenau. Over the entrance gate of the concentration camp was emblazoned the slogan, "Freedom through work." The gas chambers with crematoria ovens were disguised as public showers for the purpose of disinfection. More than 1.1 million human beings, 90% of them Jews, were murdered at Auschwitz, which has become a symbol of the Holocaust.

Auto-da(de)-fé. Literally "act of faith," a public ceremony in which judicial sentences of the Inquisition were pronounced and carried out in Spain and Portugal. The condemned heretic was brought to a principal church or the central square of a town in the presence of the chief dignitaries and great crowds, and an eminent cleric preached a fiery denunciatory sermon. The most severe penalty was public burning of the guilty party, though this did not strictly form part of the *auto-da-fé* since the Church did not want to be formally associated with the shedding of blood.

Autopsy. Whether autopsies are permitted is an extremely controversial issue among traditional Jews, bringing into direct opposition two fundamental principles – *kavod ha-met* (reverence for the human body after death) and *pikuach nefesh* (the preservation of life). Many rabbis have argued that the biblical requirement for burial as soon as possible (Deut. 21:22-23), combined with the prohibition against desecrating the corpse (see *nivul ha-met*), forbids mutilation of the body for post-mortem examination. However, the trend among modern halachists is that reverence for the corpse must yield to the superior value of life and its preservation, which overrides all but three commandments of the Torah (against idolatry, adultery, and murder). There is a universal consensus of opinion permitting autopsies in the case of violent or accidental death, or when a crime is suspected.

Av. The 5th month of the Jewish calendar (July/August). The 9th of Av (see Tisha b'Av) is the saddest day in the Jewish year.

Av beit din. Literally "father of the law court," this Hebrew title is conferred on the head of a Jewish religious court. During the Second Temple period, it referred to the vice president of the Supreme Court (see Sanhedrin) in Jerusalem. In geonic times, *av beit din* designated the assistant to the head of a Babylonian academy.

Av ha-Rachamim (Father of Mercy). Opening Hebrew words of a memorial prayer for Jewish martyrs and martyred communities, anonymously composed during the First Crusade that began in 1096. Rather than a prayer for sufficient strength to avenge the fallen martyrs, it requests that God choose how and when to exact punishment upon those who forced Jews to die *al Kiddush ha-Shem*.[9] It was originally recited only on the Sabbaths preceding Shavuot and Tisha b'Av, and at the conclusion of the *Yizkor* memorial service. In the Orthodox Ashkenazic tradition, however, the prayer has become a regular part of the Sabbath morning service, recited after the Torah reading before the scroll is returned to the ark.

Avadim (servants). Minor tractate added to the Talmud that deals with the laws regarding servants and the mutual obligations between slave and master.

Avadim Hayinu (We were slaves [to Pharaoh in Egypt]). Opening Hebrew words of the paragraph (often sung) that begins the telling of the story of the Exodus at the Passover seder. It stresses that, had God not redeemed our ancestors, we and our descendants would still be the slaves of Pharaoh. It also declares that, regardless of how learned, we nevertheless must relate the story of the Exodus, for whoever expands upon its telling is considered "praiseworthy." This is emphasized by the following paragraph, which tells of five talmudic scholars who stayed up all night discussing the Exodus from Egypt.

Aveilut. The period of mourning after the burial of a parent, child, sibling, or spouse (see mourning).

Avelei Zion (Mourners of Zion). Groups of Jews who mourned the destruction of the Second Temple and prayed for the redemption of Zion. The Talmud terms them *perushim* (ascetics), because they abstained from meat and wine as a sign of mourning. Refusing to engage in either commerce or trade, the Avelei Zion lived in great poverty and depended on the charity of Diaspora communities and pilgrims. Many of the Karaites who settled in Jerusalem in the early 9th century conducted their lives according to the customs of the Avelei Zion.

Avenger of blood – see Blood avenger.

Averah (sin). A violation of Jewish law that represents a transgression against the will of God. (See *sin*.)

Avinu Malkeinu (Our Father, our King). Opening Hebrew words of a penitential prayer that originated on fast days as a plea for rain. It now is found in an expanded version after the repetition of the *Amidah* in the morning and afternoon services during the Ten Days of Repentance from Rosh Hashanah through Yom Kippur. In the Ashkenazic tradition, *Avinu Malkeinu* is not recited on Shabbat (except during the concluding *Ne'ilah* service on Yom Kippur), both because penitential prayers are not said on that day and because its original association with fast days make it unsuitable for the Sabbath, which is dedicated to joyful experiences.[10] The core of *Avinu Malkeinu* is an appeal to God to "inscribe" (and on Yom Kippur, "seal") us in the book of (a) a good life and for (b) redemption and salvation; (c) sustenance and prosperity; (d) merit; and (e) forgiveness and pardon – not because of our personal merits, but rather on behalf of the martyrs of Israel and because of

God's own unfailing compassion.

Avinu she-ba-Shamayim (Our Father in Heaven). Rabbinic name of God that opens the modern prayer for the State of Israel.

Aviv (spring). One name for Passover is *Chag ha-Aviv* (Festival of Spring). Tel Aviv (lit., "Hill of Spring"), which was founded in 1909 as the first all-Jewish city, is now the commercial and cultural center of Israel.

Avodah. Literally "work" or "service," this Hebrew word originally referred to the sacrificial service in the Temple and the awesome ritual carried out by the High Priest on the Day of Atonement. During the talmudic period, the term was used to denote "prayer" or "worship" (i.e., service of God). Thus, Simeon the Pious said in *Pirkei Avot* (1:2), "The world depends on three things – Torah (study), *avodah* (service [of God]), and *gemilut chasadim* (acts of lovingkindness)." On Yom Kippur, "*Avodah*" is the term applied to the portion of the *Musaf* (additional) service that vividly describes the sacrificial ritual in the Temple on the Day of Atonement (based on Lev. 16 and Mishnah Yoma 1-7). *Avodah* is also the name of the 17th blessing in the weekday *Amidah*, which calls on God to "be favorable toward your people Israel and their prayer and restore the service to the Holy of Holies of Your Temple…[and accept their] fire-offerings."

Avodah Zarah (1) – see Idolatry.

Avodah Zarah (Av. Zar.) (2). The 8th tractate of Nezikin (damages) in the Mishnah, it deals with laws concerning the prohibition of idolatry.

Avon. Hebrew word denoting a sin of lust or uncontrollable emotion, done knowingly but not to defy God.

Avot (1) – see *Pirkei Avot*.

Avot (2). Literally "the fathers," the collective name for the Patriarchs – Abraham, Isaac, and Jacob. The term is applied to the first introductory blessing of the *Amidah*, which praises God for establishing the covenant with these ancestors of the Jewish people. It requests that our prayers be answered, not on the basis of our own unworthy accomplishments, but because of "the merits of the fathers" (*zechut avot*).

Avot de-Rabbi Natan (ARN). Minor tractate of the Talmud, a commentary on the Mishnah tractate Avot. (Avot has no Gemara, presumably because it does not focus on Jewish law.) Avot de-Rabbi Natan also contains substantial midrashic material. It has traditionally been ascribed to Nathan, the 2nd-century son of a

Babylonian Exilarch, who moved to Palestine and was the chief halachic adversary of Judah the Prince (though they had great respect for each other). However, most scholars now believe that it was composed much later (about 500 C.E.). Two very different versions (A, B) are extant today.

Axed heifer – see *Eglah arufah.*

Ayin. The 16th letter of the Hebrew alphabet, with a numerical value of 70.

Ayin ha-ra – see Evil Eye.

Azazel. Name either of a demon or the place to which one of the goats was sent as part of the Temple service on Yom Kippur. The Bible states that Aaron would cast lots upon two goats to select one as a sin-offering for the Lord and the other for Azazel (Lev. 16:8-10). Because this ritual took place only *after* the people had been forgiven, it appears that the goat for Azazel was merely a symbolic rite, emphasizing a cleansing of sins that had already taken place. Although the biblical text mandates that the goat sent to Azazel be set free, during talmudic times it was hurled to its death from a rocky precipice and the scarlet thread attached to its horns miraculously turned white, indicating that God had accepted the atonement of the people of Israel.[11]

Azharot. Liturgical poems (*piyyutim*) by various authors that focus on explanations and enumeration of the 613 commandments in the Torah. The one by Solomon ibn Gabirol is recited by Sephardim before the Torah reading on Shavuot.[12]

Az Yashir – see *Shirat ha-Yam.*

B

Baal. Canaanite and Phoenician god of fertility, portrayed as a man or bull. Influenced by Canaanite cults after entering the Promised Land, some Israelites lapsed into idolatry and the worship of Baal. King Ahab of the Northern Kingdom permitted Jezebel, his wicked Phoenician queen, to build a pagan altar and sanctuary to Baal. Elijah prophesied drought as a punishment for this idolatry and, when it came, even a public outcry failed to convince Ahab to forbid idol worship. In a dramatic confrontation on Mount Carmel (1 Kings 18), Elijah issued a challenge to the 450 priests of Baal – the deity who sent down fire from heaven to consume the sacrifice would be accepted as the true God. When the "fire of the Lord" consumed Elijah's sacrifice, the awe-struck people fell on their faces chanting, "The Lord He is God; the Lord, He is God;" then a heavy rain fell and the drought ended. Though some Baal worship persisted, it did not supplant traditional Jewish observances.

Baal ha-bayit. In addition to its literal meaning, "master of the household," this Hebrew term has been applied to denote a rich person or a married, dues paying male member of a congregation.

Baal korei. Literally "master of reading," the Hebrew term for the official Torah reader at a public prayer service. Originally, each person called to the Torah read his own portion. As Torah learning among the lay people declined, some were prevented from ever having an *aliyah*. One solution was to allow such a person to merely recite the appropriate blessings, while a knowledgeable official of the synagogue read the Torah selection. However, this practice publicly humiliated some members of the congregation by showing that they were so unlearned that they required a substitute to read for them. To solve this dilemma, the Rabbis decreed that an official Torah reader would read for everyone. With the person called to the Torah now only required to recite the prescribed blessings, the privilege of having an *aliyah* is available to all.[13]

Baal nes. Literally "master of the miracle" (miracle worker), this Hebrew title was given to several sages for their ability to perform miracles or because seemingly miraculous occurrences befell them. The most famous was the 2nd-century R.

Meir, who established his school in Tiberias and is usually associated with the tomb of "Meir Baal ha-Nes" in that city.

Baal Shem. Literally "master of the Name [of God]," this Hebrew term was used in the Middle Ages to refer to a Jewish miracle-working rabbi who could bring about cures and healing and had the mystical power to foresee or interpret events. Because of their good deeds, these individuals were deemed to have a close relationship with Heaven and the ability to invoke Divine mercy and compassion upon suffering human beings. The most famous was the Baal Shem Tov (Master of the Good Name), the charismatic 18th-century founder of Hasidism, who taught that all creation is imbued with the spirit of God and that even the most humble person could experience the Divine Presence.

Baal tefillah. Literally "master of prayer," a Hebrew term for the person leading the communal worship (see *shaliach tzibbur*).

Baal tekiah. Literally "master of blowing," the Hebrew title of the person who sounds the shofar during synagogue services on Rosh Hashanah and at the conclusion of Yom Kippur.

Baal teshuvah. Literally "master of return" and derived from a Hebrew word translated as "repentance," this term typically refers to a non-observant Jew who adopts a traditionally observant Jewish lifestyle. The quintessential *baal teshuvah* was Franz Rosenzweig. Ready to convert to Christianity, Rosenzweig attended an Orthodox service on Yom Kippur and was inspired to intensively study the Jewish tradition as well as write books that would draw other assimilated Jews to an appreciation and love for what he termed the "inner fire of the Jewish star of redemption." Stressing that fulfilling the commandments is a gradual process of personal growth, Rosenzweig's response when asked about those *mitzvot* he did not keep was "not yet."

Babel, Tower of. In the generation after the Flood, when all people spoke the same language and were clustered in the same place, they decided to rebel against God and build a tower (like the Babylonian *ziggurat*) that would reach all the way to Heaven. Incurring Divine fury, the tower was destroyed and human beings were scattered across the earth and forced to speak many different languages. One moral of the story is that rebellion against God also leads to the separation of human beings from one another. The biblical text derives the name "Babel" from the Hebrew word "*balal*" (confuse), because "there the Lord confounded the speech of the whole earth" (Gen. 11:1-9).

Babi Yar. A ravine on the outskirts of Kiev, where in 1941 more than 33,000 Ukrainian Jews were machine-gunned to death by a special SS unit aided by

Ukrainian collaborators. This event has come to symbolize Jewish martyrdom at the hands of the Nazis in the Soviet Union. By the end of German rule over Kiev, Babi Yar had become a mass grave for some 100,000 Nazi victims, mostly Jews. The massacre at Babi Yar was memorialized in an impassioned poem by Yevgeni Yevtushenko, which was later set to music by Dmitri Shostakovich in his 13th Symphony.

Babylonia. Named for its capital city, this ancient state in southern Mesopotamia (modern Iraq) combined the territories of Sumer and Akkad. Its most famous ruler was Hammurabi, who issued his famous Code of Laws in about 1750 B.C.E. Years of domination by Assyria ended when the Babylonians rebelled in the late 7th century, sacking Nineveh, the Assyrian capital, in 612. Under Nebuchadnezzar, Babylonia conquered Jerusalem in 586 B.C.E., destroying the First Temple and carrying off the Israelites into captivity. Within a half century, the Persian Empire under Cyrus defeated the Babylonians, and the Israelites were permitted to return to Jerusalem and rebuild the Temple.

Babylonian Exile. After the conquest of Jerusalem and the destruction of the First Temple in 586 B.C.E., much of the population of Judah was exiled to Babylonia. "By the rivers of Babylon there we sat down, yea, we wept, as we remembered Zion" (Ps. 137:1). In time, however, the Israelites developed their own traditions and institutions in this strange land. The Babylonian rulers gave them autonomy in religious and spiritual matters, which resulted in the emergence of the synagogue and words of comfort from the prophets Ezekiel and Deutero-Isaiah. The Jews were allowed to engage freely in agriculture and trade. When Cyrus of Persia defeated the Babylonians in 539 B.C.E., he fulfilled Isaiah's prophecy by permitting the exiled Israelites to return to Jerusalem and rebuild the Temple. However, the majority remained in their adopted land, where they had maintained their religious identity while reaching a standard of living never known previously. This vibrant community was critical to Jewish survival during subsequent eras, when few Jews remained in the Land of Israel.

Babylonian Talmud. A compendium of the wide-ranging discussions and elaborate interpretations of the Mishnah by scholars known as *amora'im* (Aramaic for "explainers") in the great academies of learning in Babylonia. In general usage, the term "Talmud" refers to the Babylonian Talmud (*Talmud Bavli*), which tradition dates from the first half of the 3rd century (Rav and Samuel) to its editing by Rav Ashi and Ravina around 500 (though the final editing was probably completed by the middle of the 6th century by the *Savora'im*, the disciples of the last *amora'im* and their immediate successors). The Babylonian Talmud is a monumental work, aptly termed the "sea of Talmud," which consists of approximately 2.5 million words on 5,894 folio pages. Far more extensive than its Palestinian counterpart, the Babylonian Talmud is regarded as the most authoritative compilation of the

Oral Law. It deals with a wide array of topics ranging from religion and ethics to politics and social problems.

Bachur. Literally "young man," this Hebrew term refers to a fighter in the Bible and to an unmarried man in rabbinic literature. In the Middle Ages, *bachur* denoted an advanced yeshiva student.

Badchan. Literally "joker" or "merrymaker," this Yiddish world was applied to itinerant entertainers who performed at Eastern European weddings, singing songs and reciting poems composed specially for the bride and groom. They also entertained at Chanukah and Purim celebrations, telling comic stories and making jests based on verses from the Bible and tales from the Talmud.

Badge, Jewish. Distinctive sign, usually a cloth badge (especially yellow), which Jews were forced to wear to denote their subordinate social status relative to members of the dominant religion. In Muslim countries, Jews (and Christians) were required to don special clothes and hats. The "Jewish hat" was also popular in Christian lands, where the Fourth Lateran Council (1215) mandated that Jews be physically distinguished from members of the majority religion. In Nazi Germany beginning in the fall of 1941, Jews were required to wear a yellow Star of David with the letter "J" or the word "*Jude*" inside.

Bagel. Once a characteristically Jewish food, in the United States the bagel has become omnipresent. One explanation for the name of this yeasted roll is that it comes from a German word meaning "ring" or "bracelet," which describes its shape. The unique texture of a bagel comes from being boiled in water before baking, which produces a crisp crust and moist, chewy interior. In medieval Europe, bagels were given to women about to give birth, as well as to the midwives who attended them, to drive away evil spirits and demons. In the United States, bagels are commonly sliced and served with cream cheese and lox, toppings that were never combined with bagels in Europe.[14]

Bahir – see *Sefer ha-Bahir*.

Bailee. If property entrusted to someone's care was lost, stolen, or damaged, the liability of the custodian varied according to whether the guardian was compensated for the task and whether what occurred was reasonably foreseeable. An unpaid custodian, who kept the property of his neighbor without deriving any benefit from it, was only responsible for damages resulting from negligence. A paid custodian, or one who paid for using the property (hirer), was expected to be more vigilant and thus had more liability (since he, as well as the owner, was profiting from it). The paid custodian or hirer was generally responsible for loss or theft, because he should have protected the property more diligently. However, the owner bore the risk if the occurrence was an unpreventable accident or due to unforeseen circumstances. A borrower who was keeping the property solely for his own advantage was responsible for every type of loss, unless it occurred in the course of its normal use.

Balabusta. Yiddish term that literally means "mistress of the house." This complimentary term describes an efficient housewife who graciously and creatively manages the multiple chores of running a household.

Balagan. Slang Hebrew word that can be translated as "mess, confusion, or chaos."

Balak. The 7th *parashah* in the Book of Numbers (22:2-25:9), it narrates the tale of Balak, the Moabite king, who hires the prophet Balaam to curse the Israelites, but Balaam ends up blessing them instead. It concludes with the idolatrous orgy at Baal-Peor and the zealous act of Pinchas.

Balfour Declaration. Letter from Arthur James Balfour, British Foreign Secretary, to Lord Lionel Walter Rothschild, president of the Zionist Federation of England, sent on November 2, 1917. The Balfour Declaration included the famous sentence: "His Majesty's government view with favor the establishment in Palestine of a national home for the Jewish people." The Declaration followed years of intensive negotiations that Chaim Weizmann and other leaders of British Jewry held with the British government in an attempt to obtain a charter sanctioning and legalizing Jewish settlement in Palestine, which had been vainly sought by Theodor Herzl.

Bal taschit (do not destroy). Derived from the biblical prohibition against destroying fruit-bearing trees when laying siege to a city (Deut. 20:19), the Rabbis expanded this concept to forbid the wanton destruction of anything valuable to human existence, including vessels, clothing, buildings, springs, and food. Destruction for a positive purpose, such as cutting trees to construct a dwelling, is permitted.

Bameh madlikin (with what may we light). The 2nd Mishnah of the tractate Shabbat, which is read immediately following the *Kabbalat Shabbat* prayers on Friday evening. It details the permitted and prohibited wicks and oils for the Sabbath lamps. This section also tangentially mentions the *eruv*, which allows carrying from one domain to another on the Sabbath, and the tithes that provided food to the Levites and made the remaining food permissible to eat.[15]

Bamidbar (1). Literally "in the wilderness," the Hebrew name for the 4th book of the Bible (see Numbers).

Bamidbar (2). The 1st *parashah* in the Book of Numbers (1:1-4:20), it describes the census in the wilderness; the arrangement of the tribes in the Israelite camp; and the census and duties of the Levites.

Bamot – see High places.

Ban – see *Cherem*.

Bar. Aramaic word meaning "son of," which occurs as a part of male personal names (e.g., Bar Kochba, "son of a star"). It also can denote a member of a class, as in the term "bar mitzvah" (i.e., a boy who is now old enough to be among those obligated to fulfill the commandments).

Bar Giora. Secret organization of young Jewish "irregulars" who guarded the early settlements in the Land of Israel when it was under Ottoman rule. Founded in 1907 and named for Simon bar Giora, the Zealot leader in the war against Rome (67–70 C.E.), its members eventually merged with the new defense body, Hashomer.

Bar Ilan University. Only American-chartered university in Israel, founded by the American Mizrachi movement in 1955 in the Tel Aviv suburb of Ramat Gan. It was named in honor of Rabbi Meir Bar Ilan (Berlin), a spiritual leader who raised traditional Judaism from the ashes of the Holocaust to rebirth and renaissance in the Land of Israel. Today Israel's largest academic center, Bar Ilan University blends high-quality secular training in liberal arts and sciences with traditional Jewish religious teachings.

Bar Lev Line. Series of underground forts, mine fields, and observation posts running for about 100 miles, which was constructed along the east bank of the Suez Canal following Israel's victory in the Six Day War (1967). Named for its creator, General Haim Bar-Lev, the line was completed in 1969 and designed to provide both early warning of any Egyptian attack and stiff resistance to it. However, during the Yom Kippur War of 1973, the undermanned and overestimated defensive line could not resist the advancing Egyptian army.

Bar mitzvah (lit., "son of the commandment"). Celebration of a boy's 13th birthday according to the Jewish calendar, when he officially attains his legal and religious maturity. Upon reaching this age, he is obliged to fulfill all the commandments and observe the religious duties incumbent on a Jew. As part of the bar mitzvah ceremony, which usually takes place on a Sabbath morning (but can occur on a Monday or Thursday or a Saturday afternoon when the Torah is also read), the boy is called up to the Torah for his first *aliyah* to read the *maftir* portion and then chant the *haftarah*. He usually delivers a *devar Torah* and, following the service, a festive *kiddush* is held in his honor.

Bar mitzvah, adult. It has now become common for Jews who were denied religious training in their childhood to celebrate a bar mitzvah (or bat mitzvah) as adults as a symbol of their full membership in the Jewish community. Although these ceremonies can be moving experiences, and the extensive preparatory study should be encouraged and praised, it is important to remember that the essence of the bar mitzvah (or bat mitzvah) is only the *age* of the individual; the transition to legal and religious responsibility is automatic and does not depend on any special initiation rites.

Baraita. An Aramaic word meaning "outside," a *baraita* is a piece of legal, historic, or *aggadic* tradition that was not included in the Mishnah of Judah the Prince. *Baraitot* are attributed to rabbinic teachers who lived in the Land of Israel at or before the time of the Mishnah. The *amora'im* in the Babylonian Talmud employed *baraitot* for supplementary, comparative, corroborative, or critical purposes, or for solving newly raised problems. When a *baraita* contradicted a *mishnah*, the latter usually was considered more authoritative. In the Talmud, a *baraita* is introduced by the formula "*teno rabbanan*" (the Rabbis taught) or *tanya tena* (it was taught). A collection of *baraitot* arranged according to the order of the Mishnah is called the Tosefta.

Barchi nafshi (Praise [the Lord], O my soul), opening words of Psalm 104 and the title by which it is known. A superb example of ancient Hebrew poetry, the psalm glorifies God as the Creator of the beautiful and majestic universe. It is recited on Rosh Chodesh and, according to traditional Ashkenazic custom, also on Sabbath afternoons between Sukkot and Passover along with the 15 "Songs of Ascent" (see *Shir ha-Ma'alot*). (During the rest of the year, these psalms are replaced by the recitation of *Pirkei Avot*.)

Barchu (Let us praise). Ceremonial call to worship by the prayer leader at the formal beginning of the daily morning and evening services. It is recited while standing and only in the presence of a *minyan*. After the prayer leader recites the invocation *Barchu et Adonai ha-mevorach* (Praise the Lord, who is [to be] praised), which includes bending the knee and bowing at the waist, the congregation responds *Baruch Adonai ha-mevorach l'olam va-ed* (Praised is the Lord, who is [to be] praised for ever and ever). *Barchu* is also recited by each person who is called up for an *aliyah* during the reading of the Torah, and is followed by the same congregational response.

Barley. Grain used in the bread, cakes, and porridge that formed the staple of the Israelite diet during biblical times. The importance of barley can be seen from the injunction that the valuation of a field was determined according to the amount of this grain that could be sown in it (Lev. 27:16). When wheat became more plentiful and the preferred flour of choice in mishnaic times, barley was relegated to food for the poor and for livestock. As the first grain to ripen, barley was a symbol of spring (Ruth 1:22). The first *omer* of barley was reaped on the second day of Passover, marking the beginning of the spring harvest season (Lev. 23:9-15). The end of the barley harvest is associated with the festival of Shavuot, when the Book of Ruth, which takes place during the barley harvest, is read in synagogue.

Barrenness. A recurrent theme in the Bible is the motif of the barren wife. In the ancient world, where the major role of a woman was to be a wife and mother, infertility was devastating. Its source was assumed to be the woman, although the will of God was deemed the ultimate cause. Three of the four Matriarchs experienced difficulty conceiving and bearing children. Sarah and Rachel were forced to resort to having their maidservants, Hagar and Bilhah, produce a child for Abraham and Jacob, respectively (Gen. 16:2-3; 30:3-4). The mothers of two other famous biblical figures – Samson (Judg. 13:2-3) and Samuel (1 Sam. 1-2) – also had difficulty bearing a child. In both of these cases God intervened, sending a messenger to announce to the couple the impending birth of a child who would become a major figure in Israelite history. The Rabbis taught that supporting and teaching a child was tantamount to fulfilling the *mitzvah* of procreation (Sanh. 19b).

Baruch (1). Opening word of all blessings. Although often translated as "blessed," in context the word is the equivalent of "praised," for it would be impossible for humans to add anything to God's powers or possessions.

Baruch (2). Apocryphal book attributed to the secretary and confidant of the prophet Jeremiah. It describes how this 7th-century B.C.E. Israelite scribe wrote down Jeremiah's words in the biblical book that bears his name. There are also various versions of an apocalyptic work attributed to Baruch, which relate his experiences before and after the destruction of Jerusalem and his subsequent journey through the heavens.

Baruch ata Adonai (Praised are You, O Lord). Opening three words of all blessings (*brachot*). When the blessing occurs at the beginning of a prayer, the words *Eloheinu melech ha-olam* (our God, King of the Universe) are added. Blessings for experiences of enjoyment conclude with a reference to the experience that called for the blessing. Thus, in the blessing over bread, one adds *ha-motzi lechem min ha-aretz* (Who brings forth bread from the earth); for wine, the blessing concludes *borei peri ha-gafen* (Who creates the fruit of the vine). Blessings for the privilege of performing religious commandments have an expanded formula — *asher kidshanu be-mitzvotav ve-tzivanu* (Who has sanctified us with commandments and commanded us to ...) — and conclude with the specific *mitzvah* that is about to be performed. Thus, when ritually washing the hands, one adds *al netilat yadayim*. An exception is lighting the candles on Friday night, when one says the blessing and adds *le-hadlik ner shel Shabbat* before kindling the Sabbath lights.

Baruch ha-ba. Literally "blessed is he who comes" and meaning "welcome," it is a Hebrew greeting to a visitor or new acquaintance. At a circumcision, the guests rise and welcome the infant boy with these words. This is especially appropriate since in Hebrew the numerical value of "*ha-ba*" is eight, and the celebrants are effectively welcoming "the eight-day-old."

Baruch ha-Shem (praised is the Name [of God]). Expression of thanksgiving, equivalent to "thank God," which is said upon hearing good news. It is especially used in response to the question "How are you?" to indicate that the person is doing well.

Baruch Hu u-varuch Shemo (praised is He and praised is His Name). Traditional congregational response to the mention of God's name in the first part of a blessing. The response to the second half is "amen."

Baruch she-Amar (Praised is He who spoke [and the world came into being]). Prayer that opens the *Pesukei de-Zimra* section of the morning service in the Ashkenazic tradition. (In the Sephardic tradition, verses and psalms precede it.) It praises God as Creator of the world and stresses the concept of Divine mercy. Combining the second line (*baruch Hu*, "praised is He") and the final line (*baruch shemo*, "praised is His Name") of this prayer results in *baruch Hu u-varuch* *Shemo* (praised is He and praised is His Name), the traditional congregational response whenever the name of God is recited in any blessing.[16]

Baruch shem k'vod malchuto l'olam va-ed (Praised be the name of His glorious kingdom forever and ever). Blessing recited after the first verse of the *Shema*. Although said aloud in Temple times, today it is spoken in an undertone except on Yom Kippur, when it is said aloud in remembrance of the response of the people as they prostrated themselves when the High Priest uttered the Holy Name of God (*YHVH*, the Tetragrammaton) after each of his three confessions. It remains a custom in some communities for worshipers to completely bow down on the floor of the synagogue when this part of the *Avodah* service is read.

Baruch she-petarani. After the bar mitzvah boy concludes the second Torah blessing, it is customary in Orthodox synagogues for his father to declare: "Praised is [God] who has relieved me from punishment because of this child [when he misbehaved]" (Gen. R. 63:10). The reason for saying this blessing is that before age 13, it is the responsibility of the father to make certain that his son studies

Torah and performs *mitzvot*. However, once the boy reaches the age of maturity, this becomes the son's personal responsibility. Thereafter, if the son fails to pursue Torah studies, the father is exempt from any spiritual punishment resulting from this sin of omission.[17]

Basel. City in Switzerland that hosted the First Zionist Congress, a convocation called by Theodor Herzl in 1897. This symbolic Parliament for those in sympathy with the implementation of Zionist goals consisted of about 200 attendees from 17 countries, 69 of whom were delegates from various Zionist societies and the remainder individual invitees.

Basel Program. Declaration of the goals of the new Zionist movement. In brief, it stated: "Zionism seeks to establish a home for the Jewish people in *Eretz -Israel* [Land of Israel] secured under public law." This would entail (1) the settlement of Jewish farmers, artisans, and manufacturers; (2) the organization and uniting of the whole of Jewry by means of appropriate institutions, both local and international; (3) the strengthening and fostering of Jewish national sentiment and national consciousness; and (4) preparatory steps toward obtaining the consent of governments, where necessary, in order to reach the goals of Zionism.

Bashert. Literally "fate" or "destiny," this Yiddish term refers to a destined spouse or perfect mate. According to the Talmud, marriages are preordained by Heaven. "Forty days before the birth of a child, a voice in heaven announces: 'The daughter of so-and-so will marry the son of so-and-so'" (Sot. 2a). The mystical *Zohar* maintained that each soul is created both male and female, divided before birth and ultimately reunited when a man and woman marry.[18] In addition, *bashert* can also refer to any fortuitous coincidence that seems to have been fated to occur.

Bastard – see *Mamzer*.

Bat. Hebrew word meaning "daughter of."

Bat ko*l*. Literally "daughter of the voice," this Hebrew expression is commonly used in the Talmud to denote a heavenly voice or the voice of God, which is heard by individuals or groups of people. Distinct from a prophetic communication, it often functions in the context of giving approval to a halachic decision.

Bat mitzvah (lit., "daughter of the commandment"). In Orthodox Judaism, where women do not have the same ritual obligations and privileges as men (such as being counted in the *minyan* or being called up to the Torah for an *aliyah*), there was no need for girls to have a formal ceremony like the bar mitzvah.[19] Nevertheless, by the 19th century some families celebrated a girl's 12th birthday, according to the Jewish calendar, with a special meal (*se'udat mitzvah*) and other non-synagogue rituals.[20] The first bat mitzvah to be celebrated in conjunction with a worship service occurred in 1922 and featured Judith Kaplan, the daughter of Rabbi Mordecai Kaplan, then a professor at the Jewish Theological Seminary and later the founder of the Reconstructionist movement. In contemporary Conservative and Reform congregations, young women at age 13 have a ceremony identical to the bar mitzvah for boys.

Bat mitzvah, adult – see Bar mitzvah, adult.

Batlanim. Literally "ten men of leisure," the Hebrew term for individuals who were highly respected for their piety and learning and constituted the core of the permanent congregation in larger communities. Alleviating the problem of finding a *minyan* for synagogue services, the presence of these ten men was one of the identifying features of a "big city" as opposed to a town or village.[21] (See *minyan men.*) In Yiddish, "*batlan*" refers to an unemployed or lazy man who has no trade or regular means of earning a living.

Bava Batra (BB). Third section of the first tractate of Nezikin (damages) in the Mishnah, it deals with property law (real estate, inheritance, sales, and partnerships) and such issues as beautification and protection of the environment and honest business practices. The term *bava* (gate) was used to denote a section of a book, and this is the last of the three sections.

Bava Kamma (BK). First section of the first tractate of Nezikin (damages) in the Mishnah, it deals with torts (damages to person and property). It requires wrongdoers to ask for forgiveness and injured parties to grant it.

Bava Metzia (BM). Second section of the first tractate of Nezikin (damages) in the Mishnah, it deals with civil law (lost and found property, fraud, usury, bailments, relations with workers). It is characterized by a deep concern for the welfare of the poorest and weakest members of society.

Bavli (Babylonian). Shorthand term indicating the Babylonian Talmud.

B.C.E. (acronym for "**B**efore the **C**ommon **E**ra"). This neutral term is used by Jews and biblical scholars to denote the period traditionally labeled "B.C." (before [the birth of] Christ) by Christians.

Be fruitful and multiply (*p'ru ur'vu*). The first commandment in the Bible (Gen. 1:18), it requires human beings to procreate so that God's creation will be continuously replenished with new life.

Beard. In biblical times, the beard was regarded as a symbol of manly beauty and virility and a natural feature distinguishing men from women. Shaving the head and beard were considered signs of mourning and great sorrow. Ironically, since many Jewish men are now clean-shaven, growing a beard – as opposed to shaving – has become a sign of mourning. The Torah prohibits shaving the "side-growth of your beard" (see *payot* and shaving).

Bechor – see Firstborn.

Bechorot (Bech.). The 4th tractate of Kodashim (holy things) in the Mishnah. Literally meaning "firstlings," it deals with the laws relating to firstborn children and animals.

Bechukotai. The 10th and final *parashah* in the Book of Leviticus (26:3-27:34), it contains the list of blessings and curses that would be the rewards and punishments of the Israelites for respectively obeying and disobeying God's laws (see *Tochachah*). This section also describes the laws regarding valuations, firstlings, and some tithes.

Bedeken di kallah (covering of the bride). Yiddish term for an ancient Jewish tradition in which the groom lets down the veil over the face of his bride before the marriage ceremony. The major reason for the *bedeken* ceremony is that it permits the groom to clearly identify his bride before she is veiled, so that he is not fooled as was Jacob when his conniving father-in-law Laban substituted Leah, his elder daughter, for Jacob's beloved Rachel (Gen. 29:23–38).

Bedikah (search). Hebrew term for the detailed examination of the carcass of a kosher-slaughtered animal. It is performed by the ritual slaughterer (see *shochet*) to detect any defect of the major organs that would render the animal *treif* and thus forbidden for consumption by Jews.

Bedikat chametz – see *Chametz*, search for.

Bedtime prayers. Before going to sleep, the traditional Jew recites prayers that are built around the *Shema* and were considered protection against the dangers of the night (Ber. 5a). The final prayer is *Adon Olam*, the last verse of which is: "Into God's hand I shall entrust my spirit when I go to sleep – and I shall awaken! With my spirit shall my body remain, God is with me, I shall not fear." After reciting the bedtime prayers, the Jew can sleep peacefully. Should he not awaken from sleep, he has the comforting assurance of having finished his mortal existence with the traditional affirmation of the unity of God.[22]

Be'er Sheva. Capital of the Negev. The Hebrew name of this ancient town can be translated as either "well of the seven" or "well of the oath," referring to the biblical account of the pact that Abraham made with Abimelech over a well that the Patriarch had dug in the desert. The phrase "from Dan to Be'er Sheva" occurs frequently throughout the Bible, indicating the northern and southern boundaries of Israelite territory. In Roman and Byzantine times, Be'er Sheva was a prosperous station on the route from the Red Sea to the Mediterranean. The pride of Israel's modern city of Be'er Sheva is the Ben Gurion University of the Negev.

Beha'alotecha. The 3rd *parashah* in the Book of Numbers (8:1-12:16), it describes the lighting of the Menorah; the second Passover; the manna and quail; and Miriam and Aaron speaking "against Moses because of the Cushite woman he had married."

Be-har. The 9th *parashah* in the Book of Leviticus (25:1-26:2), it details the laws concerning the Sabbatical Year when the land would rest, and the Jubilee Year of emancipation and restoration.

Beheimah. Derived from a Hebrew word for "animal," this Yiddish term refers to someone who exhibits uncouth, boorish behavior.

Beheimot. King of the land beasts that, according to tradition, was created on the fifth day. Like its adversary Leviathan, the sea monster, Beheimot was destined to feed the righteous at the messianic banquet at the End of Days following a titanic struggle between them.

Beilis case. Notorious 1913 ritual murder (see blood libel) trial in Kiev, Russia. Mendel Beilis was accused of killing a Russian Christian boy, whose body had been found near the brick factory where Beilis worked. Although an investigation soon established that non-Jewish thieves had murdered the boy, the Beilis case dragged on for more than two years. As a way of publicly indicting the entire Jewish people, the anti-Semitic Czarist Russian regime accused Beilis of committing this crime to use the boy's blood for the baking of *matzot* for Passover. At the trial, Russian "experts" gave false testimony and the judge was prejudiced. Nevertheless, Beilis was acquitted by a jury of simple Russian peasants, thanks to his brilliant team of defense lawyers and intense international protests. *The Fixer*, a dramatic fictionalized account of the Beilis case, earned the Pulitzer Prize for author Bernard Melamud.

Bein adam la-chavero ([transgressions] between one human being and another). For these sins, Yom Kippur does not secure atonement unless one has sought forgiveness from the other person and redressed the hurtful behavior. If necessary, one must attempt three times to seek forgiveness from another person. If forgiveness is not granted – itself a grave sin – the burden of seeking exoneration is removed from the transgressor.

Bein adam la-Makom ([transgressions] between human beings and God). For these sins, Yom Kippur brings pardon for sin if there is repentance. However, the forgiving quality of Yom Kippur is ineffective if one thinks: "I will sin and the Day of Atonement will procure atonement." Similarly, the person who says: "I will sin and repent, and sin again and repent" will not be afforded any opportunity to do so.

Bein ha-arbayim. Literally "between the evenings," the time between sunset and dark (see twilight). This was the time mandated by the Torah (Exod. 12:6) for slaughtering the paschal lamb.

Bein ha-meitzarim. Literally "between the straits," the Hebrew term for the three-week period of mourning that extends from the 17th of Tammuz through Tisha b'Av. It commemorates the period leading up to the destruction of the First and Second Temples in Jerusalem. Traditional Jews do not schedule any festive occasions during this period.

Beit chaim. Literally "house of the living," a euphemistic Hebrew term for a cemetery (See *euphemism.*)

Beit din. Literally "house of judgment," the rabbinic term for a Jewish court of law. Classically composed of three rabbis who arbitrated disputes among Jews on a variety of issues in civil law, today it primarily focuses on religious matters, such as the granting of a *get* (divorce) or decisions regarding conversion.

Beit El. Israelite town, situated 10 miles north of Jerusalem, where Abraham built an altar to the Lord (Gen. 12:6-9) and Jacob dreamed of a ladder connecting earth and heaven with angels of God ascending and descending it (Gen. 28:1-20). After the conquest of Canaan, the Tabernacle and the Ark were placed in Beit El (Judg. 20:26-27). The importance of Beit El decreased after Solomon built the Temple in Jerusalem. However, with the division of the monarchy after his death, Beit El became a major town in the Northern Kingdom. Jeroboam erected a shrine with a golden calf in Beit El to serve as a substitute for the *cherubim* in the Temple, thus attempting to dissuade the people from making pilgrimages to Jerusalem in the rival Southern Kingdom.

Beit ha-mikdash. Literally, "house of holiness," this Hebrew term referred to the Sanctuary or Temple.

Beit Hillel. With Beit Shammai, two schools of Pharisaic rabbinic sages during the late 1st century B.C.E. and early 1st century C.E. In general, the talmudic Rabbis decided the *halacha* in accordance with the opinions of Hillel and his school, which were more lenient and easier for the people to understand. According to tradition, in messianic times the *halacha* will revert to the stricter opinions of the House of Shammai, since people then will be able to understand and appreciate his great insights into matters of Torah.

Beit knesset. Literally "house of assembly," this Hebrew phrase is used to refer to a synagogue, which is a gathering place for the Jewish community.

Beit midrash. Literally "house of study," in talmudic times this Hebrew term was used to describe an academy for the study of Jewish religious texts that was presided over by a legal scholar. Today, it refers to an independent religious school or one located in a synagogue.

Beit olam. Literally "house of eternity," a Hebrew term for a cemetery.

Beit sefer. Literally, "house of [the] book," this Hebrew term refers to a religious school.

Beit Shammai – see Beit Hillel.

Beit She'arim. Town in southern Galilee that was the location of the Jewish necropolis during the Roman period. Founded during the reign of King Herod at the end of the 1st century B.C.E., after the destruction of Jerusalem in 70 C.E. Beit She'arim served as a site of the Sanhedrin and the residence of Judah the Prince, the editor of the Mishnah. However, Beit She'arim is best known for its large cemetery, where many Jews both in the Land of Israel and the Diaspora were buried during the 3rd and 4th centuries. The work of cutting a complex network of catacombs and burial caves into the slopes of the hills southwest of the town was apparently an important part of the economy of Beit She'arim.

Beit tefillah. Literally "house of prayer," one of the Hebrew terms for a synagogue.

Beitzah (1). Hebrew term for the roasted egg placed on the Passover seder plate. Representing the special festival offering (*chagigah*) of each Jew going up to the Temple in Jerusalem, it is also a symbol of mourning for the destruction of the Temple (the first day of Passover is always on the same day of the week as Tisha b'Av) as well as of life, birth, fertility, and regeneration.

Beitzah (2). The 7th tractate of Mo'ed (festivals) in the Mishnah, it deals with general laws regarding the festivals. The first two chapters focus on the controversies between Beit Hillel and Beit Shammai.

Belzec. Polish town in the Lublin district of Nazi-occupied Poland, which was the site of a Nazi death camp established in the spring of 1942. Extermination was by means of gas issuing from diesel engines. Several hundred thousand Jews perished in Belzec, and there was only one post-war survivor.

Ben. Hebrew word meaning "son of," which occurs as a part of male personal names (e.g., Ben Gurion).

Ben adam. Phrase used almost 90 times to denote the prophet Ezekiel in the biblical book that bears his name. Although often translated literally as "son of man," it simply means "human being." According to Hebrew grammar, the root "*ben*" in a compound word does not mean "son of," but rather implies class membership (i.e., a member of the group known as "man"). Similarly, *B'nai Yisrael* means Israelites, rather than the literal "Children of Israel."

Ben Sira, Wisdom of – see Wisdom of Ben Sira.

Bene Israel. Literally "Sons of Israel," the largest sector of the Jewish community in India. They claim to be descended from Jews who escaped the Galilee during the persecution by Antiochus Epiphanes in the 2nd century B.C.E. Although resembling the non-Jewish Maratha people in appearance and customs, an indication of intermarriage between Jews and Indians, the Bene Israel maintained the practices of the Jewish dietary laws, circumcision, and observance of the Sabbath as a day of rest. Some 40,000 Bene Israel now live in Israel; fewer than 5,000 remain in India.

Benediction – see Blessing.

Bentsch. Yiddish word meaning "bless," it usually refers to saying the Grace after Meals. The Sephardic term is *bencao.*

Bentsch licht. Yiddish phrase meaning "bless the light," it refers to kindling the candles for the Sabbath or a festival.

Bentscher. Yiddish term for a small booklet containing the *Birkat ha-Mazon* (Grace after Meals) and other prayer and songs (*zemirot*) associated with a meal. Often distributed after the festive meal to those attending a bar/bat mitzvah or wedding, it is usually personalized with the name and date of the celebration.

Berachot (Ber.). The 1st tractate in Zera'im (seeds) and the initial tractate in the entire Mishnah, it deals with blessings and prayers, illustrating the central role these play in Jewish life.

Bereshit (1). Hebrew term for the Book of Genesis. The first word in the Bible, it can be translated as "in the beginning" or "when [God] began to create."

Bereshit (2). The 1st *parashah* in the Book of Genesis (1:1-6:8), it describes the Creation, the Garden of Eden, and the narratives of Adam and Eve and Cain and Abel, before concluding with a list of genealogies.

Bergen-Belsen. Nazi concentration camp near Hanover in Germany. It opened in July 1943 as a "transit camp" for those that the German government wished to exchange for their soldiers taken prisoner by the Allies. The conditions in the camp deteriorated, and by early 1945 thousands of prisoners had arrived from camps in the east that had been evacuated because of the advance of the Russian Army. About 40,000 people, including Anne Frank, died in Bergen-Belsen before it was liberated by British troops. From 1945 to 1950, Bergen-Belsen became the largest displaced persons camp in Europe.

Beri'ah (creation). In kabbalistic lore, the next-to-the highest of the four worlds or levels of creation. At a Tu b'Shevat seder, this world is symbolized by fruits that have neither pits on the inside nor shells on the outside and thus are totally edible (even though they have small seeds) – grapes, figs, apples, *etrogim* (citrons), lemons, pears, raspberries, blueberries, carobs, and quinces.

Bermuda Conference. Anglo-American sponsored conference that convened in April 1943, during the time of the Warsaw Ghetto uprising, to discuss various methods of rescuing the victims of Nazi persecution. However, with the United States unwilling to relax its immigration laws and Great Britain adamant against allowing more Jews into the Land of Israel, the conference was doomed to failure. It did not save a single Jew from the Holocaust and was bitterly condemned by world Jewry.

Besamim (spices). Hebrew word for the fragrant spices, used in the *Havdalah* ceremony, that serve to refresh and revive the spirit, dispelling the sadness related to the conclusion of the Sabbath day. A more mystical reason is that the spices either provide spiritual compensation for the additional soul that each Jew figuratively possesses on the Sabbath day[23] (which Rashi defined as a unique feeling of rest and contentment) or symbolize the spiritual farewell "feast" for that extra soul.[24] In ancient times before forks came into use, it was customary to cleanse the hands after a meal by passing them over spices on hot coals. On the Sabbath, this custom could not be performed. However, after the third Sabbath meal (see *se'udah shlishit*) that was eaten at dusk, the spices could be brought in and thus became associated with *Havdalah*.[25]

Best man/maid of honor. Roles that have an ancient precedent in Judaism, dating back to the angels Gabriel and Michael, who according to legend attended the wedding of Adam and Eve. These friends of the groom and bride may be in charge of holding the wedding ring and the *ketubah* during the ceremony.

Bestiality. The Bible prohibits both men and women from having sexual intercourse with animals (Lev. 18:23). Unlike almost all of the other forbidden relationships, which involve natural activity though with prohibited mates, bestiality is an unnatural and perverse practice that is termed an "abomination." The Hebrew word *tevel* (perversion) is derived from a root meaning "to mix," implying that sexual relations with beasts is a forbidden "mixture" of species.[26]

Bet. The 2nd letter of the Hebrew alphabet, with a numerical value of 2.

Beta Israel (House of Israel). Black ethnic group from Ethiopia that practices a form of Judaism based on the Bible, the Apocrypha, and other post-biblical Scripture. They have a strong monotheistic belief in the God of Israel, return to Israel, the World to Come, and the resurrection of the dead. Claiming descent from Menilek I, son of King Solomon and the Queen of Sheba, they were declared Jews by the Israeli rabbinate in 1975 and most have emigrated to Israel. Often known as "falasha," they deem this term to be pejorative.

Betar. Revisionist Zionist youth movement. With an ideology deeply influenced by Vladimir Jabotinsky, Betar played an important role in Zionist education and in teaching methods of self-defense. An abbreviation of *B'rit Trumpeldor*, in honor of the martyred hero of the defense of Tel Hai, Betar also was the town near Jerusalem that was the last fortified stronghold of Bar Kochba in the unsuccessful rebellion against Roman rule (132-135 C.E.). Each member of Betar swore an oath to "devote my life to the rebirth of the Jewish State, with a Jewish majority, on both sides of the Jordan." Betar also developed a Jewish sports organization, founded in 1924, that was affiliated with the Revisionist Movement. During World War II, many Betar members in Palestine fought with the Jewish Brigade in the British army; after the founding of the State, a number joined the army of Israel.

Bethlehem. Town in the Judean Hills about 5 miles south of Jerusalem. It is the burial place of Rachel (see Rachel's Tomb), the wife of Jacob (Gen. 35:19); the setting of the Book of Ruth; and the birthplace of David and ancestral home of the royal family of Israel.

Betrothal – see *Kiddushin*.

Bezalel Academy of Arts and Design. Named for the leader of the skilled artisans who constructed and decorated the Tabernacle in the wilderness according to a detailed Divine plan communicated to Moses on Mount Sinai, the Bezalel Academy was founded in Jerusalem in 1906 by sculptor Boris Schatz. Its mission was to develop useful arts and crafts among Jews in the Land of Israel, thereby decreasing the dependence on charity, while at the same time inspiring art and design students to create a Jewish national artistic style.

B'ezrat ha-Shem (with the help of the Name [of God]). Hebrew expression of hope or trust in Divine assistance. Traditional Jews write the abbreviation for this phrase (*b"h*) at the beginning of letters.

Bialik Prize. Prestigious Israeli award for Hebrew literature. It is named for Chaim Nachman Bialik, who is generally considered the father of modern Hebrew poetry.

Bialy. Flat, round breakfast roll with a depression (but not a hole) in the middle, sprinkled with cooked onions (and sometimes garlic). The name comes from the Polish city of Bialystok, where this product was a specialty.

Bible. This English word derives from the Greek *biblios*, the vernacular translation by the Greek-speaking Hellenistic Jews of the Hebrew term *ha-Sefarim* (The Books). Today, the most frequently employed Hebrew term for the Bible is the acronym *Ta-Na-Kh* (or *Tanach*), derived from the initial letters of the names of its three major divisions – **T**orah; **N**evi'im, (see Prophets); and **K**etuvim (see Writings). The Christian term "Old Testament" is not accepted in Jewish tradition because it expresses the belief that there is a "New Testament" that has somehow superseded the special Divine relationship with the Jewish people.

Bible, canonization of the. The books that constitute the Bible clearly were only a portion of the literary achievements of ancient Israel. At some point, some of these works were selected as being Divinely inspired and worthy of being included in an authoritative body of sacred writings. This process of "canonization" derives from a Hebrew root meaning "measuring rod" (Ezek. 40:5), which later became a Greek word for "rule" or "standard of excellence." Scholars generally agree that the Pentateuch (Five Books of Moses) assumed its final form during the Babylonian Exile. The prophetic canon probably closed during the Persian era (about 323 B.C.E.). Indeed, the Rabbis regarded the post-exilic Haggai, Zechariah, and Malachi as the last of the prophets, for when they died "the Holy Spirit [Divine inspiration] departed from Israel."

Bible commentary. At the end of the 13th century, the biblical scholar Bahya ben Asher concluded that there are four ways of interpreting Scripture. These came to be known by the acronym *pardes,* a Hebrew word meaning "orchard" or "Paradise," which is a mnemonic for the initial letters of the words: ***P**eshat* (plain, literal meaning of the verse in its context); ***R**emez* (allegorical or symbolic meaning only hinted at in the text); ***D**erash* (homiletic interpretation to uncover an ethical or moral lesson thought to be implicit in the text, and ***S**od* (secret, esoteric, or mystical interpretation, emphasized by the kabbalists). *Peshat* and *derash* are the more popular methods of exegesis, since they are comprehensible to most students of the Bible.

Bible criticism. For centuries, the Divine origin of the Five Books of Moses in their entirety was an unequivocal belief of Jews and Christians. During the medieval period, various scholars raised questions regarding whether Moses had written every line of text (e.g., the description of his death). The major figure in the critical analysis of the authorship of the Bible was Julius Wellhausen, who in the 19th century developed a model of source documents that became known as the Documentary Hypothesis. This posits that the Five Books of Moses were edited from four major strands of literary tradition, known as J, E, D, and P (see individual sections).

Bible translations. Except for portions of Daniel, Ezra, and Jeremiah, the Bible was written in Hebrew. Major early translations of the Bible are the Targum (Aramaic), the Septuagint (Greek), and the Vulgate (Latin). Saadia Gaon translated the Bible into Arabic in the 10th century, Moses Mendelssohn translated it into German in the 18th century, and the Jewish Publication Society of America translated it into English in the 20th century.

Bikur holim (visiting the sick). An aspect of righteous living that constitutes a part of the fundamental Jewish concept of *gemilut chasadim* (acts of lovingkindness). According to the Rabbis, it derives its importance from God's visiting Abraham while the Patriarch was recovering from his circumcision. Consequently, human beings are required to follow this Divine example, and *bikur holim* is classified as one of the precepts for which "a man enjoys the fruits in this world while the principal remains for him in the World to Come" (Shab 127a).

Bikurim (Bik). The 11th and final tractate of Zera'im (seeds) in the Mishnah, it deals with the ceremony and laws relating to the offering of the first fruits at the Temple.

Biltmore Program. Official policy adopted by the world Zionist movement meeting in May 1942 at the Biltmore Hotel in New York. It condemned the British White Paper of 1939 as effectively rescinding the Balfour Declaration of 1917 and demanded open immigration of Jews to the Land of Israel and the founding of a "Jewish Commonwealth integrated in the structure of the new democratic world." The Biltmore Program became the basis of the 1943-1948 struggle to found a Jewish State.

BILU. A Hebrew acronym of *Beit Ya'akov Lechu ve-Nelchah* ("House of Jacob, come let us go!"; Isa. 2:5), BILU was an organized group of young Russian Jews who pioneered the modern return to the Land of Israel. They represented the earliest wave of the First Aliyah (1882–1903), individuals and small groups, mostly from Eastern Europe, who fled pogroms, czarist repression, and grinding poverty to establish settlements in Palestine. Brimming with exuberant energy, but with little money and experience, the *Bilu'im* found life extremely difficult. They were unable to cope with the swamp-filled valleys, stony hillsides, and burning desert sands, nor the hostility of the Turkish rulers and the implacable hatred of their Arab neighbors. Some *Bilu'im* returned to Russia or went on to the United States; others remained faithful to the ideal of settling the Land of Israel, and some *Bilu'im* later became leaders in the public life of the country.

Bimah (elevated place). Raised platform that contains the table on which the Torah scroll is placed when it is read. It is traditionally located in the center of the synagogue, emphasizing the central role of the Torah in the worship service. In Sephardic synagogues, the prayer leader conducts most of the service from the *bimah*, which is known as *teivah* (box). In some Ashkenazic synagogues, there is a separate reading stand immediately in front of the *bimah* and facing the ark, from which the *hazzan* leads the service. In the 19th century, the Reform movement introduced the radical innovation of locating the *bimah* in front of the ark, a plan modeled on the church pulpit. This is now the dominant style in North America among liberal and even many Orthodox congregations.

Binah (wisdom/understanding) **(1)**. The 4th blessing of the weekday *Amidah*: "You graciously endow a human being with wisdom and teach insight to a frail mortal. Endow us graciously from Yourself with wisdom, insight, and discernment. Praised are You, O Lord, gracious Giver of wisdom."

Binah (2). The 3rd of the *sefirot* and first female emanation, representing Divine wisdom. After receiving the seed of *Chochma*, *Binah* (the "supernal mother") gave birth to her children, the lower *sefirot*.

Binding of Isaac – see *Akedah*.

Binyan av. Third principle of hermeneutics of Ishmael ben Elisha. It states that a general law drawn from one specific case in a group can be applied to all the cases in the group.

Binyan Yerushalayim (rebuilding of Jerusalem). The 14th blessing of the weekday *Amidah*, it calls for the speedy rebuilding of the city and the establishment of the Throne of David within it, praising God as "the Builder of Jerusalem."

Birkat David. The 15th blessing of the weekday *Amidah*, it asks God to "speedily cause to flourish the offspring of your servant David [i.e., the Messiah] and enhance his pride through salvation."

Birkat ha-Chamah – see Blessing of the sun.

Birkat ha-Chodesh – see New Moon, announcement of the.

Birkat ha-Gomel – see *Gomel.*

Birkat ha-Kohanim – see Priestly Blessing.

Birkat ha-Mazon – see Grace after Meals.

Birkat ha-Minim (against heretics). The 12th blessing of the weekday *Amidah*: "And for slanderers [see *minim*] let there be no hope, and may all wickedness perish in an instant; and may all Your enemies be cut down speedily. May you speedily uproot, smash, cast down, and humble the wanton sinners – speedily in our days. Praised are You, O God, Who breaks enemies and humbles wanton sinners."

Birkat ha-Shanim (Who blesses the years). The 9th blessing of the weekday *Amidah*, it prays that God "give dew/rain for a blessing on the face of the earth and satisfy us with Your bounty, and bless one year like the best years."

Birkot ha-Shachar – see Morning blessings.

Birkot ha-Torah – see Torah blessings.

Birobidjan. Far-eastern province of the former Soviet Union, which was set aside for Jewish colonization in 1928 and officially declared an autonomous Jewish area six years later. Yiddish was to be the official language in all educational, cultural, and legal institutions. Hailed by Jewish communists and sympathizers throughout the world as a great Soviet contribution to the solution of the "Jewish problem," the experiment proved unsuccessful. In contrast to Israel, this isolated and desolate region had no national appeal to the masses of Jews. Jews remained a distinct minority in the region, never numbering more than 20,000.

Birth – see Childbirth.

Birth control. According to the Midrash, the practice of birth control is ascribed to the evil generations before Noah. The only biblical reference to birth control relates to Onan, who was condemned to death because he "spilled his seed on the ground" to prevent the birth of a child from his levirate marriage to Tamar, the wife of his deceased brother (Gen. 38:9-10). The Talmud and numerous *responsa* deal with the issue. Among traditional Jews, birth control may be used solely by the wife if she would face substantial medical risk during pregnancy and nursing. More liberal views tend to leave the decision on birth control to the conscience of the individual, taking into consideration social and economic factors as well as medical issues.

Birthright (1). The privilege of the firstborn son in ancient Israel to lead the family and receive a double share of the inheritance. In the Bible, Esau sold the birthright to Jacob, his younger twin, for a stew of lentils (Gen. 25:29-34).

Birthright (2). Program founded in 2000 by Charles Bronfman and Michael Steinhardt, in cooperation with the Israeli government, private philanthropists, and Jewish communities around the world, which has sent more than 100,000 Jewish young adults aged 18-26 from all over the world to Israel on short, fully paid educational trips. The self-declared goals of this extensive project are to "diminish the growing division between Israel and Jewish communities around the world; to strengthen the sense of solidarity among world Jewry; and to strengthen participants' personal Jewish identity and connection to the Jewish people."

Bitter herbs – see *Maror*.

Bittul ha-yesh (lit., "the annihilation of that which is"). This kabbalistic concept describes a state of obliteration of the ego and complete loss of self-consciousness, through profound meditation and contemplation that everything exists in God, which is a necessary step to achieve *devekut* – cleaving to and losing oneself in God.

Bittul zeman. Literally "wasting time," the Hebrew term refers to time engaging in any activities that could be better spent studying Torah.

Black Death. Mid-14th century bubonic plague, caused by a bacterium carried by flea-infested rats, which devastated Europe and killed up to 35 million people (about half of the population). The Jewish traditions of washing hands (see *netilat yadayim*), promptly burying the dead (see burial), and keeping away from sewage in order to recite blessings and study Torah offered some protection (though Jews still were horribly affected). Virulent anti-Semitism caused Jews to be blamed for the plague, with Jewish physicians accused of poisoning the wells and polluting the drinking water in a deliberate effort to kill Christians.

Black Hundreds. Popular name for the Union of the Russian People. This organization of the most reactionary monarchists and nationalists, which was formed after the abortive revolution of 1905, had the support of Czar Nicholas II and employed criminal terror against liberal revolutionaries. Strongly anti-Semitic, the Black Hundreds were the chief instigators of government-sponsored pogroms against Jews in Russia. In certain respects, the Black Hundreds can be seen as precursors of the Nazis.

Blasphemy. Uttering a curse against God, which if done willfully, with warning, and validated before witnesses was punishable by being stoned to death. (In the absence of witnesses or warning, blasphemy was not punishable by an earthly court, but resulted in *karet*) Later in Jewish history, blasphemy was punishable by excommunication. Penance by the blasphemer could bring about reconciliation with God.

Blemishes. All offerings of cattle and sheep for Temple sacrifice had to be unblemished animals, the best that the owner possessed (Lev. 22:21). The Rabbis extended the scope of this law by requiring that the oil, wine, flour, and incense offered in the Temple must be of the highest quality. Similarly, *kohanim* with bodily blemishes were not allowed to perform the Divine service, because those with physical defects were thought to also have underlying spiritual defects. According to one commentator, because ordinary people tend to lack confidence in a leader who is physically disabled and requires assistance, the presence of a handicapped *kohen* would destroy the idea of perfection in the Temple.[27] The Rabbis also discussed moral blemishes at length.

Blessing. Fundamental component of prayer. The Hebrew word *bracha* (pl., *brachot*), which comes from a verb that means to bow or bend the knee (*berech*), indicates an act of submission to God. The sequence of prayers and blessings was standardized under Rabban Gamaliel II at Yavneh at the end of the 1st century C.E. However, the precise wording of individual *brachot* and their basic requirements were fixed only during the talmudic period. (For further information, see individual blessings.)

Blessing of children. On Sabbath eve, it is a custom for fathers, or both parents, to bless their children with the Priestly Blessing, after saying either "May God make you like Ephraim and Menashe" (for sons) or "May God make you like Sarah, Rebecca, Rachel, and Leah" (for daughters). The parent(s) typically places both hands on the head of the child while reciting the blessing.

Blessings after eating – see Grace after Meals.

Blessings and curses – see *Tochachah*.

Blessings before eating. Based on the biblical verse, "the earth and all it contains is the Lord's" (Ps. 24:1), the Rabbis taught, "to enjoy [the pleasures of] this world without reciting a blessing is like robbing the Holy One [i.e., stealing from God]" (Ber. 35b). Rather than thanking God, as in the Grace *after* Meals, the blessings *before* eating and drinking effectively request permission to use these Divine gifts. All of the blessings before eating or drinking begin with the same classic benediction formula – "*Baruch ata Adonai Eloheinu melech ha-olam*" –

and differ only in the description of the actions of God relative to the specific item to be consumed. There are special blessings for (a) *bread* baked from the flour of wheat, barley, oats, rye, and spelt, the five grains mentioned or alluded to in the Torah as indigenous to the Land of Israel (*ha-motzi lechem min ha-aretz*; Who brings forth bread from the earth); (b) foods *other than bread* made from the flour of these grains (*borei minei mezonot*; Who creates various kinds of nourishment); (c) all other food that grows from the earth (*borei peri ha-adamah*; Who creates the fruit of the earth); (d) all food that does *not* grow from the earth (*she-hakol nih'yeh bid'varo*; through Whose word all things were called into being); (e) fruit from a tree (*borei peri ha-etz*; Who creates the fruit of the tree); and (f) grapes and wine (*borei peri ha-gafen*; Who creates the fruit of the vine).

B'li ayin ha-ra (without the Evil Eye). Hebrew equivalent of the Yiddish *Keyn ayen horeh*, an expression used to prevent the damage from the Evil Eye that might result from praise or admitting good fortune. According to folklore, this phrase draws away the attention of the evil spirits.

B'li neder (without a vow). Because of the biblical commandment that all oral obligations must be fulfilled, traditional Jews generally add this Hebrew phrase to qualify their promises to carry out any commitment, just in case for some unexpected reason it might be impossible to perform.

Blintzes. Thin pancakes that originated in the Ukraine and are relatively modern descendants of the ancient Russian buckwheat pancakes known as *blinis*. As with other wrapped foods, blintzes provided an excellent way of transforming leftovers into a special dish while stretching scarce resources. They are commonly filled with cheese, mashed potatoes, kasha, ground meat, or fruit. In Ashkenzic communities, cheese blintzes topped with sour cream or fruit sauce are frequently served on Shavuot, during the meatless week before Tisha b'Av, and on other occasions when it is customary to eat dairy dishes. They are especially appropriate on Shavuot, which commemorates the giving of the Torah, since two blintzes placed side by side resemble the tablets that Moses received at Mount Sinai.[28]

Blood. The biblical prohibition against the consumption of blood (Lev. 7:26–27; 17:10–14)[29] is the basis for the process of *kashering* meat. Before meat is consumed, it is necessary to remove all traces of blood – by soaking and salting the meat, or by broiling or roasting it over an open flame. In the Temple, blood was sprinkled on the Altar as a symbol of atonement. The blood of sacrificial offerings had to be treated with respect and covered with dust, equivalent to the reverent burial of a dead body.

Blood avenger (*go'el ha-dam*). Next of kin of a murdered person who, in biblical times, was responsible for avenging the murder (Deut. 19:6). A more accurate translation of the Hebrew term is "redeemer of blood," since by putting the murderer to death the avenger expiated the blood that polluted the land (Num. 35:33). If the killer fled to a city of refuge and was found guilty at trial, the court was responsible for the execution of the convicted murderer.

Blood libel (blood accusation). Allegation that Jews used the blood of murdered Christian children to bake *matzot* and prepare wine for Passover and other rituals. Since the 12th century, these blood libels have been used as an excuse for vicious pogroms and massacres in which many Jews were killed. Though entirely false and denounced by popes and rulers, this pernicious folk belief was used in Nazi propaganda and still persists. (See *Beilis case*.)

Blue Box – see Jewish National Fund.

B'nai Akiva. Orthodox youth movement founded in 1929 by the Mizrachi (Religious Zionist) movement. It is the largest youth group in Israel and plays an active role in communal youth activities in 37 countries.

B'nai Brith. Literally "Sons of the Covenant," the world's oldest and largest Jewish service organization. It was founded in 1843 as a social and philanthropic organization of American Jews of German descent. B'nai Brith sponsored Americanization classes to acculturate Eastern European Jews who came to the country in the closing decades of the 19th century, as well as trade schools and relief programs. When anti-Semitism in the United States increased prior to World War I, B'nai Brith founded its Anti-Defamation League (ADL) to protect the status and rights of Jews. Other organizations established under the auspices of B'nai Brith include the Hillel Foundation, which serves the religious, cultural, and social needs of university students on campuses throughout the United States and around the world, and the B'nai Brith Youth Organization (BBYO), which offers a broad range of activities for Jewish teenagers. B'nai Brith has been a strong supporter of Israel and has helped Jews throughout the world.

B'nai Elohim – see Sons of God.

B'nai mitzvah. Plural form of bar mitzvah (also used when referring to both bar and bat mitzvah).

B'nai Noah (lit., "children of Noah") – see Noahide laws.

B'nai Yisrael. Although often translated literally as "Children of Israel," the term in best rendered simply as "Israelites." According to Hebrew grammar, the root "*ben*" in a compound word does not mean "son of," but rather implies class membership (i.e., a member of the group known as "Israel."). Similarly, "*ben adam*" means a human being, rather than "son of man."

Bo. The 3rd *parashah* in the Book of Exodus (10:1-13:16), it describes the final three plagues (locusts, darkness, killing of the firstborn); the sacrifice of the paschal lamb and the laws concerning the festival of Passover; the beginning of the Exodus from Egypt; and the regulations concerning the redemption of the firstborn (*pidyon ha-ben*) and the donning of *tefillin*.

Body. The vessel for the soul and the instrument through which one worships God and carries out the Divine will. As such, taking proper care of the body is a religious duty, for only a healthy body is capable of sustaining a holy soul. The inviolability of the body is reflected in Judaism's insistence on speedy burial after death.

Boethusians. Jewish sect in late Second Temple times that may have been a branch of the Sadducees. Both groups, associated with the aristocracy and the high priesthood, denied the immortality of the soul and the resurrection of the body because neither of these doctrines was contained in the Written Torah.

Book of Creation – see *Sefer Yetzirah*.

Book of Life. According to tradition, three books are opened in heaven on Rosh Hashanah: one for the completely wicked, whose bad deeds definitely outweigh their good; one for the completely righteous; and one for the intermediate (average persons). The completely righteous are immediately inscribed in the Book of Life, while the completely wicked are immediately inscribed in the Book of Death. The judgment of all others is suspended from Rosh Hashanah to Yom Kippur, because one can merit being inscribed in the Book of Life through prayer, repentance, and charity. Consequently, it is customary to greet friends on Rosh Hashanah with *leshanah tovah tikateivu* (may you be inscribed [in the Book of Life] for a good year). On Yom Kippur, the greeting is *g'mar chatimah tovah* (may the final sealing be good).

Book of the Covenant. Earliest collection of biblical law (Exod. 21:1-23:29). The name comes from two steps in the process of ratifying the series of laws given by God to the Israelites at Mount Sinai – "Moses then wrote down all the commands of the Lord" (24:4), and "he took the book of the covenant [*sefer ha-b'rit*] and read it aloud to the people," who declared: "All that the Lord has spoken we will faithfully do!" (24:7). Beginning with the statement, "These are the rules [*mishpatim*] that you shall set before them" (21:1), the Book of the Covenant can be divided stylistically into two sections. The first part (21:2-2:16), composed in a casuistic format, has great similarity to other legal collections from the ancient Near East. The remainder has few analogies to other legal systems and consists of a series of commands and prohibitions reflecting more religious, social, ethical, and moral sentiments, with no penalties attached. Unlike the crimes and civil wrongs in the first section, which are routinely judged in a court of law, many of the offenses in the second section are private matters that cannot be punished by the judicial system and must be abjured by internalized moral and ethical values based on their being the dictates of the Divine will.

Book of the Wars of the Lord. Mentioned in a single biblical verse (Num. 21:14), but with no copy extant, it is thought to represent a separate early anthology of victory songs describing the battles of the Israelites at the beginning of their national existence, which were fought with the help of God.

Booths – see Sukkah.

Boundary markers – see Landmarks.

Borscht. Russian and Yiddish term for an Eastern European soup that is usually made with beets (and often topped with sour cream in dairy versions) and served hot or cold.

Borscht Belt. Term for the resort hotels in the Catskill Mountains of New York that catered primarily to Jews. Known for their excellent kosher cuisine (hence the name "borscht"), they featured nightclub entertainment with major Jewish comedians and musicians.

Bracha (brachot) – see Blessing.

Bread. Often called the "staff of life," the Hebrew word *lechem* also is used in the Bible to refer to food in general. In biblical times, bread was prepared from wheat or barley. Dough to which leaven was added was called *chametz*, to differentiate it from unleavened *matzah*. For the Rabbis, bread was an essential element of every meal and had to be treated with respect. Consequently, they introduced a special blessing to be recited before eating bread from one of the five species of cereals grown in the Land of Israel (wheat, barley, spelt, oats, rye). Popularly known as *ha-Motzi*, it thanks God, "Who has brought forth bread from the earth." After eating bread at least the size of an olive, a full *Birkat ha-Mazon* (see Grace after Meals) must be said.

Breaking of the vessels (*shvirat ha-keilim*). Concept in Lurianic Kabbalah of a primordial catastrophe that occurred during the Creation of the universe. The Divine light originating from *Ein Sof* flowing from orifices in the head of *Adam Kadmon* was trapped in vessels (*keilim*), representing the *sefirot*. However, these vessels (especially the lower seven) were too weak to contain the light of the *Ein Sof* and broke. Many of the Divine sparks fell and were trapped by the realm of darkness in shells (*klipot*) caused by sins. Therefore, the task of human beings is to perform *mitzvot* and good deeds to redeem these sparks, thus allowing the sparks to return to their original source and repair the world (*tikun olam*).

Breaking the glass. Custom at the conclusion of a Jewish wedding ceremony in which the groom crushes a glass under his right foot. The most popular explanation is that this is in remembrance of the destruction of the Temple in Jerusalem. In folklore, glass was broken to create a loud noise to frighten away evil spirits. The broken glass is also interpreted as symbolic of the mystical concept of the shattered vessels (see above), a tangible reminder of the need for the new couple to engage in the *mitzvah* of *tikun olam*, the repairing of our imperfect world.[30]

Breastplate. Known in Hebrew as *hoshen mishpat* (breastplate of decision; Exod. 28:13-30) and worn by the High Priest, the breastplate was a square pocket or pouch adorned with 12 semi-precious stones, each engraved with the name of one of the tribes of Israel. Within the pouch were the *Urim* and *Thummim*, flat stones used for the casting of lots that could be used on behalf of the leader of the people to decide matters of vital national importance. Today, the term breastplate refers to the silver ornament adorning the front cover of the Torah scroll in Ashkenazic congregations.

Bribery. The Bible forbids a judge to accept gifts (bribes) from litigants (Exod. 23:8), even if he renders a judgment that "acquits the innocent and condemns the guilty" (*Sifrei*). The mere suspicion of bribery damages the integrity of the judicial system. However, a judge who was not paid by the community for his services, and was forced to take time off from his usual occupation to preside over a court, was permitted to accept a fee as long as it was paid equally by both parties in the litigation (i.e., considered as just compensation rather than a bribe).[31] In time, it became customary to pay the judge from communal funds. However, the Talmud permitted the bribing of non-Jewish rulers, officials, and judges, since they were considered to be prejudiced against Jews.

Bridal veil – see *Bedeken*.

Bride – see *Kallah*.

Bride-price – see *Mohar*.

Bris. Ashkenazic pronunciation of the term *brit* (see circumcision), an abbreviation of the Hebrew *brit milah*.

Brit – see Covenant.

Brit bat. Literally "daughter of the covenant," a contemporary celebration to welcome the birth of a daughter.

Brit milah – see Circumcision.

B'rit Shalom. Literally "Covenant of Peace," a small but vocal political movement in pre-Israel Palestine that called for a bi-national Arab-Jewish state with equal rights for all its citizens. The members of B'rit Shalom opposed Zionism from its outset because they believed that political power would corrupt the Zionist enterprise and lead to injustice toward the Arab population. The Six Day War, which resulted in Israeli occupation of Judea, Samaria, and Gaza and the need to rule another people, caused many left-wing Zionists in Israel and elsewhere to question the morality of the occupation, despite Arab rejection of a compromise solution. (See also *post-Zionism*.)

British Mandate. Enacted by the League of Nations in 1922, it authorized Great Britain to create the political, administrative, and economic conditions that would enable the establishment of a Jewish homeland in Palestine as promised in the Balfour Declaration of 1917. To appease budding Arab nationalism, Britain removed two thirds of Mandatory Palestine to create the separate Arab territory of Transjordan. A series of White Papers was then issued to curtail Jewish immigration into Palestine, despite the increasing persecution of German Jews under the Nazi regime. This culminated in the severely restrictive White Paper of 1939. Following World War II, Jewish military resistance to British rule grew steadily as the Jewish community in Palestine sought to bring the survivors of the Holocaust to the Land of Israel. Underground extremists carried out sabotage operations and direct attacks on British military and government installations. Jews and Arabs engaged in armed clashes. Eventually, the British grew weary of the challenge of Palestine, and on May 14, 1948, the Mandate ceased to operate. The British administration left the land, and the new State of Israel was born.

Bronze (brazen) serpent – see *Nechushtan*.

B'shalach. The 4th *parashah* in the Book of Exodus (13:17-17:16), it describes the Exodus from Egypt, the parting of the Sea of Reeds, and the Song at the Sea (see *Shirat ha-Yam*); the grumbling of the people in the wilderness; the bitter waters at Marah; the miraculous gifts of manna and quail; and the battle with Amalek.

Bubbe. A Yiddish word meaning "grandmother," this term of endearment can be applied to any affectionate, grandmotherly older woman.

Bubbe meise. Literally meaning "grandmother's story," this Yiddish term is frequently translated as "old wives' tale."

Bubkes. Literally meaning "beans," this Yiddish word indicates something that is worthless or falls far below expectations.

Bund. Jewish Ashkenazic socialist and anti-Zionist party, founded in Vilna in 1897. Both a trade union and political party working for social justice and Jewish cultural tolerance and respect, the organization spread from its roots in Poland and Lithuania to Russia, elsewhere in Eastern and Central Europe, and the United States. The Bund was devoted to secular Jewish nationalism, a commitment to the Yiddish language, and the securing of a guarantee of minority rights within Eastern Europe and elsewhere.

Burglary. A homeowner was permitted to kill a burglar to save his own life, but not if only his property was at risk (Exod. 22:1-2). A burglar who entered a house in the dead of night was presumed to have no hesitation about killing the owner; a homeowner who killed this apparent "pursuer" (see *rodef*) would not be guilty of murder but rather be deemed to have acted in self-defense. However, if a burglar broke into a home in broad daylight, it was assumed that the intruder was not planning to physically harm the householder, since he would surely be apprehended. Because in this scenario only his property was at risk and it was not necessary to take a life to protect himself, the homeowner was forbidden to kill the burglar.

Burial. Jewish tradition insists on prompt burial as a matter of respect for the dead (see *kavod ha-met*). Therefore, Jewish law generally requires that burial take place within 24 hours after death. However, proper "honor of the dead" – to allow for preparation of a coffin and for shrouds to be made, or to await the arrival of close relatives – may justify some delay, but never for more than three days. Certain delays are unavoidable, since funerals may not take place on the Sabbath, on Yom Kippur, or, in many communities, on the first day of festivals. Members of the *chevra kadisha* prepare the body for burial in accordance with Jewish customs. Although bodies once were dressed in costly garments, since early talmudic times it has become customary to bury all Jews in simple shrouds. Traditional Jews are buried in plain wooden coffins.

Burial society – see *Chevra kadisha*.

Burning Bush. Desert shrub at the foot of Mount Horeb, from which God first appeared to Moses and ordered him to go to Pharaoh and tell him to "free My people, the Israelites, from [bondage in] Egypt." Although all aflame, "the bush was not consumed" (Exod. 3:2-10). The Burning Bush has been interpreted as a symbol of Israel.

Burnt offering. Known in Hebrew as "*olah*" (that which ascends), the purpose of this voluntary offering to the Temple was to raise the owner from the status of sinner and bring him to a state of spiritual elevation. By bringing this sacrifice, a person expressed his desire and intention to devote himself entirely to God and to place his life totally in the Divine service. The burnt offering was completely consumed on the Altar, and it was forbidden for anyone to eat the meat from it. It was brought by a person who (a) failed to fulfill a positive commandment or who had intentionally committed a sin for which the Torah did not prescribe a specific punishment; (b) was guilty of sinful thoughts that had not led to action; (c) came to Jerusalem for one of the three pilgrimage festivals; or (d) wished to feel closer to God.[32]

Business ethics. Traditional Judaism does not condemn the pursuit and acquisition of wealth, as long as it operates within the parameters established by Jewish law, morality, and custom and does not detract excessively from the time that a Jew should dedicate to Torah study. All wealth is a gift from God; therefore there is an obligation to conduct business affairs in accordance with the Divine will. Consequently, dishonesty in business is not merely a legal crime, but more importantly a religious transgression. Judaism rejects the concept of "let the buyer beware." Instead, it places the full responsibility for disclosing defects and other shortcomings on the seller, even in the absence of a written guarantee. Based on the biblical injunction against "placing a stumbling block in the path of the blind" (Lev. 19:14), the Rabbis required that all customers be fully informed about the quality of merchandise (no false advertising). Today, this applies to the dangers in such inherently harmful products as cigarettes, liquor, drugs, and weapons not used solely for self-defense. (See *false weights and measures*.)

Butinsky. Yiddish term for a busybody who specializes in minding someone else's business.

Buying and selling. The Talmud established a uniform set of procedures for the buying and selling of goods, as well as rules for what constituted a valid sale. For example, a buyer who had taken possession of goods, but had not yet paid money to the seller, could not cancel the transaction. Conversely, a buyer who had paid for his purchase, but not yet received the goods from the seller, could escape from the deal and get his money back. Nevertheless, the Rabbis appear not to have endorsed these practices, warning that God would take vengeance on a person who does not stand by his (spoken) word.

C

Caesarea. Named by King Herod in honor of Augustus Caesar, this seaside town midway between Tel Aviv and Haifa was once the headquarters of Roman rule in Palestine. Extensive archeological excavations have uncovered ruins from the Roman, Byzantine, and Crusader periods, including a magnificent 5,000-seat amphitheater that is now a venue for summer concerts. Just north of the city is a great Roman aqueduct almost six miles long, though most of it has been buried by the shifting sands.

Calendar. The Jewish calendar is based on 12 lunar months (of 29 or 30 days), whose names are of Babylonian origin and came into use among Jews only after the destruction of the First Temple. The months are Nisan, Iyar, Sivan, Tammuz, Av, Elul, Tishrei, Cheshvan, Kislev, Tevet, Shevat, and Adar. Because the lunar calendar is about 11 days less than the solar year, without any adjustments the festivals would "wander" and be shifted from their appointed seasons of the year. To prevent this, an additional month (Second Adar) is added 7 times in every 19 years. During Temple times, the Sanhedrin was responsible for keeping track of discrepancies in length between the solar and lunar years, intercalating an extra month when needed according to agricultural conditions. As the Sanhedrin was about to be disbanded (mid-4th century), the Patriarch Hillel established a permanent Jewish calendar based on astronomical calculations to adjust the solar and lunar years. The numbering of years in the Jewish calendar is based from the "time since the Creation of the world." To calculate this, the Rabbis combined the life spans of the early generations listed in the Bible – starting with Adam – with the time that had elapsed since then. To determine the current Jewish year, it is only necessary to add 3760 to the year in the civil calendar (for dates between Rosh Hashanah and the end of December, another year is added). A Jewish day begins and ends at sunset. A Jewish week consists of seven days, which are named consecutively as first day, second day, and so forth, ending with the seventh day, Shabbat. Each month of the Jewish year begins with Rosh Chodesh (New Moon).

Calendar, lunar – see Lunar calendar.

Calf worship. Ancient Semitic peoples considered calves or young bulls as symbols of fertility and strength. Traces of this tradition of calf worship can be found in the Bible in the infamous incident of the Golden Calf and the golden calves placed in the temples built at Beit El and Dan by Jeroboam, ruler of the Northern Kingdom after the division of the monarchy following the death of Solomon.

Camel. One of the first animals domesticated by man and often called "the ship of the desert," the camel was specifically prohibited as food in the Bible (Lev. 11:4; Deut. 14:7). Although it chews the cud, the camel does not have completely cloven hooves. (Anatomically, it is cloven-footed, but this cannot be appreciated from the outside due to the cushions covering its feet.)

Camps, concentration and extermination. Initially developed by the Nazis to imprison opponents of their new regime, they greatly expanded as part of the "Final Solution." Jews from all over occupied Europe were deported by train in sealed boxcars to the east, to be methodically gassed and then cremated in the six specially constructed death-factories of Auschwitz, Treblinka, Belzec, Sobibor, Maidanek, and Chelmno. Some of the concentration camps also had forced labor facilities, where Jews were abused until they died from starvation or disease. (See individual entries on these six camps and also Theresienstadt.)

Canaan. The land between the Jordan River and the Mediterranean Sea, which God promised to Abraham and his descendants (Gen 17:8). After the Exodus from Egypt, Moses sent a delegation of 12 spies to "scout the land of Canaan" (Num.13). Ten admitted the richness of the land that "flowed with milk and honey," but argued that the Israelites would be unable to conquer its powerful inhabitants. Only Joshua and Caleb maintained that they could gain possession of it. When the frightened Israelites were determined to return to Egypt, God decreed that all those who were aged 20 or older (except for Joshua and Caleb) would be prohibited from entering the Promised Land. The Israelites were condemned to wander 40 years in the wilderness, one year for each day the spies scouted the land.

Canary. Yiddish term derived from the German *kein* (no) and the Hebrew *ayin* (eye) and *ha-ra* (evil), it is used in the context of giving someone the "Evil Eye" (e.g., "he's giving me a canary").

Candelabrum – see Menorah.

Candlelighting. The kindling of lights has long been viewed as adding to the joy of the Sabbath and festivals. Traditionally, the woman of the house ushers in the Sabbath by lighting at least two candles on Friday evening, corresponding to the slightly different wording in which the Fourth Commandment is phrased – "remember" (Exod. 20:8) and "observe" (Deut. 5:12) the Sabbath Day – two phrases that the Talmud relates were miraculously pronounced together by God. So as to not desecrate the Sabbath by miscalculating the precise time that night falls and the seventh day begins, it is customary to light the candles 18 minutes before sunset on Friday evening. Kindling the Sabbath lights is not a biblical commandment, but rather one of the seven ritual *mitzvot* legislated by the Rabbis

(Shab. 25b). It is generally regarded as one of the three "women's commandments," along with observing the laws of family purity through immersion in a ritual bath (see *mikveh*) and separating out a portion of dough (see *challah*) when baking bread. The kabbalists regarded the flame of the candle as the light of the soul, a reflection of Divine light.

Candles. Jews light candles to mark special occasions. They are kindled to usher in the Sabbath and festivals (see above), at *Havdalah*, and in the *chanukiah*. A popular custom in the wedding procession is to have lit candles held by those who escort the bride and groom to the *chuppah*. However, the lighting of candles also can reflect a sorrowful time. Candles are placed at the head of a deceased person, and a memorial candle is kept burning in a house of mourning throughout the seven-day *shiva* period (even on the Sabbath, when no demonstrable mourning is observed). Memorial candles are lit on the anniversary of a death (*yahrzeit*) and on the eve of Yom Kippur.

Canopy, wedding – see *Chuppah*.

Cantillation – see *Trope*.

Cantor (*hazzan*). The synagogue official who leads the congregation in prayer and song. During Temple times, the *levi'im* and *kohanim* participated in thanksgiving prayers with choirs and instrumental music. In the synagogue, any knowledgeable member could lead the services. As the liturgy became more complex and general knowledge of Hebrew decreased during the geonic period, the role of *hazzan* transformed into that of a permanent *shaliach tzibbur* (emissary of the congregation). The first half of the 20th century has been described as the "Golden Age of *Hazzanut*," with celebrated cantors filling synagogues to overflowing and being equated with great opera stars. This has changed dramatically in the last half century, with a strong trend toward active congregational singing. Both the Conservative and Reform movements have admitted women to the profession, despite the traditional prohibition against hearing the singing voice of a woman (*kol ishah*) lest it be too provocative for male worshipers. Contemporary cantors often perform educational and pastoral tasks as well as musical duties.

Capital punishment. In the Torah, the death penalty was prescribed for a multitude of offenses, including murder, adultery, blasphemy, profaning the Sabbath, idolatry, incest, striking one's parents, false prophecy, witchcraft, and giving false testimony in capital cases. The Bible specified three types of capital punishment (stoning, burning, and hanging), and rabbinic law added slaying by the sword and strangulation. The Rabbis, however, were generally opposed to capital punishment and made it very difficult to sentence someone to death. According to talmudic law, two eyewitnesses must testify to the crime, and the perpetrator must have been previously warned concerning both the crime and its punishment.[33] The modern State of Israel has no capital punishment except for participation in genocidal activities and under certain conditions of warfare. The only person ever put to death in Israel was Adolph Eichmann in 1962, for his crimes against humanity and the Jewish people during the Holocaust.

Captives – see Ransom of captives.

Carmel. Mountain range on the northernmost coastal plain of Israel. In the time of King Ahab, Mount Carmel was the scene of the famous contest in which Elijah confronted the priests of Baal (1 Kings 18). The cave of Elijah at the foot of the hill is sacred to Jews, Christians, and Muslims. Before the expansion of the city of Haifa in the 20th century, the mountain area was only thinly populated with several Druze villages. Today, the Jewish suburbs of Haifa, particularly Hadar ha-Carmel, have expanded to the mountain's northern slope, though most parts of Mount Carmel have been earmarked as nature reserves and recreation areas. In 1953, the Israel Institute of Technology began the move from its original building in midtown Haifa to a 300-acre campus on Mount Carmel, popularly known as Technion City.

Carob. Known as *charuv* in Hebrew and *bokser* in Yiddish, this slow-growing evergreen tree bears rich, chocolate-like fruit. According to the Talmud, carob was so nutritious that it sustained Shimon bar Yochai and his son for 12 years while they hid in a cave from the Romans in the 2nd century C.E. Because of the association between this reputed author of the mystical *Zohar* and Lag ba-Omer, carob is traditionally eaten on this holiday.

Carrying. One of the restrictions on the Sabbath is carrying any object (even a house key or handkerchief) outside a private domain, though carrying is permitted inside a private residence or a synagogue. An ingenious way to circumvent this restriction is to convert an object that is usually carried into something that can be worn, such as converting a house key into a tie clip. The prohibition against carrying is especially difficult for mothers of infants or young children. Forbidden to carry a child outside the house, they are effectively confined to their homes on the Sabbath.[34] To overcome these restrictions, under certain circumstances the Rabbis permitted the establishment of an *eruv*.

Castration. The ancient Israelites prohibited emasculation of both men and animals. The Bible forbade the use of castrated animals as sacrifices on the Altar (Lev. 22:24). Similarly, a man whose reproductive organs were so severely crushed or maimed that he was impotent was prohibited from marrying a Jewish woman (Deut. 23:2). (If, however, the disability arose through natural means – such as birth defect or illness – it was considered an "act of God" and this prohibition did not apply.) One who was voluntarily sterilized or castrated was subject to this injunction, since this action indicated that he had no intention of fathering children.[35]

Casuistic. Conditional form in which the vast majority of legal prescriptions in the ancient Near East were written. Beginning with the words "if" or "when," an initial statement of the legal circumstances (the "facts of the case") was followed by a recital of the legal consequences. These laws were conditional formulations of general principles that reflected the verdicts of actual trials and were guides to settling legal disputes in subsequent cases with similar fact patterns. Similarly, much of biblical law uses the casuistic style, describing hypothetical situations from daily life and presenting the legal consequences of various actions. However, the Bible also makes substantial use of apodictic (absolute) law, terse statements of prohibition or command.

Cave of Machpelah. Gravesite in Hebron purchased by Abraham from Ephron the Hittite as a place to bury his wife, Sarah (Gen. 23). All of the Patriarchs and Matriarchs, with the exception of Rachel (see Rachel's Tomb), are buried in this "Tomb of the Patriarchs," which is housed in a fortress build by Herod that was converted into a mosque following the Muslim conquest of Palestine. Today, the site is open to both Jews and Arabs on a complex shared basis.

Caveat emptor (let the buyer beware). Concept rejected by Judaism, which instead places the full responsibility for disclosing defects and other shortcomings on the seller, even in the absence of a written guarantee. (See *business ethics*.)

C.E. (acronym for "**C**ommon **E**ra"). This neutral term is used by Jews and scholars to denote the period traditionally labeled "A.D." (*anno Domini*; in the year of the Lord [i.e., Jesus]) by Christians.

Cedar. Mentioned more than 70 times in the Bible, the majestic cedar was renowned for its strength, fragrance, hardiness, and longevity and described as "the tree of the Lord" (Ps. 104:16). In biblical times, cedar trees covered extensive areas of the mountains of Lebanon, and its wood was used in the construction of both the First and Second Temples (Ezra 3:7). The fine-grained, reddish wood of the cedar is resistant to water and was used to construct royal palaces, the walls and ceilings of houses, and the masts of ships (Ezek. 27:5). In the Talmud, a great sage is compared to the cedar, while the common people are likened to the lowly hyssop (MK 25b).

Celibacy. Unlike the Christians of the rabbinic era, who regarded celibacy as the ideal and marriage as merely a concession to humankind's weakness and libidinous nature, the Rabbis championed marriage, including its sexual aspects, as the essential human relationship. Sexual desire, when properly channeled in marriage, was considered a powerful positive force, rather than an emotion that was inherently shameful or evil. The person at risk for transgression was rather the unmarried man, who "spends all his days in sinful thoughts" (Kid. 29b). Indeed, the Rabbis condemned the man who rejected his normal human impulses and failed to produce children, charging that it was "as if he shed blood, diminished the image of God, and made the *Shechinah* depart from Israel" (Shab. 31a).

Cemetery. During the biblical era, Jews generally buried their dead in family plots on their own property, either in caves (Land of Israel) or in the earth (Babylonia). The primary impetus to the development of communal cemeteries was the traditional laws of ritual purity, which forbid *kohanim* from touching a corpse or coming within four cubits (about six feet) of a grave. A *kohen* may only enter a cemetery for the burial of a close relative – parent, child, wife, brother, or unmarried sister (Lev. 21:2–4). A widespread custom among Orthodox Jews, which has persisted to this day, is visiting cemeteries on public fast days to offer prayers at the graves of the departed. Visiting the cemetery is especially observed on Tisha b'Av, during the month of Elul before the High Holy Days, and on the days before Yom Kippur. In conjunction with each visit, one traditionally places a stone on the grave and makes a contribution to charity. It is the responsibility of the Jewish community to ensure a proper burial place for the indigent and any unclaimed bodies.

Census. The Bible records that God twice commanded Moses to take a census of the Israelites to determine the number who were age 20 and older and thus eligible for military service (Num. 1, 26). However, when David ordered an unauthorized census merely "so that I may know the size of the population" (2 Sam. 24), a severe plague befell the Israelites and 70,000 perished.

Central Conference of American Rabbis (CCAR). The rabbinical association of Reform Judaism in the United States, the CCAR was founded in 1889 by Isaac Mayer Wise as the successor to the Reform rabbinic councils in Germany. One key goal of the CCAR is to uphold the principle of separation of church and state, both in the United States and in Israel.

Chabad. Acronym for ***Ch**ochmah, **B**inah, **D**a'at* (Wisdom, Understanding, Knowledge) and the popular name for the Hasidic movement founded by Shneur Zalman of Liadi. In his masterwork, *Tanya*, Shneur Zalman developed a systematic theosophical doctrine on the conceptions of God and the world, and of man and his religious obligations, based on the Kabbalah of Isaac Luria (see Lurianic Kabbalah) combined with the Hasidism of the Ba'al Shem Tov and the Maggid of Mezhirich. Chabad emphasizes the significance of intellectual effort to promote religious understanding and deepen religious emotions. The most recent *rebbe* of the movement, Menachem Mendel Shneerson, who aroused messianic expectations among some of his followers, built a worldwide network by sending young Chabad families as emissaries of Judaism (*shlichim*) throughout the globe. Their primary purpose is to promote Jewish education among all Jews, regardless of background; to establish contact with and retrieve alienated Jewish youth; and to inspire the observance of the Torah as a daily experience.

Chad Gadya (One kid). The initial phrase and name of a popular Aramaic song that traditionally concludes the Passover seder. Composed of 10 stanzas, the song relates what happens to a little goat that was bought by a father for two coins (*zuzim*). The goat was eaten by a cat, which was bitten by a dog, which was beaten by a stick, which was burned by fire, which was quenched by water, which was drunk by an ox, which was butchered by the slaughterer, who was killed by the Angel of Death, who in punishment was destroyed by God. Each stanza repeats the previous verses and closes with the refrain, "*chad gadya, chad gadya*." One interpretation of the song is as an allegory of the fate of Israel among the nations. With God's triumph over death at the end of the song, the seder concludes on a positive, jubilant note.

Chag (holiday) – see Festivals.

Chag ha-Asif. Literally "Festival of the Ingathering [from the threshing floor and winepress]," a biblical name for Sukkot.

Chag ha-Aviv (Festival of Spring). A biblical name for Passover.

Chag ha-Bikurim. Literally "Festival of the First Fruits," a biblical name for the festival of Shavuot. On this holiday, joyful pilgrims would march to the Temple in Jerusalem to offer up baskets of their first ripe fruits and bread baked from the newly harvested wheat.

Chag ha-Katzir. (Festival of the Harvest). A biblical name for Shavuot.

Chag ha-Matzot. (Festival of the Unleavened Bread). A biblical name for Passover.

Chag ha-Pesach. A biblical name for Passover.

Chag sameach. Literally "happy holiday," the Hebrew greeting used on Jewish holidays.

Chagigah (1). Special festival offering of each Jew going up to the Temple in Jerusalem for one for the three pilgrimage festivals.

Chagigah (Chag.) (2). The 12th tractate in Mo'ed (festivals) in the Mishnah, it deals with the special sacrifices for the three pilgrimage festivals.

Chai. Literally meaning "life," this Hebrew word is made up of the letters *chet* and *yud*, which together have a numerical value equal to 18. Many Jews wear the word *chai* as a pendant or good luck charm and give charity in multiples of 18. (See also *l'chaim*.)

Chaim Yankel. Combination of two masculine names – Chaim (from *chai*) and Yankel (Yiddish for the Hebrew Ya'akov, or Jacob) – that is the equivalent of the English expression, "Joe Blow" (i.e., a "nothing"). Thus, the Yiddish term has the connotation of a "nobody" or simpleton.

Chair of Elijah. Usually richly carved and ornamented with embroideries, this special chair was traditionally left unoccupied and symbolically meant for Elijah the Prophet at the circumcision ceremony. In some communities, it is now occupied by the *sandek* (godfather). Elijah is depicted as the protector of the Jewish child, probably based on the biblical story in which he revived the son of a widow (1 Kings 17:17–24). Another reason for the symbolic presence of Elijah at every circumcision is the traditional belief that the prophet will ultimately announce the crowning of the Messiah to redeem humankind. Therefore, he must appear at each circumcision in order to determine whether this child will be the long-awaited messianic figure.

Chalalah. One of the women a *kohen* was forbidden to marry (Lev. 21.7). Generally translated as "desecrated" or "profaned," Rashi maintained that this term referred to a woman who was forbidden to marry a *kohen* but had previously married one anyway (such as a divorcée who had married a *kohen* or a widow who had married a *Kohen Gadol*), or to any daughters born of such unions.[36] If a *kohen* married one of these women, however, the marriage was binding and a legal divorce was required if the *kohen* later wanted to be separated from his wife.[37]

Chalav Yisrael. Literally meaning "milk of Israel," it refers to milk that is obtained and bottled under the supervision of a Jew. Only the milk of clean animals (cows, sheep, goats) is permitted for consumption. The Talmud prohibited Jews from consuming "milk which a heathen milked without an Israelite watching him," because of the fear that the former may have inadvertently mixed it with milk from an unclean animal. Only if a Jew were present at the time of milking could it be used. Today, some strictly observant Jews drink only *chalav Yisrael*, though many modern authorities permit the consumption of milk even if Jews did not supervise the milking, since the law of the land forbids the adulteration of milk.

Chalitzah. Literally meaning "taking off the shoe," this Hebrew term refers to the biblical ceremony performed on a man who refused to marry his brother's childless widow (levirate marriage). In the presence of the elders, the widow would take off the man's shoe (a symbol of mourning, because his failure to perform levirate marriage meant that his brother was now irrevocably dead) and spit on the ground in front of him (a symbol of contempt), declaring that "so shall it be done to the man who does not build up his brother's house" (Deut 25:10). From then on, the widow was free to marry anyone (except for any of the brothers of the deceased or a *kohen*). This ceremony is now obligatory in Israel, where marriage between a man and his brother's widow is not permitted.

Challah (1). Braided bread baked for the Sabbath, which is often made in special shapes for the festivals. For each Sabbath meal, two whole loaves of bread are placed on the table and covered with a cloth. These are reminiscent of either the double portion of manna that fell on Friday and sustained the Israelites over the Sabbath or the two rows (12 loaves) of the Showbread eaten on the Sabbath by the *kohanim*.

Challah (2). Small portion of dough (1/24 for an individual; 1/48 for a baker) that was to be set aside when baking bread and then offered to the *kohanim* in the Temple. Because *kohanim* can no longer observe the laws of priestly purity and thus are disqualified from eating anything related to a holy sacrifice, in observant households and kosher bakeries where bread is baked, an olive-sized *challah* portion is removed and burned.

Challah (Chal.) (3). The 9th tractate of Zera'im (seeds) in the Mishnah, it deals with the dough offering to the *kohanim* (see *challah* [2]).

Challah, festival. The familiar braided bread for the Sabbath is frequently baked in special shapes for the festivals. On Rosh Hashanah, the *challah* is typically round to symbolize the annual cycle and the hope for an abundant year of peace and goodness. Raisins are often included in the dough to emphasize the desire for a sweet year. In some communities, the *challah* is shaped like a crown to suggest the King of kings who created the universe; a ladder to signify the hope that our prayers for forgiveness will ascend swiftly to heaven; or a bird's head as a symbol of God shielding Jerusalem "like a bird hovering over its young." On Hoshana Rabbah, the top of the *challah* may be in the shape of a hand reaching up, symbolizing our receipt of the Divine judgment that was decreed on Yom Kippur but not confirmed until this last day of Sukkot.[38] Some *challot* are shaped like a menorah on the Sabbath of Chanukah, while on Purim the bread may be molded into a single giant braid representing the long rope used to hang Haman, or into small triangular loaves to symbolize Haman's ears.[39]

Chaloshes. Yiddish expression for something that is disgusting or in bad taste. It may be applied to food or drink, or to conduct.

Chalutz (pioneer). Jewish settler in Palestine before the establishment of the State of Israel. These ardent Zionists (*chalutzim*) built roads, battled malaria, drained swamps, planted trees, and founded collectivist agricultural communities throughout the land. (See also *Hechalutz*.)

Chametz. Hebrew term for leavened products, which are explicitly prohibited on Passover (Exod. 12:19-20; 13:3). This is a remembrance of the Exodus, when the Israelites "took their dough before it was leavened" (Exod. 12:34) and left Egypt in great haste. The criterion for rendering grain *chametz* is that it "ferments" on decomposition. The Rabbis deemed that this characteristic applied to the five species of grain indigenous to the Land of Israel – wheat, barley, oats, rye, and spelt. While the prohibition of most forbidden foods is nullified if it is accidentally mixed in more than 60 times its volume of permitted food, this does not apply to *chametz* on Passover. Even the minutest amount of *chametz* renders everything with which it has been mixed forbidden. In addition to the obvious breads, pasta, pastries, and cereals, *chametz* can be found as ingredients in candy and gum, vinegar, spices, processed meats, ice cream, whiskey, medicines, cosmetics, baby powder, toothpaste, mouthwash, and many other products. Because pots in which *chametz* has been cooked absorb and retain some of it – "imparting a flavor" into any other food cooked in them – those that have been used during the year are forbidden for use during Passover unless they have been rigorously cleansed in accordance with halachic requirements. For the same reason, separate dishes must be used for Passover; however, this is not required for non-permeable glass, which can be soaked and washed in order to be permissible for Passover use.

Chametz, search for (*bedikat chametz*). Formal search for leaven in the home, which is conducted on the last night before Passover. Traditionally carried out by candlelight, the search is now often performed with a flashlight for safety's sake, using a feather and a wooden spoon to collect any remaining *chametz*. Before the search, it is customary to deposit small pieces of bread (10 pieces, according to kabbalistic lore) in rooms throughout the house where *chametz* may have been used during the year. An Aramaic statement is recited declaring any remaining *chametz* "nullified and ownerless as the dust of the earth." The crumbs are burned or thrown out the next morning after the last meal of *chametz*.

Chametz, selling of (*mechirat chametz*). The mere possession of *chametz* during Passover is forbidden. However, its disposal could produce serious financial hardship when large quantities of foodstuffs are involved, or where *chametz* is used for business purposes. To alleviate this problem, the rabbis devised the legal formula of "selling" the *chametz* to a non-Jew before Passover and then "buying" it back after the festival had concluded. Although initially involving the physical transfer from Jew to non-Jew "in the market place," today all that is required is signing a composite document that grants power of attorney to sell the *chametz* to an agent, usually the local rabbi, who in turn arranges the contract with the non-Jewish buyer. After Passover, the agent buys back the *chametz* and symbolically restores it to the original owners.

Chametz, symbolism of. The Rabbis regarded *chametz* as the symbol of the evil inclination (see *yetzer ha-ra*). The "yeast in the dough" (the evil impulse that causes a ferment in the heart) prevents human beings from carrying out the will of God. *Chametz* also represents human haughtiness and conceit. Just as leaven puffs up dough, so human arrogance causes us to believe that we, not God, control our destiny. Keeping away from *chametz* during Passover reminds Jews that they once languished in Egyptian bondage before being redeemed by God "with a mighty hand and with an outstretched arm."[40]

Chametzdik. Yiddish term for any food containing prohibited leaven (*chametz*), which may not be eaten on Passover.

Chamim – see *Cholent*.

Chamisha Chumshei Torah. Literally "the five fifth-parts of the Torah," this rabbinic term for the Five Books of Moses became popularly abbreviated as *Chumash*.

Chanukah. Literally meaning "dedication," this joyous eight-day festival that begins on the 25th of Kislev (December) commemorates the victory of Judah Maccabee and his followers over the army of the Syrian ruler, Antiochus Epiphanes, and the rededication of the defiled Temple in 165 B.C.E. Each night, an increasing number of candles are kindled in the *chanukiah*. It is traditional to eat foods cooked in oil, like latkes (potato pancakes) or *sufganiyot* (Israeli jelly donuts) and play dreidel. The Rabbis sought to deemphasize the military aspect of the festival and focus on the survival of the Jewish religion in the face of pagan oppression.

Chanukat ha-bayit. Literally meaning "dedication of the home," the ceremony of affixing a *mezuzah* to the outer door of a new home, traditionally done immediately after moving in but at least within 30 days.

Chanukiah. The major ritual associated with Chanukah is the lighting of this eight-branched candelabrum, also called a "Chanukah menorah." Typically, there is also space for a ninth candle, called the *shamash* (servant), which is placed higher or to one side to differentiate it from the others. Since its only role is to kindle the other candles, the light of the *shamash* can provide illumination for reading, thus preventing any accidental use of the light of the eight primary candles, which may not be used for practical purposes. Two blessings are recited for lighting the Chanukah candles. The first relates specifically to the commandment to kindle the lights (*le-hadlik ner shel Chanukah*), while the second refers to the miracle itself ("Who performed miracles for our ancestors, in those days, in this season"). The current practice is to insert the candles in the *chanukiah* from right to left (newest addition on the left), but to light them from left to right (newest addition kindled first). On Friday night, the Chanukah candles are lit before the candles that usher in the Sabbath. It is customary to place the *chanukiah* by a window "to publicize the miracle" so that passersby can see the lights. In some cities, Chanukah lights are lit in large menorahs erected in public places to commemorate the miracle.

Chaplain. Clergyman serving the religious needs of soldiers in the military, patients in hospitals, and prisoners in penitentiaries. In the United States, the first Jewish military chaplains were appointed soon after the beginning of the Civil War (1862) following the personal intervention of President Lincoln. In Israel, there is a Chief Rabbi of the Israel Defense Forces, and chaplains are appointed throughout the armed forces of the Jewish State.

Chariot mysticism – see *Merkava* mysticism.

Charity – see *Tzedakah*.

Charity box – see *Kuppah*.

Charity, eight degrees of. According to Maimonides, the highest level is giving money to prevent another person from ever becoming poor, such as by offering him a loan or employment or investing in his business. The second highest level of charity is the rabbinic ideal of giving to the poor in such a way that neither the donor nor the recipient knows the identity of the other. In descending order, the next levels of charity are: the donor knows the recipient, but the recipient does not know the donor; the recipient knows the donor, but the donor does not know the recipient; giving directly to a poor person without being asked; giving only after being asked; giving cheerfully but less than one should; and giving grudgingly.

Charoset. Paste made of fruit, nuts, spices, and wine that is placed on the Passover seder plate and is symbolic of the mixture of clay and straw from which the enslaved Jews made bricks. The ingredients of *charoset* vary widely among different communities. Ashkenazic Jews typically use ground apples, chopped walnuts, cinnamon, and red wine; Sephardim tend to use ingredients that grew in the Land of Israel during biblical times, such as dates, figs, and almonds. North Africans also include pine nuts, hardboiled eggs, and spices such as ginger and cinnamon. Yemenites add chili pepper, whereas some Israelis mix in dates, bananas, candied orange peel, and orange juice.[41] For the second dipping at the seder, the *maror* (bitter herb) is dipped into the *charoset*.

Chastity. The Bible and subsequent Jewish law forbid sexual relations outside of marriage, such as adultery, premarital sex, prostitution, and incest (see marriages, prohibited).

Chatat – see Sin offering.

Chayei Sarah. The 5th *parashah* in the Book of Genesis (23:1-25:18), it begins with the death of the first Matriarch and her husband Abraham's purchase of the Cave of Machpelah as her gravesite. Abraham then sends his servant Eliezer to Haran to find a wife for his son from among his relatives, and Eliezer returns with Rebecca as a bride for Isaac.

Chazer. Literally meaning "pig," which Jews are forbidden to eat, this derogatory Yiddish term is often applied to a person who is greedy or a glutton.

Chazerai (**chozerai**). Relating to the pig, which has no practical value for the Jew, this Yiddish term refers to worthless trinkets and cheap junk. It also can refer to something that is disgusting or loathsome, unhealthy, or non-kosher food.

Chazeret. Additional *maror*, typically Romaine lettuce, which is used for the *korech* sandwich and is placed on the seder plate on Passover.

Cheder (room). Small elementary school where boys were taught the basics of Judaism. In the *shtetls* of Eastern Europe, the *cheder* literally was a room, often in the house of the private teacher known as a *rebbe* or *melamed*, who was paid by the parents. Three classes for different age groups were generally held at the same time, with the teacher instructing one while the others reviewed their lessons. The basic subjects were prayers, Torah with Rashi, and Talmud; no secular studies were taught.

Cheese. As a dairy product, cheese cannot be eaten with meat according to the laws of *kashrut* (see mixing meat and milk). One is generally permitted to eat meat almost immediately following a milk meal after thoroughly rinsing the mouth and eating a piece of bread or some other "neutral" solid. After eating hard cheese, it is customary to wait a longer period (up to six hours in some traditions). The Talmud prohibits eating cheese made by gentiles, because the rennet used to curdle the milk might have come from the stomach of a non-kosher animal; a kosher animal that had not been slaughtered according to the requirements of the dietary laws; or one that was sacrificed as part of an idolatrous rite. This prohibition did not extend to cottage and other soft cheeses, for which rennet is not used.

Cheilev (fat). The fat portions attached to the stomach and intestines, which were sacrificed on the Altar in biblical and Temple times and forbidden for consumption (Lev. 7:23). This prohibition applied to the abdominal fat of oxen, sheep, or goats, but it was permitted to eat the fat (*shemen*) of the deer, hart, and other kosher wild animals that could not be used for sacrificial offerings.

Chelm. Polish town settled by Jews in the 12th century. In Jewish folklore, the inhabitants of Chelm are portrayed as fools ("wise men of Chelm"), and Chelm became a synonym for a group of simpletons. During the Holocaust, most of the Jews of Chelm were murdered in the death camp at Sobibor.

Chelmno. Nazi extermination camp 37 miles from Lodz. The first of the Nazi death camps to begin operations (December 8, 1941), the victims at Chelmno were murdered by carbon monoxide and their corpses dumped into mass graves in a nearby forest. Tens of thousands of Jews, as well as Soviet prisoners of war and gypsies, perished at Chelmno; only two Jews survived the camp.

Cherem. Literally "separated," in the Bible this term was applied to any person or item that was separated from common use or contact, either because it was proscribed as an abomination or was consecrated to God (such as the prohibition against the personal use of the spoils of war, which had to be destroyed). A later meaning of *cherem* was "shunning," in which a person and his family would be subject to economic and social isolation as punishment for refusing to obey rabbinic authority. Finally, *cherem* became the Hebrew word for "excommunication." Famous excommunications include that of the philosopher Baruch Spinoza in 17th-century Amsterdam and the mutual 18th-century excommunications in the bitter dispute between the Vilna Gaon (the foremost talmudic scholar and *halachic* authority of his age) and adherents of the new Hasidic movement.

Cherubim. Supernatural creatures with human, animal, and birdlike features. After Adam and Eve were expelled from the Garden of Eden, God stationed east of it "the *cherubim* and the flame of the ever-turning sword, to guard the way to the Tree of Life" (Gen. 3:24), thus preventing human beings from ever achieving immortality. In the Tabernacle in the wilderness, two golden *cherubim* faced each other with outstretched wings turned upward. They sheltered the *kapporet*, the slab of pure gold that covered the Ark, which contained the Ten Commandments and formed a throne for God when the Divine Being descended to earth (Exod. 25:18-22). Every commandment that God gave Moses to convey to the Israelites was spoken "from above the cover, from between the two *cherubim* that are on top of the Ark of the Tablets of the Testimony." In Ezekiel's famed prophecy of the Divine Chariot, the prophet depicted four mythical creatures of human form, each of which had four faces (man, lion, bull, eagle) and four wings, which transported the Throne of God.

Chesed (1) – see *Gemilut chasadim*.

Chesed (2). The 4th of the *sefirot*, representing unconditional Divine love and grace that is only limited by its opposing emanation, *Din* (Divine justice). These complementary polar opposites must be kept in proper balance. Were justice not tempered and balanced by love and mercy, our world would be subject to harsh punishments. If love and mercy were not held in check by justice, anarchy would reign. According to the kabbalists, this balance is achieved through an intermediary that contains elements of both – *Tiferet* (glory).

Chesed shel emet (the true kindness). Hebrew term used for the respect demonstrated in preparing the body of the deceased for burial (*chevra kadisha*) and escorting the dead (especially scholars) to their last resting place – acts of genuine selflessness since one can expect no reciprocation.

Cheshbon ha-nefesh. Literally "accounting of the soul," this Hebrew term refers to the self-inventory that each Jew is to perform in the month of Elul and especially during the Ten Days of Repentance from Rosh Hashanah through Yom Kippur as the first step in the process of *teshuvah* (repentance). Based on personal ethical standards and an understanding of the teachings and commandments of the Jewish tradition, Jews are supposed to evaluate themselves and make critical decisions about how to improve their lives.

Cheshvan. The 8th month of the Jewish calendar (October-November). It is often called "Mar Cheshvan," based on either of two meanings of the Hebrew word *mar* – "bitter" and "mister." One tradition is that because Cheshvan contains no holiday or special observance, it has a taste of bitterness to it. A more endearing explanation is that the Rabbis felt sorry for the month of Cheshvan, with its lack of any special day, and therefore gave it some honor by calling it "Mister Cheshvan."[42]

Chess. Many of the great grandmasters and chess champions were Jews. They include Wilhelm Steinitz, Emanuel Lasker, Mikhail Tal, Boris Spassky, Bobby Fischer, Anatoly Karpov, and Gary Kasparov.

Chet (1). The 8th letter of the Hebrew alphabet, with a numerical value of 8.

Chet (2). From a Hebrew word meaning "to miss the mark," an unintentional sin.

Chevra kadisha. Aramaic term (lit., "holy society") for the group that is charged with the responsibility of preparing the body for burial in accordance with Jewish customs. Membership in a *chevra kadisha* is considered a great communal honor, bestowed only on those who are truly pious and can display the proper respect for the deceased. Most communities with a significant Jewish population have a *chevra kadisha*. For reasons of modesty, the *chevra* is divided according to gender.

Chewing on thread. A popular *bubbe meise* (old wives' tale) is chewing on a piece of thread whenever one is wearing a garment upon which someone is actively sewing – such as attaching a button or repairing a seam. This practice may relate to the Yiddish phrase *mir zollen nit farnayen der saychel*, meaning that one should not sew up the brains (or common sense). Another explanation is that burial shrouds are sewn around the remains of the deceased. Actively chewing while another is sewing on one's garments is a clear indication that one is quite alive and not yet a candidate for the grave.

Chickpea. The chickpea (garbanzo bean), one of the earliest-known cultivated plants, has long been a staple in the Jewish diet. Hummus, a thick puree of chickpeas and sesame paste (tahini), is a staple dip in Israel, while felafel (spicy chickpea croquettes) are sold by street vendors and kiosks.[43] Both are eaten with pita, a round, hollow, flat bread that is puffed up and separated into two layers by steam while it is baked in a very hot oven. Chickpeas are traditionally eaten on the first Friday night after the birth of a son (*shalom zachar*) and at the third Sabbath meal (see *se'udah shlishit*). They are also consumed on Purim, because of the legend that Queen Esther observed the laws of *kashrut* in the palace of King Ahasuerus by eating only vegetarian foods, specifically beans, peas, and grains.

Chiddushim – see Novellae.

Chief Rabbi. Title given in several countries to the principal religious leader of the Jewish community. Some cities with a large Jewish community, especially in Israel, also have a Chief Rabbi. In Great Britain, the Chief Rabbi represents the interests of British Jewry before Parliament and the Crown. In Israel, there are two Chief Rabbis, one Ashkenazic and one Sephardic, who each serve for a single 10-year term. Each large city in Israel also has an Ashkenazic and Sephardic Chief Rabbi. There is no Chief Rabbi in the United States.

Chilazon. Mediterranean sea snail that was the source of the expensive blue dye used to color the blue thread (*techeilet*) that was to be combined with seven white ones to fulfill the biblical command of the *tzitzit* (fringes). After the destruction of the Second Temple, the secret of obtaining this exact shade was lost, and the use of the blue thread in the fringes was discontinued. Recently, researchers have discovered a close relative of the snail, and *tallitot* with blue fringes are now available. The blue stripes woven into many *tallitot* symbolize this ancient *techeilet*.

Child, rebellious – see Rebellious son.

Child sacrifice. The Bible strictly prohibited child sacrifice, derived from the verse forbidding the Israelites to "allow any of your children to be given [offered up] to Molech" (Lev. 18:21), a Canaanite fire deity. Nevertheless, King Solomon constructed a shrine for "Molech the abomination of the Ammonites" for "his foreign wives who offered and sacrificed to their gods" (1 Kings 11:7-8), thus incurring Divine wrath. Several of his successors were explicitly accused of causing their own sons to "pass through the fire of Molech," whose "sacred precinct" just outside Jerusalem was destroyed by the reforming King Josiah (2 Kings 23:10).

Childbirth. The birth of a child is a joyous event in Judaism. In addition to reflecting the participation of the parents in the ongoing process of creation, childbirth is also the fulfillment of the first mitzvah in the Torah, to "be fruitful and multiply" (Gen. 1:28). The ceremonies associated with the birth of a male child include circumcision (*brit milah*) and the redemption of the firstborn (*pidyon ha-ben*), but these do not take place until 8 and 31 days after birth, respectively. Traditional Judaism has developed virtually no rituals for the process of childbirth. The Torah relates the pain associated with giving birth to the disobedience of Eve in the Garden of Eden (Gen. 3:16), and references to the severe intensity of the pangs of the birth process are frequently found in the prophetic books. Because of the significant danger previously inherent in childbirth, many customs surrounding birth were adapted from local non-Jewish traditions to protect the mother and child from evil spirits. These included placing charms and amulets above the labor bed and on the doorposts of the room against the demonic Lilith. With deliveries now usually taking place in hospitals, most of these traditional protective customs have disappeared, particularly since they were primarily based on medieval folklore. With the rise of the Jewish feminist movement, creative prayers surrounding childbirth have been formulated.

Childbirth, impurity after. A woman is considered ritually impure (*niddah*) after giving birth to a child (Lev. 12:1-8) for a period that depends on the gender of her offspring. According to the Torah, a woman who gives birth to a son is a *niddah* for seven days (like a menstruating woman), but she must wait for an additional 33-day period of purification before being permitted to bring a sacrifice to the Temple and regain her ritual purity. Following the birth of a girl, the mother is a *niddah* for 14 days and then must wait an additional 66 days before she is purified. Therefore, a woman is deemed ritually impure for 40 days after the birth of a son and twice that (80 days) after the birth of a daughter. The prolonged postpartum period of ritual impurity is related to the fact that bleeding often continues for four to six weeks after giving birth. However, the reason for doubling the impure period after the birth of a girl is unclear. One possibility is that the newborn daughter will one day herself menstruate and give birth. Another is that the normal period of ritual impurity following childbirth is two weeks, but is reduced after the birth of a son to allow the mother to attend the circumcision in a state of ritual purity, or because the *brit milah* on the eighth day is a purifying rite.[44]

Children of Israel – see *B'nai Yisrael.*

Chillul ha-Shem. Literally, "profaning the Name of God," the Rabbis considered desecration of the Divine Name to be one of the most serious of all transgressions. The biblical verse, "You shall not profane My Holy Name" (Lev. 22:32), is the negative correlate of the positive commandment to sanctify the Name of God (see *Kiddush ha-Shem*). Each Jew must scrupulously avoid any misdeed toward a non-Jew, lest his actions negate and sully the lofty moral standards of Judaism. The offense of a single Jew can bring shame on the entire House of Israel, as well as reflecting adversely on the Name of God, their Father and King.[45]

Chirik – see Vowels.

Chivuv mitzvah (love of the *mitzvah*). The classic example of this virtue is not to bargain over the price when buying something pertaining to a *mitzvah*, but rather to pay at once whatever the seller asks. This is done to show that the love of God is greater than any attachment to material goods. Similarly, one demonstrates love of the *mitzvah* by performing a commandment personally, even when the law permits it to be delegated to others. The Talmud relates that, in preparation for the Sabbath, the distinguished Rabbis of the Talmud showed their love of the *mitzvah* by performing such menial tasks as fanning the fire, salting fish, cutting up beet roots, chopping wood, and carrying heavy loads in and out of the house (Shab. 119a).

Chmielnicki Rebellion. Peasant revolt against Polish rule in the Ukraine, which began in 1648 and was led by this leader of the Cossacks. Whipped into a frenzy of violence and vengeance, the peasants struck out at the most accessible object of their oppression – the Jewish tax collectors, moneylenders, and estate managers who they believed represented all the injustice of the Polish system. Grateful for the opportunity to allow the rabble to vent their anger against the Jews, the Polish nobility did nothing to defend them. Tens of thousands of Jews were killed and hundreds of Jewish communities were destroyed. The massacres shocked the Jewish world and spurred messianic longing, which may have helped lead to the rise of Shabbetai Tzevi (see false messiah).

Chochma (1). Literally a wise or profound saying, this Yiddish term is often used to describe a clever remark or action, especially by a child.

Chochma (knowledge) **(2)**. The 2nd of the *sefirot* and the first male emanation. According to the *Zohar*, *Chochma* (the "upper father") builds a palace that is transfigured into a womb (*Binah*) in which he implants his seed. Also known as the "supernal mother," *Binah* gives birth to her children, the lower seven *sefirot*.

Chok – see *Chukim*.

Chol ha-mo'ed. Hebrew term for the intermediate days of the weeklong holidays of Passover and Sukkot. Except for laws governing the additional sacrifices (cited in the *Musaf* service), the Torah says nothing about how to observe these "mid-festival" days. Essential work may be done, but marriages may not take place (since according to the Talmud two types of rejoicing should not be mixed) and mourning is forbidden. It is customary to greet people by saying *mo'adim l'simcha* (joyous times).

Cholam – see Vowels.

Cholent. Yiddish term for a slow-cooked bean stew that may contain meat, potatoes, and other vegetables. *Cholent* is a Shabbat delicacy among Ashkenazim, since its flavor is enhanced by being prepared the day before and cooked overnight on a low flame, thus observing the prohibition against kindling a light on the Sabbath. Sephardim also have a traditional slow-simmered bean stew for Sabbath lunch, known as either *chamim* (from the Hebrew word for "hot") or *adafina* (from the Arabic word for "covered").

Choleria. Literally "cholera," this Yiddish word is a curse that means "a plague."

Chosen People. The concept of being a "Chosen People," with a unique relationship to God that imposes special responsibilities, has been a central tenet of Jewish thought throughout the centuries. It derives from the series of Divine choices throughout the biblical narrative – the selection of one man (Abraham) to spread the word of the One God, one family (the Children of Israel) to carry on that tradition, one High Priest (Aaron) and family of priests (Levites), one king (David, after the failure of Saul), one land (Israel), and one permanent site for the Sanctuary (Jerusalem). Each of the chosen individuals and groups are responsible for certain tasks and are required to assume particular roles. As Moses stated to the Israelites in his farewell address: "For you are a people consecrated to the Lord your God, who chose you out of all the nations on earth to be His treasured people [or 'special possession'])" (Deut. 7:6). Israel is to be "a light unto the nations" (Isa. 49:6), spreading the ideas of monotheism, God's relation to humanity, and Divine salvation to the ends of the earth. The selection of Israel, which was sealed by several covenants, was not motivated by its size and strength ("the smallest of peoples"), but solely by Divine love (Deut. 7:7–8). However, there is no concept of a relationship between chosenness and national origin, since King David and ultimately the Messiah himself are descendants of Ruth, the Moabite who converted to Judaism. For much of the non-Jewish world, the ironic notion that the despised Jews could conceive of themselves as the Chosen People was summed up in Hilaire Belloc's jingle, "How odd of God to choose the Jews," to which later was added the retort, "It was not odd – the Jews chose God!"

Chronicles (Chron.). Final two books of the Bible, part of the Writings, known in Hebrew as *Divrei ha-Yamim* (stories/events of the days). They contain genealogical lists from Adam through David (1 Chron. 1-9), accounts of the reigns of David (1 Chron. 10-29) and Solomon (2 Chron. 1-9), and a history of the Kingdom of Judah until its destruction by the Babylonians (2 Chron. 10-36). There are almost no references to the Northern Kingdom of Israel. Chronicles affirms the belief that the Israelite king was not above the law and that each generation must answer only for its own sins and not those of previous ones.

Chukat. The 6th *parashah* in the Book of Numbers (19:1-22:1), it contains the laws concerning the red heifer, relates the death of Miriam, and continues the narrative of the wanderings of the Israelites.

Chukat ha-goy. Literally "law of the gentile," this Hebrew expression is used to refer to any non-Jewish practice that a religious Jew should avoid.

Chukim (sing., *chok*). Commandments for which the reason is not obvious, such as the dietary laws, *sha'atnez*, and the red heifer, which must be obeyed as expressions of Divine sovereignty. They are distinguished from *mishpatim*.

Chullin (Chul.). The 3rd tractate of Kodashim (holy things) in the Mishnah, it deals with the ritual slaughter of animals and the dietary laws.

Chumash. Book containing the Five Books of Moses (Torah), the first of the three divisions of the Bible. In Hebrew, the name of each individual book reflects its initial (or first significant) word – *Bereshit* (in the beginning), *Shemot* (names), *Vayikra* (and He [God] called), *Bamidbar* (in the wilderness), and *Devarim* (words). The English names for these five books – Genesis, Exodus, Leviticus, Numbers, and Deuteronomy – have their origins in the titles prevailing among the Greek-speaking Jews, who translated the Hebrew designations in use among their co-religionists in the Land of Israel. These names are descriptive of the contents or major themes of the respective books. (See sections on individual books under their English names.)

Chuppah. Hebrew word referring either to the wedding canopy, which is usually made of beautiful fabric and supported by four poles, or to the marriage ceremony itself. During the biblical period, the *chuppah* was the groom's room or tent in which the marriage was consummated. According to the Talmud, "it was customary when a boy was born to plant a cedar tree and when a girl was born to plant a pine tree. When they married, the trees were cut down and a canopy (*chuppah*) made of the branches" (Git. 57a). Thus, the *chuppah* represented the fulfillment of the parents' hopes for their children. Even today, children receiving their Hebrew names are blessed with the hope that they will grow to "Torah, the wedding canopy (*chuppah*), and good deeds (*ma'asim tovim*)."[46]

Chutz la-aretz. Literally "outside the land," the collective Hebrew term denoting every place outside the territorial limits of the Land of Israel

Chutzpah. Yiddish term variously translated as impudence, nerve, unmitigated audacity, and unbelievable gall. A classic humorous example is the man who murders his mother and father and then throws himself on the mercy of the court because he is an orphan!

Circumcision. Termed *brit milah* in Hebrew and popularly pronounced in its Yiddish form, *bris*, this ceremony of removing the foreskin of the penis on the eighth day of life is the first life-cycle ritual commanded in the Torah (Gen. 17:11-12). The Hebrew word "*brit*" means "covenant," and this procedure symbolizes the entry of the infant boy into the covenant that God made with the patriarch Abraham almost 4,000 years ago. Judaism has long regarded circumcision as the primary symbol of male membership within the Jewish people. Circumcision was performed in many ancient cultures, primarily on adolescents as a puberty rite symbolizing a boy's sexual maturity and marking the passage from childhood to adulthood. In contrast, the Jewish practice of performing circumcision in infancy reflects a sanctification of his body to the Divine service. It symbolically commits the newborn male to control his sexual urges and channel them toward providing for the perpetuation of his people. Judaism prohibits female circumcision.

Cities, levitical – see Levitical cities.

Cities of refuge. The Israelites were commanded to establish six cities of refuge (three on each side of the Jordan) to which a person could flee if he unintentionally killed another individual. This injunction also required the building of wide, level roads with appropriate directional signs to these cities, as well as the removal of any obstacles that might hinder the fugitive in his flight (Num. 35:9-34). Every person who killed another, "whether unintentionally or with intent," would immediately flee to a city of refuge to escape the blood avenger. From the city of refuge, the individual would be sent to the court for trial. If the killing had been completely accidental, the perpetrator would be absolved of any responsibility and set free (and the blood avenger had no right to harm him). If the killing had been intentional, the murderer properly warned in advance, and his act witnessed by two reliable individuals, the court would order his execution by beheading. If the act was unintentional but associated with some culpable carelessness (i.e., involuntary manslaughter), the perpetrator would be exiled to a city of refuge. The court would be responsible for providing safe passage so that the blood avenger could not kill him on the way. A person who had been exiled to a city of refuge by the court was required to remain there until the death of the High Priest.

City, apostate. If a city that was so spiritually corrupt that all or most of its citizens worshiped idols, the Israelites were commanded to slay all the inhabitants of the city and burn all its property (even that of the non-sinners), leaving it a desolate ruin never to be rebuilt (Deut. 13:17). According to Maimonides,[47] this law was virtually impossible to invoke because of the strict conditions limiting its application. For example, when a report of idolatry in any city in Israel was received, the Great Sanhedrin in Jerusalem was obliged to send two sages to warn the population to repent. If those who continued their idolatrous practices constituted less than a majority, the entire city would not be destroyed; only individual idolaters would be subjected to the penalty of death by stoning.[48]

City gate. In ancient times, the center of public activity because it was often the most open area in an otherwise crowded city, a place that people constantly passed through on their way in and out of town. The city gate was often where lawsuits were heard and legal sentences executed, as well as a site for commercial transactions. The original meaning of the command to "inscribe them on the doorposts [*mezuzot*] of your house and on your gates" (Deut. 6:9) referred to the gates of the city (homes rarely had gates), since this would be the most effective way of publicizing the Divine teachings.[49]

City of David. Although this term is generally used as a synonym for Jerusalem, it more precisely refers to the ancient City of David, which was located on a narrow ridge south of the current Old City. On the east it bordered the deep Kidron Valley, the site where the Gihon Spring (its water source) is located. Under King Solomon, the city was extended northward and the lateral valley separating the City of David from Mount Moriah was filled in. This area became the site of many new palaces, and the Temple was built on the summit of Mount Moriah. By medieval times, the southern wall of Jerusalem had been built along the line of the present Old City wall. This excluded the City of David and left the site of biblical Jerusalem uninhabited. Archeological exploration of the City of David began in the middle of the 19th century and continues to this day.

Clean animals. Animals whose flesh may be eaten and whose milk may be drunk according to Jewish law (Lev. 11; Deut 14). To qualify as kosher (see *kashrut*), a quadruped must both chew the cud (ruminant) and have hoofs that are completely cloven (divided). Fish must have both fins and scales. Although the Torah specifically names 20 non-kosher species of birds, all birds of prey and those that eat carrion are prohibited. Noah was commanded to take into the ark seven pairs of every *clean* beast (but only a pair of all *unclean* animals; Gen. 7:2), with the underlying rationale presumably being that the clean animals were suitable for sacrifice.

Cleaving (to God) – see *Devekut*.

Cochin. City and former state on the Malabar Coast in southwest India that was home to a vibrant Jewish community. The so-called "black Jews" claim to descend from Jews who settled there during the reign of King Solomon and the early years of the divided monarchy. The "white Jews" came later as exiles from Europe, especially Spain and Portugal, Holland, and Germany. The third group was composed of freed slaves. The three groups maintained separate houses of worship and a traditional synagogue-centered life. Influenced by the Indian caste system, they did not intermarry. The Cochin community flourished under Dutch rule in the 17th and 18th centuries, with Jews arriving from the Middle East and North Africa. Although several thousand Cochin Jews have made *aliyah* to Israel, a small community remains.

Codes – see Law codes.

Coffin (*aron*). Coffins were not used by the ancient Israelites. The deceased was simply buried on a bed of intertwined reeds, literally fulfilling the requirement of the biblical verse, "for dust you are, and to dust you shall return" (Gen. 3:19). The only reference to a coffin in the Bible is the one in which the embalmed body of Joseph was kept (Gen. 50:26), reflecting an Egyptian custom and serving the purpose of preserving the body until it could be brought back to the Land of Israel for burial many years later. The use of elaborate coffins during talmudic times led to a ruling, followed by traditional Jews to this day, of having a plain wooden coffin – with no nails, metal, or any decoration – usually made of pine or other inexpensive soft wood that decomposes more rapidly than a hard wood like oak.

Coins. The earliest coins found on the soil of the Land of Israel date back to about 500 B.C.E. They are Greek coins that probably were brought by merchants visiting the country. The consecutive history of ancient Jewish coinage begins after the establishment of the independent Hasmonean dynasty in the 2nd century B.C.E. The bulk were bronze coins of small denomination and, in accordance with the Second Commandment, they contained no likeness of humans or animals. The emblems found on the coins (e.g., cornucopia, wreath, anchor, flower, star, helmet) were copied from those issued by the Seleucids. All Hasmonean coins bear Hebrew words (those of Alexander Yannai and Mattathias Antigonus also have writing in Greek), and almost all are undated. The first silver coin struck by Jews in antiquity was the *shekel*, with a Hebrew inscription and the image of a chalice with a pearl rim and three pomegranates. The last Jewish coin series in antiquity was issued during the Bar Kochba War (132-135 C.E.). After the fall of Jerusalem in 70 C.E., the Romans issued coins depicting the defeated Jews as a forlorn woman sitting in mourning beneath a palm tree, with the Latin inscription "*Judea capta est*" (Judea is conquered).

Columbus Platform. Declaration issued in 1937 by rabbis of the American Reform movement meeting in this Ohio city. It supported the use of traditional ceremonies and Hebrew in the liturgy and re-emphasized the idea of the Jewish people, a dramatic revision of the Reform principles stated a half century earlier in the Pittsburgh Platform.

Columns of Jachin and Boaz. The two pillars set up by Solomon at the entrance to the Temple in Jerusalem (1 Kings 7:15-22). Images of these columns are often embroidered onto the mantle covering the Torah scroll or the *parochet* in front of the ark.

Commandments – see *Mitzvot.*

Compassion – see *Rachamim.*

Complementary polar opposites. A major distinction between Greek and classical Jewish thought is the law of exclusion. Aristotle maintained that something may be *either* P or not P. In contrast, Jewish thought posits that something may be *both* P and not P, so that everything exists in terms of complementary polar opposites (e.g., male-female; up-down; heaven-earth; good-bad). For example, in Greek thought, God cannot be both transcendent and immanent at the same time, while in Jewish thought this presents no difficulty. In the standard Jewish blessing formula, God is addressed in both the second person ("praised are You") and the third person ("Who…"). Greek logic is restrictive; Jewish logic is embracive. In Greek thought there is only one dimension of meaning in a text (i.e., what it says), whereas in Jewish thought there can be multiple levels of meaning (see *eilu v'eilu*).

Concentration camps – see Camps, concentration and extermination.

Concordance, biblical. Alphabetical index with definitions of all the words in the Bible. It provides citations to, or even the full text of, the biblical verses in which individual words occur.

Concubine. In the ancient Near East, childlessness due to the wife remaining barren after a certain number of years of marriage has always been regarded as sufficient grounds for divorce. To prevent this, the wife was often willing to give her husband a maidservant as a concubine, since the children of the concubine could be regarded as those of the legal wife. Consequently, Rachel gave Jacob her handmaiden, Bilhah, as a concubine, so that Jacob could cohabit with her "that she may bear on my knees and that through her I too may have children" (Gen. 30:3-4). In ancient times, this action was tantamount to adoption, so that Bilhah would be a surrogate mother whose offspring (Dan and Naphtali) Rachel would accept as her own.

Confession of faith – see *Shema.*

Confession of sin. According to Jewish tradition, the confession of sin is the first step toward atonement. Therefore, the Rabbis included confessions of sins in each of the five services on Yom Kippur, the Day of Atonement. There are two prescribed forms of confession that are recited today – *Al Chet* and *Ashamnu.* Both of these confessions are expressed in the plural, as is customary in Jewish liturgy, in keeping with the concept of collective responsibility of Jews for one another (Shev. 39a). Each Jew confesses not only those sins that he or she has committed personally, but every transgression that may have been committed by anyone in the congregation. At the mention of each transgression, all worshipers symbolically express their remorse by tapping their chests, since the heart was thought to be the seat and source of sin. Those near death also are encouraged to confess their sins. All confessions of sins in Judaism are made directly to God with no intermediary.

Confirmation. In the 19th century, the early Reform congregations in Germany attempted to replace the bar mitzvah with a ceremony termed "confirmation," a Jewish adaptation of Christian church practice. Unlike bar mitzvah, confirmation was conceived as a group ceremony celebrated by both male and female religious school students at the completion of their studies at age 16 or 17. Today, especially in the United States, confirmation has been adopted in Reform, Reconstructionist, and most Conservative synagogues as a supplement to, rather than a substitute for, the bar/bat mitzvah ceremony. The main intention of confirmation is to extend Jewish education by several years, enhancing the commitment of young people to Judaism. Some religious schools attempt to have confirmation around age 18 to coincide with the senior year of high school. The ceremony is generally held on Shavuot, the holiday celebrating the giving of the Torah on Mount Sinai, since confirmation students symbolically accept the Torah during the ceremony and publicly declare their devotion to Jewish ideals. Before the bat mitzvah ceremony became widespread, confirmation provided an opportunity for adolescent Jewish girls to participate in a public religious rite of passage.

Congratulations. The most common expression of congratulations at a wedding, bar/bat mitzvah, or other celebration is "*mazel tov*" (lit., "good star") among Ashkenazim and "*siman tov*"(good omen) among Sephardim. In the United States, the two expressions are often joined together in the song *siman tov u-mazel tov*. In Ashkenazic synagogues, other worshipers typically congratulate the person returning from having an *aliyah* with the Yiddish phrase *yasher ko'ach* ("may you grow in strength" or "may your strength be directed in the right path."), to which the reply is "*Baruch t'hiyeh*" (may you be blessed). Among Sephardim, the expression used is "*Hazak u-varuch*" (be strong and be blessed) or "*Baruch t'hiyeh*" (may you be blessed), to which the person returning from having an *aliyah* replies, "*Hazak ve-ematz*" (be strong and of good courage).

Consecration. The act of making something or someone holy, dedicated to a specific function. During the biblical period, this was usually accomplished by anointing with oil. The festival of Chanukah celebrates the rededication (consecration) of the Temple Altar by the Maccabees. Today, newly built synagogues are consecrated for sacred use. The ceremonies of bar and bat mitzvah can be viewed as consecrating the boy or girl to a life of observance of the *mitzvot*.

Conservative Judaism. Modern denomination of Judaism that arose in the United States in the early 1900's. Known in Israel as "Masorti Judaism," Conservative Judaism has its roots in the Positive-Historical Judaism developed by Zechariah Frankel in Germany in the 1850's as a reaction to the more liberal religious positions taken by Reform Judaism.Conservative Judaism is committed to a non-fundamentalist view of *halachah* (Jewish law) and a positive view toward modern culture. It accepts both traditional rabbinic modes of study and modern scholarship and critical analysis when considering Jewish religious texts. Conservative Judaism emphasizes Jewish peoplehood and commitment to the Land of Israel and the Hebrew language. The major academic institution of Conservative Judaism is the Jewish Theological Seminary of America in New York City; the smaller University of Judiasm is in Los Angeles. The Solomon Schechter day schools are affiliated with the movement, as are the Ramah camps and United Synagogue Youth (USY).

Contract. Legally binding agreement between two or more parties. The only standard contracts in Jewish law are related to marriage (see *ketubah*) and divorce (see *get*).

Controversies, religious. As with all religions, Judaism has been beset by sectarian disputes. Examples include the differences between the Pharisees and Sadducees in the late Second Temple period; the Rabbinites and Karaites in the 8th century; and the Hasidim and *mitnagdim* in the 18th century. Today, there are conflicts between the ultra-Orthodox and more liberal Jewish movements (Conservative, Reform, Reconstructionist). One particularly divisive controversy concerns the Reform movement's acceptance of patrilineal descent, which has been totally rejected by Orthodox and Conservative Jews.

Conversion. Throughout its history, Judaism has always been open to accepting converts. The conversion process consists primarily of a period of study, ranging from several months to a few years, which includes private or group classes on Jewish history, beliefs and prayers, holidays, life-cycle ceremonies, and home rituals. Many rabbis require that a convert learn basic Hebrew; in Orthodox conversions, there is an emphasis on the specific requirements of Jewish law. In addition to study, prospective converts begin to adopt a Jewish lifestyle, such as attending synagogue services; observing the Sabbath, festivals, and dietary laws;

and performing acts of *tzedakah* and *gemilut chasadim*.[50] Traditionally, the prospective convert appears before a *beit din*, a court of three rabbis, which asks the candidate a variety of questions to test basic Jewish knowledge and commitment to Jewish beliefs, ethics, and ritual observances. In Orthodox and Conservative conversions, the next steps in the process are the rituals of circumcision for males and immersion in the *mikveh* (ritual bath) for both men and women. If a man has already been circumcised, a drop of blood is taken from the penis as a symbol of circumcision (see *hatafat dam brit*). Neither circumcision nor immersion in the *mikveh* is required by the Reform movement. In Israel, conversions may be performed only by Orthodox rabbis.

Conversion, forced. For centuries, Jews have been compelled to forsake Judaism and convert to another religion on pain of death. The most famous were the *Conversos* in Spain and Portugal, who were forced to convert to Catholicism. Less well-known were Jews forcibly converted to Islam in Spain and North Africa during the 12th century and in Mashad (Persia) during the 19th century. Like the *Conversos*, these "New Muslims" lived a double life and observed their Judaism in secret.

Conversion from Judaism – see Apostate.

Conversos. Term for the tens of thousands of Jews and their descendants in Spain and Portugal who were forcibly converted to Christianity in the late Middle Ages but continued to practice their Judaism in secret. Those "crypto-Jews" who were caught by the Inquisition, the church body charged with uprooting heresy, were ruthlessly tortured and then burned at the stake in a ceremony known as the *auto-da-fé*. *Converso* is preferred to the more frequently used, but disparaging, term *Marrano*, which comes from a Spanish word meaning "swine." Some *Conversos* lived in Spain and Portugal for centuries.

Converts, attitude toward. It is forbidden to taunt converts by reminding them of their non-Jewish past and suggesting that this makes them unfit to study God's Torah. The Tanhuma praises those who have converted to Judaism as "dearer to God than all of the Israelites who stood at Mount Sinai. Had the Israelites not witnessed the lightning, thunder, quaking mountain, and sounding trumpets, they would not have accepted the Torah. But the convert, who did not see or hear any of these things, came and surrendered to God and accepted the yoke of heaven. Can anyone be dearer to God than such a person?" A tendency to increase the honor of converts may be reflected in the tradition that traces the origins of great rabbinic personalities to evil non-Jewish forebears. Nevertheless, some authorities were extremely opposed to the concept of conversion, expressing concern about the true motivation of potential converts. During times of war and revolt, some converts and their offspring became renegades and informers, often slandering their new religion and denouncing the Jewish community and its leaders to foreign rulers. The Midrash urged that Jews "not trust a convert, even to the 24th generation, because the inherent evil is still within him." One sage went so far as to state that, "converts are as hard for Israel [to endure] as a sore" (Yev. 47b). Today, the non-Jewish partners of mixed marriages are encouraged to convert to Judaism.

Copper Scroll. One of the Dead Sea Scrolls, discovered in Qumran in 1952, it is the only one written on metal (almost pure copper with about 1% tin). Rather than a literary work, it is an inventory listing the locations where the gold and silver treasures of the community were buried or hidden when it was disbanded in the 1st century C.E.

Corporal punishment. In biblical times, whipping with a strap was the penalty for transgressions of negative commandments that involved a physical act and could not be rectified by a monetary payment or by performing a subsequent positive commandment.[51] According to tradition, the maximum number of strokes that could be inflicted on a man liable to whipping was 39; the minimum was three. However, no person was subjected to corporal punishment until an estimate was made of the number of strokes he could bear (based on his age, temperament, and physique). Rather than the infliction of pain, the goal of lashes was to allow the guilty party to atone for past transgressions and to discourage him from engaging in similar activity in the future.

Corpse. According to biblical law, a dead human body was the most potent source of ritual impurity. Thus, a person who had come into contact with a corpse was prohibited from entering the Temple or eating sanctified food. The corpse conveyed ritual uncleanness to anyone or anything that entered or remained under the same roof with it (including household utensils and wearing apparel), even if the person or thing had no direct contact with the dead body. In biblical times, this uncleanness required purification by the ashes of the red heifer.In rabbinic law, the restrictions concerning contact with a corpse only affected priests, who were forbidden from defiling themselves for any dead person other than those specified in the Torah (mother, father, son, daughter, unmarried sister). Proper care of the corpse (see *kavod ha-met*) has been regarded as a *mitzvah* of the highest order.

Cossacks. In the 1630s, a series of Cossack uprisings in the Ukraine sparked a wave of unrest throughout Eastern Europe, culminating in the Chmielnicki Rebellion in 1648.These warlike descendants of Russian serfs were renowned for their skill as horsemen and recruited by the kings of Poland in the 16th century to repel the Tartar invaders from Crimea to the east. When the Cossacks were victorious and the Tartar threat eliminated, the Polish government revoked the privileges and autonomy it had granted the Cossacks as payment for their services.

Council of the Four Lands (*Va'ad Arba Aratzot*). Collective term for the central institutions of Jewish self-government in Poland and Lithuania from the middle of the 16th century until 1764, a period during which the Jewish community in these lands gained a substantial degree of autonomy. Although formally only bodies that negotiated and then collected the taxes of Jews for the secular government of the country, they also directed many social, economic, ethical, and legal aspects of Jewish life, as well as framing the laws regulating the affairs of the communities and the conduct of their leaders. The councils also controlled religious education and granted approval to books published in their communities. They stressed the establishment of *yeshivot* and exempted scholars from paying tax. The councils ceased operation when the Polish *Sejm* (parliament) established a different system for collecting the Jewish poll tax.

Counting. Based on the catastrophe that followed David's unauthorized census of the people (see census), the Talmud decreed: "Israel must not be counted [using numbers], even for religious purposes." Therefore, several different counting customs developed to determine the presence of a *minyan*.Some use verses from Psalms that consist of 10 Hebrew words – *Hoshia et amecha u-varech et nachalatechah u-r'eim v'nas'eim ad olam* (Save Your people and bless Your inheritance, tend them and elevate them forever; Ps. 28:9); *Einay chol eilecha y'sabeiru, v'ata notein la-hem et achlam b'ito* (The eyes of all look to You with hope, and You give them their food in its proper time; Ps 145:15); and *Va'ani b'rov chasdechah avo veitechah, eshtachaveh el heichal kodshechah b'yiratechah* (As for me, through Your abundant kindness I will enter Your house, and bow low toward Your holy Temple in awe of You; Ps. 5:8). A different approach is to say "not one, not two ...," thus pretending that one is not actually counting.

Court Jews. Term applied to financial or other agents of absolute European rulers from the end of the 16th century. Along with their Christian counterparts, they made significant contributions to financial, commercial, and industrial undertakings in their realms. Among the special privileges they enjoyed were permission to live wherever they chose and exemption from wearing the Jewish badge. Many used their influential positions to secure additional rights for their fellow Jews.

Courts – see *Beit din* and Sanhedrin.

Covenant. The concept of covenant (*brit* in Hebrew), a special relationship between God and the Jewish people, is a major foundation of the theology of Judaism (see Chosen People). The classic covenant between God and Israel took place at Mount Sinai, less than two months after the Exodus from Egypt (Exod. 19). Periodic renewal of the covenant was a major biblical motif at times of important historical events. In addition to the ceremonies before the entry of the Israelites into the Promised Land and after its conquest, formal renewals of the covenant occurred under Solomon at the dedication of the Temple; Josiah after the discovery of the Book of Deuteronomy and as part of his sweeping religious reforms; and Nehemiah after the return of the people to Zion from Babylonian Exile. Each of these was characterized by a "reaffirmation of faith" – a long sermon to the entire nation that served as a tool to educate the people and renew their connection with both the One God and their national history. At the renewal ceremony before entering Canaan, Moses emphasized the continuity of the covenant throughout the generations, stressing that at Sinai "it was not with our fathers that the Lord made this covenant." Rather, it was made "with us, the living, every one of us who is here today" (Deut. 5:2-3) and thus was binding upon the Jewish people for all time. Covenants also were made between God and specific human beings – Noah (Gen. 6:18, 9:9-11), and Abraham (Gen. 15). Circumcision is the primary outward sign testifying to the validity of the covenant.

Covenant, conditional. Mutual agreement between God and Israel stipulating that when the people perform the will of God they will enjoy Divine blessings; however, if they disobey the law of God, fail to fulfill the commandments, and lapse into idolatry they will be cursed and suffer natural and political disasters. This concept of national reward and punishment, associated with the covenant at Mount Sinai and elucidated in painstaking detail in the *Tochachah*, is the traditional explanation for the destruction of the First Temple and the Babylonian Exile.

Covenant, unconditional. Unilateral pledge, as in the Divine promise to David that his dynasty will be everlasting. God assures the king that his son will "build a house for My name and I will establish his royal throne forever. I will be a father to him, and he shall be a son to Me. When he does wrong, I will chastise him with the rod of men and the affliction of mortals, but I will never withdraw My favor from him...Your house and your kingship shall ever be secure before you; your throne shall be established forever" (2 Sam. 7:12-16). According to Jewish tradition, the fulfillment of this Divine promise will be the coming of the Messiah, who will be a descendant of King David.

Covering the head – see *Kippah* and Head covering, women.

Coveting. The prohibition against the envious desire for possessing that which belongs to one's neighbor is the last of the Ten Commandments (Exod. 20:14; Deut. 5:18). Ibn Ezra observed that one who has complete faith in God should realize that the property of his neighbor was not Divinely intended to be his.[52] Although coveting can lead to hatred and is a root cause of many sins, Judaism maintains that one may master one's desires. As noted in *Pirkei Avot* (4:1), "Who is rich? One who is happy with his lot."

Creatio ex nihilo (creation from nothing). Theological doctrine that God created the universe from nothing, a polemic against the idea in ancient myth and philosophy that the universe was created by the gods from some primordial matter that had always existed. For the medieval Jewish mystics, this creation from nothing (in Hebrew, *yesh mei-ayin*) began with the emanation of *Chochma* from *Keter* (*ayin* or "nothing") and thus represented an unfolding of the Divine personality from within itself.

Creation. The biblical account of Creation in Genesis is substantially different from the myths of other peoples in the ancient Near East. Rather than the pagan idea of a primordial realm that contained the elements of all being and led to the birth of sexually differentiated gods who then procreated to produce the full panoply of deities, in the Israelite view there is a single God who is the source of all being and by fiat caused everything to appear from nothing (*creatio ex nihilo*) according to God's exclusive will. This idea excluded both dualism and pantheism.In both the biblical and Babylonian accounts, the final act of the creative process is man. However, unlike the Babylonian myth in which human beings are created merely to build shrines and worship the gods, attending to their every physical need, the Bible views man as the pinnacle of Creation, a creature who represents a unique combination of animalistic traits with the nobility of a soul that elevates him to be created in the image of God. In the Babylonian epic of creation, the deities relaxed after their creative activities and held a huge feast, whereas in Genesis, God's rest set an orderly pattern for the future conduct of mankind, making the Sabbath holy.

Creation, Book of – see *Sefer Yetzirah*.

Creed. Authoritative statement of religious belief. Although popular in Christianity, a concise formula expressing a fundamental system of beliefs is not a basic idea in Judaism, which places supreme value on observance of the commandments. A person is judged by actions rather than on professions of belief. The closest to an accepted "creed" in Judaism are the Thirteen Principles of Faith of Maimonides. These fall into three general categories – the nature of belief in God; the authenticity of the Torah; and the responsibility of human beings and their ultimate reward. (See also *dogma*.)

Cremation. Disposal of a dead body by burning is not a Jewish custom, and cremation is prohibited because it interferes with natural bodily decay. According to traditional practice, cremated ashes may not be buried in a Jewish cemetery. Furthermore, those who choose not to be buried in the ancient Jewish manner, as a final defiance of tradition, are not to be mourned.[53] Although more liberal Jewish denominations also discourage cremation in favor of the traditional practice of burial, many of their rabbis will officiate at a memorial service for a person who has been cremated and permit the ashes to be buried in the cemetery.[54]

Crusades. Series of holy wars in the 11th-13th centuries, undertaken by European Christians to redeem the Holy Land from the Muslims. The Crusades provoked religious passion that produced anti-Jewish sentiments, resulting in the massacre of numerous European Jewish communities as the armies marched toward the Land of Israel. This marked a turning point in the history of the Jews of Christian Europe, ushering in a period of increased Christian anti-Semitism. Many Ashkenazic Jews willingly embraced martyrdom, choosing death over conversion. When the Crusaders conquered Jerusalem in 1099, they ruthlessly murdered all the Jews in the city.

Crypto-Jews. Jews who remained faithful to Judaism in secret, while outwardly practicing another religion to which they had been forced to convert. The most famous of these were the *Conversos* in Spain and Portugal.

Cubit. Biblical measurement of length, based on the distance between the elbow and the tip of the middle finger, which in an average man equals about 18 inches (1.5 foot or 45 cm.).

Cultural Zionists – see Zionists, cultural.

Cup of Elijah. Large ornate goblet that is filled with wine at the Passover seder and placed on the table, but not drunk. It is prepared in the hope that the prophet will come soon – perhaps even on this Passover night – as the herald of the Messiah. Once the Cup of Elijah has been poured, it is customary to open the front door and recite a prayer asking God to "Pour out Your wrath upon the nations that do not recognize You and upon the kingdoms that do not invoke Your Name." This custom dates back to the Middle Ages, when the Passover season was an especially difficult time for Jews because of the proximity to Easter and the threat of a blood libel. During this period of danger, Jews would constantly open their doors to foil such a plot.

Curse. In ancient times, a curse was more than an expressed wish for evil. Often pronounced in the name of a pagan god or demon, a curse was considered a method of making a potential harm become a reality. The penalty for cursing one's father or mother was death (Exod. 21:17). The Bible also expressly prohibited cursing God, judges (Exod. 22:27), authorities (chief of a clan or a tribe in the period before the monarchy; Exod. 22:27), and the deaf (Lev. 19:14). The Rabbis extended this to a prohibition against cursing any Israelite, for if a person was forbidden to curse one who cannot hear it and thus would not be angered or embarrassed by the curse, how much more is it forbidden to curse one who would react with anger or shame and might even resort to violence in a moment of uncontrollable passion.

Cursing God – see Blasphemy.

Custom – see *Minhag*.

D

D. According to the Documentary Hypothesis (see Bible criticism), one of the four major strands of literary tradition edited to form the Five Books of Moses. Also known as the Deuteronomist, it consists of most of the Book of Deuteronomy as well as the "Deuteronomist history," which includes Joshua, Judges, 1 and 2 Samuel, and 1 and 2 Kings. D stresses the primacy of the central shrine in Jerusalem. Some scholars associate the D source with the reforms undertaken by King Josiah of Judah in the 7th century B.C.E., hypothesizing that Deuteronomy might be the law book found during the repair of the Temple.

Daf Yomi. Literally, "page of the day," this term refers to a monumental program in which Jews throughout the world study an identical page of the Talmud each day. Initiated by Rabbi Meir Shapira in 1923 at the First World Congress of Agudat Yisrael in Vienna, this program results in communal completion of the study of the entire Talmud every seven and a half years. The *daf yomi* has become an accepted part of Orthodox study, and the current 12th cycle of study began March 2, 2005. The term "*daf yomi*" is related to the experience of the great talmudic sage, R. Akiva, who was tossed into a stormy sea when his ship was wrecked and given up for lost. As he later described his miraculous rescue: "*A daf* (plank) from the ship suddenly appeared as a salvation, and I just let the waves pass over me." Writing between the two World Wars, Rabbi Shapira explained the significance of his undertaking by paraphrasing R. Akiva: "*A daf* is the instrument of our survival in the stormy seas of today. If we cling to it faithfully all the waves of tribulation will pass over us."

Dagesh. Diacritical mark in Hebrew that appears as a dot within a consonant. In its most common form, the *dagesh* indicates that the consonant (*bet*, *gimel*, *dalet*, *kaf*, *pei*, *tav*) is to be pronounced with a hard sound. Less frequently, it means that the consonant, though written only once, is to be pronounced as if it were doubled.

Dairy foods – see *Milchig* and Mixing meat and milk.

Dalet. The 4th letter of the Hebrew alphabet, with a numerical value of 4.

Damages. Despite the famous biblical verse mandating an "eye for an eye" (see *lex talionis*) for bodily injury, under Jewish law a person who injures another willfully or by gross negligence must pay the monetary equivalent to the person he has harmed. Although the Torah speaks only of compensation based on time lost from work and the cost of medical treatment, the Rabbis expanded it to include payment for physical disability, pain, and the "indignity inflicted" (humiliation and mental anguish) (BK 83b).

Damascus affair. When a Franciscan friar and his servant disappeared in Damascus in February 1840, not long before Passover, the Turkish governor and French consul believed accusations of ritual murder associated with blood libel.Leading Jews were tortured and a confession was obtained. More than 60 Jewish children were held hostage, and mobs attacked Jewish communities throughout the Middle East. After widespread international protest, the murder charge was eventually dropped and the surviving Jewish prisoners were released. The Damascus affair prompted French Jews to establish the Alliance Israélite Universelle to safeguard Jewish rights and to promote Jewish well-being.

Dan. Town in the territory of the tribe of Dan, the fifth of Jacob's children, near the headwaters of the Jordan River. Dan was considered as the northernmost limit of the Land of Israel, whose north-south span was described by the popular phrase "from Dan to Be'er Sheva" (Judg. 20:1).

Dance. As in other ancient cultures, dance in Judaism dates back to the earliest recorded times. After the Israelites crossed the Sea of Reeds, in which the army of Egypt drowned, Miriam and other women performed a victory dance praising God. By the Middle Ages, most Jewish communities in Central and Eastern Europe had a wedding house in which dancing took place. On Simchat Torah, it became customary to dance with the Torah scrolls in the synagogue. With the rise of Hasidism in the mid-18th century, dance assumed a religious role as a way of expressing love and devotion to God. The Zionist movement in the Land of Israel developed a series of folk dances, including the *hora*. Indeed, dancing helped the early pioneers in Palestine develop a group spirit and overcome hardship.

Daniel (Dan.). The 9th book of the Writings section of the Bible. Daniel was carried off to Babylonia and educated in the court of Nebuchadnezzar, where he was trained for the king's service. At a great royal banquet, Daniel interpreted the four strange words (*mene mene tekel upharsin*), written silently by a mysterious hand silently across the palace wall, as foretelling the downfall of the King Belshazzar, whose arrogant actions had earned the wrath of God. That very night, the king was killed and Darius became ruler of the land. Despite a royal decree prohibiting the presentation of a petition to any god or man other than the king, Daniel continued to pray and give thanks to God three times a day (Dan. 6:11). As punishment, he was cast into a den with seven famished lions, miraculously remaining there unharmed for six days. Thus, Daniel serves as a role model for a

Diaspora Jew who can maintain his faith in the face of opposing religious demands. The last half of the Book of Daniel, written in Hebrew (the rest is in Aramaic), contains mystical revelations about the end of days, the Day of Judgment when the wicked world powers will be destroyed and the Jewish people restored to their home.

Darshan (preacher) – see *Derash.*

Date palm – see Palm tree.

Dati. Hebrew word meaning "religious," used by Israelis for modern Orthodox Jews. Unlike the ultra-Orthodox *haredim*, who try to completely isolate themselves from secular culture and learning, the modern Orthodox live within the framework of contemporary society while engaging in strict religious observance.

Daughter(s) of Zion. Biblical phrase respectively referring to the city of Jerusalem or the entire Jewish people.

Daven. Yiddish word meaning "to pray," which is used among Ashkenazim. Traditional Jews *daven* three times a day (morning, afternoon, evening) in private or preferably with a *minyan* (quorum of 10) at synagogue services.

David, melech Yisrael, chai v'kayam (David, King of Israel, lives and endures). Lyrics of a popular song that are repeated three times during the ceremony of *Kiddush Levanah* (Sanctification of the Moon) as a symbol of Israel's renewal and national redemption. This code message relating the rebirth of the moon, the Davidic dynasty, and the perpetual existence of the Jewish people developed during the talmudic era. When the Romans abrogated the authority of the rabbinical court in Jerusalem to consecrate the day of the New Moon, this ceremony had to be carried out clandestinely. Judah the Prince sent an emissary to the place where the *beit din* met, instructing them to sanctify Rosh Chodesh on the 30th day. The return message, indicating that this mission had been accomplished, contained the watchword *David, Melech Yisrael, chai v'kayam*.

David's Tomb – see Mount Zion.

Davka. A Hebrew expression of defiance. It means "in spite of," or perhaps even "because of a certain obstacle, one is prepared to move forward."

Day of Atonement. English term for Yom Kippur.

Day of Judgment (*Yom ha-Din*). A rabbinic term for Rosh Hashanah, when God weighs the deeds of every person and decides the fate of each one for the coming year (see *U-netaneh Tokef*). According to tradition, however, the final judgment is not "sealed" until Yom Kippur, allowing for a 10-day period (see Ten Days of Repentance) of intensive soul searching and reconciliation with the Divine that may influence God to reconsider an unfavorable decision and "avert the severity of the decree." The Bible also refers to an eschatological Day of Judgment (Day of the Lord) at the end of the world when the enemies of Israel will be destroyed, a time when the righteous receive their eternal reward and the wicked get the endless punishment they merit.

Day of the Lord – see Day of Judgment.

Dayan. Judge of a rabbinic court (see *beit din*).

Dayan ha-Emet (the True Judge). Those present when a person dies recite the blessing *Baruch Ata Adonai, Dayan ha-Emet* (Praised are You, Lord, the True Judge), indicating submission to the will of God. According to the Talmud, one must also say a blessing for sad news, praising the Divine Name even at a time of personal loss (Ber. 59b).

Dayenu. Hebrew word that literally means "it would have been enough for us [sufficient]." The refrain of a popular song of thanksgiving at the Passover seder, it begins with the words, "How many acts of kindness God has performed for us," and enumerates 15 (in some versions 16) stages of the redemption of the Israelites from Egyptian bondage. These include their miraculous survival in the Sinai wilderness, receiving the laws of the Sabbath and the entire Torah, and finally being led into the Land of Israel and building the Temple. The sages stressed that "*Dayenu*" does not imply that the Jews would have been content had they not received all of these blessings, especially the final ones of Sabbath, Torah, Land of Israel, and Temple. Instead, the meaning is that any one of these gifts would have been sufficient to require infinite expressions of gratitude. In colloquial Hebrew and Yiddish, the term "*dayenu*" is often used ironically to mean "That's enough" or "I've had enough."

Days of Awe. *Yamim Nora'im* in Hebrew, this term refers to the inclusive 10-day period of introspection and repentance from Rosh Hashanah through Yom Kippur. (See *High Holy Days*.)

Dead Sea. Large inland lake in the lower part of the Jordan Valley, which lies between the hills of Moab to the east and Judea to the west. The lowest point on earth at about 1,300 feet below sea level, it derives its Hebrew name (*Yam Hamelach*; lit., "Salt Sea") from the huge quantities of minerals it contains. Six times as salty as the ocean, the waters are so heavy that they hold the human body buoyant and it is virtually impossible to sink. Israelis and foreign tourists alike flock to area spas for therapeutic black mud applications and sulfur and mineral baths. The Dead Sea Works has been established to commercially exploit the millions of tons of salt, potash, and bromides of these mineral-rich waters. The Dead Sea Scrolls, probably the greatest archeological discovery of the 20th century, were found by a Bedouin boy in a cave near the northwestern shore of the Dead Sea.

Dead Sea Scrolls. Collection of ancient manuscripts that were discovered in the mid-20th century in various caves west of the Dead Sea. Written in Hebrew and Aramaic, they primarily date from 150 B.C.E. to 68 C.E., when the Romans destroyed the Qumran community that collected them. Probably written by the Essenes and currently housed in the Shrine of the Book in Jerusalem, the Dead Sea Scrolls contain at least fragments of all the books of the Bible except Esther. In addition, there are texts from the Second Temple period that may relate to the Bible. The Dead Sea Scrolls also contain ancient documents that cast a light on a turbulent and critical period in Jewish history, when Judaism was divided into three major and conflicting groups – Pharisees; Sadducees; and Essenes.The scrolls also aid scholars in understanding the Jewish roots of Christianity.

Death and dying. In Jewish thought, both life and death are part of the Divine plan for the world. In view of the high value attached to life as the highest good (see *pikuach nefesh*), the most baffling phenomenon is death, which puts an end to human achievements. The account of Adam's sin (Gen. 2) is the biblical attempt to deal with the problem, but it raises the difficult issue of explaining the death of children. Some of the sages echoed the biblical concept of death as a punishment, but others maintained that death was an appropriate termination for a finite creature and had been preordained at the time of Creation. A response to the fear of death was the concept that individuals survive as incorporeal spirits. Related to this was the belief in retributive judgment, with the righteous rewarded with eternal bliss in Paradise while the wicked are punished in Gehenna.The final mitigation of the terror of death in rabbinic literature was the belief in the resurrection of the dead and the existence of a World to Come (see *olam ha-ba*). Some contemporary thinkers emphasize naturalistic immortality, the continuation of an individual's memory; others speak about the eternal soul.

Death penalty – see Capital punishment.

Death, time of. A precise definition of the moment of death is a major issue in obtaining permission for organ transplantation among Orthodox Jews. According to classical Jewish sources, two criteria determined when death occurred. The majority rule was the breath test, in which a feather was placed beneath the nostrils and lack of movement signified death. A minority view in the Talmud maintained that the cessation of heartbeat was also required. Later codifiers insisted on both respiratory and cardiac manifestations of death. Moses Isserles, acknowledging the difficulty of accurately distinguishing death from a fainting spell, argued that even after the cessation of breath and heartbeat one should wait a period of time before assuming that a person is dead. In a 1988 ruling approving heart transplantation, the Chief Rabbinate of Israel effectively accepted the modern definition of death as a completely flat electroencephalogram (both cortical and brainstem function), which indicates the cessation of spontaneous brain activity.

Debt. Several biblical laws attempted to ease the burden of Israelites in debt. For example, it was forbidden to exact interest from a fellow Jew, and all debts were automatically cancelled every seventh (Sabbatical) year.As the Israelites moved from an economy based on agriculture to one increasingly based on business and commerce, in which the release of debts contracted in trading became onerous, the situation was modified when Hillel (1st century C.E.) enacted the *prosbul.*

Decalogue. Literally meaning "ten words," this linguistically accurate Greek term is often used for the Ten Commandments.

Declaration of Independence (Israel) – see *Yom ha-Atzmaut.*

Dedication – see Consecration.

Deed. Formal written document, attested by two witnesses, that confirms a variety of civil transactions ranging from the conveyance of property to a marriage contract (see *ketubah*) and a writ of divorce (see *get*). Known in biblical Hebrew as *sefer*, in rabbinic sources the term *shetar* is used.

Deism. 18th-century theological conception of the complete transcendence of God, a distinction between the Creator of all that exists and Nature, which proceeds by its own laws without Divine intervention. This idea posited God as the maker of a machine-like universe, which then was left to function by itself with only an occasional check by the maker to see if the machine were functioning properly (i.e., God is apart from the world). Deism was attacked by theists, who believed in Divine providence, solicitude, and intervention. Deism was also challenged in the *Tanya*, which maintained that Nature would "naturally" revert to nothingness if not for the hand of God, which keeps Nature permanently suspended over the void. According to this view, it is absurd to speak of Nature left to its own devices, for if Nature were "left alone" by God, it would become "no-Nature," vanishing into the abyss from whence it came.

Deluge – see Flood.

Demai (Dem.) The 3rd tractate in Zera'im (seeds) in the Mishnah, it deals with the requirements for tithing produce when there is doubt whether proper tithes have been given.

Democracy. Ancient Israel was not a democracy. Nevertheless, the Bible contains such democratic moral values as the creation of all human beings in God's image and the idea that no person, not even the king, is above the law. For centuries, Jews in the Diaspora were not involved in the political systems of the countries in which they dwelled. Among Ashkenazim since the Middle Ages, the autonomous *kehilla* was an oligarchy run by the wealthy members of the community. With the advent of the Emancipation in the 19th century, European Jews championed the cause of representative democracy, inspired in part by their previous persecution by tyrannical authorities and consequent desire for safeguards against arbitrary rule. The modern State of Israel is a vibrant democracy in which all citizens can vote for members of the Knesset based on party lists, though there is no direct election of the Prime Minister.

Demons. Evil spirits mentioned in both the Bible and Talmud. Demons play a prominent role in Jewish folklore and legend, and a variety of amulets, charms, magic formulas, and superstitions developed to counteract their malevolent influence. The Kabbalists envisioned the universe as being divided into two spheres, the demonic and the Divine.

Derash (1). From a Hebrew word meaning "to seek," it refers to a popular homiletic method of biblical interpretation that strives to uncover an ethical or moral lesson thought to be implicit in the text. Rather than the literal meaning of a verse in its context (*peshat*), *derash* offers a subjective approach to discover hidden meanings within it. This entails a detailed and often ingenious analysis of unusual spelling, vocabulary, and other elements in the sparse biblical text, as well as cross-references to other parts of the Bible.

Derash (2). Religious discourse. Soon after the return from Babylonian Exile, Ezra assembled the whole people, read the Torah, "and caused them to understand the reading" (Neh 8:8), presumably through explanations and homilies. By the end of the Second Temple period, a *derash* in the vernacular was regularly delivered in synagogues after the Torah reading on Sabbaths and festivals. Coming from a Hebrew root meaning "to search," it was offered by a *darshan* (preacher) who delved into the Torah portion for novel insights that could shed new light on the problems of the day. The Pharisees and their rabbinic descendants were masters of the art of preaching, though they had no formal training in composing and delivering sermons. Medieval rabbis, however, were so focused on their scholarly and judicial activities that their competence as preachers suffered. Consequently, they generally delivered only two annual addresses to the congregation – on the Sabbath before Passover (see Shabbat ha-Gadol) and on the Sabbath before Yom Kippur (see Shabbat Shuvah). (See also *sermon*.)

Derech eretz. Literally "way of the land," this Hebrew term is used to describe proper behavior that is in keeping with accepted social and moral standards. In rabbinic literature, it refers both to appropriate conduct[55] and a worldly occupation. The motto of Modern Orthodoxy, as expounded by Rabbi Samson Raphael Hirsch, is "Torah together with *derech erertz*" (i.e., the general culture).

Derech Eretz Rabbah. Minor tractate added to the Talmud that deals with proper manners and behavior, including laws related to forbidden marriages and a list of activities that pose a danger to life.

Derech Eretz Zuta. Minor tractate added to the Talmud that is addressed to scholars and is a collection of maxims urging modesty and self-examination. It recommends a life of patience, temperance, gentleness, forgiveness, and respect for the elderly.

Desecration of the host. Defilement of the consecrated bread or wafer used in the Christian sacrament of the Eucharist. According to the doctrine of transubstantiation adopted by the Fourth Lateran Council (1215), the bread becomes the body of Christ. Throughout the Middle Ages in Europe, accusations of desecration of the host were frequently leveled against the Jews and used as a pretext for massacres and expulsions, especially in southern Germany during the late 13th century.

Detention camps. Facilities set up by the British Mandatory Government in the 1940s where "illegal" immigrants to the Land of Israel (see *Aliyah Bet*) were kept in prison-like conditions. They also housed political prisoners arrested for engaging in anti-governmenty activities. The major detention camp was Atlit on the Mediterranean coast, where in October 1945, the prisoners were freed in a daring action by members of the Palmach.After the end of World II, most "illegal" immigrants (some 50,000) were imprisoned on the British-controlled island of Cyprus and only released with the establishment of the State of Israel.

Determinism. Philosophical concept that all events, as well as personal choices and actions, are pre-ordained by Divine decree or are the necessary and inevitable results of previous causes. Judaism accepts a belief in the foreknowledge of God, but emphasizes that each individual possesses free will, which is seen as indispensable for a religious and moral life and compatible with Divine omniscience.

Deutero-Isaiah. Scholarly name for the second half of the Book of Isaiah (chapters 40-66).[56] Unlike the first half of the book, written by a prophet who lived in Jerusalem in the 8th century B.C.E., the second half is by an unnamed author who lived at the end of the Babylonian Exile during the 6th century. The first half of Isaiah is a stern warning of impending judgment against the Israelites, whereas Deutero-Isaiah predicts the demise of Babylonia and attempts to provide comfort to an exiled, suffering, and despairing people. It assures them that God will send a servant who will lead Israel from darkness to light, and that Israel will become a "light unto the nations" (49:6). Despite the identification of the so-called "suffering servant" (Isa. 52:13-53:12) with Israel, Christian theology interprets this portion as a precursor to Jesus.

Deuteronomy (Deut.). English name for the 5th and final book of the Torah. The name derives from a Greek word meaning "repetition of the law," since it contains (along with much new material) a repetition or reformulation of many of the laws found earlier in the Bible. Deuteronomy is a series of disources in which Moses recounts the history of the Israelites after they received the law at Mount Sinai. It presents a series of Divine commandments and ethical injunctions and calls for the centralization of sacrificial worship. The book concludes with the death of Moses, after he blesses the Twelve Tribes as they prepare to cross the Jordan River and enter the Promised Land. Some scholars believe that Deuteronomy was the book found by Hilkiah, the Temple High Priest, in 621 B.C.E. during the reign of King Josiah of Judah.

Deuteronomy Rabbah (Deut. R.) – see Midrash Rabbah.

Devar Torah. Literally meaning "word of Torah," this Hebrew term usually refers to a talk explaining the Torah portion that is being read that week in the synagogue. It also may apply to brief remarks at the opening of a Jewish-related meeting.

Devarim (1). Hebrew term for the Book of Deuteronomy. Literally meaning "words," it comes from the phrase, "These are the words," which opens the book.

Devarim (2). The 1st *parashah* in the Book of Deuteronomy (1:1-3:22), it again relates the episode of the spies who brought back an evil report concerning the Promised Land. The acceptance of this report by the Israelites led to them being condemned to 40 years of wandering in the wilderness, the beginning of which is narrated in this portion.

Devekut. Literally "cleaving [to God]," this Hebrew word refers to a spiritual state of communion with God that is achieved by prayer and meditation. A major concept in Kabbalah and Hasidism, the mystics developed the idea of *devekut* as the highest rung on the spiritual ladder. In its most intense form of this approach, the human being reaches the goal of a mystical union with God, which the kabbalists likened to a drop of water being absorbed in a great sea or to a ray of light in the sun. The term comes from the biblical verse commanding the Israelites "to love the Lord your God, to walk in all His ways, and to cleave to Him" (Deut. 11:22).

Devil – see Satan.

Dew, prayer for. Recited on the first day of Passover by Jews throughout the world, it asks God to end the winter rains in Israel and to send dew to a land that depends on this source of moisture during the long, dry summers. In the Ashkenazic ritual, the prayer for dew is recited during the reader's repetition of the *Amidah* during the *Musaf* (additional) service. The six-stanza invocation ends, "For You are the Lord our God, who makes the wind blow and the dew descend," followed by the plea: "For a blessing and not for a curse; for life and not for death; for plenty and not for famine." (See also *morid ha tal.*)

Dhimma. Arabic term applied to the legal status of Jews and Christians ("people of the book") in Muslim lands. Although the state protected their lives and property and guaranteed them religious freedom, *dhimmis* were treated as second-class citizens who were required to pay a special poll tax and not insult Islam, convert Muslims, or betray the ruling Muslim government. However, sources have indicated that, with the exception of the fiscally important poll tax, the restrictive laws including a ban on holding office were enforced irregularly and sporadically. Nevertheless, the *dhimma* status could be humiliating and demoralizing.

Diaspora. From a Greek word meaning "dispersion," the term refers to Jews and their communities living outside the Land of Israel. It was first used in the 6th century B.C.E., when the Temple was destroyed and the Israelites were forced into exile in Babylonia. Over the centuries, persecutions have forced Jews to repeatedly leave their homes and become scattered throughout the world. Nevertheless, the synagogue, prayer, Jewish law, Torah study, Jewish communal structure, anti-Semitism, and the hope of eventual return to Zion helped them maintain their Jewish identity and way of life.

Dietary laws – see *Kashrut.*

Din (1). Literally meaning "judgment," this Hebrew term is applied to a legal decision on religious law or a verdict on civil litigation that is handed down by a religious (or even secular) court.

Din (2). One name for the 5th of the *sefirot*, also known as *Gevurah* (strength), which is the second female emanation and represents Divine justice. *Din* is identified with limitation and restriction, while *Chesed* is associated with freedom and flow. A balance between these two emanations is essential to avoid catastrophe and chaos.

Dina d'malchuta dina. Aramaic phrase meaning "the law of the state is the law." This halachic rule was enunciated by Samuel, a prominent 3rd-century Babylonian sage, who argued that even though Jews had their own civil courts, it was a religious duty for them to obey the laws of the country in which they lived. The only exceptions to this idea were laws that contradicted fundamental Jewish beliefs, such as those advocating murder or theft (Git. 10b, BK 113b).

Discipline Scroll. Also known as the "Manual of Discipline" and the "Community Rule," this Dead Sea Scroll contains a set of regulations ordering the lives of the members of a sect who lived communally and accepted strict rules of conduct. It cites the admonitions and punishments to be imposed on violators of the rules, the method of joining the group, the relations between the members, their way of life, and their beliefs.

Discrimination. Special, usually unequal, treatment of an individual or group on the basis of race, religion, color, or national origin. For centuries in Muslim and Christian countries, Jews were subjected to discrimination by both civil and religious authorities. Even in the United States, until the last half of the 20th century, Jews were discriminated against in housing and employment. There were quotas for Jews attending prestigious universities and professional schools, and numerous private clubs refused them admission. Today, legislation has eliminated the most flagrant manifestations of discrimination, though some private discrimination persists.

Dispensation (*heter*). Permission to modify or eliminate rules to relieve hardship. Examples include *heter iska*, the technique for circumventing the biblical prohibition against lending or borrowing at interest from a fellow Jew; and *heter me'ah rabbanim* and *heter nisuin*, which allow a husband to remarry if his wife is mentally incompetent, refuses to accept a *get*, or disappears without a trace. In recent times, an example of a *heter* is the dispensation given by the Chief Rabbinate of Israel permitting land to be worked under certain conditions during the Sabbatical Year.

Displaced persons. People forced to flee or deported from their homes due to war or natural disaster. From the end of World War II until 1952, more than 250,000 Jewish displaced persons lived in camps and urban centers in Germany, Austria, and Italy that were administered by the victorious Allied authorities and the United Nations Relief and Rehabilitation Administration. About 80,000 emigrated to the United States and 136,000 to Israel (mostly after the establishment of the State in 1948, when the strict British limits on the immigration of Jews were lifted). During the immediate post-war years, the birthrate in displaced persons camps was the highest in the Jewish world.

Disputation. Formal debate between the adherents of different religious faiths and philosophies. In the Middle Ages, disputations were commonly held between major rabbis and Christian theologians concerning such controversial topics as alleged messianic references in the Bible and the virgin birth and divinity of Jesus. A famous disputation took place at Barcelona in 1263, in which Nachmanides (Ramban) was compelled by King James I of Aragon to debate whether the Messiah had already arrived, or was yet to appear to redeem the world from its state of misery and suffering. The Ramban's arguments were so persuasive that they even convinced the reluctant king of the validity of the great Jewish scholar's views. However, the victory enraged his adversaries, the Dominican priests, who accused the Ramban of insulting the Christian faith and compelled him to flee from Spain. Forced disputations became a recurring problem for medieval Jews during the following centuries.

Dittographic. Error in writing a Torah scroll in which the scribe writes the same letter or word twice.

Divination. The Bible unequivocally forbids various pagan practice of communicating with supernatural forces to predict the future and thus determine what action to take or avoid. "There shall not be found among you one who practices divinations, an astrologer, one who reads omens, a sorcerer, one who casts spells, one who inquires of the *ob or yid'oni*, or one who consults the dead" (Deut. 18:10). These techniques included pouring oil on water (to see the shapes and forms the oil made) and examining the innards of animals before sacrifice (especially the liver). Nevertheless, the High Priest used the *Urim* and *Thummin* and Saul consulted the witch of En Dor to speak to the spirit of the dead Samuel (1 Sam. 28:5-25). Indeed, popular belief in omens and oracles was common in both early and medieval Jewish history, despite official condemnation.

Divine attributes – see God, attributes of.

Divine Chariot (*Merkava*). The most esoteric passage in the Bible is the first chapter of the Book of Ezekiel, in which the prophet has an incredible vision of the Divine Presence seated on a throne on a four-wheeled conveyance carried by four *cherubim*, each with four faces (of a man, lion, ox, and eagle). It constitutes the *haftarah* for the festival of Shavuot, possibly because of the tradition that the Divine Chariot descended on Mount Sinai when God gave the Ten Commandments to Israel on that day. The vision of the Divine Chariot was the basis of *Merkava* mysticism.In medieval Judaism, the study of this mystical section was discouraged, except by mature individuals with an extensive grounding in the study of traditional Jewish texts.

Divine Presence – see *Shechinah.*

Divine punishment. Even though the Israelites were granted the authority to inflict penalties in certain prescribed cases, God retained the ultimate power of imposing punishment upon the people. At various times, God punished whole peoples (Sodom and Gomorrah [Gen. 18]; Egypt), individuals (Cain [Gen. 4:10-15], two sons of Aaron [Lev. 10:1-2]; Korach and his company [Num. 16]), and all of humanity in the Flood (Gen. 6). God even reserved the right to punish a person's descendants, by visiting "the guilt of the fathers on the children, upon the third and fourth generations of those who reject Him" (Exod. 20:5; Deut. 5:9). The prophet Ezekiel, however, condemned any form of vicarious Divine punishment (18:20). For numerous offenses, the only punishment noted in the biblical text is the Divine penalty of *karet*.

Divorce. The dissolution of a marriage in Jewish law is a formal legal procedure with a host of specific details that must be observed. The biblical ideal of marriage was a permanent union, with divorce only countenanced under exceptional circumstances (primarily when the marriage produced no children) or if the husband "finds some unseemly thing" (see *ervat davar*) in his wife (Deut. 24:3), a phrase that was interpreted in various ways by the talmudic rabbis. Divorce is initiated by the husband and requires a formal document (see *get*) that is signed by the husband and then delivered to his wife. If this is not received, the woman is unable to remarry under Jewish law (see *agunah*). Unlike many other legal systems, in Jewish law the mutual consent of the parties is sufficient for dissolution of the marriage and delivery of the *get*, and there is no requirement for a court to become involved in the process. Rabbinic law does not recognize civil divorce unless it is supplemented by a *get*; however, the Reform movement has eliminated this formal religious document.

Divorce, consequences of. Men and women who divorce are generally free to remarry anyone they please, unless it is halachically forbidden. A divorced woman is not permitted to marry a *kohen*, nor is she allowed to marry a man with whom she is suspected of having committed adultery. Furthermore, she may not marry any person who served as a witness at the delivery of her *get*, or any man within a period of 90 days following the divorce (lest there be doubt as to the paternity of a first child from her second marriage).[57] The husband is required to pay his ex-wife her dowry and the money stipulated in the *ketubah*, unless she has forfeited it as in the case of adultery, but he no longer has any legal obligation to maintain her.

Divrei ha-Yamim – see Chronicles.

Documentary Hypothesis – see Bible criticism.

Dogma. Religious doctrine that is established as authoritative and beyond dispute. Unlike most Christian denominations, Judaism has never developed a single binding catechism, instead permitting a spectrum of different formulations of belief as long as they are compatible with the overall Torah system of the Written and Oral Law. Rather than expressing obedience to a creed, traditional Judaism stresses performance of *mitzvot*. During the Middle Ages, several rabbinic authorities attempted to establish a set of uniformly accepted beliefs. By far the most enduring has been the Thirteen Principles of Faith developed by Maimonides in the 12th century. (See also *creed*.)

Domain. In determining the laws of permissible carrying on the Sabbath, the Talmud distinguishes four domains based on how they are enclosed and used. There is no limitation on transferring objects to or from an "exempt area," which is defined as being at least three hand-breadths higher than the ground and having an area less than four hand-breadths by four hand-breadths. A second type is a semipublic ("neutral") area that is neither strictly public nor private (e.g., fields and oceans). In the private domain, which must be clearly set off and defined (e.g., the interior of a house), carrying is permitted. Carrying is forbidden in the public domain, which is defined as an open area that is always used by the public (e.g., highways, deserts, and forests). The detailed laws regarding whether objects may be transferred from one domain to another on the Sabbath are explained in the talmudic tractate Shabbat. (See also *eruv*.)

Donkey. Although Jewish folklore often considered the donkey the epitome of foolish or stubborn behavior, ancient Jewish sources regarded the animal as a symbol of patience and understanding. The most famous incident involving the animal is the story of the talking donkey of Balaam (Num 22:21–35), which three times sees an angel and takes evasive action to save her master's life. Having neither perceived the presence of the angel nor realized the danger, Balaam strikes the donkey on all three occasions. Miraculously, the donkey has the power of speech to reprove Balaam for his own obstinacy and quick temper. As God uncovers his eyes, Balaam finally understands the situation, bows his head, and prostrates himself on the ground. The Rabbis observe that if God could allow a beast to speak intelligently, surely Balaam could only speak in accordance with the Divine Will and thus could not carry out Balak's plan to curse the Israelites.[58] According to legend, the talking donkey was one of the 10 miraculous things created at twilight on the sixth day of Creation, just before the onset of the first Sabbath.

Dough offering – see *Challah* (2).

Dove (*yonah*). Universal symbol of peace, purity, beauty, vulnerability, and innocence. The first and most famous dove mentioned in the Bible was the one that Noah sent out from the ark. She returned to the ark with an olive leaf in her mouth (according to tradition, plucked from the Mount of Olives in Jerusalem), so that "Noah knew that the waters had decreased on the earth" (Gen. 8:8-11).

The dove holding an olive branch in its mouth is a well-known symbol of peace. During Temple times, doves and turtledoves were brought as sacrificial offerings by the poor (Lev. 5:7) because they were the least expensive animal offering; by a Nazirite after the completion of his vow (Num. 6:10); by a woman after her days of purification following childbirth (Lev. 12:6); and as part of the purification ritual of a poor person who had been afflicted with the skin disease *tzara'at* (Lev. 14:22).

Dowry. Property that a wife brings to her husband at marriage and reverts to her upon divorce or his death. The practice of providing a dowry has disappeared among most contemporary Jews.

Dream. Almost all ancient peoples, including the Israelites, considered dreams as passageways to realms that were otherwise inaccessible to the conscious thought of a wakeful mind. They served as an insight into the will of Heaven, the world of evil spirits, or the future. The basic biblical view of dreams was that they were Divine communications, presages or omens that may subsequently be actualized in historical fact. In the Bible, Joseph was the master of dream interpretation. The Talmud offers diverse views on the significance of dreams, and interest in dream interpretation remains important among Hasidim and kabbalists. A major work of Sigmund Freud, the "father of psychoanalysis," was his *The Interpretation of Dreams* (1900).

Dream fast (*ta'anit chalom*). Based on the statement, "fasting is potent against a dream," some sages observed a "dream fast" after a bad dream. This took place even on the Sabbath or a festival, if the dream was especially troubling.

Dream, remedying the (*ha-tevet chalom*). Intriguing ritual based on talmudic teaching, in which the dreamer asks three close friends to gather on the morning after an apparent bad dream to encourage the dreamer to interpret the dream for good. The three friends open the ritual by reciting in unison, "Do not interpretations belong to God?" This is followed by the responsive recitation of various verses, some of which are repeated three times. It is recommended, but not required, that the dreamer fast and repent on the day of the ritual.[59]

Dreck. Literally "excrement," this Yiddish term is used to describe any cheap or worthless thing than can be compared to junk or garbage, as well as artistic performances that are of grossly inadequate quality.

Dreidel. Yiddish word for a four-sided top that is one of the best-known symbols of Chanukah and the name of a popular game of chance played on this holiday. Derived from medieval German gaming dice, a dreidel is inscribed with the Hebrew letters *nun*, *gimel*, *hei*, and *shin*, which is an acronym for the phrase *nes gadol* *hayah sham* (a great miracle happened there). Respectively, the letters represent the words *nichts* (nothing), *ganz* (all), *halb* (half), and *shtell arein* (put in). In Israel, the letter *pei* (here) is substituted for the letter *shin* (i.e., a great miracle happened *here*). After spinning the dreidel, the player performs the action indicated by the letter that appears face upward.

Dress. Specific modes of dress have distinguished Jews throughout the ages. The Bible mandated the wearing of *tzitzit* on the four corners of a garment. From the Middle Ages, Jews were often required to wear Jewish badges, hats, or other distinctive clothing. The *kippah* is a hallmark of religious Jews, and on the Sabbath Hasidim and other ultra-Orthodox from Eastern Europe wear long kaftans and wide, fur-trimmed black hats (see *streimel*). Traditional Yemenite dress is distinguished by intricate silver and gold embroidery, while beautiful stitching also characterizes Bukharan and North African Jewish dress.

Drey a kop. Literally "to turn a head," this Yiddish term refers to something that makes one's head spin with difficulty or is confusing because of its noise or tumult. It also can be something that "turns one's head" related to a compliment or flattery.

Dreyfus Affair. Named for the trial and subsequent attempts at exoneration of Alfred Dreyfus, a Jewish officer on the French General Staff, whose 1894 court-martial for treason, conviction, and final acquittal developed into a political event that had repercussions throughout France and the Jewish world. The son of a wealthy, assimilated family, Dreyfus was falsely accused and found guilty of writing documents divulging French military secrets to Germany and sentenced to life imprisonment on Devil's Island. The Dreyfus affair increasingly developed into a *cause célèbre* involving all strata of French society. Those on the political right generally believed in Dreyfus' guilt, while most on the left considered him innocent. More than a decade later, Dreyfus was cleared of all charges, restored to the army, raised to the rank of major, and decorated with the Legion of Honor. Jews everywhere were shocked that the affair could take place in liberal France and that so many of its citizens harbored such virulent hatred toward them. The Jewish victim in this case was completely assimilated, seeming to prove clearly that this was no defense against anti-Semitism. For Theodor Herzl, the Dreyfus affair led him to embrace Zionism.

Drink offering – see Libation.

Drunkenness. Under Jewish law, a person under the influence of alcohol is legally responsible for his actions (unless he has virtually lost consciousness). The first person described as becoming drunk was Noah, who planted a vineyard, "drank of the wine and became drunk, and [losing control of himself] he uncovered himself within his tent." His eldest son, Ham, saw his father and derisively reported his condition to his brothers, Shem and Japheth, who respectfully covered Noah with a cloth. Recovering his senses, Noah blessed Shem and Japheth but cursed Ham, through his son Canaan (Gen. 9:20-27). While hiding in a cave and fearing that they were the only human beings remaining on earth after the destruction of Sodom and Gomorrah, Lot's two daughters made their father drunk and then had intercourse with him. In this way, Lot became the ancestor of the nations of Moab and Ammon (Gen. 19:30-38). Although the Bible forbade an intoxicated priest from officiating at the Temple service, Rav said that a person should get so drunk on Purim that "he cannot tell the difference between 'Cursed is Haman' and 'Blessed is Mordecai'." (See *ad lo yada.*)

Druze. Distinct religious community, based mostly in Syria, Lebanon, and Israel. Their religion is a sect of Islam but is influenced by other faiths and philosophies, such as Judaism and Christianity. In modern Israel, Druze are full citizens who vote in elections and serve in the army. The name of the religion derives from one of its founders, Muhammad ibn Ismail al-Darazi (d. 1019). Druze believe in the transmigration of souls and in the ultimate perfection of humanity.

Dry Bones. Classic prophesy of Ezekiel (37) of a valley filled with dry bones, long separated from one another, that are knitted together through the Divine breath. It is a parable for the Israelites, long dead in exile, who will be raised up by God from their desperate straits to become alive, fully healed, and restored to the Land of Israel.

Dualism. Zoroastrian (Persian) theological concept proposing the existence of two gods, one good (light) and the other evil (dark), and a cosmic struggle between them. Gnosticism also preached a form of dualism. In the Hellenistic and medieval periods, a philosophical dualism that originated with Plato and opposed spirit to matter had some influence on Jewish religious thinking.

Duchaning. Recitation of the Priestly Blessing by the *kohanim* in traditional synagogues. Each morning and evening immediately after the daily offering in the Temple, the *kohanim* would ascend a special raised platform (*duchan*), place their *tallitot* over their heads, raise their arms, spread out their fingers in a special fanlike gesture (forming the Hebrew letter *shin*, the first letter of *Shaddai*, one of the names of God), and pronounce these three blessings that include the major name of God (*YHVH*, the Tetragrammaton). In traditional synagogues today (local customs differ as to the place in the service), the *kohanim* ascend the *bimah* and recreate this ancient rite, repeating the Priestly Blessing in a haunting and mysterious tone, word for word after the prayer leader.

Duress. Under Jewish law, no punishment is imposed on a person who has committed a sin under compulsion This was deduced by the talmudic Rabbis based on two biblical situations in which a betrothed virgin has sexual intercourse (Deut. 22:23-26). "If a man finds her in the city and lies with her," both are condemned to death – the man because he "afflicted the wife of a fellow," and the woman because she did not cry out. Since the attack occurred in the city, where there presumably would have been other people around to hear her shouts and save her, the Torah attaches some degree of complicity to the woman's failure to scream for help. However, "if a man discovers her in open country and attacks her," only he is executed, giving the betrothed girl the benefit of the doubt that she cried out but there was no one to help her.

Duty (*hovav*). One of the three basic categories of Jewish law, *hovav* is an obligatory action that one is required to perform, rather than something that is commendable but not necessary (see *reshut*). In his classic *Duties of the Heart*, the first book of Jewish philosophy (written in Spain in 1040), Bahya ibn Pakuda distinguished between "duties of the limbs" (involving practical and ceremonial obligations) and "duties of the heart" (involving the spiritual life and inner moral obligations).

Dybbuk. Disembodied spirit that possesses a living body with its own soul. Representing an alien personality, the *dybbuk* may speak through the mouth of the possessed and cause mental illness. A *dybbuk* is often considered to be the soul of a person who has recently died and is seeking revenge for some evil that was done to it while it was alive (as in the classic play by Anski). At times, it may merely be lost and enter a body to seek a rabbi who can help it on its proper way to the hereafter. According to folklore, *dybbuks* can be exorcised from the people they possess by conjuring the Divine Name, legendary feats attributed to Isaac Luria and his fellow kabalists and to wonder-working Hasidic *tzadikim*.

Dying process. Jewish tradition emphasizes respect for the dying and the dead, as well as deference and adherence to the last wishes of those who are on their deathbed. Thus, the final requests of Jacob (Gen. 49:29) and Joseph (Gen. 50:25) to have their remains taken out of Egypt and buried in the land of their fathers were respectfully followed. The verbal instructions of a dying person (see *goses*), even a deathbed change of last will and testament, are legally binding. Family members should be present when death is imminent, because it is a matter of great respect and comfort, as well as a religious act, to watch over a person passing from this world to the next. According to the Talmud, sick persons nearing their end should be encouraged to confess their sins (*vidui*) before God (Shab. 32a).

E

E. According to the Documentary Hypothesis (see Bible criticism), one of the four major strands of literary tradition edited to form the Five Books of Moses. Also known as the Elohist or Ephraimitic source, it uses *Elohim* as the Divine name (until after Exod. 3:6, when it begins to also use *YHVH*). Like "J," some scholars date it back to the time of the divided kingdom after the death of Solomon (late 10th century B.C.E.) and the Northern Kingdom of Israel."E" employs more refined speech patterns about God, who communicates with human beings through dreams, and uses the name "Horeb" (rather than Sinai) for the mountain of the Revelation.

Easter. Major Christian festival that celebrates the resurrection of Jesus. Since the Middle Ages, Jews were often attacked at Easter to "avenge" Jesus' death. Because of its proximity to Passover and the false accusation that Jews used Christian blood to bake *matzah*, the carnage was commonly related to the charge of blood libel against the Jews.

Ebla. Important city in northern Syria in the late 3rd millennium and later again in the 18th and 17th centuries B.C.E. Numerous cuneiform tablets found at the site, today known as Tel Mardikh, were written in Eblaite, a previously unknown Semitic language similar to Akkadian.

Ecclesiastes (Eccles.). One of the five *megillot* (scrolls) in the Writings section of the Bible, it is read in the synagogue on Sukkot. Although its composition is traditionally ascribed to King Solomon in his old age, when he was frustrated and despondent, linguistic analysis and content suggest the 3rd century B.C.E. as its likely date. The name "Ecclesiastes," which is derived from the Septuagint (Greek translation of the Bible), means "Assembler" or "Convoker" and is a reasonably accurate rendering of *Kohelet*, the Hebrew name for the book. The author observes that although human beings cannot predict the phenomena of nature nor their personal fate, they are determined in advance by God: "For everything there is a season, a time for every activity under heaven. A time to be born and a time to die, a time to plant and a time to uproot ... a time to love and a time to hate, a time for war and a time for peace" (3:1-8). Looking back at the end of his life on his many accomplishments and his amassing of numerous possessions, the author grimly concludes that "vanity of vanities...all is vanity" (1:2) and "everything was emptiness and chasing after wind, of no profit under the sun" (2:11). Nevertheless, the book ends with the affirmation of an ultimate purpose to life – "Fear God and obey His commandments, for this is the whole of man" (12:13).

Ecclesiastes Rabbah. Post-talmudic (7th or 8th century) aggadic midrash on the Book of Ecclesiastes.

Ecclesiasticus – see Wisdom of Ben Sira.

Echad Mi Yode'a (Who knows one?). Classic "counting song," in which each of the 13 stanzas consists of the question "Who knows ..." followed by the corresponding answer. The reply to each succeeding question also repeats the previous answers. By the final verse of this medieval song, the aim is to rapidly race through all the answers from 13 back to one. This verse reads: "Who knows thirteen? I know thirteen. Thirteen are the attributes of God; twelve are the tribes of Israel; eleven are the stars (in Joseph's dream); ten are the commandments; nine are the months of pregnancy; eight are the days to circumcision; seven are the days of the week; six are the orders of the Mishnah;[60] five are the books of the Torah;[61] four are the Matriarchs;[62] three are the Patriarchs;[63] two are the tablets of the covenant; One is our God in heaven and on earth."

Ecology. The Jewish attitude to nature is based on the belief that the universe is the work of the Creator and its natural order reflects the Divine covenant with God's creations. Love of God includes love of all aspects of Divine creation, encompassing all humanity, plants and animals, and the inanimate world. When God placed Adam in the Garden of Eden, the first man was commanded to "work it and guard it." The deep Jewish concern for ecology is exemplified in the regulations concerning the Sabbatical Year and the prohibitions against wanton destruction (see *bal taschit*) and cruelty to animals (see *tza'ar ba'alei chaim*). The need to preserve the natural balance of creation is the underlying rationale for forbidding the mingling of fabrics (see *sha'atnez*). A famous comment of R. Yochanan ben Zakkai (1st century C.E.) illustrates the importance with which the Rabbis viewed preservation of the natural world: "If you are planting a tree and you hear that the Messiah has come, finish planting the tree and then go greet him."

Edah. A Hebrew word meaning "community," the Torah applies it to the 10 Israelite spies (termed a "wicked community") who gave a negative report on the land of Canaan (Num. 14:27), thus condemning the Israelites to 40 years of wandering in the wilderness. This is one source for the talmudic rule that 10 are required for a *minyan*, a quorum for congregational worship.

Edah heredit. Literally "community of tremblers [before God]," a term for ultra-Orthodox anti-Zionist Jews.

Eden, Garden of – see Garden of Eden.

Edom. Ancient Semitic kingdom in the southeastern part of the Land of Israel, between the Dead Sea and the Gulf of Aqaba. According to the Bible, the Edomites were descendants of Esau and one of his Canaanite wives. Edom is often portrayed as the bitter enemy of Israel and Judah (Amos 1:11, Obad. 1:1-16). The Talmud used Edom as a symbol of the oppressive government of Rome, while in medieval Jewish sources Edom represented Christian Europe.

Education. The Bible emphasizes the importance of education: "You shall teach them [the Divine commandments] diligently to your children" (Deut. 6:7). Parents, Levites, scribes, and scholars engaged in this important enterprise. In the 1st century C.E., the High Priest, Yehoshua ben Gamla, instituted universal education for boys from age 6 and appointed many teachers throughout the land. The Rabbis even forbade a Jew to remain in any place that had no Hebrew teacher for the young. Consequently, Jews became known as "the people of the Book." Although in the traditional *cheder* the curriculum was narrowly limited to Jewish studies (secular studies were only introduced in the 19th century), almost every Jewish male over the age of 6 could read and write. Today, there has been a dramatic increase in the number of Jewish day schools (for girls and boys), which teach both Jewish and secular subjects and are fully accredited according to state educational standards. Nevertheless, most Jewish children in the Diaspora attend supplementary synagogue-related schools. In recent decades, especially in the United States, programs in Jewish Studies have appeared in colleges and universities.

Eduyot (**Eduy**.). The 7th tractate of Nezikin (damages) in the Mishnah, it primarily deals with various rabbinic teachings (testimonies, *eduyot* in Hebrew) of later sages on the legal controversies and rulings of earlier authorities, such as those between Beit Hillel and Beit Shammai.

Egg. Based on the talmudic dictum, "that which emerges from a clean animal is clean and that from an unclean animal unclean" (Bek. 1:2, 5b), it is an established principle that the eggs of clean birds are permitted for food, whereas those of unclean birds are forbidden (see *kashrut*). Even the eggs of permitted birds are forbidden if they have been fertilized. For Jews, the egg has long been a sign of mourning and consolation, consumed by mourners at the meal given to them when they return from the cemetery after the burial (see *se'udat havra'ah*). (For the major role of the egg at the Passover seder, see *beitzah* [1].) The egg was also an important standard of measurement in talmudic times.

Eglah arufah (axed heifer). Young heifer that had to be slain in an uncultivated valley with a stream by the elders of the nearest town when the corpse of an unwitnessed murder was found lying in the open. In conjunction with this public ritual, the elders would testify that they were neither directly nor indirectly culpable for the person's death. Had they only known of his existence, they would have provided the traveler with food and accompanied him safely on his way. Moreover, they would never have allowed a known murderer to wander in their land. The valley where the heifer was slain could never be tilled or sown again. As the Rabbis observed, "Let the heifer that has never produced fruit have its neck broken in a spot which has never produced fruit, to atone for one [the death of a man] who was not allowed to produce fruit [i.e., have future children]" (Sot. 46a).[64]

Egypt – see *Mitzrayim*.

Eh'yeh Asher Eh'yeh. Literally "I am Who I am" or "I will be Who I will be," the name by which God was revealed to Moses at the Burning Bush (Exod. 3:14). It was given in response to Moses asking how he should reply to the Israelites when they would ask the Divine name – not seeking merely an appellation but rather some concept of the essential nature of God. *Eh'yeh Asher Eh'yeh* indicates that God is timeless and eternal, the God of Creation and their ancestors (past) who is cognizant of their suffering in Egyptian slavery (present) and will soon redeem them from bondage (future).

Eichah – see Lamentations.

Eichmann trial. Celebrated trial of the Nazi who facilitated and managed the logistics of mass deportation of Jews to ghettos and extermination camps in occupied Eastern Europe during World War II. Captured by Mossad agents in Argentina in 1960 and brought for trial to Israel, Eichmann's defense that he was only following orders was refuted by evidence that he acted on his own initiative in a criminal manner. Eichmann was convicted of crimes against humanity and executed by hanging in 1962. The trial revealed to Jews and others throughout the world the extent and horror of what had happened to European Jewry during the "Final Solution," raising the status of survivors in Israel society and magnifying the importance of the Holocaust as a key element in Jewish identity.

Eidut. One of several biblical words for "laws" (Deut. 4:45) and usually translated as "testimonials," it refers to those religious rituals and rites that remind Jews of historic moments and serve as testaments to cardinal beliefs of the Jewish faith. Examples include the observance of the Sabbath, the celebration of Passover, and the affixing of a *mezuzah* on the doorpost.

Eight (*shemoneh*). Circumcision, the first life-cycle ritual that a Jewish male undergoes, occurs on the eighth day of life (Gen. 17:11-12). There were eight garments worn by the *Kohen Gadol;* eight days of Chanukah; and Maimonides listed eight degrees of charity.

Eighteen (*shemoneh esrei*). The core of the weekday prayer service is the 18 blessings of the *Amidah,* which is also known as the *Shemoneh Esrei* (lit., "the 18," though now there are actually 19 blessings). On Passover, the entire process of preparing the *matzah*, from kneading to final baking, may not exceed 18 minutes. Sabbath candles are lit 18 minutes before sundown. Eighteen is the numerical value of *chai* (life).

Eighteen Benedictions – see *Amidah.*

Eilat. Israel's southernmost city (at the tip of the Negev), Eilat is a leading winter resort. Blessed with fine beaches, coral reefs filled with exotic fish, and year-round sunshine, Eilat lies on the Gulf of Aqaba, a finger of the Red Sea where the borders of Israel, Egypt, Jordan, and Saudi Arabia meet. About 950 B.C.E., Solomon built the twin cities of Eilat and Ezion-Geber for his navy and copper industry, but they were abandoned with the discovery of a sea route around Africa to India. Modern Eilat was founded in 1949 near the ruins of the biblical city. It was developed by Israel both as a tourist mecca and as a seaport window to East African and Asian markets.

Eileh Ezkerah (These I will remember). Medieval *piyyut* (liturgical poem) dealing with the Ten Martyrs, which is part of the Yom Kippur liturgy.

Eilu v'eilu. Talmudic term that is short for "*eilu v'eilu, divrei Elohim hayim,*" which literally means "these and these are both words of the Living God" (Er. 13b). According to Jewish thought, a search for "truth" requires that an issue be viewed from all sides, rather than a dry analysis of restrictive definitions. Whereas Greek thought tries to arrive at a final answer by means of *à priori* proof through deductive logic, the Talmud starts with the premise that it is necessary to investigate all arguments (measures of truths) – not through deductive logic but through open investigation – and not coming to a final conclusion but instead exploring all aspects of the issue. Frequently, two opposite views (*eilu v'eilu*) are presented as "words of the Living God" (i.e., both P and not-P are true; see complementary polar opposites), because Divine truth may reside in multiple opinions. Discussions often end with "*teiku*"(literally, "it remains standing," meaning that we await the final answer). Thus, in analyzing a biblical or mishnaic text, the goal is not to attain the absolute truth, but rather to understand its various meanings; not to freeze the biblical text as a conclusion, but to open it to many interpretations.

Ein Keloheinu (There is none like our God). Popular hymn of praise recited at the end of the *Musaf* (additional) service on Sabbaths and festivals by Ashkenazim and on weekdays after the morning service by Sephardim. God is designated by four different names, which are arranged in the order in which they appear in the Torah: (a) *Elohim* (God), from the first verse describing the Creation in Genesis;

(b) *Adon* (Master), first used by Abraham (Gen. 15:2); (c) *Melech* (King), implied in the phrase "the Lord will *reign* for ever and ever" (Exod. 15:18) but first used directly later (Num. 23:21); and (d) *Moshi'ah* (Deliverer), which is implied when Israel is termed "a people *delivered* by the Lord" (Deut. 33:29).[65] The opening letters of the five verses are an acrostic for the Hebrew words, "Amen, praised be You."

Ein Sof. Literally "limitless" or "without end," this kabbalistic term refers to the hidden aspect of the infinite God, the essence of the Divine that is completely spiritual, incorporeal, and beyond the reach of human comprehesion and relationship. *Ein Sof* is sometimes described as *Ayin* (no-thing), because it cannot be compared to anything else since humans have no basis either intellectually or experientially for grasping its nature.[66] Therefore, God can be understood only as manifested in the 10 *sefirot* (Divine emanations), which come forth from *Ein Sof*.

Einsatzgruppen. Mobile units that first carried out mass murders of civilians in occupied Poland. After the invasion of Russia, the Einsatzgruppen, headed by members of the Gestapo, carried out the murder of Jews by shooting on a massive scale, with about 1.5 million victims. Strenuous efforts were made to keep these operations secret to prevent them from being used for anti-Nazi propaganda in the West.

Eirev rav – see Mixed multitude.

Ekev. The 3rd *parashah* in the Book of Deuteronomy (7:12-11:25), it begins and ends with a description of the blessings that the Israelites will receive for obeying the commandments and warns of their dire fate should they fail to fulfill them. It repeats the episode of the Golden Calf (and other shameful occurrences) and how Moses soothed the Divine anger before receiving the second set of tablets engraved with the Ten Commandments.

El. Oldest of the names of God, it is often incorporated in biblical names as the first element (Elijah, Elisha, Elihu) or more commonly at the end (Israel, Ishmael, Samuel). It also appears as the first element in compound names of the Divine, such as *El Elyon* (Most High God) and *El Shaddai* (God Almighty).

El Al. National airline of Israel. Initially established in 1948 to transport immigrants to the new Jewish state, El Al has become a major airline with flights throughout the world.

El Malei Rachamim (God full of compassion). Opening words and title of the prayer for the departed that is recited with a haunting chant at the funeral service, on visiting the grave of a relative, and after being called up to the reading of the

Torah on the anniversary of the death of a close relative. In some Ashkenazic synagogues, it is also a part of the *Yizkor* memorial service on Yom Kippur and on the last days of the three pilgrimage festivals (Passover, Shavuot, Sukkot). *El Malei Rachamim* is a plea that the soul of the departed be "granted perfect rest under the wings of Your Presence" and reside forever in *Gan Eden* (Paradise). It originated in the Jewish communities of Europe, where it was recited for the martyrs of the Crusades and then those of the Chmielnicki massacres.

El melech ne'eman (God, faithful king). Phrase interposed at times between *Ahavah Rabbah* or *Ahavat Olam* and the recitation of the *Shema*. The Rabbis taught that the 248 positive commandments equal the number of organs in the human body, symbolizing that the purpose of physical existence is to obey the precepts of the Torah and to dedicate one's entire body to the service of God. Because the total number of words of the *Shema* (together with *baruch shem k'vod*) is 245, in public worship it is customary for the prayer leader to repeat the last two words of the *Shema* (*Adonai Eloheichem*; The Lord, your God) and the first word of the following benediction (*emet*; true) to bring the total number of words up to 248. When the *Shema* is recited in private, or if there is no *minyan*, the total of 248 is achieved by first reciting *El melech ne'eman*. These three words were chosen because their initial Hebrew letters (*aleph*, *mem*, *nun*) spell "amen," literally meaning "it is true." Therefore, it indicates that the worshiper is firmly convinced that the words about to be recited are completely true.[67]

Elderly. The verse, "You shall rise in the presence of an old person" (Lev. 19:32), mandated that the Israelites show respect for the elderly, who in ancient times were honored for their wisdom and life experiences. The rabbinic attitude to the elderly is well expressed in *Pirkei Avot*: "A person who learns from the young is compared to one who eats unripe grapes and drinks wine from a vat, whereas a person who learns from the old is compared to one who eats ripe grapes and drinks wine that is aged" (4:26). However, one must not always defer to the views of the elderly. When considering a halachic issue, the most important factor is the strength of a person's proof and analysis, because "a decision of law depends not on the teacher's age but on his reasoning"(BB 142b).[68]

Elders. Known in Hebrew as *zekeinim* (lit., "old ones"), this term was applied to the leaders of the confederation of the Twelve Tribes of Israel. These heads of families formed a sort of representative council and judicial body in every community. At critical points in the narrative of the Book of Exodus, Moses was ordered to assemble and instruct the elders, who were God-fearing, trustworthy, and honest. After the Revelation at Sinai, Moses appointed 70 elders to assist him in governing the Israelites. Gathering "at the city gate," the elders acted as a judicial body in issues of family law, such as the cases of the rebellious son (Deut. 21:18-21), the husband who accused his new wife of not being a virgin (Deut.

22:13-21), and the man who refused a levirate marriage (Deut. 25:8-10). In the talmudic, medieval, and early modern periods, the term "elders" often referred to scholars and sages.

Elders of Zion, Protocols of the – see Protocols of the Elders of Zion.

Elephantine. Island in the middle of the Nile River where a military garrison of Jewish soldiers was stationed during the Persian occupation of Egypt. The Elephantine papyri – a store of legal documents and letters written in Aramaic and dealing with such material as marriage and divorce, commerce, and inheritance – document this flourishing community, which maintained its own temple. Even after the expulsion of the Persians from Egypt, the Jewish garrison continued to serve on Egypt's southern frontier.

Elijah, Chair of – see Chair of Elijah.

Elijah, Cup of – see Cup of Elijah.

Eliyahu ha-Navi (Elijah the Prophet). Popular song expressing the hope that "quickly, in our day, he [Elijah] will bring the Messiah, son of David." It is sung at the Passover seder, when the door is opened to welcome the prophet, and after the *Havdalah* ceremony that marks the conclusion of the Sabbath or a festival.

Elohai neshamah (My God, the soul [You placed within me is pure]). Prayer in the *Birkot ha-Shachar* (see morning blessings) that expresses gratitude to God for graciously restoring our souls when we awake. The Rabbis drew a parallel between death and sleep – "sleep constitutes one-sixtieth of death" – observing that the human soul is not functional when asleep and only becomes reactivated upon wakening. *Elohai neshamah* confidently suggests that our daily reawakening anticipates the restoration of our souls in the World to Come. In stark contrast to the Christian concept of human beings born in "original sin," this prayer stresses the Jewish belief that "just as God is pure, so the soul [of man] is pure."[69]

Elohim. One of the two major biblical names of God, it is a plural word in Hebrew. Used more than 2,000 times in the Bible to refer to the God of Israel, it is often preceded by the definite article as "*ha-Elohim*" (the [true] God). The paradoxical use in Hebrew of a plural noun to designate the One God of Israel illustrates the idea of the innumerable examples of God's majesty and the many facets of the Deity.

Elul. The 6th month of the Jewish year (August-September). The entire month is a preparation for the High Holy Days, with its themes of repentance and renewal. The shofar is blown daily after the morning service on weekdays, and special penitential psalms (see *selichot*) are recited when a *minyan* is present.

Emanations, Divine – see *Sefirot*.

Emancipation. Removal of political and civic restrictions from Jews, resulting from ideas of the Enlightenment and the French Revolution (1789), which stressed equality and social reform and the integration of subgroups into the nation state. Natural results of the Enlightenment and Emancipation were acculturation and, in some cases, total assimilation.Many Jews abandoned their faith once permitted to adopt the secular culture and professions of their gentile neighbors. Emancipation was achieved in Western and Central Europe during the 19th century, and in Eastern Europe with the fall of the Russian Empire in 1917. It resulted in a breakdown of Jewish communal and religious authority and led to the development of the Reform, Conservative, and neo-Orthodox movements.

Embalming. Egyptian practice associated with mummification of the dead and not an Israelite custom. Embalming is mentioned twice in the Bible as a purely practical measure to preserve the body for burial in the cases of Jacob (who was to be buried far from the place where he died; Gen. 50:2-3) and Joseph (who was to be reburied years later in the Land of Israel; Gen. 50:26).

Embezzlement. Fraudulent conversion of money or property, entrusted to the care of a person, to that individual's own personal use. Unlike theft, the embezzler has lawful possession of the property. Under biblical law, an accused embezzler could take an oath denying any guilt. However, if the charge was later proven to be true, he was required to restore the property plus one fifth of its value and bring a guilt offering as a sacrifice.

Emet (truth). God is often described as the "true King" or the "true Judge." The latter phrase (see *Dayan ha-Emet*) is recited by those present when a person dies and by close relatives before the funeral service. *Emet* is also one of the Thirteen Attributes of God.

Emet v'Emunah (True and faithful). Opening words of the prayer following the *Shema* in the evening service. In both this prayer and the one listed below, the worshiper affirms a belief in the teachings of the Torah and thanks God for redeeming Israel from Egyptian bondage. Included are three verses from the victorious *Shirat ha-Yam* (Song at the Sea) – "Who is like You among the gods, O Lord" (*Mi-chamocha ba-Eilim Adonai*); "This is my God (*Zeh Eili*)," and "The Lord shall reign forever and ever" (*Adonai yimloch li-olam va-ed*)."

Emet v'Yatziv (True and certain). Opening words of the prayer following the *Shema* in the morning service (see above).

Emor. The 8th *parashah* in the Book of Leviticus (21:1-24:23), it describes some limitations regarding the priesthood; sacred donations; the pilgrimage festivals of Passover, Shavuot, and Sukkot; laws relating to kindling the Menorah and the Showbread; and the case of the blasphemer who was stoned to death.

Emunah (faithfulness). Hebrew term indicating a deep, unshakable belief in God and the Torah.

En. Literally meaning "well," a common component of place names in the Land of Israel in both biblical and modern times (e.g., En Dor, En Gedi, and En Gev).

Encyclopedias, Jewish. The first large Jewish encyclopedia in alphabetical arrangement was the 13-volume *Pachad Yitzchak*, compiled by Isaac ben Samuel Lampronti in the 18th century (and finished posthumously), which traced the history of each topic through the rabbinic literature until his day. The first comprehensive Jewish encyclopedia was published between 1901 and 1906. The massive Encyclopedia Judaica first appeared in 1972, and a new edition was published in 2006.

End of Days – see Afterlife.

Engagement – see *Kiddushin.*

Enlightenment (*Haskalah*). Era of great social and cultural changes that began in Western Europe in the late 17th century. An age of rationalism and unparalleled scientific achievement, it led philosophers in England and France to question the existing order dominated by the Church, the State, and the privileged aristocracy. It introduced new concepts of freedom, natural human rights, religious tolerance, equality, and reliance on reason rather than tradition. Jewish proponents of this movement (*maskilim*) eagerly welcomed this opportunity to adopt the language, manners, and culture of their gentile neighbors and immerse themselves in secular knowledge. Others challenged this belief, attacking it as a threat to Jewish traditions and institutions. Indeed, acceptance of Enlightenment thinking did result in widespread assimilation in Western and Central Europe, as large numbers of Jews decided that the opening of new opportunities required them to renounce their Judaism. Some even became baptized as Christians, considering this their ticket to societal advancement in the arts and the professions. The Enlightenment also resulted in modern research tools being applied to the investigation of Judaism and Jewish history (see *Wissenschaft des Judentums*) and in Jewish educational reforms, as well as a renewal of interest in the Hebrew language. In Eastern Europe, the *Haskalah* resulted in the development of modern Yiddish and Hebrew literature and aided the rise of the Zionist and Jewish socialist movements.

Enoch, Book of. Apocryphal work attributed to Enoch, the father of Methuselah and great-grandfather of Noah. The biblical text notes that Enoch "walked with God; then he was no more for God took him" (Gen. 5:23). This has traditionally been interpreted as meaning that Enoch did not die naturally, but instead was transported to heaven because of his righteousness. Usually dated to the period of the Maccabees (mid-2nd century B.C.E.), it describes the ascent of Enoch through the seven heavens, his return to earth to speak to his son, and his second ascent. The second and third books of Enoch also describe his heavenly pilgrimage.

Envy – see Coveting.

Ephah. Ancient Hebrew dry measure, ten times larger than an *omer* and equal to one tenth of a *homer*.

Ephod. Ornamented long vest worn by the High Priest over the blue robe (Exod. 28:6-12). It consisted of four elements: the main body of the garment, two shoulder straps, and a richly decorated band "of gold, of blue, purple, and crimson yarns, and of fine linen." Attached to the ephod was the breastplate containing the *Urim* and *Thummim*.

Epitaph. Commemorative inscription that, since First Temple times, has marked the place of a Jewish burial. During the Middle Ages, the use of Hebrew in epitaphs became universal. In most Western countries today, the vernacular has become more common. The inscription is generally headed by the letters *pei nun* (standing for *po nikbar*) for a man and *pei tet* (short for *po timunah*) for a woman, both of which mean "here is buried." Sephardim use the letters *mem kuf*, which stand for *mikom kevurat* (the place of burial of). At the bottom of the tombstone are engraved the letters *tav nun tzadi vet hei*, the abbreviation of the phrase *ti-hee nishmato (nishmatah) tzerurah bitz'ror ha-chaim* (May his [her] soul be bound up in the bond of eternal life).[70]

Eppis. A Yiddish word meaning "something."

Eretz Yisrael (Land of Israel). The name of the land promised by God to Abraham and his descendants. The initial description of this Promised Land extended "from the river of Egypt to the great river, the river Euphrates" (Gen. 15:18). Different boundaries are given in later biblical and talmudic sources. Today, the Hebrew term *Eretz Yisrael* refers to the geographic area of the State of Israel.

Erev (evening). Term used in the context of the evening of the Sabbath or a festival, as the Jewish day begins and ends at sunset.

Erusin – see *Kiddushin*.

Eruv. Literally meaning "blending" or "intermingling," a rabbinically permitted way to overcome the restrictions on carrying and travel on the Sabbath while preserving the sanctity of the day. The establishment of an *eruv* takes advantage of the legally mandated permission to carry inside a private domain by converting a large public area into a huge "private domain." For example, it is forbidden to carry an object from one house to another. However, if all the tenants living around a large courtyard contribute food and place it at a central point before the Sabbath, the entire area is symbolically transformed from a series of individual private dwellings into one common group dwelling that belongs to the entire community. Today, a common way of making an *eruv* is to extend a wire or nylon cord around the perimeter of a community, by connecting it to telephone or utility poles. This transforms the entire area into a single domain, in which it is permitted to carry and push baby carriages. In Israel, *eruvim* have been constructed in all cities. In the United States, they have been established in many cities that have a substantial traditional Jewish population.

Eruv tavshilin. While preparation of holiday meals is permitted on festivals, it is forbidden to prepare food for another day. Strictly speaking, if a festival occurs on Friday, one would not be permitted to prepare food for the Sabbath. To overcome this problem, the Rabbis instituted the *eruv tavshilin*. On the day before the festival, one prepares a special dish consisting of two items of food (such as bread and a piece of fish) for the Sabbath. In this way, a "blending" (*eruv*) of the Sabbath and festival foods occurs, making it permissible to prepare food on Friday for the Sabbath.[71]

Eruvin (Er.). The 2nd tractate of Mo'ed (festivals) in the Mishnah, it deals with the permissible limits for carrying on the Sabbath.

Ervat davar. Biblical term for the grounds for divorce (Deut. 24:1). Generally translated as "something obnoxious" or "a matter of indecency," the precise meaning was the subject of a talmudic debate. Beit Shammai argued that it meant adultery, so that the only proper grounds for divorce was sexual impropriety. Beit Hillel disagreed, maintaining that "something obnoxious" might refer to any act that made the husband unhappy, even something as minor as his wife's cooking.[72] Although Beit Hillel prevailed in the law of divorce, the concept of Beit Shammai still has influence. Whereas in the case of "something obnoxious" the husband has the *right* to divorce his wife, in the case of sexual transgression he has an *obligation* to do so, even if he would prefer to forgive her.[73] R. Akiva took a different approach, interpreting the biblical verse as including two separate statements regarding the grounds for divorce. For him, the exact nature of *ervat davar* is immaterial, for the first part of the clause – "she finds no favor in his eyes" – stands as an independent justification. Thus, a man was permitted to divorce his wife "if he finds another woman more beautiful than she is."

Eschatology. From a Greek root meaning "end," the speculative study of the final events in the history of the world. In traditional Jewish belief, the "end of days" is intimately associated with the Messianic Age, an era of peace and prosperity for both the living and the resurrected dead. At that time, the enemies of Israel will be defeated and the scattered exiles will be gathered in the Land of Israel, where the Third Temple will be built in Jerusalem. On the eschatological Day of Judgment at the end of the world, the righteous will receive their eternal reward and the wicked the endless punishment they merit. The Messianic Age is seen as a time when human beings will realize their potential to live in peace, harmony, and prosperity.

Eshet Chayil (Woman of Valor). Alphabetical acrostic poem taken from Proverbs (31:10-31) that enumerates the qualities of the virtuous woman. It is traditionally recited or chanted by the husband, alone or together with the children, prior to the *Kiddush* on Friday evening, a custom originated by the 16th-century kabbalists. In *Eshet Chayil,* the woman of valor is praised for being dignified, respected, practical, hard-working, and charitable, speaking with wisdom and kindness and facing life with optimism and confidence. The ideal wife, she is trusted and praised by her husband and beloved by her children. The poem concludes with the lines: "Grace is deceitful, beauty is vain, but a woman who fears the Lord, she shall be praised; give her of the fruit of her hands, and let her works praise her in the [city] gates"[74] Initially, the singing of *Eshet Chayil* was a kabbalistic ritual, and the intended object of the song was the *Shechinah* – the Divine Presence and a mystical feminine symbol. Verses of *Eshet Chayil* are often recited at the funerals of pious women and appear as inscriptions on their tombstones.

Essenes. Pietistic, ascetic Jewish sect of the late Second Temple period. They lived in segregated communities in less populated regions, often in the Judean Desert. Sworn to maintain the secrecy of their sect from outsiders, the Essenes emphasized strict adherence to communal rules, ritual purity, and communal property, with each new member (accepted after a prolonged period of candidacy) turning over his assets to the group. They avoided luxury, espoused moderation, and were required to be celibate after becoming members (though some scholars debate this last point). Like the Pharisees, the Essenes accepted a belief in the immortality of the soul.Many scholars believe that the Dead Sea sect at Qumran were Essenes. They participated in the war against Rome, but when the revolt was crushed, they disappeared from the stage of history.

Esther (**Esth**.). The last of the five *megillot* (scrolls) in the Writings section in the Bible, the book is read in the synagogue on the festival of Purim. Written in the 5th or 4th century B.C.E., it relates how Esther, the Jewess, married King Ahaseurus of Persia and saved her people from the nefarious plot of Haman, the chief royal counselor. According to Jewish legend (Meg. 15a), the heroine of the Purim story was one of the four most beautiful women in the world, of perfect height like a myrtle, with a necklace of lovingkindness strung around her neck. Although her Hebrew name was Hadassah (myrtle), non-Jews called her Esther, a name that was derived from Ishtar (the Persian equivalent of Venus), the goddess of beauty

(Meg. 13a). Some have suggested that the name Esther came from the Hebrew word *seter* (hidden), a foreshadowing of her ability to disguise her Jewish identity until she had won the heart of King Ahasuerus so that she was in a position to save her people from destruction. There was opposition to the canonization of the Book of Esther because God is not mentioned in it. For persecuted Jews in the Diaspora, the Book of Esther had a strong appeal, since it ends with the Jews triumphing over their enemies.

Esther, Fast of – see Fast of Esther.

Esther Rabbah. Aggadic midrash on the Book of Esther, dating from the late talmudic period.

Eternal light – see *Ner tamid.*

Ethical will. Written testament of moral and ethical instructions to children and other descendants. Although there are references to more ancient documents, the writing of ethical wills became a frequent practice among Jews in the Middle Ages, when they were also common among Muslims and Christians. Not only do ethical wills reflect the moral and ethical views of pious Jews living in particular countries during specific periods, they also are valuable historical sources that offer insights into the cultural and social life of the time.

Ethics. Jewish ethics is a unique mode of thinking that differs from western philosophical thought in terms of its basic premises and assumptions. This often leads to disparate conclusions as to whether an act is deemed moral or immoral. Jewish ethics is a form of religious or theological ethics, "derived from a Divine source and communicated to human beings in acts of revelation." Therefore, Jewish ethics presupposes that morality ultimately has its origins in a source other than ourselves. This is in contrast to secular ethics, which maintains that "ethics is derived from and is justified by autonomous human origins, such as human reason, human emotion, human intuition, and social mores. Secular ethics rejects the proposition that any guidance from beyond the human or natural realm is either possible or necessary." In contrast, Jewish ethics allows "the possibility of justifying ethical behavior on the basis of humanistic criteria…Moral principles conveyed by revelation may be understood, interpreted, embellished, and applied by utilizing God-given abilities, such as intellect, intuition, experience and emotion."[75] Ultimately, however, Jewish ethics rests on theological presuppositions. In modern times, Jewish ethical concerns have been expanded to such areas as business and medicine.

Ethics of the Fathers – see *Pirkei Avot.*

Ethnarch. Literally "head of the people," the title bestowed on John Hyrcanus II and his sons in the Land of Israel by official decree of Julius Caesar in 47 B.C.E. The term "ethnarch" was also used to designate the head of the Jewish community of Alexandria.

Etiquette. The proper conduct expected of a Jew at home and in society, encompassed by the Hebrew term *derech eretz*.This includes appropriate speech, clothing, eating and drinking, interpersonal relations, and treatment of spouse and children.

Etrog. Traditionally identified as "the fruit of a goodly tree" (*peri etz hadar*; Lev. 23:40), it is one of the four species used as part of the celebration of the festival of Sukkot. Known as "citron," this yellow citrus fruit is usually larger than a lemon and has tangy taste and smell, symbolically representing those Jews who have both learning and good deeds to their credit. During Sukkot, it is customary to protect the *etrog* and its fragile stem (*pitom*) in an ornamental container. Some legends suggest that the *etrog* was the forbidden fruit eaten by Adam and Eve in the Garden of Eden. During the Second Temple period, the *etrog* was a popular design on Israelite coins, synagogue walls, and mosaic floors.

Etz Chaim – see Tree of Life.

Etzel. Hebrew acronym for ***Irgun Zeva'i Leumi*** (National Military Organization; see Irgun).

Eulogy. Central part of the funeral service, in which a speaker praises and laments the deceased. The Talmud stresses that the eulogy should be truthful and neither exaggerate the qualities and accomplishments of the person who has died nor fail to give them their just due (Ber. 62a). Although normally offered by the officiating clergy, family members or close friends may elect to speak. In traditional circles, the eulogy is omitted when the funeral takes place on festivals or other days when *Tachanun* is not recited.

Euphemism. A neutral word that is substituted for one that is indelicate, blasphemous, or taboo. Among common euphemisms in the Bible and Talmud are the use of the verb "to know" instead of "have sexual intercourse;" "house of the living" to mean a cemetery; and various expressions to avoid the verb "to die."

Euphrates. Longest river in Western Asia, mentioned as one of the four that watered the Garden of Eden (Gen. 2:14). The Euphrates was the northern boundary of the land promised to the Israelites in the Bible (Gen. 15:18; Deut. 11:24; Josh. 1:4). During talmudic and geonic times, Jewish communities flourished along the Euphrates, including such centers of Babylonian scholarship as Sura, Nehardea, and Pumbedita.Among the many cities built near the Euphrates was Ur, described in the Bible as the birthplace of Abraham.

Euthanasia. Also known as "mercy killing," this Greek word denotes "the action of inducing gentle and easy death." A complicated concept in Judaism, the general halachic rule is that although a person is forbidden to do a positive act to *hasten* death, one is also prohibited from performing an act that would *delay*, by artificial means, the death of a *goses* who has no hope of living. In modern practical terms, most Jewish authorities would permit the withholding or disconnecting of artificial respirators and other machines that maintain the vital bodily functions of a *goses* but do not offer any reasonable chance of cure, on the basis that these merely prolong the dying process and do not serve the interests of the patient. This includes cardiopulmonary resuscitation, surgery, dialysis, chemotherapy, and radiation therapy if they are merely palliative, especially if they increase pain and suffering or if the patient does not consent. However, the majority would not permit the removal of artificial nutrition and hydration from one who is terminally ill and cannot (or will not) ingest food and liquids through the mouth. While there is a controversy regarding the amount of medication that can be administered to relieve pain, all traditional authorities agree that if the primary intent is to cause the death of the patient, it is forbidden to give that quantity, even at the patient's request.

Evel Rabbati – see Semachot.

Even Ha-Ezer – see *Shulchan Aruch.*

Even Shetiyah – see Foundation Stone.

Evening service – see *Ma'ariv*.

Evian Conference. International conference of 32 countries, convened in 1938 by Franklin D. Roosevelt after the German occupation of Austria, to address the growing crisis of Jewish refugees in Nazi-dominated Europe. The invitation specified that no country would be expected to receive more immigrants than was permitted by existing law. Thus, Great Britain was assured that the question of Palestine would not be considered, and the American quota system was also not up for discussion. In the end, only the tiny Dominican Republic announced its willingness to accept Jewish refugees. The Evian Conference had a devastating impact on the fate of the Jews of Europe. In addition to indicating that other nations would do nothing to protect the Jews from Nazi oppression, thus emboldening the Nazis to pursue their anti-Semitic policies, it had the practical effect of maintaining only severely restricted possibilities of the emigration of Jews from German-dominated lands on the eve of the Holocaust.

Evidence. Material produced to establish proof at trial. According to biblical law, the testimony of at least two witnesses was required in criminal cases (Deut. 19:15; 17:6). The Rabbis listed 10 categories of disqualified witnesses.In civil cases, documents were acceptable as evidence if no witnesses were available.

Evil. The existence of evil and the problem of theodicy have been vexing theological problems throughout Jewish history. Unlike polytheistic religions that posited separate deities for good and evil, the Bible clearly states that both were created by God, who is termed "the Former of light and the Creator of darkness, the Master of peace and Creator of evil" (Isa. 45:7). For the medieval philosophers, who tried to minimize the problem, evil did not really exist and was merely "the absence of the good." The mystics offered several explanations for evil, such as an intrinsic flaw in the work of Creation (due to the breaking of the vessels), and dilution of the Divine flow from *Ein Sof* to our world, where God's presence is represented by the *Shechinah* rather than the omnipotent Divine Being of the philosophers. Following the Holocaust, philosophers and theologians sought to grapple anew with the problem of evil. While some reformulated traditional explanations, others took a more radical course, even advancing new ideas of the nature of God.

Evil Eye (*ayin ha-ra*). The traditional folk belief in the ability of the Evil Eye to injure or cast a spell on another person led to the development of numerous practices to prevent or counteract it. Believing that jealousy was the most frequent cause of the Evil Eye, the Rabbis warned against excessive praise, especially of children, and ostentatious displays of riches (see *Keyn ayen horeh*).

Evil inclination – see *Yetzer ha-ra* and *Yetzer ha-tov*.

Evil speech – see *Lashon ha-ra*.

Evil spirits – see Demons.

Evolution. Theory promoted by Charles Darwin that all plant and animal species have successively progressed from lower to higher forms through a struggle for survival accompanied by a series of mutations, natural selection, and survival of the fittest. Initially, traditional Judaism utterly rejected this theory as incompatible with the biblical description of God creating the world in six days (Gen. 1). However, some Orthodox scholars have reconciled evolution and the account in Genesis by figuratively interpreting the six days of Creation, while more liberal scholars have argued that evolution is part of the Divine plan.

Excommunication – see *Cherem*.

Exegesis – see Bible commentary.

Exilarch. Political head of the Jewish community in Babylonia from the 1st-13th centuries. Known in Aramaic as *Resh Galuta* (head of the exile), the office was hereditary, with the holder traditionally being a member of the House of David and wielding considerable power. Recognized by the established royal court, the exilarch was the chief tax collector among the Jews, appointed judges, and oversaw the criminal justice system in his community. The relationship between the exilarchs and the heads of the talmudic academies (*geonim*) varied from amicable to a state of bitter conflict; as the influence of the academies grew, new exilarchs had to receive their approval.

Exile – see Babylonian Exile and Diaspora.

Exiles, ingathering of the. Part of the prophetic concept of the Messianic Age, when the Jewish people will return from exile, rebuild the Temple, reinstitute the sacrificial cult, and establish God's kingdom of universal peace. This phrase has been used to denote the immigration of Jews to the State of Israel, though today the bulk of Jews outside of Israel would claim to be living in the Diaspora rather than in exile.

Exodus (Exod.) (1). English name for the 2nd book of the Torah. The first section describes the oppression of the Israelites by the Egyptians, the call of Moses to be the deliverer of his people, the ten plagues, the Exodus from Egypt, and the miraculous crossing of the Sea of Reeds. The second part deals with the Revelation at Mount Sinai, the Ten Commandments, the covenant and other Divine legislation, the building of the Tabernacle in the wilderness, and the shameful episode of the Golden Calf.

Exodus (2). Flight of the Israelites from Egypt and the birth of the nation of Israel. This paradigmatic story of freedom, redemption, and God's special choosing of the Israelites is commemorated in the spring festival of Passover, the central holiday of the Jewish people. References to the Exodus are found throughout the liturgy and the *mitzvot*. In the *Shacharit* (morning) service, Jews recount the story of the Exodus, including Moses' *Song at the Sea*.The first of the Ten Commandments links monotheism with the Divine act of saving the Israelites: "I am the Lord your God who took you out of the land of Egypt from the house of bondage" (Exod. 20:2). The Friday night *Kiddush* describes the Sabbath as "a memorial to the Exodus from Egypt." The rationales for the numerous laws requiring ethical sensitivity and compassion are based on the fact that "you were strangers in the land of Egypt, and I took you out;" just as God heard the pleas of a desperate enslaved people, so we are enjoined to heed the call of the downtrodden and disenfranchised among us. Finally, we are reminded of the Exodus in the *tzitzit, mezuzah*, certain rules of *kashrut*, and laws pertaining to the harvest.[76]

Exodus 1947. Name of a ship carrying more than 4,500 Jewish refugees to Palestine under the auspices of the Haganah.Seized by the British in the Mediterranean after a bloody battle, its passengers were forcibly returned to Hamburg in Germany and then transferred to a detention camp in that country. This incident, which aroused world opinion against Britain's policy of closing the gates of Palestine to survivors of the Holocaust, played a major role in gaining widespread sympathy for the Zionist cause.

Exodus Rabbah (Exod. R.) – see Midrash Rabbah.

Exorcism. The expulsion of a spirit (soul of the dead) that is possessing a living person (see *dybbuk*).

Expulsion. During ancient times, Jews were expelled from the Land of Israel by the Assyrians and Babylonians. Diaspora Jews under Christian rule experienced numerous expulsions. Duing the Middle Ages, they were expelled from England (1290), France (1306, 1394), and many areas in Central Europe and Russian-controlled territory (15th century to 1772). The most famous expulsion was from Spain in 1492, followed by one from Portugal in 1497. Ironically, on the same day the Spanish edict of expulsion took effect (Tisha b'Av), three small ships sailed from the Spanish port of Cadiz on an expedition largely supported by Jews and *Conversos*–the voyage of Christopher Columbus to the land that would one day be the home of the largest Jewish community in the world.

Extermination camps – see Camps, concentration and extermination.

Eye for an eye – see *Lex talionis*.

Ezekiel (Ezek.). The 3rd of the major prophets. A member of the priestly family of Zadok, Ezekiel was carried off to Babylonia by Nebuchadnezzar along with the king and the Judean aristocracy in 597 B.C.E following the first capture of Jerusalem (2 Kings 24:12). The first half of his book denounces Judah and Jerusalem for their sinfulness and prophesies their inevitable destruction. Ezekiel believes in each person's individual responsibility to God and calls for personal repentance to avert the otherwise inevitable catastrophe. He stresses that guilt is not passed on from generation to generation, arguing that all people are responsible for their own sins. The final part of the book provides a vision of the New Jerusalem and its restored Sanctuary, to which the Glory of God will return. Ezekiel's prophecies have great poetic beauty and are often steeped in mystical images. His vision of the Divine Chariot (*Merkava*), which is the *haftarah* for the first day of Shavuot (1:1-28), formed the basis of early mystical speculation. In his symbolic vision of a valley of dry bones that were resurrected and rise again (Ch. 37), Ezekiel envisions the rebirth of Israel and the ingathering of the exiles.

Ezra. The 10th book of the Writings section of the Bible, it relates the story of the return of the Jews from exile in Babylonia to the Land of Israel during the 6th century B.C.E. Together with Nehemiah, Ezra received permission from the Persian ruler to lead the Jewish exiles back to Jerusalem and rebuild the Temple. Ezra instituted religious reforms, such as periodic readings (with explanations) of the Torah to the people, and promoted the observance of the Sabbath and the Sabbatical Year.

Ezrat Nashim (Court of the Women). Section of the Second Temple in Jerusalem. Situated at the east of the Temple Court, before the Courts of the Israelites and the Priests, it was a square 135 cubits long on each side. In each of its four corners were 40 x 40 cubit chambers – for the Nazirites (southeast) and lepers (northwest), and for the storage of oil (southwest) and wood (northeast). A balcony surrounded the area, from which the women used to watch the celebrations of the Feast of the Water-Drawing (*Simchat Beit ha-Sho'evah*) on Sukkot. From the Court of the Women, men could ascend to the Court of the Israelites (*Ezrat Yisrael*). The term *Ezrat Nashim* was later applied to the section of the synagogue where women sit during the service.

Ezrat Yisrae*l* (Court of the Israelites). Section of the Second Temple in Jerusalem. It represented that portion of the Court of the Priests open to all male Jews. Both of these courts were enclosed by an inside wall 20 meters high, on top of which were exhibited enemy spoils taken by the Hasmoneans and Herod. The Court of the Israelites was long and narrow (135 x 11 cubits). This small area was especially filled on Passover, as well as on Sukkot at the close of the Sabbatical Year, when the king used to stand upon a wooden platform to read the biblical portion traditionally assigned to him.

F

Falasha. Amharic word literally meaning "stranger" or "immigrant," it is often used to denote Ethiopian Jews. Considering the term "falasha" to be pejorative, they prefer to call themselves Beta Israel (House of Israel).

Fall of man. After Adam and Eve ate the forbidden fruit, they were expelled from the Garden of Eden. Men were forced to work for their bread, women were fated to suffer pain in childbirth, and human beings became mortal. However, Jews (and Muslims) reject the Christian doctrine of "original sin," which maintains that the "fall of man" caused a fundamental change in human nature, so that all Adam's descendants are born in sin and can only be redeemed by Divine grace. (Christians believe that Jesus, who was without sin, died on the cross as the ultimate redemption for the sin of humankind.) Instead, Jews believe in the concept of reward and punishment, which is repeatedly expressed in the Torah and rabbinic literature and maintains that God will reward those who observe the Divine commandments and punish those who intentionally disobey them.

False accusations. The most vicious form of slander (*lashon ha-ra*) is false accusations made to a ruling authority *(malshinut)* with the intent of endangering a person's livelihood and even his life. Through their slanderous allegations, informers sometimes jeopardized entire Jewish communities. The Talmud even declared that the destruction of Jerusalem resulted from false charges brought to the Roman authorities by a disgruntled individual who was insulted by his neighbor (Git. 55b-56a). These especially vicious slanderers were placed in the category of persons who commit assault with intent to kill, so that putting them to death was authorized. If their intention to slander was clear, death was sanctioned even before the crime was committed. The extent to which Jewish communities were harassed by slander led to the inclusion in the daily *Amidah* of the prayer: "And for slanderers (*minim*), let there be no hope."

False weights and measures. The Torah expressly prohibits the use of false weights and measures (Lev. 19:35). On Rosh Hashanah, the traditional belief is that God decides each individual's income for the year. By using false weights, a person unfairly increases his income and thus interferes with the Divine plan. Weights should be made of materials that cannot rust, because rust adds weight.[77] A grain merchant was required to wipe his measuring vessels clean at least once every 30 days, so that he always sold the exact measure and not less. Jews were prohibited from keeping false weights in their pockets or home (Deut. 25:14), even though they did not use them for purposes of trade. As Sforno observed, "God abhors not only the actual practice of dishonesty, but also the instruments that enable one to commit it."[78]

False witness. The biblical prohibition against bearing false witness is the ninth of the Ten Commandments (Exod. 20:13). The rabbis extended this injunction to prohibit testimony even in cases when a witness was convinced that something took place but did not actually see it. A person may not present hearsay (not personally witnessed) testimony even if he heard it from an apparently impeccable source. In addition to the literal meaning of giving false testimony in court, this passage was extended by the Rabbis to also prohibit gossip, slander, and misrepresentation. According to the Bible, the punishment for violating this commandment was: "You shall do to him as he conspired to do to his fellow" (Deut. 19:19).

Family. "Be fruitful and multiply" (Gen. 1:18), the first of the 613 commandments, was interpreted by the Rabbis as the duty to raise a family. The basic nucleus of the Israelite family in biblical times was the "house of the father" (*beit av*), which consisted of a husband, his wife (or wives), his unmarried daughters and sons, and his married sons with their wives and children. Children were to honor their parents and provide for their needs; disobedience and disrespect were severely punished (see parents and rebellious son). The paterfamilias was the highest authority within the family and its representative to the society at large. As head of the family, he exercised the power of life and death and was required to educate his sons and prepare them for a useful trade. Women were to be modest, submissive, and always comport themselves in a proper manner, generally remaining in the background in the private parts of the house. Halachic rules governed marital relations. Monogamy was considered the ideal by talmudic times, and polygamy was outlawed by the *takanah* of Rabbi Gershom in the 11th century. Jewish tradition values a close-knit family and encourages domestic harmony (*shalom bayit*).

Family purity – see *Taharat ha-mishpachah.*

Farblondjet. Yiddish term meaning "completely lost."

Farbrengen. Literally "spending time together," this Yiddish term also refers to a lively gathering of Hasidim. When the Rebbe leads a *farbrengen*, there is a more formal atmosphere when he addresses his assembled followers, communicating Torah thoughts and his messages for the Jewish world at large.

Farfel. Yiddish word for small noodle-like pieces of dough used in soups or served as a side dish like rice. Farfel is especially popular as a seasonal item in Passover dishes, when it is made from crumbled *matzah* and used a substituted for forbidden *chametz*.

Farmisht. Yiddish term meaning "mixed up" or "confused."

Farpitzed. Yiddish term meaning "all dressed up," often with the connotation of being overly gaudy or made-up.
Farshtay. Yiddish word meaning "to comprehend," it is usually followed by a question mark and means "Did you understand that?"

Fascism. Term used to describe a political philosophy that flourished in Europe, Japan, and elsewhere after World War I. Fascism is characterized by chauvinistic ultra-nationalism, subordination of the individual to an all-powerful totalitarian state, and the embrace of militarism, violence, and expansionism. Italy under Benito Mussolini was the first fascist state, and Nazism was a racist variant of fascism.

Fast days. The Jewish calendar contains several fast days relating to specific holidays. "Minor" fast days, which last only from sunrise to sunset (rather than including the previous night) and on which work may be performed, include the 17th of Tammuz, Tzom Gedaliah, the 10th of Tevet, the Fast of Esther, and the Fast of the Firstborn. The "major" fast days – on which eating and drinking are prohibited the entire day, work is forbidden, and other restrictions are in place – are Yom Kippur and Tisha b'Av.There are also fasts held on private occasions, such as the fast of a bride and groom on their wedding day until the marriage ceremony.

Fast of Esther (*Ta'anit Esther*). Minor fast observed on the 13th of Adar, the day preceding Purim. It recalls the three-day fast by the Jews of Persia (Esth. 3:12; 4:16) to lend support to Queen Esther as she prepared to enter King Ahasuerus' presence unsummoned, an act punishable by death. Ironically, this fast, which is mentioned in the *Megillah*, actually took place during Passover of the previous year, rather than just before the climactic events in the Purim story. When the day of fasting falls on a Sabbath, it is moved back to Thursday – since fasting is not permitted either on the Sabbath (except on Yom Kippur), a day of joy, or on Friday, when one is preparing for the Sabbath.

Fast of Gedaliah – see Tzom Gedaliah.

Fast of the Firstborn (*Ta'anit Bechorim*). Minor fast observed on the 14th of Nisan, the day before Passover. It commemorates and expresses gratitude to God for sparing the firstborn Israelites during the tenth plague in Egypt (Exod. 13:1). Many of those firstborn who observe it take advantage of the halachic principle that Torah study can supersede and cancel the fast. Whenever the study of a body of Jewish text is completed, such as a tractate of the Talmud, it is customary to have a *siyum* – a celebration of the special occasion with food and drink. Therefore, the tradition has evolved to finish the study of a tractate of Talmud on the morning before Passover, when a festive meal (*se'udat mitzvah*; meal in honor of a *mitzvah*) is arranged in the synagogue. For those firstborns who participate, the meal associated with the *siyum* concludes the fast.[79]

Fear of God. The Hebrew term *yirat ha-Shem*, also translated as "awe" of God, is the closest biblical equivalent for the English concept of "religion." Psalms (111:10) and Proverbs (9:10) call *yirat ha-Shem* "the beginning of wisdom." After grimly concluding that his lifetime of amassing possessions was merely "emptiness and chasing after wind, of no profit under the sun" (1:11), the author of Ecclesiastes ends his book with the affirmation that there is an ultimate purpose to life—"Fear God and obey His commandments, for this is the whole of man" (12:13). Indeed, the term *yirat ha-Shem* has come to define pious Jews, who are convinced that by performing the Divine commandments they are fulfilling the will of God.

Feast of Booths – see Sukkot.

Feast of Tabernacles – see Sukkot.

Feast of the Commandment – see *Se'udat mitzvah.*

Feast of Unleavened Bread – see Passover.

Feast of Weeks – see Shavuot.

Feasts – see Festivals.

Feh. Yiddish expression of disgust.

Felafel. Spicy, deep-fried chickpea croquette, usually served in pita bread with salad, pickles, and tahini. In Israel, felafel sandwiches are sold by street vendors and kiosks as the Middle Eastern equivalent of fast food.

Feminism. In a Jewish context, according to Susannah Heschel, feminism encompasses "attaining complete religious involvement for Jewish women; giving Jewish expression to women's experiences and self-understanding; and highlighting the imagery, language, and rituals already present within Jewish tradition that center around the feminine and women." Moreover, Jewish feminism deals with "changing or eliminating aspects of Jewish law, customs, and teachings that prevent or discourage women from developing positions of equality to men within Judaism as well as bringing new interpretations to bear on the tradition." New feminist rituals include bat mitzvah and *simchat bat*; counting women in the *minyan*, calling women for *aliyot*, and allowing them to read from the Torah. The Reform, Conservative, and Reconstructionist movements have ordained women as rabbis and cantors. Feminism has dramatically influenced the language of prayer, with gender-neutral terminology becoming increasingly prevalent in liberal congregations. One version of the *Amidah* includes the "*imahot*" (Sarah, Rebecca, Rachel, and Leah) in addition to the traditional *avot* (Abraham, Isaac, and Jacob). Jewish feminism became prevalent in the United States during the 1970's and has spread to Israel and elsewhere.

Fence around the Torah – see Torah, fence around the.

Festival of First Fruits – see Sukkot.

Festival of Lights – see Chanukah.

Festivals. The generic Hebrew term for the festivals is *chagim* (sing., *chag*), which comes from a verb meaning "to celebrate." Also termed *mo'adim* (appointed times or seasons) or simply *yom tov* (good day), the festivals allow Jews to recognize the role of God in nature and history, to identify with the Land of Israel and the holy city of Jerusalem, and to vicariously experience both the triumphs and the tragedies of their people over the millennia.[80] The festivals can be divided into those commanded by the Torah (major) and those that were added later (minor). The Torah-mandated festivals include the three pilgrimage festivals (Passover, Shavuot, and Sukkot), Shemini Atzeret, Rosh Hashanah, and Yom Kippur. Those festivals that were added later include Purim, Chanukah, Simchat Torah, Lag ba-Omer, Tisha b'Av, Tu b'Shevat, and the modern commemorations of Yom ha-Atzmaut (Israel Independence Day) and Yom Yerushalayim (Jerusalem Day). Ironically, Tisha b'Av, the national day of mourning, is also regarded as a festival, since according to tradition it will become the greatest festival with the coming of the Messiah. (For more information, see separate entries for individual festivals.)

Festivals, second day of. In the Diaspora, an extra day is added to each of the biblical festivals of Passover, Shavuot, Sukkot, and Rosh Hashanah. This practice originated because of uncertainty in the Diaspora as to the day on which the Sanhedrin in Jerusalem announced the New Moon (see Rosh Chodesh). Thus a second day was added to each festival to prevent any chance of the people mistakenly failing to celebrate it on the proper date. Even after a fixed Jewish calendar (still used today), based on precise mathematical and astronomical formulations, was established in about 360 C.E. so that everyone knew the precise day of the festival in advance, the sages decided to continue the long-standing custom of celebrating second days of festivals in the Diaspora. Yom Kippur was the sole exception, since a double fast day was considered too difficult (though some observed it). Rosh Hashanah, on the other hand, gradually came to be observed as a two-day festival even in the Land of Israel.[81, 82]

Festivals, special prayers for. Changes in the liturgy generally correspond to the importance of the festival. In Temple times, on festivals there was an additional (*Musaf*) offering particular for the day. Today, this constitutes the *maftir* portion of the Torah reading for each festival, which is read in a second scroll from the relevant verses in Numbers 28-29. During the *Musaf* service, a recitation of the required offerings for that specific festival effectively serves as a replacement for the additional offerings that were brought to the Temple on that day. It is customary to read one of the *megillot* on certain festivals (The Song of Songs on Passover; Ruth on Shavuot; Lamentations on Tisha b'Av; Ecclesiastes on Sukkot; and Esther on Purim). Special prayers are inserted into the *Amidah* and the Grace after Meals, and *Hallel* is recited.

15th of Av – see Tu b'Av.

15th of Shevat – see Tu b'Shevat.

Fig. One of the seven species of agricultural produce that symbolize the fertility of the Land of Israel, the fig is the first fruit mentioned in the Bible (Gen. 3:7). Adam and Eve covered themselves with the broad leaves of a fig tree when they became ashamed of their nakedness after eating the forbidden fruit of the Tree of Knowledge in the Garden of Eden. Throughout the Bible, the fig (and vine) symbolizes the ideal of peace and security in the Land of Israel. In his vision of the future Messianic Age, the prophet Micah promised that "each man will dwell under his own vine and fig free, and none will be afraid" (4:4).

Fin. From the Yiddish word *finf*, meaning "five," an American slang term for a $5 bill.

Final solution. Euphemistic term employed by the Nazis for the killing of all the Jews of occupied Europe. This entailed the deporting of Jews from their countries of origin by train in sealed boxcars to extermination camps in Poland, where they were methodically gassed and then burned in specially constructed crematoria. Two of the extermination camps (Auschwitz-Birkenau and Maidenak) also had forced labor facilities, where Jews were humiliated and abused until they died from starvation or disease.

Finding of property. A person is required to return lost property to its owner. He is responsible for caring for the lost article he has found (talmudic examples include unrolling and reading a scroll and shaking a garment every 30 days) until it is claimed by its owner, and he is not permitted to "shut his eyes" to lost property. The Talmud brands as a thief any person who finds a lost object or animal and does not attempt to return it to its rightful owner. The finder must make a public announcement and return the item to a person who can describe its identifying signs or provide evidence of ownership. If the lost property lacks identifying marks and is found in a public place, or if it appears abandoned (e.g., spilled fruit along a road), it is deemed ownerless and can be taken by the finder.[83, 84]

Fines. In four specific cases, the Bible mandates the payment of money to an aggrieved party – 30 *shekels* for killing a slave with an ox (Exod. 21:32); 50 *shekels* for raping (Deut. 22:29) or seducing (Exod. 22:16) an unbetrothed virgin; and 100 *shekels* for falsely accusing one's new wife of premarital unchastity (Deut. 22:19). The talmudic Rabbis interpreted the biblical concept of "an eye for an eye…" (*lex talionis*; Lev. 24:19-20) as meaning that an individual who injured another must pay the monetary equivalent to the person he has harmed. The Rabbis also decreed that fines could be imposed only on the evidence of two witnesses. Later, Jewish communities imposed statutory fines on their members as punishment for such offenses as absence from religious services or community meetings and refusing community office or synagogue honors.

Fire. In addition to the general forbidding of all manner of work on the Sabbath, there is a special prohibition against making a fire (Exod. 35:3). The Rabbis considered this to include everything that pertains to the kindling of light, even if no actual work is involved. In modern times, there is a controversy as to whether the switching on of electric lights and appliances is equivalent to making a fire. First, switching on a light does not create electric power; the power exists already. Second, there is no combustion in the filament of an electric light. Nevertheless, Orthodox Jews do not use electrical appliances on the Sabbath. An exception is the refrigerator, which may be opened and closed provided the interior light bulb is unscrewed for the Sabbath. Lights that have been kindled before the Sabbath, such as the Sabbath candles, are allowed, as are burners and an oven for keeping water and previously cooked food warm. Similarly, it is permitted to leave an electric appliance running during the Sabbath and to use a timer to automatically turn an appliance on or off, as long as the timer is set before the Sabbath begins.

Firstborn. The Bible (Deut. 21:17) endorsed the principle of primogeniture, meaning that the firstborn of the father received a double share in the estate. This may have reflected the requirement that the eldest son provide for his mother and any unmarried female members of the family. Nevertheless, the father could choose a son other than the firstborn for leadership – an option that occurred frequently in the stories of the Patriarchs. Thus Abraham selected Isaac over Ishmael, and Isaac gave the primary blessing to Jacob rather than Esau (albeit through a skillful subterfuge engineered by his wife, Rebecca). In turn, Jacob gave the primacy of the tribes to Judah rather than Reuben, his firstborn, and Joseph arranged for Ephraim to be favored over the older Menashe. (See also *birthright*.)

Firstborn, fast of the – see Fast of the firstborn.

Firstborn, redemption of the – see *Pidyon ha-ben.*

First fruits (*bikurim*). Once the Israelites settled in Canaan, they were commanded to bring their first fruits to the Temple in Jerusalem (Exod. 23:16, 19; 34:22; Num. 28:26). Although no specific fruits or grains are mentioned in the biblical text, R. Akiva declared that they were the seven species.After presenting his basket of first fruits to the *kohen*, the farmer was commanded to recite a brief synopsis of Jewish history – humbly thanking God for treating Jacob mercifully in his hour of need, delivering the Israelites from slavery in Egypt, and bringing the Jewish people to their Promised Land flowing with milk and honey (Deut. 26:1-11). Beginning with words that can be translated as either "A wandering Aramean (Jacob) was my father" or "An Aramean (the deceitful Laban) tried to destroy my forefather (Jacob)," these verses became an important part of the Passover Haggadah. When the First Temple was destroyed and the first fruits could no longer be brought, acts of charity served as a substitute.

First Temple. Central Israelite shrine for worship and sacrifice in ancient Jerusalem. Built by King Solomon in the 10th century B.C.E., the First Temple came to be accepted as the only legitimate place for sacrifices to the God of Israel. The First Temple was destroyed by the conquering Babylonians under Nebuchadnezzar in 586 B.C.E.

Fiscus judaicus. Latin term for the "Jewish tax" levied by Vespasian after the destruction of the Second Temple (70 C.E.). This tax was directed to Rome to pay for the reconstruction of the Temple of Jupiter. During the reign of Vespasian's son, Domitian, the tax was especially harsh and humiliating. The imposition of the *fiscus judaicus* persisted for at least 200 years.

Fish (*dag*). According to the laws of *kashrut*, only fish that have scales and fins are permitted for consumption (Lev. 11:9-11). Unlike meat, there is no requirement for fish to be slaughtered ritually (see *shechitah*) and their blood is not prohibited. Fish has long been a favorite food for all three meals on the Sabbath, as the numerical value of the Hebrew word for "fish" equals seven. There is a custom among Sephardic Jews to eat fish heads on Rosh Hashanah so that they rise to the "head" of the community in righteousness and good deeds.

Five (*chamesh*). There are Five Books of Moses (see Torah) and five *megillot*, five species of grain indigenous to the Land of Israel (wheat, barley, spelt, oats, and rye), and five Hebrew letters that have a final letter (*kaf, mem, nun, pei, tzadi*). The five-fingered hand, in the form of a *hamsa*, is a popular amulet to ward off the ill effects of the Evil Eye.

Five Books of Moses – see Torah.

Five Scrolls – see *Megillot.*

Flag (*degel*). During their wanderings in the wilderness after the Exodus from bondage in Egypt, the Jewish people raised banners and flags in their camps to signify their tribal identities (Num 2:2). According to the Midrash (Num. R. 2:7), each tribal prince had a flag of a unique color, corresponding to one of the 12 precious stones in the breastplate of Aaron, the High Priest.The flag of the State of Israel consists of "a white rectangle with two blue stripes along its entire length and a Star of David in the center made up of six stripes forming two equilateral triangles."[85]

Fleishig. Yiddish term meaning "meat," it applies to beef, poultry, and their byproducts (such as chicken broth and fat, but not eggs), as well as to utensils and dishes used for cooking, eating, and serving meat products. According to the laws of *kashrut*, it is forbidden to mix meat and milk. Traditional Jews wait 1 to 6 hours, depending on custom, after consuming meat before eating dairy products.

Flogging – see Corporal punishment.

Flood. As recounted in the Book of Genesis (6:5-7), because of the rampant lawlessness and immorality on earth, God decided to send a great flood to destroy the entire human race. Only a single blameless and righteous man named Noah, who "walked with God," was to be saved together with his family. God gave Noah detailed instructions for building an ark that would preserve his family, a male and female of every "unclean" species of living creature (to allow for their regeneration), and seven pairs of each type of "clean" animal (needed for sacrifices after the flood). After 40 days and nights of torrential rains, the waters subsided and the ark came to rest upon the mountains of Ararat. Upon leaving the ark, Noah erected an altar to God and sacrificed one of every species of clean animal. In accepting this offering, God promised never again to send a universal flood and symbolized this covenant with the rainbow.

Forgiveness. An essential element of the Thirteen Attributes of Mercy, Divine forgiveness requires a combination of genuine remorse for the wrong committed plus evidence of changed behavior. For sins committed against a fellow human being, atonement can only be secured by seeking forgiveness from the other person and redressing the wrong done to the injured party. Because human beings have free will, a famous saying states "to err is human, to forgive Divine." Therefore, human beings must strive to emulate this attribute of God, and failure to grant forgiveness to one who is truly penitent is a grave sin.

Forty (*arba'im*). In the Bible, a measurement of substantial time, as in 40 days and 40 nights of rain in the story of Noah (Gen. 7) and the 40 years the Israelites were condemned to wander in the wilderness after the episode of the spies.Moses remained on Mount Sinai twice for 40 days, while receiving the first and second tablets of the Ten Commandments (Exod. 24:18; Deut. 10:10). King David ruled for 40 years (2 Sam. 5:4), as did his son Solomon (1 Kings 11:42).

Foundation Stone (*Even Shetiyah*). Rock projecting on the summit of the hill in Jerusalem on which the Temple was built. According to tradition, it was the site where the world was founded and where Abraham bound Isaac as he prepared to sacrifice his only son (see *Akedah*). The Mishnah describes the Foundation Stone as the location of the Ark and the Tablets of the Law in the First Temple and the support of the censer in the Second Temple. According to Islamic tradition, Mohammed ascended to heaven from the Foundation Stone, over which the Mosque of Omar now stands.

Four (*arba*). There were four biblical Matriarchs (Sarah, Rebecca, Rachel, and Leah), and Jacob had four "wives" (Rachel, Leah, Bilhah, and Zilpah, although the last two are more generally termed "maidservants" or "concubines") who gave birth to the Twelve Tribes, the ancestors of the Jewish people. The holiest name of God consists of four letters (*YHWH*, the Tetragrammaton). At the Passover seder there are four questions, four cups of wine, and four kinds of children (see all below). The Tu b'Shevat seder also has four cups of wine that represent both the changing seasons and the four worlds according to the Kabbalah. There are four sections in the *Shulchan Aruch*, the most authoritative Code of Jewish Law.

Four cups of wine (*arba kosot*). Each participant at the Passover seder is required to drink four cups of wine. They are consumed at the following times: (1) after recitation of the *Kiddush* at the start of the seder; (2) the conclusion of the main part of the Haggadah, which ends with the blessing for redemption (*ge'ulah*); (3) the end of the Grace after Meals; and (4) the conclusion of *Hallel* (after the hymn *Nishmat kol chai*). It is customary to drink each of the four cups of wine while leaning to the left and reclining on a pillow, since in Roman times reclining was a sign of a free person. The general consensus among the Rabbis was that the four cups of wine reflect the four different expressions of Divine deliverance used in the Torah in relation to the redemption of Israel (Exod. 6:6-7).[86] Four cups of wine are also drunk at the Tu b'Shevat seder.

Four questions. The four questions asked at the Passover seder are popularly known by the first words of the introductory line – *Mah nishtanah* (What is different [about this night from all other nights?]). These questions come at the beginning of the recital of the Haggadah and are asked by the youngest participant. According to the Ashkenazic ritual, the questions come in the following order:

"(1) On all other nights we eat either *chametz* or *matzah*. Why, on this night, do we eat only *matzah*? (2) On all other nights we eat all kinds of vegetables. Why, on this night, must we eat bitter herbs? (3) On all other nights we do not usually dip vegetables even once. Why, on this night, do we dip twice? (4) On all other nights we eat sitting upright or reclining. Why, on this night, do we eat reclining?" The order of the four questions among Sephardim is dipping, *matzah*, bitter herbs, and reclining.

Four sons (children). The Passover Haggadah speaks of four children – wise, wicked, simple, and one who does not know how to ask. It stresses that by listening closely to the way in which a person asks a question or makes a statement, one can gain an insight into the individual's character and prepare a suitable reply.[87] (See sections on the individual children.)

Four species (*arba minim*). Plants mandated by the Torah as part of the celebration of Sukkot (Lev. 23:40) – *etrog* (citron), *lulav* (palm tree), myrtle (*hadas*), and willow (*aravah*). Three myrtle and two willow branches are bound to the *lulav* with strips of palm (the myrtle on the right and the willow on the left) and held in the right hand, while the *etrog* is taken separately in the left hand. The four species (often called merely *lulav* and *etrog*) are waved in all four directions of the compass, as well as up and down, to demonstrate that God is omnipresent. They are then carried in procession around the synagogue during the festival (except on the Sabbath). The Midrash offers several moral and homiletic interpretations of the symbolic meaning of the four species. They are said to correspond to the human body (the *etrog* resembles the heart, the *lulav* is like the spine, the *myrtle* resembles the eyes, the *willow* is like the lips) and to the four types of Jews that differ with respect to scholarship (taste) and good deeds (pleasant aroma) but must be united in the community of Israel, so that the failings of one are compensated for by the virtues of the others.

Four worlds. According to the Kabbalists, there were four levels of creation – *asiyah*, *yetzirah*, *beri'ah*, and *atzilut*.These are symbolized by fruits and nuts at the Tu b'Shevat seder.

Frankincense. An aromatic resin that was the fourth ingredient of the incense (*ketora*) offered up with the burned sacrifices at the Temple. The Hebrew name *levona*, meaning "white," was derived from the color of the fresh sap ("pure frankincense"). Frankincense was expensive because it had to be brought a great distance from southern Arabia and northern Somalia. Therefore, it was kept in a special storeroom in the Temple (Neh. 13:9). Prisoners condemned to death were given frankincense mixed with wine before their execution so that they might not feel pain.

Fraternal societies. Organizations providing mutual aid for members that developed in the 19th century. Particularly active in the United States in the early 20th century, these Jewish organizations provided a broad range of educational, health, insurance, and funeral services as well as a venue for leisure activities. Initially, many were composed of immigrants from the same area (see *landsmanschaft*). The oldest and largest is B'nai B'rith.

Fraud. Jewish law prohibits any deliberate deception or cheating to gain an advantage, with the injured party entitled to annul the contract and have his money refunded. The Bible expressly forbids the use of false weights and measures.

Freedom. The deliverance of the Israelites from bondage in Egypt to freedom is the central theme of the Passover seder. Although slavery existed in biblical times, an Israelite slave could serve a maximum of six years before being released (see slavery). The war of the Maccabees against the Syrian Greeks was the first recorded fight for religious freedom. The Founding Fathers of the United States drew inspiration from the Torah in their fight for American freedom.

Freemasonry. Secret order, founded in London around 1717, to promote brotherhood, mutual aid, and religious tolerance. It arose at the dawn of the Enlightenment, when the idea of the national rights and rationality of all people regardless of their religion was slowly permitting Jews to participate in activities from which they had long been barred. Many Jews viewed joining the Freemasons as part of their personal "emancipation" from former legal and social disabilities. There are many common themes and ideals in Masonic and Jewish rituals, words, and symbols (including the Temple of Solomon). Belief in God, prayer, immortality of the soul, charity, and acting respectfully to all people are essential elements of Freemasonry as well as Judaism.

Free will. Theological doctrine that all individuals have the ability to make choices that are not predetermined, and that they are morally responsible for these choices. The biblical concept of reward and punishment is based on this principle. According to the Bible, the Israelites would receive blessings for obeying the Divine commandments, but suffer curses if they failed to follow them (Deut. 11:26). The Hebrew prophets presupposed free will, as did the Pharisees and most of the medieval Jewish philosophers.

Free-will offering – see Voluntary offering.

Freilach. Yiddish term meaning "happy" or "cheerful," which is often used in reference to music at weddings and other joyous occasions (*simchas*). The word "*freilach*" is also applied to a specific type of lively dance or tune.

Fress. Yiddish word meaning to devour food in great quantities. A *fresser* is one who eats a huge amount.

Friendship Societies (with Israel). Organizations established for the promotion of social and cultural relations between their countries and Israel. They organize lectures, seminars, Israeli art exhibitions and concerts, and receptions for Israeli personalities. Some friendship societies arrange annual study tours to Israel for their members and publish material on life in the country.

Fringes – see *Tzitzit*.

Frontlet. Term for the gold plate worn by the High Priest on the forehead over the headdress and bearing the inscription, "Holy to the Lord." According to the Talmud, this was to remind the High Priest to direct his thoughts to God when he served in the Sanctuary and to prevent him from having feelings of excessive pride. Today, the word "frontlet" is used for the *tefillin* worn on the head, which also serves the purpose of focusing the concentration of the worshiper on God during morning prayers.

Frum. Yiddish term referring to a person who is observant of Jewish law.

Funeral – see Burial.

Funeral service. Ceremony designed to pay tribute to the departed and to console the mourners. For centuries, funerals took place either at the residence of the deceased or at the cemetery. Today, the service is often held in a funeral chapel or at the graveside. The service typically begins with one or more psalms, followed by one or more eulogies, and concludes with the chanting of *El Malei Rachamim*.

Funeral procession. After the funeral service, the body is transported to the cemetery, where relatives and close friends are honored by being pallbearers carrying the coffin to the gravesite. Escorting the dead (*levayat ha-met*), especially deceased scholars, to their last resting place is considered an extremely important symbol of respect that even warrants interrupting the study of Torah. It was called "the true kindness" (*chesed shel emet*), an act of genuine selflessness since one can expect no reciprocation. The minimum duty is to rise as the funeral cortege passes and symbolically accompany it by walking in the direction of the hearse some six to eight feet to indicate respect for the deceased and sympathy for the mourners.

G

Gabbai. Hebrew word for each of the two synagogue members who serve as an "honor guard" on either side of the Torah scroll as it lies on the reading table. The plural term (*gabba'im*) originally referred to a pair of individuals who aided in the collection of taxes and charitable contributions from the community, but now designates those who supervise the synagogue services. One *gabbai* is responsible for calling people up to the Torah and reciting the special *Mi she-Berach* prayer after each *aliyah*. The other typically covers the Torah scroll after the second Torah blessing of one *aliyah* is completed and then removes the covering when the next person called for an *aliyah* is ready to begin the first blessing. However, the major duty of the two *gabba'im* is to closely follow the Torah reading from a printed text and quietly correct any mistakes. Such errors are easy to make, since the scroll has neither punctuation nor vowel signs.[88]

Gadna. Acronym of *Gedudei No'ar* (Youth Corps), a voluntary pre-army youth movement that trains Israeli teens in defense and national service. Functioning in high schools and youth clubs, Gadna provides firsthand knowledge of the geography and topography of Israel as well as courses stressing physical fitness, marksmanship, scouting, field exercises, comradeship, teamwork, and mutual aid. When reservists were mobilized for active duty during previous conflicts, Gadna members took their places in civilian jobs in the postal system, civil defense, schools, hospitals, agriculture, and industry.

Galilee. Northern part of the Land of Israel. The Galilee extends from the Jezreel Valley in the south to the foothills of Lebanon in the north, from the Mediterranean Sea in the west to the Jordan River and the Sea of Galilee in the east. With the division of the monarchy, the Galilee became part of the Northern Kingdom of Israel, which was later captured by the Assyrians. The Galilee came under the rule of the Hasmoneans under Judah Aristobulus I and rapidly became completely Jewish. During the war with Rome, the defense of the Galilee was delegated to the historian Josephus, who lost it to Vespasian in 67 C.E. After the fall of Jerusalem, the national authority of the Patriarchate was reconstituted in the Galilee in the 2nd century, and the Sanhedrin finally settled in Tiberias, the largest town in the region. Today, numerous Christian Arabs and Druze also form part of the population of the region.

Galitzianer. A Jew from Galicia, a province of southern Poland that for many years was part of the Austro-Hungarian Empire. Galicia was a seat of talmudic learning with numerous important *yeshivot*. Galitzianers and Litvaks were natural rivals, each claiming superiority over the other.

Galut (exile). Hebrew expression for the condition of the Jewish people in the Diaspora, usually connoting a situation in which Jews were degraded by their neighbors and persecuted by the ruling authorities. Zionists applied the term *galut* to the history of the Jewish people from the destruction of the Second Temple in 70 C.E. to the founding of the State of Israel in 1948.

Galveston Plan. Project initiated in 1907 by Jacob Henry Schiff, a wealthy New York Jewish financier, to encourage Eastern European Jews immigrating to the United States to move to the Southwest rather than congregating in ghetto conditions in the urban Northeast. It was named for the southern Texas city where the project was first established. By the outbreak of World War I, 10,000 Jews had settled in Galveston.

Gam zu le-tovah (this is also for the best). This Hebrew expression of faith in Divine providence in response to whatever adversity would befall him (Taan. 21a) was the famous motto of Nahum of Gimzo, a 1st-2nd century C.E. teacher of R. Akiva.

Gambling. The Rabbis traditionally forbade gambling as a waste of time that could be better spent on Torah study. Nevertheless, they relaxed their strictness on Chanukah, the joyous festival on which playing dreidel was permitted. During the rabbinic period, gamblers were considered among the wicked persons who were undisciplined, not committed to religious observance, and thus not fit to testify as witnesses in court. In modern Israel, there is a national lottery.

Gan Eden (Garden of Eden). The idyllic place where Adam and Eve lived and from which they were expelled after disobeying God and eating the forbidden fruit. The early prophets figuratively depicted the end of days as a return to the original peace and joy of the Garden of Eden before the sin of Adam and Eve (Isa. 11:6–9, 51:3; Ezek. 36:35), rather than the "heavenly" abode of God. In the traditional Jewish view of the afterlife, only the souls of the extremely righteous go directly to *Gan Eden*; the less virtuous must spend up to a year in *Gehenna* before ascending to this Paradise. According to the talmudic sage Rav (Ber. 17a): "In *Gan Eden* there is no eating, no drinking, no cohabitation, no business, no envy, no hatred or ambition; but the righteous sit with crowned heads and enjoy the luster of the *Shechinah* [Divine Presence]."

Gaon (pl., *geonim*). Formal title of the heads of the academies of Sura and Pumbedita in Babylonia from the 6th-11th centuries. The term is derived from the phrase *g'on Ya'akov* ("the pride of Jacob"; Ps. 47:5). Known for their scholarship and wisdom, the *geonim* were considered the intellectual leaders of the entire Diaspora, and their decisions in all religious matters had absolute legal validity in most Jewish communities. Similar weight was given to their *responsa*, replies to written questions sent to them from all parts of Babylonia and throughout the world. The first Gaon was Hanan of Pumbedita in 589; the last was Hai Gaon in 1038. After falling out of use for more than 500 years, the term "Gaon" was later revived as an honorific title for any rabbi or scholar who had a great knowledge of Torah, such as the Vilna Gaon (1720-1797). The *geonim* helped to develop talmudic law and elevate the Babylonian Talmud to its position of authority. The greatest of the *geonim* was Saadia ben Yosef, who became head of the Sura academy in 928.

Garden of Eden – see *Gan Eden.*

Garlic (*shum*). Along with its relatives onion and leek, garlic is listed as one of the foods that the Israelites had eaten as slaves in Egypt and for which they were nostalgic while wandering through the wilderness (Num. 11:5). Considered a remedy for intestinal worms, the alleged aphrodisiac qualities of garlic led to the Talmud recommending that it be eaten on Friday evenings since "it promotes love and arouses desire."

Gartel (gartl). From a Yiddish word literally meaning "to bind," a black silk or wool belt worn around the midsection by Hasidic Jews at prayer (or at all times), in fulfillment of the commandment to separate the upper and lower halves of the body when praying. *Gartel* is also another name for a wimpel, the long band of material that encircles and holds together the two rolls of a Torah scroll.

Gaza Strip. Thin, rectangular land (including the modern city of Gaza) that extends for 22 miles along the Mediterranean coast northward from the eastern border of Egypt. During the 1948-1949 War of Independence, the invading Egyptian army occupied the Gaza Strip, which was put under Egyptian administration by the armistice agreement of 1949. Israeli forces captured the Gaza Strip during the 1967 Six Day War, but it was handed over to the Palestinian Authority in a unilateral "disengagement" in 2005.

G-d. Alternative form of writing the name of the Deity, used by many traditional Jews to avoid writing God's name (even in the vernacular) on paper or something else of a temporary nature that might be discarded or erased. Out of respect, documents and sacred texts containing the Hebrew name of God are buried rather than merely thrown away (see *genizah* and *sheimot*).

Gedaliah, Fast of – see Tzom Gedaliah.

Gefilte fish. A Yiddish word literally meaning "stuffed," *gefilte* refers to deboned, ground up fish mixed with onions and matzah meal and poached to produce what became the quintessential Sabbath dish in Eastern Europe. It originated around the 14th century as a way to avoid the need to remove bones from a piece of fish on the Sabbath (which would violate the prohibition against "winnowing"). Although one may eat around the bones of a non-filleted piece of fish, the tedious task of deboning impinged on the joy of the Sabbath meal. The solution was to prepare in advance a boneless piece of fish that could be eaten without fear of violating the Sabbath laws or choking on a bone.

Gehenna. Greek form of the Aramaic "*Gehinnom*" (the Valley of [the sons of] Hinnom), the ravine in the southern part of ancient Jerusalem (Josh. 15:8, 18:16). Defiled by being the site of the cult of Molech, which involved the burning of children, *Gehenna* was cursed by Jeremiah, who predicted that the Babylonian destruction of Jerusalem would fill this valley with the corpses of the city's inhabitants, who would burn there and rot like "dung upon the face of the earth" (Jer. 8:2). The traditional rabbinic view of *Gehenna* was a purgatory, where even the worst of sinners would spend only a year. There was some scholarly support for a doctrine of eternal punishment, but modern Jewish thought has essentially abandoned this notion and virtually eliminated the entire concept of *Gehenna* as a place of torture for one's sins.

Gehinnom – see *Gehenna*.

Gelilah. Hebrew word for rolling up and tying the Torah scroll and replacing its cover and ornaments. These action are performed by the *goleil*.

Gelt. Yiddish for "money," it is most commonly used in the context of "Chanukah *gelt*."

Gemara. An Aramaic word that literally meaning "study," it refers to the vast rabbinic legal and ethical commentary on the Mishnah that was compiled over the span of three centuries. Together, the Mishnah and Gemara comprise the Talmud.

Gematria. Interpretive device whereby words are understood through the numerical value of their letters. The letters *aleph* to *tet* represent the digits one to nine; *yud* to *tzadi* from 10 to 90; and *kuf* to *tav* from 100 to 400. The kabbalists went to fantastic lengths in applying *gematria* as an exegetical device, employing complex substitution and other techniques in an attempt to discover hidden truths within the biblical text.

Gemilut chasadim. Literally "the giving of lovingkindness," a core social value that the Rabbis considered a quintessential and distinctive attribute of the Jew. The Talmud specifies six traditional kinds of *gemilut chasadim* – clothing the naked, visiting the sick, comforting mourners, extending hospitality to strangers, providing for a bride, and accompanying the dead to the grave. During the Middle Ages, the broad concept of *gemilut chasadim* became restricted to the granting of interest-free loans to the needy. In the modern period, the term has again been expanded to refer not only to free-loan societies but also to a wide variety of communal welfare organizations. As Shimon the Just declared in the opening lines of *Pirkei Avot* (1:2), "On three things does the [continued] existence of the world depend – Torah, *avodah* [initially the Temple service, later prayer], and *gemilut chasadim*." *Gemilut chasadim* is enumerated among the things "that have no fixed measure," for which "man enjoys the fruits in this world, while the principal remains for him in the World to Come" (Pe'ah 1:1).

Genealogy. As in other ancient Near Eastern historical records, the Bible contains genealogical lists. For example, there are lists of the 10 generations from Adam to Noah (Gen. 5)[89] and from Noah to Abraham (Gen. 11:10–27).[90] There are also genealogies that trace the descendants of major biblical figures and tribal genealogies from census lists in the Book of Numbers, as well as an extensive list tracing the Jewish people from the Patriarchs in the initial eight chapters of the First Book of Chronicles. Records of priestly descent were important in the Second Temple period to verify their ancestry. During the Middle Ages, distinguished family genealogy conferred special status, and in the Hasidic movement descent from a *tzadik* (charismatic leader) has special significance.

Genesis (Gen.). English name for the 1st book of the Torah. Opening with an account of the Creation of the universe by God, it describes such famous episodes in the origin of humanity as Adam and Eve in the Garden of Eden, Noah and the Flood, and the Tower of Babel. The remainder of the book narrates the story of the Patriarchs and Matriarchs during the earliest generations of the Jewish people, before concluding with the Joseph story.

Genesis Rabbah (Gen. R.) – see Midrash Rabbah.

Genizah. Literally meaning "hidden away," this Hebrew term refers to a special storeroom in a synagogue that is set aside for the disposition of torn prayer books, Bibles, and other holy texts, as well as religious articles such as *tefillin* and *tzitzit* that have deteriorated and can no longer be used, so as to show respect for the name of God contained within them. The contents of the *genizah* are removed periodically and reverently buried in the cemetery. An ancient tradition, the most famous *genizah* was in Cairo, which also held a wide variety of "secular" documents that revealed otherwise unknown aspects of the economic, social, and family life of Jews in medieval Egypt. The oldest known work in Yiddish (14th century) was also found in this *genizah*.

Genocide. The systematic and planned extermination of a national, racial, political, ethnic, or cultural group through coordinated acts that lead to the group's destruction, in whole or in part. The term was coined by Raphael Lemkin from the roots *genos* (Greek for family, tribe, or race) and *–cide* (Latin for massacre). After the Holocaust, the most horrific genocide in human history, the Convention on the Prevention and Punishment of the Crime of Genocide was adopted by the UN General Assembly in December 1948. It was finally ratified by the United States Senate in 1988.

Gentile. Any person (especially a Christian) who is not a Jew. Unlike "*goy*," the Yiddish term for a non-Jew, the word "gentile" has no negative connotation. In Jewish tradition, gentiles are divided into two major categories: idolaters/pagans and those who adhere to belief in one God.

Genug shoyn. Yiddish expression meaning "enough already."

Ger – see Conversion and Love the stranger.

Ger toshav. Literally "resident alien," the biblical term for a non-Jew permitted to live in the Land of Israel. Considered a "righteous gentile," a *ger toshav* promised before a rabbinical court to uphold the seven Noahide laws. By formally indicating that he was on a righteous path, a *ger toshav* was entitled to certain legal protections and even financial aid from the community.

Gerim. Minor tractate added to the Talmud that deals with Jewish law concerning conversion and the acceptance of converts.

Gerushin. Literally "driving out" or "banishment," the Jewish legal term for "divorce." The word also refers to the 16th-century kabbalistic practice of praying and meditating on the graves of righteous leaders (see *tzadikim*), in order to spontaneously elevate one's contemplative powers and achieve mystical illumination through sharing in the exile of the *Shechinah*.

Gestapo. Abbreviation of the German phrase for "Secret State Police," it was the main Nazi instrument of persecution, oppression, and destruction of political enemies and a symbol of the terror and horror associated with the regime. Following the Nazi seizure of power in 1933, the Gestapo was initially run by Hermann Göring and then led by Reinhard Heydrich when it merged with other police units under Heinrich Himmler, the head of the SS. Along with the SD, the intelligence service of the SS, the Gestapo was in charge of uncovering, arresting, interrogating, and imprisoning "enemies of the Reich," and as such it was one of the primary agencies for the persecution of the Jews. With the adoption of the

"Final Solution," the Gestapo was responsible for the roundup and deportation of Jews to the death camps.

Get. Talmudic term for a formal divorce document that is signed by the husband and then delivered to his wife. Just as a Jewish marriage is entered into by a contract between husband and wife (see *ketubah*), it can be terminated only by a legal document nullifying the original contract. A *get* may not be issued until a civil divorce is first obtained, just as a Jewish marriage ceremony may not be conducted without first fulfilling all civil requirements. Like all legal documents of the mishnaic and talmudic periods, a *get* is written in Aramaic, the everyday language of the time. The document follows a standard formula and must be handwritten by a scribe, as representative of the husband. After the formal ceremony of handing over the *get*, the wife is officially divorced from her husband and both are free to marry again. However, the wife must wait a minimum of 90 days; if she is pregnant, this will eliminate questions about the paternity of the child.[91]

Get, compelled delivery of. For a divorce to be valid, the husband must voluntarily give a *get* to his wife. Therefore, it is invalid if the husband is of unsound mind or under duress "contrary to law." A wife can appeal to the rabbinical court to compel her husband to grant her a divorce on the basis of his offensive physical condition, violation of marital obligations, or "unworthy conduct." However, this is an inherently problematic procedure because it violates the requirement that a *get* be given with the husband's "full consent." Rabbis have used a variety of tortuous arguments to escape this conundrum, essentially maintaining that, although the husband initially did not wish to divorce his wife, once ordered to do so by a court he is under legal obligation to follow its command. According to Israeli law, the rabbinical courts have the authority to appeal to the civil courts and the police to request the incarceration of a recalcitrant husband. Even within the Orthodox world in the Diaspora, civil authorities are not infrequently requested to force a stubborn husband to grant a divorce. Rather than appealing to a court to compel the husband directly, the approach is to use threats of other legal actions against him, particularly an investigation of tax evasion.[92]

Get, conditional. In exceptional cases, a *get* may be written and delivered conditionally, designed to take effect only if a specific event occurs. This is usually applicable only in times of severe persecution (such as pogroms or the Holocaust) or war, when husband and wife may become separated, and there is a danger of her becoming an *agunah* if the husband does not return and no one can unequivocally attest to the fact that he has died. Consequently, a soldier preparing for war may issue a conditional *get* that would be effective if he failed to return by a certain date, thus permitting his wife to remarry.[93] A conditional *get* may also be written if the husband of a childless couple becomes seriously ill. Such a document would free the wife from the law of levirate marriage.The husband may give his wife a *get* on condition that it become effective only if he dies from his present illness; if so, she would be considered divorced on the day she received the *get.*[94]

Ge'ulah (redemption). The 7th blessing of the weekday *Amidah*, it requests deliverance from individual hardships and troubles: "Behold our affliction, take up our grievance, and redeem us, speedily for Your Name's sake, for You are a powerful Redeemer. Praised are You, O Lord, Redeemer of Israel."

Gevalt. Yiddish word that can mean a desperate expression of protest; an exclamation of fear, astonishment, or amazement; or a cry for help. It is frequently preceded by the word "*oy*."

Gevurah (strength). The 5th of the *sefirot*, also known as *Din*, which brings strict justice into the world. The term is usually understood as God's mode of punishing the wicked and judging humanity based on absolute adherence to the letter of the law. This is tempered by *Chesed*, which represents mercy and forgiveness.

Gevurot (powers). The 2nd blessing of the *Amidah*.It describes God as "eternally mighty," Who "sustains the living with kindness, resuscitates the dead with abundant mercy, supports the fallen, heals the sick, releases the bound, and maintains God's faith for those asleep in the dust…[and] causes death and restores life and makes salvation sprout." The prayer concludes by praising God, "Who resuscitates the dead."

Gezer. Ancient strategic military site, about 20 miles northwest of Jerusalem, which has been the subject of extensive excavations.

Gezerah. A law instituted by the rabbis to prevent people from accidentally and unintentionally violating a Torah commandment. For example, the Torah prohibits work on the Sabbath, but a *gezerah* mandates that one is forbidden from even handling an implement that is used to perform prohibited work (see *muktzeh*) lest he violate the Sabbath. From the point of view of a traditional Jew, there is no difference between a *gezerah* (or a *takanah*) and a *mitzvah* in the Torah. Both are equally binding and neither can be disregarded on a whim. The difference is generally in the degree of punishment. For example, desecrating the Sabbath was punishable by death under Torah law, while violating a *gezerah* merited a lesser penalty.

Gezerah shavah. The second principle of hermeneutics of Ishmael ben Elisha. Using verbal analogy, it posits that if the same word or phrase occurs in two places in the Torah, and a specific law is found in one place, then one can infer that the law also applies in the second place (even if not explicitly stated). In *aggada*, this technique is employed to understand an ambiguous expression (i.e., by seeing how it is used in the other verse, where the meaning is clear); in *halacha*, it aids in determining the law.

Gezundheit. Yiddish term meaning "be healthy," it is most commonly used as the response when someone sneezes.

Ghetto. Compulsory residential quarter of a city or town, generally walled, where Jews were required to live. The term derives from the foundry (*geto*) section in Venice into which Jews were segregated about 1516. During the 16th and 17th centuries, ghettos were established throughout Central and Southern Europe. Although Jews in ghettos enjoyed some autonomy, were free to practice their religion, and enjoyed a strong sense of community, the physical barriers separating them from the rest of the population seriously limited their educational, economic, and political opportunities. Moreover, as the ghettos became increasingly overcrowded and Christian rulers imposed heavier taxes, the Jews were reduced to desperate poverty. Ghettos largely disappeared as Jews were steadily emancipated in the 19th century, but were reimposed in some towns and cities (such as Warsaw) under Nazi rule. These overcrowded, unsanitary, disease-ridden ghettos became "death boxes." Today, the word "ghetto" refers to a section of a city occupied by a particular ethnic or minority group, which usually has a lower socioeconomic status though it is not separated by any physical barrier.

Gid ha-Nesech. Hebrew term for the "sinew of the thigh vein" (see sciatic nerve).

Gilgul – see Transmigration of the soul.

Gimel. The 3rd letter of the Hebrew alphabet, with a numerical value of 3.

Gittin (Git.). The 6th tractate of Nashim (women) in the Mishnah, it deals with the laws of divorce.

Glass, breaking of the – see Breaking of the glass.

Glatt kosher. Although the *halacha* permits certain abnormalities in animal lungs that have been determined to be harmless, those Jews who are strictest in their observance declare as kosher only those animals with smooth, lesion-free lungs. This super-inspected meat is called *glatt kosher*, from the Yiddish word for "smooth."[95] Although the term literally refers only to meat, it has been expanded to apply to food or restaurants that meet the most exacting standards of *kashrut*.

Gleanings. Produce of the fields and vineyards required to be left for the poor. When reaping the harvest, the ancient Israelite farmer was commanded to leave a corner (*pe'ah*) of the field for those in need (Lev. 19:9). He also left single ears of corn that fell to the ground at the time of reaping, the forgotten sheaf of grain in the fields (Deut. 24:19), and single grapes that fell to the ground in the vineyard (Lev. 19:10), as well as undeveloped twigs in which single grapes had not formed clusters (Lev 19:10). The Rabbis took these laws seriously: "He who places a basket under the vine when he is gathering the grapes [so that no single grapes fall to the ground] is robbing the poor" (Peah 7:3). Rashi said: "He who leaves the gleanings, the forgotten sheaf, and the *pe'ah* for the poor is considered as if he had built the Temple and offered his sacrifices there."

Gloss. Short explanation or interpretation of a word or phrase that is added to a manuscript or text. Commentators on the Bible and Talmud often explained difficult words by giving their equivalents in the vernacular language, written in Hebrew script.

Gluttony. The Rabbis prohibited eating and drinking to excess. For Maimonides,[96] "intemperance in eating, drinking, and sexual intercourse ... counteract the ultimate perfection of man ... and generally disturb the social order of the country and the economy of the family." He noted that the "rebellious and stubborn son," who is described in the Bible as "a glutton and drunkard" (Deut 21:20), was to be put to death "lest he grow up in this character and kill many good men by his great lust." Rashi echoed these sentiments, observing that in view of the high cost of meat and alcoholic drinks, the boy must have stolen money from his parents to pay for them. This indicates that he likely will grow up to become a vicious robber to finance his voracious appetite.[97]

G'mar chatimah tovah (may the final sealing be good) – see Book of Life.

Gnosticism. Derived from the Greek word for "knowledge," a complex system of mystical thought and practice that dates back to late Second Temple times. It is based on the concepts that matter is evil and that salvation can be achieved only through esoteric knowledge of spiritual truth.

Goat. In biblical Israel, the goat was a vital part of the economy. In addition to serving as a valuable source of meat and milk, its hides and hair were used for clothing, parchment, tents, water vessels, and the curtains of the Tabernacle. The goat was the most common sin offering, and on Yom Kippur the sins of Israel were symbolically transferred to a goat (scapegoat) in the rite of *Azazel*.The ancient practice of boiling a kid in milk as part of idolatrous fertility ceremonies may have been the underlying source of the prohibition against "seething a kid in its mother's milk."In the popular *Chad Gadya* sung at the conclusion of the Passover seder, the kid is the symbol of the Jewish people. This animal also is featured in a prophetic image of the Messianic Age of peace, when "the leopard shall lie down with the kid" (Isa. 11:6).

God. Divine Creator and Ruler of the universe. The fundamental essence of Judaism is a belief in One God, who is omniscient, omnipresent, omnipotent, and the Creator of everything in existence. This is clearly stated in the first of the Ten Commandments, "I am the Lord your God, who brought you out of the land of Egypt..." (Exod. 20:2). Belief in One God is a prerequisite for the acceptance of all of the other commandments, for a denial of the existence of God would render observance of the other Divinely mandated commandments irrelevant. The existence of God is the first of Maimonides' Thirteen Principles of Faith, and he maintained that any Jew denying this belief is an apostate who does not merit a portion in the World to Come. In the presence of God, one feels awe and love. God is both transcendent and immanent, beyond human understanding yet accessible to the humblest human being. In Jewish thought, there is a special relationship between God and Israel (see Chosen People), though God is Ruler of the universe.

God, attributes of. According to Maimonides and the medieval Jewish philosophers, there are three basic problems they make it impossible to define the attributes of God. As an incorporeal Being, God is unique and mortals have no conceptions to use for comparison. Assuming that God is perfect (and thus static), describing God in more than one way would "change" God into an imperfect Being. Since the highest form of existence is intellectual, God must be "pure intellect" without emotions, which intrude on the intellect. Therefore, Maimonides declared that there are only two ways of speak about God – in terms of negative attributes (what God is not) and attributes of action (what God does). An obvious theological problem with this philosophical idea of God is that it fails to address the issue of how a perfect God can create an imperfect world and have a relationship with imperfect humans. (See *Thirteen Attributes of Mercy*.)

God, fear of – see Fear of God.

God, love of – see Love of God.

God, names of. The numerous names of God reflect the various ways in which the Divine manifestations have been perceived by human beings at different times. The major biblical names are *El*, *El Shaddai*, *Elohim*, and *Adonai* (*YHVH*; see Tetragrammaton). The Rabbis of the Talmud developed a number of additional names for God, including *ha-Kadosh baruch hu, Ribbono shel Olam*, *ha-Makom*, *ha-Rachaman*, *Avinu Malkeinu*, *Avinu she-ba-Shamayim*, *Melech ha-Olam* and *Shechinah*. The Rabbis prohibited writing the name of God, except in sacred texts, lest any paper on which it was casually written might later be defaced, obliterated, or destroyed accidentally by someone who did not know any better.

Go'el ha-dam – see Blood avenger.

Gog and Magog. As described in an apocalyptic vision of Ezekiel (34-39), these names refer either to two persons or to one person (Gog) and a land (Magog). The utter defeat of the satanic Gog and Magog by God and Israel in eschatological warfare will, according to rabbinic tradition, precede the coming of the Messiah.

Golah – see Diaspora.

Golan Heights. Large hilly region east of the Jordan River, which was captured by Israeli forces during the Six Day War. After the establishment of the State of Israel, the Syrians covered the Golan with a network of artillery positions and fortifications to harass Jewish settlements in Upper Galilee and the area of the Sea of Galilee. During the last two days of the 1967 war, virtually the entire population (except for the Druze) fled, along with the Syrian army. Since that time, Jewish settlements have sprung up on the Golan and agriculture, industry, and tourism have been developed.

Golden Calf. Idol fashioned by Aaron at the demand of the Israelites when they feared that Moses would not return from Mount Sinai to lead them (Exod. 32). In its honor, the Israelites celebrated a wild festival with eating, drinking, and frenzied dancing. Hearing the tumult below, Moses immediately descended from the mountain, carrying in his hand the two stone tablets of the Ten Commandments, which he smashed on the ground. Moses grabbed the Golden Calf and threw it into the fire until it melted. Then he ground the metal into powder, mixed it with water, and forced the Israelites to drink the potion. Tradition maintains that the tribe of Levi did not take part in this idol worship and was rewarded with the priesthood.

Golden rule. Term for the moral principle attributed to the statement of Jesus in the gospels, "Do unto others as you would have them do unto you" (Matt. 7:12). A negative formulation appears in the earlier incident involving the heathen scoffer who asked Hillel to condense the entire Law in the shortest form possible, while standing on one foot. The sage replied, "What is hateful to you do not do to your neighbor," followed by "this is the whole Torah, the rest is commentary; now go and learn!" (Shab. 31a). A well-known biblical verse expressing a similar sentiment is "You shall love your neighbor as yourself" (Lev. 19:18).

Goldene medina. Literally meaning "golden country," this Yiddish term was used by impoverished Jews in Eastern Europe to refer to America, where the streets were thought to be paved with gold.

Goleil – see *Gelilah*.

Golem. Legendary creature made of dust and clay by human hands in a magical, artificial way to serve its creator. The legend of the *golem* became fully developed during the Middle Ages, under the influence of non-Jewish European folklore and Kabbalah. According to *Sefer Yetzirah* and other mystical books, it is possible, using a detailed set of instructions, to create living beings out of earth by using secret combinations of the letters of the Hebrew alphabet, the names of the 10 *sefirot*, and the secret Name of God. However, making a *golem* was considered a hazardous endeavor, which should be attempted only by those who were extremely pious and deeply immersed in the Divine mysteries. The fear was that the creator would lose control of the *golem*, which would then run amok. The most famous *golem* legend involved the 16th-century Rabbi Judah Loew of Prague, who created one to protect the Jews of his city against a false charge of blood libel.

Gomel (He who bestows [good]). Thanksgiving blessing (*Birkat ha-Gomel*) that is recited by a person who has been saved from a life-threatening situation. According to the Talmud, it must be said by anyone who has completed a sea voyage or a hazardous land journey, has recovered from a major illness, or has been released from prison or captivity (Ber. 54b). It is ideally said in the presence of a *minyan*, to publicly acknowledge God's saving deed, and within three days of the event. It is customary, but not required, that the person recite the blessing when called to the Torah for an *aliyah*. The accepted text for *Birkat ha-Gomel* is: "Praised are You... who bestows good things upon the undeserving, and who has bestowed every goodness upon me." The congregation responds: "Amen. May He who has bestowed goodness upon you continue to bestow every goodness upon you forever."[98]

Gonif. Literally meaning "thief," this Yiddish term may also be used to denote a shady character or dishonest businessman.

Gornisht. Yiddish word meaning "nothing," often used sarcastically as the answer to the question, "what benefit did you get from it?"

Goses. A person who is moribund and expected to die within 72 hours, described as a flickering candle that cannot be moved for fear of extinguishing life. Although it is strictly forbidden to *hasten* death, one is also prohibited from performing an act that would *delay* the death of a *goses* by artificial means when there is no hope of living. In his *Sefer Hasidim*, Judah the Pious (12th century) recognizes the right to "remove the impediment" – any object or action that prevents the *goses* from dying (e.g., a woodchopper in the vicinity of a dying person, if the noise is preventing the soul from departing). The prohibition against needlessly prolonging the dying process is dramatically illustrated by the ruling that those attending at the moment of death are forbidden to cry, lest the noise restore the soul to the deceased. In view of modern medical interventions (e.g., artificial respirator), which can keep even a moribund patient alive for far longer than 72 hours, the very concept of the *goses* is now somewhat problematic.

Goshen. Area in northeastern Egypt, east of the Nile Delta, where the river empties into the Mediterranean Sea. The Israelites settled in this fertile grazing area after Jacob was finally reunited with his long-lost son, Joseph (Exod. 45:10). Just east of Goshen is the Sinai Peninsula.

Gossip – see *Lashon ha-ra.*

Government, prayer for the. Based on the talmudic principle of *dina d'malchuta dina* (the law of the state is the law), a prayer for the welfare of the government is recited during the morning service, immediately after the prayers for the congregation that are said prior to returning the Torah scroll to the ark. In most congregations, a prayer composed by Israel's Chief Rabbinate for the welfare of the State of Israel has also been included in the series of prayers recited after the Torah reading. In Israel, this prayer for the state is accompanied by one that invokes God's blessing upon the soldiers who are serving in the Israel Defense Forces.[99]

Goy. Hebrew word meaning "nation" or "people," which occurs commonly in the Bible. Indeed, just before the Revelation on Mount Sinai, God promises Moses that, by fulfilling the terms of the covenant, the Israelites would become "a kingdom of priests and a holy nation [*goy kadosh*]" (Exod. 19:6). Today, the term "*goy*" refers (often disparagingly) to someone who is not a Jew.

Grace after meals (*Birkat ha-Mazon*). The complete prayer, recited after a meal where bread has been eaten, consists of four blessings that (1) praise God for providing food for all creatures; (2) express thanks for the good land (of Israel) that God has given us, the redemption from Egypt, the covenant of circumcision, and the revelation of the Torah; (3) plead for God's mercy, the rebuilding of Jerusalem, and the restoration of the ancient Temple and the Davidic kingdom; and (4) offer thanks for God's eternal goodness to us and include a request for sending Elijah the Prophet, as well as blessings upon the house in which one has eaten and upon all who shared the meal. If bread is not eaten, a shorter form of the Grace after Meals is recited.

Grace before meals – see Blessings before meals.

Grain offering – see Meal offering.

Grapes. One of the seven species, since ancient days the grapevines of the Land of Israel have been celebrated for their quality and abundance. The grapevine is the first cultivated plant mentioned in the Torah, in connection with Noah – "he drank of the wine and became drunk" (Gen. 9:20-24). When the 12 spies returned from Canaan, two of them were needed to bear a single cluster of grapes on a pole (Num. 13:23) – an image used in advertisements promoting tourism in modern Israel. Along with the fig, the vine symbolizes the fertility and peace of the land

and evokes the image of messianic redemption. (See also *wine.*)

Grave, decorating the. The custom of decorating graves with flowers is strongly opposed by Orthodox rabbis, who considered this merely an imitation of gentile practice. However, planting flowers and shrubs in the cemetery does not bother non-Orthodox Jews, who view it simply as a manifestation of reverence for the dead.

Grave, filling in the. Mourners and all others who attend a burial help fill the grave with dirt so that they can physically take part in the *mitzvah* of burying the dead. The practice is usually only symbolic, with each person adding just a small amount of dirt. In some communities, however, those attending the burial add enough dirt to cover the coffin or even completely fill the grave.[100] If a shovel is used, it is customary for each person to place it in the pile of dirt, rather than hand the shovel to the next person. This is a silent symbolic gesture expressing the prayer that the tragedy of death not be "contagious," and a hope that the surviving family and friends may live long and peaceful lives.[101]

Gravestone – see Headstone.

Graveyard – see Cemetery.

Great Assembly. Group of 120 sages who led the Jewish people at the beginning of the Second Temple era. They included the last three prophets (Haggai, Zechariah, Malachi; see individual entries), Mordecai (of the Purim story), Ezra, and Nehemiah.As the first verse of *Pirkei Avot* states, "Moses received the Torah from Sinai and transmitted it to Joshua, Joshua to the Elders, the Elders to the Prophets, and the Prophets to the Men of the Great Assembly." The Men of the Great Assembly fixed the biblical canon, determining which books would be included in the Bible, and laid the foundations of the liturgy (including the *Amidah*) and the formalization of prayer. They are also said to have decided upon the division of the Oral Law into the fields of *midrash*, *halacha*, and *aggada*.

Great Hallel (*Hallel ha-Gadol*). Talmudic term that refers to Psalm 136, which is recited during *Pesukei de-Zimra* at the morning service on Sabbaths and festivals (Pes. 118a). This psalm praises God for mercifully sustaining all creatures, and for saving the Israelites from both Egyptian bondage and mighty kings who sought to destroy the people. Each of its 26 short lines is followed by the refrain, "*ki l'olam chasdo*" (for His kindness endures forever). In ancient days, the Great *Hallel* was also recited on Passover eve when the sacrificial lamb was eaten, and therefore it is now said at the seder.[102]

Great Sanhedrin – see Sanhedrin.

Greetings. The most common Hebrew greetings are "*Shalom*" and "*Shalom aleichim*." Another customary welcome is "*Baruch ha-ba*." On the Sabbath, one wishes another a "*Shabbat shalom*" or the Yiddish "*Gut Shabbos*;" at the conclusion of the Sabbath, one says "*Shavuah tov*" or the Yiddish "*Gut voch*." Greetings used on festivals include "*Chag sameach*," "*Mo'adim le-simcha*," and the Yiddish "*Gut yontif*." The greeting for Rosh Hashanah is "*Le-shanah tovah tikateivu*," and on Yom Kippur it is "*G'mar chatimah tovah*" (see Book of Life). The person who returns from an *aliyah* to the Torah is greeted with "*Yasher ko-ach*" among Ashkenazim and *Hazak u'varuch* among Sefardim. "*Le chaim*" is said for a toast. On birthdays, one says "*Ad me'ah v'esrim shanah*."

Greiger (grager). From a word meaning "rattle," the Yiddish term for the noisemaker used during the reading of the Book of Esther on Purim to drown out the name of Haman, the villain of the story. While any kind of noisemaking device, including booing and stamping one's feet on the floor, is acceptable, it is traditional to use a *greiger* for this purpose each of the 54 times that the name of Haman is read in the *Megillah*. This fulfills the biblical commandment to "blot out the name of Amalek" (Deut. 25:19), the ancestor of Haman.

Gribenes. Yiddish term for the fatty skin of a chicken or goose that is cooked with onions, *shmaltz* (fat), and salt until crispy and brown.

Grudge, bear a – see Revenge.

Guardian of property – see Bailee.

Guide of the Perplexed (*Moreh Nevuchim*). Major philosophical work of Maimonides (1190).

Guilt offering (*asham*). Brought by a person who had committed one of the most serious types of sins (Lev. 5:14-26), the sacrifice was always a ram, which was more expensive than any other type of offering.

Gush Emunim. Literally "Bloc of the Faithful," an Israeli political movement that was formally established in 1974 (following the Yom Kippur War) as an organization dedicated to increasing Jewish settlement on the land that had been captured during the Six Day War in 1967. Closely associated with the National Religious Party, the ideology of Gush Emunim is based heavily on the teaching that the coming of the Messianic Age can be hastened by Jews settling throughout the territory alloted to them in the Bible.

Gut Shabbos. Literally meaning "Good Sabbath," the Yiddish greeting after lighting the Sabbath candles and at the end of services.

Gut voch (good week). Traditional Yiddish greeting after the *Havdalah* ceremony at the conclusion of the Sabbath. (See also *Shavuah tov*).

Gut Yontif. Literally "good festival," the generic Yiddish greeting on a holiday.

H

Ha'aretz (1) – see *Eretz Yisrael.*

Ha'aretz (2). Israeli daily newspaper, first published in 1919 in Jerusalem as *Hadashot ha-Aretz* (News of the Land).

Ha'azinu. The 10th *parashah* in the Book of Deuteronomy (32:1-52). In poetic form, it is a portion of Moses' farewell address. *Ha'azinu* summarizes the themes of this final book of the Torah – the greatness and benevolence of God, contrasted with the stubbornness and faithlessness of the Israelites.

Habad – see Chabad.

Habakkuk (Hab.). The 8th of the minor prophets (7th century B.C.E.). In the first chapter of his 56-line book, Habakkuk foresees the Chaldean invasion of Judea. In the second, he cries out against injustice, while in the third the prophet presents the terrifying vision of God on a storm chariot with dramatic imagery of the Divine power to devastate the natural world. Habakkuk's message highlights the problem of theodicy, and his dictum, "the righteous shall live by faith" (2:4), is an apt summary of biblical instruction.

Habimah (stage). First professional Hebrew theater, founded in Moscow in 1918. It had achieved an international reputation before making its permanent home in Palestine in 1928, with the declared objective of acting as a cultural bridge between the Jews of the Land of Israel and those in the Diaspora. Thirty years later, Habimah was officially recognized as the Israel National Theater. Its repertory includes Israeli and Jewish plays, as well as classic and contemporary works.

Habiru. Ancient group of people living in the Fertile Crescent in the second millennium B.C.E. who, though of varied origin, shared a common and inferior social status. The appearance of this name on the Tel el Amarna tablets and other documents has led some scholars to identify this group with the ancient Hebrews, but it is unclear whether there is any link between the two.

Habonim (the builders). International Zionist youth movement, founded in 1929, which helped establish collectivist settlements in the Land of Israel.

Hacham (1). A wise, learned, or clever person. At times, the word is used sarcastically to denote a person who pretends to be wise but does something foolish or disastrous.

Hacham (2). Literally meaning "wise man," among Sephardic Jews this Hebrew term came into use instead of "rabbi."

Hacham (3). The wise child (the first of the four children mentioned at the seder) who asks insightful questions, seeking a deeper understanding of the proper way to observe the commandments related to Passover. This child should be answered with precise and explicit information that satisfies a quest for knowledge.[103] Although the biblical text reads, "What are the statutes, laws, and ordinances that the Lord our God has commanded you (*etchem*)" (Deut. 6:20), the Jerusalem Talmud changed the last word to *otanu* (us) in order to sharpen the difference between the wise child, who unequivocally stands with the community, and the wicked child who does not.[104]

Hacham Bashi. Title of the Chief Rabbi of the Turkish Empire. The term also was used to refer to the Chief Rabbi of provincial towns in the empire.

Hachnasat kallah. Literally "bringing in the bride," the traditional Jewish duty to provide a dowry for poor and orphaned brides and to rejoice at their weddings. During the Middle Ages and later, communal societies were established for this purpose. The term has been extended to a general obligation to rejoice with the bride and groom on their wedding day. Indeed, according to the Midrash, the angels themselves danced and played musical instruments at the wedding of Adam and Eve (PdRE 12).

Hachnasat orchim (hospitality). Literally "welcoming strangers," hospitality is a major ethical value in Jewish tradition. It was practiced in exemplary fashion by Abraham (the first Jew) and his wife Sarah, whose dwelling place was always open to strangers. The Jewish emphasis on hospitality is ultimately related to the historical experience of the Israelites as being "strangers in a strange land" (Lev. 19:34). According to the Talmud, a lack of hospitality led directly to the destruction of the Second Temple (Git. 55b-56a).

Had Gadya – see *Chad Gadya*.

Hadas – see Myrtle.

Hadassah (Women's Zionist Organization of America). The largest women's and Jewish membership organization in the United States, Hadassah was founded in 1912 by Henrietta Szold. According to its constitution, this voluntary, non-profit organization is dedicated to "the ideals of Judaism, Zionism, American democracy, healing, teaching, and medical research." From its inception, it sought to elevate the health standards in the Land of Israel. Its American and international members participate in fund-raising for health care, education, and Zionist youth programs in Israel, as well as national educational activities. The Hebrew University-Hadassah Medical Center in Jerusalem is the largest state-of-the art diagnostic, research, and treatment center in the Middle East. Hadassah is also the Hebrew name of the biblical Esther.

Haftarah. Literally meaning "concluding portion," a selection from the biblical books of the Hebrew prophets that is read after the Torah reading on Sabbaths, major festivals, and fast days. Unlike the continuous Sabbath Torah readings, which consist of successive portions of the Five Books of Moses without any omission, the *haftarot* are generally scattered parts of the prophetic books. There apparently were two major criteria for the selection of a particular *haftarah*. When no other considerations prevailed, the choice was determined by a thematic connection between the contents of the prophetic portion and the weekly Torah reading. However, about one-third of the Sabbath *haftarot* are determined either by the calendar or by historic circumstances. For example, during the ten successive weeks from the Sabbath before the 17th of Tammuz until the Sabbath before Rosh Hashanah, there are three *haftarot* of tribulation and then seven of consolation.

Haftarah blessings. The person chanting the *haftarah* recites five blessings, one before and four after it. These symbolize the Five Books of Moses, whose ethical and moral teachings were stressed by the prophets. The single blessing before the *haftarah* notes that God has chosen "prophets of truth and righteousness" to continually guide Israel. The four blessings after the *haftarah* deal with a variety of praises, supplications, and thanksgivings, including prayers for a return of the Jewish people to Zion (Jerusalem) and the restoration of the House of David at the time of messianic redemption. They conclude with a blessing for God having sanctified the Sabbath or festival on which the *haftarah* is being read.[105]

Haftarot of consolation. The seven sections from the prophetic books that are read each week from the Sabbath immediately following Tisha b'Av (see Shabbat Nachamu) until Rosh Hashanah. They prophesy the redemption of Israel, restoration to its Land, and the coming of the Messianic Age of peace and justice.

Haganah. Underground military organization of the *yishuv* in Palestine from 1920 until the establishment of the State of Israel in 1948. It carried out underground military training and manufactured arms for protection against hostile Arabs, especially during the years of the Arab rebellion (1936-1939). After World War II, the activities of the Haganah were focused on encouraging and facilitating the "illegal immigration" (see *Aliyah Bet*) of refugees into Palestine and attempting to force the British to rescind the anti-Zionist White Paper of 1939 that prevented more Jews from entering the land. During World War II, the Haganah established its crack commando unit, the Palmach.Within weeks after the onset of the War of Independence, the Haganah was transformed into the Israel Defense Forces (IDF) – the national army of the State of Israel.

Hagbah (lifting). Hebrew word for the honor of raising the Torah in the synagogue (by the *magbi'ah*) after it has been read, so that the congregants can see the writing on the parchment scroll.

Haggadah. Literally meaning "telling" (of the Exodus), this book contains the prayers and blessings, stories, legends, commentaries, psalms, and songs that are traditionally recited at the Passover seder. The word derives from the phrase "*ve-higad'ta [le-vincha]...*" (and you shall *tell* [your child on that day, it is because of that which the Lord did for me when I came forth out of Egypt]) (Exod. 13:8). The oldest published version of the Haggadah is in the prayer book of Saadia Gaon (10th century). Beginning in the 13th century, lavishly decorated Haggadahs began to appear, many of which are considered masterpieces of illuminated manuscripts. The Haggadah has been a favorite focus of the Jewish creative spirit, and it is estimated that almost 3,000 editions have appeared since the 15th century.[106]

Haggai. The 10th of the minor prophets. Living in the post-exilic period, his existing prophecies consist of only 38 verses and date from the second year of the reign of Darius I, King of Persia (520 B.C.E.). They deal mainly with the construction of the Second Temple and the great events that the nation will experience as a result of it. Haggai urged Zerubavel, governor of the Jews after the return from Babylonian Exile, to rebuild the Temple, prophesying that it would be even more beautiful that the first and would eventually be honored by all the world. However, Haggai reaffirmed the characteristic prophetic admonition that moral and ethical behavior is of supreme importance and must lead to good and honorable deeds.

Hagiographa – see Writings.

Ha-Gomel – see *Gomel.*

Haifa. Israel's principal port and third largest city. The capital of the north overlooking a stunning bay, Haifa extends over the foot, slopes, and crest of Mount Carmel. Like a triple-decker sandwich, the city is divided into three tiers – a lower industrial area fringing the harbor; the central business area (Hadar); and the upper Carmel district, a verdant residential section with panoramic vistas. Haifa's most impressive tourist attraction is the domed Baha'i Temple with its majestic gardens. Known for its example of peaceful coexistence between Jews and Arabs, the city has two major institutions of higher learning, the Technion and the University of Haifa, which contribute to the hi-tech industries in the city.

Haimish. From a word meaning "home," this Yiddish term denotes a warm, comfortable manner. Some synagogues boast of their *haimishness*, which makes members "feel at home." It is the opposite of snobbish, fancy, or putting on airs.

Hak a chainik. Literally "strike a teapot," this Yiddish expression means to chatter constantly, usually talking nonsense.

Ha-Kadosh baruch Hu (the Holy One, praised be He). One of the additional names for God developed by the Rabbis in the talmudic period, it most often is used in prayers.

Hakafah (hakafot). Literally meaning "circuit," this Hebrew term refers to the ceremonial procession in which the prayer leader and members of the congregation march around the synagogue, recalling the procession around the Altar in the Temple during biblical times. On Sukkot, one carries the four species in a single circuit each day (except for the Sabbath). On Hoshana Rabbah, seven circuits are made with the four species. For the seven *hakafot* on Simchat Torah, all the Torahs are removed from the ark and joyfully carried around the synagogue.

Ha-Kohen. Literally "the *kohen*," the title placed at the end of a son's (child's) name if the father is of priestly descent.

Ha lachma anya (This is the bread of affliction [that our ancestors ate in Egypt]). Opening words of an Aramaic paragraph that is recited near the beginning of the seder and invites all who are needy to join those assembled and partake in the Passover meal. In this way, the joyous celebration of Passover is tempered with the sobering reality that hunger still persists in our unredeemed world.[107] The passage ends with a hope for the return to Israel and Jerusalem ("This year we are slaves, next year we will be free").

Halacha. Literally meaning "walking," this all-inclusive term refers to the body of law (rules, prohibitions, requirements) that govern every aspect of Jewish life and constitutes the essence of Jewish religious and civil practice. It reflects commandments in the Torah as they were interpreted by the Rabbis during the talmudic period and further developed in *responsa* by the *geonim* and their rabbinic successors. *Halacha* is distinct from *aggada*, the non-legal aspects of the Talmud and Midrash. Following the Emancipation of the Jews, the Reform, Conservative, and neo-Orthodox movements each took substantially different approaches to *halacha*.

Halachot Gedolot. Literally meaning "Great Laws," this codification of talmudic law arranged according to the order of the tractates of the Mishnah was compiled in Babylonia by Simon Kayyara in the 8th century. It represented the first attempt to precisely enumerate each of the 613 commandments, though it included some *mitzvot* that were established only by rabbinic ordinance.

Halevai (may it be so). Yiddish word generally translated as "if only" or "would that," expressing the hope that some desirable outcome will come true.

Ha-Levi. Literally "the Levite," the title placed at the end of a son's (child's) name if the father is of levitical descent.

Halilah. Short for *has v'halilah*, a Yiddish expression that can be translated as "God forbid that should happen." It is said immediately before or after a prediction (or even a statement of fear or mere possibility) that something bad might occur. In context, the term most often comes right before the dire event (e.g., "he should not *halilah* get sick").

Hallel (praise). The recital of six psalms (113-118) immediately after the morning *Amidah*, which is the hallmark of the festival liturgy. Expressing thanksgiving and joy for Divine redemption, they are recited on each festival and to commemorate times of national redemption from peril. *Hallel* is not said on Rosh Hashanah and Yom Kippur, because the Rabbis deemed it inappropriate to sing psalms of joy when one's fate and destiny are being decided. It also is omitted on Purim because, despite the miracle of the day, the Jewish people remained in exile as servants of King Ahasuerus. The deliverance of the Jews was only partial, for they did not gain complete freedom. The jubilance and celebration expressed in *Hallel* make it most appropriate for days of national rejoicing in Israel, such as Yom ha-Atzmaut (Israel Independence Day) and Yom Yerushalayim (Jerusalem Day).

Hallel, "half." In the Temple, *Hallel* was chanted by levitical choirs only on the first day of Passover and not on Rosh Chodesh.Beginning in the third century C.E., Babylonian Jews initiated the practice of reciting *Hallel* on the last six days of Passover and on the New Moon. To distinguish these new occasions from those on which *Hallel* had been traditionally recited, they omitted the first 11 verses from Psalm 115 and all of Psalm 116. This resulted in the current distinction between the "full" and "half" *Hallel*.[108] The Midrash offers an ethical, humanitarian explanation for limiting the *Hallel* on the last six days of Passover. God is pictured as rebuking the ministering angels who wished to sing praises to celebrate the deliverance of the Israelites: "My creatures are drowning in the sea, and you would sing to Me!" Thus, the abridged *Hallel* reflects the mitigation of Israel's joy because of the death of the Egyptians who had pursued them.

Hallel ha-Gadol – see Great *Hallel*.

Hallelujah. A composite of the Hebrew words *hallelu* (praise) and *yah* (short form of *YHVH*, the Tetragrammaton, the most common biblical name for God), it is usually translated into English as "[Let us] praise the Lord." Hallelujah is the beginning or ending word in the refrain of several psalms, some of which are recited as part of the *Hallel*.

Halukah. Donations from Jewish communities in the Diaspora for the financial support of poor Orthodox Jews and religious scholars living in Jerusalem and elsewhere in the Land of Israel (primarily the holy cities of Hebron, Safed, and Tiberias).

Halvah. Literally meaning "sweetmeat," this flaky confection from the eastern Mediterranean area has a distinctive texture and is made from ground and sweetened sesame seeds and often enriched with chocolate, pistachio nuts, or almonds.

Ha-Makom. One of the additional names for God developed by the Rabbis in the talmudic period, it literally means "the place" but is usually translated as "the Omnipresent."

Ha-Makom yenachem (may God comfort you). Opening words of the expression of consolation given to mourners both before they leave the cemetery after a burial, and by visitors when they leave a house of mourning during the *shiva* period. The full expression is: "May God comfort you among the other mourners of Zion and Jerusalem." This reinforces the concept that *all* Jews are mourners since the destruction of the Temple.

Hamantashen. Literally "Haman's hats," the Yiddish term for the triangular pastries that are traditionally eaten by Ashkenazic Jews on Purim. Although they may be stuffed with dried fruits, hamantashen are traditionally filled with *mohn* (Yiddish for "poppy seeds"), a word that sounds reasonably close to the Hebrew pronunciation of the second syllable of the name of the villain of the Purim story. Medieval depictions of this ancient Persian often anachronistically portray him wearing a three-cornered hat popular in Europe at that time.

Hamavdil (Who distinguishes). Hymn sung at the conclusion of the *Havdalah* ceremony at the close of the Sabbath. It asks the God who differentiates between the holy and the profane to pardon our sins and to multiply our offspring (and our wealth), making them as numerous "as the sand and as the stars in the night." This is the same biblical symbol for limitlessness that was expressed in God's promise to Abraham concerning his descendants (Gen. 22:17).

Hammurabi. Babylonian ruler (18th century B.C.E.) whose classic code is the longest, most comprehensive and sophisticated, best organized, and best preserved of the cuneiform legal collections in the ancient Near East. There are important similarities between the Code of Hammurabi and the biblical legislation found in the Book of the Covenant. Reflecting a highly stratified society, the Code of Hammurabi contains a large number of capital offenses, provides for vicarious punishment and bodily mutilations, and demonstrates great concern for the protection of private property.

Ha-Motzi. Name for the blessing recited before eating bread baked from the flour of wheat, barley, oats, rye, and spelt – the five grains mentioned or alluded to in the Torah as indigenous to the Land of Israel. It concludes with the words *ha-motzi lechem min ha-aretz* (Who brings forth bread from the earth). Saying the blessing for bread at the beginning of a meal suffices for everything eaten as part of the meal, except wine and fresh fruit, which require separate blessings. When pronouncing this blessing, it is customary to place both hands on the loaf of bread (both loaves on the Sabbath).

Hamsa. From a Semitic root meaning "five" (*chamesh* in Hebrew, and used in this context to refer to fingers), a hand-shaped amulet worn to ward off the Evil Eye. Symbolically representing the protective hand of God and long popular in Mediterranean cultures, in Muslim lands it has also been termed the "hand of Fatima" (after the daughter of Muhammed) or even "the hand of Miriam." A *hamsa* frequently has a single eye embedded in the middle of the palm, either symbolic of the ever-vigilant eye of God or as a means to repel the Evil Eye. Magical hand-shaped amulets are still commonly used by Jews originating in Muslim countries; through the influence of Sephardim in Israel, *hamsas* also have become popular among Jews in the West.[109]

Hana'ah min ha-met (deriving benefit from a dead body). The halachic prohibition of the use of a cadaver for some other purpose or extraneous benefit (Av. Zar. 29b) has been used by the ultra-Orthodox as a rationale for opposing organ donation for transplantation.Modern rabbis have advanced arguments to show that organ donation and transplantation are consistent with Jewish law. For example, the prohibition was designed to ensure a timely burial that would prevent dishonoring the cadaver, so that once the bulk of the remains have been properly buried, individual organs can be used for transplantation without violating the original prohibition. Moreover, once an organ has been transplanted, it is no longer considered as dead tissue, since it literally has been revitalized in the body of the recipient.

Hands, washing the – see *Netilat yada'im.*

Ha-nerot hallahu (These lights). Opening words of a short prayer that is traditionally recited after kindling the Chanukah lights.

Hanging. Although not used as a form of capital punishment, those executed for certain transgressions (blasphemy, idolatry) were subsequently hanged after death (Deut. 21:22). According to the Talmud, this hanging could apply only to a man and was to last for only for a few moments, with the body not allowed to remain hanging overnight. The prohibition against allowing the body of a criminal to remain unburied overnight was extended to also apply to those who died naturally, who should be buried within 24 hours (see burial). Both of these practices demonstrate a reverence for the human body after death (see *kavod ha-met*).

Hapax legomenon. A word that appears in a text only once. There are about 1,500 of these in the Bible.

Haplographic. Error in writing a Torah scroll in which the scribe omits one or two identical letters or words that should follow each other.

Hapo'el (the worker). Sports organization of Israeli workers, founded in 1926 as an affiliate of the Histadrut.Unlike the Maccabi movement, which emphasized competitive sports and has devoted its energies to organizing them on a national basis (as well as introducing Israel to the international sports arena), the main objective of Hapo'el initially was to provide opportunities for physical education and sport for the masses of Israeli youth and to involve them in the labor movement. The Hapo'el Games are sports festivals held every four years.

Ha-Po'el ha-Mizrachi – see Zionists, religious.

Ha-Rachaman. One of the additional names for God developed by the Rabbis in the talmudic period, it derives from "*rechem*" (womb) and means "the All-Merciful." It is used particularly in the Grace after Meals.

Haredim. Literally meaning "those who tremble [in fear of God]," this Hebrew term refers to various groups of ultra-Orthodox Jews. Separating themselves from the secular world and shunning many elements of modern life, *haredi* men are characterized by their black hats and coats, untrimmed beards, and *payot* (see sidecurls). *Haredi* women dress modestly and, once married, keep their hair covered.

Harvest festivals – see Pilgrimage festivals.

Has v'halilah – see *Has v'shalom*.

Has v'shalom. Literally meaning "have mercy, and peace," this Hebrew term is actually a fervent expression of hope that something terrible will not occur, as in the English "God forbid!" (A popular alternative is *has v'halilah.*)

Hasaneh. Derived from the Hebrew word for "bridegroom," the Yiddish term for a wedding.

Hasbara. Literally "explaining" in Hebrew, this term is used by the State of Israel and independent Israel advocacy groups to describe their efforts to explain the policies of the Israeli government and promote Israel to the world at large.

Ha-Shem. Literally "the Name," a Hebrew term used by traditional Jews to avoid pronouncing in secular conversation the sacred name *Adonai* (itself a substitution for *YHWH*, the Tetragrammaton), which is only said in prayer. It is found in such phrases as *Baruch ha-Shem* (Praised is God), *B'ezrat ha-Shem* (with the help of God), and *Im yirtze ha-Shem* (God willing).

Hashgacha. Kosher certification (see *mashgi'ach*).

Hashkama. From a Hebrew root meaning "to get up early in the morning," the term for an alternative early service that finishes before the official morning prayers in the synagogue.

Hashkava. Literally meaning "lay in rest," the Sephardic term for the memorial prayer that corresponds to the Ashkenazic *Yizkor*.

Hashkiveinu (Let us lie down [to sleep in peace]). Opening word of the second blessing after the *Shema* in the evening service, in which the Jew prays for Divine protection against the terrors of the darkness and the evil forces of the night. In isolated communities in Babylonia during the talmudic period, nighttime violence was common and such phrases as "guard our going forth and our coming in" and "remove our adversary from before us and from behind us" were most appropriate at this time of day. In the morning, the fears of physical danger were minimal, and thus there was no parallel prayer.[110]

Hashomer (the watchman). First organized self-defense group of the Jewish settlers in the Land of Israel. It was founded in 1909 by pioneers of the Second Aliyah, many of whom had been active in revolutionary movements and Jewish self-defense in Russia and were critical of the use of non-Jewish guards to protect life and property in the Jewish settlements. The members of Hashomer spoke Arabic, wore a mixture of Arab and Circassian dress, and carried modern weapons. Some became expert horsemen and were romantic figures throughout the *yishuv*, creating for the first time the image of the modern Jewish fighter that inspired

Jewish youth in the Land of Israel and in the Diaspora. The small body of professional watchmen carefully studied Arab methods of fighting, trying to outdo their enemy in organizational ability, discipline, and force of arms.

Hashomer ha-Tza'ir. Literally "Young Guard," a Zionist-socialist youth movement (established in Galicia in 1913 and reorganized in Vienna four years later) that played an important role in the Third Aliyah.Many of its members who immigrated to the Land of Israel championed the Hebrew language as well as socialist and collectivist ideals, promoted the joint organization of Arab and Jewish workers, and urged the formation of a bi-national state. During the Holocaust, movement activists played a major role in the Jewish resistance. In 1948, Hashomer ha-Tza'ir joined with other leftist factions to form Mapam.

Hasidei Ashkenaz. German pietist movement during the Crusades in the 12th and 13th centuries. This was a terrifying time for the Jews, who were killed as "infidels" when the Christians marched to the Holy Land. Not understanding why they were suffering, some of the Hasidei Ashkenaz had an almost neurotic need to invent some sins that they must have perpetrated. They then devised an array of severe punishments, including self-flagellation, as repentance for real or imagined transgressions. The Hasidei Ashkenaiz compiled liturgical commentaries and ethical and mystical treatises. One school developed new methodologies for biblical exegesis.

Hasidism. Mystical religious movement, founded in Poland by the charismatic 18th-century Baal Shem Tov (lit., "master of the good name" or "miracle worker"). Finding his religious feelings within the marvels of the natural world, which he perceived as physical manifestations of the all-pervasive Divine spirit, the Baal Shem Tov stressed devotion to God and fervent prayer. He taught that joyful, enthusiastic, and sincere worship, even that of an unlearned person, finds more favor in the eyes of God than elite scholarship and knowledge of the Law. He held the kabbalistic belief that the duty of every Jew is to seek out and redeem the sparks of Divine Light scattered in the material world. These teachings had great popular appeal, and Hasidism increasingly spread throughout Eastern European Jewry. However, this stress on emotions rather than traditional scholarship, as well as giving Kabbalah precedence over halachic studies, incited strenuous objections from the Vilna Gaon, the major figure of the *mitnagdim* (those opposed [to Hasidism]). Eventually, Hasidism began to place more emphasis on study and halachic observance. After a period of decline in the late 19th and first half of the 20th centuries, Hasidism has enjoyed renewed popularity. Lubavitch Hasidism (Chabad), inspired by Menachem Mendel Schneerson, has become an international movement. Today, the ultra-Orthodox Hasidim are distinguished by their modest dress, exuberant worship, and devotion to a leader known as a *tzadik* or a *rebbe*.

Haskalah – see Enlightenment.

Haskamah. Literally "approval," a written sanction from a rabbinic authority that is printed at the beginning of a Jewish book and attests to the scholarship and orthodoxy of what it contains. The practice of securing approval of Hebrew books by the local Jewish authorities began in 16th-century Italy as a means to avoid censorship by the civil powers.

Hasmoneans. Priestly dynasty founded in the 2nd century B.C.E. by Mattathias of Modi'in near Jerusalem. With Judah Maccabee and his other four sons, he led the struggle against Antiochus Epiphanes and Jewish Hellenizers to free Judea from Syrian-Greek oppression. The Hasmoneans established an autonomous Jewish state (which was often divided by internecine conflicts), annexed the most important regions of the Land of Israel, and absorbed a number of neighboring Semitic peoples into the Jewish people. The successful rebellion of the Hasmoneans assured the continued existence of the Jewish religion and contributed to the decisive influence of monotheism in Western culture and history. The Hasmonean dynasty ended with military defeat by the Romans in 37 B.C.E., which paved the away for the unchallenged rule of Herod the Great.

Hatafat dam brit. Literally "shedding the blood of the covenant," the ritual drawing of a single drop of blood from the penis that is performed by a *mohel* as part of the conversion process of a male who was already circumcised at birth.

Hatan (bridegroom). According to the Torah, a bridegroom must devote himself to his new wife, bringing her happiness and rejoicing with her for a full year after their wedding day (Deut. 24:5). In biblical times, during this period the newly married man was forbidden to take a journey, go to war, or be encumbered by any public duties and responsibilities. This year-long limitation on a bridegroom's activities applied to all marriages except remarrying one's divorced wife, so as to prevent a man from gaining deferrals from military and civic duties by divorcing and then remarrying her.

Hatan Bereshit. Literally "bridegroom of the beginning," the Hebrew designation for the person called up for the reading of the opening portion of Genesis (1:1-2:3) on Simchat Torah. This honor is traditionally given to the president of the congregation or a distinguished lay member. In some Sephardic and Oriental communities, it is customary to honor an actual bridegroom of the past year.

Hatan Torah. Literally "bridegroom of the Law," the Hebrew designation for the person called up for the reading of the final portion of Deuteronomy (33:27-34:12) on Simchat Torah. This honor is traditionally given to the rabbi of the congregation or a scholar.

Hatarat nedarim (absolution of vows). Traditional practice in which Jews ask forgiveness from each other on the day before Rosh Hashanah. One person asks three others to serve as a *beit din* (religious court) to grant forgiveness for any unfulfilled vows from the past year. In turn, each of the four asks the other three to serve as the *beit din.*[111]

Ha-Tefillah. Literally "The Prayer," a rabbinic term for the *Amidah*, the core of the Jewish prayer service.

Hatikvah (The Hope). National anthem of the State of Israel. The words come from the poem *Tikvateinu* (Our Hope), written in 1887 by Naphtali Herz Imber, who had moved to the Land of Israel five years previously. The music was arranged by Samuel Cohen, an immigrant from Moldavia, based on an Eastern-European folk song *Carul cu Bo* (Cart and Ox). The same melody had previously been used by the classic Czech composer Bedrich Smetana in *The Moldau*, part of his suite "My Fatherland." The simple text of *Hatikvah* is a stirring expression of the age-old Zionist dream, to which the Jewish people clung during their almost two millennia of dispersion in the far-flung Diaspora: "As long as deep in the heart, the soul of a Jew yearns, so long as the eye looks eastward toward Zion, our hope is not lost – the 2,000-year hope to be a free people in our land, the land of Zion and Jerusalem" – a hope that which was finally realized with the birth of the State of Israel in 1948.

Hatra'ah. Caution or warning that must be given to those who are about to commit a crime to make them liable to corporal or capital punishment for their actions. Because many people sin through ignorance or error, the talmudic Rabbis required that a prior warning be given to prove guilty intention, which alone can make a person subject to the full penalty for his crime. The caution must be administered immediately before the commission of the crime and name the particular punishment that it entails; if the crime warrants capital punishment, the particular mode of death must be mentioned.

Hatred. The verse "You shall not hate your kinsman in your heart" (Lev. 19:17) prohibits a person from nursing a grievance against one's fellow man, even without giving it outward expression. In order to prevent smoldering enmity, Maimonides[112] said that when a man sins against another, "the injured party should not hate the offender and keep silent." Instead, he should ask the reason for the sin. "If the offender repents and pleads for forgiveness, he should be forgiven." However, it is permitted to hate evildoers and the enemies of God, as well as to hate "the sin" rather than "the sinner." According to rabbinic tradition (Yoma 9b), destruction of the Second Temple was due to causeless hatred (*sinat chinam*).

Hatred, causeless – see *Sinat chinam*.

Hatzi Kaddish. Literally "half *Kaddish*," it is recited by the prayer leader after each subdivision of the synagogue service. In the morning, it is included after the introductory psalms (*Pesukei de-Zimra*), the *Amidah* – or *Tachanun* when that is said – and after the Torah reading.

Hatzor. Ancient Canaanite fortified city in Upper Galilee. The site of one of the major archeological discoveries of our time that revealed the presence of several ancient civilizations, Hatzor was the inspiration for James Michener's *The Source*, a historical novel about Jews and Israel.

Hava Nagila (Come let us rejoice). Traditional Jewish melody, often played at celebrations with guests dancing the *hora*.

Havdalah. Literally meaning "separation," an ancient ritual ceremony that marks the conclusion of the Sabbath (or a festival) and is rich in symbols and religious significance. Traditionally observed when three stars appear in the sky (42 minutes after sunset), *Havdalah* consists of three blessings – over wine, sweet-smelling spices, and light – followed by the major benediction that deals with the separation or distinction that God has made "between the holy and the profane, between light and darkness, between Israel and the other nations, and between the seventh day and the six working days." At the end of a festival that does not fall on a Saturday night, only the blessing over wine and the major *Havdalah* blessing are said. If the end of the Sabbath coincides with the onset of a festival, *Havdalah* is still recited but the blessing for the spices is omitted, since the festival is regarded as sufficient "fragrance" to compensate for the loss of the Sabbath.[113]

Havdalah candle. Braided multi-wick candle that produces a compound light, in keeping with the blessing *borei me'orei ha-esh* (Who creates the flaming lights). While reciting the blessing for the light, it is customary to spread one or both hands toward the flame and examine the palm of the hand or the nails of the fingers. Unlike Sabbath, festival, and memorial candles, the *Havdalah* candle is extinguished at the end of the ceremony.[114]

Haver. Hebrew word meaning "friend" or "comrade."

Havineinu (Grant us understanding). Initial word of the middle section of an abbreviated version of the *Amidah*, which can be used when there is not enough time to recite the full text. It consists of the first and last three paragraphs plus a brief restatement of the main ideas of the other paragraphs.

Havlagah. Literally "self-restraint," the Hebrew term given to the policy of the Jewish Agency and the Haganah during the Arab revolt in the Land of Israel (1936-1939). This concept limited military actions to self-defense and precluded attacks on Arabs not known to be involved in the violence against the Jews. After the establishment of the State of Israel, the word was applied sarcastically to any policy of "restrained and stately protest" when direct action was deemed necessary.

Havurah (friendship circle). Hebrew term for a group that meets informally for Jewish study, worship, and celebrations. Originally applied to a counterculture movement of Jews not affiliated with synagogues, who focused on creative, non-traditional interpretations of prayers and holiday rituals, many *havurot* are now sponsored by synagogues for members who have particular interests in common. The first *havurah* was founded near Boston in 1968. Others emerged in the 1970's and new groups proliferated in the 1980's. The *havurah* movement reflects a renewal of interest in more personal Jewish intellectual and spiritual experiences.

Hazak. According to Jewish custom, the completion of any of the Five Books of Moses is marked in the synagogue by the congregation rising and exclaiming, "*Hazak, hazak, ve-nit'hazek* (Be strong! Be strong! And let us be strengthened [in our efforts]). In the Sephardic tradiition, a person returning after an *aliyah* to the Torah is greeted with the expression *Hazak u'varuch* (Be strong and blessed).

Hazakah. Hebrew word literally meaning "possession," this legal term relates to the means whereby one acquires or proves the ownership of property

Hazal. An acronym for *Hachmeinu zichronam li-verachah* (our sages of blessed memory), which refers to the teachers of the talmudic era.

Hazamah (discreditation). Talmudic term for the unmasking of witnesses who had planned to submit false testimony.

Hazer – see *Chazer*.

Hazkarat neshamot – see *Yizkor*.

Hazzan – see Cantor.

Hazzanut. Florid style of cantorial singing characteristic of Ashkenazic synagogues in Eastern Europe. The first half of the 20th century has been described as the "Golden Age of *Hazzanut*." In the late 19th and early 20th centuries, nearly 2 million Eastern European Jews immigrated to the United States. Even if the immigrants did not maintain their religious standards, they generally retained a deep emotional attachment to the synagogue and a love for classic Eastern European *hazzanut*, which thus was firmly transplanted into America. Large congregations vied with each other to entice one of the big names among the cantors, who became major celebrities, filled their own synagogues to overflowing, and even made regular guest appearances at other synagogues and in concert halls. Combined with the development of sound recordings, this allowed these brilliant musicians to create international reputations of legendary proportions. The best cantors were considered on a par with opera stars, and some even had major operatic careers.[115] However, the last half of the 20th century saw the virtual demise of classic *hazzanut*.

Head covering, women. Although there are no explicit biblical references to the tradition of women wearing head coverings, by talmudic times it was accepted practice. Currently, only strictly Orthodox married women cover their hair in public. Nevertheless, many married women still wear a head covering in synagogue. (For head coverings for men, see *kippah.*)

Headstone. Since ancient times, graves have been marked with a stone or monument. During the biblical period, the primary purposes of the monument were to protect the body from wild beasts and to identify the position of the grave so that a *kohen* could avoid approaching too close and becoming ritually unclean. Today, the monument also serves to identify the grave so that relatives can find it when they visit the cemetery and to honor the memory of the departed.[116] Sephardic tombstones typically lie horizontal on the grave and often portray events connected with the biblical character whose name was borne by the deceased. In contrast, Ashkenazim have traditionally used symbols illustrating the religious status or occupation of the departed. A recent trend, especially among the Orthodox, is to use simple tombstones to emphasize that all are deemed equal in death.[117] (See also *matzevah* and *unveiling*.)

Health. Numerous biblical and talmudic laws deal with the preservation of life and health. In Jewish thought, the concept of "health" entails physical, emotional, and spiritual well-being – health of both the body and the soul. This "holistic" view is evident in the word *shleimut* (completeness), one of the Hebrew terms for health. Another word for health is *beri'ut* (from the root "to create"), which associates health with creating one's life as a work of art. This implies that one can have a disability, such as an amputation or deafness, and yet be considered healthy in terms of productivity and the ability to contribute to society. The Hebrew word for physician (*rofeh*) comes from a root meaning "to ease," indicating that the doctor treating a "dis-ease" is effectively removing some impediment that is preventing the patient from proceeding further in the creation of a whole and fulfilling life. Judaism teaches that each person is responsible for taking those steps necessary to preserve health, for seeking qualified medical care when needed, and for not endangering himself through lifestyle choices. Maimonides, a physician as well as the most illustrious medieval Jewish philosopher, offered a 6-point plan for preventing disease and preserving health, citing the importance of clean air (anti-pollution); diet (high-fiber, low-fat); exercise; regular excretion; ample sleep; and regulation of emotions (direct link between body and soul).[118]

Heave offering – see *Terumah.*

Heaven. According to traditional cosmology, the uppermost sphere of the universe, where God is surrounded by the celestial court of angels and the souls of the righteous. The term is also used as a substitute for "God," as in such phrases as "fear of Heaven," "for the sake of Heaven," and "kingdom of Heaven." Some modern Jewish thinkers conceive of "Heaven" as a spiritual state rather than a specific place.

Heavenly bodies – see Moon, Stars, and Sun.

Hebrew. Semitic language of the Bible, commonly known as "the holy tongue" (*lashon ha-kodesh*) in rabbinic literature. It was spoken by the ancient Israelites until the 2nd century B.C.E., when it was replaced by Aramaic for everyday speech. Hebrew remained the language of prayer and was revived as a literary language during the Enlightenment.The revival of Hebrew as a spoken language was deeply impacted by the rise of the modern Zionist movement in the late 19th and early 20th centuries. The use of Hebrew for daily use, after more than 2,000 years, was championed by Eliezer Ben Yehuda, known as the "father of the modern Hebrew language," who established the first Hebrew-speaking home in the Land of Israel. With the founding of the State of Israel in 1948, Hebrew (in the Sephardic pronunciation) became the national language, together with Arabic and English

Hebrew Free Loan Association. Organization in all American cities with a substantial number of Jews that offers interest-free loans in accordance with the biblical precept, "When you lend money to any of My people, even to the poor person who is with you, you shall not exact interest" (Exod. 22:24). Interest-free loans are available for emergencies, personal financial challenges, tuition and education-related costs, debt consolidation, starting a small business, adopting a child, and special medical needs. Loans are also made to Jewish organizations and synagogues. Borrowers typically agree to a specified repayment plan, ranging from two to five years.

Hebrew Immigrant Aid Society – see HIAS.

Hebrew school. General name for a synagogue-based Jewish religious school, usually attended by students outside of regular school hours on weekday afternoons or evenings and Sunday morning. The curriculum can include Hebrew language and Jewish prayers, Bible, Jewish history, holidays, rituals, and values, as well as preparation for bar/bat mitzvah and confirmation.

Hebrew Union College (HUC). The oldest rabbinical seminary in the United States, it is dedicated to the training of Reform rabbis. Founded by Isaac Meyer

Wise in Cincinnati in 1875, in 1952 it merged with the Jewish Institute of Religion (JIR) in New York. Additional campuses are in Los Angeles and in Jerusalem, where rabbinical students study for a year. In recent decades, HUC has ordained female rabbis, and women today constitute a majority of its enrollment.

Hebrew University. A major school of higher learning in Israel, with Jerusalem campuses on Mount Scopus and in Givat Ram. It was officially opened by Lord Balfour in an impressive ceremony in 1925. At its founding, Albert Einstein predicted: "In the course of time, this institution will demonstrate with greatest clearness the achievements of which the Jewish spirit is capable." His words were prophetic, and today the Hebrew University ranks as one of the leading universities in the world – an outstanding center of modern Jewish learning and scholarship and the repository of the world's most comprehensive collection of Judaica.

Hebrews. Name given to the Israelites and Judeans before the Babylonian Exile.Some scholars identify the people known as Habiru with the ancient Hebrews. In the 19th century, the term "Hebrew" was frequently used in place of Jew, as in the Young Men's Hebrew Association (YMHA) and Hebrew Union College.

Hebron. Ancient city southwest of Jerusalem that is the site of the Cave of Machpelah.King David reigned for seven years and six months in Hebron before establishing his capital in Jerusalem. Under Ottoman rule, Hebron became an important spiritual center and, along with Jerusalem, Safed, and Tiberias, one of the four holy cities in Judaism. In more recent times, Arabs massacred Hebron's 700 Jews in the 1929 riots. After the War of Independence, Hebron came under Jordanian rule, but was captured by Israel in the Six Day War. Today, conflict often erupts between the large Arab majority and Orthodox Jews living either in a small community in the heart of Hebron or in the nearby settlement of Kiryat Arba (a biblical name for Hebron; Gen. 23:2).

He-Chag. Literally "the holiday," a biblical name for Sukkot.The term indicates that Sukkot was the major festival of the year and the occasion for the consecration of Solomon's Temple (1 Kings 8).

Hechalutz (the pioneer). International association of Jewish youth that trained its members to settle in the Land of Israel. The Hebrew word is used in the Bible (Josh. 6:13) to describe the vanguard that marched in front of the seven priests blowing their *shofars* as Joshua and his army circled the walled city of Jericho. The movement had its origin in the national awakening of Russian Jewry following the pogroms of 1881. Joseph Trumpeldor joined the movement in 1918 and published an influential Russian-language pamphlet entitled "*Hechalutz*." Inspired by the ideal of rebuilding Palestine as a Jewish homeland, young pioneers came from countries ravaged by war and revolution to form the bulk of the Third Aliyah (see aliyah, third) of immigrants to the Land of Israel. They undertook the most difficult tasks – building roads, draining swamps, and establishing settlements.

Hefker (ownerless property). Property may become ownerless if the owner renounces it (e.g., putting it in the trash) or has given up hope of recovering something that has been lost (e.g., a dollar bill accidentally dropped in a public place), or if it remains unclaimed for a specific period of time. According to Jewish law, any person may acquire such property by taking possession of it (see *hazakah*).

Hei. The 5th letter of the Hebrew alphabet, with a numerical value of 5.

Heichal (palace). Biblical term for the outer sanctuary of the Temple in Jerusalem. Today, it is used by Sephardim to denote the ark in the synagogue. Until 1998, Heichal Shlomo was the building in Jerusalem that housed the headquarters of the Chief Rabbinate.

Heichalot (palaces). Collection of Jewish mystical midrashic literature that contains ecstatic experiences and descriptions of ascents to Heaven to view the Divine Chariot (*Merkava* mysticism), heavenly palaces, and the Throne of Glory, as well as the "dangers" the soul might encounter on this mystical journey. Many motifs of later Kabbalah are based on the *Heichalot* texts. Some of the hymns in praise of God found in the *Heichalot* literature have been incorporated into the Ashkenazic liturgy for the High Holy Days.

Hekdesh. Consecrated property (including animals for sacrifice) that was dedicated to the needs of the Temple. It could be redeemed by paying its value plus an additional fifth to the Temple treasury. In post-talmudic times, the term *hekdesh* came to denote property set aside for charitable purposes or for the fulfillment of any other *mitzvah*.

Heksher. A symbol on packaged food, coming from the same Hebrew root as the word "kosher," it indicates that the product has been certified kosher by a specific rabbi or organization. The letter "P" is a special *heksher* indicating that a product contains no *chametz* and thus is kosher for Passover. The term *heksher* also can refer to a certificate posted in a restaurant to guarantee that the food served is kosher.

Hell – see *Gehenna*.

Hellenism. The classical Greek civilization that spread across the Mediterranean and much of the known world after the conquests of Alexander the Great in the

4th century B.C.E. The Maccabees rebelled against those Jews who wanted to Hellenize their society in the 2nd century B.C.E., and their victory is celebrated as the festival of Chanukah.Nevertheless, within a century Greek influences pervaded Jewish life both in the Land of Israel and much of the Diaspora, including a Greek translation of the Torah (see Septuagint) and the introduction of numerous Greek words into the Hebrew language.

Henna. Ritual celebrated the night before the wedding in most Middle Eastern communities. In this strictly feminine ceremony, relatives and friends of the bride gather at her home to paint her hands with red henna to ward off the Evil Eye.

Hereditary diseases. As an isolated and inbred community, the Ashkenazic Jewish population has a relatively high incidence of specific hereditary diseases. These include Tay-Sachs disease, Gaucher's disease, cases of breast and ovarian cancer due to a specific gene (BRCA 1 and 2), and several rare neurologic disorders. Consequently, genetic counseling and testing are recommended when both prospective parents are of Ashkenazic ancestry.

Heresy. Opinion or doctrine contrary to that of the orthodox precepts of a religion. As a faith without an official fixed creed or formal dogma, Judaism has no precise definition of heresy. Nevertheless, rabbinic Judaism considers as heretics those unbelievers who openly reject the teachings of the Torah and the rulings of the rabbis and fail to obey the commandments. One punishment for heresy was *cherem*.(See also *apikoros*.)

Hermeneutics. Method of biblical interpretation developed by the Rabbis of the talmudic period. The first formulation was by Hillel (1st century B.C.E.), who listed seven hermeneutical principles. These precepts were subsequently expanded by R. Ishmael into 13 principles (found in modern prayer books), and finally by R. Eliezer into 32 rules.

Hermon. Mountain range in Lebanon, Syria, and, after the Six Day War of 1967, in Israel. Its impressive peak, the highest in Israel with a 9,230-foot summit, is situated on the northeast border of the land. Israel has erected a recreation and winter sports center on Mt. Hermon.

Herodian. Palace-fortress built by King Herod about eight miles south of Jerusalem in the 1st century B.C.E. Standing on a hill rising more than 2,000 feet above sea level, Herodian had a breathtaking view, overlooking the Judean Desert and the mountains of Moab to the east and the Judean Hills to the west.

Herut (freedom). Israeli political party founded by Revisionist Zionists and members of the Irgun and Betar. Based on the ideas of Vladimir Jabotinsky and established in July 1948, Herut was led by Menachem Begin. The slogan of the party was "there are two banks to the Jordan," advocating a State of Israel on both sides of the river. Favoring economic liberalism and free enterprise, Herut championed the cause of the Mizrachi (Eastern) Jews, whom they charged were being discriminated against by the ruling socialist Labor Party. Herut eventually merged with other right-wing parties to form the Likud, which swept into power in 1977 with Begin serving as prime minister.

Hesder yeshiva. Literally meaning "arrangement," the *hesder* program is a five-year commitment in which advanced talmudic studies are combined with a shortened period of military service in the Israel Defense Forces within a national religious framework (see National Religious Party). It enables religious Zionists to fully participate in the defense of Israel while decreasing the risk that Orthodox young men might assimilate into the surrounding secular society during their military service.

Hessah da'at. Literally "removal of the mind," this Hebrew term denotes a lack of attention when performing religious duties, which causes the action to become invalid.

Hester panim. Literally "hiding the face," the concept behind this Hebrew term is that there are times when the Divine Presence seems to be absent from the world. The phrase is often used in reference to the question of theodicy, especially the apparent "silence" of God during the Holocaust. It gives rise to the idea that God often relates to the world in a hidden, imperceptible manner, leading some human beings to believe that God is not really there. Because the name of God does not appear in the Book of Esther, the story of Purim has been used as a model of God's hidden hand in history.

Heter iska. Technique for avoiding the biblical prohibition against lending or borrowing at interest from a fellow Jew. As the agrarian society was transformed into a more urban economy, lending money at interest became necessary to preserve the financial well-being of the Jewish community. An ingenious approach was the *heter iskah* (permission to form a partnership). Using a standardized and witnessed legal form, the "lender" would agree to supply a specified amount of money to the "borrower" as a joint venture. The borrower alone would operate the business, pledging to pay a fixed minimum profit (i.e., interest) and guaranteeing the lender's capital against loss. At the agreed time of maturity, the lender would recover the initial investment (loan) plus the promised minimum profit as stipulated in the deed.

Heter me'ah rabbanim. Literally "permission of 100 rabbis," a legal document permitting a husband who wishes to remarry to escape the consequences of his wife being mentally incompetent and unable to accept a *get*.In this procedure, a document is drawn up by a *beit din* and circulated to the other rabbis for their signatures. Traditionally, these rabbis should be from at least three different countries; in North America today, it is generally accepted that the rabbis can be from three of the U.S. states or Canadian provinces.[119]

Heter nisuin. Legal document permitting a husband who wishes to remarry to escape any consequences for his wife's refusal to accept a *get* or her disappearance without a trace. Although the first marriage remains valid, the court has the power to release the husband from the prohibition against bigamy by granting him exceptional permission to contract an additional marriage.

Hevruta. From the same Hebrew root as *haver* (friend) and *havurah* (friendship circle), the traditional study of Jewish texts in pairs.

Hexagram. Six-pointed star formed by two interlocking equilateral triangles, one pointing upward and one pointing downward. A popular symbol in Europe and the Middle East since ancient times, the earliest known Jewish use of the hexagram was on a seal from the 6th century B.C.E. (See *Magen David*.)

HIAS. Acronym for **H**ebrew **I**mmigrant **A**id **S**ociety, the oldest Jewish refugee resettlement agency in the United States. Formed in New York City in 1909, it eventually became international in scope. For more than a century, HIAS has had an extraordinary impact on millions of Jews by providing essential lifesaving services of food, shelter, and other aid to endangered Jewish refugees migrating to the United States and Israel.

Hibbat Zion – see Lovers of Zion.

Hiddur mitzvah (glorifying the *mitzvah*). By going beyond the call of duty in fulfilling a *mitzvah*, a Jew can reflect glory upon the One who commanded its observance. Based on the verse "This is my God and I will glorify Him" (Exod. 15:2), the Talmud suggests that one should spend up to an extra third of the cost of a *mitzvah* on its adornment. Thus, on Sukkot the Jew should purchase the best *etrog* possible and bedeck the sukkah with the most beautiful decorations. Other examples of glorifying the mitzvah include buying the most beautiful *tefillin*, *shofar*, and *tallit*, as well as employing the finest clear ink, best quality pen, and most skilled scribe with superb script in the writing of a Torah scroll.

High Holy Days. Inclusive term applied to Rosh Hashanah, Yom Kippur, and the Ten Days of Repentance between them. Also known as the "Days of Awe [*Yamim Nora'im*]," during this solemn period of introspection, repentance, and prayer the Jew endeavors to merit being inscribed and sealed in the Book of Life for the coming year.

High places (*bamot*). Sites of worship built on hills or mountains, originally Canaanite shrines, which were commonly used by the Israelites until the Divine service was centralized in the First Temple in Jerusalem. In addition to a sacrificial altar, the high place usually had a stone pillar (see *matzevah*), a symbol of masculine divinity in Canaanite religion, and a wooden post (see *asherah*), which represented the mother-goddess of fertility. Despite the Hebrew prophets continually railing against it, worship at the high places persisted in popular religion throughout the monarchy until they were destroyed during the reigns of Hezekiah (8th century) and Josiah (7th century).

High Priest – see *Kohen Gadol*.

Hillel (1). Greatest sage of the Second Temple period. A brilliant scholar and leader of the Pharisees and the liberal school of interpretation of Jewish law, Hillel served as the president of the Sanhedrin for 40 years (30 B.C.E. - 10 C.E.). He and Shammai were the last of the pairs of scholars (see *zugot*), and each led a famous school of Rabbis (see Beit Hillel). In general, the talmudic sages decided the *halacha* in accordance with the opinions of Hillel and his school, which were more lenient and easier for the people to understand. In messianic times, however, the *halacha* will supposedly revert to the stricter opinions of the House of Shammai, since people then will be able to understand and appreciate his great insights in matters of Torah. Humble and tolerant, Hillel urged Jews to "be among the disciples of Aaron, loving peace and pursuing peace, loving people and bringing them closer to the Torah" (Avot 1:12). (See also *Golden Rule*, *hermeneutics*, and *prosbul*).

Hillel (2). Also known as "The Foundation for Jewish Campus Life" and established in 1923, the B'nai B'rith Hillel Foundation serves the religious, cultural, and social needs of college and university students on campuses throughout the United States and around the world.

Hillel sandwich (*korech*). Sandwich made of *matzah* and *maror* that is eaten at the Passover seder just before the festive meal. It is a reminder of Hillel's practice in Temple times, based on the verse: "They shall eat it [the Passover sacrifice] with unleavened bread and bitter herbs" (Num. 9:11).

Hiloni. Hebrew word used by Israelis to denote secular Jews. This concept is also expressed by the phrase *lo dati*, which literally means "not religious."

Hin. Ancient Hebrew unit of liquid capacity, mentioned several times in the Bible, which was equal to about 3.7 liters (a little smaller than an American gallon).

Hineni (Here I stand, [devoid of deeds]). Opening word of a special prayer recited by the *hazzan* before the *Musaf Amidah* on Rosh Hashanah and Yom

Kippur among Ashkenazim. This Hebrew word, also translated as "Here I am," was the simple answer given by Abraham in the story of the *Akedah* when summoned by God to sacrifice his son (Gen. 21:1); when asked by Isaac where was the lamb for the offering (Gen. 21:7); and when commanded by the angel not to slay his son (Gen. 21:11). In simple words but chanted with a stirring melody, the *hazzan* expresses feelings of trepidation and humility and, despite shortcomings in conduct, voice, memory, and devotion, prays to be worthy to serve as the representative of the congregation to bring its supplications before God.

Histadrut. Acronym for a Hebrew phrase meaning "General Federation of Labor in Israel." Founded in 1920, the Histadrut became the largest labor union in Israel as well as the most powerful non-governmental organization in the country. Members pay dues to the federation and in return receive full medical coverage through *Kupat Holim* (Workers' Sick Fund), old age and disability benefits, and the right to participate in all its educational, cultural, and social activities and elections. The Histadrut also initiated and developed many economic enterprises, some in the form of autonomous cooperative societies and others owned directly and collectively by the entire membership. Arabs and members of other minority communities in Israel are accorded full membership in the Histadrut.

Hittites. Ancient people of Asia Minor who spoke an Indo-European language and established a kingdom in the 18th century B.C.E. that reached its height in the 14th century and disintegrated two centuries later. The Covenant between God and Israel has a form that closely parallels ancient treaty documents that were first developed by the Hittites for administering conquered kingdoms. These "suzerainty" treaties specified the relationship between a feudal lord (suzerain) and the vassal state he controlled.

Hod (splendor). The 8th of the *sefirot*, the source of prophecy and anthropomorphically viewed as the left leg of God.

Hoda'ah (thanksgiving). General name for the last three blessings of the *Amidah*, which include an expression of the hope that God will accept the prayers of the congregation (*avodah*; worship); thanksgiving for God's past, present, and future kindnesses and the miracles of daily living; and a prayer for peace.

Holidays – see Festivals.

Holiness (*kedushah*). Complex concept implying a state of separation from (and elevation above) the common or profane. It denotes some relation to the sphere of the Divine and, in the ethical sense, an ideal of moral purity and perfection incapable of sin and wrong. Some individuals were "separated" from the rest of mankind to serve the Divine, with the priest called "holy to God" (Lev. 21:6-7). Similarly,

God selected the entire people of Israel from among all those on earth to be "a kingdom of priests and a holy nation" (*am kadosh*; Exod. 19:6) and God's "holy people" (Isa. 42:2). In rabbinic literature, the term "the Holy One, blessed be He" is the most common epithet for God, who is to be venerated as the perfection of righteousness and goodness and whose holy attributes are to be emulated by human beings.

Holiness Code. Constituting the last half of the Book of Leviticus (16-27), this priestly document is characterized by the recurrent theme, "You shall be holy, for I, the Lord your God, am holy" (Lev. 19:2). It stresses that every act an Israelite does should be performed in a conscious striving to imitate the holiness of the Divine. The Holiness Code includes regulations regarding the priesthood, sacrifices, and the funding of the Sanctuary; prohibited sexual relations; the Sabbatical and Jubilee Years; miscellaneous moral and religious laws (including "love your neighbor"); and an epilogue of blessings for obeying its precepts and curses for disobeying them (see *Tochachah*).

Holocaust. The deliberate murder of 6 million European Jews by the Nazis and their collaborators during World War II. The term "Holocaust" comes from a Greek word meaning "wholly burnt offering/sacrifice."[120] An alternative Hebrew term is "Shoah."

Holocaust Remembrance Day – see Yom ha-Shoah.

Holy City – see Jerusalem.

Holy Days – see Festivals

Holy Land – see *Eretz Yisrael*.

Holy of Holies. Innermost portion of the Temple, which housed the Ark of the Covenant.A windowless 10-meter cube, the Holy of Holies was entered only once a year, by the High Priest on Yom Kippur.

Holy places. The Western Wall, the Herodian retaining wall of the Second Temple, is generally considered the holiest site in Judaism. Other special locations for Jewish prayer are the graves of biblical figures and of renowned sages from the mishnaic period to the present day.

Holy Spirit (*ru'ach ha-kodesh*). Unlike the Christian view of a separate aspect of the trinity, the Hebrew term refers to a Divine power that inspires human beings, especially in the context of the gift of inspired speech conferred on the prophets. Jewish thought links communion with the Holy Spirit to the striving for moral and spiritual perfection through religious study, prayer, and the performance of deeds of loving-kindness.

Homer. Ancient Hebrew dry measure, equal to 10 *ephahs*.

Homiletics. The art of preaching and giving sermons.

Homoioteleutonic. Error in writing a Torah scroll in which the scribe mistakes a word for the next time it appears in the passage and thus fails to include everything in between.

Homosexuality, female. The Torah does not mention female homosexuality, either because lesbianism was not widely practiced or because it was considered merely a minor offense. The Talmud considered it as indulging in obscene practice, and Maimonides stated that a husband should prevent his wife from associating with women known to engage in lesbian activities.

Homosexuality, male. Considering it an unnatural and depraved activity, the Bible is unequivocally explicit on the subject of male homosexuality: "You shall not lie with a man as one lies with a woman" (Lev. 18:22). This verse comes at the conclusion of the list of prohibited sexual relationships, but is the only one (other than bestiality) that uses the harsh term "abomination" (*to'eivah*). According to some commentators, this stresses the special repugnance in which God holds those who engage in these unnatural practices, for all the other prohibited relationships involve normal sexual activity, though with prohibited mates.[121] The Rabbis considered homosexuality an unnatural perversion, defying the very structure of the anatomy of the sexes (which they deemed as obviously designed for heterosexual relationships) and frustrating the procreative purpose of sex. Since the 1980s, the rise of the gay pride movement has forced the Jewish community to confront the issue of homosexuality. Synagogues have been established by and for homosexuals, attempts have been made to accept homosexuality as an alternative lifestyle, and some liberal rabbis have performed same-sex commitment ceremonies. The Reform, Reconstructionist, and Conservative movements now admit students who are openly gay or lesbian to their rabbinical seminaries.

Homunculus – see *Golem*.

Honey. One of the seven species, the biblical description of Israel as "a land flowing with milk and honey" (*chalav u-devash*; Exod 13:5) refers to a syrup made from dates, figs, or grapes, rather than bee's honey, which was much less common in the area. Only in the talmudic period did honey come to refer specifically to that produced by a bee. Based on the principle, "that which goes forth [issues] from the unclean is unclean," the honey of a bee should be forbidden, since the bee is considered an unclean insect. However, the Rabbis permitted its use on the grounds that honey is not the product of the bee, but instead is merely stored in its body. Along with leaven, honey was prohibited in burnt offerings (Lev. 2:11) because the pagans considered it the food of their gods. At the festive meal on Rosh Hashanah, it is traditional to dip the *challah* over which the blessing has been recited into honey, instead of the usual salt, to symbolize the hope for a sweet year. For the same reason, many Jews also dip apple slices in honey.

Honored Citizen of Jerusalem – see *Yakar Yerushalayim*.

Hora. A traditional Romanian circle dance, it became popular in Palestine after World War I and is now the national dance of the State of Israel. A favorite at bar/bat mitzvah and wedding celebrations, it is often danced to the song *Hava Negila*.

Horayot (Hor.). The 10th tractate of Nezikin (damages) in the Mishnah, it deals with erroneous decisions (*horayot*) made by the court on matters of religious law (and how to correct them). Its final words reflect the Jewish belief in the superiority of scholarly accomplishment over inherited rank.

Horeb. Term used in Deuteronomy for Mount Sinai, it is also the name of the place where Moses encountered the Burning Bush.Horeb is the title of a major work on the philosophy of Jewish laws and observances by Rabbi Samson Raphael Hirsch, the 19th-century founder of neo-Orthodoxy, which responded to the challenges posed by the emerging Reform movement and the opportunity afforded Jews to engage with the wider world.

Hosafot (additional). On Sabbath mornings, some congregations take advantage of a provision in Jewish law that permits dividing the Torah portion into more (but not less) than the required number of *aliyot*. (This is not permitted on Mondays, Thursdays, or other midweek occasions such as Rosh Chodesh, Chanukah, and fast days, because of the principle of *bittul melachah*, wasting the time of people who have to go to work.) Termed *hosafot*, these extra *aliyot* allow one or more additional persons to have the honor of being called up to the Torah.[122] Other congregations reject this practice because it lengthens the service, insisting on limiting the number to the prescribed seven *aliyot*.[123]

Hosea (Hos.). The 1st of the minor prophets. He lived in the turbulent days of the idolatrous Northern Kingdom when it was at the height of its power under the rule of Jeroboam II (8th century B.C.E.). Hosea's prophesies are oracles of doom, thundering against moral, religious, and political evils as offenses against God. Hosea likened the infidelity of his wife, Gomer, to Israel's disloyalty to God. He predicted the devastation of Israel as just punishment for its idol worship and social injustice. Nevertheless, he stressed that God's love for Israel will never cease. Through punishment, God will purify Israel and lead His people to repentance. The surviving remnant of Israel will no longer worship alien gods or seek foreign help, but will rely solely on God, who will preserve them and eventually restore Israel to its former glory. The verses from Hosea that open the *haftarah* for the Sabbath of Repentance (see Shabbat Shuvah), between Rosh Hashanah and Yom Kippur, presage Maimonides' doctrine that true repentance requires an intellectual awareness of sin, confession and appeal for Divine mercy, and the resolve never to engage in such practices again. The ideal of love is the central theme of Hosea, who compares God to a loving father and faithful husband to the Jewish people.

Hoshana (Save, I pray). Single-word refrain sung after the *hoshanot.*

Hoshana Rabbah. Literally "the Great Hoshana," the seventh day of the Sukkot festival. On this day, seven circuits (see *hakafot*) are made around the synagogue (in Temple times, the Altar) with the fours species, rather than the single circuit performed on the other days of Sukkot. After the final circuit, a bundle of willow branches (or those from the four species) are beaten against the ground or a chair. Some traditions consider Hoshana Rabbah as the end of the High Holy Day period, the last time that unfavorable judgments can be averted before the final seal is placed on the Books of Life and Death. In accordance with this concept, the prayer leader in some synagogues wears a *kitel* (white robe) as on the High Holy Days.[124]

Hoshanot. Prayers recited on Sukkot by all congregants who have the four species as they circle the synagogue in procession. This is omitted on the Sabbath, when the four species are not carried. One circuit is made each day, except for the seventh day (Hoshana Rabbah), on which seven circuits are made. The word *hoshanot* is derived from the Hebrew word *hoshana* (or *hoshi'a na*; "Save, I pray"), the refrain sung after the six prayers for deliverance that are usually written as alphabetical acrostics or in reverse alphabetical order. These prayers are derived from biblical and midrashic sources and are recited in a particular sequence, depending on the day of the week. The *hoshanot* depict the destructive forces of nature and beseech Divine protection of both animal and plant life, based on the merit of the Patriarchs, Matriarchs, 12 tribes of Israel, Moses and Aaron, prophets, and kings who demonstrated their courage and faithfulness to God. They contain an array of appeals, ranging from requests for sufficient water and good crops to prayers for the return of the Jewish people from exile and the ultimate redemption.

Hoshen Mishpat – see Breastplate and *Shulchan Aruch.*

Hospitality – see *Hachnasat orchim.*

Hospitals. In the Middle Ages, small buildings supported by community charity were established both as places to care for the sick and to house poor travelers. Hospitals exclusively devoted to healing the sick developed in Europe during the 18th century. Jews Hospital in New York was founded in 1852, and other Jewish hospitals were subsequently established in cities throughout the United States. In the early decades of the 20th century, when anti-Semitism was widespread in the country, Jewish hospitals provided professional opportunities for Jewish physicians. With the decline of anti-Semitism, service to the community at large became the rationale for Jewish hospitals.

House of the Lord – see Temple.

Hovah – see Duty.

Hovevei Zion – see Lovers of Zion.

Hozeh – see Contract.

Humanistic Judaism. Established by Rabbi Sherwin Wine in 1963, the movement "embraces a human-centered philosophy that combines the celebration of Jewish culture and identity with an adherence to humanistic values and ideas… [and] offers a non-theistic alternative in contemporary Jewish life…Humanistic Jews value their Jewish identity and the aspects of Jewish culture that offer a genuine expression of their contemporary way of life. Humanistic Jewish communities celebrate Jewish holidays and life cycle events with inspirational ceremonies that draw upon but go beyond traditional literature."[125] The International Federation of Secular Humanistic Jews was founded in 1985.

Humility. A major Jewish virtue, the Bible glowingly describes Moses as "a very humble man, more so than any other man on earth" (Num. 12:3). The prophet Micah declared: "What does the Lord require of you? Only to do justice, and to love goodness, and to walk humbly with your God" (6:8) – a verse that, according to the Talmud, contains within it the entire Torah. Humility should not be confused with servility or any form of self-hatred.

Humor. There is a long tradition of humor in Judaism dating back to the Bible and the Midrash. However, the term "Jewish humor" generally refers to the verbal, self-deprecating, and often anecdotal humor that originated in Eastern Europe in the 19th century and spread to the United States. Beginning with vaudeville and continuing through radio, stand-up comedy, film, and television, a disproportionately high percentage of American comedians have been Jewish. Jewish humor tends to be anti-authoritarian, and in Jewish jokes the disadvantaged often come out triumphant. Especially popular topics are food, family, health, survival, business, wealth, poverty, and anti-Semitism. No subject is so sacrosanct that it is immune from the often-biting satire of Jewish humor, which is highly aware of the short distance that separates the rational from the absurd.

Humus. Thick puree of chickpeas and sesame seed paste (tahini) that is a popular dip in Israel and other Middle Eastern countries.

Husband, obligations toward wife. According to Jewish law, a man who marries becomes obligated to his wife for 10 things in addition to the statutory *ketubah*. Of these, three are biblical in origin – food, clothing, and conjugal rights (Exod. 21:10). The other seven obligations are rabbinic: "to treat her if she falls ill; to ransom her if she is captured; to bury her if she dies; to provide for her maintenance out of his estate after his death; to let her dwell in his house after his death for the duration of her widowhood; to let the daughters sired by him receive their maintenance out of his estate until they become espoused; and to let her male children sired by him inherit her *ketubah,* in addition to their share with their half brothers in his estate."[126] The relationship between husband and wife is one of the fundamentals of the Jewish way of life. Spousal love and respect cause the Divine Presence to enter the home.

Hygiene. Judaism teaches that each person is responsible for taking those steps necessary to preserve health and for seeking qualified medical care when needed (see physicians). Because the body is viewed as a vessel for the soul and the instrument through which one worships God and carries out the Divine will, taking proper care of the body is a *mitzvah*, for only a healthy body is capable of sustaining a holy soul. As the "caretaker" of a body on loan from God, it is incumbent on each person to keep the Divine vessel clean. Indeed, the Talmud explicitly states that a Jew may not live in a town without a bathhouse. In the Middle Ages, the emphasis on cleanliness and sanitation led to Jewish having lower rates of illness than the general population. During the Black Death, this led to the accusation that Jews were poisoning the wells and infecting the gentiles with plague. Throughout Jewish history, there is abundant evidence of a high level of personal cleanliness among Jews.

Hymns, table – see *Zemirot*.

Hyssop. Small, strongly aromatic shrub that grows in rocks and stone walls. In the Bible (1 Kings 5:13), the hyssop is contrasted with the lofty cedar of Lebanon, both of which were used in preparing the ashes of the red heifer. Just prior to the Exodus, the Israelites were commanded to use hyssop to smear blood on their doorposts so that they would remain unharmed while the firstborn of Egypt were killed during the tenth plague (Exod. 12:22). The Samaritans still use this plant for sprinkling blood at the ceremony of slaughtering the Passover sacrifice.

I

I-Thou relationship. Philosophy of dialogue propounded by Martin Buber, in which he viewed all of human existence in terms of two fundamentally different kinds of relations: I-It and I-Thou. An I-It relation is the normal everyday way in which a human being relates towards the things surrounding him. Most of the time, one considers another as "It," viewing the person from a distance, like a thing and as a part of the environment. Radically different is the I-Thou relationship, which a person enters into with his innermost and whole being, with both partners engaging in a real dialogue. For Buber, the I-Thou relationship is a reflection of the deep human encounter with God.

ICA – see Jewish Colonization Association.

IDF – see Israel Defense Forces.

Idolatry (*avodah zarah*). The worship of idols by the ancient Israelites was forbidden by the Bible as an unpardonable breach of the covenant with God. The second of the Ten Commandments explicitly states, "You shall have no other gods beside Me" (Exod. 20:3). Nevertheless, idolatry must have been widely practiced considering the frequent prophetic denunciation of this activity. The Babylonia Exile (586-538 B.C.E.) did much to lessen idolatrous practices. The Rabbis devoted a tractate of the Mishnah (see Avodah Zarah) to prohibitions concerning contact with idolaters. Jews were forbidden to eat with idolaters or consume their bread, oil, or wine, as well as to sell or lease land or houses in the Land of Israel to them. Death by martyrdom was preferable to being forced into idolatry. In Maimonides' list, the first 59 of the 365 negative commandments relate directly in some way to the prohibition of idolatry, which can also be understood as extending to the worship of wealth, power, and fame.

Illegal immigration – see *Aliyah Bet*.

Illegitimacy – see *Mamzer*.

Ilui. Literally "prodigy," this Hebrew term is applied to a young talmudic scholar of extraordinary ability.

Im yirtzeh ha-Shem. Hebrew phrase meaning "God willing."

Ima. Familiar form of the Hebrew word for "mother," equivalent to "mommy."

Image of God. The Torah explicitly states that the human being was created "in the image of God" (Gen. 1:27). The concept includes the individual as a creative creature ("God's partner in the work of creation"), as well as a moral agent with free will and the ability to sanctify (i.e., make things holy). God created only one human being to show that each individual is unique and irreplaceable, a quality every person shares with the One God. The medieval philosophers stressed that each individual was an intellectual being, like the Divine. For the mystics and Hasidim, the human soul was an actual part of God from the spiritual realm.

Imitation of God. The Talmud figuratively interpreted the biblical verses, "Follow none but the Lord Your God" (Deut. 13:5) and "You shall be holy, for I, the Lord your God, am holy" (Lev. 19:2), as indicating that the essence of morality is to act in a "God-like" manner toward other human beings. In emulation of God's actions of *gemilut chasadim*, Jews also should clothe the naked, visit the sick, comfort the mourners, and bury the dead. Similarly, in interpreting the verse, "This is my God and I will glorify Him" (Exod. 15:2), the Jew can do justice to the glory of God only by aspiring to the Divine level of mercy and compassion.

Immanence. The continual involvement in human history, despite being remote, of the transcendent God who created the universe. According to the Bible, God chose the Jewish nation as his people, freed them from bondage in Egypt, revealed the Divine Law to them at Mount Sinai, brought them into the Promised Land, and always guides their destiny. In Jewish mystical and Hasidic thought, the attributes of God are reflected in the soul and body of human beings. Therefore, the more aware we become of our innermost selves, the more aware we will be of God.

Immersion. Based on the verse, "He shall bathe all his flesh in water" (Lev. 15:16), immersion was required to cleanse the Israelites of any ritual impurities that would prevent them from bringing sacrifices to the Sanctuary. These included contact with a dead body, various skin disorders, normal and abnormal bodily discharges, and women after childbirth. Ritual immersion also was performed by the *kohanim* during their consecration ceremony (Exod. 29:4; Lev. 8:6) and by the *Kohen Gadol* prior to the Yom Kippur rituals (Lev. 16:4). Today, it is an essential part of the conversion ceremony. Initially, ritual immersion took place in a natural, flowing body of water (*mayim chaim*, lit. "living water") – a river, stream, lake, pond, or ocean. However, these venues were not available for Jews living in all locations, nor in some climates where bodies of water freeze for part of the year. This led to the development of an alternative place to perform ritual immersion, the *mikveh*.[127]

Immigration – see *Aliyah.*

Immortality of the soul. During the Second Temple period, the idea of heavenly immortality of the soul, either for all Israel or for the righteous alone, vied with the Pharisaic ideal of bodily resurrection as the dominant theme of the afterlife. Eventually, the idea developed that individual souls would be judged after death, go temporarily to *Gehenna* to expiate their sins, then proceed to heaven and at last to the final judgment. In the medieval period, the concept of a disembodied afterlife of the soul was especially strong among the Jewish philosophers, who were heavily influenced by the Greek traditions of Platonism and neo-Platonism. As the part of a human being that is most like God, the soul was considered the seat of the intellect, spirituality, creativity, and the Divine spark. Thus the soul can survive bodily death, being transported to a spiritual realm beyond the dimensions of time and space, where it enjoys eternal repose. Traditional Judaism has maintained a consistent belief in both some form of immortality of the soul after death and its eventual reuniting with the body at the time of the future resurrection of the dead as part of the messianic redemption. An unequivocal belief in the survival of the soul after death is implicit in the various prayers said in memory of the dead and in the custom of mourners reciting the *Kaddish*. Many Enlightenment and post-Enlightenment Jewish thinkers defended the idea of immortality of the soul while rejecting the notion of bodily resurrection. Others have taken a more metaphorical approach to immortality of the soul, suggesting that we live on in the memory of our loved ones.

Imprisonment. In the Bible, Joseph was put into prison in Egypt and Samson was confined by the Philistines. During the talmudic period, suspects were detained prior to trial and convicted murderers were held pending execution. From the 14th century onward, influenced by non-Jewish penal systems, imprisonment became used as a form of punishment – for a person who had repeatedly (three or more times) committed an offense for which the punishment was *karet*, and for a murderer who could not be executed because of legal technicalities. Imprisonment was also used by the court as a means of compelling a husband to grant a bill of divorce (see *get*) and for failure to comply with a court order. Additional causes for imprisonment developed in the Middle Ages and subsequent eras. Jewish law stipulated that prisoners awaiting trial were to be kept under better conditions of detention than those already convicted of a crime.

Impurity – see Ritual impurity.

In mitn/mitske drinen. Literally meaning "in the middle of the thing," this Yiddish phrase describes something that "comes out of the blue," all of a sudden and for no apparent reason.

Incense (*ketoret*). Burned after the daily morning sacrifice, the incense was compounded from 11 spices. Four are specifically mentioned in the Torah (Exod. 30:34) – stacte, onycha, galbanum, and frankincense; the identity of the other seven spices (myrrh, cassia, spikenard, saffron, costus, aromatic bark, and cinnamon) has been passed down in the Oral Law. Many of these were rare, and some could only be obtained in exotic and distant lands. (See *pitum ha-ketoret.*) It was forbidden to make incense using the identical ingredients in the same relative weights as that used in the Sanctuary, even for private or non-sacred use (Exod. 30:37-38). The art of making the incense was the special skill of members of the house of Avtinas in Jerusalem, who refused to divulge its secret and were censured for this by the Rabbis (Yoma 3:11, 38a). The use of incense has declined over the centuries, though the memory of it is found in the ceremony of *Havdalah* that concludes the Sabbath.

Incest – see Marriages, prohibited.

Inclinations, Good and Evil – see *Yetzer ha-ra* and *Yetzer ha-tov*.

Incorporeality. The concept that God has no material body or form, a basic tenet of Judaism. The numerous anthropomorphic statements in the Bible ascribing physical attributes to God are considered mere metaphors attempting to describe an otherwise incomprehensible Deity, thus enabling human beings to address and pray to a transcendent Being.

Indemnity. Financial compensation for injury to a person or loss or damage to his property, which is required under Jewish law. (For damages related to personal injury, see p. 000.) However, since two penalties cannot be imposed for a single offense, a person who pays an indemnity was not traditionally subject to additional punishment.

Independence Day (Israel) – see Yom ha-Atzmaut.

Informers (*malshinim*). Jews who denounced individual fellow Jews or the Jewish people in general to non-Jewish authorities, thus promoting Jewish insecurity and vulnerability and undermining Jewish solidarity. Unequivocally condemned by the Talmud, according to one tradition the number of informers increased to such an extent that a special blessing (see *minim*) was added to the *Amidah* to identify them. During the Middle Ages, social and political conditions led to Jews volunteering privileged information about the property, lives, and religious beliefs of their fellows to the non-Jewish authorities. This often caused disastrous results, prompting Jewish leaders to try and convict the offenders, excommunicate them, and even impose capital punishment upon them.

Ingathering of the exiles – see *Kibbutz galuyot.*

Inheritance. In biblical times, the right of primogeniture (double portion for the firstborn) was accepted, and the case of the five daughters of Zelophehad (Num. 27:8-11) established that daughters could inherit if there were no sons (though they were required to marry within the tribe). As developed by later Jewish law, the order of inheritance is as follows: (1) sons and their descendants; (2) daughters and their descendants; (3) the father; (4) brothers and their descendants; (5) sisters and their descendants; (6) the father's father (grandfather); (7) the father's brothers (uncles) and their descendants; (8) the father's sisters (aunts) and their descendants; (9) the great-grandfather and his collateral descendants, and so on.[128] A husband is heir to his wife's property. The converse, however, is not true – a wife does not inherit her husband's estate, though she receives her dowry. From the talmudic period onward, there were various rabbinic rulings that sought to mitigate the bias of inheritance law toward the male line.

Innocence. In Jewish law, a person is presumed innocent until proven guilty. This presumption cannot be overturned by hearsay or circumstantial evidence, and self-incrimination is not permitted.

Inquisition. Tribunal of the Roman Catholic Church established for the investigation of heresy.As far as Jews were concerned, the cruelest occurred in Spain beginning in 1481 and lasted for nearly 350 years. It focused on the *Conversos*, Jews who had converted either under duress or out of social convenience and were suspected of secretly practicing the Jewish faith. Many "crypto-Jews" who were caught by the Inquisition were ruthlessly tortured to admit their heresy and then burned at the stake in a ceremony known as the *auto-da-fé*. The Inquisition soon moved to Portugal and then to Spanish and Portuguese colonies in the New World. The victims of the Inquisition numbered in the tens of thousands.

Inspiration, Divine – see *Ru'ach ha-Kodesh.*

Insult – see Shame.

Intent – see *Kavanah.*

Interest. Jews are forbidden to lend (Lev. 25:36-37) or borrow (Deut. 23:20) at interest from a fellow-Jew. In addition, Jews are prohibited from even taking part in a transaction between borrower and lender involving a loan at interest – whether as surety, witness, or notary drawing up the contract between them for payment of the interest on which they have agreed (Exod. 22:24). Maimonides maintained that it was a *command* to exact interest from non-Jews to whom one lends money, while virtually all other commentators believed it was merely *permitted* to do so. Giving a loan to a fellow Jew without any expectation of profit was considered one of the highest forms of charity, because it preserved the self-respect of the borrower and allowed him to rebuild his own financial stability so that he would no longer be dependent on others.[129] Kli Yakar observed that the lender actually derives a greater benefit from his generosity than the borrower does from the loan. The borrower is helped only in this world; however, by generously helping the poor on earth, the lender receives a reward in the World to Come.[130] (For a technique to circumvent this prohibition, see *heter iska.*) During the Middle Ages, the Roman Catholic Church prohibited Christians from charging interest on loans to other Christians. However, they permitted Jews to practice this occupation, thus leading to the Jews being stereotyped and disparaged as moneylenders.

Interfaith dialogue. Term referring to positive and cooperative interaction between people of different religious faiths at both the individual and institutional level, leading to tolerance and mutual respect without any attempt to convert each other. Interfaith dialogue between Jews and Christians has substantially increased in the past half century, and efforts are underway to extend this dialogue to the Muslim community. Conservative, Reform, and Reconstructionist rabbis generally engage in interfaith religious dialogue; the Orthodox community has been more reluctant to take part. However, Rabbi Yosef Dov Soloveichik, the leading 20th-century rabbinic figure in American Modern Orthodoxy, endorsed interfaith dialogue focused on social issues of common concern.

Intermarriage (mixed marriage). Marriage between a Jew and a non-Jew, which has been opposed since biblical times as a danger the family (a key aspect of the essential core of Judaism), is invalid under Jewish law. From the time Abraham sent his servant, Eliezer, to choose a wife for Isaac from among his own people, through Ezra's expulsion of the non-Jewish wives of the Jews who returned from Babylonian Exile to establish the Second Commonwealth, to the practice of severing all ties with and even observing a period of mourning for intermarried children, marrying out of the faith has been one of the most strenuously discouraged and forcefully condemned acts that a Jew could perform. Orthodox and Conservative rabbis will not officiate at a mixed marriage ceremony; a growing number of Reform and Reconstructionist rabbis are willing to do so. In recent decades, intermarriage rates among Diaspora Jewry have soared. Among liberal Jewish denominations and organizations, there are attempts to reach out and embrace the intermarried spouse in the hope that (a) the children of intermarried couples will be raised as Jews and (b) the non-Jewish spouse will convert to Judaism.

Intermarriage, status of children. According to Jewish law, the status of children from a mixed marriage is determined exclusively by the faith of the mother. If the mother is Jewish and the father non-Jewish, the children are considered Jewish in every respect; if the father is Jewish but the mother is not, the children are not considered Jews. The Reform movement now recognizes patrilineal descent, deeming children of a Jewish father and a non-Jewish mother as Jewish.

Intermediate days of festivals – see *Chol ha-mo'ed.*

Irgun. Popular name for the *Irgun Zeva'i Leumi* (National Military Organization; acronym *Etzel*), an underground military force founded in 1931 in pre-state Israel that was ideologically linked to the Revisionist movement and accepted the authority of its leader, Vladimir Jabotinsky. Led by David Raziel and, after his death, by Menachem Begin, it rejected the "self-restraint" policy (see *havlagah*) of the Haganah and carried out armed reprisals against Arabs during their 1936-1939 uprising. After the publication of the 1939 White Paper that virtually banned the immigration of Jews into Palestine, the Irgun directed its activities against the British authorities, sabotaging government property and attacking security officers. During World Was II, Irgun members aided the British in the war against Nazi Germany, but in 1944 they resumed attacks on British forces in the Land of Israel. These activities culminated in 1946 with the blowing up of a wing of the King David Hotel that housed the administrative headquarters of the Mandatory government. Severe British reprisals followed, but this only increased Jewish resistance, in which the Irgun played a prominent role. After the birth of the State of Israel, the Irgun sought to maintain its separate identity and clashed with the government. Several months later, after the Altalena affair, the Irgun joined the national army (Israel Defense Forces).

Isaiah (**Isa**.) The 1st of the major prophets. The son of Amoz, Isaiah prophesied in Judah during the 8th century B.C.E. and attacked the idolatry, moral laxity, and injustice of his time. In a passage read today in synagogues as the *haftarah* on Yom Kippur morning (57:14-58:14), Isaiah railed against those who piously fast and then oppress their neighbors, arguing that God is more interested in social justice for the weak and the poor than in the offering of sacrifices in the Temple. Isaiah envisioned a messianic era of world peace at the end of days, when "the lion shall lie down with the lamb" (11:6-9) and "nation shall not lift up sword against nation; neither shall they learn war any more" (2:4). The words he uttered during his ecstatic vision (6:3) are part of the *Kedushah* prayer.The first 39 chapters of the Book of Isaiah contain material from this 8th-century prophet. The remainder of the book is considered the work of a 6th-century "Deutero-Isaiah," although some scholars have suggested that a third prophet (see "Trito-Isaiah") was responsible for chapters 56-66.

Islam. Monotheistic religion that is marked by both Jewish and Christian influence. It is based on the Koran, the sacred book that adherents believe was revealed by

God to Mohammed (570-632), the final Divine prophet. As with Judaism, Islam is uncompromisingly monotheistic and has an oral tradition (*hadith*) of the teachings of Mohammed that are indispensable in interpreting the Koran. Like Judaism, Islam is grounded in religious law (*Sharia*), which commands circumcision and prohibits the consumption of blood and pork. Islam began in Arabia in the 7th century and rapidly spread by religious conversion and military conquest. It soon developed two major strands: Shi'ite and Sunni. Shi'ites believe that legitimate religious authority comes only from the direct descendants of Mohammed, whereas Sunnis maintain that religious authority rests with the representatives of the community of the faithful. The "five pillars" of Islam (in order of priority) are: (1) The Testimony of Faith (a declaration that Allah is the one God and Mohammed is His prophet); (2) prayer five times a day; (3) giving charity to the poor; (4) fasting from dawn to sunset during the month of Ramadan (the ninth month of the Muslim lunar year); and (5) the pilgrimage to Mecca (Haj), which is compulsory once in a lifetime for all who have the ability to do it. Jihad, interpreted by some as "holy war" and by others as a struggle against one's evil inclination and to find God, is a command but not a pillar. Jews and Christians were recognized as *dhimmi*, tolerated but second class subjects. During the Middle Ages, Islamic thinking had an impact on Jewish philosophy, poetry, and mysticism. At times, Jews fared better under Islamic than Christian rule, but in the 20th century the growth of Zionism and the establishment of the State of Israel, along with the rise of Islamic fundamentalism, have led to a deterioration of Muslim-Jewish relations.

Israel. Name used to describe the Land of Israel (see *Eretz Yisrael*, the Northern Kingdom of Israel (see below), and the modern State of Israel. It is also the term for the descendants of Jacob (see Israelites).

Israel, Kingdom of (Northern Kingdom). Following the death of Solomon and the refusal of his son and successor (Rehoboam) to ease the unbearable burden of taxation and forced labor due in part to the construction of the First Temple, the 10 northern tribes declared their political independence from the House of David. They established the Kingdom of Israel (c. 930 B.C.E.) and appointed Jeroboam as their king (1 Kings 12:1-20). Jeroboam rebuilt and fortified Shechem as his capital and erected two golden calves in Dan and Beit El (near the northern and southern borders of his kingdom, respectively), transforming these sites into holy shrines in competition with Jerusalem so that the people would have no need to make pilgrimages to worship in the Davidic capital. The dynasty of Omri (882-871) was Israel's most successful, but its history was marked by assassinations, palace revolts, and civil wars. Its most notorious king was Ahab (873-852), whose Phoenician wife, Jezebel, introduced the worship of Baal. In 721 B.C.E., the Assyrians conquered the Kingdom of Israel and dispersed its inhabitants throughout their empire (see Ten Lost Tribes).

Israel, Land of – see *Eretz Yisrael.*

Israel, State of. The modern democratic State of Israel was proclaimed on May 14, 1948, with David Ben Gurion as the first Prime Minister and Chaim Weizmann as the first President. Ten minutes after the proclamation of statehood and the reading of its Declaration of Independence, President Harry Truman extended *de facto* American recognition of the new State. However, the fledgling nation immediately had to overcome a coordinated attack from land, sea, and air by the military forces of the five surrounding Arab nations (Egypt, Iraq, Jordan, Syria, Lebanon). Although enormously inferior in numbers and military power, Israel was able to defeat the Arab armies, and an armistice ending the conflict was signed in 1949. However, Jordan remained in control of the Old City, which was liberated in the Six Day War of 1967 with the united city of Jerusalem becoming the capital of Israel. Today, Israel has a Jewish population of some six million, about 80% of the inhabitants of the State. Its religious establishment is exclusively in Orthodox hands. The official languages are Hebrew, Arabic, and English. Israel is proud of its absorption and assimilation of Jewish immigrants from many diverse lands, its dynamic high-tech economy, and its strong military (Israel Defense Forces), which helps guarantee the security of the nation in the face of unrelenting conflict with the Arab world.

Israel Defense Forces (IDF, *Tzahal*). The army of the State of Israel, which was established in 1948. A true citizens' army, the IDF has a relatively small number of career soldiers and is essentially based on reserve service of the civilian population, retaining much of the pre-state character of a popular militia. Because almost all the Jewish youth of the country have to pass through its ranks, the IDF has proved to be one of the most important factors, together with the school system, in integrating new immigrants as well as the various cultural elements of the population of Israel. Most *yeshiva* students, married women, and mothers are exempted from the draft. Women from strictly Orthodox homes who have religious objections to serving in the army must perform national service as teachers or nurses. Israeli Arabs are also exempt, but Druze men are drafted at their own request. Following their term of national service, men and women without children remain in the reserves, and men generally report each year for various periods of training. This arrangement enables able-bodied citizens to be mobilized for combat within hours if there is a national emergency.

Israel Museum. Founded in 1965 as the national museum in Jerusalem, it houses extensive collections of Jewish art, modern sculpture, and archeological artifacts, including the Dead Sea Scrolls, as well as ancient Hebrew and Aramaic manuscripts. It serves as a repository for some of the most important cultural and artistic treasures of the Jewish people.

Israel Philharmonic Orchestra (IPO). There was little organized musical life in the Land of Israel until the 1930s, when the immigration of Jews from Central Europe swelled potential audiences and brought many professional musicians. The Palestine Orchestra (1936) was the vision of violinist Bronislaw Huberman, who saw it as a rescue operation for musicians persecuted by the Nazis as well as a contribution to the cultural life in Palestine. Known as the Israel Philharmonic Orchestra since the establishment of the State in 1948, it became recognized as one of the great international ensembles under long-time maestro Zubin Mehta.

Israel Prize. Most prestigious award given by the State, it is presented annually in Jerusalem on the eve of Israel Independence Day (see Yom ha-Atzmaut). The recipients of the prize are Israeli citizens (or sometimes organizations) who have displayed exemplary excellence in their particular field or have contributed strongly to the culture of the State of Israel. The winners are selected by committees of judges, who pass on their recommendations to the Education Minister.

Israelites (1). The descendants of the Patriarch Jacob, collectively known in the Bible as the "Children of Israel" (see *B'nai Yisrael*). The night before Jacob was to meet his brother Esau after spending 20 years outside the Land of Canaan, "a man [angel of God] wrestled with him [Jacob] until the break of dawn" (Gen. 32:24-33). This titanic battle resulted in Jacob's name being changed to Israel, since he had "struggled with God." The attacker injured Jacob's thigh, resulting in a residual limp. Jews commemorate this event by not eating the sciatic nerve.

Israelites (2). The vast majority of Jews, those who are not descended from the *kohanim* or the *levi'im*. When allocating *aliyot* to the Torah at the Sabbath morning service, the first is given to a *kohen* and the second to a *levi*, while the third through seventh are distributed among the "Israelites" (i.e., the rest of the congregation).

Ivrit. Hebrew word for the Hebrew language.

Ivrit b'Ivrit. Literally "Hebrew in Hebrew," an educational method of teaching Hebrew by immersing students in the spoken word and speech patterns of the language. This total immersion approach, used in *ulpanim* in Israel, has proven to be a most effective technique for successfully raising the level of Hebrew comprehension.

Iyar. The 2nd month of the Jewish calendar (April-May). Holidays in the month of Iyar include Yom ha-Atzmaut (5th), Lag ba-Omer (18th), and Yom Yerushalayim (28th).

J

J. According to the Documentary Hypothesis (see Bible criticism), one of the four major strands of literary tradition edited to form the Five Books of Moses. Also known as the Jahwist or Jerusalem source, it uses *YHVH* (see Tetragrammaton) as the name of God. Like "E," some scholars date it back to the time of the divided kingdom after the death of Solomon (late 10th century B.C.E.) and believe it represents the tradition preserved in the Southern Kingdom of Israel."J" is characterized by its anthropomorphic speech about God, who walks and talks with human beings, and uses the name "Sinai" for the mountain of the Revelation.

Jabbok. Eastern tributary of the Jordan River that arises in the mountains of Gilead and served as a natural boundary and political border throughout almost all historical periods.[131] The first biblical reference to the river occurs in connection with Jacob, who forded it on his way to meet Esau following his departure from Haran. After crossing the river repeatedly to transport his people and possessions to the other side, Jacob remained alone and experienced his struggle with the man/angel that lasted until the break of dawn (Gen. 32:23-25) and resulted in his name being changed to Israel.

Jachin – see Columns of Jachin and Boaz.

Jaffa. Now an integrated component of the sprawling Tel Aviv metropolitan area, Jaffa has a long and colorful history as a port city dating back to biblical times. King Hiram of Tyre floated the cedars of Lebanon down to Jaffa for the building of Solomon's Temple, and Jonah sailed from this port en route to his encounter with the whale. Ashkenazic and Sephardic Jews came to Jaffa as part of the First and Second Aliyot, but it was then a predominantly Arab town until captured during the War of Independence, when most of the Arabs fled and Jaffa was incorporated into Tel Aviv. The "Jaffa orange," developed in the coastal area of Israel, has become internationally famous.

JDL – see Jewish Defense League.

Jehovah. Christian name for God that represents a mistaken reading of *YHVH*, the consonants of the Tetragrammaton.After the destruction of the Temple, this name lost its vocalization. The term *Adonai* was generally substituted for *YHVH*, as is still the custom in the standard prayer formula (see *Baruch Ata Adonai*). In the early Middle Ages, when vowel points were introduced into the purely consonantal text of the Bible to preserve the traditional reading (see Masoretes), the four consonants of *YHVH* were vocalized with vowels borrowed from *Adonai*, resulting in the erroneous reading by Christian scholars.

Jeremiah (**Jer**.). The 2nd of the major prophets (c. 645-582 B.C.E). Son of Hilkiah, a priest of Anatot, Jeremiah witnessed the tragic events that ended in the destruction of Jerusalem. Jeremiah severely castigated the people for forsaking God and the Torah and turning to idolatry. Using the relationship of husband and wife as an analogy to that between God and Israel, Jeremiah accused Israel of being unfaithful to God, like a wife betraying her husband for a lover. Therefore, he exhorted the people to repent and worship the Lord, stressing individual responsibility for one's acts. Jeremiah's prophecies foretold the disaster of the Babylonian conquest that would befall the people as punishment for their sins, but they rejected his doom-laden words. Some considered him a traitor for urging them to submit to Babylon, and there was considerable opposition against Jeremiah even as he verbally attacked false prophets. Although a prophet of destruction due to Divine judgment, Jeremiah lamented the suffering of his people. He consoled them with the assurance that God would redeem them from captivity, enabling a righteous Israel to eventually dwell in safety in its own land. Jeremiah died in Egypt, where he had been taken by force.

Jericho. Oldest town in the Land of Israel, situated five miles north of the Dead Sea and 820 feet below sea level. A rich tropical oasis in the salt-encrusted plain, the walled city of Jericho was the strategic key to the land of Canaan from the east and was successfully stormed by Joshua and the Israelites when they entered the Promised Land.

Jerusalem. National capital of the Jewish people ever since King David conquered the city and made it the center of his kingdom about 3,000 years ago. Also known as the "Holy City" and "City of David," Jerusalem is now the capital of the modern State of Israel. From a Hebrew root meaning "peace" or "whole," Jerusalem was the unending object of Jewish longing throughout the centuries of dispersion. As they wept in exile by the rivers of Babylon, the Jews cried out, "If I should forget you, O Jerusalem, let my right hand lose its cunning" (Ps. 137:5). Each year at the end of the Passover feast and the Yom Kippur fast, Jews throughout the world fervently hope for "Next year in Jerusalem!" (see *Le-shanah ha-ba'ah bi-Yerushalayim*).

Jerusalem Post. Israel's independent English-language daily newspaper. Founded in 1932 by Gershon Agron, and until 1950 known as the Palestine Post, the

Jerusalem Post is a highly regarded publication and the major English-language source for authoritative news in the region.

Jerusalem Talmud. Much smaller than the more authoritative Babylonian Talmud, this commentary on the Mishnah was actually produced in the Galilee and completed in the early 5th century by Palestinian *amora'im*. Unlike the numerous tangents and extraneous material in the Babylonian Talmud, which frequently delves into topics in great depth, the discussions in the Jerusalem Talmud are shorter and to the point, but its language and style are at times obscure. The Jerusalem Talmud is primarily concerned with mishnaic interpretation and contains much less *aggadic* material, reflecting the fact that in the Land of Israel the *aggadic* element was assembled in special collections out of which later evolved the Midrash.

Jeshurun. Poetic name for Israel, occurring four times in the Bible (Deut. 32:15; 33:5, 26; Isa. 44:2).

Jew. Member of the Jewish community. The word derives from the Latin "*Judaeus*," which in turn comes from the Hebrew "*Yehudah*" (Judah, the fourth son of Jacob). Traditionally, a Jew is defined as a person whose mother is Jewish (matrilineal descent) or who has converted according to Jewish law (see who is a Jew?). In 1983, the Reform movement broke with this tradition and formally adopted the principle of patrilineal descent, extending the definition of a Jew to one who has only a Jewish father.

Jew-by-Choice. Term for a person who has converted to Judaism.This stresses freedom of choice to join the Jewish people and avoids the words "convert" and "proselyte," which some view as derogatory or as being associated with Christianity.

Jewish. Generic term for something relating to, or characteristic of, Jews or Judaism.

Jewish Agency. International non-governmental body, centered in Jerusalem, which is the executive and representative of the World Zionist Organization, whose aims are to assist and encourage Jews throughout the world to help in the development and settlement of Israel. Prior to the establishment of the State of Israel, the Jewish Agency organized the *aliyah* and absorption of immigrants, fostered settlement on the land, took part in the development of the Jewish economy, and promoted educational and social services. After the White Paper of 1939, the Jewish Agency fought restrictions on land purchase and immigration, mainly by organizing the "illegal" immigration (see *Aliyah Bet*) of survivors from Europe in the face of determined British and Arab opposition. After 1948, the Jewish Agency relinquished many of its functions to the newly created government of Israel. However, it continued to be responsible for the absorption of huge numbers of immigrants, land settlement, youth work, and other activities financed by voluntary Jewish contributions from abroad. The Jewish Agency maintains a department of education and culture that functions both in Israel and the Diaspora.

Jewish Brigade. Independent infantry unit in the British Army during World War II, made up mainly of Jews from Palestine. The Jewish Brigade had its own emblem, a gold Star of David on a background of blue and white stripes, bearing the inscription *Chayil* (the Hebrew word for soldier and the initials of its Hebrew name, Jewish Brigade Group). After the war, members of the Jewish Brigade worked to assist Jewish survivors reach the Land of Israel.

Jewish calendar – see Calendar.

Jewish Colonial Trust. The bank of the Zionist Organization, incorporated in London in 1899 in accordance with a policy endorsed at the First and Second Zionist Congresses. The bank invested in Jewish financial and business ventures in Palestine.

Jewish Colonization Association (ICA). Organization established by philanthropist Baron Maurice de Hirsch to facilitate the mass emigration of Jews from Russia and their settlement in agricultural colonies in the Americas, particularly in Argentina and Brazil, as well as in the Land of Israel.

Jewish Community Center. American Jewish communal institution, eventually subsidized by Jewish Federations throughout the United States. It was initially organized "to promote the religious, intellectual, physical, and social well-being and development of Jewish young men and women." In the 1930s, the role of the Jewish Community Center was greatly influenced by the views of Mordecai Kaplan, who envisioned it as an all-embracing agency serving the religious, cultural, and recreational needs of the entire Jewish community.

Jewish Defense League (JDL). Founded in the United States in 1968 and inspired by the charismatic Rabbi Meir Kahane, this often-militant organization is dedicated to fighting anti-Semitism and defending Jewish interests. It has been condemned as extremist by mainline Jewish organizations. Referring to the Holocaust, the motto of the Jewish Defense League is "Never Again!"

Jewish ethics – see Ethics, Jewish.

Jewish Federations. Local organizations in most North American cities that oversee Jewish social services and fund-raising. In addition to supporting a broad spectrum of local activities in their communities, Jewish Federations also underwrite similar programs in Israel. Many American Jews make a single donation to their local federation, which then distributes the funds among many charitable agencies. In 1997, the Council of Jewish Federations merged with the United Jewish Appeal and the United Israel Appeal to form an umbrella organization known as the United Jewish Communities.

Jewish Forward. Launched as a Yiddish-language daily newspaper in 1897 under founding editor Abraham Cahan, the Forward became known as the voice of the Jewish Eastern European immigrants to America and the conscience of the immigrant community. It fought for social justice, helped several generations of immigrants to enter American life, broke some highly significant news stories, and was among the nation's most eloquent defenders of democracy and Jewish rights. By the early 1930s, the Forward had become one of America's most influential metropolitan dailies, with a nationwide circulation topping 275,000. One its most popular aspects sections was "A Bintel Brief," (lit., 'a bundle of letters'), which dispensed shrewd, practical, and fair-minded advice to its readers. As the number of Yiddish speakers declined, the Forward became a weekly publication. In 1990, a weekly English-language Forward was established.

Jewish identity. One theological definition of Jewish identity based on classical sources is: "a member of the covenant community known as the people of Israel, who is bound to its collective consciousness shared through memories of its historical experience."[132] Numerous other factors determining Jewish identity have been suggested throughout history, including racial, physiological/genetic, ethnic, nationalistic, religious, cultural, and sociological (belonging to a Jewish organization). (See also *who is a Jew?*, *patrilineal descent*, and *intermarriage, status of children*.)

Jewish law – see Law, Jewish.

Jewish Legion. Jewish volunteer unit that fought in the British army during World War I to liberate Palestine from Turkish rule.

Jewish National Fund (JNF). Land purchase and development fund of the World Zionist Organization. Founded in 1901 at the Fifth Zionist Congress, its Hebrew name (*Keren Kayemet Le-Yisrael*) comes from the talmudic statement about good deeds, "the fruits of which a man enjoys in this world, while the capital abides *(ha-keren kayemet)* for him in the World to Come." The JNF's initial principles, which were greatly influenced by the agricultural laws of the Bible, provided that the land it purchased must remain the inalienable possession of the Jewish people. It cannot be sold or mortgaged and may be leased only to individual pioneers or groups of settlers for a normal rental period of 49 years, renewable only by the original contractor. By 1947, the JNF had bought and controlled more than half the total Jewish property in Palestine, and the UN Partition Plan of that year drew

Israel's borders along the lines of JNF land holdings. During its first century, the Jewish National Fund planted more than 200 million trees and reclaimed about 250,000 acres. Since the founding of the State of Israel, the emphasis of JNF activity shifted from land purchase to land improvement and development, as well as the planting of forests and the preservation and development of water resources. For years, funds for the JNF came from coins and bills placed by Jews around the world in the "Blue Box," which has remained a popular Zionist symbol.

Jewish oath. Special oath, accompanied by certain ceremonies, that Jews were required to take in European courts of law. Dating back to the Christian Middle Ages in Central and Eastern Europe, it remained in effect in some countries until the 20th century. The oath was typically sworn on a Torah scroll or *tefillin* and invoked curses on anyone who took it in vain.

Jewish people – see *Am Yisrael.*

Jewish Publication Society (JPS). Oldest publisher of Jewish titles in the English language. Its mission is "to enhance Jewish culture by promoting the dissemination of religious and secular works of exceptional quality, in the United States and abroad, to all individuals and institutions interested in past and contemporary Jewish life." It was founded in 1888 "to provide the children of Jewish immigrants to America with books about their heritage in the language of the New World." Members' dues support the publication of books that "broaden and deepen understanding of the Jewish heritage and advance Jewish scholarship."[133]

Jewish Renewal. Trans-denominational, egalitarian movement founded in the United States in the 1970's and "grounded in the prophetic and mystical traditions of Judaism," it "seeks to bring creativity, relevance, joy, and an all embracing awareness to spiritual practice, as a path to healing our hearts and finding balance and wholeness," as well as helping "to heal the world by promoting justice, freedom, responsibility, caring for all life and the earth that sustains all life."[134]

Jewish star – see Magen David.

Jewish studies. Traditionally based in *yeshivot* (see *yeshiva*), it involved the study of codes and talmudic precedents as preparation for rabbinic ordination. In early America, the Bible was an important area of study in Christian denominational colleges (especially the Ivy League). Hebrew was mandatory, both because of the idea that to be a cultured person one needed to learn the major classical languages (Latin, Greek, and Hebrew) and because knowing biblical Hebrew increased one's ability to understand the Hebrew Bible (which was considered the basis for understanding Christianity). Modern Jewish studies has been profoundly influenced by the "Science of Judaism" (see *Wissenschaft des Judentums*), which utilized critical methods and such scholarly tools as demography and social and economic history. In the first half of the 20th century, Jewish studies in the United States was confined primarily to such Jewish institutions as rabbinical seminaries and Hebrew colleges. With the rise of "ethnic studies" in the 1970s, Jewish studies became recognized as an academic field of interest in major American universities. It now has expanded to include such areas as Jewish history and literature, religious studies, Near Eastern languages, and Jewish arts.

Jewish Telegraphic Agency (**JTA**). International news agency, founded in 1917, that serves Jewish community newspapers and media throughout the world. Headquartered in New York, it collects and disseminates news among and affecting the Jewish communities of the Diaspora as well as Israel.

Jewish Theological Seminary of America (**JTSA**). Educational and spiritual center of Conservative Judaism and the major institution for the training of its rabbis. Opened in New York is 1887, it became a major academic institution under the leadership of Solomon Schechter, who engaged outstanding Jewish scholars (such as talmudist Louis Ginzburg) to serve on its faculty. To reach the rapidly growing Jewish community on the West Coast, in 1947 the seminary opened the University of Judaism in Los Angeles, which is now a separate institution. In the 1980's, it began to ordain women rabbis. The Seminary also trains cantors and Jewish educators and boasts a superb library. Congregational support for the Seminary is provided by the United Synagogue of America.

Jews for Jesus – see Messianic Jews.

Jezreel Valley. Extending across the breadth of the Land of Israel between Mount Carmel, Mount Gilboa, and the hills of Lower Galilee, the Jezreel Valley was the site of some of the great battles in biblical history – between Deborah and Jabin, king of Hatzor (Judg. 4-5); Saul and the Philistines (1 Sam. 29:1; 31:1); and Josiah and Pharaoh Necho (2 Kings 23:29:30). With the establishment of the British Mandate following World War I, the Jewish National Fund acquired large tracts of land in the Jezreel Valley, drained the swamps, and set up settlements that were showpieces of Zionist pioneering.

JNF – see Jewish National Fund.

Job. The 3rd book of the Writings section of the Bible, its pious title figure confronts the basic question of theodicy – if God is just, benevolent, and omnipotent, why do good people suffer? A blameless and upright man who had sired seven sons and three daughters and possessed immense wealth, Job became the wager in a bet between God and Satan. The latter cynically maintained that it was easy for a rich man to love and revere God, but if Job were to lose all he had, he would renounce and curse God. However, even when his children were killed and he lost his vast possessions, the patient Job did not reproach God. Instead, he declared God's act to be just, saying: "The Lord gave, and the Lord has taken away; blessed be the name of the Lord" (1:21). Even after Job himself was afflicted with painful sores, he refused to curse God. Most of the Book of Job consists of a poetic dialogue between him and three friends who hear of the calamities that have befallen Job and come to mourn with and comfort him. However, Job refuses to accept their traditional argument that he must have been guilty of some transgression, based on the idea that the righteous cannot perish and only the wicked suffer in just measure for their sins. Finally, God enters the scene and chastises the three friends for their arrogant assumption that they could fathom the Divine will. At the end of the book, God vindicates Job and restores his health and wealth, and Job also sires a new family. Although never revealing the reason for Job's suffering, which remains a Divine mystery, God does communicate directly with Job and assure him of His Presence.

Joel. The 2nd of the minor prophets (late 6th-early 5th century B.C.E.). The Book of Joel gives a vivid description of a plague of locusts of unprecedented severity that destroyed fields and vineyards and deprived the people of food. It calls on the people to repent and seek the Lord's mercy to save themselves from the kind of impending punishment that will befall the nations that had oppressed Judah. The final part of the book portrays an apocalyptic battle in which the enemies of God will be destroyed, followed by a golden age when God will restore His exiled people to their land, which will be blessed with great fertility. The book concludes with the promise that "Judah shall abide forever, and Jerusalem from generation to generation" (4:20).

Jonah (Jon.). The 5th and most famous of the minor prophets. The son of Amitai, Jonah was commanded to go to the Assyrian capital of Nineveh and announce to its inhabitants that God would destroy the city because of their wickedness. He attempted to flee by sea in the opposite direction, was cast overboard during a savage storm, and swallowed by a "great fish" (often mistranslated as a whale). After spending three days and nights in the fish's belly praying to God in repentance, Jonah was spewed out onto dry land. At last, Jonah obeyed God's will and went to Nineveh to prophesy its destruction. The people repented and God renounced the planned punishment. Because of its message of Divine forgiveness in response to true repentance, the entire Book of Jonah is the *haftarah* read in synagogue during the afternoon service on Yom Kippur.

Jordan (Hashemite Kingdom of). Portion of Mandatory Palestine lying east of the Jordan River (almost 80% of the total area of the Mandate), which in 1921 was made into an autonomous political division granted to the Hashemite Emir Abdullah (elder son of an Arab ally of Britain in World War I). Jordan was made an independent kingdom in 1946. Although Jordan fought against Israel in several wars, the two countries signed a peace treaty in 1994.

Jordan (River). From a Hebrew word meaning "to descend," this largest river in the Land of Israel arises from headwaters in the Lebanese mountains, flows south through the Sea of Galilee (*Kinneret*), and empties into the Dead Sea, the lowest point on earth. The Israelites under Joshua crossed the Jordan River from the east to reach the Promised Land of Canaan (Josh. 3-4). The waters of the Jordan became sacred to Christians because it was the site where John the Baptist preached and performed his ritual immersions (Matt. 3:5; Mark 1:5).

Josephus. Jewish historian and soldier (1st century C.E.) Commander of the Jewish forces in the Galilee during the rebellion against Rome, Josephus surrendered to the Roman general Vespasian and was taken prisoner. For the remainder of the war, Josephus assisted Titus, Vespasian's son, in understanding the Jewish nation and negotiating with the revolutionaries. Called a traitor and unable to persuade the defenders of Jerusalem to surrender to the Roman siege, Josephus instead became a witness to the destruction of the city and the Holy Temple. His major books, *The Jewish Wars* and *The Antiquities of the Jews* (whose purpose was to diminish anti-Jewish prejudice by teaching non-Jews about the Jewish people), provide valuable insight into Jewish life at the end of the Second Temple period.

Joshua (Josh.). The 1st book of the Prophets, named for the lieutenant and successor of Moses, it describes the story of Israel's military conquest of the Land of Canaan and its allocation among the various tribes. After the capture of Jericho, whose great walls came tumbling down (Josh. 6), Joshua fulfilled the command from Deuteronomy (27:11-13) to proclaim a series of blessings and curses on Mounts Gerizim and Ebal, representing the Divinely imposed consequences of fulfilling or disobeying the terms of the Covenant.

Jubilee Year (*yovel*). According to the Bible, every 50th year cultivation was prohibited, slaves were freed, and all landed property purchased since the previous Jubilee reverted to its original owner. The Jubilee Year was ushered in with a blast of the *shofar* on Yom Kippur (recalled today by the final long sounding of the ram's horn [*yovel*] at the end of the concluding *Ne'ilah* service on that day), which was designed to "proclaim liberty throughout the land and to all the inhabitants thereof" (Lev. 25:10). These words were selected by the American patriots to be inscribed on the Liberty Bell, which announced the signing of the Declaration of Independence and the birth of their new free land.

Jubilees, Book of. Part of the Apocrypha dating back to the middle of the Second Temple period, it claims to be the secret revelation of the Angel of the Divine Presence to Moses on his second ascent to Mount Sinai. It is a significant reworking of the biblical books of Genesis and Exodus and reflects the views of traditional Jews opposed to the influences of Hellenistic culture, which they considered an existential threat to Judaism.

Judah, Kingdom of. Also known as the Southern Kingdom, it was composed of the two remaining tribes of Judah and Benjamin after the other ten tribes broke off to form the Northern Kingdom following the death of Solomon (late 10th century B.C.E.). With only one exception, the monarchy passed peacefully from father to son in the House of David. Jerusalem served as the capital of Judah throughout its history. Major religious revivals occurred during the reigns of Hezekiah (8th century) and Josiah (7th century), the latter when the "Book of the Law" (thought to be a large part of the current Book of Deuteronomy) was discovered by the high priest Hilkiah during repair work on the Temple. After the first capture of Jerusalem by Nebuchadnezzar in 597 B.C.E., the Judean aristocracy was carried off to Babylon. In 586 B.C.E., Jerusalem and the First Temple were destroyed and the Babylonian Exile began. The Davidic monarchy was never restored.

Judah Maccabee. Third son of Mattathias of Modi'in, who initiated the successful guerilla war against the Syrian-Greeks that is celebrated in the festival of Chanukah.After his father's death, the leadership of the band passed to Judah, who waged a brave and brilliant campaign that eventually led to the defeat of the forces of Antiochus Epiphanes, the liberation of Jerusalem, and the rededication of the Temple (165 B.C.E.). Judah was given the name "Maccabee," which may have derived from the Hebrew word *makav* (hammer) and thus have been a testament to his great strength. Another explanation is that Maccabee is an acrostic for the first letters of the Hebrew words *Mi chamocha ba'elim Adonai* ("Who is like You, O Lord, among the mighty"; Exod. 15:11), which is recited daily before the morning and evening *Amidah* and as part of the Song at the Sea (see *Shirat ha-Yam*). Judah eventually fell in battle and was succeeded by his brother, Jonathan.

Judaica. General term for Jewish books and ritual objects.

Judaism. Monotheistic religion originating with the Divine call to the Patriarch Abraham (Gen. 12) almost 4,000 years ago and expressed through the idea of a Covenant with God elaborated in the Divinely revealed Torah. Throughout the centuries, various groups have claimed that their beliefs and practices represented authentic Judaism. The synagogue replaced the Temple as the focus of Jewish ritual life, and rabbis supplanted priests as its spiritual leaders. The most authoritative rabbinic text is the Talmud.In the Middle Ages, Maimonides formulated his Thirteen Principles of Faith, which are still generally regarded as the basic tenets of the religion. Jewish liturgy stresses the themes of Creation, Revelation, and Redemption. Jewish observance is shaped by a religious calendar and the obligation to fulfill *mitzvot*.Today, numerous denominations ranging from ultra-Orthodox to extremely liberal all maintain that they reflect valid forms of Judaism.

Judaism, Positive-Historical. Intellectual forerunner to Conservative Judaism, which developed as a school of thought in the 1840s and 1850s in Germany. Its principal founder was Rabbi Zechariah Frankel, who had broken with German Reform Judaism over its rejection of the primacy of the Hebrew language in Jewish prayer. As head of the new Jewish Theological Seminary of Breslau, Frankel taught that Jewish law was not static, but rather has always developed in response to changing conditions. He called his approach towards Judaism "Positive-Historical," meaning that Jews should have a positive attitude towards accepting Jewish law and tradition as normative, yet always be open to changing the law as it has always developed in response to evolving historical circumstances. Frankel was sympathetic to the then-current trends in critical Jewish scholarship, as reflected in the "Science of Judaism" (see *Wissenshaft des Judentums*). He rejected the innovations of Reform Judaism as insufficiently based on Jewish history and communal practice, but his acceptance of modern methods of historical scholarship in analyzing Jewish texts and developing Jewish law set him apart from the neo-Orthodox Judaism of Rabbi Samson Raphael Hirsch.

Judea. This Latin form of the name Judah was the Roman title for the mountainous southern part of the historic Land of Israel when it was a client state of their empire. The most famous of these vassal rulers was Herod the Great (1st century B.C.E.), who imposed heavy taxes to pay for his massive building projects and lavish decoration of the Second Temple. After a Jewish rebellion was crushed by the Roman legions in 70 C.E., Jerusalem fell and the Temple was destroyed.

Judea and Samaria (*Yehudah v'Shomron*). Ancient Hebrew terms used among Israelis living in the region that is commonly known as the "West Bank."

Judea capta est (Judea is conquered). Latin inscription on coins issued by Vespasian, the Roman Emperor, after the fall of Jerusalem in the 1st century C.E. These depicted the defeated Jews as a forlorn woman sitting in mourning beneath a palm tree.

Judean Desert. Just east of Jerusalem, the Judean desert is a land of rugged splendor – hot, dry, and inhospitable, but rich in history. Jericho, the oldest inhabited city on earth, surrounds an oasis deep within this desert. In the Judean Desert, Lot's wife cast her last unfortunate glance back toward the burning cities of Sodom and Gomorrah and turned into a pillar of salt; Jacob laid his head on a rock to dream of angels; Moses gazed on the Land of Canaan he was never to reach from the top of Mount Nebo (today within Jordan); and the tribes of Israel streamed through the craggy heights of this wilderness on their way into the

Promised Land. The Judean desert is also the site of the Dead Sea, Herod's mighty fortress of Masada, and Qumran, where the Dead Sea Scrolls were discovered.

Judenrat. German for "Jewish council," the administative body that the Germans imposed on the Jewish communities of Nazi-occupied Europe. Though commonly thought to represent the Jewish leadership of this period, this view is inaccurate. The Nazi authorities exerted substantial influence on the composition of the councils, and Jewish leadership continued to exist outside of them. The councils were established to serve German goals, but they also carried out a variety of Jewish communal services. In the ghettos of Eastern Europe these included security, health and sanitation, construction and housing, food supply, education, and culture. Until the massive deportations to the death camps in 1942, most Eastern European councils believed that they could help the Jews survive by acceding to German demands for forced labor. In the immediate post-war decades, the councils were harshly criticized. However, subsequent research has shown that the behavior of the various councils varied from determined resistance to compliance with some Nazi directives to complete acquiescence to German demands in the hope that at least some Jews could be saved.

Judenrein. German for "free of Jews," this term was used by the Nazis to apply to any area from which Jews had been expelled. The ultimate aim of the Nazis was a "Europe free of Jews," which would be brought about by the "Final Solution of the Jewish Question" (i.e., genocide).

Judenstaat, Der (The Jewish State). Short pamphlet, published in 1896 by Theodor Herzl, the founder of political Zionism, that became the manifesto of the Zionist movement. After outlining the "plight of the Jews," he suggested "the restoration of the Jewish State" as its solution. Herzl discussed in depth the needs of the state, which would provide a safe haven for those threatened with anti-Semitic persecution. The next year, Herzl issued a call for the first Zionist Congress.

Judeo-Christians. Members of a Jewish sect during the 1st century C.E. who believed that Jesus was the Messiah, but insisted on the ongoing validity of Jewish law. However, the early Church, following the teaching of Paul that belief in the divinity of Jesus made the law obsolete, rejected the Judeo-Christians and they disappeared.

Judeo-Spanish – see Ladino.

Judge. During the wanderings of the Israelites after the Exodus from Egypt, Moses exercised judicial power over the people. When the task became too overwhelming, he followed the advice of his father-in-law, Jethro, and delegated some of this authority to appointed "chiefs of thousands, hundreds, fifties, and tens ... the difficult matters they would bring to Moses, and all the minor matters they would decide themselves" (Exod. 18:25-26) According to the Torah, judges were to be "capable men who fear God, trustworthy men who spurn ill-gotten gain" (Exod. 18:21), as well as "wise, discerning, and experienced" (Deut. 1:13). Warned not to be "partial in judgment," judges were required to "hear out low and high alike [and] fear no man, for judgment is God's" (Deut. 1:16–17). After the conquest of the Promised Land and its division among the various tribes, judges were appointed in every settlement (Deut. 16:18). (See also *beit din*, *justice*, and *Sanhedrin.*)

Judges (Judg.). The 2nd book of the Prophets section of the Bible. The title "judge" was applied to the 12 leaders of the Israelites after the death of Joshua until the beginning of the monarchy.[135] In a recurring cycle, the people "did evil in the sight of the Lord" by praying to the gods of the Canaanites. These actions provoked Divine wrath, and God angrily delivered the Israelites into the hands of enemies who ruled over them harshly. Repeatedly, God then brought judges at these times of crisis to save the Israelites from their oppressors. However, as soon as each judge died, the people quickly went astray, bowing in worship to other gods and becoming even more corrupt. The Book of Judges describes the period until the time of Eli and Samuel and relates stories about such well-known figures as Deborah, Gideon, Jephthah, and Samson.

Judgment – see *Din.*

Judgment, Day of – see Day of Judgment.

Judith. Historical narrative of the Apocrypha, dating from Second Temple times, that relates how the title character saved the Jewish people. When the Assyrians under Holofernes laid siege to Bethulia, a small but strategic fortified town, Judith asked permission to descend to the enemy camp. Captivated by her beauty, Holofernes invited Judith to a feast. When the general, overcome with wine, fell asleep, Judith took his dagger, cut off his head, and returned with her trophy. Deprived of their commander by Judith's courageous deed, the panic-stricken Assyrian soldiers fled when the Jews attacked. After securing their victory, the Jews gave thanks to God.

Junior congregation. Worship services that are specially arranged for children of school age and are often conducted entirely or partially by them. These abridged services include the central core of prayers and are most commonly held on Saturday mornings in some Reform and Conservative congregations.

Justice. *Tzedek, tzedek tirdof* ("Justice, justice, shall you pursue;" Deut. 16:20) is a major ethical cornerstone of Judaism. It is a foundation of biblical legislation and the prophetic demands for social justice. Establishing fair and impartial courts of justice is one of the seven Noahide laws, which constitute the basic requirements for any civilized society. The Torah strictly prohibits anything that perverts justice, or even gives the appearance of injustice. Consequently, a judge must be scrupulously fair and honorable to preserve the integrity of the judicial system, not departing from the Torah-mandated principles of guilt and innocence. As the Talmud observed, "He who does not deliver judgments in perfect truth causes the Divine Presence [*Shechinah*] to depart from the midst of Israel" (Sanh. 7a). Nevertheless, the Rabbis recognized that strict justice must at times be tempered by mercy.

K

K. When surrounded by a circle, a star, or a square, a symbol of kosher certification found on prepared food in a package.

Kabbalah. A Hebrew word derived from a root meaning "to receive," Kabbalah is the Jewish mystical tradition. Developed and nurtured within Judaism, it is inextricably bound to classical Jewish texts, teachings, theology, and religious practices. Although kabbalistic ideas can offer wisdom and enlightenment outside the orbit of Jewish faith, life, practice, and community, there is no authentic Kabbalah outside or detached from Judaism.[136] Various forms of Kabbalah endeavor to achieve a mystical union with God (see *devekut*), repair the damage to the realm of the *sefirot*, or draw down Divine grace upon the world through prayer, deeds of lovingkindness, or various magical practices.

Kabbalah, Christian. During the Renaissance, Kabbalah influenced philosophical trends and spawned a Christianized version that attempted to merge certain Jewish mystical and Christological ideas. Some of these teachings eventually influenced concepts and rites of groups like the Freemasons, who influenced the ideas of the founders of the American republic.[137]

Kabbalah, ecstatic/prophetic. As expounded by the 13th-century mystic Abraham Abulafia, the use of combinations and permutations of the letters of the Hebrew alphabet (particularly of the names of God) to achieve a heightened state of awareness that induced "prophecy" and afforded the practitioner personal illumination and redemption as well as an experience of the World to Come. Rather than based on the observance of *mitzvot*, "ecstatic mysticism" emphasized the performance of highly technical mystical exercises that result in altered states of consciousness. The "ecstatic mysticism" of the charismatic Abulafia exerted substantial influence on later Jewish kabbalists.

Kabbalat panim. Literally "receiving faces," the Hebrew term for welcoming guests prior to the wedding ceremony.

Kabbalat Shabbat (Welcoming the Sabbath). Set of introductory prayers in which the congregation welcomes the Sabbath before the main Friday evening service. In 16th-century Safed, Isaac Luria and his disciples used to form a procession every Friday afternoon and go to the outskirts of the town to receive the Sabbath

Bride with songs and praise. This mystical ceremony spread to other communities, where the Sabbath Bride was welcomed not in the fields but in the synagogue. Eventually, the *Kabbalat Shabbat* was standardized to consist of six psalms that correspond to the regular days of the week (Ps. 95-99; 29) and *Lecha Dodi*, followed by *Mizmor Shir*, the psalm (92) for the Sabbath day. Some congregations open the service with the singing of *Yedid Nefesh* (Beloved of the soul).

Kaddish. Aramaic prayer that closes every public service as well as the individual sections within it. Recited only in the presence of a *minyan*, the *Kaddish* proclaims God's greatness and holiness and expresses the hope for the speedy establishment of the Divine kingdom on earth. For the Rabbis, the essential element of the prayer was the congregational response: Y'*hei Shmei rabba mevorach, l'olam u-l'olmei ulmaya* (May the great Name of God be blessed forever and unto all eternity). The *Kaddish* is first mentioned as part of the prescribed synagogue daily prayers in about the 6th century. Subsequently, two Hebrew verses were added for those who did not speak Aramaic – the explanatory passage *Yitbarach v'yishtabach* (Blessed and praised…) following the congregational response, and the concluding passage *Oseh shalom bim'romov* (He who creates peace above…).

Kaddish de-Rabbanan (*Kaddish* of the Rabbis). Initially, the *Kaddish* was not even a part of the synagogue service but rather the formal dismissal that was recited by the preacher or teacher at the conclusion of a discourse on the Torah. The ancient custom of dismissing the assembly with the words of the *Kaddish* is still preserved in the *Kaddish de-Rabbanan*, which is recited in the synagogue after communal study. However, instead of being uttered by the teacher, it is now recited by those mourners who are in attendance. Instead of the *titkabeil* verse (see *Kaddish Shalem*, below), the *Kaddish de-Rabbanan* includes several lines praying for the teachers of Israel, their disciples, and all who study the Torah.

Kaddish, Hatzi – see *Hatzi Kaddish*.

Kaddish Shalem ("full" *Kaddish*). Prayer recited by the prayer leader after the *Amidah* that virtually concludes each service. It contains a special verse beginning with the word *titkabeil* (Let be accepted [the prayers and supplications of the whole house of Israel by their Father in heaven; and let us say "amen"]) as well as two prayers for peace (the first in Aramaic, the second in Hebrew).

Kaddish Yatom (lit., "orphan's *Kaddish*") – see *Mourner's Kaddish*.

Kadimah (forward). First Jewish national students' association, established in Vienna in 1882 with the goal of "struggling against assimilation and fostering Jewish peoplehood" as a "barrier against the destruction of Judaism." Today, Kadimah is the name of the centrist political party in Israel that was founded in 2006 by Prime Minister Ariel Sharon.

Kaf. The 11th letter of the Hebrew alphabet, with a numerical value of 20.

Kaf Tet (29th) b'November. The date (November 29, 1947) on which the General Assembly of the United Nations voted in favor of the partition of Palestine and the creation of a Jewish State, thereby affording it international legitimacy. Five months later, the British withdrew from Palestine. On May 14, 1948, the State of Israel was proclaimed in Tel Aviv, with David Ben Gurion reading its Declaration of Independence.

Kaftan. Full-length garment with elbow-length or long sleeves, worn by Mediterranean and Eastern European Jews.

Kahal (congregation/community) – see *Kehilla*.

Kalam. Arabic word meaning "speaking," which refers to the Islamic tradition of seeking theological principles through dialectic, discussion, and reasoning through dialogue. This practice profoundly influenced the development of Jewish philosophy in the Middle Ages.

Kalikeh. Literally a "cripple," this Yiddish term is generally used to describe a clumsy person, or someone who is incapable of performing a task properly (e.g., a performer who sings off key or a waiter who spills the soup).

Kallah (1). Hebrew word for "bride," to which the Sabbath is compared in the refrain of the Friday night hymn, *Lecha Dodi*: "Come, my beloved, to greet the bride (*likrat kallah*); let us welcome the Sabbath Presence."

Kallah (2). Minor tractate of the Talmud that deals with betrothal, marriage, chastity, and moral purity. A longer version is known as Kallah Rabbati.

Kallah (3). Courses of study during the talmudic and geonic periods that took place at the major Babylonian academies of Sura and Pumbedita during the months of Elul (August-September) and Adar (February-March), when the demands of agricultural work were minimal and thus students had time to gather together to learn a tractate of the Talmud. Today, the term is applied to a program of several days devoted to learning, often organized by a synagogue.

Kalut rosh. Literally "lightheadedness," this Hebrew term denotes a spirit of levity and undignified behavior. In the context of disrespect to the dead, avoiding *kalut rosh* requires the wearing of a head covering in a cemetery and abstaining from eating, drinking, and smoking. Care must be taken not to tread on a grave or lean on a headstone; a path through a cemetery cannot be used as a shortcut, and animals are not permitted to graze there. It is inappropriate to wear *tallit* or *tefillin* or read a Torah scroll in a cemetery, lest one "shame" the dead who are no longer able to perform these *mitzvot*. The danger of *kalut rosh* was also invoked as a rationale for the separation of men and women in the synagogue (see *mechitzah*).

Kal v'homer. Literally meaning "light and heavy," the name of the first principle of hermeneutics of Hillel and Ishmael ben Elisha. It proves a point by arguing that if the law is stringent in a case where it usually is lenient, it is certainly so in the more stringent case (and vice versa). For example, if an action is forbidden on a festival (minor), it certainly is forbidden on the Sabbath (major); conversely, if an action is permitted on the Sabbath (major), it certainly is permitted on a festival.

Kametz – see Vowels.

Kaparos. Literally "atonements," but in the sense of "ransom," the Yiddish term for the custom on the day before Yom Kippur in which the sins of a person are symbolically transferred to a fowl (a cock for a male; a hen for a female). While the fowl is swung around the head three times, a prayer is recited to transfer any misfortune that might otherwise befall the person in punishment for sins. These birds, never offered in the Temple, were selected so that no suspicion would arise that one was attempting the strictly forbidden practice of recreating a Temple sacrifice. After the ceremony, it is customary to donate the fowl to the poor. Today, many people have substituted money for the live bird. Many major rabbinic authorities, both medieval and modern, have strenuously opposed the *kaparos* ceremony, attacking it as a superstitious ritual and decrying the belief that one may substitute the death of an animal for one's own life. Nevertheless, the ceremony appealed strongly to the masses and has survived in traditional households. [138]

Kapote. Long black coat worn by ultra-Orthodox Jews.

Karaites. Jewish sect founded in the late 8th century by Anan ben David. It rejected the authority and legitimacy of the rabbinic formulation of talmudic law (Oral Law) and based its religious life on the literal meaning of the Bible. For example, Karaites interpreted the biblical prohibition against making a fire on the Sabbath as requiring that all lights be extinguished before the Sabbath, thus spending the day without heat or light. In direct opposition to this ritual, the *geonim* inserted into the Friday night service a recitation of a talmudic passage (*bameh madlikin*; with what may we light) that discusses which types of wick and oil should be used to provide the home with light on the Sabbath – indicating unequivocally that having lights burning in one's dwelling was not merely permitted but a positive commandment.[139] Karaite communities were established in Babylonia, Persia, Egypt, and the Land of Israel. In the 13th century, many Karaites settled in the Crimea in Russia and spread from there to Lithuania and Galicia. Since the establishment of the State of Israel, many of the remaining Karaites have moved there, founding several settlements and tending to draw nearer to normative Jews.

Karet (extirpation). Hebrew term for punishment "at the hands of Heaven," in cases when a person cannot be convicted by an earthly court because of the absence of witnesses. The Bible indicates *karet* as the penalty for such deliberate transgressions as idolatry, desecration of the Sabbath, the eating of *chametz* on Passover, incest, and adultery.

Karpas. Fresh green vegetable, typically parsley or celery, that is placed on the seder plate on Passover. It represents the seasonal rebirth that takes place in the spring (the time of Passover in Israel and elsewhere in the Northern Hemisphere) as well as the renewal of hope for redemption. The *karpas* is dipped in salt water as a reminder of the tears the Israelites shed while slaves in Egypt. This practice may date back to ancient Rome, where banquets would begin with hors d'oeuvres.

Kasha. Buckwheat groats, used like a grain, which was a staple of the diet of Eastern European Jews and traditionally served as an accompaniment to meats, in pilafs, or mixed with noodle "bow-ties" to make a dish called *kasha varnishkes*.

Kashe. Literally meaning "difficult," this Yiddish term is applied to a question or an intricate talmudic issue. On Passover, the four questions are known in Yiddish as the "*Fir Kashes*."

Kashering. The process of preparing meat to comply with the biblical proscription against the consumption of blood (Lev. 7:26–27; 17:10–14). Before meat is cooked, it is necessary to remove all traces of blood by soaking and salting it in a prescribed fashion. Meat that is to be broiled does not need to be *kashered*, because the broiling process drains off at least as much blood as is removed by soaking and salting. Nevertheless, some people do sprinkle salt on meat before broiling. Salting is not considered effective enough to *kasher* the blood-saturated liver, which must be pre-broiled on a rack to allow the juices to drain before further cooking.[140] Today, most packaged kosher meat comes already *kashered* and is ready to be cooked. The term *kashering* can also be applied to the process of heating and cleaning utensils and dishes so that they may be used for kosher cooking, or for removing all traces of *chametz* to make an entire kitchen ready for the preparation of Passover meals.

Kashrut (dietary laws). From a Hebrew root meaning "fit" or "proper," the collective term for the Jewish regulations and customs that specify what types of food are permitted for consumption and how they are to be prepared. All fruits and vegetables are allowed and may be consumed with either meat or dairy. Therefore, the dietary laws (derived largely from Lev. 11) are concerned with what animals, birds, and fish may be eaten, how they may be slaughtered (see *shechitah*) and prepared for consumption (see *kashering*, above), and the fact that meat must not be consumed or cooked together with dairy products (see mixing milk and meat). To qualify as kosher, a quadruped must both chew the cud (ruminant) and have hoofs that are completely cloven (divided). Fish must have both fins and scales. Although the Torah specifically names 20 non-kosher species of birds, in general all birds of prey and those that eat carrion are prohibited. Insects and "swarming creatures that swarm on the earth" are forbidden. Some portions of kosher animals are prohibited, such as the sciatic nerve in the hindquarters of any quadruped and the fat attached to the stomach and intestines (see *cheilev*). The Rabbis regarded the laws of *kashrut* as Divine legislation, which was sufficient reason to observe them. In addition to fostering self control and mastery of one's appetite, obedience to the laws of *kashrut* have strengthened Jewish identity and reinforced devotion to the Divine will.

Kav. Biblical liquid measure, equal to four *logs* or approximately 40 fluid ounces (1.23 liter).

Kavanah. Hebrew word meaning "devotion, intent, conscious purpose," which describes the state of mind required for praying or performing a *mitzvah*. When a *mitzvah* entails the performance of a specific act (such as eating unleavened bread), one who merely performs the act without conscious purpose technically fulfills the obligation. However, where no specific act is required, there must be a conscious awareness of fulfilling one's duty. In a talmudic example, "If a man is passing behind a synagogue, or if his house adjoins the synagogue, and he hears the sound of the *shofar*, or the reading of the Scroll of Esther, then if he listens with attention he fulfills his obligation, but otherwise he does not" (RH 27b). The blessing recited before performing a *mitzvah* not only offers praise to God, but also reminds the individual of the importance of the sanctified act. In the context of prayer, *kavanah* implies total concentration on the act of prayer and the intent to come ever closer to God. When reciting the *Shema*, it is customary to place the right hand over the eyes while saying the first verse so as to prevent any distractions that would hamper full concentration on the meaning of the words and the direction of one's thinking towards God.

Kavod. A Hebrew word meaning "honor," it refers to the respect owed to specific people as well as to the general requirement of mutual regard for the dignity of others. The Fifth Commandment (Exod. 20:12; Deut. 5:16) is to "honor" your father and mother (see parents). One is also enjoined to honor scholars and the aged (Lev. 19:32). With the accent on the first syllable of the word (Yiddish pronunciation), *kavod* has the connotation of "paying respects," especially to the leader of an organization or community or to a person who has successfully accomplished some valuable task.

Kavod ha-met. Literally "honor for the dead," this requirement to show reverence for the human body after death is the basis for all Jewish burial customs, such as prompt burial, ritual cleansing of the body (see *tahara*) and the use of a *shomer* to keep watch over the body until the funeral. It is the opposite of *nivul ha-met* (desecration of the corpse). (See also *kallut rosh*.)

Kavod ha-tzibbur. Literally meaning "honor of the community," this Hebrew phrase is the basis of the controversial issue of whether a woman who is not required to fulfill a certain commandment, but assumes it as her duty (such as reading the Torah), can perform it on behalf of men. Except for a few recent opinions, the traditional consensus has been that women may not discharge men's obligations for *mitzvot* they have taken upon themselves, because they are fulfilling them voluntarily rather than as a Divinely mandated responsibility. According to the concept of *kavod ha-tzibbur*, having a woman perform a *mitzvah* for men would cast doubt on the education and piety of the male members of the congregation, putting them to shame by implying that none was capable of performing this function. Nevertheless, in non-Orthodox synagogues, women are permitted to read from the Torah and lead prayer services.

Kazatske. Famous Russian Cossack dance in which one squats and alternately kicks each leg out.

Kedoshim. The 7th *parashah* in the Book of Leviticus (19:1-20:27) and the center of the Torah, it contains numerous commandments predicated on the concept that the Israelites "shall be holy because I, the Lord your God, am holy."

Kedushah (1). A Hebrew word meaning "holiness" or "sanctification," it refers to the proclamation of God's holiness and glory in the third blessing that is recited during the repetition of the *Amidah* when a *minyan* is present. Although there are different forms of the prayer depending on the service at which it is included, the nucleus of the *Kedushah* consists of three biblical verses – *Kadosh, Kadosh, Kadosh* ("Holy, holy, holy [is the Lord of hosts; the whole world is full of His glory]"; Isa. 6:3), which is taken from the prophet's vision of the angels surrounding the Divine throne and proclaiming the holiness of God; "Blessed is the glory of the Lord from His place," from Ezekiel's vision of Heaven (3:12) in which the rushing winds carry the angelic praise of God; and "The Lord shall reign forever, Your God, O Zion, from generation to generation, Hallelujah" (Ps.146:10), which was declaimed by human beings and not by angels, but was considered to be a fitting climax for the proclamation of God's holiness and eternal sovereignty. The mystics who developed this prayer during the rabbinic period in Babylonia then provided appropriate introductions and connecting sentences for these three verses in an effort to recapture the spirit and ecstasy reflected in their biblical contexts.

Kedushah (2) – see Holiness.

Kedushat ha-Shem. Literally "holiness of the Name [of God]," the 3rd blessing of the *Amidah*.

Kehilla. Ashkenazic community structure, developed in the Middle Ages, which was based strictly on "tradition" (i.e., Torah as interpreted by the rabbis). The *kehilla* was a paradigmatic insular community that had minimal interaction with the outside world, except for the *stadlan* who served as the official "ambassador" to the non-Jewish population. Granted a charter by the civil authorities, the *kehilla* was responsible for keeping order and providing taxes through its officials and the regulations they imposed. It had the power to impose *cherem* (shunning) that would subject an offender and his family to economic and social isolation as punishment for refusing to obey rabbinic authority. Except for the position of rabbi, which was open to even a poor boy with a superb mind who could marry into the oligarchic leadership of the community, the *kehilla* system prevented all other possibilities for upward mobility, leading to stagnation and an oppressive society. Especially burdensome was the arbitrary and often-inequitable taxation faced by Jews in the *kehilla*. With the development of nation-states and Jews becoming subject to their laws, the *kehilla* was no longer granted autonomy within the larger community and thus lost its civil authority and its reason for existence.

Kelai ha-kerem. Biblical prohibition against sowing a field with a mixture of different kinds of seeds, such as grain or vegetables in a grape vineyard (Deut. 22:9). According to Maimonides, this commandment was in opposition to the heathen custom of sowing barley and grape seeds together in the belief that this was the only way that the vineyard would thrive. If a Jew followed this practice, both the barley and the produce of the vineyard would be burned.

Kelim (Kel.). The 1st tractate in Tohorot (purity) in the Mishnah, it deals with the laws of the ritual purity of utensils.

Kemach. Literally "flour," this Hebrew word served as a metaphor for a person's earnings that provide sufficient funds for his bodily needs, which are essential for the more important task of study. A popular song derived from *Pirkei Avot* recognizes the interrelation of the physical and spiritual aspects of life, observing that "without flour, there is no Torah; without Torah, there is no flour" (3:21).

Keren Hayesod (Palestine Foundation Fund). The financial arm of the World Zionist Organization with its head office in Jerusalem, Keren Hayesod coordinates operations in countries outside the United States, including the State of Israel. In addition to establishing and developing more than 800 villages and towns in Israel, funds collected through Keren Hayesod have helped to finance such important enterprises as the General Mortgage Bank, Israel Land Development Corporation, Mekorot Water Company, Rassco (Rural and Suburban Settlement Company), Solel Boneh (the Histadrut's building and contracting company), the Palestine (Israel) Electric Corporation, the Palestine Potash Works (Dead Sea Works), the Anglo-Palestine Bank (now Bank Leumi), Amidar Housing Corporation, Zim Navigation Company, and El Al Airlines. In the early 1990s, Keren Hayesod achieved unprecedented results from its fund-raising campaigns to support the massive exodus of Russian Jews to Israel and the dramatic rescue of Ethiopian Jews in Operation Solomon.

Keren Kayemet Le-Yisrael – see Jewish National Fund.

Keri and ketiv. Literally "reading and writing," the Hebrew phrase for the notation system used by the Masoretes to correct spelling errors in the scroll that were regarded as deviations from the original biblical text and could occasionally alter its meaning. Believing that the Torah had been dictated by God, the Masoretes left the original text intact, but indicated in the margin how the word should be properly spelled. According to Jewish law, the Torah reader must follow the *keri*, not the *ketiv*, when reading the Torah; thus it is necessary to study the masoretic notes in printed texts before reading from the scroll.

Keriah. Ritual tearing of a garment as a sign of grief, which is a traditional Jewish mourning custom. It is performed before the funeral of one of the seven relatives for whom mourning is decreed – father, mother, child (at least 30 days old), brother, sister, husband, wife. A rent of at least four inches long is made in the lapel of an outer garment. Among non-Orthodox Jews, it is common to cut and tear a black ribbon, which is pinned to a garment of the mourner as a substitute for destroying the garment itself. According to the Talmud, *keriah* should be done at the moment of death, but today the general practice is to defer *keriah* until just before the funeral service or burial.

Keri'at ha-Torah – See Torah reading.

Keritot (Ker.). The 7th tractate of Kodashim (holy things) in the Mishnah, it deals with the biblical punishment of *karet* and lists the offenses to which it was applied.

Keter (crown). In Kabbalah, the transition between *Ein Sof* and the *sefirot* (Divine emanations). *Keter* is the attribute of Divine Will, the beginning of the unfolding of God's personality. In the mystical telling of this unfolding, a point (*nikudah*) shoots forth from *Keter* and this becomes *Chochma* (Divine Knowledge), the seed for the rest of the *sefirot*.

Keter malchut (crown of royalty). Another term for *Keter* and the mark of Divine sovereignty, which is recognized by angels and human beings by "crowning" God with praise.

Keter Torah. Large silver crown (*keter*), which fits completely over the two wooden rollers (see *atzei chaim*) to which the Torah scroll is affixed and is frequently encircled with silver bells. Originally, the crown may have been used only on special occasions, such as when the scroll was officially consecrated and on Simchat Torah.[141] The *keter Torah* is a reminder of the sovereignty of God.

Keter yitnu. Literally "A crown shall be ascribed to you [the heavenly angels above, with Your people Israel assembled beneath]," the opening words of the *Kedushah* in the third blessing during the repetition of the *Amidah* in the *Musaf* (additional) service for Sabbath and festivals according to the Sephardic, Yemenite, and most Hasidic traditions.

Ketiv – see *Keri* and *ketiv*.

Ketsele. Literally "little cat" or "kitten," a Yiddish diminutive term of endearment.

Ketubah. Literally meaning "written document," it is the Jewish marriage contract. Written in Aramaic, it stipulates the obligations of the husband toward his wife, including his duty to "maintain, honor, and support her as it is fitting for a Jewish husband to do." The *ketubah* sets forth in detail the financial obligations that a husband undertakes toward his wife as to her inheritance should he die, or as to her alimony should he divorce her. If either of these events occurred, the woman would have money and resources of her own and not become destitute without any financial support. Today, a standardized *ketubah* is read before the bridegroom and two witnesses and signed by them. Just as the bridegroom is forbidden to cohabit with his bride after marriage unless he has written and delivered the *ketubah* to her, so the husband is forbidden to live with his wife for even one hour if she no longer has it in her possession. Therefore, if the *ketubah* is lost or destroyed, the husband is obliged to write a new one with the same terms as in the original. From the Middle Ages to the present day, the *ketubah* has often been a work of art, with the calligraphic text decorated with an illuminated border and prized for generations as a family heirloom. In recent decades, egalitarian *ketubot* have been written omitting traditional legal and financial terms and specifying mutual obligations.

Ketubot (Ket.). The 2nd tractate in Nashim (women) in the Mishnah, it deals with the mutual rights between husband and wife as detailed in the marriage contract (*ketubah*).

Ketuvim – see Writings.

Keva. Literally meaning "fixed," this Hebrew word refers to the fixed structure of individual prayers and their order in the service. The inherent tension between *keva* and *kavanah* (proper intention) must be balanced, since both are essential requirements for prayer.

Kever avot (grave of the fathers). This Hebrew term refers to the custom of visiting the graves of parents and close relatives and praying there, both for the peaceful eternal rest of the deceased and for Divine aid to the living based on the pious deeds performed by their ancestors. So as not to encourage the practice of praying to the deceased, it was limited to special occasions such as anniversary of the death (see *yahrzeit*). The Talmud relates the tradition of visiting the graves of saintly individuals so that "the departed will intercede for mercy on behalf of the living" (Taan. 16a).

Kevutzah. Hebrew term for the first collective settlement in the modern Land of Israel, Degania Aleph, which was founded by a group of pioneers in 1909. Within a decade, 29 *kevutzot* had been established on land purchased by the Jewish National Fund under the responsibility of the Zionist Organization.The early *kevutzot* had limited memberships based upon the idea that the community should be small enough to constitute a kind of enlarged family. However, as the number of immigrants rose after World War I, larger, self-sufficient villages were established that combined agricultural pursuits with industrial enterprises to increase employment opportunities, lessen the dependence of the settlements on the cities, and raise the standard of living (see *kibbutz*).

Keyn ayen horeh. Yiddish phrase meaning "without the Evil Eye," often shortened to "*keynahora*" or "*kinehora*," which is used to temper any praise and ward off bad luck.

Khazars. Semi-nomadic Turkish tribe from Central Asia. At some point in the 8th century, the Khazar royalty and nobility converted to Judaism. Part of the general population followed, and Judaism became the state religion. *The Kuzari,* a philosophical work written by Judah Halevi in the 12th century, depicts an imaginary discussion at the court of the Khazar king in which a philosopher, a Christian, a Muslim, and a Jew present reasons for the superiority of their beliefs. Upon hearing of the many miracles that God had performed for the Israelites throughout their history, including the Exodus from Egypt and the Revelation on Mount Sinai, the Khazar king is convinced and converts to Judaism. The power of the Khazars declined in the 10th and 11th centuries, and they disappeared from history following the Mongol invasion of 1237.

Ki anu amecha (For we are Your people). Favorite *piyyut* that is recited at all services on Yom Kippur. In a series of poetic parallels, the close relationship between Israel and God is analogized to that between children and parents, servants and masters, sheep and shepherd, vineyards and their keepers, and lover and beloved. Although based on a midrash that interprets the verse the verse from Song of Songs (6:3), "I am my beloved's and my beloved is mine" (see *ani le-dodi ve-dodi li*), as a love poem describing the intimate relationship between God and Israel, the *piyyut* quickly departs from this idyllic description by contrasting the stark difference between humanity and the Divine. It notes that we are "arrogant, stubborn, laden with sin, and ethereal as a passing shadow," whereas God is "gracious and merciful, patient, abounding in compassion, and eternal."[142]

Ki hinei ka-chomer (Behold, like clay). Prayer for the evening service on Yom Kippur. This *piyyut* by an unknown author is based on the verse from Jeremiah (18:6): "Just like clay in the hands of the potter, so are you in My hands, O House of Israel," implying that God has the power to mold, create, or destroy the Jewish people. In succeeding stanzas, God is compared to various craftsmen (masons, smiths, glassblowers, weavers, and smelters) and human beings are likened to the materials that they use (stone, iron, glass, cloth, and silver, respectively). The poet implores God to use us for creative, not destructive, purposes. Each couplet ends with the plea, "Recall Your covenant and do not regard our [evil] inclination," a direct reference to the Thirteen Attributes of Mercy.[143]

Ki Lo Na'eh (For to Him praise is proper). Song in alphabetical acrostic form with a tongue-twisting refrain, which is sung at the end of the Passover seder in the Ashkenazic tradition.

Ki Tavo. The 7th *parashah* in the Book of Deuteronomy (26:1-29:8), it describes the ceremony of offering the first fruits, reminds the Israelites of their covenantal duties, orders ceremonies to mark the arrival of the Israelites in the Promised Land, and details the blessing for obeying the commandments and the extensive list of curses for failing to fulfill them (see *Tochachah*).

Ki Teitzei. The 6th *parashah* in the Book of Deuteronomy (21:10-25:19), it contains a variety of laws ranging from fair treatment of slaves and laborers, as well as strangers, widows, and orphans, to the punishment of the rebellious son, the prompt burial of an executed criminal and payment of vows, levirate marriage, honest weights and measures, laws preventing cruelty to animals and the prohibitions of adultery, prostitution, and lending at interest.It closes with the command to "remember what Amalek did to you" and to "blot out the memory of Amalek from under heaven."

Ki Tissa. The 8th *parashah* in the Book of Exodus (30:11-34:35), it continues the instructions for the building of the Tabernacle and the Divine service and notes the appointment of Bezalel as chief architect of the Tabernacle and Oholiab as his assistant. The bulk of this *parashah* deals with the apostasy of the Golden Calf, which resulted in Moses angrily smashing the first stone tablets of the Ten Commandments; the successful efforts of Moses to appease God's wrath; Moses' second ascent of Mount Sinai; and his return bearing the second set of tablets.

Kibbitz. From the German name for a lapwing plover, a bird reputed to be especially inquisitive and noisy, this Yiddish term means to give unsolicited, unwanted, but good-natured advice (classically describing the actions of someone watching a card game) or to make jokes or wisecracks while others are trying to work or be serious.

Kibbush avodah. Literally "conquest of labor," the Hebrew slogan and program adopted by the early 20th-century pioneers in the Land of Israel. It called for a return of Jews to manual and agricultural work rather than trades and professions, as well as the preference of Jewish workers over Arab laborers in Jewish farms and industries in Palestine. This emphasis on Jewish labor was a central tenet of the Hashomer and Histradrut movements.

Kibbutz. Voluntary collective community, generally of an agricultural nature, established by pioneering Zionist youth devoted to building the Jewish National Home and creating a basis for the socialist society of the future. The *kibbutz* represented a unique community dedicated to mutual aid and social justice – a socioeconomic system based on the principle of joint ownership of property, with equality and cooperation of production, consumption, and education, so as to fulfill the ideal of "from each according to his ability, to each according to his needs." A true participatory democracy, the general assembly of all its members formulates policy, elects officers, authorizes the budget, and approves new members, as well as offering a forum where all members may express their views. Originally, meals were eaten communally and children often slept apart from their parents in special houses. *Kibbutzim* have played a major role in the economic, political, and cultural life of the country, as well as making vital contributions to the security of the nation. In recent decades, *kibbutzim* have experienced a drop in membership as the appeal of the collectivist ideal and agricultural values has declined.

Kibbutz galuyot (1). Literally meaning "ingathering of the exiles," the return of the Jewish people to the Land of Israel is one component of the longed-for Messianic Age, which would also see the rebuilding of the Temple and the re-establishment of Jewish sovereignty under a descendant of King David. In modern times, *kibbutz galuyot* became a cornerstone of the secular Zionist dream and the political philosophy of the State of Israel.

Kibbutz galuyot (2). The 10th blessing of the weekday *Amidah*, it asks God to "sound the great *shofar* for our freedom and raise the banner to gather our exiles together from the four corners of the earth."

Kibbutznik. Yiddish term for a person who currently lives on a *kibbutz* or was born or raised on one.

Kichel. Yiddish term for an egg cookie. Made of unsweetened dough with a sprinkling of sugar, it is often eaten at Jewish celebrations with a glass of wine or *schnapps*.

Kiddush (sanctification). Prayer recited over a cup of wine in the home and the synagogue to consecrate the Sabbath or a festival. The Friday evening *Kiddush* begins with an introductory biblical paragraph (*va-yechulu ha-shamayim*) describing the seventh day of Creation (Gen. 2:1-3). This is preceded by the words *yom ha-shishi* (the sixth day), the last two words of the preceding verse (Gen. 1:31), so that the first four letters spell out *YHVH* (the Tetragrammaton). The blessing over the wine (*borei peri ha-gafen*) is then recited, followed by the blessing for the sanctification of the day. Concluding with "Blessed are You, O Lord, Who hallows the Sabbath," the core of this longer blessing refers to both the Creation of the world and the Exodus from Egypt. On festivals falling on weekdays, the introductory Scriptural passage is omitted; all that is recited are the blessings over wine and for the sanctification of the day, which ends "Who hallows Israel and the festive seasons." In modern times, the Saturday morning *Kiddush*, which follows the prayer service, has assumed new importance and serves as a communal social hour.

Kiddush, Great. Exaggerated title for the minor *Kiddush* recited before the noon meal on the Sabbath or a festival. Essentially only the customary blessing over wine, to provide more substance some have added an appropriate scriptural verse before the blessing. For the Sabbath, one says: "Therefore the Lord blessed the Sabbath day and hallowed it" (Exod. 20:11). For festivals, the additional verse is: "So Moses declared to the Israelites the set times of the Lord" (Lev. 23:44). Some further enhance the stature of the Great *Kiddush* on the Sabbath by adding the prayer *Ve-Shamru*. Strong drink other than wine may be used for this *Kiddush*, for which the name "great" may originally have referred to the amount of drink rather than the length of the prayer.[144]

Kiddush ha-Shem. Literally "sanctification of the Name [of God]," this command was originally addressed to the priesthood, obligating them to fulfill their duties to God as guardians of the Sanctuary (Lev. 22:32). The requirement to sanctify God's Name was later extended to the entire Jewish people, who were to be "a kingdom of priests and a holy nation" (Exod. 19:6). All Jews, great or small, have the privilege and responsibility of sanctifying the Name of God through their behavior (whether among Jews or gentiles) – by studying Torah and performing the commandments, and by treating others kindly, considerately, and honestly – for people inevitably judge Judaism by the conduct of Jews. The ultimate expression of *Kiddush ha-Shem* is martyrdom, giving up one's life rather than desecrate the Name of God (see *Chillul ha-Shem*). Notable examples of martyrdom for *Kiddush ha-Shem* occurred in the period of Roman persecution following the destruction of the Second Temple, during the Crusades, and at the time of the Chmielnicki massacres of Polish and Ukrainian Jewry in the 17th century.

Kiddush Levanah (Sanctification of the moon). Prayer of thanksgiving recited at the monthly reappearance of the crescent moon. The moon symbolizes the regenerative capacity of the Jewish people, for just as it remains in the skies even though temporarily absent from our view, so the throne of David will eventually reappear with the coming of the Messiah. As a ceremony stressing God as the Creator and Israel's rebirth, *Kiddush Levanah* should be recited joyously, preferably at the conclusion of the Sabbath. Ideally, it should be said with a *minyan* under the open sky, when the moon is clearly visible and not hidden by clouds. It is customary to delay recitation of *Kiddush Levanah* until after Tisha b'Av (9th of Av) and Yom Kippur (10th of Tishrei), because the gloom of Av and the trepidation associated with the Day of Judgment (Rosh Hashanah) and the Day of Atonement are not conducive to the requisite joy.

Kiddushin (1). Although this Aramaic term is often translated as "betrothal," it does not correspond to the modern conception of the word. Instead, *kiddushin* creates a special legal and personal relationship between a man and woman before the actual marriage that can be dissolved only by divorce or the death of either party. During *kiddushin*, cohabitation between the couple is strictly prohibited and the formal duties between husband and wife are not yet incumbent upon them. The prospective bridegroom is not liable for the maintenance of his future bride, and she has no *ketubah*. *Kiddushin* is accomplished by the bridegroom transferring to the bride something with a value of at least one *perutah* (the lowest coin). Today, this is usually an unadorned ring (see wedding ring).

Kiddushin (Kid.) (2). The 7th tractate in Nashim (women) in the Mishnah, it deals with the laws of betrothal and marriage (including prohibited marriages).

Kidnapping. According to the Talmud, the eighth of the Ten Commandments (Exod. 20:13) applies specifically to only one kind of thief – a kidnapper who forced his victim to work for him and then sold him into slavery. Because the two prohibitions in the Ten Commandments that precede it are against the capital offenses of murder and adultery, the Rabbis reasoned that "you shall not steal" must refer to kidnapping, the only theft for which the perpetrator was liable to the death penalty.[145]

Kidron. Valley northeast of the Old City of Jerusalem that separates it from the Mount of Olives.It contains three major tombs: Yad Avshalom (Absalom, the rebellious son of King David); the tomb of the prophet Zechariah; and the tomb of members of the Hezir family, who had served as priests in the Temple and were buried in the rock-hewn tomb below.

Kilayim (1). Literally "mixed species," this Hebrew term refers to various combinations of "mutually exclusive kinds" that are prohibited by the Torah in the verse, "You shall not let your cattle mate with a different kind [animal]; you shall not sow your field with two kinds of seeds; and you shall not wear garments made of a mixture of two kinds of materials [fibers]" (Lev. 19:19). (See *sha'atnez* and *kelai ha-kerem*.) One possible explanation for the prohibition against *kilayim* is the often-repeated statement of God's having created each species "according to its kind" (Gen. 1), suggesting that mixing species is thus a sin against the Divinely ordered pattern of Creation.

Kilayim (Kil.) (2). The 4th tractate in Zera'im (seeds) in the Mishnah, it deals with prohibitions against "diverse kinds" – crossbreeding and mingling of varied species of plants, animals, and clothing. (See *sha'atnez* and *kelai ha-kerem*.)

Killing – see Murder.

Kindling of lights – see Candlelighting and Candles.

King. Throughout the ancient Near East, the king was viewed as a divine or semi-divine being. Often an object of worship and a lawgiver whose authority derived from the gods, the king combined secular rule with priestly rights and duties. He was considered essential to the fertility of the land and the welfare of the society. In contrast, the Bible pictures a king who is neither divine nor sacred. Rather than being responsible for executing justice, the king was just as subject to God's law as any Israelite. When seated on his royal throne, the king kept a copy of the Law so that he might be faithful to the Divine commands and not act haughtily toward his subjects (Deut. 17:18-20). The Israelite king was to be a limited monarch, explicitly restricted from having too many wives (i.e., foreign spouses who would "turn his heart astray" toward their idolatrous practices) or amassing great personal wealth (Deut. 17:16-17). Despite these admonitions, King Solomon felt no qualms about violating these restrictions on royal privilege because he was certain that his incomparable wisdom would protect him from the consequences indicated in the biblical verses. However, Solomon was mistaken. His foreign wives led the people to idol worship, and the heavy taxes he imposed led to a split of the kingdom after his death. The Torah rejected any combination of royal and priestly roles in Israel, describing the Divine punishment imposed on King Uzziah for attempting to do so (2 Chron. 26:16-20).

Kingdom of Heaven. Eschatological concept, found in the late books of Chronicles and Daniel, of a future state of worldly perfection and peace in which God will intervene to restore the nation of Israel to its own land and return to rule over them forever through a descendant of the House of David, the Messiah.

Kings. The 5th and 6th books of the Prophets section of the Bible. They relate the history of the Kingdoms of Israel and Judah during the more than 400-year period from the death of David through the fall of Jerusalem, the destruction of the Temple, and the liberation of King Jehoiachin of Judah in the 37th year of the Babylonian Exile. Key sections in Kings are the narratives concerning the prophets Elijah and Elisha. These books seek to explain the fall of the Kingdoms of Israel and Judah and the destruction of the First Temple through the traditional theology of Divine reward and punishment. Thus these national disasters could serve a positive purpose if they renewed the fidelity of the Jewish people to the covenant with God.

Kings of Israel. The first three kings of Israel were Saul (11th century B.C.E), David (c. 1000-960), and Solomon (c. 960-931). After the death of Solomon, the 10 northern tribes revolted and established the Northern Kingdom of Israel.The remaining two tribes remained loyal to the son of Solomon (Rehoboam) and formed the Southern Kingdom of Judah.Israel fell to the Assyrians in 721 B.C.E.; Judah survived until 586 B.C.E., when the Babylonians captured Jerusalem and destroyed the First Temple.

Kinneret. From a root meaning lyre or violin, the Hebrew name for the Sea of Galilee, a harp-shaped, fresh-water lake about 13 miles long and seven and a half miles wide at its broadest point. Surrounded by the hills of Galilee and the Golan in northern Israel, the *Kinneret* is about 700 feet below sea level and is filled from the north by the Jordan River. A rich fishing ground, the Sea of Galilee is encircled by such towns and villages as Tiberias, Capernaum, Migdal, Ginossar, and En Gev. Israel's victory over Syria in the Six Day War, followed by its occupation of the Golan Heights, moved the border with Syria away from the *Kinneret*, where Israeli fishermen had suffered from Syrian harassment.

Kinnim (**Kin**.). Literally "birds' nests," this 11th tractate of Kodashim (holy things) in the Mishnah deals with bird offerings.

Kinot (lamentations). Medieval dirges, recited on Tisha b'Av, which recount and bemoan the destruction of the Temple and the sins of the Jewish people. The term also applies to elegies recited at funerals and on other days of mourning in biblical and talmudic times.

Kinyan (acquisition). In ancient Israel, trade agreements that are now frequently sealed by a handshake were instead confirmed by passing a piece of cloth from seller to buyer. Today, this "acquisition" of a woman is symbolized among traditional Jews by the handkerchief ceremony before the wedding. One of the witnesses represents the bride and holds up a handkerchief. The bridegroom takes hold of the handkerchief and raises it, thus formally completing the "transaction" and indicating his agreement to fulfill the obligations of the *ketubah* (marriage document).[146] The witnesses then sign the marriage document; in many communities, including the State of Israel, the groom also signs.

Kippah. Head covering worn by Jews in modern times. Also known by its Yiddish equivalent *yarmulke* (skullcap), it has become a universally recognized symbol of Jewish identity. There is no explicit biblical commandment to cover one's head for prayer or other religious functions. In ancient Rome, free men went bareheaded, and the wearing of a head covering stigmatized a person as a servant. To stress that they were loyal servants of the Lord, Jews adopted the practice of covering their heads in a House of God, while reciting prayers, and during any activity when blessings including the Divine name were said (such as eating). Eventually, Jews began to cover their heads at all times to demonstrate their awesome respect for God.[147] Others wear *kippot* only on formal religious occasions, primarily at synagogue services and while studying Torah. *Kippot* come in various materials and weaves, from simple cloth to satin, velvet, crochet, and leather. The style of head covering often provides a clue as to the type of religious observance of the wearer – from the stringent "black hat" of the ultra-Orthodox to the knitted *kippah* of the modern Orthodox. The early Reform movement virtually eliminated the practice of covering the head during services, but now the wearing of a *kippah*, though considered optional, is increasingly encouraged.[148] (See also *head covering, women.*)

Kiryat Shmona. Literally meaning "Town of the Eight," the name of this Upper Galilee community refers to Joseph Trumpeldor and his seven comrades who died at nearby Tel Hai defending the settlement from Arab attackers in 1920. Founded in 1950, Kiryat Shmona currently has a population of about 20,000.

Kishka. Also known as "stuffed derma," this Yiddish term refers to a mixture of ground meat or vegetables, flour, and spices stuffed into intestine casing and baked. The plural, *kishkes*, is a slang term for "belly" or "innards."

Kishon. River in northern Israel that arises on Mount Tabor and flows across the Jezreel Valley before entering the Mediterranean Sea just north of Haifa. In the Song of Deborah, the "torrent Kishon" is praised for having swept away the Canaanite forces (Judg. 5:21). On its shore, Elijah slew the priests of Baal (1 Kings 18:40).

Kislev. The 9th month of the Jewish calendar (November-December). The first day of Chanukah falls on the 25th of Kislev.

Kissing holy objects. This widespread custom, though not a religious duty, expresses a depth of reverence and spiritual devotion. The two ends of the *atarah* of the *tallit* are kissed just before putting on the prayer shawl. *Tefillin* are kissed when taken out or returned to their bag. The *tzitzit* (fringes) are kissed at the end of *Baruch she-Amar* and during the recitation of the final portion of the *Shema*. The curtain on the ark (see *parochet*) is kissed before it is opened and after it is closed (i.e., when the Torah is taken out and then returned), and the Torah mantle is kissed when it passes by in procession in the synagogue. The Torah scroll is kissed before one recites the blessings over it, either with the intermediary of the edge of a *tallit* or the sash used to tie the scroll together, but never with the bare hand. A *siddur* (prayer book) and *Chumash* (Five Books of Moses) are kissed before putting them away or if they are accidentally dropped on the floor. Finally, the *mezuzah* on the doorpost is kissed when entering or leaving a house.

Kitel. A Yiddish word meaning "gown," it refers to the white garment that once was worn every Sabbath and is now used in some Ashkenazic communities by worshipers on special occasions and as a shroud. The white color, representing purity and forgiveness of sin, makes the *kitel* appropriate for worshipers on the High Holy Days (Rosh Hashanah and Yom Kippur). Among some traditional Jews, a *kitel* is also worn by a groom on his wedding day, by a father at the circumcision of his son, by the person conducting the Passover seder, and by the prayer leader during the solemn prayers for dew on Passover and rain on Shemini Atzeret.

Kitniyot. Group of foods, generally translated as "legumes," that Ashkenazic authorities (but not Sephardim) have forbidden for consumption on Passover. These include beans, peas, corn, lentils, buckwheat, and, according to some authorities, peanuts. One reason for this ruling is to prevent possible confusion if flour made from these substances were stored near *chametz* flour. The question of what constitutes *kitniyot* – and the proper treatment of liquids and oils produced from them – has been the subject of much debate in the rabbinic literature, with most authorities forbidding the use of all derivative products (such as corn syrup to sweeten soft drinks).

Klaf. Hebrew word for the parchment on which a *sofer* writes a Torah scroll. The parchment must come from specified sections of the hide of a kosher animal, though not necessarily one that has been slaughtered according to Jewish ritual law. Individual leaves of parchment are sewn together with thread (see *giddim*). The term "*klaf*" also refers to the handwritten scroll, containing the first two paragraphs of the *Shema*, which is rolled up and enclosed in the wood or metal case of the *mezuzah*.

Klal Yisrael. Literally meaning "the whole of Israel," this Hebrew phrase refers to the Jewish people in the context of their social unity, mutual responsibilities, and shared values.

Klezmer. Derived from the Hebrew phrase *k'li zemer* (vessels of song) and initially referring to musical instruments, this Yiddish term now is applied to a lively Eastern European style of instrumental music. It dates back to itinerant musicians who traveled to villages playing a variety of popular folk melodies and dance tunes. Enjoying a revival in the recent past, *klezmer* generally features a clarinet accompanied by a spectrum of other musical instruments. It has an improvisational style and a repertoire largely composed of dances for weddings and other celebrations.

Klipot. Literally "shells" or "husks," in Lurianic Kabbalah this Hebrew term refers to the base material that has trapped the holy sparks of Divine light that were released during the breaking of the vessels at the beginning of time. Through repentance and good deeds, Jews are able to assist God in the elevation of the trapped holy sparks, which eventually will usher in the Messianic Age to complete and perfect the work of Creation.

Klop. Yiddish word meaning "hit" or "smack."

Klutz. Yiddish word for a clumsy or awkward person.

Knaidel (pl., *knaidlach*). Yiddish word for a dumpling made of *matzah* meal, these "*matzah* balls" are often served in chicken soup on the Sabbath and at the Passover seder on Ashkenazic menus.

Knesset. Parliament of the State of Israel. Composed of 120 representatives, Knesset members (MKs) are chosen in nation-wide elections from party lists. Since no party has ever won a majority of seats, a coalition must be formed to govern the country. Regularly scheduled elections are held every four years, but a vote of no confidence approved by a majority of Knesset members (61 votes) can cause the government to fall and precipitate a new election. Israel has the only truly democratic government in the Middle East, with all citizens over the age of 18 having the right to vote. Jews, Arabs, and Druze all serve as members of the Knesset. This law-making body meets in a striking building with mosaics and tapestries by Chagall. Opposite the Knesset is a large menorah, the symbol of the country.

Knesset Gedolah – see Great Assembly.

Knesset Yisrael. Literally "assembly of Israel," a classic rabbinic term for the entire Jewish community. Under the British Mandate's Jewish Community

Regulations of 1927, the *Va'ad Leumi* was required to maintain a register of the Jews in the Land of Israel who were at least 18 years of age and members of "Knesset Yisrael," the official Jewish community that included about 95% of the Jews in the land. The small percentage of Jews who did not belong to Knesset Yisrael was composed almost exclusively of members or supporters of Agudat Yisrael or other ultra-Orthodox elements.

Knish. Yiddish word for a small baked savory pastry, classically filled with mashed potato. Other popular fillings include meat, spinach, and kasha.

Knocker. Yiddish term for a "big shot" or "show-off."

Knocking on wood. This superstition to protect one from evil is a completely non-Jewish practice, even though many Jews do it. Some connect this action to Christian belief, relating wood to slivers of the cross that were thought to bring good luck. However, this practice has a more universal, pantheistic origin. Long before the time of Jesus, cultures regarded trees as gods, with believers convinced that touching (or knocking on) wood could produce magical results.

Ko'ach. A Hebrew word meaning "strength," it is most commonly used in the expression *yasher ko'ach* ("may you grow in strength" or "may your strength be directed in the right path"), the customary greeting by fellow congregants in Ashkenazic synagogues to a person returning from having an *aliyah*. This custom may reflect the belief in talmudic times that intense study of the Torah, symbolized by the Torah reading, "weakens the strength of a person" (Sanh. 26b).
Kodashim (holy things). The 5th order of the Mishnah, its 11 tractates are Zevachim, Menahot, Chullin, Bechorot, Arachin, Temurah, Keritot, Me'ilah, Tamid, Midot, and Kinnim.Kodashim deals primarily with the sacrificial cult and Temple activities, *tzitzit* and *tefillin*, and the regulations concerning firstborn children and animals.

Kohelet – see Ecclesiastes.

Kohen. Member of the hereditary priestly caste (*kohanim*) established when the Tabernacle was built. The priests were the descendants of Aaron and exclusively male. They were to be shown honor and deference because they were consecrated to God and offered the sacrifices to the Lord (Lev. 21:8). During biblical times, the *kohanim* performed four sacred functions: (1) serving the cultic center; (2) deciphering signs and messages from God (i.e., revealing God's will, somewhat like a diviner in other traditions); (3) treating defilement (purification) and diseases (resulting from impurities); and (4) dispensing justice and teaching the law. A *kohen* was forbidden to come in contact with a dead body (except for one of his close relatives) and prohibited from marrying a divorced woman. Even after the destruction of the Temple, the Rabbis insisted that those of priestly descent continue to be treated as holy. Today, the custom in traditional synagogues is to give a *kohen* the honor of the first *aliyah* to the Torah. (See also *Priestly Blessing* and *duchaning*.)

Kohen Gadol (High Priest). On Yom Kippur, after conducting the daily cultic rituals dressed in gold-embroidered garments, the *Kohen Gadol* would change to white linen vestments to perform the confessionals and sacrifices of atonement – first for himself and his family, then for the tribe of Aaron (the *kohanim*), and finally for all Israel. Every time the *Kohen Gadol* uttered the Holy Name of God (*YHVH*, the Tetragrammaton), which was spoken only on Yom Kippur, the people prostrated themselves and responded: "Praised is His Name, whose glorious kingdom is forever and ever" (see *Baruch shem kavod*). The *Kohen Gadol* then drew lots to determine which of the two male goats was sent off to the wilderness "for *Azazel*," and which would be sacrificed as "a sin-offering for the Lord." On Yom Kippur, the *Kohen Gadol* went beyond the veil into the Holy of Holies where he made a special incense-offering, the only time it was entered during the year. The *Kohen Gadol* was commanded to marry, but could only wed a virgin.

Kohen Gadol, garments of the. According to the Torah (Exod. 28), the following eight special garments were worn by the High Priest – *ephod*; breastplate; golden head plate (inscribed "Holy to the Lord;" see frontlet, miter (possibly a type of turban), robe (long blue garment adorned with pomegranate-shaped balls and golden bells, worn under the *ephod*); tunic; girdle (sash); and breeches.

Kol ha-kavod. Literally meaning "all the honor," this Hebrew phrase is used idiomatically to express praise or congratulations for an achievement.

Kol isha. Literally meaning "voice of a woman," this Hebrew term was used in the context of the prohibition against men hearing a woman singing, which was deemed too provocative for male worshipers. This traditionally precluded the possibility of a woman leading the congregation in prayer. Today, however, the Conservative, Reform, and Reconstructionist movements have accepted women as cantors.

Kol Nidre*i* (All vows). Opening words of the declaration of the annulment of vows that begins the evening service on Yom Kippur. The Aramaic words, chanted by the *hazzan* in a dramatic and beloved melody, proclaim that all personal vows, oaths, and promises made to God unwittingly, rashly, or unknowingly – and which cannot be fulfilled – be considered null and void. Early rabbis criticized *Kol Nidrei* as an invalid practice that made light of vows. This primarily related to the initially accepted version of the prayer, which invoked Divine pardon, forgiveness, and atonement for those sins "from the *previous* Yom Kippur until *this* Yom Kippur" (i.e., the *past* year). In the 12th century, Rabbenu Tam reworded this phrase to read "from *this* Yom Kippur until the *next* Yom Kippur" (i.e., the *coming* year). Ashkenazim have adopted this formulation of Rabbenu Tam, while Sephardim generally accept the earlier version. *Kol Nidrei* assumed special significance during the time of the Spanish Inquisition, when Jews at pain of death were forced to give up their faith and convert to Catholicism. For the many Jews who continued to practice their religion in secret, *Kol Nidrei* provided a welcome opportunity for solemnly renouncing those vows they had made under duress.[149] Anti-Semites often pointed to *Kol Nidrei* as evidence that Jews could not be trusted and their oaths meaningless. To combat this, rabbis took great pains to stress that the *Kol Nidrei* formulation relates to vows and promises *only* to God and was never meant to apply to oaths taken before secular courts of law.

Kol tuv. Literally meaning "all good," a Hebrew expression of good wishes.

Kolel. Institute of advanced talmudic studies for married students (the term "*yeshiva*" has traditionally been applied to similar centers for students who are not married).

Korach. The 5th *parashah* in the Book of Numbers (16:1-18:32), it details the rebellions of Korach and of Dathan and Abiram and their 250 cohorts against Moses and Aaron, which resulted in their being swallowed up by the earth and consumed by Divine fire, respectively. In Jewish tradition, Korach is seen as the prototypical demagogue who lusts for power and is concerned only about himself, rather than service to the people.

Korban. Often translated as "offering" (see sacrifices), it derives from a Hebrew root meaning "to come close," implying that by giving a gift to God we draw nearer to the Divine Presence. This is a striking contrast to contemporaneous pagan religions, in which sacrifices were offered to nourish or bribe their gods.

Korech – see Hillel sandwich.

Kosher. In addition to denoting food that Jews are permitted to eat (see *kashrut*), the term can be used to indicate the ritual fitness of an object used in a Jewish observance (e.g., Torah scroll, *tefillin*, *shofar*).

Kosher for Passover. Certification on processed, packaged food indicating that the product contains no *chametz* and thus may be consumed on Passover.

Kotel. Literally meaning "wall" and short for *Kotel ha-Ma'arivi* (Western Wall), it is part of the Herodian retaining wall surrounding and supporting the Temple Mount. It was formerly called the "Wailing Wall" by European observers, because for centuries Jews came here to bewail the loss of their Temple. The holiest of Jewish sites, the Western Wall is a major venue for prayers day and night. Many of the faithful place private petitions on bits of paper stuffed into the cracks of the massive yellow-white stone blocks.

Krechtz. From a German word meaning "to croak or caw," this Yiddish term means to grunt or groan from some minor pain or discomfort, or to fuss and complain with associated sound effects.

Krenk (kraink). Yiddish term for an illness.

Kreplach. Triangular or square pockets of boiled noodle dough, filled with chopped meat, vegetables, or cheese. They are often served in soup and are variations of Italian ravioli or Chinese wonton.

Kristallnacht. Literally "night of [broken] glass," the Nazi government-sponsored pogrom that occurred all over Germany and Austria on November 9-10, 1938. Nazi-led mobs looted some 7,500 businesses and destroyed about 200 synagogues. Torah scrolls and prayer books were burned, and more than 100 Jews were murdered. The authorities arrested 30,000 Jewish males and sent them to concentration camps. The *Kristallnacht* pogrom marked a crucial milestone in the Nazis' actions against the Jews, an escalation of violence that culminated in the Holocaust.In the wake of *Kristallnacht*, the Jews of Germany and Austria realized that they had to flee, but very few countries in the world would give them sanctuary.

Kubutz – see Vowels.

Kuf. The 19th letter of the Hebrew alphabet (pronounced 'koof'), with a numerical value of 100.

Kugel. Traditional Jewish side dish or dessert for the Sabbath and festivals. A baked pudding, commonly with a noodle or potato base, it can be sweet or savory and made with countless variations.

Kumsitz. Informal sing-along, often related to a camp experience. Derived from the Yiddish "come and sit," it encourages a sense of community and belonging.

Kuppah (charity box). Institutions for providing charitable assistance developed at an early period in medieval Jewish communities. The major method of relief was the donation of money through the *kuppah*. Coins were placed in boxes in private homes, in the synagogue just before the start of major festivals (including gifts to the poor on Purim), and even in the cemetery. This practice continues today, with various charities supplying boxes for money to support their organizations. One of the most famous has been the "Blue Box" of the Jewish National Fund.

Kupat Holim. The first health insurance institution in Israel. Founded in 1911 by a small group of agricultural workers, it was taken over in 1920 by the Histadrut.The largest countrywide fund, which insures more than 70% of the population, Kupat Holim covers workers in town and country, manual laborers and professionals, salaried and self-employed, Israeli-born veterans and new immigrants, all on a basis of mutual aid. Kupat Holim operates its own clinics and hospitals, laboratories, pharmacies, and convalescent homes.

Kutim. Minor tractate added to the Talmud that deals with laws regarding the Samaritans. This term also was used generically to denote any person or group that rejected the Oral Law.

Kvater and **kvaterin**. Polish-Yiddish corruptions of German words meaning "godfather" and "godmother," respectively. As a prelude to the circumcision ritual, the *kvaterin* takes the child from his mother and carries him into the room in which the circumcision is to be performed. This intermediate step is required because the father is not permitted to take the child directly from the mother, who is still in a state of ritual impurity from childbirth.

Kvell. Yiddish word meaning to beam (literally "gush") with pride or pleasure, especially over the accomplishments of one's children or grandchildren.

Kvetch. Yiddish word meaning to complain, usually about some relatively minor issue. It also can be used as a noun to describe one who gripes or frets about everything.

L

L'chaim. Literally meaning "to life" in Hebrew, a popular Jewish toast said over wine or liquor.

L'hitraot. Modern Hebrew word of farewell meaning "see you again."

Labor. Both the Bible and the Talmud stress the physical and moral value of physical labor. Even esteemed Rabbis participated in menial tasks, rejecting the belief that certain types of labor were beneath one's dignity, and until the Middle Ages they earned their living from their occupations. Jewish law mandates prompt payment for laborers after they have completed their work, and the biblical rights of the laborer were reinforced in the Talmud. The early Zionist movement exalted the dignity of manual labor in the numerous collective agricultural settlements it established in the Land of Israel.

Labor Party. Center-left party with socialist roots that dominated the political scene in Israel from the establishment of the State (1948) until 1977. Known as Mapai from the initials of its Hebrew name, the Labor Party took a pragmatic rather than ideological approach to socialism. The Labor Party was instrumental in the struggle to establish a Jewish State during the British Mandate. Its best-known member was David Ben Gurion, the first Prime Minister of Israel. Other Labor Party luminaries include Golda Meir, Moshe Dayan, Yitzhak Rabin, and Shimon Peres.

Labor Zionism – see Zionists, labor.

La-bri'ut. Literally "to your health," this is a typical Hebrew response to hearing a person sneeze, like "*gezundheit*" in Yiddish or "bless you" in English.

Lachish. Canaanite city-state southwest of Jerusalem that was conquered by Joshua in about 1230 B.C.E. Later it was the scene of Samson's heroic deeds and David's victory over Goliath. A link in the chain of fortresses built by King Rehoboam to guard the southern approaches to Jerusalem, Lachish was captured by the Assyrians (701 B.C.E.) and destroyed by the Babylonians (588).

Ladino. Judeo-Spanish language that was primarily spoken among Sephardic Jewish communities in Spain, Portugal, Turkey, the Balkans, and Morocco, as well as by Spanish and Portuguese-speaking Jews in Central and South America. Written in Hebrew script, it is a form of 15th-century Castilian Spanish, with many words and phrases borrowed from Hebrew, Arabic, Turkish, and Greek. Ladino is also used as a term for the music and culture of Sephardic Jews.

Lag ba-Omer. 33rd day of the counting of the *omer*, which occurs on the 18th of Iyar. According to tradition, the terrible "plague" that afflicted the students of R. Akiva ceased on Lag ba-Omer, a day of celebration amidst the period of semi-mourning between Passover and Shavuot.Relating Lag ba-Omer to Shimon bar Yochai, the reputed author of the mystical *Zohar*, kabbalists and Hasidim in Israel hold a festive celebration at the sage's grave in the village of Meron, near Safed, studying mystical texts and singing and dancing around bonfires. It also is traditional to eat foods made from carob on this day. Because marriages and cutting one's hair are generally prohibited during the Omer period, on Lag ba-Omer many weddings are performed and it became customary for three-year-old boys to have their first haircut.

Lamed. The 12th letter of the Hebrew alphabet, with a numerical value of 30.

Lamed-vavniks. According to ancient tradition, in every generation there are 36 righteous people (*tzadikim*), unknown to the world and even to themselves, for whose sake the world is sustained. They often are called the "*lamed-vavniks*," since the numerical values of the Hebrew letters *lamed* and *vav* are 30 and 6, respectively.

Lamentations (*Eichah*). The 3rd of the *megillot* and the 6th book in the Writings section of the Bible. It describes the Babylonian destruction of Jerusalem in 586 B.C.E. and the exile of the Jewish people from their land. The Book of Lamentations is recited in a haunting melody on Tisha b'Av.The next-to-last verse – "Turn us back, O Lord, and let us return; renew our days as of old" (5:21) – is repeated by everyone so that the book ends on a hopeful note. This same verse is the final line sung as the ark is closed after the scroll has been returned to it following the Torah reading.

Lamentations Rabbah (Lam. R.). An aggadic midrash on the Book of Lamentations, it contains homiletic interpretations of the text as well as many stories about the destruction of the First Temple.

Land boundaries. The Bible prohibited the stealthy moving of a landmark with the intent to fraudulently enlarge one's property at the expense of a neighbor (Deut. 19:14). Infringing on the property rights of another showed contempt for God's grand design. Just as God apportioned the Promised Land among the Twelve Tribes of Israel, so all individual holdings of land are ultimately Divine gifts that may not be seized covertly or by force.[150] The rabbis extended this commandment to forbid any unfair encroachment on the honor or livelihood of another person. They also applied it to the attributing of the opinion of one person to another.[151] In modern times, this commandment also prohibits copyright and patent violations.[152]

Land of Israel – see *Eretz Yisrael*.

Land of Israel movement. Founded immediately after the stunning victory in the Six Day War, it urged the permanent retention by Israel of Judea and Samaria (West Bank), the Golan Heights, and the Gaza Strip. The Land of Israel movement was supported by political elements of the Left and Right, and its leaders included high-ranking army reserve officers, heads of commerce and industry, university teachers, rabbis, and members of the various *kibbutz* movements. It stressed that the entire area of the Land of Israel, as circumscribed by the cease-fire lines of June 1967, should become the permanent borders of the State. This was justified not only on military and defense grounds, but also because the area had been the historical possession of the Jewish people. They argued that no Israeli government had a mandate for surrendering any part of this inalienable trust, and that these areas should be integrated into the rest of Israel by increased immigration and intensive settlement.

Landsman. Yiddish word for a person whose ancestors came from the same *shtetl* or area in Eastern Europe. It is most commonly used more colloquially to describe a fellow Jew.

Landsmanschaft. Mutual aid society made up of immigrants from the same *shtetl* or area in Eastern Europe who came to the United States in the late 19th and early 20th centuries. It provided members with valuable financial benefits and offered an opportunity to maintain the social relations and traditions of the Old World while adjusting to the chaos of immigrant life. One of the most important functions of the *landsmanshaft* was the purchase of cemetery plots, because having a proper Jewish burial was a critical issue for Jewish immigrants.

Lashon ha-ra. Literally "evil speech" but translated as "gossip," the term refers to any derogatory or damaging statements against an individual (even when the slanderous or defaming remarks are true), which if publicized to others would cause the subject physical or monetary damage, anguish, or fear. The Rabbis cited numerous biblical verses emphasizing the seriousness of the prohibition against *lashon ha-ra*, which they asserted destroys three persons – "he who relates [the slander], he who accepts it, and he about whom it is told" (Ar. 15b). Slander was considered tantamount to murder: "Many have been killed by the sword, but not so many as by the tongue" (Ecclesiasticus 28:18). The most vicious form of slander is false accusations made to a ruling authority. In the 19th century, the Chafetz Chaim (Israel Meir ha-Kohen) gained wide recognition for his writings stressing the gravity of the sin of *lashon ha-ra*.

Lashon kodesh (holy language) – see Hebrew.

Latke (pancake). On Chanukah, latkes (especially the potato variety) serve as a reminder of the miracle of the oil on the Ashkenazic menu.

Lavadores. Sephardic term for members of the communal burial society (see *chevra kadisha*).

Laver. Basin in the Tabernacle and the Temple used by the priests for their ritual ablutions. Today, the vestibule of a traditional synagogue contains a pitcher and washbasin to enable worshipers to pour water over their hands. By physically cleansing themselves, they are reminded of their duty to be pure in conduct: "Who may ascend the mountain of the Lord? Who may stand in His holy place? He, who has clean hands and a pure heart ..." (Ps. 24:3-4).[153] *Kohanim* also wash their hands before giving the Priestly Blessing.

Law codes. Since the Talmud is a huge work without an index, knowing what it says about a given subject effectively requires one to read it completely through. This prohibitive task led some rabbis to prepare extensive summaries of specific legal topics and eventually comprehensive codes. In the Middle Ages, by far the greatest of these legal codes was the *Mishneh Torah* of Maimonides. In this massive 14-volume work, Maimonides discussed every conceivable topic of Jewish law in an impressively logical sequence. The most influential code in modern Jewish life – and the last comprehensive one to be written – is the *Shulchan Aruch* of Yosef Karo.

Law, Jewish. Unlike Anglo-American law, in which issues are framed in terms of *rights*, Jewish law is based on *obligations*. In a system of rights-based law, it is necessary to first determine the rights of each of the involved parties and assess what happens when these rights conflict. In contrast, under Jewish law the decision in each case must fall into one of three basic categories – obligatory (*hovah*), in which one must do something (see *duty*); (b) prohibited (*asur*), in which one is strictly forbidden from doing something; and (c) permitted (see *reshut*), in which one has the option of doing something as long as there is some precedent in Jewish law allowing the action. (See also *halacha*)

Law, Oral – see Oral Law.

Law, reading of the – see Torah reading.

Law, Tablets of the – see *Luchot ha-brit*.

Law, Written – see Written Law.

Law of Return. The first law passed by the Knesset after the establishment of the State of Israel, it guarantees all Jews throughout the world the right to immigrate to Israel and become a citizen of the country. Adopted five years after the Holocaust, when Jews trying to escape the Nazis were denied entry to virtually all countries (including the United States and, because of the British White Paper, even to Palestine), the Law of Return provided a haven for persecuted Jews throughout the Diaspora. A vexing issue has been the question, "Who is a Jew?" A 1970 amendment to the Law of Return defined a Jew as "a person born of a Jewish mother or who has been converted to Judaism and is not a member of another religion."[154] The Chief Rabbinate in Israel has consistently refused to recognize as Jews those who have converted under the auspices of non-Orthodox rabbis. However, according to the Law of Return as interpreted by the Supreme Court of Israel, all converts must be registered as Jews on their identity cards and in the population registry.

Laying on of hands – see *Semichah*.

Leaven – see *Chametz*.

Leaven, search for (*bedikat chametz*) – see *Chametz*, search for.

Lech Lecha. The 3rd *parashah* in the Book of Genesis (12:1-17:27), it opens with the Divine command to Abram to leave his home and journey "to the land that I will show you." It narrates the adventures of Abram and Sarai in Egypt, the Patriarch's rescue of his nephew Lot, the Covenant between the Pieces (in which Abram is promised land and offspring) sealed with the *mitzvah* of circumcision, the birth of Ishmael and his banishment (with his mother, Hagar), and the change of the names of Abram and Sarai to Abraham and Sarah. The term "*Lech lecha*," which literally means "go to yourself," has been interpreted as a command for Jews to search for their authentic selves, similar to the process whereby Abraham discovered that he was a child of the One God who created and governed the world.

Lecha Dodi (Come, my beloved). Poem that is the climax of the *Kabbalat Shabbat*, the set of prayers in which the congregation welcomes the Sabbath before the official Friday evening service. It was composed by Solomon ha-Levi Alkabetz, the best-known liturgical poet of the Safed circle of kabbalists in the early 16th century, whose name (Shlomo ha-Levi) is formed by the initial letters of the first eight stanzas. In the Torah, there are two different versions of the fourth commandment – "remember" and "observe" the Sabbath day to keep it holy (Exod. 20:8; Deut. 5:12). The first stanza of *Lecha Dodi* opens with the talmudic statement that God simultaneously spoke these words to link them forever in the mind of the Jewish people. When reciting the final stanza of *Lecha Dodi* – "Enter in peace …come, O bride" – it is customary to turn around to face the rear of the synagogue (traditionally facing westward in the direction of the setting sun that signals the arrival of the Sabbath), bowing slightly to symbolically welcome the Sabbath Bride.

Lechem oni (bread of affliction) – see *Matzah.*

Lechem panim (bread of the Presence) – see Showbread.

Lechu neranena (Come, let us sing). Opening words of Psalm 95, the first of the six psalms (symbolizing the six weekdays) that begin the *Kabbalat Shabbat* that precedes the official Friday evening service.

Legend – see *Aggada.*

Le-hayim – see *L'chaim.*

Lehi. Hebrew acronym for ***Lohamei Herut Yisrael*** (Fighters for the Freedom of Israel), an extremist right-wing splinter faction that in 1940 broke off from the Irgun.Its members believed that the Irgun was not aggressive enough in its fight against British rule in Palestine when it declared a truce with the Mandatory authorities for the duration of the war against Nazi Germany. Led by Avraham (Ya'ir) Stern, Lehi (often termed the "Stern Gang") resorted to terror tactics, including assassination, in its struggle to drive the British out of the country.

Lehrhaus. Literally meaning "house of learning" in German, the name was first applied to a school for Jewish studies founded by philosopher Franz Rosenzweig in Frankfurt in 1920. Attracting scholars such as Martin Buber, Shai Agnon, Abraham Joshua Heschel, Gershom Scholem, and Erich Fromm, the original Lehrhaus (until its closure by the Nazis) was the focal point of a Jewish intellectual revival between the wars. Today, the name "Lehrhaus" has been adopted by numerous institutes for adult Jewish learning that are open to the general public.

Leil Shimurim (Night of Watching). Home ceremony the night preceding a circumcision. It probably developed because friends and relatives, who were visiting the new parents, commonly joined the *mohel* on his rounds as he checked on the health of the infant. Later, this custom reflected the perceived need to guard the newborn throughout the night against malevolent spirits, especially Lilith.In the glow of candlelight (because evil spirits were said to avoid light), a festive meal featuring cooked beans and peas (to scare away demons) was eaten, and the participants held a vigil around the crib reciting prayers and studying Torah. Before departing, all recited the *Shema* near the mother. *Leil Shimurim* is also the name given to the night of the Exodus from Egypt (Exod. 12:42) and hence the first night of Passover.

Leining. Yiddish word for reading from the Torah scroll.

Le-mishpechoteihem (to their families). Longest word in the Torah (Gen. 8:19). In talmudic times, the word contained 10 Hebrew letters, but in modern texts it is spelled without a *vav* and has only nine. Its significance is that, as a simple guide, the Rabbis recommended that the length of a line in a Torah scroll must be such that it could accommodate the word three times.

Lentil. The basic ingredient of the red porridge for which the famished Esau sold his birthright to Jacob (Gen. 25:29-34). Lentils are traditionally eaten by Jewish mourners. According to one talmudic explanation, just as the lentil "has no mouth," so the mourner should remain silent in the face of death and not speak of ordinary subjects. Another is that "just as the lentil is round, so mourning comes round to all the inhabitants of the world [i.e., all are mortal]."

Leprosy – see *Tzara'at.*

Le-shanah ha-ba'ah bi-Yerushalayim (Next year in Jerusalem). The concluding statement of the Passover seder, it expresses the hope that by next Passover the Messiah will have come, leading to the ingathering of all Jews throughout the Diaspora to Jerusalem.

Le-shanah tovah tikateivu (May you be inscribed for a good year [in the Book of Life]). The customary greeting among Jews on Rosh Hashanah.

Levanah. See Moon and *Kiddush Levanah.*

Levantadores. Literally meaning "master lifters [of the Torah scroll]," designated individuals in Western Sephardic congregations who were exclusively honored with the role of *hagbah* so as to minimize the danger of dropping the scroll or handling it in a degrading way.[155]

Levayat ha-met (escorting the dead) – see Funeral procession.

Levi (levi'im) – see Levites.

Leviathan. Derived from a Hebrew root meaning "to coil or twist," a gigantic sea monster upon which the righteous will feast at the end of days. The Bible relates that when the sea monsters rebelled against the Divine authority, God utterly destroyed them (Ps. 74:13-14; Isa. 27:1). This scenario is similar to pre-biblical myths of a primordial combat between the creator deity and the forces of the sea for control of the universe.

Levirate marriage (*yibbum*). Obligation of a surviving brother to marry the widow of his brother if he died without having sired children (Deut. 25:5-6). The corollary is that the widow must marry a brother-in-law rather than anyone outside the family. The oldest of the surviving brothers had the first obligation to perform this commandment, which also allowed him to inherit all his dead brother's property. The explicit purpose of this commandment was to have the surviving brother produce an heir to perpetuate the name of his dead brother, so that it would not "be blotted out of Israel." The most famous story about levirate marriage in the Bible is that of Tamar (Gen. 38), who was an ancestress of King David. After the death of his older two sons, who had both married Tamar, Judah refused to allow his third son to perform the levirate obligation. Eventually, Judah himself fulfilled the commandment unknowingly when he had sexual relations with Tamar, and she subsequently gave birth to a child. Today, levirate marriage is no longer permitted and the alternative *chalitzah* is required.

Levites (*levi'im*). Descendants of the tribe of Levi (third son of Jacob and Leah), who were consecrated by Moses to serve in the Tabernacle and Temple as gatekeepers, musicians, teachers, and assistants to the priests (*kohanim*). In honor of their ancient service, in traditional synagogues a Levite (*levi*) is the second person called for an *aliyah* to the Torah. A ewer and basin or musical instruments may be carved on the tombstone of a Levite as a symbol of the ancient duties of their tribe.

Levitical cities. The 48 cities, dispersed throughout the land, which God commanded Moses to set aside for the tribe of Levi because, unlike the other tribes, they were not allotted any specific territory in the Promised Land (Num. 35). Among these were the six cities of refuge.

Levitical priests. Terminology used in the Book of Deuteronomy to refer to the *kohanim*, noting that they are descended from the tribe of Levi.

Leviticus (Lev.). English name for the 3rd book of the Torah, known in Hebrew as *Vayikra* ("He [God] called;" the first word) or *Torat ha-Kohanim* (Law of the Priests). For centuries, little children began their biblical studies with Leviticus because it was deemed appropriate for pure children to study the laws of purification. The book deals with the laws of sacrifice (1-7), the installation of the priests (8-10), physical purity and the laws of *kashrut* (11-16), moral instruction (18-22), the weekly Sabbath and annual festivals (23), and such topics as the Sabbatical and Jubilee years. It also contains a series of blessings and curses for fulfilling or disobeying the Divine commandments. The most famous verse in Leviticus is, "Love your neighbor as yourself. I am the Lord" (19:18).

Leviticus Rabbah (Lev. R.) – see Midrash Rabbah.

Lex talionis. The classic law of retaliation ("eye for an eye"; Exod. 21:24, Lev. 24:20, Deut. 19:21), which mandates that the punishment inflicted for bodily injury be precisely the same as the harm caused. This concept was common to all

Semitic peoples and well developed by the time of the Code of Hammurabi. Rejecting a literal interpretation, the Rabbis declared that the law required an individual who injured another to pay the monetary equivalent to the person he had harmed.

Lexicon. As it relates to the Hebrew Bible, a book that lists (in Hebrew alphabetical order) the roots and definitions of all the Hebrew words used, including their various prefixes and suffixes.

Libation. Drink offering of wine that accompanied animal sacrifices. (Meal offerings were mixed with oil.) According to the Bible, the amount of the libation varied with the type of animal – a fourth part of a *hin* for a lamb, a third for a ram, and a half for a bullock (Num. 15:5-9). The Israelites were strictly forbidden from drinking libation-wine that had been used in connection with idol worship (see *yayin nesech*).

Liberal Judaism – see Reform Judaism.

Library, Jewish National. Main library in Israel, which also serves as the library of the Hebrew University. In addition to rare manuscripts and prayer books and special collections on Jews in medicine and Jewish autographs and portraits, the Jewish National Library also houses the personal archives of Ahad ha-Am (see Zionism, cultural), Martin Buber (see I-Thou), Joseph Klausner, Stefan Zweig, and Shmuel Yosef Agnon.

Life. The sanctity of human life is a supreme value in Judaism. It is based on the biblical concept of humans being created "in the image of God" (Gen. 1:27) and the talmudic dictum that "one who destroys a single soul is regarded as having destroyed an entire world, and one who preserves one life is as if he preserved an entire world" (Sanh. 4:5, 37a). Every second of human life is unique and of equally infinite value. Desecration of the Sabbath is permitted for the preservation of life (see *pikuach nefesh*). According to the Rabbis, if a Jew is forced to transgress any of the commandments (except those against murder, adultery, and incest) at pain of death, he may violate the law rather than surrender his life. This is in accordance with the principle, "You shall therefore keep My statutes, and My ordinances, which if a man do he shall *live* by them" (Lev. 18:5).

Life, danger to – see *Pikuach nefesh*.

Lifnim mishurat hadin. Talmudic phrase that denotes going beyond the strict letter of the law in serving God and in helping other individuals. Rather than a person acting only out of a sense of obligation or to earn a reward, this indicates a sincere wish to effectuate the Divine will. One who contributes the minimum amount to charity, behaves toward his parents and teachers with only the barest respect, or sets aside only a minuscule portion of his day for learning Torah, may indeed be fulfilling the letter of the law, but the Rabbis believed that he could certainly do better. A superb example of acting *lifnim mishurat hadin* is the story of a man who approached the Brisker Rav before Passover and asked, "May I use milk instead of wine for the four cups at the seder?" The Brisker Rav removed five rubles from his pocket and gave the money to the man. His puzzled wife did not begrudge the man the gift, but wondered whether one ruble would not have been more than enough money to buy wine. "Perhaps," replied her husband, "but from his question it was obvious that he lacked money for meat as well, since one cannot eat meat and use milk for the four cups at the same time. I therefore gave him sufficient money for both wine and meat for his meal."

Light. The first creation of God (Gen.1:3-4), light in Jewish tradition is a symbol of life, blessing, knowledge, goodness, peace, and the soul. Jews mark joyous occasions by lighting candles, and light played an important role as a metaphor for God and Torah in Jewish mystical practice.

Lightning (*barak*). Along with thunder (*ra'am*), awesome natural phenomena viewed as manifestations of Divine power. The Talmud mandated the recitation of the blessing "Whose strength and might fill the world" (Ber. 9:2) after experiencing lightning and thunder (as well as viewing shooting stars and feeling an earthquake).

Lights, Festival of – see Chanukah.

Likud. Israeli right-wing political party, a coalition of the former Herut and Liberal parties, which was established in 1973. Four years later, the Likud won the most seats in the Knesset and its leader, Menachem Begin, became prime minister and organized Israel's first right-wing cabinet.

Lilith. According to Jewish folklore, the female evil spirit and natural enemy of newborns. The first wife of Adam, Lilith was the mother of the demons who resulted from this union. To guard against Lilith, a variety of amulets were placed above the bed of a new mother and on the doorposts of her room, and an attempt was made to keep her awake for the first three days after birth. Jewish feminists have viewed Lilith in a more positive light because she, like Adam, was created from the earth. When she demanded equality with Adam he refused, and Lilith ran away and united with "the great demon."

Liturgy – see Prayer, Prayer services, *Siddur*, *Machzor*, and citations for individual prayers.

Litvak. Yiddish term for a Lithuanian Jew. Lithuania was renowned as an outstanding cultural center for Jewish scholarship (the site of great *yeshivot* and the home of the Vilna Gaon), and Litvaks were characterized by their rational approach to learning and highly organized community life. The term has the connotation of an erudite but pedantic individual who is dry and humorless. When used in a derogatory manner by a Galitzianer, it means a person who is a sharp trader and willing to cut corners. About 95% of the Litvak community was destroyed during the Holocaust.

Loans - see Interest, Sabbatical Year, and *Prosbul.*

Loch in kop. Literally meaning "hole in the head," this Yiddish phrase connotes something that one does not need.

Lo dati (not religious) – see *Hiloni.*

Log. Biblical liquid measure, approximately equal to 10 fluid ounces (0.3 liter).

Lokshen. Yiddish word for "noodles."

Lord of Hosts. General translation of *YHVH Tzeva'ot*, one of the Names of God. "Hosts" refers to an army or other military group, and thus the name is a manifestation of Divine Sovereignty. It does not occur in the Five Books of Moses, but is common in the prophetic books and found extensively in the Psalms.

Lost property – see Finding of property.

Lots. In the Book of Esther, the villain (Haman) cast lots (*purim*) to determine when the slaughter of the Persian Jewish community would take place (3:7). In the Book of Jonah, the sailors cast lots to establish who was responsible for the terrible storm – "and the lot fell upon Jonah" (1:7). Lots also were used to determine God's will in the division of the Promised Land among the tribes.

Love of God. The biblical verse, "And you shall love [*v'ahavta*] the Lord your God... " (Deut. 6:5), means performing God's commandments out of pure love – an intense desire to fulfill the Divine will and the highest level in the human being's relationship with God – rather than because of fear of punishment or the inducement of a reward. People who are motivated by fear may abandon a task if it becomes too difficult to perform, whereas those who act based on love are prepared to make substantial sacrifices for the objects of their affection.[156, 157] The mutual love of the people of Israel and God was metaphorically described by the prophets (Isaiah, Jeremiah, Hosea) as the love between a bride and groom. The Song of Songs was interpreted as an allegory of the love between God and the Jewish people, which begins with the Exodus from Egypt on Passover and is "consummated" with their "marriage" – the giving of the Torah at Mount Sinai seven weeks later, which is celebrated on the festival of Shavuot.[158]

Love of neighbor. "You shall love your neighbor as yourself" (Lev. 19:18; see golden rule) is the commandment to let the honor, property, and desires of other human beings be as dear to you as your own. R. Akiva declared this commandment a "fundamental principle of the Torah," and Maimonides observed that it was the foundation of such activities as visiting the sick, consoling the mourners, attending to the dead, escorting guests, dowering the bride, cheering the bride and groom, and providing what they needed for their life together.[159] Love of God and love of one's fellow human beings form the foundation of Jewish ethics.

Love of stranger. "You shall love the stranger (*ger*), for you were strangers in the land of Egypt" is a commandment found 36 times in the Torah. This required the Israelites to protect the alien who was born elsewhere but residing in the land. The explicit reason for this commandment was that Jews – because of their bitter experience in Egypt, long history of persecution, and desire to remain a holy people – should be especially sensitive to the suffering of aliens and therefore obliged to love them simply because they are fellow human beings and creations of God.

Lovers of Zion (*Hovevei Tzion*). 19th-century Jewish nationalist movement, organized by Russian Jewish students, which called for the large-scale settlement of Jews in the Land of Israel. Its first president was Dr. Leon Pinsker. Initially, *Hovevei Tzion* also urged political support of the major powers for this purpose. However, when *Hovevei Tzion* members established the first Jewish agricultural settlements in Palestine, primarily in the wake of the Russian pogroms in the early 1880's, they focused their efforts toward encouraging *aliyah* and establishing and strengthening settlements, rather than concentrating their efforts in the political arena.

Loving-kindness – see *Gemilut chasadim.*

Lox. Yiddish term for smoked salmon. The sugar-cured variety is known as "nova" (short for Nova Scotia) lox.

Lu'ach – see Calendar.

Lubavitch – see Chabad.

Luchot ha-brit (Tablets of the Covenant). The two tablets containing the Ten Commandments, which were engraved "by the finger of God" and included the conditions of the Covenant between God and Israel (Deut. 4:13). Outraged over the blasphemy of the Golden Calf, Moses smashed the first pair of tablets (Exod. 32:19; Deut. 9:17). Again ascending the mountain, Moses remained another 40 days pleading on behalf of the people. After God forgave the Israelites, Moses was ordered to prepare a second pair of stone tablets identical to the first. God commanded that these be placed inside the Ark of the Covenant, which was housed first in the portable *Mishkan*, later in the Tabernacle at Shiloh, and ultimately in the Temple in Jerusalem. While the biblical text gives no indication of how the commandments were distributed on the two tablets, it is commonly assumed that they were arranged vertically, five on each. Representations of the two tablets containing the Ten Commandments are popular decorations in synagogues. Instead of including the full text, most have only the initial letters of the Hebrew alphabet (representing the numbers one through ten) inscribed on the two tablets. Another approach is to simply use the first Hebrew word of each commandment.[160]

Lulav. Branch of the date palm that is part of the four species used on Sukkot. Its fruit has a taste but no aroma, and thus the *lulav* symbolizes a scholar who is deficient in good deeds. The four species, collectively called "*lulav*" from its largest member, are shaken three times in all six directions (east, south, west, north, up, down) to acknowledge that the Dominion and Presence of God extends to the four corners of the universe as well as to heaven and earth.

Lunar calendar. The basis of the Jewish calendar, it consists of 12 months. The time span between one new moon and the next is approximately 29 days, 12 hours, 44 minutes, and 3 1/3 seconds. Since a month must be composed of complete days, in the Jewish calendar they vary between 29 and 30 days. Five months (Nisan, Sivan, Av, Tishrei, and Shevat) have 30 days; five (Iyar, Tammuz, Elul, Tevet, and Adar) have 29 days; and two (Cheshvan and Kislev) have either 29 or 30 days. However, the 12 lunar months add up to approximately 11 days less than the solar year (365 days, 48 minutes, and 46 seconds). Without any adjustments (see calendar), the festivals would "wander" and be shifted from their appointed seasons of the year. Therefore, a leap month (Second Adar) is added 7 times every 19 years.

Lurianic kabbalah. System of Jewish mysticism based on the teachings of Isaac Luria, the 16th-century master of Kabbalah who settled in Safed. Luria described a concept in which the present world has arisen out of two dramatic cosmic events – the contraction of God (*tzimtzum*) to allow space for the creation of a finite world; and the breaking of the vessels, in which Holy Sparks flew off in all directions and were trapped in shells of impurity (see *klipot*). The trapped sparks can be freed by human prayers and good deeds, as well as by faithful observance of the commandments, making it incumbent on every Jew to perform these actions to elevate these sparks to their state of pre-Creation unity and thus repair the world (see *tikun olam*).

Luz. According to the Talmud, a small indestructible bone at the base of the spine. Only found in Jews, it will be the basis for regeneration of the body at the time of the resurrection at the end of days.

Lying. Forbidden in the Bible (Lev. 19:11), the Talmud says that a liar who "speaks one thing with his mouth and another in his heart" is as evil as a person who worships idols (Sanh. 92a) and is one whom God hates (Pes. 113b). The Rabbis repeatedly condemn lying, noting that the penalty for being branded a liar is that one is not believed even when speaking the truth (Sanh. 89b). In some circumstances, however, lying is permitted to preserve family harmony.

M

Ma'abarah. Hebrew word meaning "transit camp," referring to the temporary primitive villages, often consisting of huts and tents, constructed to meet the needs of the mass immigration of Jews (many from Arab lands) to the newly established State of Israel. The newcomers eventually were provided with permanent housing.

Ma'amadot. System by which the general public was represented at the Temple during the offering of the daily sacrifices (Num. 28:1), even though they could not perform any of the priestly or levitical duties. The Land of Israel was divided into 24 districts, each of which sent a delegation of eminent and pious men to represent it at the daily public offerings for one week every six months. These men were known as the *anshei ma'amad* (men of standing), because their task was to "stand by" and observe the Temple ritual. Those *anshei ma'amad* unable to travel to Jerusalem for the week refrained from work and assembled each day to recite prayers, which mostly corresponded to the psalms being said at the Temple and ended at the same time as the services in Jerusalem. Eventually, these local gatherings attracted large crowds, who joined the *anshei ma'amad* in prayer. After the destruction of the Temple, some devout men would remain in the synagogue after daily services to read the same verses from Genesis that the *anshei ma'amad* had formerly recited. Some modern editions of the *siddur* still include a section (*ma'amadot*) that contains these Scriptural passages from what may have been the origin of the synagogue service.[161]

Ma'apilim ("illegal" immigrants) – see *Aliyah Bet*.

Ma'ariv (1). The evening service. According to the Rabbis, this was instituted by Jacob as he was fleeing from the wrath of his brother Esau. The Patriarch prayed before going to sleep on his stone pillow and dreamed of angels ascending and descending a ladder connecting the earth to heaven (Gen. 28:11). The *Ma'ariv* service consists of a short reading from Psalms, the *Shema*, with two blessings before and two after, the *Amidah*, *Aleinu*, and the *Mourner's Kaddish*.

Ma'ariv (2). Major Hebrew daily in Israel, founded in 1948, which describes itself as an "independent Zionist" newspaper that espouses an editorial policy generally reflecting a liberal approach.

Ma'aseh Bereshit. Literally "Work of Creation," a mystical tradition based on the first chapter of Genesis (see *Sefer Yetzirah*). It attempts to understand the essence of cosmology (how the world came into being) so as to provide the mystic with a means to better cleave to God (see *devekut*).

Ma'aseh Merkava. Literally "Work of the Chariot," a tradition based on the vision of the Divine Chariot (see *Merkava* mysticism) in the first chapter of Ezekiel, which formed the basis of early mystical speculation. It describes the ascent of the mystic to Heaven, where he views the Divine palaces and the Throne of Glory and personally experiences the Divine Presence. Devotees of this form of mysticism attempted to seek an ecstatic vision of the Divine Throne.

Ma'aser – see Tithe.

Ma'aser Sheni (**Ma'as. Sh.**). The 8th tractate in Zera'im (seeds) in the Mishnah, it deals with the second tithes.

Ma'aserot (**Ma'as.**). The 7th tractate in Zera'im (seeds) in the Mishnah, it deals with tithes for the Levites and the poor.

Ma'asim tovim. Literally meaning "good deeds," it is one of the three blessings given to children when they receive their Hebrew names – that they grow up to "Torah, *chuppah* [the wedding canopy], and *ma'asim tovim*."

Maccabees (1). Band of Jewish revolutionaries, under the leadership of Judah Maccabee, who defeated the Syrian-Greek forces in 165 B.C.E – a victory celebrated during the festival of Chanukah.The name is also applied to the Hasmonean dynasty, which continued to rule for more than a century.

Maccabees (2). Four books of the Apocrypha that deal with the time before and after the Jewish revolt led by Judah Maccabee.

Maccabi. First Jewish sports organization, founded in response to Max Nordau's speech before the Second Zionist Congress in 1898 that called for the Jewish people to develop an interest in sports and physical fitness. Initially affiliated with the General Zionist movement, the Liberal party that subsequently became a partner in the Likud, the Maccabi movement quickly became depoliticized, unlike the Hapo'el and Betar sports organizations.

Maccabiah Games (Maccabiah). Often termed the "Jewish Olympics," these international athletic events are recognized and approved by the International Olympic Committee and open to all Jewish athletes. First held in 1932 in Tel Aviv, since 1953 the Maccabiah Games have been held regularly every four years, with an ever-increasing participation of athletes from more than 30 countries. The program includes festive opening and closing ceremonies under the patronage of the president and prime minister of the State of Israel, with contingents parading under their national flags.

Macher. Literally meaning "maker" or "doer," this Yiddish word is applied to an important person in an organization, or to an "operator" who can use his connections to make something happen.

Machetunim. Yiddish word that means "in-laws" but can also refer to the extended members of a spouse's family.

Machloket. Literally meaning "division," this Hebrew word is used in the Talmud to refer to a disagreement between sages that is a central feature of rabbinic discussion.

Machoza. Town in Babylonia, on the shores of the Tigris, which was an important Jewish center and site of a major talmudic academy after the destruction of Nehardea in 259 C.E. In the early 4th century, many scholars from the academy of Pumbedita moved to Machoza, but this center of learning was destroyed in 363.

Machpelah, Cave of – see Cave of Machpelah.

Machshirin. The 8th tractate in Tohorot (purity) in the Mishnah, it deals with liquids and foods subject to ritual uncleanness.

Machzor. Prayer book used on the major festivals of the Jewish year. The best-known *machzor* is the one for the High Holy Days (Rosh Hashanah and Yom Kippur). It is especially enriched with *piyyutim*, a sampling of the thousands of prayer-poems composed by *hazzanim* who were deeply inspired by the liturgy of these days There is also a joint *machzor* for the three pilgrimage festivals (Passover, Shavuot, Sukkot), as well as separate prayer books for each. The Hebrew word means "return" or "cycle," appropriate since each of these festivals occurs once a year.

Machzor Vitry. First Ashkenazic *siddur* (prayer book). Compiled in the 11th century by Simcha ben Samuel, a Vitry resident and pupil of Rashi, this work contained the text of all the regular prayers in accordance with the rite of northern France, which was close to that of Germany. In addition, there was a running commentary that included both notes on the prayers and the laws pertaining to life-cycle events. Consequently, this constituted a comprehensive manual containing almost everything a Jew needed to live a full religious life. It even included material that had not previously been considered inherent parts of the liturgy, such as the mishnaic tractate *Pirkei Avot* (Ethics of the Fathers) and the Passover Haggadah, along with commentaries for each.[162]

Madaba map. Oldest known representation of the city of Jerusalem. The Byzantine-era (6th century) Madaba map is actually a mosaic floor (25 by 5 meters), made up of two million stones, which illustrates the entire eastern Mediterranean region and has a detailed depiction of Jerusalem at its center.

Maftir. Literally meaning "one who concludes," the person who is called up for the final *aliyah* on the Sabbath and festivals. On the Sabbath, the *maftir* portion consists of a repetition of a few verses from the end of the seventh portion. On festivals, Rosh Chodesh, and the four special Sabbaths before Passover, the *maftir* portion is a special reading from a second Torah scroll (Numbers 28-29). After the Torah is raised and bound, the *maftir* chants the *haftarah*, the reading from the prophets.

Magen Avot (Shield of [our] fathers). Opening words of an abridged form of the intermediate blessings of the *Amidah*, which is recited aloud by the prayer leader at the Friday evening service. It summarizes the seven blessings said quietly by each congregant. In talmudic times, when synagogues were generally outside the town limits, it was dangerous to walk home alone after dark. Some scholars have suggested that reciting this extra prayer gave latecomers time to complete their prayers so that all the worshipers could return to town together.

Magen David. Literally "Shield of David" and popularly known as the "Star of David" or "Jewish Star," it has become the most common and universally recognized symbol of Judaism and Jewish identity. The Magen David is a six-pointed star (hexagram) formed by two equilateral triangles that share the same center and are placed in opposite directions. It was adopted by the First Zionist Congress as its symbol in the 19th century and is featured on the national flag of the State of Israel. A yellow Star of David was employed as a Jewish identity badge by the Nazis. Today, the Star of David is widely used on religious articles and in the décor of many synagogues, as well as on necklaces and other jewelry as a secular sign of Jewish identity.

Magen David Adom. Literally "Red Shield of David," the name and emblem of the Israeli equivalent of the Red Cross. Founded in 1930 as Israel's emergency medical first aid society, it operates emergency response, ambulance, and mobile intensive care services and national blood banks, as well as providing instruction in first aid.

Maggid (1). Literally "one who tells," a popular, usually itinerant, Ashkenazic preacher who wandered from town to town attracting an audience through a combination of the parables, folk tales, and quotations from biblical and rabbinic sources that he wove into his text and the oratorical flourishes of his delivery. The *maggid* generally was forced to subsist on the meager collections from those who attended his sermon on a weekday evening or on a Saturday afternoon (of course, paid after the Sabbath ended). Neither an ordained rabbi nor a trained preacher, the *maggid* relied upon a natural flair for the poetic and dramatic, an innate talent for preaching, and a fervent desire to teach the will of God. It was the *maggid* who helped spread the teachings of Hasidism in the 18th century. In Kabbalah, the term "*maggid*" denotes a heavenly force that communicates supernatural illumination to the kabbalist.

Maggid (2). Literally "telling," the narrative of the Exodus from Egypt in the Passover Haggadah that is recited at the seder.

Magic. Technique to control the demonic forces (both benevolent and hostile) in the universe that are above and beyond ordinary human power. Practitioners of magic employ a variety of incantations to change realities and confuse or circumvent the evil powers (e.g., altering their direction so that they are unable to find and wreak havoc on the individual or nation they are seeking). The Talmud differentiates between beneficent "white magic" and deleterious "black magic," the former being used to provide protection against the harm that could be caused by the latter. Jewish rationalist thinking dismissed magic as simple-minded superstition.

Mah nishtanah – see Four questions.

Mah Tovu (How goodly [are your tents, O Jacob, your dwelling places, O Israel]). Initial words of the opening prayer of the morning service, which is recited upon entering the synagogue. This biblical verse (Num. 24:5) was initially uttered by the gentile prophet, Balaam, who was hired by Balak to curse the Israelites but blessed them instead. According to tradition, Jacob's tents refer to houses of prayer, while Israel's dwellings represent houses of study. Balaam also was amazed at how the Israelite encampment was constructed so that everyone's privacy was respected, with no one able to see into his neighbor's home.[163]

Mahal. Acronym for ***Mitnadvei Hootz L'****aretz* (volunteers from outside the land), the Hebrew term for foreign volunteers who enlisted in the Israel Defense Forces (IDF) during the War of Independence. Rather than fighting in separate formations, these 3,500 mostly Jewish volunteers were absorbed into IDF units according to the need for reinforcements. Their contribution was not in numbers but in quality and experience – most necessary in a new army whose fighting tradition was that of an underground movement – as well as in the development of the air force and medical corps. After serving Israel in her hour of greatest need, most of the volunteers returned to their home countries. However, about 500 stayed or returned soon after and decided to make Israel their home.

Mahamad. Term used in Sephardic communities for the governing board of a synagogue and later applied to the executive body of an autonomous Jewish community. It is an alternative transliteration of the Hebrew word "*ma'amad*" (see *Ma'amadot*).

Maidanek. Nazi concentration and death camp on the outskirts of Lublin, Poland. The camp had seven gas chambers that used Zyklon B and carbon monoxide to murder the inmates, which included more than 125,000 Jews.

Maideleh. Endearing Yiddish term for a young girl or unmarried woman, often in the expression "*shayna maidele*" (pretty young girl).

Maimuna. Daylong celebration of Moroccan Jews, which begins immediately after sundown at the conclusion of the Passover holiday. Maimuna is characterized by an extraordinary show of hospitality, in which Jews open their doors to friends and neighbors. In every home, the table is set with a white tablecloth and adorned with flowers, branches of fig trees, stalks of wheat, and a fishbowl that usually contains a live fish as a symbol of fertility. Dairy foods are eaten, especially pancake-like wafers of fried dough (*muflita*) spread with butter and honey. In Israel, Jews of Moroccan descent celebrate the day after Passover with communal picnics, and a large central gathering is held in Jerusalem.

Major prophets. The three prophets – Isaiah, Jeremiah, and Ezekiel – whose writings are substantially longer than the combined output of the 12 so-called "minor" prophets.

Majority. Based on the verse, "You shall not follow a multitude to do evil" (Exod. 23:2), the Rabbis deduced that one *should* follow the majority when it is a matter of doing "not evil" (i.e., the good). Therefore, one is required to follow the majority if there is a difference of opinion among the rabbis regarding any of the laws of the Torah, and litigants must accept the majority view if there is a difference of opinion in a private lawsuit. However, if the majority of judges or witnesses are agreed on an opinion that another judge knows is unjust, he should not abandon his own view in order to fall in line with the others. Automatically accepting the reasoning of another judge, however brilliant, without arriving at the same conclusion through independent thinking, would establish the dangerous situation in which the opinion of a single judge dictates the decisions of an entire court.[164] In a court, a single person who has honestly and accurately analyzed the case and arrived at the correct opinion, in consultation with God, represents the true majority.

Makkot (Mak.). The 5th tractate in Nezikin (damages) in the Mishnah, it deals with the rules governing flogging (see corporal punishment, false witnesses, and the cities of refuge.

Malach ha-Mavet – see Angel of Death.

Malachi (**Mal.**). The 12th (last) of the minor prophets. Malachi lived in Jerusalem in the mid-5th century B.C.E., probably about 50 years after the rebuilding of the Temple by the Jewish exiles who had returned from Babylonia. Malachi stresses obedience to ritual and law, but his message also speaks of the universality of God's moral rule and the natural worth of all people. The prophet fiercely condemns moral and social offenses and emphasizes the concept of the unity of all Jews under one Supreme Being. Malachi also foresees a Day of Judgment when the righteous would be rewarded and the wicked punished. According to the Talmud, after the death of Malachi, "the Holy Spirit [of prophecy] departed from Israel."

Malchut (sovereign). The 10th of the *sefirot,* also known as *Shechinah.*In rabbinic literature, *Shechinah* represents the Divine immanence, God's closeness to the world and humankind. As the first aspect of God that we encounter, it is our portal to the Divine realm. The creation of our world is described as the result of an erotic relationship between *Shechinah* and *Tiferet.* When these two emanations are in balance, the Divine flow into the world causes blessing. Blockage of the flow impedes the flow of Divine grace, which results in adverse effects on our world. When enhanced by good deeds, *Shechinah* joins with *Tiferet* in sacred intercourse that increases the Divine flow; conversely, it is decreased by human sins.

Malchuyot (sovereignty). First of the three long intermediate blessings in the *Musaf Amidah* on Rosh Hashanah, it deals with God's universal sovereignty and stresses the optimistic view of the eventual Divine rule over the entire world. It opens with the *Aleinu,* which eloquently expresses the hope that all humanity will eventually realize the oneness and sovereignty of God. During the rest of the year, the prayer leader and congregants slightly bend their knees and hips and bow their heads when saying, "We bend the knee, bow in worship, and give thanks." However, when recited aloud during the *Musaf Amidah* on Rosh Hashanah and Yom Kippur, the *Aleinu* is traditionally accompanied by complete prostration, in which one falls to the hands and knees and touches the head to the floor to physically demonstrate total obeisance to God.[165]

Malshinim – see Informers.

Mammeloshen (mother tongue) – see Yiddish.

Mamzer. Contrary to popular misconception, a *mamzer* (often mistranslated as "bastard") is not someone born out of wedlock. Instead, a *mamzer* is the child of a sexual relationship between a man and woman whose marriage could never be valid under Jewish law. Examples include (1) a child born to a married woman by some man other than her lawful husband (see adultery); (2) a child born of a woman who had remarried without having obtained a valid divorce (see *get*) from her first husband; and (3) the child of an incestuous relationship. According to the Bible, a *mamzer* and all of his or her descendants may never marry a Jew. However, a marriage between two *mamzerim* is permitted. Realizing that this law was overly harsh and unfair to both *mamzerim* and their descendants, the Rabbis eventually allowed a *mamzer* to marry a convert as a way of becoming more quickly integrated into the Jewish community. It should be noted that, according to Jewish law, a child born out of wedlock is not considered a *mamzer* and retains unimpeachable legal status. Except in regard to marriage, the personal status of a *mamzer* is not adversely affected in any way. He can be called up to the Torah, has equal rights of inheritance as other heirs, and can hold public office. The Mishnah even states that, "a *mamzer* who is a scholar takes precedence over a High Priest who is an ignoramus."

Mandate, British – see British Mandate.

Mandelbread (Mandelbrot). Twice-baked crisp cookie ("Jewish biscotti") that is usually dunked in tea.

Mandlen (sing., *mandel*). Known as "soup nuts," a cracker-like garnish used to accompany soup. The Yiddish word literally means "almonds," because *mandlen* are formed into nut-sized balls and baked until golden. A popular Yiddish lullaby is *Rozinkes mit mandlen* (raisins and almonds).

Manna. Food that nourished the Israelites during their 40 years of wandering in the wilderness. The Bible describes manna as "a flaky substance, as fine as frost on the ground" (Exod. 16:14). "Like coriander seed, and in color like bdellum" (a pale yellow or white aromatic resin), manna is described as tasting like rich cream (Num. 11:7-8) or wafers in honey (Exod. 16:31). On each of the first five days of the week, God supplied the required amount of manna (an *omer* per person; Exod. 16:16). The Israelites would go out and gather it, grind it between millstones or pound it in a mortar, boil it in a pot, and make it into cakes. They only took what they needed, for anything left over "became infested with maggots and stank" (Exod. 16:20). On Friday they collected a double portion, which would remain fresh over the Sabbath when work was forbidden (Exod. 16:22-26).

Manslaughter – see Cities of refuge.

Mantle. Covering of the Torah in the Ashkenazic tradition. This sheath of satin, velvet, or other fine material is usually embroidered with gold or silver threads and may be richly decorated with images of lions, crowns, pomegranates, the columns of Jachin and Boaz, and various implements of the Temple service. The mantle is open at the bottom and closed at the top, except for two circular openings though which protrude the two staves on which the scroll is rolled (see *atzei chaim*). On the High Holy Days, it is traditional to use a white mantle.

Manual of Discipline. Also called "Rule of the Community," one of the most important of the Dead Sea Scrolls.It described the requirements for anyone who sought to join the community of Essenes at Qumran.These included: "to live according to the communal rule: to seek God; to do what is good and upright in His sight, in accordance with what He has commanded through Moses and through His servants the prophets; to love all that He has chosen and hate all that He has rejected; to keep far from evil and to cling to all good works; to act truthfully and righteously and justly on earth and to walk no more in the stubbornness of a guilty heart and of lustful eyes, doing all manner of evil; to bring into a bond of mutual love all who have declared their willingness to carry out the statutes of God."

Maot hittim. Literally "money for wheat," during the talmudic period this Hebrew term referred to a compulsory communal tax before Passover that ensured a sufficient supply of flour for the poor to make *matzah.* Today, *maot hittim* refers to a charitable collection to supply the needs of the poor for *matzah*, wine, and other special foods required for observance of the holiday.

Maoz Tzur (Mighty Rock [of my salvation]). Most popular of the Chanukah songs traditionally sung after kindling the festival lights. Composed in 13th-century Germany, the opening stanza is a plea for the reestablishment of the Temple, the rededication of the Altar, and the restoration of the sacrificial rites. Concluding with the phrase *chanukat ha-Mizbeach* (dedication of the Altar), this stanza is the only one known by most Jews. However, *Maoz Tzur* is an acrostic poem of five stanzas, with the first Hebrew letter of each spelling Mordecai (presumably the name of the poet). The first stanza thanks God for deliverance from our oppressors. The next three stanzas relate the story of the Exodus from Egypt, and the liberation from Babylonia, Persia, and Syria; the final stanza recounts the story of Chanukah.

Mapai. Acronym for *Mifleget Po'alei Eretz Israel* (Land of Israel Workers' Party), a moderate Labor Zionist political party that became the dominant political faction during the period of the British Mandate and in the Jewish labor movement. Mapai was the major party in the First Knesset and its leader, David Ben Gurion, became the first prime minister.

Mapam. Acronym for *Mifleget Po'alim Me'uchedet* (United Workers' Party), a left-wing Marxist-Zionist political party that was the second largest party in Israel until the mid-1950s. Mapam later joined with its former rival Mapai, which in 1968 merged with Ahdut ha-Avodah and Rafi to become the Israeli Labor Party, in an electoral alliance known as the Labor Alignment.

Mappah. Literally "tablecloth," this Hebrew word may refer either to the protective cloth on the stand where the Torah is read or to the decorated fabric strip (see wimpel) used as a binder around the Torah scroll. *Mappah* also was the name of the 16th-century commentary of Moses Isserles (Rema) on the *Shulchan Aruch* (Set Table) of Yosef Karo. This major code of Jewish law reflected the Sephardic background of the author and was initially not accepted as authoritative by Ashkenazim, since it completely ignored the halachic decisions and customs among the Jews of Germany and Poland. With the inclusion of the *Mappah* detailing the distinctive customs of the Jews of Central and Eastern Europe, the *Shulchan Aruch* gained universal acceptance, and this composite work has become the functioning code for observant Jews to the present day.[166]

Mar. Literally "master," the title given to some Babylonian *amora'im* and especially to the exilarchs.

Mar Cheshvan – see Cheshvan.

Mare de-atra. Literally, "the master of the place," the Aramaic title of the rabbi of a community. In early medieval times, the leaders of the Babylonian academies (*geonim*) appointed the local scholars who judged matters related to Jewish law. As their power declined and Jewish communities developed in far-flung regions, there was a substantial increase in the authority and responsibilities of the local rabbi (and autonomy of the local community in selecting him), making him the preeminent decision maker.

Mari. Ancient Semitic city-state that rivaled Babylon in its influence over the northern portion of Mesopotamia in the 18th century B.C.E. Scholars have discovered evidence in Mari of what has been termed "a forerunner of biblical prophecy." Rather than responding to a royal request to obtain signs from a god, as elsewhere in the ancient Near East, these "intuitive" prophets were said to have articulated "spontaneous" prophesies resulting from "the experience of divine revelation." The Mari archives shed light on the structure, organization, and institutions of the tribal society of ancient Israel.

Maror (bitter herbs). The Torah stipulates that the festival of Passover is to be observed by eating the Passover offering (see paschal lamb), *matzah*, and *maror* (Exod. 12:8; Num. 9:11). *Maror* is eaten at the seder to remember the bitterness that the Israelites experienced during their period of slavery in Egypt. The Bible does not specify the plant by name, and most Jews today use horseradish for *maror*. The Rabbis preferred Romaine lettuce as a bitter herb because, like the experience of the Jews in Egypt, it begins as a sweet taste and then turns bitter.[167] (See also *Hillel sandwich*.)

Marranos – see *Conversos*.

Marriage. The Jewish tradition views marriage as the ultimate social, religious, and moral ideal and basic to a healthy life. As the Talmud observes, "One who does not have a wife lives without joy, without blessing, and without goodness," as well as without Torah, protection, and peace. Marriage was established by God at the time of Creation, both to provide humans with warm companionship and to allow them to fulfill the Divine plan for procreation (Gen. 1:28). It is considered a holy covenant between a man and woman, with God as the intermediary. As the mystical *Zohar* notes, "God creates new worlds constantly. In what way? By causing marriages to take place." The Song of Songs is usually interpreted as an allegory of the relationship between God and Israel, which is analogous to the marriage bond.

Marriage ceremony. A wedding is the public union of a man and a woman who enter into a covenant of mutual responsibility, protection, and caring.[168] The Jewish marriage ceremony is a complex series of formalities and customs that have developed over the centuries. It consists of two separate acts – *kiddushin* and *nisuin.*

Marriage ceremony, day of. In the West, Sunday is a popular day for weddings because of its convenience for the guests. Orthodox couples often select Tuesday, because the phrase "And God saw that it was good" occurs twice in the biblical account of the Creation on that day (Gen. 1:10-12). Conversely, Monday was generally avoided because this phrase does not appear. However, any day of the week is valid except the Sabbath, when legal transactions are forbidden and work and travel are not permitted. In addition, two celebrations (Sabbath and wedding) should be observed individually and not combined with each other, based on the talmudic principle that "we should not mix joy with joy." Weddings also are not celebrated on festivals, the three-week mourning period between the 17th of Tammuz and Tisha b'Av, and the *sefirah* period between Passover and Shavuot (with the notable exception of Lag ba-Omer). Rosh Chodesh traditionally was considered a propitious time for weddings, since the waxing moon was a symbol of growth and fertility.

Marriage, levirate – see Levirate marriage.

Marriages, prohibited. All the relationships forbidden in the Torah are termed "incestuous." The two people could not be considered married under Jewish law, no document of divorce (see *get*) would be required for the dissolution of their relationship, and any children would be considered *mamzerim.* As listed in Leviticus (18:6-17, read during the afternoon service of Yom Kippur), a man is specifically prohibited from marrying the following relatives: mother; step-mother; sister (whether born of a legal marriage or out of wedlock); half-sister; granddaughter (daughter is not specifically mentioned, but is obviously included); aunt (sister of his mother or father or the wife of his father's brother); daughter-in-law (either after divorce or his son's death); sister-in-law; and wife's sister (while the wife is still alive). A marriage between a Jew and a non-Jew is also void under Jewish law (see intermarriage).

Marriages, prohibited, secondary. The Rabbis expanded the primary forbidden relationships in the ascending and descending line. Just as a man was forbidden to have relations with his mother, so was he forbidden to marry his grandmother or great-grandmother. Similarly, since his step-mother was forbidden, so was his grandfather's wife; as his daughter-in-law was prohibited, so was his grandson's wife. Unlike primary prohibited marriages, which are void, marriages of the secondary prohibited degree must be dissolved by a divorce and any children are legitimate.[169]

Martyr. Throughout the centuries, Jews have been willing to die for their faith as the ultimate expression of *Kiddush ha-Shem* (Sanctification of the Name [of God]). Martyrdom was seen as the ultimate example of the biblical injunction to "love the Lord your God with all your soul" (Deut. 6:5). According to the Rabbis, if a Jew is forced to transgress any of the negative commandments on pain of death, he may violate the law rather than surrender his life (with three exceptions). Martyrdom is preferred only if the choice is between death and committing idolatry, unlawful sexual intercourse, or murder. In addition, one must sacrifice one's life rather than be forced to publicly violate any religious law, if a reasonable onlooker would deem such an action as meaning that one was renouncing Judaism. The Talmud distinguishes between a Jew being compelled to light a fire in a church (permitted, since the motivation was merely to provide warmth, rather than force him to be associated with idolatrous worship) and one ordered to cut grass to feed cattle on the Sabbath (forbidden, because the intention was to force the Jew to violate his religion). Widespread martyrdom occurred during the Crusades, when whole communities allowed themselves to be killed rather than submit to baptism.

Martyrs Forest. The single largest memorial to the Holocaust in the world. Situated near Jerusalem, the Martyrs Forest is truly a living memorial that is comprised of six million trees – 4.5 million pine trees representing the adults who died in the Holocaust and 1.5 million cypress trees symbolizing the children who perished.

Masada. Magnificent palace and fortress complex built by King Herod in the Judean wilderness on an isolated mountain plateau that rises to 1,440 feet above the western shore of the Dead Sea. In 73 C.E., three years after the fall of Jerusalem, Masada was the last stand of the Jewish Zealots in the war against Rome. The Romans launched a massive attack with siege engines, flaming torches, rock bombardments, and battering rams, but Masada remained in Jewish hands. At last, it became clear that the end was near. As the historian Josephus reports, Zealot leader Eliezer Ben-Yair made an impassioned speech that persuaded the 900 men, women, and children who inhabited Masada to accept death bravely on their own terms, rather than surrender to the Romans. Ten men chosen by lot served as executioners; one of these then killed the other nine before falling on his own sword. This tragic, yet heroic, stand has inspired the confident slogan of modern Israel – "Masada shall not fall again!" The reconstructed Masada has become one of the premier tourist sites in Israel.

Masei. The 10th and final *parashah* in the Book of Numbers (33:1-36:13), it continues the description of the wandering of the Israelites in the wilderness and brings the people to the threshold of the Promised Land. It details the boundaries of the Promised Land and the system to be used to divide it among the tribes, the levitical cities, the cities of refuge, and the distinction between the treatment of the intentional murderer and one who killed accidentally. The *parashah* concludes with the decision to the challenging problem posed by the daughters of Zelophehad (see inheritance).

Mashal. Most commonly translated as "parable," the rabbis made extensive use of this device for teaching moral and ethical lessons in the Talmud and especially in the Midrash. One of the most frequent motifs is the king, representing God, with Israel as his wayward but beloved son or wife. Also popular were parables taken from the animal world, especially fox fables.

Mashgiach. Religious overseer, appointed by a rabbinic authority, who supervises observance of the laws of *kashrut*. A *mashgiach* must be pious and trustworthy and is employed by restaurants, butchers, food manufacturers, and supermarkets that, once certified, receive a certificate (*hekshe*r) indicating that the food is kosher.

Mashiach. Literally "anointed one" in Hebrew, it reflects the practice in ancient Israel, as elsewhere in the Near East, of anointing kings and priests with olive oil. In Judaism, this term came to refer to a Divinely appointed redeemer (see Messiah), who would rule over a restored kingdom of Israel where the dispersed Jews would be gathered at the end of days.

Mashiv ha-ru'ach u-morid ha-geshem (Who causes the wind to blow and the rain to fall). Hebrew phrase added at the beginning of the second blessing during the recitation of the *Amidah* from Shemini Atzeret, when the prayer for rain is recited, until the first day of Passover, when the prayer for dew is said.

Maskilim. Literally, "enlightened ones," the Hebrew term for Eastern Europeans Jews who were followers of the *Haskalah* (see Enlightenment). They advocated breaking down the barriers between traditional life in the *shtetl* and the wider secular world, as well as revival of the Hebrew language and Jewish Emancipation. When used by Orthodox Jews, the term "*maskil*" had a negative connotation.

Masoretes. From a Hebrew root meaning "tradition" or "that which has been transmitted," textual scholars of the 6th–9th centuries who determined and preserved the authentic (masoretic) text of the Torah. From earliest times to this day, Torah scrolls have contained only the consonants of the text. The proper vowels, accentuation, and melody to be used when chanting the text were handed down orally to each generation. The Masoretes developed a system of vowel-points designed to ensure the correct pronunciation of the individual words. They also introduced cantillation marks (see *trope*) that indicate the proper way of accenting the words, where sentences begin and end, and the correct musical patterns to be used when chanting the text.[170] Manuscripts with these masoretic notations were designed only for study and could not be used at public Torah reading services. (See also *keri* and *ketiv*.)

Masorti. From a Hebrew root meaning "tradition" or "that which has been transmitted," the name for the Conservative movement in the State of Israel.

Massechet. Literally "woven fabric," the Hebrew term for a tractate of the Mishnah or other rabbinic work, such as the Talmud or Tosefta.

Matchmaker – see *Shadchan*.

Matmid. Literally "diligent" or "one who persists," this Hebrew term denotes a scholar who is devoted to studying Talmud. Bialik wrote a poem entitled *Ha-Matmid* (The Talmud Scholar), and Matmid is also the name of the El Al frequent flier program.

Matriarchs. Collective term for Sarah, Rebecca, Rachel, and Leah (the wives of the Patriarchs – Abraham, Isaac, and Jacob), the four "mothers" of the Jewish people. They are now included along with the Patriarchs in daily prayers in many non-Orthodox congregations.

Matrilineal descent. Traditional Jewish custom in which the status of the children of a mixed marriage depends solely on the faith of the mother. (In contrast, see *patrilineal descent*.)

Mattan Torah (giving of the Torah). Hebrew term for God giving the Torah to Moses on Mount Sinai, the key act in establishing the Divine covenant with the Jewish people. During rabbinic times, when Shavuot became observed as the anniversary of this event, this festival became referred to in the liturgy as *Zeman Mattan Torateinu* (The Time of the Giving of Our Torah).

Mattanot le-evyonim. Literally "gifts to the poor," they are traditionally sent on Purim to at least two needy people so that they also can share in the joy of the festival. This giving of Purim gifts is usually done through the various charities that assist indigent Jews.[171]

Mattot. The 9th *parashah* in the Book of Numbers (30:2-32:42), it opens with laws concerning the annulment of vows and oaths made by women, once again emphasizing the power and importance of the spoken word. There is then an account of the war against Midian and the settlement of Transjordan by the tribes of Reuben and Gad and half the tribe of Menashe.

Matzah. Unleavened bread that is made from flour and water and is the quintessential symbol of Passover.[172] Only grains capable of fermentation are valid for the manufacture of *matzah*. This applies to the five species indigenous to the Land of Israel – wheat, barley, spelt, rye, and oats – although wheat is most commonly used. Exquisite care is taken to ensure that the entire process from kneading to final baking does not exceed 18 minutes, the time when fermentation is traditionally thought to begin. *Matzah* has a paradoxical symbolism in the Passover story. The flat shape is a reminder that the former Israelite slaves left Egypt for freedom so quickly that their bread did not have time to rise (Exod. 12:39). Conversely, *matzah* is described as "*lechem oni*" (bread of affliction; Deut. 16:3), the minimal food provided for the Jewish slaves when they labored for Pharaoh. Two blessings are made over the *matzah* at the seder – one for its use as "bread," and the other related to the positive commandment to eat unleavened bread on the festival. One half of the broken middle *matzah* on the seder plate becomes the *afikoman*, which is eaten to finish the meal.

Matzah ball. Served with soup during the Passover seder, *matzah* balls are a popular alternative to noodles or dumplings made with forbidden *chametz* flour (see *knaidel*). *Matzah* balls are shaped by hand and dropped into a pot of salted, boiling water, where they swell up and become either feather-light or dense, depending on the way the recipe was prepared.

Matzah brei. Popular breakfast treat during Passover. Sheets of *matzah* are broken into small fragments and sprinkled with boiling water to soften, then combined with eggs and fried. *Matzah brei* is often served with cinnamon and sugar, honey, or preserves.

Matzah meal. Finely crumbled *matzah* that is used as a substitute for flour in cooking during Passover.

Matzah, shmurah. Literally meaning "guarded" *matzah*, it is preferred by some Jews for Passover use. The preparation of *shmurah matzah* is closely supervised from the time the wheat is harvested until it reaches the oven. This is in contrast to ordinary Passover *matzah*, which is supervised only beginning with the milling of the wheat. Rather than the uniform square sheets of manufactured *matzah*, handmade *shmurah matzah* is uneven and round, resembling the *matzah* baked in ancient times. It is generally more expensive because of the labor involved.[173]

Matzevah. Literally "monument," the Hebrew word for a headstone.In the Bible, the term is used for the monument that Jacob erected over the grave of his beloved wife Rachel (Gen. 35:20). Initially, a *matzevah* was pile of stones, a pillar, or merely a distinctive sign served to indicate the site of a grave. Only during the Hasmonean period, under Greek and Roman influence, did the custom develop of erecting ornate monumental tombstones for the nobility, such as *Yad Avshalom* (Monument of Absalom) and the sepulcher of Zechariah in the Kidron Valley in Jerusalem. (See also *ohel*.)

Maiven. From a Hebrew root meaning "to understand," a Yiddish term for a person who has special knowledge or expertise in a particular area. It also connotes a good judge of quality, a connoisseur.

Mayim. The Hebrew word for "water," it is the name of a popular Israeli song and dance. The text comes from Isaiah (12:3): "Joyfully you shall draw water from the fountains of salvation."

Mayim acharonim. Literally "last water," the ritual washing of the hands after a meal containing bread before saying *Birkat ha-Mazon* (Grace after Meals). According to the Talmud, this was to remove any salt adhering to the fingers that could cause serious injury to the eyes. Unlike the more common hand washing before the meal (*mayim rishonim* [first water]), this is done as a precautionary health measure rather than as a religious obligation, and no blessing is recited.

May Laws. So-called "Temporary Regulations," enacted on May 15, 1882 by the Russian Empire after the assassination of Czar Alexander II, which stayed in effect for 35 years. They constitued a systematic policy of discrimination that reduced the area of the Pale of Settlement where Jews could live by 10%, resulting in local expulsions, overcrowding, and economic restrictions. Jews were prohibited from buying or renting property outside their prescribed residences, denied jobs in the civil service, and forbidden to trade on Sundays and Christian holidays. Strict quotas were placed on the number of Jews allowed into secondary and higher education and many professions. The May Laws provided an impetus for the mass emigration of more than two million Jews from the Russian Empire.

Mazel. Literally "star, constellation, or sign of the Zodiac" in Hebrew, the word has been transformed from its astrological association to mean "good luck" (see below).

Mazel tov. Literally "good star," the phrase hearkens back to biblical and talmudic times, when it was widely believed that a person's fate depended on the positions of the stars. Today, it is the most common expression of congratulations and best wishes used by Jews on happy occasions (*simchas*). Among Ashkenazim, it is traditional to shout *mazel tov* to the bride and groom at the conclusion of the wedding ceremony.

Mazik. Literally meaning "one who causes harm," a Yiddish term in Jewish folklore that refers to a mischievous demon or evil spirit. Having the connotation of ingenuity and creativeness, it often is used endearingly to describe a clever child.

Mazuman. From a Hebrew root meaning "fixed" or "prepared," a Yiddish expression for "money" (as in the American slang term, "ready cash").

Meal of consolation (*se'udat havra'ah*). The community has an obligation to provide a meal of condolence for the mourners on their return from the cemetery. It is customary to serve foods that are round to symbolize the cyclical and continuous nature of life. Among the most common are hard-boiled eggs (a symbol of the close connection between life and death), lentils, garbanzo beans, and even bagels. Lentils are especially significant because, unlike most beans, they have no "eye" – symbolic of the deceased no longer being seen. Also, just as lentils have no "mouth," so mourners are forbidden to open their mouths to greet people. The critical importance of the *se'udat havra'ah* to the mourners is that it is served by friends and other family members who care deeply for them. In modern times, guests now share in this meal, but it was once limited to those in mourning.[174]

Meal offering (*mincha*). One of the sacrifices brought to the Temple, it consisted of finely ground wheat flour, oil, and frankincense (usually with water added), which could be merely a mixture of these ingredients or be cooked or baked in one of four different ways (Lev. 2:1-16). A meal offering was inexpensive and thus was most likely brought by a person who was too poor to afford anything more, but still wanted to express gratitude, homage, and reverence for God, or to invoke Divine favor. Indeed, the word used in the Torah to refer to the person who brought a meal offering is "*nefesh*" (soul), which Rashi interpreted to mean that God would regard it as if the individual had offered his very soul. A portion of the meal offering was burnt on the fire of the Altar, but the rest was eaten by the *kohanim*. Communal meal offerings were brought on Passover (the Omer), Shavuot, and the Sabbath (the twelve loaves of Showbread).

Meat – see *Fleishig*.

Mechayeh. Literally meaning "resurrection" (see below), this Yiddish word denotes a feeling of delight or relief. It typically is used in the context of physical pleasure after a sensation of discomfort, such as cooling off on a sweltering day or loosening one's belt after a huge meal.

Mechayei ha-meitim. Literally "Who resuscitates the dead," the conclusion of the second blessing of the *Amidah* (see *gevurot* and resurrection of the dead).

Mechilta. Halachic midrash on the Book of Exodus. There are two separate versions: *Mechilta de-Rabbi Ishmael* and the fragmentary *Mechilta de-Rabbi Shimon bar Yochai*. The former, completed around 400 C.E., was based on the mode of interpretation of Rabbi Ishmael ben Elisha and his school (1st-2nd century C.E.), which advocated the plain sense of the biblical text as the only reliable guide to proper interpretation. Consequently, he developed a set of 13 hermeneutical rules for halachic exegesis that were universally adopted by his successors and are still found in traditional prayer books.

Mechirat chametz – see *Chametz*, selling of.

Mechitza. Literally "partition," the physical separation in an Orthodox synagogue between the space reserved for men and that for women. Contrary to popular belief, the separation of the sexes in the synagogue is not an ancient tradition. The Jerusalem Temple had a special Women's Court (see *Ezrat Nashim*), but this generally was open to both men and women. The sole exception was the Water-Drawing ceremony on Sukkot, when the sexes were separated lest the ecstasy of the occasion lead to promiscuity. By the 13th century, separate sections for women in the synagogue were widespread, and this practice soon became the universally accepted rule everywhere.[175] In the early 19th century, the Reform movement abolished the *mechitzah*, arguing that the Bible does not command the separation of men and women during public worship or assemblies. In Conservative, Reform, and Reconstructionist synagogues today, there is no *mechitzah* and men and women sit together.

Mechutan. Yiddish term for a relative by marriage.

Medicine – see Physicians.

Meggido. Fortified town in the Jezreel Valley on the ancient highway linking Egypt in the south to Syria and Assyria in the north, Megiddo was the scene of numerous major battles. The word "Armageddon" may derive from the Hebrew phrase *Har Megiddo* (Mountain of Megiddo).

Megillah (1). Hebrew word meaning "scroll," it usually refers to *Megillat Esther*.

Megillah (2). Derived from *Megillat Esther*, which is read in its entirety on Purim, this Yiddish term refers to a long involved story. It is especially used in the slang expression *gantze megillah* (the whole *megillah*), meaning that it contains every detail from start to finish.

Megillah (Meg.) (3). The 10th tractate of Mo'ed (festivals) in the Mishnah, it deals with the reading of the Scroll of Esther on Purim. It also lists the scriptural readings for special Sabbaths, festivals, and fast days, as well as rules for taking care of synagogues and sacred objects.

Megillat Esther. The Book of Esther, the reading of which is the main feature of the festival of Purim. This melodramatic tale of court intrigue opens with the banishment of the proud Queen Vashti by the somewhat dim-witted King Ahasuerus and the choice of Esther, the winner of a beauty contest, to be the new queen. When Mordecai, Esther's cousin and foster father, refuses to bow down to Haman, the grand vizier, the latter decides to take out his fury on all the Jews. He convinces Ahasuerus with a classic anti-Semitic argument to consent to a decree calling for the genocidal massacre of Jewish communities throughout the kingdom. Under Mordecai's urging, Esther invites Haman to a private gala banquet, where she reveals that she is Jewish and pleads for Ahasuerus to save her people. The king agrees, Haman is hanged, the Jews are given permission to defend themselves against their enemies, and Mordecai and Esther institute Purim as an annual holiday.[176] Hiddenness and reversal of fate are key elements of the Purim plot, which has a number of ironic moments and serendipity.

Megillot. Literally "scrolls," the collective term for the 4th through 8th books of the Writings section of the Bible. They are often grouped together because of the custom of reading them on festivals – The Song of Songs on Passover; Ruth on Shavuot; Lamentations on Tisha b'Av; Ecclesiastes on Sukkot; and Esther on Purim.

Me'il. Literally "robe" or "cloak," the Hebrew term for the richly embroidered mantle that covers the Torah scroll in the Ashkenazic tradition. In the Bible, the term was applied to the robe worn under the *ephod* (see *Kohen Gadol*, vestments of the) and the cloak worn by the prophet Elijah.

Me'ilah. The 8th tractate in Kodashim (holy things) in the Mishnah, it deals with sacrilege (profane use) of Temple property.

Melachah – see Work.

Melamed. Hebrew teacher in a *cheder*.In Eastern Europe, a *melamed* had little training and low status, but was often the best possible instructor for a town that was too small to afford a rabbi or a teacher with higher credentials.

Melaveh malkah. Literally "escorting the Queen," the festive meal at the close of the Sabbath on Saturday evening. Throughout the ages, many Jews have preferred to eat their main meal after *Havdalah*, when they could have freshly cooked food. Since the rabbis could not prevent this practice, they insisted that this meal be considered a farewell feast in honor of the departing Sabbath Queen. This Saturday evening meal is also associated with King David, the ancestor of the Messiah. The Talmud relates that in answer to his plea, "Lord make me know my end" (Ps. 39:5), David was informed that his death would occur on a Sabbath. Therefore, after the conclusion of each Sabbath, King David would celebrate because he knew he would live for at least one more week.[177]

Melikah. Procedure for killing the bird of a sin offering. Rather than severing its head with an instrument (Lev. 5:8), which rendered the offering invalid, the *kohen* was required to nip with his fingernail close by the nape and cut through the neck bone until reaching and cutting the windpipe and gullet. Because severing the head of the bird would make the offering appear smaller, this prohibition was designed so as not to diminish the offering of a poor person, who could not afford to sacrifice a four-legged animal.

Mem. The 14th letter of the Hebrew alphabet, with a numerical value of 40.

Memorial service – see *Yizkor*.

Menahot (Men.). The second tractate in Kodashim (holy things) in the Mishnah, it deals with the preparation of meal offerings, *tzitzit*, and *tefillin*.It opens with an emphasis on the requirement of intention (see *kavanah*) related to offerings, because directing one's thoughts to God was considered more important than the size or quality of the offering itself.

Mene mene tekel u-pharsin. Four strange words in an unknown language that appeared on the wall during the feast of the Babylonian King Belshazzar. Daniel interpreted them as meaning: *mene* – "God has numbered the days of your kingdom and will bring it to an end;" *tekel* – "You have been weighed in the balance and been found wanting;" and *pharsin* – "Your kingdom has been divided and given over to the Medes and Persians." This interpretation proved accurate when the Persian ruler Cyrus conquered the Babylonian Empire.

Menorah. Seven-branched candelabrum that once stood in the Jerusalem Temple. One of the most beloved and enduring symbols of Judaism, the menorah is the emblem of the State of Israel. In the portable Tabernacle (*Mishkan*), the Menorah was placed in front of the curtain (see *parochet*) on the south side against the Table. The lights of the Menorah had to be kindled even on the Sabbath, when lighting other fire was forbidden, just as burnt offerings also were brought on that day. The Arch of Titus in Rome depicts the Romans sacking Jerusalem and carrying a menorah out of the Temple. The menorah was a common symbol during the rabbinic period, especially in synagogue mosaics and in various amulets, seals, and rings. For the kabbalists, the menorah symbolized the Tree of Life and its seven branches the lower seven *sefirot*; the oil in the menorah was seen as a symbol of Divine abundance flowing to humankind. Today, menorahs are often prominent features in decorations for Torah mantles and the ark. In Israel, the menorah is reproduced frequently on stamps, coins, and souvenirs. A large sculptured menorah depicting major events of Jewish history stands outside the Knesset in Jerusalem, a symbol of the miraculous rebirth of the Jewish people after almost 2,000 years of exile. The term "Chanukah menorah" is also applied to the eight-branched *chanukiah*.

Mentsch. Literally meaning "human being," this Yiddish word denotes a particularly kind, decent, and responsible person who possesses admirable qualities that one would seek in a trusted colleague or a dear friend.

Menstruation – see *Niddah*.

Mercy – see *Rachamim*.

Mercy killing – see Euthanasia.

Meretz. Zionist social-democratic, left-wing, and dovish political party in Israel. Founded in 1992, Meretz is part of the Socialist International and views itself as the political representative of the Israeli peace movement.

Merits of the fathers – see *Zechut avot*.

Merkava mysticism. Jewish mystical practice in the early talmudic period that focused on visions of the heavenly world based loosely on Ezekiel's vision of the Divine Chariot. Treatises on this subject depict the Divine Throne as located in the innermost of seven concentric palaces or temples (see *heichalot*), with doors guarded by terrifying angels. Only by knowing the correct passwords, consisting of mystical names of God, could the practicing mystic get past these angelic gatekeepers and enter into the throne room to gaze upon God's glory and join the celestial choir in declaring the Divine holiness. The Talmud labeled the teachings and practices of *Merkava* mysticism as dangerous, but they persisted well into the Middle Ages, especially among the kabbalists.

Meron (Merom). Village in Upper Galilee near Safed and the gravesite of R. Shimon bar Yochai, the reputed author of the mystical *Zohar*.Today, kabbalists and Hasidim in Israel hold a festive celebration in Meron on Lag ba-Omer, the traditional date of bar Yochai's death. Thousands gather to study mystical texts and to sing and dance around large bonfires.

Meshugge. Yiddish word meaning "crazy." Variant terms are *meshuggener* (crazy person) and *mishegas* (craziness).

Mesorah (tradition). The transmission of knowledge from generation to generation, which is a central pillar of Judaism. This tradition consists of the Written Law and the Oral Law. Not merely a compendium of law, *mesorah* encompasses everything of worth from the Jewish past that relates to the social, moral, and intellectual development of a person, the sum total of the experience of the Jewish people throughout the millennia. The term is also used to refer to the commonly accepted official text of the Torah, which was developed by the Masoretes and includes a system of vowel-points (see vowels and *trope*).

Messenger, Divine. An angel in human guise assigned to perform a specific act on earth. Examples include the three who visited Abraham after his circumcision and announced that the elderly Sarah would have a child (Gen. 18), the two who continued on to save Lot and his daughters from the destruction of Sodom and Gomorrah (Gen. 19), and the one who appeared to Manoah and his wife telling of the upcoming birth of their son, Samson (Judg. 13).

Messiah. Human agent of Divine redemption. The concept of a divine or semi-divine "savior," whose self-sacrifice will save mortals from the punishment merited by their sins, is a purely Christian idea that has no foundation in Jewish thought. Absolute trust in the ultimate coming of the Messiah is a core belief in Judaism and one of Maimonides' Thirteen Principles of Faith. Faith in, and hope for, the Messiah sustained Jews throughout centuries of suffering and persecution. Yearning for the coming of the Messiah plays a major role in Jewish festivals and liturgy. The Sabbath has always been considered a foretaste of the Messianic Age and the World to Come. Jews traditionally eat fish on the Sabbath as a symbol of Leviathan, the great sea monster that will be part of the messianic meal for the righteous. The song *Eliyahu ha-Navi* (Elijah the Prophet, the herald of the Messiah) is sung at *Havdalah*, when according to tradition the Messiah will come; at every circumcision, since this Jewish child may be the long-awaited Messiah; and at the Passover seder, the festival of redemption. Today, many liberal Jews view the Messiah not as a human agent but in more figurative terms as a time when justice, mercy, and peace will prevail throughout the world.

Messiah, coming of the. Normative Judaism teaches that one should work actively to hasten the arrival of the Messiah by doing everything possible to perfect the world (see *tikun olam*), rather than simply waiting passively for him to come. Even the advent of the Messiah will not relieve human beings of responsibility for taking care of the world. This is perfectly illustrated by the statement of R. Yochanan ben Zakkai: "If you are planting a tree, and you hear that the Messiah has come, finish planting the tree and then go greet him." The Talmud teaches, "The Messiah will come if every Jew observes the Sabbath twice in a row" (Shab. 118b). According to tradition, the Messiah will only come when we are ready. The Talmud relates that R. Joshua ben Levi found Elijah the Prophet, disguised as a filthy beggar, sitting at the gates of Rome. He asked, "When will you come and proclaim the Messiah?" Elijah replied, "Today, if you will only hear his voice" (Sanh. 98a).

Messiah, false. Throughout the Middle Ages and early modern times, Jews speculated extensively on the apocalyptic end of days, attempting to determine exactly when the Messiah would appear. Periodically, self-proclaimed "messiahs" attracted thousands of followers, whose hopes were subsequently dashed when their messianic claims proved to be false. The most infamous was Shabbetai Tzevi in the 17th century, who proclaimed himself the Messiah in the synagogue at Smyrna (today in Turkey) and attracted thousands of followers. With the Jewish world in a frenzy of excitement, Shabbetai Tzevi traveled to Constantinople to claim his kingdom from the sultan. Promptly arrested, he converted to Islam under threat of death. This apostasy was a devastating blow, and many disillusioned Jews converted with him; others were left depressed and demoralized.

Messianic Age. Era of universal peace and justice, described as a time when "the wolf shall live with the sheep, and the leopard lie down with the kid; the calf with the young lion shall grow up together, and a little child shall lead them" (Isa. 11:6). It will be a time when "every man shall sit under his vine and under his fig tree, and none shall make him afraid" (Micah 4:4). According to traditional Jewish belief, the Messiah will be a descendant of King David. Under his rule, the city of Jerusalem and the Temple will be rebuilt and all Jews throughout the world will be gathered to the Land of Israel. In the prayer for Israel in most prayer books, the establishment of the State in 1948 is called *reishit tz'michat g'ulateinu* (the dawn of our redemption). Contemporary religious Zionists have embraced this idea, viewing the establishment of the State of Israel as the inauguration of the messianic process.

Messianic Jew. A person who was born Jewish or converted to Judaism and acknowledges his Jewish ethnicity, but believes that Jesus is the Messiah.This view is completely opposed to traditional Judaism.

Met mitzvah. The speedy burial of a corpse found unattended. This duty, which indicates the importance of reverence for the human body after death (see *kavod ha-met*), was incumbent even on the High Priest, who was otherwise forbidden to become ritually unclean through contact with the dead.

Metatron. Most important angel in the heavenly hierarchy according to the aggadic and kabbalistic literature. One version of the myth indicates that Metatron came into being when God created the world and immediately assumed many of the Divine responsibilities. Another associates Metatron with the biblical Enoch, a pious man who ascended to Heaven and was transformed into a fiery angel who served as the scribe of the Divine court, recording the deeds of men.

Metziah. From a Hebrew word meaning "find," this Yiddish term means a bargain or a lucky break.

Metzora (1). A person afflicted with the skin disease *tzara'at*, who was deemed to be ritually unclean and was forced to make himself recognizable so that people could keep away from him. The *metzora* had to rend his clothes, allow the hair of his head to go loose, cover his upper lip, and cry "unclean, unclean" (Lev. 13:45). It was forbidden for affected individuals to cut out or cauterize the physical signs of *tzara'at* in order to change their appearance. The cleansing of the *metzora* was a complex process involving shaving the head, washing clothes, and immersion in a ritual bath, as well as bringing an offering to become completely pure for ritual purposes.

Metzora (2). The 5th *parashah* in the Book of Leviticus (14:1-15:33), it details the purification rites (see previous section) for individuals recovering from the skin disease *tzara'at*.It concludes with a description of abnormal discharges from the sexual organs and the normal menstruation of women and seminal emissions of men.

Meturgeman. When the Jews returned from exile in Babylonia, where the vernacular was Aramaic, Hebrew was no longer the spoken language of the masses. The custom developed of having a special synagogue official (*meturgeman*; "interpreter" in Aramaic) provide a verse-by-verse translation of the Torah reading. This was a challenging task because the translator was prohibited from having any written material in front him, since the translation was regarded as part of the Oral Law. The *meturgeman* was "not permitted to translate word by word, lest he distort the sense of the Torah reading, nor was he permitted to elaborate on the text. His was to be a free, though exact, translation. If he took any liberties with the translation, he was to be 'silenced and admonished'."[178] Many centuries later, this gave rise to *Targum Onkelos*, the official Aramaic version of the Torah.[179]

Mevushal. Literally "boiled" and meaning "pasteurized," this Hebrew term refers to wine that is heated to the boiling point so that air bubbles are brought to the surface with some loss of liquid due to evaporation. This is required according to the laws of *kashrut* for a wine to retain its kosher status (see wine, kosher) once it has been opened and poured by a non-Jew, such as a waiter. Thus, a wine that is produced in this manner retains its religious purity regardless of who opens or pours it.

Mezonot. Foods other than bread (such as cakes, cookies, cereals, and pasta) made from the flour of wheat, barley, oats, rye, or spelt, the five grains mentioned or alluded to in the Torah as indigenous to the Land of Israel.

Mezuzah (1). The distinctive mark of a Jewish home and a reminder of the Divine Presence. It consists of a piece of parchment, made from the skin of a clean animal, upon which a scribe has written the first two paragraphs of the *Shema* (Deut 6:4-9 and 11:13-21). Both of these include the commandment, "And you shall write them upon the doorposts [*mezuzot*] of your house and upon your gates" (Deut. 6:9, 11:20). The parchment is rolled up and enclosed in a special wood or metal case, since it has the status of a Torah scroll and cannot be touched directly. The case is fastened at an angle (upper end pointed inward) to the upper third of the doorpost on the right side of the outside door, as well as to the doorpost of every living room in the house (excluding bathrooms, storerooms, and kitchen). The Hebrew word *Shaddai* (Almighty) is written on the back of the parchment, which is inserted into the case in such a way that the word can be seen through a small opening near the top of the container. A Jew who moves into a new home places a *mezuzah* on the outer door immediately, or at least within the first 30 days. When securing the *mezuzah* to the door, a special blessing is recited. A Jew who sells or rents a home to a fellow Jew is required to leave the *mezuzot* in place, but must remove them if the purchaser or lessee is a non-Jew.

Mezuzah (2). Minor tractate added to the Talmud that deals with the laws regarding the writing and use of the *mezuzah.*

Mi Chamochah (Who is like You [among the gods]). Verse from the victorious Song at the Sea (see *Shirat ha-Yam*), which is included in the blessing after the *Shema* that immediately precedes the recitation of the *Amidah.*

Mi she-Berach (1). Literally "May He Who blessed [our forefathers, Abraham, Isaac, and Jacob])," this third prayer after the Torah reading on Sabbath morning invokes God's blessings on those individuals who provide funds for the general welfare. It calls for special blessings to those "who give lamps for illumination and wine for *Kiddush* and *Havdalah*, bread for guests and charity to the poor; and all who involve themselves faithfully in the needs of the community."[180] Although written in Hebrew, it is often read in the vernacular because it clearly enunciates the fiscal and ethical responsibilities incumbent on members of the congregation.[181]

Mi she-Berach (2). Initial words of a prayer formula that invokes God's blessings on individuals and the community. For example, each person called for an *aliyah* generally receives a personal *Mi she-Berach*, though in some congregations a collective blessing is recited after the completion of the entire Torah portion. Those celebrating a special occasion, such as a bar/bat mitzvah, forthcoming marriage, or birth of a child, receive a special version of the prayer that makes reference to the event. The *Mi she-Berach* formula is also used as the introduction to the prayer for those who are sick. In Israel, an additional *Mi she-Berach* is recited for the welfare of members of the Israel Defense Forces.

Micah (Mic.). The 6th of the minor prophets. In the 8th century, he railed against the social corruption of the cities, the injustice of the rulers, and the oppression of the poor in both Judah and Samaria. He predicted the downfall of Samaria and the eventual destruction of the Temple and the beloved city of Jerusalem. According to Micah, what the Lord requires of a human being is only "to do justice, to love mercy, and to walk humbly with your God" (6:8). His appeal to God to "cast out (*tashlich*) all our sins into the depths of the sea" (7:19) is the basis for the ceremony of Tashlich on the first day of Rosh Hashanah. Micah prophesied an era of universal peace and justice at the end of days, when "every man shall sit under his vine and under his fig tree, and none shall make him afraid (4:4)."

Microcalligraphy. The art of using minuscule Hebrew script, usually of verses from the Bible, traditional liturgy, or kabbalistic texts, to create abstract shapes or figurative designs.

Midot (1). Jewish moral values that enable a person to live a good life according to God's will. Playing with the similarity in Hebrew between the words *midot* and *mitzvot*, Nachmanides (13th century) argued that the purpose of a human being is to become a *baal midot* (virtuous person) by fulfilling the *mitzvot*, which can be understood as vehicles for the formation of proper character.

Midot (Mid.) (2). The 8th tractate of Kodashim (holy things) in the Mishnah, it deals with the architecture, organization, and measurements of the Second Temple.

Midot (3). Rabbinic term for the collection of hermenteutical rules of biblical interpretation.

Midrash. Deriving from a Hebrew root meaning "to search out," the word can refer to either the process of interpreting the Bible or to the genre of rabbinic literature that has collected these interpretations (see midrashic literature, below). One reason for the development of the Midrash is to fill in the gaps of the terse biblical narrative, which provides little information as to the thoughts and feelings of the characters or the motivations behind their actions. The Bible is an ancient document that reflects its time of origin, the world of the early history of Israel. By the time of the Rabbis, the social and political situation had dramatically changed and was heavily influenced by Hellenic culture. Thus, the Midrash provided an opportunity for the Rabbis to reread the biblical text, rendering it meaningful to their contemporaries.

Midrash Rabbah. Literally "The Great Midrash," a 10-part collection of aggadic *midrashim* on the Five Books of Moses (see *Chumash*) and the five *megillot*. Despite the similarity in their names, this set does not represent a cohesive work since the individual books were written by different authors, in different locales, and in different historical eras (from the 5th–12th centuries).

Midrash Tanhuma – see Tanhuma.

Midrashic literature. There are three basic types of Midrash: exegetical, homiletic, and narrative. An *exegetical* midrash contains short comments on each chapter, every verse, and even individual words of an entire book of the Bible (e.g., Genesis Rabbah, Exodus Rabbah, and Lamentations Rabbah; Mechilta, Sifra, Sifrei). A *homiletic* midrash (e.g., Leviticus Rabbah and Deuteronomy Rabbah; Tanchuma; Pesikta de-Rav Kahana) is more discursive and is structured around sermons expounding on verses from the weekly Torah portion or the readings for special Sabbaths and festivals. Each chapter or section of these *midrashim* constitutes a collection of homilies and sayings on one specific topic that seem to combine into one long homily. A *narrative* midrash (e.g., Pirkei de-Rebbe Eliezer) does not attempt to explicate the Bible in a direct or orderly manner, but instead is a collection of stories and legends about individual Rabbis or biblical characters. Midrash can also be divided into the more common *midrash aggadah*, which contains stories and legends that are concerned with ethical teachings or other topical issues of non-legal parts of the Bible, and *midrash halacha*, which expounds upon the legal aspects and implications of the biblical text. Probably the best-known collection of midrashic literature is the Passover Haggadah. Although it contains prayers, instructions for the Passover rituals, and biblical verses, most of the seder before the festive meal is pure midrash. Although classic midrashic literature ceased by the end of the 12th century, there has been a resurgence of this genre in recent times.

Midwives. Women who assist in the birth process. After Pharaoh's order to kill all the newborn Israelite boys, two Hebrew midwives named Shiphrah and Puah[182] bravely refused to obey the royal decree. They explained to Pharaoh that the Hebrew women were not like their Egyptian counterparts: "Before the midwife can come to them, they have given birth" (Exod. 1:15-19). The midwives had the courage to challenge Pharaoh because their consciences answered to a higher authority.

Miketz. The 8th *parashah* in the Book of Genesis (41:1-44:17), it narrates Joseph's interpretation of Pharaoh's dreams of the seven fat and scrawny cows, and the seven full and shriveled ears of corn, as both indicating seven years of prosperity followed by seven years of famine. Joseph, the former slave, is declared vizier of Egypt, second only to Pharaoh, and he implements his successful plan to store grain during the years of plenty so that it would be available during the seven years when the crops failed. It also describes the two meetings of Joseph with his brothers, who were sent by their father Jacob to purchase food in Egypt. As the result of a stratagem devised by Joseph to test his brothers' family loyalty, the second encounter ends with Benjamin accused of theft and sentenced to remain Joseph's slave.

Mikrah. Literally "reading," this popular Hebrew term for the Bible stresses the central role of the public reading of Scripture in synagogue services.

Mikra'ot Gedolot. The "Great Rabbinic Bible" published in 1524-1525 in Venice by the Christian printer Daniel Bomberg. This version is generally considered the "official" masoretic text of the Hebrew Bible and has been the model for all future editions.

Mikva'ot (Mik.). The 6th tractate in Tohorot (purity) in the Mishnah, it deals with the regulations concerning the *mikveh.*

Mikveh. Literally "a collection [of water]," the Hebrew term for a ritual bath. Initially a natural, flowing body of water, today most are located indoors and look like small swimming pools, though they are filled with either rainwater or water from a spring or stream. A *mikveh* must contain forty *se'ah* (about 200 gallons) of clear water and be deep enough to cover the entire body of the person undergoing immersion. Prior to entering the *mikveh*, it is essential to wash thoroughly. This indicates, both literally and symbolically, that the purpose of immersion is ritual purity rather than physical cleanliness. No object can be interposed between the body and the water of the ritual bath. Therefore, before entering the *mikveh* it is necessary to remove all jewelry, makeup, and even nail polish.[183] Today, the *mikveh* is most frequently used by a woman before resuming sexual relations with her husband after completing the period of separation related to her menstrual cycle (see *niddah*). An unmarried woman does not go to the *mikveh* for purification, and she typically performs *tevilah* for the first time before her wedding (rather than after her first menses). Immersion in the *mikveh* is also indispensable in the conversion of both male and female non-Jews to Judaism. Some Orthodox Jewish men immerse themselves in the *mikveh* on Fridays and before Jewish holidays (especially Yom Kippur) to stress the transition between regular weekdays and the Sabbath and festivals.[184]

Mikveh Israel (Hope of Israel). First agricultural school in Israel, and for many years the only one in the land. Situated southeast of Tel Aviv, Mikveh Israel was founded in 1870 by the Alliance Israélite Universelle on the initiative of Charles Netter, in response to an appeal to help Jews in the Holy Land learn a productive occupation. The first Bilu pioneers trained at Mikveh Israel immediately upon their arrival in the country, and the school became an important education center for Youth Aliyah. Mikveh Israel has been instrumental in developing novel techniques in citrus and other agricultural branches, introducing avocado cultivation and the acclimatization of many livestock strains.

Milchig. Yiddish term meaning "milk," it refers to all dairy products – such as butter, cheese, and fresh and sour cream – that cannot be cooked or consumed with meat (*fleishig*; see mixing meat and milk). Because processed foods can contain unsuspected dairy ingredients – buttermilk, non-fat dry milk, whey, or dairy-derived additives – *kashrut*-observers always read labels carefully and buy products with a kosher certification (see *heksher*). (See also *chalav Yisrael.*)

Milk – see *Milchig* (above).

Mincha (1). The afternoon service, which the Rabbis maintained was instituted by Isaac, who went out "to meditate in the field toward evening" (Gen. 24:63). It consists of a brief introduction, composed primarily of the *Ashrei*, *U'va le-Zion Go'el* (only on Sabbath and festivals), *Amidah*, *Tachanun* (not on Sabbath, festivals, fast days, and other occasions), Torah reading (only on Sabbath and fast days), *Aleinu*, and *Mourner's Kaddish*. *Mincha* is often combined with the *Ma'ariv* service in the late afternoon or early evening.

Mincha (2) – see Meal offering.

Minhag (custom). This Hebrew word usually refers to a practice that over time became binding with the force of *halacha*. It also refers to local community (or even individual) religious practices that have become a tradition. As an example, because meat takes a long time to digest, or due to residual meat particles caught in the teeth or its taste remaining on the palate, Jewish law rules that one must wait a designated period after eating a meat meal before ingesting milk products. Customs range from an hour for Jews of Dutch ancestry to three hours for German Jews and six hours for those from other European countries

Minim (1). Hebrew word for sectarians such as the Sadducees, Essenes, Gnostics, and especially the early Judeo-Christians, who posed a threat to the precarious existence of the Jewish people. When the *Amidah* was put into its final form by Rabban Gamaliel II and his colleagues at Yavneh after the destruction of the Second Temple, they added an additional 19th blessing designed to attack the *minim*. Any reader who failed to recite this blessing, or any worshiper who failed to respond to it with the customary "amen," was immediately recognized as a heretic; in this way these sectarians were effectively eliminated from the synagogue.[185] Although the specific sects against whom it was addressed no longer existed, the Rabbis retained the blessing against *minim* in the *Amidah* because the danger of nonbelievers and heretics persists in every generation.[186] (See next entry and *false accusations*.)

Minim (2). The 12th blessing of the weekday *Amidah*, it asks the God who "breaks enemies and humbles wanton sinners" to ensure that there be "no hope" for slanderers and that "all wickedness perish in an instant."

Minor prophets. Term for the following 12 prophets – Hosea, Joel, Amos, Obadiah, Jonah, Micah, Nahum, Habakkuk, Haggai, Zephaniah, Zechariah, and Malachi (see individual listings). The popular epithet "minor" has solely a quantitative connotation and is not necessarily an indication of relative importance.

Minor tractates (of the Talmud). Essays from the *tannaitic* period or later works dealing with topics for which there is no formal tractate in the Mishnah. The minor tractates, which are usually printed at the end of Nezikin (the 4th order of the Mishnah), include the following (briefly described in separate sections): Avot de-Rabbi Natan; Soferim (Scribes); Semachot (or Evel Rabbati); Kallah; Kallah Rabbati; Derech Eretz Rabbah; Derech Eretz Zuta; Perek ha-Shalom; Sefer Torah; Mezuzah; Tefillin; Tzitzit; Avadim; Gerim; and Kutim.

Minyan. Literally "number," the term for the quorum necessary for congregational worship and certain other religious ceremonies. Traditionally composed of 10 adult males (13 years of age or older), a *minyan* is required for the following sections of the public synagogue service: *Barchu*, repetition of the *Amidah* with *Kedushah*, reading the Torah and *haftarah*, Priestly Blessing, and *Kaddish*. A *minyan* is also necessary for the rites of comforting the mourners, the recital of the *Sheva Berachot* at wedding ceremonies, and the special invitation (*zimun*) including the word *Eloheinu* preceding the *Birkat ha-Mazon* (see Grace after Meals). Orthodox congregations do not count women as part of the *minyan*, because they are not required to attend public prayer services – an exemption related to their essential time-dependent responsibilities toward home and family. In Reform, Reconstructionist, and most Conservative synagogues today, in which women have full religious equality with men, the requirement is for 10 *persons* to constitute the *minyan* needed for a public prayer service.

Minyan men. Paid functionaries, frequently elders, who received a dole from the community in exchange for always being available to make the required quorum of 10 men for a synagogue service.[187] (See *batlanim*.)

Miracles. Termed "signs" (*ot*; *mofetim*) and "wonders" (*fele*; *nifla'ot*) in the Bible, any extraordinary events attributed to Divine intervention in which an omnipotent God sets aside the established order of nature. *Pirkei Avot* (5:9) lists 10 miraculous things that were created at twilight on the sixth day of Creation, while the medieval Jewish philosophers attempted to give rational explanations for the biblical miracles. The Rabbis emphasized that, though often unaware, we are surrounded by miracles on a daily basis. The workings of the human body, the beauty and harmony of nature, and the very gift of life are miraculous.

Miriam's Cup. At Passover seders in households with a strong feminist bent, a new tradition has developed of adding a cup (parallel to the Cup of Elijah) as a symbol of the contributions of Miriam, the sister of Moses and a prophetess. Miriam's Cup is filled with water, rather than wine, and symbolizes the miracle of Miriam's well.

Miriam's Well. Mysterious well that, according to legend, was created at twilight as the sixth day of Creation drew to a close. It brought forth water to sustain the Israelites for 40 years during their wandering in the wilderness after the Exodus. With the death of Miriam, the guardian of the well, it promptly disappeared. One tradition maintains that Miriam's Well now lies hidden in the Sea of Galilee, waiting for the arrival of Elijah and the Messiah.

Mishegas (craziness) – see *Meshugge*.

Mishkan. Often translated as "Tabernacle," the portable tent-like structure for the Divine Presence that the Israelites were commanded to build in the wilderness so that God might "dwell among them." It consisted of an outer court, enclosed by curtains, and the Sanctuary proper, which was divided into two chambers by a hanging curtain (see *parochet*). The outer chamber contained the Table of the Showbread, the Menorah, and the Golden Altar for incense. The inner chamber (see Holy of Holies) was entered only once a year by the High Priest on the Day of Atonement. The sole object within the Holy of Holies was the Ark of the Covenant, which held the two stone tablets on which were written the Ten Commandments. Rather than a dwelling place for God, the *Mishkan* was considered by most commentators as a central focus where the people could worship God and receive Divine inspiration,[188] or as a symbol of the historic experience on Mount Sinai (i.e., a "portable Mount Sinai" because it was ringed by the tribes and topped by the cloud of God's Presence). The portable Sanctuary was replaced by a permanent structure when King Solomon built the First Temple in Jerusalem.

Mishlo'ach manot. Often abbreviated as *shalach manot*, this Hebrew phrase refers to the tradition of sending gifts (lit., "portions") to friends and acquaintances on the holiday of Purim. Because the word *manot* is in the plural, it became traditional to send at least two kinds of food to at least two people.

Mishmeret. One of several biblical words for "law" and coming from a Hebrew root meaning "watch" or "guard," *mishmeret* (Lev. 8:35) is usually translated as "observance."

Mishnah. Literally meaning "repetition" or "teaching" in Hebrew, the earliest major rabbinic book and the basis for the Talmud. It was compiled in the early 3rd century by Judah ha-Nasi (Judah the Prince, known simply as "Rabbi"), who sifted through, evaluated, and edited the vast number of legal opinions constituting the Oral Law that had been expressed over the centuries in the academies of learning, primarily in the Land of Israel. The Mishnah is divided into six "orders" – Zera'im (seeds), Mo'ed (festivals), Nashim (women), Nezikin (damages), Kodashim (holy things), and Tohorot (purities). Each order is divided into *massechot* (see tractates). (See entries for individual orders of the Mishnah and the tractates within them.)

Mishneh Torah (1). By far the greatest medieval legal code, which was compiled by Maimonides in the 12th century. In this massive 14-volume work – also known as *Yad*, since the numerical value of the letters *yud* (10) and *dalet* (4) equal 14 – this renowned rabbinic scholar discussed every conceivable topic of Jewish law in an immensely logical sequence. He collected and digested all talmudic sources relevant to any given subject and then wrote down a simple statement of the law in the clearest possible language, without any summary of the ancient discussions. Maimonides wrote that the purpose of his code was to make the study of the Talmud unnecessary for those who merely wanted to know the law and how to live their lives as observant Jews. For this arrogance, Maimonides was condemned and denounced as a threat to traditional Judaism. Nevertheless, the *Mishneh Torah* became recognized as an exemplary work of Jewish law and a significant source for subsequent codes (see *Shulchan Aruch*).

Mishneh Torah (2). Literally "Repetition of the Torah," a Hebrew term for the Book of Deuteronomy.

Mishpachah. Literally "family," this Hebrew term can denote a nuclear family or be extended to include relatives by blood and marriage. As a technical term related to biblical times, the word refers to one of the divisions of the tribes of Israel ("clan"), which was larger than a single household (*beit av*).

Mishpat (1). The 11th blessing of the weekday *Amidah*, which asks the God who "loves righteousness and judgment" to "restore our judges as in earlier times" and to "reign over us with kindness and compassion."

Mishpat (2). One of several biblical words for "law," *mishpat* (Num. 9:14) is usually translated as "ordinance." It often has the connotation of a judgment in a court case (see *Mishpat Ivri*, below). In contrast to *chukim*, *mishpatim* are laws whose rationales are evident (such as the prohibitions against theft and murder) and thus would have been followed even if God had not commanded them.

Mishpat Ivri. Literally "Jewish Law," this Hebrew term refers to those halachic matters that are not related to specifically religious issues, but are similar to those subjects within the purview of other modern legal systems – relations among human beings (contracts, torts, family relations, criminal law) and not between man and God. *Mishpat Ivri* recognizes a strong link between law and morality and contains examples of the conversion of moral imperatives into norms with legal sanction. It is also the name of a major four-volume textbook on Israeli law by Menachem Elon.

Mishpatim. The 6th *parashah* in the Book of Exodus (21:1-24:18), it contains the Book of the Covenant, the earliest legal code in the Bible. It includes the religious, moral, and civil laws that provided the foundation for a just society in ancient Israel.

Miskeit. Yiddish word meaning "homely."

Mission to Israel. Group visit to the Land of Israel sponsored by a synagogue, Jewish communal agency, or charitable organization. In addition to sightseeing, most missions include briefings by political and religious leaders, visits to projects supported by the organizer of the group, and fund-raising activities.

Mitah yafah (beautiful death) – see Euthanasia.

Mitnagdim. Literally "opponents," the term is specifically applied to those who opposed the Hasidic movement in 18th-century Eastern Europe. The major figure was the Vilna Gaon, a semi-legendary intellectual giant who towered over the Lithuanian (see Litvak) community. He strenuously objected to the singing of wordless melodies (see *nigunim*) in prayer services and other new customs of the Hasidim, attacking their stress on simple piety rather than traditional scholarship, the seemingly excessive veneration of their leaders, and their according kabbalist teachings precedence over halachic studies. The Vilna Gaon and other *mitnagdim* stressed the strict observance of all the details and minutiae of *halacha*, convinced that the undermining of a single precept of the Written or Oral Law was a blow to the foundations of the Torah as a whole. The *mitnagdim* issued several bans of excommunication against the Hasidim.

Mitpachot. Scarves that Orthodox women use to cover their hair (see head covering, women). The Hebrew term also refers to the kerchiefs used to wrap the Torah scroll after reading (see wimpel).

Mitzrayim. Hebrew word for Egypt, the country in northeastern Africa known as "the gift of the Nile" that Abraham visited; where Joseph became grand vizier and invited his father Jacob and the Israelites to dwell to escape the famine (see

Goshen); which enslaved the Israelites for more than two centuries; and from which they were redeemed by God in the Exodus. After the conquest of Egypt by Alexander the Great, numerous Jewish immigrants settled there (see Elephantine). Coming from a Hebrew root meaning "narrow," the idea of "being in *Mitzrayim*" was interpreted metaphorically as a spiritual and religious constriction due to the idol worship and overemphasis on the afterlife in that country.

Mitzvah (pl., ***mitzvot***). Derived from a Hebrew root meaning "to command," the term is applied to a religious obligation. In common usage, *mitzvah* has also come to mean a "good deed." The 613 *mitzvot* (see *taryag mitzvot*) in the Torah are traditionally divided into 248 positive requirements and 365 negative prohibitions. There also are seven rabbinic *mitzvot* that were not based on any biblical verses in the Torah. The *mitzvot* provide the foundation for Jewish law and guidelines for Jewish behavior.

Mitzvah ha-ba'ah b'averah. Literally one that "comes with sin," it means that a *mitzvah* must never be performed with the profits of a transgression. For example, one does not fulfill the obligation of taking up the four species on Sukkot by using a stolen *lulav*. As the Talmud asks, "If one has stolen a measure of wheat and has ground, kneaded and baked it, and set apart the *challah*, how can he recite a blessing over it? It would not be a blessing, but rather a blasphemy!" (Sanh. 6b).

Mitzvot, obligation of women to perform. The great majority of *mitzvot* apply equally to men and women. Obvious exceptions are those that are gender-based, such as circumcision and *mikveh*.Women are obligated to observe virtually all the negative commandments. With respect to the positive commandments, both men and women are required to perform all that are independent of time. However, for those commandments that are time-bound, "men are obligated and women are exempt." The most common explanation for this distinction is that it reflects the traditional domestic role of women in society. Imposition of time-bound *mitzvot* would be an unreasonable burden on a busy housewife and mother. The Talmud lists five specific time-bound positive commandments for which women are not obligated – dwelling in a sukkah and taking up the four species on Sukkot, hearing the *shofar* on Rosh Hashanah and Yom Kippur, wearing *tzitzit* (fringes), and putting on *tefillin*. Conversely, women are exempt from some positive commandments that are not time-bound, such as the study of Torah and the redemption of the firstborn son (see *pidyon ha-ben*). Issues of intense controversy are whether women "may" perform *mitzvot* for which they are "exempt" and, if so, whether they can perform commandments on behalf of men (see *kavod ha-tzibbur*).

Mitzvot, performance of. The Rabbis stressed that the performance of the commandments is not merely a mechanical action or the discharge of a burdensome obligation, but rather an infinitely rich and rewarding experience within the reach of every individual. Instead of being a thoughtless matter of routine, religious observance requires constant and careful consideration, since the greater the devotion with which the *mitzvot* are carried out, the more the reward and spiritual satisfaction.[189] These include glorifying the mitzvah (see *hiddur mitzvah*), love of the mitzvah (see *hivuv mitzvah*); joy in the mitzvah (*simcha shel mitzvah*); alertness (*zerizut*); conscious purpose (see *kavanah*); and doing the *mitzvah* for its own sake (*lishmah*) without any expectation of a reward. *Mitzvot* may not be performed with disrespect (see *bizui mitzvah*) or with the fruits of sin (see *mitzvah ha-ba'ah b'averah*).

Mitzvot, rabbinic. The Rabbis established seven *mitzvot* that were not based on any verses in the Torah. These include: washing hands before eating; lighting Sabbath candles; reciting the *Hallel* psalms of praise (Ps. 113-118) on festival days; lighting Chanukah candles; reading the Scroll of Esther on Purim; making an *eruv* to alleviate some Sabbath restrictions concerning the limitation of movement and transfer of objects; and saying a blessing of thanksgiving before experiencing pleasure in worldly items (such as for specific foods, see *blessings before eating*). (For differences in the manner in which rabbinic and biblical commandments are performed, see *Mitzvot de-oraita* and *de-rabbanan*.)

Mitzvot, reasons for observing – see *Ta'amei ha-Mitzvot*.

Mitzvot de-oraita (biblical commandments) and ***de-rabbanan*** (rabbinic *mitzvot*). Although the performance of these two major categories of *mitzvot* is preceded by reciting a blessing of sanctification, there are substantial differences in the manner in which they are observed. Commandments based on Torah verses (*de-oraita*) must be observed with the greatest possible strictness; the *mitzvah* must be repeated if there is any doubt as to whether it has already been performed. In contrast, a similar uncertainty as to whether one has fulfilled a rabbinic commandment (*de-rabbanan*) would not obligate the individual to repeat the *mitzvah*. According to Jewish law, conscious purpose (see *kavanah*) is an unequivocal requirement for fulfilling most biblical commandments, but is not strictly necessary (though strongly recommended) in the case of rabbinic *mitzvot*.[190]

Mitzvot kallot and **chamurot**. Although these refer to commandments that are, respectively, "less important" (lit., "light" or "easy") and "more important" (lit., "severe"), the Rabbis stressed that Jews should "be as scrupulous in performing a 'minor' *mitzvah* as a 'major' one, for you do not know the reward given [for the respective *mitzvot*]" (Avot 2:1).

Mitzvot sichliyot and **shimiyot**. Differentiation made by the medieval Jewish philosophers between those commandments that were, respectively, "rational" and "revealed." The former would include forbidding murder and stealing, while the latter would include the prohibition against *sha'atnez* and the rite of the red heifer, seemingly irrational commandments that could be given only through Revelation. Maimonides argued that all the commandments had underlying reasons and useful purposes, even if they could not yet be understood by the human mind.

Mixed marriage – see Intermarriage.

Mixed multitude (*eirev rav*). Various groups of forced laborers who took advantage of the chaos surrounding the Exodus to flee with the Israelites from Egypt (Exod. 12:38). According to rabbinic tradition, these non-Jews were the major troublemakers who continually complained during the 40 years of wandering through the wilderness.

Mixed species – see *Kilayim*.

Mixing meat and milk. The prohibition against mixing milk and meat[191] derives from the verse, "You shall not seethe a kid in its mother's milk." Since it became impossible to determine which baby goat and which mother's milk were related, the law was extended so that no animal (meat) could be cooked in any milk (dairy). The Rabbis interpreted the threefold repetition of this verse (Exod. 23:19, 34:26; Deut. 14:21) as defining three distinct prohibitions – cooking meat and milk together; eating such a mixture; and deriving any benefit from it (such as savoring the aroma or feeding it to a pet). In order to create a "fence around the Torah," the Rabbis decreed that the separation of meat and milk must be as complete as possible. Thus, it is necessary to use separate utensils (pots, pans, dishes, and flatware) for dairy foods and meat, which are known respectively in Yiddish as *milchig* and *fleishig*. Classic Reform rejected the prohibition against mixing milk and meat, along with other dietary laws, but in recent years the movement has urged its members to learn about these regulations so they can make individual choices whether to integrate them into their daily lives.

Mizbeach – see Altar.

Mizmor le-David (A Song of David). Phrase that introduces several of the psalms, indicating that their authorship is attributed to King David. Examples include Psalm 29, which is recited during the procession following the reading of the Torah on Sabbath morning, and the well-known Psalm 23. A variant is *Tehillah le-David*, which introduces Psalm 145 (see *Ashrei*).

Mizmor shir (*l'yom ha-Shabbat*). Thanksgiving hymn of praise to God that is the "Psalm for the Sabbath day" (92). In answer to the ancient theodicy problem of the apparent prosperity of evildoers and the misery of those who are virtuous and honorable, it unequivocally asserts that the wicked are doomed to destruction, while God will cause the righteous to "flourish like a date palm and grow mighty like a cedar in Lebanon."[192] Although this psalm makes no mention of the Sabbath except in its title, Rashi taught that it refers not to the weekly Sabbath but to the World to Come, when humanity will achieve the spiritual perfection that can now only be hinted on the seventh day.[193]

Mizrach (east). Calligraphic or ornamental design that hangs on the eastern wall in many Jewish homes and synagogues to indicate the direction in which to pray and to aid in meditation. The Hebrew word comes from a root meaning "to cast forth rays," as the sun does every morning when it rises in the east. From Temple times to the present, Jews have faced Jerusalem in prayer. Consequently, the term *mizrach* really only applies to locations west of Jerusalem. In addition to biblical, liturgical, or kabbalistic verses, many *mizrachim* are decorated with images of animals, pictures of holy places, or kabbalistic symbols, sometimes rendered in microcalligraphy or as paper-cuts.

Mizrachi (1). Religious Zionist movement, founded by Isaac Reines in Vilna in 1902. The World Mizrachi Movement, based in Jerusalem, sends out 120 *shlichim* (sing., *shaliach*) each year throughout the Jewish world to work with members of the movement and teach in Jewish day schools. The motto of Mizrachi is "the land of Israel for the people of Israel according to the Torah of Israel."

Mizrachi (2). Hebrew term for a Sephardic Jew of Middle Eastern origin.

M'lechet avodah. Generally translated as "laborious or servile work" and prohibited on festivals, it contrasts with the more restrictive prohibition, "you shall do no work," that applies to the Sabbath and Yom Kippur. According to Rashi, *m'lechet avodah* means "essential work that will cause a significant loss if it is not performed." Nachmanides considered it "burdensome" work, such as ordinary farm or factory labor; in contrast, a person may engage in "pleasurable work," such as the preparation of food.[194] Whatever the interpretation of the term, all agree that the preparation of food – including such labors as slaughtering, cooking, and baking – is permitted on festivals (other than Yom Kippur) that fall on a weekday, based on the verse, "except for what every person must eat, only that may be done for you" (Exod. 12:16).

Mo'adim. Literally, "appointed times" or "seasons," a biblical term for the festivals.

Mo'adim le-simcha. Literally "festivals for rejoicing," the Hebrew greeting used on religious holidays.

Modeh ani (I thank). Initial words of a short prayer said immediately upon waking up in the morning and welcoming anew the Presence of God. The full prayer – "I thank You, O living and eternal King, for You have returned my soul within me with compassion; great is Your faithfulness!" – does not mention any of the Divine names and thus may be said while still in bed before washing. Short and simple, *Modeh ani* is a favorite morning prayer for children who are too young to recite the ordinary daily morning service. (See also *sleep*.)

Modern Orthodox. Movement founded in the late 19th century by Rabbi Samson Raphael Hirsch as a reaction to Reform, it attempts to harmonize traditional observance (*halacha*) and values with the secular modern world. This philosophy has been termed *Torah im Derech Eretz* (Torah with the way of the Land). Its ideal is a Torah-observant Jew who is nevertheless comfortable with contemporary modes of living and is willing to play a constructive role in modern society. In the United States, the rabbinical school of the Modern Orthodox movement is Yeshiva University and its association of rabbis is the Rabbinical Council of America.

Modim of the Rabbis. The 18th blessing of the weekday *Amidah*, beginning with *Modim anachnu lach* (We give thanks to You), it gratefully acknowledges all the "miracles, wonders, and favors" that God has bestowed upon us. Each member of the congregation accepts God's sovereignty by bowing during these three words. When this section is read aloud by the prayer leader during the repetition of the *Amidah*, the congregants recite in an undertone a different prayer of thanksgiving that is usually printed in a column parallel to *Modim anachnu lach* but in smaller type.[195]

Mo'ed. The 2nd order of the Mishnah.Literally meaning "appointed time" or "season," its 12 tractates (dealing with laws concerning the Sabbath, festivals, and fast days) are Shabbat, Eruvin, Pesachim, Shekalim, Yoma, Sukkah, Beitzah, Rosh Hashanah, Ta'anit, Megillah, Mo'ed Katan, and Chagigah.

Mo'ed Katan (MK). Literally meaning "little festival," this 11th tractate of Mo'ed (festivals) in the Mishnah deals with the nature of work permitted during the intermediate days of Passover and Sukkot, as well as mourning on holy days.

Mohar. Hebrew term for "bride price," the monetary gift the groom (or his father) gave the father of the bride. Not always in cash, the *mohar* sometimes was paid in kind or in service. Eliezer, the servant of Abraham, gave "precious things" to Rebecca and her family to secure her as a wife for Isaac; Jacob worked seven years each for the hands of Leah and Rachel. As far back as biblical times, the father generally gave most or all of the *mohar* to his daughter. During the talmudic period, the *mohar* was not a gift but funds set aside as protection for the bride. Therefore, during marriage it was considered a debt that was to be paid only in case of death or divorce, and the *mohar* thus became a divorce or life insurance settlement rather than a mere marriage gift. This arrangement also enabled poor grooms to marry without any immediate monetary expenditure.

Mohel. Person specially trained in performing circumcisions in accordance with the requirement of Jewish law, who acts as a surrogate for the father. In the traditional community, a *mohel* must be ritually observant; among more liberal Jews and in remote communities where *mohalim* are not readily available, a physician may be called upon to perform the circumcision while a rabbi conducts the ritual. After reciting the blessing for circumcision and performing the procedure, the *mohel* says a blessing over wine and then one for the welfare of the child and his family. During the course of this blessing, the Hebrew name of the child is announced. Sometimes, the ritual concludes with a recitation of the Priestly Blessing.

Mohn. Yiddish term for poppy seeds, it also denotes the sweetened poppy seed paste popularly used as the filling for *hamantashen* on Purim.

Moishe pupik. Literally a combination of "Moshe" and "belly button," this Yiddish phrase is used as a put-down, ridiculing someone for being about as smart as a navel.

Molech. Canaanite fire deity. The Bible strictly prohibited "allowing any of your children to be given [offered up] to Molech" (Lev. 18:21). According to Maimonides, this idolatrous practice "consisted of kindling a fire and fanning its flame, whereupon [the father] would take some of his offspring and hand them over to a priest engaged in the service of that idol, and then cause them to pass through the fire from one side to the other." Although this would indicate that the child was not burned, many commentators disagreed, arguing that the ritual of Molech called for the child to be consumed by the flames as a human sacrifice to the idol.[196] The worship of Molech was eradicated during the religious reforms of King Josiah (2 Kings 23:10). (See also *child sacrifice*.)

Mondays and Thursdays. According to the Talmud, after the return of the Israelites from Babylonian Exile, Ezra the Scribe introduced the practice of publicly reading the Torah on the market days of Monday and Thursday. This was established for the convenience of those living in isolated areas, who were unable to attend a local prayer meeting on the Sabbath. Because farmers came to town to do their shopping and trading, the market days were a perfect time to gather the people together to teach them Torah. This practice eventually became the binding custom, even in larger towns where a regular Sabbath reading of the Torah took place. Today, the Torah is read during morning services on Monday and Thursday (with three *aliyot*), and additional prayers of penitence and supplication are recited. In Yiddish, the phrase "*Montik un Dounnershtik*" (lit., "Monday and Thursday") means "regularly" or "on a continuing basis."

Moneylending. Although Jews are forbidden to exact interest on a loan to a fellow Jew (Lev. 25:36-37), they are permitted to do so when lending money to a non-Jew. During the Middle Ages, when Jews (especially in Northern Europe) were excluded from engaging in agriculture and becoming members of craftsmen's guilds, moneylending became a necessary Jewish occupation. Like Shylock in Shakespeare's *The Merchant of Venice*, the image of the greedy, ruthless, and unmerciful Jewish moneylender demanding his "pound of flesh" became a reviled stereotype that contributed to anti-Semitism. Despite religious prohibitions, Christians eventually also became moneylenders, though it remained the Jews who were associated with the negative stereotypes of this occupation.

Monotheism. Belief in only one God, as eloquently expressed in the *Shema*.In Jewish tradition, God is both transcendent and immanent, eternal, omniscient, omnipresent, omnipotent, and all-good. The One God is Creator of the universe, both just and compassionate, answers prayer, and welcomes those who repent of their transgressions. Abraham, Moses, and the literary prophets all stressed monotheism. Rational thinkers of the Enlightenment focused on the moral aspects of Judaism rather than its ritualistic demands, leading Classical Reform to define the essence of Judaism as "ethical monotheism."

Months. The 12 months of the Jewish lunar year are Nisan, Iyar, Sivan, Tammuz, Av, Elul, Tishrei, Cheshvan, Kislev, Tevet, Shevat, and Adar. (See also *calendar* and entries for the individual months.)

Moon. God created the moon (*yare'ach* or *levanah*) on the fourth day of Creation as "the lesser light...to rule the night" (Gen. 1:16). As with the sun, the Israelites were forbidden to worship the moon, and those who defied this ban were to be stoned at the gates of the city (Deut. 4:19, 17:3-5). Nevertheless, moon worship (like sun worship) continued. The heretical King Manasseh set up altars to the celestial bodies (2 Kings 21:3-5), and during Jeremiah's time the Israelites worshiped the moon as the "Queen of Heaven." According to tradition, the moon and sun were originally created of equal size. However, when mutual jealousy led each heavenly body to claim that it should be larger than the other, the moon was reduced in size because it had unlawfully intruded into the domain of the sun by sometimes remaining visible while the sun was still above the horizon. The waxing and waning of the moon was considered a symbol of the vacillating fortune of Jewish history. (See also *New Moon*.)

Moon, blessing of the – see *Kiddush Levanah*.

Morenu. Literally "our teacher," a Hebrew title given to distinguished rabbis and talmudic scholars since the 14th century.

Morid ha-tal (Who causes the dew to descend). Hebrew words added at the beginning of the 2nd blessing of the *Amidah* from the first day of Passover, when the prayer for dew is recited, until Shemini Atzeret, when the prayer for rain is said. Originally a Sephardic custom, this practice has been widely adopted by all rites in Israel.

Morning blessings (*Birkot ha-Shachar*). Initial prayer section of the morning service. It contains a greater variety of prayers, blessings, and Torah study passages than any other part of the *siddur*. Many of the prayers and blessings were intended to be said privately at home prior to the synagogue service, to be recited with each act of rising and getting ready for the day's work. However, they became widely neglected because many Jews did not know the blessings by heart and, as part of the Oral Law, it was forbidden to write them down. Therefore, the Rabbis decided to transfer these morning blessings to the beginning of the synagogue service, where the prayer leader recited them aloud to provide an opportunity for the less knowledgeable in the congregation to hear them and respond with the traditional "amen."[197] Ashkenazim begin with the prayer *Mah tovu.* After putting on the *tallit* and donning the *tefillin* on weekdays, the hymn *Adon Olam* is recited. Other prayers said during the *Birkot ha-Shachar* include *Elohai neshamah* and the preliminary morning blessings.

Morning blessings, preliminary. The 15 blessings that are traditionally said upon arising. Each begins with the standard blessing formula – "Praised are You, Lord our God, King of the universe" – and concludes with a specific instance of the Divine role in all that one does in life and the satisfaction of every human need: (1) Who has given the rooster intelligence to distinguish between day and night (*asher natan la'sechvi vinah l'havchin bein yom u-vein lailah*); (2) Who did not make me a gentile (*she-lo asani goy*); (3) Who did not make me a slave (*she-lo asani aved*); (4) (Men) Who did not make me a woman (*she-lo asani ishah*); (Women) Who made me according to His will (*she-asani kirtzono*); (5); Who gives sight to the blind (*poke'ach ivrim*); (6) Who clothes the naked (*malbish arumim*); (7) Who releases the bound (*matir asurim*); (8); Who straightens the bent (*zokeif k'fufim*); (9) Who spreads out the earth upon the waters (*roka ha-aretz al ha-mayim*); (10) Who has provided my every need (*she-asah li kol tzorchi*); (11) Who firms man's footsteps (*ha-meichin mitzadei gaver*); (12) Who girds Israel with strength (*ozeir Yisrael big'vurah*); (13) Who crowns Israel with splendor (*oteir Yisrael b'tifarah*); (14) Who gives strength to the weary (*ha-notein la-ya'eif ko'ach*); and (15) Who removes sleep from my eyes and slumber from my eyelids (*ha-ma'avir sheinah mei-einai u-tenumah mei-afapai*). The Conservative movement has revised the 2nd through 4th blessings into affirmative statements – "Who has made me an Israelite, a free person, and in His image"[198]

Morning service – see *Shacharit*.

Mortara Case. In 1858, a six-year-old Italian Jewish boy named Edgardo Mortara, who when ill had been secretly baptized by a Catholic servant girl, became the center of an international controversy when he was seized from his Jewish parents in Bologna by the Papal authorities and taken to be raised as a Catholic on the basis of the secret baptism. Napoleon III protested against this abduction, and Moses Montefiore traveled to Rome to attempt to secure the boy's release. However, all efforts proved futile, and Mortara eventually became a professor of theology, receiving the title "Apostolic Missionary." The Mortara case resulted in severely strained relations between the Church and the Jewish community.

Moshav. Cooperative agricultural village that differs from a *kibbutz* in that each member has a home and plot of land worked by himself and his family. However, all marketing of produce and purchase of supplies is done cooperatively, and some of the machinery is communally owned by the *moshav*. The idea of the *moshav* evolved during World War I in the search for a form of settlement that would not only express national and social aspirations on the basis of collective principles like the *kibbutz*, but also provide scope for individual initiative and independent farm management. The first *moshav*, Nahalal in the northern Jezreel Valley, was founded in 1921.

Moshiach – see Messiah.

Mossad. Hebrew for "institute," the full title is "The Institute for Intelligence and Special Operations." The Mossad is responsible for human intelligence collection, covert action, and counter-terrorism in Israel.

Motzi – see *ha-Motzi*.

Mount Moriah – see Temple Mount.

Mount Nebo. When Moses was about to die, he was permitted to ascend Mount Nebo in the extreme northwest of the mountains of Moab across the Jordan from Jericho. There God showed him the entire land that constituted the Divine promise to the Patriarchs (Deut. 34:1-3).

Mount of Olives (*Har ha-Zeitim*). Mountain to the east of Jerusalem that rises about 2,500 feet above sea level. In Second Temple times, the red heifer was burned on the Mount of Olives and a bridge (or possibly two) connected its slopes with the Temple Mount.At the order of the Sanhedrin, beacons were lit on the Mount of Olives to announce the sanctification of the New Moon. Over the centuries, the Mount of Olives became a burial place for the Jews of Jerusalem, based on the belief that at the end of days the Messiah will ascend it and Ezekiel will blow his trumpet there for the resurrection of the dead. Conquered by the

Jordanian army during the War of Independence (1948), Jewish cemeteries and monuments on the Mount of Olives were vandalized by Arabs. The entire Mount of Olives was reclaimed by Israeli troops in the Six Day War (1967).

Mount Scopus. *Har ha-Tzofim* in Hebrew, the English name describes its incredible view of Jerusalem. North of the Old City, Mount Scopus was the site where the Romans planned and launched their attack that destroyed Jerusalem and the Temple in 70 C.E. Unlike most of the eastern part of Jerusalem, Mount Scopus was held by Israel after the 1948 War of Independence and remained an enclave within Jordanian territory until all of Jerusalem was liberated in the Six Day War (1967). It is the site of the major campus of the Hebrew University and a branch of the Hadassah Medical Center.

Mount Sinai. Site of the greatest single event of God's Revelation to the Israelites, which Moses ascended to receive the two stone tablets of the Ten Commandments. According to rabbinic tradition, Moses received both the Written Law and the Oral Law on Mount Sinai.

Mount Tabor. Tallest mountain in the Lower Galilee (1,800 feet), a conspicuous landmark about six miles southeast of Nazareth. At Deborah's command, Barak assembled the northern tribes of Israel on Mount Tabor. When the Canaanite forces approached, the Israelites rushed down from the slopes and destroyed them (Judg. 4).

Mount Zion (*Har Tzion*). Eastern hill of Jerusalem, which includes the Temple Mount. The name "Zion" was first used for the Jebusite fortress on the southeast of Jerusalem; when captured by King David, it was renamed the "City of David." The exact location of the biblical Mount Zion is still a matter of some dispute. Solomon brought up the Ark of the Covenant to the Temple "from the City of David, which is Zion" (1 Kings 8:1-2; 2 Chron. 5:2). In poetry, Zion became synonymous with Jerusalem as well as the messianic city of God. The sons and daughters of Zion denoted its inhabitants, and through the centuries Zion became a symbol for the restoration of the Jewish people to their original homeland. By the 10th century, the single synagogue on Mount Zion became known as the site of the grave of King David. After 1948, Mount Zion was the only section of East Jerusalem (other than Mount Scopus) to remain in Jewish hands. The reputed site of David's Tomb was once again turned into a synagogue and became an important pilgrimage center for Jews in Israel.

Mourner's Kaddish. Also known as *Kaddish Yatom* (lit., "orphan's" *Kaddish*), it contains the full *Kaddish* text except for the *titkabeil* verse.It is recited after *Aleinu* at the end of each service and may be repeated after the reading of additional psalms. Many Jews think of the *Kaddish* as the mourner's prayer, even though it contains no mention of death. Instead, it extols the sovereignty of God and ends with a prayer for peace. The practice of mourners reciting the *Kaddish* probably began during the 13th century, when Jews in Germany were suffering severe persecutions at the hands of the Crusaders. However, the origin may be related to a legend that R. Akiva rescued a soul from eternal punishment in hell by teaching the son of the departed to recite the *Kaddish* at a congregational service. Widespread belief in the efficacy of this practice led to children reciting the *Kaddish* for their parents during the year after burial (and later on the *yahrzeit*, the yearly anniversary of the death). Mourners actually recite the *Kaddish* for only 11 months, based on a talmudic statement implying that only the wicked are judged in purgatory for a full 12 months – and no child would want to designate a parent as wicked.

Mourning (*aveilut*). The expression of grief and sorrow over the death of a close relative, friend, or national leader, or in response to a national calamity. The Rabbis distinguished four stages in the mourning period: *aninut* (the period between death and burial); *shiva* (the seven days following burial); *sheloshim* (the time until the 30th day after burial); and the first year. The traditional Jewish view towards mourning is expressed in the statement, "It is forbidden to overstress mourning for the departed" (MK 27b).

Muflita. Pancake-like fried dough, spread with butter and honey, that is eaten by Jews of Moroccan descent during Maimuna, the festival that follows the conclusion of the Passover holiday.

Muktzeh. Literally meaning "set aside" or "store away," this Hebrew term refers to items that may not be handled on the Sabbath (because they may not be used on that day lest one unintentionally perform a forbidden type of work). Among the many things considered *muktzeh* are money and checks; scissors, hammers, and saws; pencils and pens; battery-operated toys and flashlights; telephones and all electronic devices; and religious objects such as *shofar*, *tefillin*, and *lulav*. Even the Sabbath candlesticks are *muktzeh* and thus should not be moved on the Sabbath after the candles have been lit.[199]

Mumar. Talmudic term for an apostate. Also called *meshumad*, the Rabbis drew distinctions between those who violate religious precepts because they are unable to withstand temptation and those who rebel in denial of Divine authority. They also defined three categories of apostates – those who disobey a single commandment; those who regularly fail to perform a specific *mitzvah*; and those who violate the entire Torah.

Mun – see *Mohn*.

Murder. The prohibition against murder is the sixth of the Ten Commandments (Exod. 20:13; Deut. 5:17). In ancient Israel, willful murder merited capital punishment, while one who committed accidental manslaughter was banished to a city of refuge. Although often incorrectly translated as "You shall not kill," Jewish law recognized that there were situations in which it was required to take a human life. These included an obligatory war against idolaters, the infliction of capital punishment based on judicial decree, and the requirement to kill a *rodef* if there was no other way to save the person being pursued. The Rabbis extended this commandment by describing many things as "equivalent to murder," such as shaming a fellow human being in public, failing to provide food and safety for travelers, causing loss of livelihood, withholding charity from the poor, tale bearing, and character assassination.

Musaf. Literally "additional," it refers to the service added after the morning service (see *Shacharit*) on those days when an additional sacrifice was offered in the Temple – Sabbath, New Moon, the three pilgrimage festivals (Passover, Shavuot, Sukkot), New Year (Rosh Hashanah), and the Day of Atonement (Yom Kippur). The *Amidah* recited during this service contains a biblical passage (from Numbers 28-29) describing the special additional sacrifices offered on that day. Besides the *Amidah*, the *Musaf* service includes several concluding prayers and the *Kaddish*. The *Musaf Amidah* on Rosh Hashanah contains three long intermediate sections that deal with Divine kingship over the entire universe (see *Malchuyot*), God's remembering Israel (see *Zichronot*); and the sounding of the *shofar* on the day (see *Shofarot*).

Musar. Orthodox movement, founded by Rabbi Israel Salanter in Lithuania during the mid-19th century, which focused on ethics, moral instruction, and self-reflection. It stressed the proper motivation that a person should have when observing the commandments. Efforts were made to identify and inculcate the right attitude that would strengthen observance through regular spiritual exercises. The Musar movement stressed the powerful role of the human tendency toward sinfulness, teaching that repentance is the persistent task of the Jew, day after day, year after year. This turning inward to scrutinize one's deeds and motives gave the follower of the Musar movement a heightened awareness. In Musar *yeshivot*, spiritual development went hand in hand with intellectual growth.

Myrtle (*hadas*). One of the four species on Sukkot. Having no taste but with an aroma, the myrtle symbolizes a person who is deficient in Torah but possesses good deeds.

Mysticism – see Kabbalah.

N

Na'amat (Women's Labor Zionist Organization). A Hebrew acronym for "Movement of Working Women and Volunteers," Na'amat was founded in 1921 as the first feminist movement in the Land of Israel. It protested a society in which women were relegated to the kitchens while men worked the land and built the country. Its goal was for women to become full partners in the life of the Labor movement, the founding of the State, and the future of the Jewish people. Branches of Na'amat developed throughout the world, with the second largest in the United States – where until 1981 it was known as Pioneer Women. Today, Na'amat operates day care centers for children, vocational training, and community institutions, as well as legal aid bureaus for women and shelters for battered women, as part of its ongoing efforts to improve the lives of women, children, and families in the Jewish State.

Na'aritzcha v'nakdishcha (We will revere You and sanctify You [according to the mystic utterance of the holy Seraphim]). Based on Isaiah 29:23, it is the introduction to the *Kedushah* for all morning and afternoon services in Sephardic and Middle Eastern congregations. Ashkenazim use it for the *Musaf* (additional) service on Sabbaths and festivals.

Na'aseh v'nishmah. Literally, "[first] we will obey [the law], then we will hear/understand it" (Exod. 24:7), the eager promise of the Israelites to fulfill the commandments of the Torah even before they were announced. The Rabbis considered this as the reason for the Israelites being selected as the Chosen People.

Nachas. Yiddish word meaning "pleasure," usually referring to the pride one has in the accomplishments of children or grandchildren.

Nagid (prince). Head of the Jewish community in Islamic countries during the Middle Ages. The most famous was Shmuel ha-Nagid (993–c.1055), vizier of Granada, statesman, poet, and scholar. His meteoric rise and political and military career mark the highest achievement of a Jew in medieval Muslim Spain. Ironically, much of his work as vizier entailed the remarkable fact of a Jew leading the army of Granada, which was occupied in constant war with Seville (also controlled by Muslims).

Nahal. Acronym of *No'ar Halutzi Loheim* (fighting pioneer youth), a special unit of the Israel Defense Forces. Its soldiers are organized in *garinim* (literally, "seeds") of pioneering youth movements in Israel and Zionist youth movements in the Diaspora that educate their members toward cooperative settlement in Israel. During their term of military service, these soldiers simultaneously participate in intensive training and social and ideological preparation toward their future as members of new or existing cooperative agricultural settlements. All members of such a potential group are mobilized together and form a single army unit. After a period of combined agricultural and military training in a *kibbutz* or at a Nahal outpost, the men generally receive advanced training in paratroop, tank, artillery, engineering, or other units. Both men and women complete their military obligation by serving in a frontier settlement. Upon conclusion of military service, those Nahal soldiers who wish to return to civilian life do so; others remain and continue to live in the settlement. When self-supporting, the settlement is separated from military control and becomes a civilian village.

Nahum (Nah.). The 7th of the minor prophets. Nahum prophesied the coming of Divine vengeance on Nineveh, the capital of the Assyrian Empire, and provided a vivid description of the city's destruction by the Babylonians and the Medes in 612 B.C.E. The book also contains promises of Divine protection for Judah.

Name. Until the Emancipation, Jews had no family names. They possessed only the Hebrew name given to a boy on the occasion of his *brit milah* (see circumcision) and to a girl when her father was honored with an *aliyah* in the synagogue shortly after her birth. A person's complete Hebrew name is his or her first name (and middle name) followed by *ben* (son of) or *bat* (daughter of) and then the first (and middle) name of the father (and in an increasing number of liberal congregations today, also that of the mother). If the father is a *kohen* or *levi*, the child's name ends with the word *ha-Kohen* or *ha-Levi*. Even today, these Hebrew names are used during Jewish ceremonies and rituals – when called to the Torah for an *aliyah*, on the *ketubah* (marriage document), and in a special memorial prayer at the funeral and later engraved on the gravestone in the cemetery.[200] Ashkenazim generally name a child for a deceased relative, both to perpetuate that person's memory and with the hope that the child will manifest the spiritual qualities of the beloved who is no longer alive. In contrast, among Sephardim it is customary to name children after living relatives, particularly the grandparents.[201]

Name, change of. When someone was gravely ill in the *shtetls* of Eastern Europe, members of the community would change the person's name as a last desperate measure. They reasoned that if, for example, God had ordained that a person by the name of David was to die, the Divine judgment might not extend to an individual by the name of Moshe. A copy of the Hebrew Scripture would be opened at random, and the sick person would be given the name of the first meritorious Jew that appeared. Charity would be donated on behalf of the invalid, along with a blessing for his/her recovery. If the patient recovered, the individual would carry the new name from then on. Although this may seem like vain superstition, it reflected the Jewish belief that God was waiting for only a loophole to extend Divine mercy.[202]

Names of God – God, names of.

Narrishkeit. Yiddish word meaning "foolishness."

Nashim (women). The 3rd order of the Mishnah, its 7 tractates are Yevamot, Ketubot, Nedarim, Nazir, Sotah, Gittin, and Kiddushin. Nashim contains laws relating to betrothal, marriage, divorces, and marital relationships.

Nasi (prince). Talmudic title for the president of the Sanhedrin, who served as the spiritual head of the Jewish people and later was also recognized as their political leader (see Patriarch) by the Roman government. In addition to presiding over the Sanhedrin, the *nasi* (together with the court) fixed the calendar by proclaiming the new month and intercalating (inserting) an extra month for the leap year, led public prayers for rain, and ordained scholars and appointed judges. The office was abolished in 425 C.E. Following the geonic period, the title *nasi* was applied to the head of Jewish institutions or communities. In modern Israel, *nasi* is the title of the largely ceremonial office of the President of the State.

Naso. The 2nd *parashah* in the Book of Numbers (4:21-7:89) and the longest in the Torah, it contains the laws of the suspected adulteress (see *sotah*) and the Nazirite; the Priestly Blessing; and the identical gifts from the chiefs of the Twelve Tribes of Israel to the newly anointed and consecrated Tabernacle.

National Religious Party (NRP). Political party that represents the religious Zionist movement in Israel. It emphasizes legislation based on Jewish law and economic policies that support the Orthodox community and their educational systems. Unlike many of the religious parties, the knitted-*kippah* supporters of the NRP join the Israel Defense Forces, with many serving in elite units and becoming officers. Today, the NRP views Jewish presence in Judea and Samaria (West Bank) as fulfilling the *mitzvah* of settling the Land of Israel.

Nationalism. Term coined in the 19th century that refers to the concept of loyalty or devotion to the nation, which is sometimes seen as the supreme value. In the late 19th century, modern nationalism was manifested in the Jewish sphere by the Zionist movement and the socialist Bund.The former advocated the establishment of a Jewish State; the latter supported Jewish autonomy within an existing nation-state.

Navi – see Prophet.

Nazir. The 4th tractate of Nashim (women) in the Mishnah, it deals with the vows of the Nazirite.

Nazirite. Literally meaning either one who was "separated" (from the temptations of the environment) or "consecrated" (to God), a person who voluntarily assumed restrictions beyond the obligatory commandments in order to reach an elevated state of holiness. The Nazirite vowed to (1) allow the hair to remain uncut during the period of the vow; (2) abstain from grapes or grape products such as wine; and (3) avoid any contact with a human corpse (Num. 6:1-21). The Nazirite vow was often taken purely for personal reasons, such as thanksgiving for recovery from illness or the birth of a child. The minimum period of the vow was 30 days, but some persisted for years.[203] The Rabbis debated why the Nazirite was required to bring a sin offering after a period dedicated to the Divine service. The most popular view was that the offering of the Nazirite atoned for the sin of rejecting the delights of the world that God had created for human beings, instead misconstruing them as sources of temptation and evil.[204] The most famous Nazirite was Samson.

Nazism. A body of political, socioeconomic, and ideological principles held and instituted by the National Socialist Party, which controlled Germany during the period of the Third Reich (1933-1945). These principles included dictatorial government centered on the person of the Fuhrer (leader), Adolf Hitler; an aggressive foreign policy that prepared the nation for war and territorial expansion; an unalterable belief in the superiority of the German people and its right and duty to rule as a "master race" over the so-called "inferior races;" and a determination to eliminate what the Nazis viewed as their main "racial" enemy, the Jews. Nazism gave rise to a regime of murderous racial annihilation.

Nebbish. Yiddish word for an ineffectual person, a loser for whom one feels sorry.

Nechushtan (copper serpent). As punishment for their rebellion in the wilderness, God sent fiery serpents to bite the people who had complained to Moses. When the people repented, God heeded their prayers and ordered Moses to make a serpent and place it on a pole, so that anyone who was bitten could look at it and recover (Num. 21:6-10). Although God did not specify the material to be used, Moses chose copper (*nechoshet*), because in Hebrew it contains the letters of the *nachash* (serpent) that was attacking the sinners (Rashi).[205] This copper serpent eventually became an object of idol worship in the Temple until it was destroyed by King Hezekiah in the 8th century (2 Kings 18:4), an action that was praised by the Rabbis (Ber. 10b).[206]

Necromancy. Magical practice that purports to foretell the future by communicating with the spirits of the dead. The Bible strictly prohibits necromancy, which it describes as "the sorcery of the *ob* and the *yid'oni*" (translated as "ghosts and familiar spirits"). Necromancy was one of the esoteric arts that were collectively disparaged as "abominations to the Lord." The only actual account of this practice occurred when King Saul consulted the witch of En Dor to summon the spirit of Samuel and learn his fate (1 Sam. 28).

Nedarim (1). Literally "vows," these promises to God were taken extremely seriously. The Rabbis explicitly stated that it was better to take no vows at all rather than to fail to fulfill them. Nevertheless, they understood the natural inclination of human beings to make rash vows in times of sickness and danger, only to forget them once they become healthy and secure. Just as oral commitments to God must be fulfilled, the Rabbis extended the obligation to fulfill all promises made to other individuals. Concern about unfulfilled vows to God was an important factor in the emergence of *Kol Nidrei* as a significant ritual on Yom Kippur. In biblical times, under certain circumstances men could annul the vows of their wives or daughters.

Nedarim (Ned.) (2). The 3rd tractate in Nashim (women) in the Mishnah, it deals with the making and annulling of vows (see above).

Nefesh. The part of the soul that is identified with the blood,[207] it is the aspect of vitality and energy that is found in both animals and human beings and ceases at death. In the Bible, the term is also used for life itself when referring to an individual person.

Nefilat apayim. Literally "falling on the face," the Hebrew term for the submissive posture of a worshiper saying *Tachanun*.This is based on the actions of Moses and Aaron in response to the Korach rebellion (Num. 16:22) and Joshua after the disastrous defeat at Ai (Josh. 7:6). In the Temple, the people knelt and prostrated themselves until their faces touched the ground, a gesture of absolute humility and total self-effacement indicating complete submission to God. In modern times, however, the prayer is recited in a seated position with head lowered and the face buried in the bend of the left forearm (or the right forearm when *tefillin* are on the left). This posture indicates the feelings of desolation and guilt that threaten to overwhelm the worshiper, but which are mitigated by the unquenchable hope that God's mercy will provide salvation from even the most desperate situation.[208]

Nega'im (Neg.). Literally meaning "plagues," this 3rd tractate of Tohorot (purity) in the Mishnah deals with *tzara'at*, a skin disease mistranslated as "leprosy."

Negev. From a Hebrew root for "dry" or "parched," the still largely uninhabited southern region that constitutes about 60% of the total area of Israel. The Negev was long a forsaken wasteland of wind-sculpted mountains, high plateaus, canyons, and wide dry riverbeds. "Making the desert bloom" has been a Zionist dream. Although the Negev is still sparsely populated, settlements have been established to grow winter crops and early vegetables. The Jewish National Fund has spurred development in the Negev, and the port of Eilat lies at its southernmost end.

Negligence. In Jewish law, people are responsible for all damage caused by their property or actions if they fail to take appropriate care to prevent them from becoming dangerous. They are also required to protect property entrusted to them against any foreseeable harm. These are excellent descriptions of the modern legal concept of negligence as a failure to meet the duty of "reasonable care."

Nehardea. City in Babylonian and site of a famous talmudic academy, which was destroyed in 259 C.E. Most of its scholars then moved to the academy at Pumbedita.Nehardea was also the seat of the exilarch and his *beit din.*

Nehemiah (Neh.). The 11th book of the Writings section of the Bible. Literally meaning "God has consoled," Nehemiah was a cupbearer to the Persian King Artaxerxes I (465-424 B.C.E.). When he learned of the poor condition of the exiles who had returned from Babylonia to Jerusalem, he obtained a commission from the Persian king to serve as governor of Judah in order to help his fellow Jews. One of Nehemiah's first tasks was to provide protection for the people by rebuilding the walls of Jerusalem. To repopulate the city, he ordered that one out of every ten Jews should take up residence in the capital. Together with Ezra the Scribe, Nehemiah rectified social injustices and enforced observance of the Sabbath and festivals and the prohibition of mixed marriages, which preserved the identity and continuity of the Jewish people.

Ne'ilah. Literally "closing [of the gates of Heaven]," this final service on Yom Kippur is the last opportunity before the end of the holiday to pray for forgiveness from sin. Beginning with the repetition of the *Amidah*, the ark remains open throughout the *Ne'ilah* service. The phrase used since Rosh Hashanah, "*inscribe* us in the Book of Life," now becomes "*seal* us in the Book of Life." As the climax of the Day of Atonement rapidly approaches, the prayer leader and congregation join in the recitation of three biblical sentences whereby they rededicate themselves to the essential theological doctrines of Judaism.[209] The first is a single recitation of the *Shema*, the quintessential affirmation of faith. This is followed by a threefold repetition of "Blessed is the Name of His glorious kingdom for ever and ever" (see *baruch shem k'vod*), the line that is usually recited as a silent response to the *Shema*. Finally, the verse *Adonai Hu ha-Elohim* (The Lord, He is God) is repeated seven times. This unequivocal denial of all idolatry and affirmation of the One and Only God was the response of the Israelites to Elijah's triumphant victory over the priests of Baal on Mount Carmel (1 Kings 18:39). This declaration is followed by a long blast of the *shofar* (an echo of the ancient practice [Lev. 25:9] of sounding the ram's horn to proclaim the beginning of the Jubilee Year, and the exclamation of *le-shanah ha-ba'ah bi-Yerushalayim* (Next year in Jerusalem).

Nekadesh (We will sanctify [Your Name in the world]). Opening word of the *Kedushah* recited in Ashkenazic congregations at both the morning and afternoon services on weekdays.

Neo-Orthodox – see Modern Orthodox.

Nephilim. Mythical offspring of the sons of God and the daughters of men, described by the Bible as "the heroes of old, the men of renown" (Gen. 6:4), who supposedly dwelled in pre-Israelite Canaan. This term may come from a Hebrew root meaning "to fall," thus relating to the later myth of the "fallen angels" (Zohar 1:58a). The Israelite spies sent by Moses to explore the Land of Canaan referred to the "men of great size" they saw there as *nephilim* (Num. 13:33).

Ner tamid. Literally "perpetual/eternal lamp," a continuously burning light in the synagogue that usually hangs in front of the ark and is a symbol of the Golden Menorah in the Temple. According to the Rabbis, the *ner tamid* symbolizes the Divine Presence, which dwells among the congregation of Israel. It may also refer to the Torah, which rests in the ark below the *ner tamid* and is associated with light.[210] Although in ancient times the perpetual light was created by a wick burning in olive oil, today an electric light is used instead.

Nes – see Miracle.

Nes gadol hayah sham (a great miracle happened there) – see Dreidel.

Nesech. Libation wine used in connection with idol worship, which the Bible forbids Jews from drinking. This prohibition was extended to apply to any wine made by gentiles, lest some of it may have been used as a libation in an idolatrous pagan ceremony. In rabbinic times, this decree remained in effect to prevent Jews from fraternizing with gentiles in social situations, which could lead to assimilation or intermarriage.[211] Kosher wine must be produced under rabbinic supervision. Only observant Jews are permitted to handle the wine or operate the wine-making equipment from grape crushing to consumption. (For an exception see *mevushal*.)

Neshamah. The part of the soul that symbolize the "breath of life" that God "blew into the nostrils" of Adam so that he "became a living being" (Gen. 2:7). Found only in human beings, it is the immortal part of a person that survives the death of the body and returns to God. Rabbinic thought did not subscribe to Hellenistic dualism, which equated matter and the body with evil and spirit and the soul with good. The talmudic sages did not view the body as the prison of the soul, but rather as the medium for its development and improvement.

Neshamah yeterah (extra soul). According to tradition, the "higher" soul" that was given by God to Abraham to elevate him on the Sabbath, and which in turn passes to all Jews on that day. A mystical reason for the fragrant spices used in the *Havdalah* ceremony that concludes the Sabbath is that they either provide spiritual compensation for the additional soul that each Jew figuratively possesses on the Sabbath day,[212] which Rashi defined as a unique feeling of rest and contentment, or that the spices symbolize the spiritual farewell "feast" for that extra soul.[213]

Netanya. Seaside Israeli town north of Tel Aviv. Founded in 1929 as a citrus center among the sand dunes of the fertile Sharon Plain, Netanya was named after American philanthropist Nathan Strauss. Perched on verdant cliffs overlooking the Mediterranean, Netanya is also the center of Israel's diamond-cutting industry, which was developed in the late 1930s by immigrants from Antwerp and South Africa.

Netilat yadayim (washing the hands). Literally "raising the hands" in Hebrew, hand washing in Judaism is performed in relation to meals, synagogue services, and other daily activities. This practice is primarily a religious, not hygienic, act and was instituted by the Rabbis to correct the condition of *tumat yadayim* – their concept of "impurity of the hands." The method of ritual washing is either by immersion up to the wrist or by pouring about one cup of water over both hands from a receptacle with a wide mouth, the lip of which must be undamaged. It is customary to alternately pour water over each hand three times (first washing the right hand by pouring water from a vessel held in the left hand). Traditional Jews ritually wash their hands with recitation of the appropriate blessing before meals, since the dining table is compared to the Altar upon which the sacrificial service was performed. In observant homes, a pitcher and basin are placed next to the bed for immediate washing of the hands after awakening. Washing the hands is also required before eating the *karpas* (greens) at the Passover seder. It is designed to restore the ritual purity of the hands after the following activities: going to the toilet; cutting nails; taking off shoes with bare hands; combing the hair; sexual intercourse; touching parts of the body that are routinely covered; bloodletting; and attending a funeral, leaving a cemetery, or departing from a house where a corpse is present.[214]

Neturei Karta. Aramaic term meaning "Guardians of the City," the name for an Israeli organization of anti-Zionist, ultra-Orthodox Jewish zealots who adamantly refuse to recognize the existence or authority of the State of Israel. Their opposition stems from a talmudic doctrine that Jews should not use human force to bring about the establishment of a Jewish state before the coming of the Messiah (Ket. 111a). Neturei Karta followers do not participate in Israeli elections or accept any aid from Social Security, and their educational institutions reject any form of financial support from the Ministry of Education. They are shunned by the great majority of Orthodox Jews.

Netzach (eternity/victory). The 7th of the *sefirot*, the source of prophecy and anthropomorphically viewed as the right leg of God. *Netzach* is considered the fraternal twin of *Hod*, and they are identified with the biblical brothers Moses and Aaron.

Nevelah. The flesh of any kosher animal that has died without ritual slaughter, which Jews are forbidden to eat. This includes not only an animal that died a natural death, but also one that has been killed by shooting or incorrectly slaughtered. Unlike the non-kosher creatures that the Torah terms "abomination," *nevelah* could be consumed by gentiles residing in the Land but was forbidden to the Israelites because it was not appropriate food for a holy people. A limb torn from a living animal, forbidden by the Noahide laws, is also considered *nevelah*.

Nevi'im – see Prophets.

New Christians – see *Conversos*.

New Jew. A concept of the Labor Zionists, who envisioned a polar opposite to the traditional ghetto Jew who was scorned as downtrodden and weak as a result of centuries in exile. This "New Jew," like the ancient Maccabees, would be strong, brave, active, and rooted in nature rather than alienated from it. Instead of a slave to the *halacha*, the rabbis, and rabbinic Judaism, the "New Jew" would be free, relying on innate abilities and strengths to construct a new secular Jewish society.

New Moon – see Rosh Chodesh.

New Moon, announcement of the (*Birkat ha-Chodesh*). Public announcement mentioning the name of the new month and the day(s) on which Rosh Chodesh will be celebrated. It is recited on the Sabbath before the New Moon, following the reading of the *haftarah*. Traditionally, the *shaliach tzibbur* (prayer leader) holds the Torah during *Birkat ha-Chodesh*. In the 18th century, Ashkenazim added an introductory prayer (*Yehi Ratzon*; "May it be Your will"). The congregation rises for *Birkat ha-Chodesh*, a custom that hearkens back to the Sanhedrin's sanctification of the New Moon, which was performed while standing. On the Sabbath preceding Rosh Hashanah (the 1st of Tishrei), *Birkat ha-Chodesh* is not recited in order to "confound the heavenly adversary."

New Year. The Mishnah (RH 1:1) designates four different days as "Rosh Hashanah," each relating to specific activities: (a) the 1st of Nisan for reckoning the reigns of Jewish kings (the date for determining how many years a king has ruled) and for establishing the order of the festivals; (b) the 1st of Elul for tithing animals; (c) the 1st of Tishrei for agriculture (Sabbatical Years, Jubilee Years), passing judgment on humankind, and marking the anniversary of the Creation of the world; and (d) the 1st (but according to Hillel, the 15th) of Shevat for trees.

Next Year in Jerusalem – *see Le-shanah ha-ba'ah bi-Yerushalayim.*

Nezikin (damages). The 4th order of the Mishnah, its 10 tractates are Bava Kamma, Bava Metzia, Bava Batra, Sanhedrin, Makkot, Shevu'ot, Eduyot, Avodah Zarah, Avot, and Horayot. Nezikin deals with a broad spectrum of legal and financial issues.

Nicanor, Gate of. Named for the wealthy Alexandrian Jew who donated the magnificent bronze doors of the gate that led to the courtyard of the Second Temple in Jerusalem. According to tradition, these gates were miraculously saved during a storm when transported by sea. In view of this history and their beauty, the doors of the Gate of Nicanor were left as is when all the other gates of the Temple were changed for golden ones. The Nicanor Gate was approached by 15 steps, on which the Levites used to stand singing and playing musical instruments (see *Shir ha-Ma'alot*).

Niddah (1). Literally "separated" or "excluded," this Hebrew term refers to a menstruating woman. The complex laws that define the status of a *niddah* are based on the two different contexts in which the menstruating woman appears in biblical law – the sexual prohibitions (Lev. 18:19), and the laws of purity and impurity (Lev. 15:19-33). The latter were designed to exclude ritually impure persons from the Temple. After the Temple was destroyed, only the sexual prohibitions related to the *niddah* remained relevant.[215] The laws of sexual separation are known as *taharat ha-mishpachah* (purity of the family).

Niddah (Nid.) (2). The 7th tractate in Tohorot (purity) in the Mishnah, it deals with family purity (menstruation and the monthly period of separation between husband and wife; see *taharat ha-mishpachah* and the ritual uncleanness related to childbirth.

Night of Watching – see *Leil Shimurim.*

Night prayers – see Bedtime prayers.

Nigun. Literally "tune," a wordless melody that is an essential component of Hasidic prayer and can capture the heights of overwhelming ecstasy or the depths of grief.[216] The Hasidic emphasis on song as a way of joyously serving God has had a profound effect across the Jewish religious spectrum, leading to the return of congregational singing as a central component in contemporary synagogue services, especially on Sabbaths and festivals. In this way, modern Jews are increasingly heeding the words of the ancient Psalmist (100:2), "Serve the Lord with gladness, come before His presence with singing."[217]

Nikudot – see Vowels.

Nili. An acronym for the Hebrew phrase *Netzakh Yisrael Lo Yishaker* ("The Eternal One of Israel does not lie"; 1 Sam. 15:29), a secret pro-British spying organization that operated under Turkish rule in Syria and Palestine during World War 1 in an effort to realize a Jewish homeland.

Nine Days. The period between the 1st and 9th of Av (Tisha b'Av, which commemorates the destruction of the First and Second Temples), during which the mourning customs observed during the Three Weeks become intensified. Eating meat and drinking wine are forbidden, except for Sabbath meals. Also prohibited are cutting hair, shaving, bathing, swimming, washing clothes, or any activities that could bring joy – such as attending a concert or the theater or redecorating a room.

Ninth of Av – see Tisha b'Av.

Nirtzah (acceptance). The concluding prayer at the seder, it expresses the hope that God has accepted our observance of Passover and will speedily send the Messiah, or provide humankind with the strength and wisdom to help inaugurate a Messianic Age. It is followed by all saying *le-shanah ha-ba'ah bi-Yerushalayim* (next year in Jerusalem) and the singing of various Passover songs.

Nisan. The 1st month of the Jewish year (March-April), known in the Bible as the month of Aviv (spring). The pilgrimage festival of Passover begins on the 15th of Nisan, and Yom ha-Shoah (Holocaust Remembrance Day) occurs on the 27th of the month.

Nishmat kol chai (The soul of every living being [shall bless Your Name]). Poetic glorification of God that is recited during Sabbath and festival morning services near the end of *Pesukei de-Zimra*.*Nishmat* consists of three major sections. The first recognizes that Jews are totally dependent on God and Divine mercy, for "without You we have no King, Redeemer, or Savior." This is followed by a passage similar to the formula of thanksgiving for abundant rain recited in the talmudic period, and a final section beginning with "From Egypt You have redeemed us." In most prayer books, the Hebrew words *ha-Melech* (the King), *Shochein*

Ad (God who abides [forever]), and *ha-El* (the God) are printed in large type, since the prayer leader starts the central part of the morning service at these places on the High Holy Days, Sabbaths, and festivals, respectively.

Nisuin. Aramaic term for the second part of the marriage ceremony. Initially separated from *kiddushin* (betrothal) by one year, during the Middle Ages the two parts of the marriage ceremony were combined and celebrated on a single day. (See also *marriage ceremony, day of, chuppah, kinyan, ketubah, bridal veil, wedding ring*, and *sheva brachot*.)

Nitzavim. The 8th *parashah* in the Book of Deuteronomy (29:9-30:20), it describes the renewal of the Covenant, foretells the evil that will befall the people for failing to fulfill its terms, and comforts the Israelites by ensuring that they will eventually be redeemed if they return from their evil ways. It contains the famous verse, "I have put before you life and death, blessing and curse. Choose life!"

Nivul ha-met (desecration of the corpse). Jewish law strictly forbids mutilation of the body after death. Some ultra-Orthodox have used this prohibition as the reason for opposing post-mortem examination (see autopsy).

Noah. The 2nd *parashah* in the Book of Genesis (6:9-11:32), it describes the narrative of Noah and the Flood and concludes with the story of the Tower of Babel.

Noahide Laws. The rabbis derived seven basic laws that were binding on all human beings and constituted the fundamental precepts required for the establishment of a civilized society. They are termed the "Noahide laws" since they are to be observed by all people on earth, whom the Torah describes as descended from the three sons of Noah (Gen. 9:19). The Noahide laws include (1) the establishment of courts of justice and the prohibition of (2) idolatry, (3) blasphemy, (4) murder, (5) incest and adultery, (6) robbery, and (7) eating flesh cut from a live animal. Although Israelites in the Land were obliged to carry out all 613 commandments in the Torah (see *taryag mitzvot*), observance of the seven Noahide laws was all that was required of non-Jews who lived among the Israelites or attached themselves to the Jewish community. In this way, non-Jews could assure themselves of a place in the World to Come.

Nobel Prize. As of 2006, persons of full or half Jewish ancestry had been awarded 23% of individual Nobel Prizes worldwide and 37% of those received by Americans. This is a remarkable achievement, considering that Jews currently make up only about 0.25% of the world's population and 2% of the population of the United States.

Normal mysticism. Term coined by Jewish scholar Max Kadushin to describe the Jewish preoccupation with reciting blessings as part of everyday life. Unlike those few individuals, generally labeled as "mystics," who attempt to achieve an intimate, powerful experience of God (see *devekut*), most people never reach such lofty spiritual heights, let alone sustain such exalted levels on a regular basis. Therefore, the Rabbis wisely developed a myriad of blessings to accompany the ordinary moments of daily life, enabling the average Jew to transform both usual and unusual activities into experiences of the Divine Presence and love of humankind.[218]

Northern Kingdom – see Israel, Kingdom of.

Nosh. Yiddish term that can be used as a noun (a "bite") or verb ("to nibble/ snack").

Notarikon. A Greek word meaning "shorthand writer," it refers to two hermeneutical principles of interpreting the Bible. In the first, a word is understood as an acronym for its real meaning (i.e., each letter of the word represents an entirely new word). For example, *Anochi*, meaning "I" (the first word of the Ten Commandments), is actually an abbreviation for "*Ana Nafshi Ketavit Yahavit*" (I, Myself, wrote and gave [them]), so that there can be no doubt that the Decalogue is the word of God (Shab. 105a). The second type consists of breaking up a word into two or more components that have meanings of their own (such as the name of Jacob's son, Reuben, which becomes *re'u ben* [see the son]).

Nothar. The meat of an offering left beyond the time assigned for its consumption, which the Israelites were forbidden to eat. Whenever the Bible states that an offering (e.g., sin, guilt, thanksgiving, Passover) must be consumed during the day of slaughtering and the following night, the duty could be performed until dawn the next morning. However, "in order to keep a man far from transgression," the Rabbis ordained that the time should extend only until midnight. Thus the last piece of *matzah* at the seder (see *afikoman*), which commemorates the Passover offering, must be eaten before midnight.[219]

Novellae (*Chiddushim*). Commentaries on the Talmud and later rabbinic literature that attempt to derive new ideas from the text. In France and Germany they were incorporated into the Tosafot, while in Spain they were published as separate works.

Nu. Yiddish word that is equivalent to the English "so?," "well?," or "what's new?"

Nudge. Yiddish term meaning to "pester" or "nag." As a noun, it is a synonym for *nudnik*.

Nudnik. Yiddish term for a person who is persistently annoying or a pest.

Numbers (Num.) (1). English word for the 4th book of the Bible. It describes the events that occurred during the 40 years of wandering of the Israelites after the Revelation at Mount Sinai to their encampment east of the Jordan River prior to entering the Promised Land. The English name reflects the two censuses of the Israelites reported in the book – the first taken at Sinai in the second year following the Exodus from Egypt, and the second made on the banks of the Jordan during the 40th year of their wandering.

Numbers (2). In the Bible, numbers are often more than just quantitative indicators and are replete with symbolic significance (see *Echad mi yode'a*). Even when numbers are used to indicate quantity, they may represent approximations or hyperboles. In *gematria*, words in the biblical text are understood through the numerical value of their letters. (See sections on individual numbers.)

Numbers Rabbah (Num. R.) – see Midrash Rabbah.

Numerology – see *Gematria.*

Numerus clausus. Latin term literally meaning "closed number," it refers to any limitation in the number of persons admitted to institutions of higher education, permitted to pursue specific professions or join professional organizations, or eligible to be appointed to positions of public office. These restrictions were often imposed on Jews, not only in Eastern Europe but also in the United States, especially during the first half of the 20th century.

Numismatics – see Coins.

Nun. The 14th letter of the Hebrew alphabet, with a numerical value of 50.

Nuremburg Laws. Two anti-Jewish statutes passed by the German Reichstag and announced at the annual Nazi party rally held in this city on September 15, 1935. The Nuremburg Laws excluded Jews from German citizenship and prohibited them from marrying or having sexual relations with persons of "German or related blood." Jews were prohibited from flying the German flag or employing a female German citizen under age 45 in their household. Legislation enacted two months later defined a Jew as one who had at least three Jewish grandparents who were full Jews "by race," or as a person descended from two full Jewish grandparents who at the time the law was passed belonged to the Jewish religious community or was married to a Jew. The Nuremburg Laws and subsequent anti-Jewish enactments humiliated and isolated German Jews, branding them as pariahs.

Nusach. Collection of musical motifs that differentiate one service from another and have been handed down through the generations. Specific modes and melodies characterize the weekday, Sabbath, festival, and High Holy Day services. Certain biblical books, such as the five *megillot* (Esther, Ruth, Song of Songs, Ecclesiastes, and Lamentations), have their own *nusach*. The musical tradition also differs from one ethnic division of Judaism to another, reflecting the secular music of the place where each group lived.

Nuzi. Ancient city in Northern Mesopotamia. Excavations at Nuzi have uncovered clay tablets that provide insights regarding the biblical texts, such as the adoption of sons in the narrative of Jacob and the value of the *teraphim* (family idols) stolen by Rachel from her father Laban, which conferred property rights on her husband Jacob.

O

Oaths – see *Nedarim*.

Obadiah (Obad.). The 4th of the minor prophets. The shortest book in the Bible (one chapter containing only 21 verses), it predicts the destruction of Edom, which not only exulted at the humiliation of the inhabitants of Judah when Jerusalem fell in 586 B.C.E., but also actively assisted their Babylonian enemies by intercepting the fugitives and occupying the Negev. The final five verses describe the reestablishment of the children of Jacob in their homeland, when Mount Zion will rule over Mount Esau (Edom).

Obligatory offerings. These consisted of the sin (see *chatat*) and guilt (see *asham*) offerings that an individual *must* bring if he had transgressed certain commandments. The obligatory offerings were designed to amend the relationship with God when it was tainted by sin, and the Torah sections describing the obligatory offerings virtually always end with the phrase "the *kohen* shall make expiation on his (the offeror's) behalf ... and he shall be forgiven." To be acceptable to God, all cattle and sheep offerings had to be unblemished animals, and salt had to be brought with every offering. (See also *voluntary offerings*.)

Offerings, additional for festivals. Constituting the *maftir* portion of the Torah reading for each festival, it is read in a second scroll from the relevant verses in Numbers 28-29. During the *Musaf Amidah*, a recitation of the required offerings for that specific festival effectively serves as a replacement for the additional offerings that were brought to the Temple on that day.

Ohel. Tent-like canopy erected over the grave of an outstanding religious leader. This practice was designed to bestow royal treatment on great sages, such as the elaborate *ohel* for Maimonides in the Tiberias cemetery in Israel.[220] Hasidim especially venerate the tombs of their *tzadikim*, where they make pilgrimages on the anniversaries of their deaths.

Ohel mo'ed – see Tent of Meeting.

Oholot (Ohol.). The 2nd tractate of Kodashim (holy things) in the Mishnah, it deals with ritual impurity related to a corpse.

Oil. Used for various ritual, ceremonial, and sacrificial practices in Jewish life (see olive oil).

Ol machut shamayim (yoke of the Kingdom of Heaven). Hebrew term for the Divine will and commandments, which the Israelites voluntarily accepted at Mount Sinai. The Rabbis viewed this acceptance as the basis for the selection of Israel as the Chosen People.

Olah – see Burnt offering.

Olam ha-ba. Literally "the World to Come," the Hebrew term for the afterlife, the eternal world of the spirit to which the soul passes after death. *Olam ha-ba* also can refer to the time when the world will be perfected following the coming of the Messiah.(See also *Kingdom of Heaven.*)

Olam ha-zeh. Literally "this world" in Hebrew, it was regarded by the Rabbis as a place where one could perform deeds of lovingkindness that would be rewarded in the World to Come (*olam ha-ba*). The *olam ha-zeh* was compared to an antechamber to the future world, where one was urged to "prepare yourself so that you may enter the palace" (Avot 4:21).

Old Testament. Christian term for the Hebrew Bible. This is not accepted in Jewish tradition because it expresses the belief that there is a "New Testament" that has somehow superseded the special Divine relationship with the Jewish people. Instead, Jews use such terms as Hebrew Bible, Hebrew Scriptures, or *Tanach*.

Oleh (pl., ***olim***). Literally "one who ascends," a person who has made *aliyah* to the Land of Israel.

Olive oil. Olive trees have always been the most prominent and extensively distributed in the landscape of Israel, growing on terraced hillsides throughout the land. One of the seven species indigenous to the Land of Israel, olives were pressed to make oil, which served as fuel for lamps and as a major element in the meal offering (see *mincha*). The Bible frequently describes the bounty of the land in terms of "corn, wine, and oil" (Deut. 7:13). Olive oil was used for anointing Israelite priests, prophets, kings, and holy places (see anointing). It also was the original source of light in the Temple Menorah and the *ner tamid*, as well as in the *chanukiah* – the menorah kindled on Chanukah, a holiday when it is traditional to eat foods fried in oil (such as potato latkes and *sufganiyot*).

Omer (1). Literally "sheaf," the measure of the newly harvested grain (traditionally barley, the first to ripen) that the Israelites were commanded to bring to the

Jerusalem Temple as a harvest offering on the second day of Passover (Lev. 23:9-16). The *kohen* took the offering and waved it in every direction, praying that God protect the harvest from "injurious winds and harmful dews."

Omer (2). Dry measure equal to one tenth of an *ephah.*

Omer, counting of the (*sefirat ha-omer*) From the second day of Passover until the festival of Shavuot, Jews are commanded to count seven weeks. For the ancient Israelites, the Omer period (*Sefirah*) was the critical time when the success of the harvest was determined. The pilgrimage festival of Shavuot at the conclusion of the Omer period was in thanksgiving for God's blessing and protection of the land and its produce. The *Sefirah* is observed each evening by reciting a special blessing and marking off each day of the Omer. To keep an accurate count of the days, special "Omer calendars" were developed. These contained movable numbers and were often embellished with folk art motifs. Except for the 33rd day of the Omer (see *Lag ba-Omer*), the Omer period is observed as a time of semi-mourning during which traditional Jews do not get haircuts, celebrate weddings, or attend concerts. Two modern holiday exceptions are the celebrations of Yom ha-Atzmaut (Israel Independence Day) and Yom Yerushalayim (Jerusalem Day), which fall during this period on the 5th and 28th of Iyar.

Ona'ah. Literally "overreaching," this talmudic term refers to fraudulent misrepresentation or unfair profit in commercial dealings. Based on the biblical verse, "When you sell anything to your neighbor, or make a purchase from the hand of your fellow, you shall not wrong one another" (Lev. 25:14), the Rabbis ruled that substantial overcharging (one-sixth or more of the market value of the goods) was grounds for canceling a business agreement, since fraud or the taking of an undue advantage would be presumed.

One (*echad*). The quintessential number of Jewish monotheism, which is best expressed in the central affirmation of faith, the *Shema.*The commentators stress that *echad* also means "unique," and that the numerical value of the Hebrew word equals 13, the traditional number of Divine Attributes.Other liturgical references to the Oneness of God include *Adon Olam*, *Yigdal*, and the messianic conclusion of the *Aleinu.*

120. A popular expression is to wish another person, whether young or old, to live "until 120" – the life span of Moses (Deut. 34:7), the greatest Jew who ever lived. To reach this age is to be granted not only the great gift of length of days, but also the supreme honor of being linked to the life of the most revered figure in Jewish history.[221]

Oneg Shabbat. Literally "delight in the Sabbath," the term is based on a verse in Isaiah (58:13), "and you shall call the Sabbath a delight [*oneg*], and the holy of the

Lord honorable." According to Maimonides, for the rabbis "delight" meant lighting candles on Friday night, enjoying special delicacies, a minimum of three Sabbath meals, cohabitation with one's spouse, general repose, and added sleep. Traditionally, "honor" implied the duties of bathing immediately before the Sabbath, wearing special Sabbath clothes, and receiving the Sabbath with joy.[222] The term "Oneg Shabbat" was coined by famed poet Chaim Nachman Bialik to describe a popular study session with the singing of Sabbath songs on Saturday afternoons that he initiated during the 1920's in Tel Aviv. This custom spread throughout Israel and the Diaspora. Today, Oneg Shabbat refers to the informal reception held in synagogue after Sabbath services on Friday night and Saturday morning.

Onen – see *Aninut*.

Ongeblozzen. Yiddish word meaning "sulking" or "angry at the world."

Ongepotchket. From a Russian word meaning to "soil" or "sully," this Yiddish word connotes something that is piecemeal or overdone. It also can be used to describe something that is garish and unaesthetic, such as jewelry and furnishings.

Onkelos – see Targum Onkelos.

Operation Ezra and Nehemiah. Also known as "Operation Ali Baba," the code name for the airlift, carried out by the Jewish Agency and the Israeli government, that brought virtually all of Iraqi Jewry (about 120,000) to Israel in 1950-1951. Before the Jews could leave Iraq, they were forced to liquidate their businesses and sell their property for tiny sums, thus becoming impoverished. They could not remain in Iraq because their lives were in danger due to virulent anti-Zionism, which morphed into anti-Semitism. This exodus from Iraq effectively ended the Jewish community in a country where it had existed for 2,500 years.

Operation Magic Carpet. Code name for the airlift, carried out by the Jewish Agency and the Israeli government, that brought 50,000 Yemenite Jews to Israel in 1949-1950. This exodus followed severe Muslim rioting in the wake of the declaration of the State of Israel. Most Yemenite Jews had previously never even seen an airplane, but they believed the biblical prophecy that God would return the dispersed Children of Israel to Zion "with wings" (Isa. 40:31).

Operations Moses and Solomon. Code name for the airlift of more than 22,000 Ethiopian Jews (see Beta Israel) to Israel in 1984 and 1991. The Beta Israel were thus able to escape a land rife with political instability, poverty, and famine and come to a land of freedom.

Ophel. Name applied by modern archeologists to the old City of David south of the Temple Mount.

Orach Hayim – see *Shulchan Aruch.*

Oral Law. The body of rabbinic discussions, expositions, and commentaries on the Torah (see Written Law) that deal with all aspects of existence from the most trivial to the sublime. According to tradition, it was part of the Revelation given to Moses and subsequently transmitted faithfully by the leaders of each generation to their successors – from Moses to Joshua, and then to the elders, the prophets, the men of the Great Assembly, the leaders of the Pharisees, and eventually to the earliest Rabbis (Avot 1:1).[223] The Oral Law consists of two major divisions: *halacha* and *aggada.* For centuries, the study of the Oral Law was essentially a matter of memorizing and recapitulation, unlike the Written Law that could be read. Eventually, the Oral Law was written down with the aid of established hermeneutical techniques, rabbinic legislation, and rational principles. It was codified in the Mishnah, and subsequent rabbinic discussions in the academies were recorded in the Babylonian and Jerusalem Talmuds. Although some sects, such as the Karaites, rejected the authority of the Oral Law, it became authoritative in normative Judaism and has been continually expanded and enriched by numerous codifiers and commentators.

Ordeal, trial by – see *Sotah.*

Ordination – see *Semichah.*

Organ. Although the ancient Israelites had a rich tradition of vocal and instrumental music, after the Temple was destroyed the use of musical instruments on Sabbaths and festivals was banned as a sign of mourning. The sages believed that no Jewish prayer service should approximate the glory of worship in the ancient Sanctuary. Musical instruments were also prohibited because they might lead to work (forbidden on the Sabbath and festivals), such as the repair of a broken string on a violin.[224] In later times, certain instruments – especially the organ – were so closely associated with worship in Christian churches that the rabbis ruled it would be a case of the prohibited "imitating of gentile customs" (see *chukat ha-goy*) to play them in the synagogue (see prayer, music in). The organ was introduced into the worship service in the early stages of the Reform movement and has been used since that time.

Organ donation. As with autopsy, this issue revolves around the often-conflicting principles of *kavod ha-met* (reverence for the human body after death) and *pikuach nefesh* (preservation of life). In this instance, however, these two basic tenets work in tandem, for it assumed that deceased persons would be honored if their organs were used to preserve the life of others. Enabling a person to live through the donation of an organ is also a supreme act of *chesed*, loving-kindness to one's fellow human being. Despite the predominant opinion that delaying burial to permit organ transplantation does not diminish respect for the dead, but rather enhances it, some rabbis have limited this practice to varying degrees. Others object based on the belief that one must be buried intact to be resurrected whole. Nevertheless, except for the most extreme branches of Orthodoxy, virtually all rabbis agree that saving life in the here and now clearly and unequivocally takes precedence over whatever one believes about future resurrection.

Original sin – see Fall of man.

Orlah (1). Literally "uncircumcised fruit," this Hebrew term refers to the fruit of a tree during its first three years, which the Bible states may not be eaten by Jews (Lev. 19:23). Ibn Ezra and Nachmanides believed that fruit from such young trees was harmful to health. Moreover, because the fruit of three-year-old trees were not mature enough to be used as offerings of first fruits for the sacred purpose of praising and thanking God, they also were forbidden for human consumption.[225] Fourth-year fruit could be eaten, but only at the site of the Sanctuary and after using it to praise God (Lev. 19:24). Only in the fifth year was the fruit of a tree available for general use.

Orlah (2). The 10th tractate in Zera'im (seeds) in the Mishnah, it deals with the forbidden fruits of young trees.

Orlah (3). The foreskin of the penis, which is cut off during circumcision.

Orphans. As some of the weakest members of society, along with widows and strangers, the Bible mandates that "You shall not ill-treat any [widow or] orphan" (Exod. 22:21), who have no human protector, lack the physical force to defend their rights, and are likely to become the victims of exploitation – like the Jews in Egypt. Maimonides wrote that one should "show them unvarying courtesy, not hurt them physically with hard toil, nor wound their feelings with harsh speech. One must take greater care of their property than of one's own. Whoever irritates them, provokes them to anger, pains them, tyrannizes over them, or causes them loss of money, is guilty of a transgression, and still more so, if one beats them or curses them."[226] The two verses that follow in the biblical text from the Book of Exodus indicate that anyone who violated this commandment should expect severe retribution from God, the Protector of orphans, whose "anger shall blaze forth" when hearing their cry and "will put you to the sword" so that "your own children shall become orphans."

ORT. Acronym for **O**rganization for **R**ehabilitation through **T**raining, a philanthropic society founded in Russia in 1880. It has become a global movement that promotes and develops vocational training opportunities for Jews in the skilled trades and agriculture, with the aim of fostering dignity and economic self-sufficiency. After the establishment of the State of Israel, ORT opened occupational courses for new immigrants and the first vocational schools in major cities. Gradually, ORT has begun to emphasize hi-tech (such as computer skills) rather than basic vocational training, so that the students receive the best possible preparation for their future occupations.

Orthodox movement. This term was first used in 1795 to differentiate "traditional" Jews from those adhering to the liberal Reform practices. Rather than a united movement with a single governing body, it contains numerous sects that are conveniently (but somewhat artificially) categorized as "modern Orthodox and "ultra-Orthodox." The unifying factor is a belief in the Divine origin of both the Written Law and the Oral Law and the need for strict adherence to Jewish law as codified in the *Shulchan Aruch* and other authoritative sources. The Orthodox regard the ceremonial precepts of Jewish law as equally important to its ethical demands.

Oseh shalom. Literally, "He who creates peace [above]," the final verse in the full *Kaddish* and the *Amidah*.It is based on the verse from Job (25:2), "He makes peace in high places." Before reciting *Oseh shalom*, the worshiper takes three steps back (starting with the left foot), and then bows to the left, right, and center, as though leaving one's teacher or departing from the presence of royalty.[227] Another interpretation is that as we bow to the left we face the angel Michael, who symbolizes God's spirit of Mercy and stands at the right of the Divine throne. The bow to our right is toward the angel Gabriel, who stands at the left of the throne and represents the Divine quality of strict justice. Finally, we bow forward, directly toward God, who alone can harmonize these two disparate Divine manifestations and establish lasting peace, both on earth and in Heaven.[228]

Ossuary. Small stone container in which the bones of the dead are placed. Ossuaries dating from the 2nd and 3rd centuries C.E. have been found with Hebrew, Greek, and Aramaic inscriptions.

Ostracon. A Greek word meaning "shard," it refers to fragments of pottery with inscriptions that were used as letters and for receipts. Ostracons found at various archeological sites within Israel and surrounding countries have offered valuable insights into life in ancient times.

Oy. Yiddish exclamation expressing a broad spectrum of emotions, ranging from surprise, joy, contentment, and relief to anguish, pain, fear, and regret. It is commonly repeated three times (*oy, oy, oy*) or combined with the words *gevalt* or *vey*.

Oysgemutchet. Yiddish word meaning to be thoroughly exhausted or worn out.

Oznei Haman. Literally "Haman's ears" in Hebrew, these fried ear-shaped cookies are popular among Sephardim on Purim. This name allegedly derived from the old practice of cutting off the ears of criminals before hanging them – appropriate since Haman was hanged "on the gallows that he had prepared for Mordecai" at the conclusion of the Book of Esther (7:10).

P

P. According to the Documentary Hypothesis (see Bible criticism), one of the four major strands of literary tradition edited to form the Five Books of Moses. This "Priestly" source is thought to have provided the first chapter of Genesis, the Book of Leviticus, and other sections dealing with genealogical information, the priesthood, and worship, always stressing the cultic approach to God. Although initially considered the latest source (sometime after the return of the Jews from Babylonian Exile in the 6th century B.C.E.), according to some recent scholars "P" may have preceded the 7th-century "D."

Pairs – see *Zugot*.

Pale of Settlement. Area within the borders of the czarist Russian Empire where Jews were officially permitted to live. Established by Catherine the Great in 1791 in response to pressure to rid Moscow of Jewish business competition and their "evil influence" on the susceptible Russian masses, the Pale of Settlement included territory of present-day Latvia, Lithuania, Ukraine, Bessarabia, Belorussia, and Poland. Subsequent czars reduced the area of the Pale. More than 90% of Russian Jews were forced to live in the poor conditions of the Pale, which made up only 4% of imperial Russia and was effectively a large-scale ghetto. Despite these hardships, from 1820-1910 the Jewish population in Russia grew from 1.6 to 5.6 million, and the Pale developed its own Jewish culture. Even within the Pale, however, Jews were discriminated against – they paid double taxes and were forbidden to lease land, operate taverns, or receive higher education. The May Laws of 1882 restricted Jews in the Pale to urban areas, which were often overcrowded and offered limited economic opportunities. These deplorable conditions, combined with a series of pogroms and boycotts, led to mass immigration to the United States. The Pale of Settlement was effectively abolished in 1915, though the laws concerning it remained in force until the overthrow of the czarist regime two years later.

Palestine. One of the names of the territory known as the Land of Israel or the Holy Land. Derived from the Hebrew *Peleshet* describing the land inhabited by the Philistines, it was initially called "Palestinian Syria" by the Greeks but later the word "Syria" was dropped. After the fall of the Crusader kingdom in the 13th century, Palestine was no longer an official designation, and during the long centuries of Ottoman rule it was part of the province of Syria. After receiving the Mandate over Palestine from the League of Nations following World War I, the British restricted the use of the term "Palestine" to the land west of the Jordan River. The State of Israel was established (1948) in the western part of Palestine; the remainder was incorporated into the Hashemite Kingdom of Jordan, so that Palestine as a political entity ceased to exist. During the Six Day War (1967), after Jordan attacked Israel and was soundly defeated, Israel took possession of all of Palestine west of the Jordan.

Palestinian Talmud – see Jerusalem Talmud.

Pallbearers. Relatives and close friends who, after the funeral service, are given the honor at the cemetery of carrying the coffin of the deceased to the gravesite.

Palm tree. The date palm (*tamar* in Hebrew; *dekel* in the Mishnah) has been a valuable tree in the Middle East since ancient times. According to rabbinic tradition, the biblical description of Israel as a "land flowing with milk and honey" (Exod. 3:8) referred to date honey, one of the seven species indicating the fertile abundance of the land (Deut. 8:8). The psalmist compared the righteous to a flourishing palm (Ps. 92:13), as did the lover in Song of Songs his beloved (7:8). The prophetess Deborah judged the people in the shade of a palm tree (Judg. 4:5), and Tamar was the name of the daughter-in-law of Judah (Gen. 38:6) and the daughter of David (2 Sam. 13:1). The palm tree with its flowing fronds was a popular ornamental design in the Temple (1 Kings 6:29) and ancient synagogues. The palm branch (see *lulav*) is one of the four species carried in the *hoshanot* processions in the synagogue during Sukkot.

Palmach. Acronym for *plugot machatz* (translated as "assault companies" or "shock troops"), the commando unit of the Haganah under the leadership of Yitzhak Sadeh. It was organized after the outbreak of war in 1941, when Axis forces had moved dangerously close to the approaches to the Land of Israel. Members of the Palmach achieved high standards in physical fitness, field training, and guerilla fighting by day and night. The Palmach carried out numerous daring missions – rescuing thousands of Jews from Nazi Europe, running the British blockades of Palestine in the "death ships" of the post-war "illegal immigration" period, and guarding the settlements and highways as the British were preparing to leave the land. During the War of Independence (1948), the Palmach was integrated in the Israel Defense Forces and its members bore the brunt of the Arab attack. Many Palmach commanders, including Yigal Allon, Moshe Dayan, and Yitzhak Rabin, became leaders of the new State of Israel.

Panentheism. Hasidic concept, especially in Chabad, which maintains that all the world is "in" God. According to this idea, the multiplicity of things we observe in the universe, as well as we ourselves, are due to the screening of the Divine light that does not permit us to observe the Infinite reality. From the point of view of God, neither creatures nor the universe exist apart from the Divinity. This theological concept is difficult for the finite mind of man to comprehend – how there can be a universe and creatures and yet only God. Panentheism attempts to resolve the paradox of Divine transcendence and immanence by declaring that God is the all; if only man learns to penetrate deeper into ultimate reality, he will see the Divine power by which all things are sustained.

Pantheism. Theological concept elaborated upon by Spinoza and other philosophers, which declares the complete immanence of God. According to this view, God and Nature are different names for the same thing. God did not "create" Nature, but "is" Nature. Neither intellect nor will can be ascribed to God, who is only "in" the world. Pantheism is opposed to classical theism, which affirms the belief in a Creator (who is above and beyond human comprehension) and a created order.

Papyrus. Plant used for paper during the biblical period. The huge stems of papyrus, often more than 10 feet high, were employed in the construction of light boats, such as the ark in which the infant Moses was placed (Exod. 2:3).

Parable – see *Mashal*.

Paradise. Greek word used by the Septuagint to translate the Hebrew word "*pardes*," which refers to the Garden of Eden (see *Gan Eden*). In this eschatological Paradise, the abode of the mystical ascent of the soul, the righteous sit at golden tables (Taan. 25a) or under elaborate canopies, participating in lavish banquets (BB 75a) and partaking of spiritual delights.

Parah. The 4th tractate in Tohorot (purity) in the Mishnah, it deals with the regulations concerning the red heifer.

Parah adumah – see Red heifer.

Parapet. Homes in the ancient Middle East had flat roofs, which were used for sleeping, walking, and other household activities. To prevent one from accidentally falling off the roof, the Bible mandated that an Israelite erect a parapet, a barrier about two cubits (three feet) high, "so that you do not bring blood on your house if anyone should fall from it" (Deut. 22:8). The Rabbis extended this verse to require the removal of all obstacles and sources of danger from both public and private property to prevent fatal accidents. Maimonides noted that this commandment also required the building of restraining devices around cisterns and trenches, which in modern terms would translate into erecting protective barriers around a swimming pool, a tall stairway, or a construction site. Similarly, people must safeguard their own lives and not place themselves in dangerous situations;[229] some modern rabbis have applied this prohibition to the practice of smoking cigarettes

Parashah (pl., *parshiyot*). Ashkenazic term for the weekly Torah portion (called *sidrah* by Sephardim). The Hebrew name of each *parashah* reflects the first significant word(s) in that portion. Although the Land of Israel used what is now called the "triennial cycle," the large and influential Jewish community in Babylonia developed the custom of completing the entire Torah in a single year, which eventually became the generally accepted practice throughout the world. The Babylonian tradition divided the Torah into 54 sections, making it inevitable that two portions be read on some occasions to complete the entire Torah during the year (especially since the regularly scheduled weekly portion is deferred for a week when a major festival falls on the Sabbath). The relatively lengthy Torah portions from the Book of Genesis are never combined, since this would extend the service unduly and violate the Jewish legal principle against imposing unnecessary inconvenience on the congregation.

Parchment. The words on the Torah scroll are written on parchment, which must be prepared from specified sections of the hide of a kosher animal (though not necessarily one that has been slaughtered according to Jewish ritual). Individual leaves of parchment are sewn together with thread (see *giddim*), and these are reinforced by thin strips of parchment pasted on the top and bottom of the page.

Pardes (1). Hebrew word that refers to the Garden of Eden (see *Gan Eden*) and is translated in English as "Paradise" or "orchard."

Pardes (2). Acronym for the four classic ways of interpreting the Bible, as developed by Bahya ben Asher at the end of the 13th century. This is a mnemonic for the initial letters of the words *peshat* (plain, literal meaning of the verse in its context), *remez* (allegorical or symbolic meaning only hinted at in the text); *derash* (homiletic interpretation to uncover an ethical or moral lesson thought to be implicit in the text), and *sod* (secret, esoteric, or mystical interpretation, emphasized by the kabbalists).

Parents. The fifth of the Ten Commandments mandates that one should "honor" (Exod. 20:12) and "revere" (fear; Lev. 19:3) your father and mother. Honoring parents is one of only two commandments for which a reward (i.e., length of days) is promised to one who observes it. According to the Rabbis, *honoring* one's parents means serving them, providing them with food and drink, clothing, and shelter, and assisting them when they are too old and infirm to walk. Respect for one's parents forbids any act that might offend them or reduce the esteem in which they are held. The traditional interpretation of this injunction was that a child may not sit in their regular places, interrupt them, insolently challenge their statements, or call them by their first names. These filial responsibilities extend beyond the grave, with the child obligated to say *Kaddish* in memory of departed parents for 11 months and on the annual anniversary of their deaths. Conversely, striking one's parents or cursing them (treating them with contempt) is expressly prohibited. Disobedience is permitted only if parents order children to transgress Torah commandments.

Pareve. A Yidddish world literally meaning "neutral," the term for food products that contain neither meat (see *fleishig*) nor milk (see *milchig*). Foods that are *pareve* include fruit, vegetables, eggs, and grains. These may be eaten together with milk or meat dishes. Fish also is a neutral food, but the Rabbis prohibited the eating of fish and meat together on the grounds that such a combination impairs health.

Parnas. Literally "provider" or "supporter," a Hebrew term for the head of the Jewish community. Today, it often refers to the president of a synagogue. In Sephardic congregations, the term applies to a member of the governing board.

Parochet. Curtain, usually elaborately decorated, that is hung in front of the doors of the ark in Ashkenazic synagogues, or inside the doors in the Sephardic tradition. This is in imitation of the curtain of "blue, purple, and crimson yarns, and fine twisted linen" (Exod. 26:31-33) that separated the Holy of Holies (in which the Ark containing the Ten Commandments was housed) from the rest of the Tabernacle (Exod. 40:21). On the High Holy Days, virtually all synagogues change the *parochet* (and Torah mantles and lectern covers) to white, a symbol of purity and forgiveness of sins. On Tisha b'Av, the *parochet* is removed from the ark to heighten the somber atmosphere of the day. Many contemporary synagogues have eliminated ark coverings, replacing them with doors that are ornately ornamented.[230] Among the most popular designs for the *parochet* are the Ten Commandments, crowns, lions of Judah (symbolizing the sovereignty of God), and representations of the Tree of Life.[231]

Parnosse. Yiddish term meaning "livelihood" or "sustenance."

Parshat ha-shavuah. Literally "portion of the week," this Hebrew phrase refers to the part of the Torah read in the synagogue during the Sabbath morning service.

Particularism. The conviction that Jewish thinking has some unique categories and that non-Jewish thinking is either inimical or superfluous to strictly Jewish thought. Inimical refers to non-Jewish concepts that are dangerous to Jewish thinking and potentially destructive to Jewish authenticity. An example is the introduction by the medieval Jewish philosophers of "harmful foreign elements" from Arab and Greek culture (e.g., *mitzvot* have no value since there are more direct routes to come close to God). Superfluous means that, if Jewish thinking is true, any true non-Jewish ideas must merely be the same, so why bother with outside views? Over the centuries, some who have sought an explanation for the various disasters that have befallen the Jewish people have adopted this concept. Adhering to the biblical notion of reward and punishment, they have considered the expulsion from Spain as Divine punishment for Jews moving away from Judaism (even though some of them actually converted and remained in Spain). In our modern day, some ultra-particularists far beyond the mainstream have used the concept of reward and punishment to argue that the Holocaust was somehow Divine retribution for Jews having been seduced by the lures of alien culture. According to the particularist view (e.g., Judah Loew of Prague), the further back the source, the higher the authority since it is closer to the Revelation at Mount Sinai (see revelation, terminal). (See also *accommodationism.*)

Partisans. Term for the estimated tens of thousands of Jews throughout Europe who participated in resistance movements against Nazi Germany during World War II. Partisan bases were located in the forests, swamps, and mountainous regions of both Western and Eastern Europe. Units composed completely of Jews were much more prominent in the East; in Western Europe, Jews played significant roles in national partisan movements. The activities and accomplishments of the Jewish partisans helped dispel the false stereotype of the "cowardly Jew."

Partition (1) – see *Mechitzah.*

Partition (2). After the British formally announced the decision to relinquish their Mandate over Palestine, a United Nations Committee of Inquiry recommended partitioning the country into separate Arab and Jewish states, with Jerusalem to be governed by an international authority. On November 29, 1947, a majority of UN members voted to approve this compromise solution, which was accepted by the *yishuv* but rejected by the Arabs of Palestine and surrounding Arab states.

Paschal lamb. The animal sacrificed on the eve of Passover from the time of the Exodus from Egypt through the destruction of the Second Temple. Shortly before leaving Israel, the Israelites were commanded to sprinkle the blood of the lamb on their doorposts to prevent the death of their firstborn sons during the tenth and final plague. The paschal lamb was roasted whole and could not be eaten by an uncircumcised person or an apostate Israelite. None of the meat could be allowed to remain until the next morning. Today, the roasted shankbone (*zero'ah*) on the seder plate is a reminder of the paschal lamb.

Passover. Spring pilgrimage festival, also known as the "Feast of Unleavened Bread," which commemorates the redemption of the Jewish people from bondage and the Exodus from Egypt. A seven-day festival in Israel and among Reform Jews (eight in the Diaspora for Orthodox and Conservative Jews) that begins on the 15th of Nisan, the name derives from the tenth plague, when God "passed over" (*pasach*) the homes of the Israelites and slew only the firstborn of Egypt (Exod. 12:27). The major Passover ritual is the seder, when Jews read the Hagaddah, drink four cups of wine, ask four questions, speak of four sons, eat *matzah* and *maror*, and finish the meal with the *afikoman* and numerous songs (see *Ki Lo Na'eh*, *Adir Hu*, *Echad Mi Yode'a*, and *Chad Gadya*). During Passover, it is forbidden to eat or possess leaven (see *chametz*).

Passover, Second (*Pesach Sheni*). Passover sacrifice offered on Iyar 14 by anyone who had been ritually impure or absent when the paschal lamb was sacrificed during Passover in the preceding month (Nisan 14) (Num. 9:6-13).

Pasuk. Hebrew term for a biblical verse (see also *perek*).

Pasul. Ritual object that is unfit for use. Any incorrect word, or even an obliterated letter, makes a Torah scroll *pasul*. Most simple errors may be corrected by scratching out the mistake with a sharp blade and pumice stone. The most serious error – the omission or misspelling of the Name of God – cannot be corrected, since the Divine Name cannot be erased, and the entire sheet of parchment must be discarded. When a mistake is found in a Torah, a cloth ribbon is tied around the mantle as a sign that it is *pasul* and cannot be used until the appropriate correction is made. A scroll that cannot be repaired must be placed in an earthenware container and buried in the cemetery.

Patach – see Vowels.

Patria. Ship carrying "illegal" Jewish immigrants that sank in Haifa Bay. On November 25, 1940, the British Mandatory Government had chartered this French liner to deport Jews arriving on steamers to the island of Mauritius. Explosives placed on board to sabotage the engines and thus prevent the deportation blew up, resulting in the deaths of more than 200 Jews.

Patriarchate. Administration under the Sanhedrin, whose president (*nasi*, or "Patriarch" as he was called in the outside world) became officially recognized as the representative of the Jewish people in its relations with the Roman authorities. The most famous patriarch, Judah the Prince (who compiled the Mishnah), was commissioned to tax all the Jews throughout the Roman Empire in order to maintain the Sanhedrin and the numerous other government functions that pertained exclusively to the Jewish people, thus effectively setting up a virtually autonomous Jewish community. Ruling a "state" and supported by the emperors with money and other privileges, Judah was criticized by other Jews for living so regally.

Over the next two centuries, the fortunes of the Patriarchate decreased. The last Patriarch was Gamaliel VI, who died in 426 leaving no heirs. This marked the end of the 400-year dynasty of the House of Hillel.

Patriarchs. Term applied to the three "founding fathers" of the Jewish people – Abraham, Isaac, and Jacob.

Patrilineal descent. Principle adopted by the Reform movement in 1983 that broke with the rabbinic tradition that the status of the children of a mixed marriage depended solely on the faith of the mother (see intermarriage, status of children). Instead it defines a person as a Jew if *either* of his parents is Jewish *and* the person is "living a Jewish life/committed to Judaism." This new definition was designed to compensate for demographic decline by broadening the definition of a Jew and extending a welcome and a sense of legitimacy to people who otherwise might be lost to the Jewish community. However, by defining Jews differently from traditional Jewish law, this practice has effectively established a new category of people who are deemed Jewish by the standards of some, but not most, Jews.

Payess. Yiddish term for *payot*.

Payot. Hebrew term (*payess* in Yiddish) for the long sidelocks of hair worn in front of the ears by ultra-Orthodox men and boys. This is in keeping with the biblical verse, "You shall not round off the corners of your heads" (Lev. 19:27), a prohibition designed to distinguish Israelite practice from that of certain pagan priests. The required length of the *payot* is not specified, but it was understood to be a line drawn from the top of the forehead to the base of the earlobe and long enough to be grasped by two fingers. The custom arose (first in Hungary and Galicia) of allowing the sidelocks to grow completely uncut. Yemenite Jews follow a similar custom, but this originated in a decree forbidding Jews to cut their sideburns in order to distinguish them from Muslims.[232]

Paytanim. Liturgical poets of the post-talmudic period, who were probably cantors and offered their communities a poetic alternative to the standard prayers. They employed sophisticated formal arrangements of rhymes, meters, refrains, and acrostics in their *piyyutim*.

Peace (*shalom*). A request for peace concludes all of the major prayers in the Jewish liturgy – the *Amidah*; *Kaddish*; Priestly Blessing; and *Birkat ha-Mazon* (see Grace after Meals). Domestic peace (see *shalom bayit*) is necessary for a home to be blessed by the Divine Presence. The Jewish vision of the Messianic Age is one of universal peace. (See also *shalom*.)

Peace offering (*sh'lamim*). Sacrifice of cattle, sheep, or goat that was brought by a person who was moved to express his love of God or gratitude for Divine goodness (such as thanksgiving for deliverance from sickness or danger, or in fulfillment of a vow made in times of distress) and to achieve a closeness to God (Lev. 3:1-17). The Hebrew word "*sh'lamim*" can also be translated as "whole" or "harmony," implying that one who offered it was motivated not by guilt or obligation, but rather by a feeling that his life was "complete" in relation to family and God.[233] Unlike the burnt offering, only a small part of the peace offering was burned on the Altar. With the exception of portions reserved for the *kohanim*, all the rest was eaten by the one who offered it, his family, and guests at a festive meal, where the person bringing the sacrifice would praise God and relate the Divine blessings that had been bestowed on him.[234] (For the thanksgiving offering, see *Gomel*.)

Peace, prayer for. The final blessing of the *Amidah*, it appears in two versions. *Sim Shalom* (Grant peace) is said by Ashkenazim in the morning service and by Sephardim in all services. *Shalom Rav* (Abundant peace), is used in the afternoon and evening services among Ashkenazim.

Pe'ah (1). When reaping the harvest, the farmer was commanded to leave a corner (*pe'ah*) of the field for the poor (Lev. 19:9), who were allowed free access to it. Although the precise size of this section was not prescribed in the Torah, the Talmud (Pe'ah 1:2) declared that it should be not less than one-sixtieth part of the harvest and always proportional to the number of the poor and the yield of the crops. The Rabbis regard *pe'ah* as a unique Jewish ethical achievement.

Pe'ah (2). The 2nd tractate in Zera'im (seeds) in the Mishnah, it deals with the setting aside of the corners of the field for the poor (see above), as well as other duties owed them.

Peel Commission. British Royal Commission that issued a 1937 report recommending the partition of Palestine into a Jewish state, an Arab state, and a British Mandatory enclave. It recommended that during the interim period no land transactions should be made that "might prejudice such a scheme," and that immigration should be limited to a total of 8,000 for next 8 months. The Peel Commission also urged as much of an exchange of populations as possible, but none of its proposals was ever implemented.

Pei. The 17th letter of the Hebrew alphabet, with a numerical value of 80.

Peki'in. Village northwest of Safed near the hills of Upper Galilee, where Shimon bar Yochai and his son Eleazar hid in a cave for 12 years during the Hadrianic persecution of Jews following the Bar Kochba War (2nd century C.E.). Totally immersed in Torah, they were sustained only by spring water and the fruit of a giant carob tree.

Pekudei. The 11th and final *parashah* in the Book of Exodus (38:21-40:38), it describes the completion and dedication of the Tabernacle.

Penitence – see *Teshuvah.*

Penitential prayers – see *Selichot.*

Pentateuch – see *Chumash.*

Pentecost – see Shavuot.

People of the Book – see *Dhimma.*

Perek. Hebrew term for a chapter in the Bible. Although the traditional text of the Torah flows unimpeded, in printed books it is subdivided into chapters and verses. This division was a 13th-century Christian innovation designed to aid missionaries and those engaged in public theological disputations with the Jews to quickly find numerous quotations to support their spurious arguments. Thus, it became necessary for rabbis to use the same system of chapters and verses so as to recognize the references used by their religious opponents and offer effective rebuttals to the Christian version of the Jewish text.[235]

Perek ha-Shalom. Minor tractate added to the Talmud that deals with the importance of fostering peace between individuals. It emphasizes that peace is one of the foundations on which the world rests.

Perjury. The act of swearing to a statement known to be false or giving false testimony under oath. As a violation of both the third and ninth of the Ten Commandments, perjury is regarded as a serious transgression.

Perpetual light – see *Ner tamid.*

Perutah. Smallest denomination of currency in talmudic times. When marriage was understood as essentially a business transaction, the groom "acquired" his bride and sealed the deal by the payment of a silver or gold coin that had a value of not less than one *perutah.* Although Yemenite Jews still use a coin at the wedding ceremony, most Jewish traditions have substituted a ring.

Pesach. Hebrew name for Passover.

Pesach Sheni – see Passover, Second.

Pesachdik. Yiddish term for something that is certified to be free of *chametz* (leaven) and thus can be utilized on Passover.

Pesachim (Pes.). The 3rd tractate in Mo'ed (festivals) in the Mishnah, it deals with regulations regarding Passover (*chametz*, *matzah*, paschal sacrifice).

Pesha. Hebrew word denoting an intentional sin committed in a spirit of rebellion, a treasonous breach in the covenantal relationship in deliberate defiance of the sovereignty of God.

Peshat. Objective method of biblical interpretation that attempts to understand the literal meaning of a passage based on its plain language and historical context. (See also *Pardes*.)

Peshitta. Literally "simple," the translation of the Hebrew Bible (and Christian Bible) into Syriac, a language similar to Aramaic. Begun in the 1st or 2nd century C.E. and intended for the use of Jews, by the 3rd century it had become the Bible of Syriac-speaking Christians.

Pesikta de-Rav Kahana. Collection of midrashic homilies on the Scriptural readings in synagogues for special Sabbaths and holidays. Sometimes called simply "*Pesikta*" (Aramaic for "section"), it was written in the 5th century in the Land of Israel.

Pesikta Rabbati. Medieval midrash on the Scriptural readings in synagogues for special Sabbaths and holidays.

Pesukei de-Zimra. Literally "verses of prayer," a collection of psalms and biblical passages that are recited immediately after the morning blessings (*Birkot ha-Shachar*). It contains a description of the Divine revelation in nature and history and is designed to permit the worshiper to achieve the required state of mind to recite the *Shema* and the *Amidah*, the core sections of the service. The origin of *Pesukei de-Zimra* can be traced back to "the pious men of old" who, according to the Mishnah, "used to wait an hour before praying in order that they might concentrate their thoughts upon their Father in Heaven" (Ber. 5:1). *Pesukei de-Zimra* remained optional for a long time and did not become an integral portion of the synagogue service until the geonic period. As a separate section of the morning service with a purpose all its own, the *Pesukei de-Zimra* is introduced with *Baruch she-Amar* and concludes with *Yishtabach.*It contains a variety of biblical prayers and passages including *Shirat ha-Yam* (Song at the Sea), the last six psalms (145-150) and Psalm 100, which were recited in the Temple whenever a thanksgiving offering was brought to the Altar. On Sabbath morning, Psalm 100 is eliminated since no thanksgiving offerings were brought on that day, but there are nine additional psalms and the prayer *Nishmat kol chai.*

Peter rechem. Hebrew phrase literally meaning "the first to open the mother's womb," it is the biblical prescription (Exod. 13:1) requiring that a firstborn son be "redeemed" (see *pidyon ha-ben*). Thus, this ritual does not apply to a boy who was delivered by Cesarean section, or to a second boy who was subsequently delivered normally. Similarly, it is not performed if the mother had previously miscarried or had an abortion of a fetus that existed more than 40 days *in utero*. The first son of a Jewish mother must be redeemed, even if he has an older half-brother born to the father from a previous marriage. Conversely, it is not necessary to redeem a son who is the firstborn of the father but not the mother. Thus, if a man marries a woman who already has a child from a previous marriage, any son issuing from their marriage need not be redeemed.

Petichah (opening). The honor of opening the doors or curtain (see *parochet*) of the ark just before the Torah is taken out to be read.

Pharaoh. Literally "great house" and originally referring to the royal palace, the title of the king in ancient Egypt. Scholars disagree as to the identity of the Pharaoh at the time of the Exodus of the Israelites from Egypt, though it may have been Ramses II (c. 1279-1212 B.C.E.).

Pharisees. One of the three major sects in Israel before the destruction of the Second Temple in 70 C.E., its teachings formed the basis of rabbinic Judaism. Representing primarily the middle and lower classes, the Pharisees viewed as authoritative what they regarded as the ancient tradition of Israel – non-biblical laws and customs handed down through the generations (see Oral Law) that supplemented the written Torah. Extremely scrupulous in observing the law, their name probably derived from a Hebrew word meaning "separate." This refers to their separation from ritually impure food and the tables of the common people, who were not as meticulous regarding the laws of levitical purity and tithes. The Pharisees raised the synagogue to a place of prayer and study rivaling the Temple. Several critical theological distinctions separated the Pharisees from their major rivals, the Sadducees. The Pharisees accepted the concepts of the immortality of the soul and reward and punishment after death, both denied by their opponents. In the debate over the relative importance of free will and Divine providence, the Pharisees took a middle ground between the Sadducees, who totally rejected the notion of Divine interference in human affairs and deemed free will to be absolute, and the Essenes, who maintained a belief in complete predestination. The Pharisees and Sadducees were also political rivals. During the reigns of John Hyrcanus and Alexander Janneus (103-76 B.C.E.), the Sadducees were in the ascendancy and the Pharisees were persecuted. This changed dramatically during the reign of Salome Alexandra (76-67 B.C.E.), when the Pharisees dominated and were in control of national policy.

Philistines. Ancient people who inhabited the southern coast of the Land of Israel in the 12th century B.C.E. and occupied the five cities of Gaza, Ashkelon, Ashdod, Ekron, and Gath. The biblical narratives of Samson, Samuel, Saul, and David include accounts of conflicts between the Israelites and the Philistines. Saul met his death at the hands of the Philistines, but David (his successor) successfully ended the Philistine threat.

Philosophy. Beginning in the Hellenistic period, Philo of Alexandria interpreted Jewish teachings in terms of Platonic and Stoic concepts in an attempt to reconcile the basic ideas of the Bible with Greek thought. In Arab lands during the Middle Ages, a revival of Greek thought deeply influenced such notable Jewish thinkers as Saadia Gaon, Bahya ibn Pakuda, Judah Ha-Levi, Joseph Albo, Isaac Abravanel, and Maimonides by giving rise to theological efforts to prove the validity of religion through rational means. Aristotelian influence was most pronounced in the work of Maimonides who, in his *Guide of the Perplexed,* sought to reconcile Judaism and philosophy. The modern period of Jewish philosophy began in the mid 18th century with Moses Mendelssohn, who combined Enlightenment thinking with traditional Judaism. Mendelssohn lived a century after Baruch Spinoza, whose place is more in the history of Western thinking than Jewish philosophy. Spinoza was excommunicated from the Jewish community of Amsterdam for what it considered his heretical ideas. In the last decades of German Jewry before the Holocaust, Franz Rosenzweig's thinking reflected Existentialist trends and Martin Buber's philosophy of dialogue impacted Christian thought. In the United States, Abraham Joshua Heschel, Yosef Dov Soloveichik, and Mordecai Kaplan have produced highly regarded philosophical works. The most notable Zionist philosopher was Ahad ha-Am, who propounded the doctrine of the Land of Israel as a spiritual and cultural center for world Jewry.

Phoenicians. Ancient people, active in maritime trading, who inhabited the coastal plain in what is now Lebanon and occupied the cities of Sidon and Tyre. Hiram, the king of Tyre (10th century B.C.E.), established political and economic relations with David and Solomon and supplied cedar and cypress trees for the building of the Temple in Jerusalem. The Phoenicians were intrepid merchants and colonizers and, according to Greek tradition, the inventors of the alphabet.

Phylacteries – see *Tefillin*.

Physicians. Based solely on the literal meaning of the biblical text, it is unclear whether human beings are even permitted to treat illness. Sickness is often described as a Divine punishment for sin – either as a specific statement ("King X did ... and he became sick") or in nonspecific terms ("If you do ..., you will be punished by ... sickness"). Thus, medical care could be interpreted as a human attempt to intervene in God's actions, a rejection of the Divine prerogative. However, the dominant Jewish view is that physicians are agents or partners of God. According to traditional Jewish thinking, physicians should never feel that their power and skill alone has resulted in a cure. The major duty of the physician is to educate the patient in ways to prevent illness and attain health. The Talmud observes that "no Jew may live in a town without a physician," and if a Jew feels ill he must immediately consult a doctor.[236] During the Middle Ages, a number of well-known Jews (such as Maimonides and Nachmanides) were physicians. In modern times, Jewish physicians have played significant roles in medical practice and research.

Pidyon ha-ben (lit., "redemption of the [firstborn] son"). As a consequence of the miracle of the tenth plague, when God killed all the firstborn males in Egypt but passed over those of the Israelites, the firstborn son was to be dedicated to God and perform religious services for the *kohanim* in the Temple (Num. 3:13). However, it was possible to free a firstborn male from this obligation by redeeming him through the payment of five *shekels* to the *kohen* (as the representative of God). *Pidyon ha-ben* takes place on the 31st day after the child's birth (with the day of birth counting as the first day), or the next day *if* the 31st day falls on the Sabbath or a festival, when all business transactions are prohibited. The father officially presents his son, usually on a special tray, to the *kohen*, who then asks if the father wants to redeem the child or leave him with the *kohen*. Responding that he wants to redeem his son, the father gives the *kohen* five silver coins, originally *shekels* but today most often five silver dollars or coins of the country. Following this transaction and prayers for the baby's long and healthy life, it is traditional to conclude with a festive meal. *Pidyon ha-ben* is performed only if the firstborn son "is the first to open the mother's womb" (see *peter rechem*). It does not apply if the father or the maternal grandfather is a *kohen* or *levi*, since in this case the child would have been obligated to serve in the Temple and could not be exempted.

Pidyon shevu'im. The Hebrew term for the ransoming of captives, an important obligation in Judaism.

Pig (*chazer*). One of the unclean animals prohibited as food for Jews. Although it has a cloven foot, it does not chew its cud (Lev. 11:7; Deut. 16:8). The pig was such a negative symbol that the Talmud often refused to mention it by name, referring to it only as *davar acheir* (another thing). Rabbinic law distinguished between items prohibited for food and those from which no benefit can be enjoyed (such as *chametz* on Passover). Therefore, although it is forbidden to eat the flesh of swine, it is permitted to wear pigskin shoes, carry a pigskin wallet, and bind religious books in pigskin.[237]

Piggul. An offering that the Israelites were forbidden to eat because the *kohen* performing the sacrificial service had an improper thought in mind. This could occur if the *kohen* intended that either the burning of the appropriate parts on the Altar or the consumption of the meat of the offering would take place after its allotted time. The law of *piggul* (Lev. 7:18) demonstrates that the sacrificial ritual in the Sanctuary required that the *kohen* have the proper inner feeling and intent and was not merely a matter of outward performance. After the destruction of the Temple, sacrifice was replaced by prayer, which also requires appropriate motivation and concentration (see *kavanah*).[238]

Pikta tava. Literally meaning a "good note" in Aramaic, the traditional greeting among Jews for Hoshana Rabbah, the seventh day of Sukkot. It expresses the wish that the person addressed will receive a favorable judicial decree from the Divine court on this day, when according to tradition the decisions made by God on Rosh Hashanah are issued as final writs of judgment.

Pikuach nefesh. Literally "preservation of life," the rabbinic term applied to the obligation to save an endangered human life. It applies both to an immediate threat, such as a severe illness, or to a less acute or serious condition that has the potential to rapidly become life threatening. The concept of *pikuach nefesh* is derived from the biblical command, "Neither shall you stand idly by the blood of your neighbor" (Lev. 19:16), and from the rabbinic interpretation of the verse (Lev. 18:5), "You shall keep My laws and ordinances, by the pursuit of which a man shall *live* [i.e., not die]." Even desecration of the Sabbath is permitted for *pikuach nefesh*, for as the Talmud reasons, it is better to violate one Sabbath in order to save a person's life, thus enabling the person to observe many others in the future. Similarly, on Yom Kippur, a sick person or pregnant woman may be required to eat when others fast. The concept of *pikuach nefesh* supersedes all laws except those prohibiting murder, idolatry, and incest (see martyr).

Pilgrimage Festivals. "Three times a year all males shall appear before the Lord your God" (Deut. 16:16) required every Israelite to come up to Jerusalem on Passover, Shavuot, and Sukkot.These three pilgrimage festivals marked the spring (barley), summer (wheat), and autumn (fruit) harvests of the agricultural cycle. They are known as the *shalosh regalim* (lit., "three feet") because most people went up to Jerusalem on foot. According to Josephus, on one occasion more than 2.5 million pilgrims appeared in Jerusalem for Passover. All males were expected to fulfill the commandment of appearing before the Lord and bringing a burnt offering on these festivals. The pilgrimage to Jerusalem was qualified by the verse, "you shall not appear before Me empty-handed" (Exod. 23:15), which the Rabbis interpreted as also requiring the bringing of a special peace offering for the specific holiday (see *chagigah*), as well as a second peace offering that could be shared by its owner, family, and guests at a festive meal.

Pilpul. From a Hebrew root meaning "pepper," the term refers to the Jewish tradition of talmudic interpretation that involves penetrating investigation, disputation, and the drawing of conclusions. It is often disparaged as "hair-splitting," debating for the sake of demonstrating one's own cleverness rather than to elucidate a difficult passage or concept.

Pinchas. The 8th *parashah* in the Book of Numbers (25:10-30:1), it opens with Pinchas being rewarded with the "everlasting priesthood" for himself and his descendants because of his zealous act in slaying the Israelite man and Moabite princess who were brazenly fornicating in view of Moses and the people. It also describes the second census of the Israelites, the question of inheritance posed by the daughters of Zelophehad, and the naming of Joshua as the successor to Moses, before closing with the calendar of public sacrifices – the source of the *maftir* portions for festivals and special Sabbaths.

Pine. The Talmud reports: "It was the custom when a boy was born to plant a cedar tree and when a girl was born to plant a pine tree, and when they married, the trees were cut down and a canopy [see *chuppah*] made of the branches" (Git. 57a). Traditional Jews are buried in simple coffins made of pine, an inexpensive wood, to symbolize the equality of all human beings in the eyes of God.[239] Over the past century, the pine has been adopted as the most important forest tree in Israel. The Jewish National Fund has planted tens of thousands of acres with pine trees because of their rapid growth, abundant shade, and ability to grow on rocky ground.

Pioneer – see *Chalutz.*

Pioneer Women. Worldwide Labor Zionist women's organization, known since 1981 as Na'amat.It was founded in New York City in 1925 to provide social welfare services for women, young adults, and children in the Land of Israel, as well as to help new immigrants become productive citizens. With its sister organization in Israel, Pioneer Women maintains a large network of welfare and cultural projects in the Jewish State. In the United States, Pioneer Women conducts Jewish educational and cultural activities and supports youth work through the Labor Zionist youth movement, *Habonim.*

Pirkei Avot (Ethics of the Fathers). The 9th tractate of Nezikin (damages) in the Mishnah. It has no halachic content, but rather consists of the moral and practical teachings of some 60 sages whose lives spanned nearly five centuries. In many traditional congregations, it is customary to study *Pirkei Avot* during the Omer period.Beginning after Passover, one of the six chapters is studied each Sabbath following the afternoon service. In this way, the final chapter dealing with the Torah is read just before Shavuot, the festival commemorating the Revelation on Mount Sinai. Most Ashkenazic congregations repeat the entire tractate three times until the Sabbath before Rosh Hashanah. *Pirkei Avot* has enjoyed great popularity and influence for centuries.

Pirkei de-Rabbi Eliezer (PdRE). Aggadic midrash on the biblical narrative (8th century). The first chapters detail the life of Eliezer ben Hyrcanus, the talmudic sage for whom the work is named.

Pisher. Literally a "bed wetter," this Yiddish term denotes a young, inexperienced person or someone who is "wet behind the ears."

Pitom. Fragile, stem-like protrusion on the *etrog*. Before the blessing over the four species on Sukkot, the *etrog* is held with the *pitom* pointed downward; after the blessing, the *etrog* is inverted so that the *pitom* faces up.

Pittsburgh Platform. Founding document of what has come to be called "Classical Reform," adopted by the Union of American Hebrew Congregations as the culmination of a meeting of American Reform Rabbis at their 1885 national conference in this Pennsylvania city. As part of a "modern" approach to Judaism, the Pittsburgh Platform called for rejection of those laws that had a ritual, rather than moral, basis (such as *kashrut*). Instead of a discrete people, it envisioned Jews as a religious community within the nation in which they resided. With Jews now supposedly accepted and at home in the United States rather than in "exile," it considered Zionism to be unnecessary. The Pittsburgh Platform affirmed that the mission of Israel was to help lead the world to a universal morality. The principles it articulated guided the Reform Movement in the United States for half a century, until superseded by the Columbus Platform. However, its call to engage in acts of social justice developed into the overriding goal of *tikun olam* (repair of the world), which inspires the Reform Movement today.

Pitum ha-Ketoret (the incense mixture). This *baraita* on the preparation of incense in the Temple is recited by Ashkenazim on Sabbaths and festivals at the end of the *Musaf* (additional) service just after *Ein Keloheinu*. Sephardim say this passage every morning and afternoon.

Piyyutim. Liturgical poems, especially from the medieval period, that have been incorporated (primarily among Ashkenazim) in the synagogue services for Sabbaths and festivals, especially for the High Holy Days.They may have short refrains and distinctive rhythmic and rhyming schemes, or be written in an acrostic style with each verse beginning with successive letters of the Hebrew alphabet or having their initial letters spelling out the name of the author. The thousands of *piyyutim* and their composers are poetic testimony to Jewish liturgical creativity.

Plagues – see Ten plagues.

Pleasing aroma (*rei'ach nicho'ach*). Anthropomorphic term used in the Bible to indicate that God has accepted a sacrifice.

Pledge. An item given by a borrower to a lender as security for a loan. The Torah was deeply concerned with preserving the dignity of a debtor and preventing the creditor from taking as pledges items that were desperately needed by their impoverished owner for making his living or preparing food (Deut. 24:6). Neither the creditor nor an agent of the Court was permitted to go into the debtor's house to collect the pledge (Deut. 24:10); instead, they were required to wait outside and allow the debtor to bring the security to them. If a borrower did not pay back a loan by the stipulated date, the lender could ask the court to order that personal effects of the borrower be given to him as collateral. In this case, however, the lender was required to return them to the borrower at those times when they would be needed (Deut. 24:12). If the item was something the borrower needed during the day (such as a tool for his trade or occupation), it must be held as security only at night and promptly restored to him by morning so as not to deprive him of its use. Conversely, an item that was needed at night (such as bedding or a garment in which he slept), had to be restored to him before nightfall.

Ploni almoni. Hebrew term meaning "an anonymous individual." In the Book of Ruth (4:1), Boaz goes to the city gate and explains to the closer relative of Ruth's late husband, whose name is given as "*Ploni Almoni*," that he has the right of first refusal to acquire land from the late husband's estate.

Plotz. Literally "to burst," this Yiddish term means to explode or collapse from embarrassment, excitement, or surprise. It also can denote being aggravated beyond endurance.

Pluralism, religious. The viewpoint that different or even contradictory religious interpretations and behaviors can and should coexist because there are equally valid understandings of religious and spiritual approaches to ultimate realities. Traditionally, Jews believe that God chose the Jewish people to be in a unique covenantal relationship, though this does not necessarily exclude the existence of a relationship between non-Jews and God (see Noahide laws). In the latter part of the Second Temple period, Pharisees, Sadducees, and Essenes lived side by side in Judea. In Alexandria, there were Hellenized Jews. The Pharisaic-Rabbinic tradition led to a certain fundamental unity centered around the study and veneration of the Talmud, but this was broken by the Karaites who rejected the Talmud's authority. Nevertheless, the two groups coexisted and intermarried. In the Middle Ages, rationalists such as Maimonides were opposed by kabbalists, yet both of these traditions have found their way into modern Judaism. Ashkenazim and Sephardim developed different religious customs, but both remained part of the Jewish faith community. In the 18th and 19th centuries, bitter disputes arose between Hasidim and *Mitnagdim*, but eventually both camps found common cause in opposition to religious reform and assimilation. Currently, Orthodox, Conservative, Reform, and Reconstructionist Jews differ over the authority of traditional Jewish law, especially when defining "Who is a Jew?", conversion, and requirements for Jewish marriage. In the United States, however, these branches of Judaism coexist (along with those who adhere to a secular Jewish identity) and religious pluralism is an established fact. In the State of Israel, unlike America, Orthodox Judaism is politically powerful and attempts to minimize the influence of the other movements, although they do have a foothold there and the validity of their conversions has often been upheld by the civil courts. Despite the power of the Orthodox establishment in matters of personal status, many Israelis embrace a secular Jewish identity that focuses more on peoplehood and nationality than on religion.

Po'alei Agudat Yisrael. Israeli Orthodox religious labor party, founded in Poland in 1922, which advocated the application of biblical social principles to daily life and the development of a Jewish society in Israel centered on *halacha*.

Po'alei Tzion (Workers of Zion). Socialist Zionist movement that originated in Russia at the beginning of the 20th century. In 1968, the left-wing Po'alei Tzion joined with two other parties to form the Israel Labor Party.

Poetry. Although having some sort of meter or rhythm, the essence of biblical poetry is parallelism, the division of a verse into two halves. In the most frequent variety of parallelism, the second half expresses the same ideas as the first but usually in different words that often intensify the meaning. In the geonic period, rhyme became an important feature of Hebrew poetry through the influence of Arabic verse. During the Middle Ages, Hebrew poetry consisted both of religious liturgical works (see *piyyutim*) and secular poems. Among the best known secular poets of the period were Judah Ha-Levi, Moses ibn Ezra, and Solomon ibn Gabirol. The massacres of Jews in the Crusades and elsewhere led to the composition of heartfelt dirges. During the Enlightenment, the *maskilim* revitalized interest in Hebrew poetry, which has flourished in modern Israel. Among the most famous modern Hebrew poets were Chaim Nachman Bialik, Saul Tchernichowsky, Zalman Shneour, Nathan Alterman, Rachel, and Yehudah Amichai.

Pogrom. Russian word meaning "devastation" or "destruction" used to denote the organized massacre of Jews by the Christian population in unprovoked attacks carried out in the Russian Empire in the late 19th and early 20th centuries. These vicious attacks involved destruction of property, looting, rape, and murder. Military and civil authorities either stood by during these attacks or provided covert support.

Polemic. An attack on, or refutation of, the opinions or principles of another. In addition to being a means of expression for worship, prayer has a polemical element. It is designed not only to articulate one's own principles of faith, but also is an attempt by the normative majority "to counter dissidents and sectarian minorities."[240] Examples of liturgical polemics in Judaism include: *Yigdal*; (b) *Elohai neshamah*; the second blessing of the *Amidah*, which repeats six times the doctrine of resurrection of the dead (denied by the Samaritans and Sadducees); (d) the verse "Who forms light and creates darkness, makes peace and creates all things," attacking the dualist Persian (Zoroastrian) religion that believed that the world was created and preserved by two opposing forces, light and darkness, which manifest their existence in good and evil; and (e) removing the Ten Commandments from the daily service, in opposition to the Pauline Christians, who accepted them but rejected the authority of other Torah laws. Several polemics were introduced against the Karaites, who followed the literal meaning of the Bible and denied rabbinic interpretation of the text. Jewish-Christian polemics reached its zenith during the Middle Ages. In the wake of the Holocaust, there has been an effort on both sides to substitute dialogue for polemics.

Political Zionists – see Zionists, political.

Poll tax. Tax levied on each person in the community. In biblical times, a poll tax of a half *shekel* was imposed on all male Israelites to pay for the upkeep of the Sanctuary (Exod. 30:12-16). The qualification that "the rich shall not pay more and the poor shall not pay less" indicated that the Tabernacle belonged to the entire community, without regard to wealth or social status, since all are equal in the eyes of God. The Mishnah reported that the Jew of the Second Temple period, whether residing in the Land of Israel or in the remotest corner of the Diaspora, cherished this commandment as a sacred privilege and a means of participating in the public offerings brought daily in the House of God in Jerusalem.[241] After the destruction of Jerusalem in 70 C.E., the voluntary contribution of a half *shekel* each year was designated for the Roman *fiscus judaicus* until the 4th century. Poll taxes on Jews were levied in the Middle Ages by the Holy Roman Empire and later by various other governments of the lands where they lived.

Polygamy. The Bible permits a man to have more than one wife, though there are indications that monogamy was preferred (see *Eshet Chayil*). Around 1000 C.E., Rabbenu Gershom, the great German talmudic scholar known as the "Light of the Exile," issued a decree forbidding polygamy that was enforced by the threat of excommunication. Although literally only affecting the Jews of his community and limited to 500 years, it has remained the law among Jews everywhere. (For rare exceptions to this rule, see *heter nisuin* and *heter me'ah rabbanim*.) In 1950, the Chief Rabbis of Israel ruled that all Jews throughout the world had to be monogamous, and Israeli law regards polygamy as a criminal offense.

Polytheism. The belief in multiple gods, who personally embody the forces of nature and express dichotomies of good and evil. Unlike the One God of Israel, these gods are divided into male and female deities who desire and mate with each other, procreate, and give birth. They are also subject to the same physical needs and maladies as mortals – eating, drinking, falling sick and requiring healing, and even dying and rising again. In polytheistic thinking, gods can be coerced by magical practices and nourished by sacrificial cults.

Pomegranate (*rimon*). One of the seven species, the pomegranate has striking red flowers and decorative fruit that has a tangy, yet delicate, sweet flavor and huge clusters of seeds. According to tradition, the pomegranate has precisely 613 seeds, representing the number of *mitzvot* in the Torah (see *taryag mitzvot*). Pomegranates are a popular fruit for Rosh Hashanah because their numerous seeds symbolize the hope for fertility and the privilege of performing abundant good deeds. The Hebrew word *rimonim* is also applied to the silver ornaments placed atop the two wooden rollers (see *atzei chaim*) of the Torah scroll.

Poor. For the Bible, poverty is an inescapable part of the social structure: "For the poor will never be absent from your land" (Deut. 15:11). Nevertheless, poverty is viewed with great sympathy, and alleviating the suffering of the poor is an essential religious virtue in Judaism (see *tzedakah* and gleanings). As the Bible commands, "Open your hand wide to your brother, to the poor and the needy of your land" (Deut. 15:11). Maimonides categorized eight degrees of charity. (See also *poverty*.)

Porge. Literally "purge," the removal of the sciatic nerve and its associated blood vessels from the hindquarters of any quadruped before the meat can be prepared for consumption under Jewish law.

Posekim (decisors). Talmudic scholars whose intellectual efforts were concentrated on determining the practical *halacha* (Jewish law). These sages often found no firm answers to legal questions in traditional sources and were forced to arrive at decisions through their own reasoning processes. Most *posekim* were heads of *yeshivot* and members of rabbinical courts, but their decisions were binding only upon those communities that accepted their authority.

Posken. To make a decision according to *halacha* (see above).

Post-mortem – see Autopsy.

Potch. Yiddish term meaning to "smack" or "spank," especially used playfully in the phrase "*potch in tuchis*" (slap on the bottom).

Potchke. Yiddish term meaning to "mess around" with something without showing expertise or making any progress, or to dawdle or waste time.

Poverty. Although the Torah recognized that poverty could not be eliminated (Deut. 15:11), numerous *mitzvot* were designed to mitigate its effect. The Sabbatical Year provided for periodic remission of debts, and the Jubilee Year mandated the return of ancestral landed properties as well as the freeing of Israelite slaves. Those who were in a better economic position were expected to treat the poor with compassion, for God was their protector, and Divine blessings to Israel were contingent upon the generous treatment the poor received. Some of the produce of the fields and vineyards (see gleanings) was left for the poor, who were designated as the recipients for the third- and sixth-year tithes. Failure to alleviate the condition of the poor drew stinging rebukes from the prophets.

Practical Kabbalah. Mystical method attempting to alter the nature of existence and change the course of events using ritualistic techniques. This may involve summoning spiritual forces, such as angels, and commanding them to perform specific acts in the real world, as well as employing a variety of magic and talismans.

Practical Zionists – see Zionists, practical.

Prayer (*tefillah*). A way for mortal humans beings to communicate with a personal Deity, a God who exists, hears, and answers. It can take the form of praise, petition, thanksgiving, or confession. In prayer we recognize our dependency upon God and realize that every blessing, even life itself, is not earned but rather a generous Divine gift. Prayers express our deepest feelings, which Abraham Joshua Heschel termed "radical amazement." As Heschel wrote, "to pray is to take notice of the wonder, to regain a sense of the mystery that animates all beings, the Divine margin in all attainments."[242] Prayer is also a means for self-examination and reflection, a way to heal and strengthen oneself and heighten communion with the Divine.

Prayer book – see *Siddur*.

Prayer, congregational. Communal worship has always been a distinctive feature of Jewish prayer. Although an individual Jew can fulfill the *mitzvah* of prayer privately, joining others as part of a congregation is a particular virtue. Consequently, many of the major parts of the worship service – including *Barchu*, repetition of the *Amidah* with *Kedushah*, Torah reading, Priestly Benediction, and *Kaddish* – require the presence of a *minyan*. The person leading the communal worship is known as the *shaliach tzibbur* (emissary of the congregation).

Prayer for the sick – see Sick, prayer for the.

Prayer for the State of Israel. This is recited on Sabbath morning in most synagogues (except some ultra-Orthodox) in Israel and the Diaspora. Although there are longer versions, all contain the following: "Our Father in Heaven, Protector and Redeemer of Israel, bless the State of Israel, the dawn of our redemption. Shield it beneath the wings of Your love. Spread over it Your canopy of peace; send Your light and Your truth to its leaders, officers, and counselors, and direct them with Your good counsel. O God, strengthen the defenders of our Holy Land; grant them salvation and crown them with victory. Establish peace in the land, and everlasting joy for its inhabitants."

Prayer, gestures in. Body gestures are normal expressions of worship. The Bible does not mandate any specific position, instead at various time citing individuals who prayed standing, sitting, kneeling, prostrated on the earth, or with head bowed, and with hands uplifted or outstretched. Today, standing is considered the formal posture for prayer. However, as the liturgy developed and the number of prayers progressively expanded, it became difficult for the average worshiper to stand for the entire service. Although there are variations among the different branches of Judaism as to when one sits and stands, as a general rule worshipers stand during *Baruch she-Amar*, *Shirat ha-Yam*, *Yishtabach*, *Barchu*, *Hallel*, the silent *Amidah* and its *Kedushah* portion during the reader's repetition, *Aleinu*, and when the Torah is taken out and returned to the ark.[243] Bowing the head and bending the knees are frequent gestures to demonstrate humility before the Divine Presence (e.g., *Barchu*, *Amidah*, *Aleinu*). Taking steps backward and forward at the beginning and end of the *Amidah* symbolize the entrance into and departure from a royal court. Symbolically falling on one's face (see *nefilat apayim*) is limited to the recitation of *Tachanun* in the presence of the Torah. Kneeling and prostration are restricted to short sections of the services on Rosh Hashanah and Yom Kippur.[244] (See also *shuckling*.)

Prayer, language of. Hebrew has always been the preferred language of Jewish prayer. The Rabbis even opposed the use of Aramaic in prayer, despite the fact that this was considered a semi-holy tongue because several of the books of the Bible (Daniel, Ezra, Nehemiah) contain significant Aramaic elements. One sage wrote that prayers in Aramaic are worthless because the Ministering Angels do not understand that language and thus cannot transmit these prayers to God! However, this extreme view did not prevail, and prayer in other languages was permitted. A number of Aramaic prayers were admitted into the liturgy, such as the *Kaddish* and *Kol Nidrei*. The Mishnah ruled that the *Shema* and the *Amidah*, which form the core of Jewish worship, may be recited in any language. Maimonides argued that the Rabbis mandated prayer in Hebrew because they foresaw the danger of Jews being dispersed throughout the world and speaking different languages. Formulating the prayers in pure Hebrew would allow all

Israelites to worship together. A Jew who can pray in Hebrew is able to attend a synagogue anywhere in the world and feel at home in the worship service.

Prayer, mourner's – see *Mourner's Kaddish.*

Prayer, music in. Music has always added to the beauty of prayer and enhanced its emotional and spiritual depth. In the Temple, a choir of Levites sang the appropriate psalms accompanied by musical instruments. After the Temple was destroyed, the use of musical instruments on the Sabbath and festivals was banned as a sign of mourning. The sages believed that no Jewish prayer service should approximate the glory of worship in the ancient Sanctuary. In later times, certain instruments – especially the organ – were so closely associated with worship in the Christian churches that it was considered a prohibited "imitation of gentile custom" (*chukat ha-goy*) to play them in the synagogue. Today, Reform and some Conservative synagogues do permit the playing of instrumental music on the Sabbath and festivals, rationalizing that the prohibition of music as a sign of mourning for the destruction of Jerusalem included vocal no less than instrumental music. Moreover, they argue that since the use of instrumental music in the church is itself a borrowing from the Temple, there is no reason to prohibit something as a "Christian" custom that was originally adapted from Jewish practice.

Prayer services. Daily Jewish worship consists of three services – morning (see *Shacharit*), afternoon (see *Mincha*), and evening (see *Ma'ariv*) – based on the biblical verse, "Evening and morning and at noon I pray and cry aloud, and He hears my voice" (Ps. 55:18). They also correspond to the daily offerings brought in the morning and toward dusk, as well as the flesh of sacrifices burnt on the Altar during the night hours. The *Shacharit* service is preceded by two preliminary services – *Birkot ha-Shachar* (see morning blessings) and *Pesukei de-Zimra* (Verses of Song). On the Sabbath and holy days (including Rosh Chodesh), a *Musaf* (additional) service immediately follows *Shacharit*. On Friday evening, the *Kabbalat Shabbat* (Welcoming the Sabbath) precedes *Ma'ariv*. The core of every service is the *Amidah*, which is read silently by each individual and then repeated out loud by the service leader (see *shaliach tzibbur*) if there is a *minyan*.

Prayer shawl – see *Tallit*.

Preacher – see *Maggid*.

Preaching – see Homiletics.

Predestination. Philosophical doctrine positing that everything is predetermined by God. According to this view, despite human beings having free will, the overall course of history is controlled by the inscrutable and unalterable Divine will. Traditional Jewish thinking takes cognizance of the paradox that, while God foresees and knows all, free will is given.

President (of Israel). Known as "*nasi*" in Hebrew, the largely ceremonial office of the Chief of State. The first President of the State of Israel was chemist and statesman, Chaim Weizmann.

Press. Newspapers in Hebrew and Yiddish, which date back to the late 17th century, provided information to Jews who could not read the languages of the countries in which they lived. The earliest Hebrew newspaper in the Land of Israel was *Halbanon*, which initially appeared in Jerusalem in 1863. Another important publication was *Ha-Shilo'ah*, a Hebrew-language literary, social, and scientific monthly. The oldest Jewish periodical still in existence is the weekly *Jewish Chronicle*, which published its first edition in London in 1841. Until the Holocaust, the largest number of Jewish periodicals was found in Europe. In Poland alone, there were some 200 periodicals and newspapers during the 1920s, reflecting the broad range of Jewish political and cultural life in the country. In Israel today, the major newspapers are the Hebrew-language *Ha-Aretz, Yediot Aharonot*, and *Ma'ariv*, and the English-language *Jerusalem Post*. Throughout the world, Jewish weekly newspapers are published in all cities with a substantial Jewish population.

Priest – see *Kohen*.

Priestly Blessing (*Birkat ha-Kohanim*). Biblical verses with which the *kohanim* conveyed the Divine blessing to the people: "May God bless you and keep you; may God shine His face on you and be gracious to you; may God lift up His countenance on you and give you peace" (Num. 6:23-26). (See also *duchaning*.) After the destruction of the Second Temple, the *Birkat ha-Kohanim* became the last significant remnant of the priestly cult. Today, local customs differ as to the time (morning or additional service) for the recital of the Priestly Blessing, which requires a *minyan*. The general Ashkenazic custom is to recite it only during the *Musaf Amidah* on the High Holy Days and the three pilgrimage festivals of Passover, Shavuot, and Sukkot (exclusive of *chol ha-mo'ed*). In Israel and among Sephardic Jews everywhere, the *kohanim* go up to recite the Priestly Blessing every day in accordance with the ancient Temple practice – during the *Amidah* of the morning service or, whenever there is an additional service, during the *Musaf Amidah*. In all communities, if the *kohanim* do not recite the Priestly Blessing, the prayer leader recites the text during the repetition of the *Amidah*, just before the final blessing. Congregants initially listened silently to the Priestly Blessing. Today, it is customary to respond with "amen" after each of the three sections when said by the *kohanim*, but with "*kein ye-hi ratzon*" (so may it be Your will) when recited by the prayer leader. On Sabbath eve, it is a custom for parents to bless their children with the Priestly Blessing, after first saying either "May God make you like Ephraim and Menashe" (for sons) or "May God make you like Sarah, Rebecca, Rachel, and Leah" (for daughters).

Priestly Blessing, hands of *kohanim* in. While chanting the Priestly Blessing, the *kohanim* cover their heads with prayer shawls and stretch both arms and hands out at shoulder height with their hands touching at the thumbs and their palms forward. The second and third fingers of each hand are separated from the fourth and fifth to produce a fanlike appearance.[245] In a later period, outstretched hands became symbolic of the *kohanim*, and it is common to find this representation engraved on tombstones of members of priestly families.

Priestly vestments – see *Kohen Gadol*, garments of the.

Primogeniture – see Firstborn.

Principles of faith – see Thirteen Principles of Faith.

Printing, Hebrew. The first Hebrew books – Rashi's commentary on the Pentateuch and Jacob ben Asher's *Arba'ah Turim* – appeared in 1475, within 20 years after the invention of printing. Daniel Bomberg established Venice as a center of Hebrew printing with the production of the first complete edition of the Talmud in 1520. The first edition of the *Shulchan Aruch* appeared in 1565. The initial books printed in the Land of Israel were in Safed, first by a short-lived press in 1577 and then on one of Israel Bak in 1831. Ten years later, Bak opened a printing house in Jerusalem, the first step toward developing the craft of printing that later became one of the city's main industries. In Israel today, the printing industry has embraced advanced modern standards and caters to an avid and well-informed readership.

Procreation. "Be fruitful and multiply [fill the earth and subdue it]" (*p'ru ur'vu*; Gen. 1:28) is the first commandment in the Torah. It obligates one to marry, build a home, and raise a family. According to the Mishnah, each married couple must have at least one son and one daughter to fulfill this commandment (Yev. 6:6). However, both law and historical practice urge Jews to have as many children as possible (Yev. 62b). Of course, couples who cannot have children naturally are exempt from the commandment; they may pursue fertility treatments, but are not obligated to do so.[246] The commandment to procreate traditionally applies only to men. Therefore, if a husband and wife both deliberately refrain from having children, it is only the man who is culpable. Similarly, only a man is obligated to marry. Whereas a woman is permitted to marry a eunuch, a man must marry a woman capable of being a mother.[247] Traditionally, if a couple was married for 10 years without children, a man was permitted to divorce his spouse and marry a second wife to be able to fulfill the commandment to procreate.

Profaning the Name of God – see *Chillul ha-Shem*.

Promiscuity. The *halacha* condemns non-marital sexuality as "promiscuity" (*zenut*). However, the Rabbis recognized the strength of the human desire for sexual gratification as a healthy force that must be properly controlled. Consequently, they advised that "18 is the proper age for marriage" (Avot 5:25). As Maurice Lamm observed, "For Judaism, the value in human sexuality comes only when the relationship involves two people who have committed themselves to one another and have made that commitment in a binding covenant recognized by God and society. The act of sexual union, the deepest personal statement that any human being can make, must be reserved for the moment of total oneness."[248]

Promised Land. Also known as Canaan, the territory indicated by God when promising the Patriarch Abraham, "I will assign this land to your offspring" (Gen. 12:7). (See *Eretz Yisrael*.)

Proof text. Biblical verse used as justification to support a legal or ethical point.

Property. In Jewish law, the acquisition of property (see *kinyan*) can be accomplished by various means. Examples include acquisition by deed (*shetar*), by taking physical possession (*hazakah*), by pulling or moving an object toward oneself (*meshikah*), by raising an object (*hagbahah*), and by inheritance. Property also may be abandoned (see *hefker*).

Prophecy, ecstatic. Phenomenon in which a person is seized with an extraordinary inner tension that causes his spirit and body to be abnormally moved. This peculiar behavior leads the individual to be perceived as a "madman" (*meshuga*),[249] a term occasionally used as a synonym for *navi*, the usual word for prophet.[250] In the Bible, ecstatic prophets typically appeared in groups, such as the 70 elders who "spoke in ecstasy" in the Israelite camp (Num. 11:25) and the "band of prophets" whom Samuel encountered at Gibeah, prophesying to the accompaniment of "lyres, timbrels, flutes, and harps" (1 Sam. 10:5). However, unlike the pagans who had an "innate ability" for ecstasy, or ingested or inhaled specific intoxicating substances or participated in wild dancing and other rites to induce this state, in Israel ecstasy could not be achieved by any "natural talent" or external stimulus. Instead, it was a "Divine effluence" that seized the prophet in its spell and could leave him at any moment.[251]

Prophet (*navi*). The biblical prophet was a messenger of God. Unlike the pagan prophet and diviner, whose primary function was to answer the inquiries of human beings and manipulate the deity on their behalf, the biblical prophet simply conveyed the Divine will to men. Even the popular prophets who were healers and wonder workers were viewed as merely performing the will of God, rather than demonstrating any inherent powers. The prophets described in vivid terms the dire consequences of failing to fulfill the Divine commandments and perpetuating injustice in Israel by neglecting the poor and the weak, countenancing the greed and corruption of the wealthy and powerful, and believing that God could be satisfied by sacrifices alone. They warned the people that violating the covenant and continuing to behave in a manner unacceptable to God would inevitably lead to destruction, captivity, and exile. Indeed, the ancient Israelites did experience these cataclysmic developments at the hands of the Assyrian and Babylonian Empires. The prophets, however, balanced their message of doom with the promise of ultimate redemption and restoration, which did occur following the Babylonian Exile. The last three prophets were Haggai, Zechariah, and Malachi; after them, the word of God was sought in the Written and Oral Law.

Prophet, false. A false prophet is one whose words are not inspired by God. Jeremiah taught that the true prophet was ready to intercede with God on Israel's behalf (27:18), whereas the false prophet would be unwilling to do so. According to Maimonides, if a prophet predicted a calamity (such as war, famine, or the death of a specific individual) that was not fulfilled, this "does not disprove his prophetic standing ... for God is long-suffering and abounding in kindness, and repents of the evil [He has threatened]." Those who were warned of impending doom may have repented and been forgiven (such as the people of Nineveh after the prophecy of Jonah), or "the execution of the sentence may have been deferred, as in the case of King Hezekiah." However, Maimonides maintained that failure of a prophecy of good fortune to occur is an unequivocal sign of a false prophet, "for no blessing decreed by the Almighty, even if promised conditionally, is ever revoked."[252]

Prophetesses. The Bible labels four women as prophetesses – Miriam (Exod. 15:20), Deborah (Judg. 4:4), Huldah (2 Kings 22:14), and Noadiah (Neh. 6:14). Rabbinic tradition added another three – Hannah, Abigail, and Esther – to round out the seven prophetesses of ancient Israel. The Talmud also replaced Noadiah with Sarah in its list of the seven prophetesses (Meg. 14a)

Prophets (*Nevi'im*). Second of the three major divisions of the Bible. In addition to the historical works of the pre-classical prophets (Joshua, Judges, 1 and 2 Samuel, and 1 and 2 Kings), it includes the three "major" classical prophets (Isaiah, Jeremiah, and Ezekiel) and the 12 so-called "minor" prophets (Hosea, Joel, Amos, Obadiah, Jonah, Micah, Nahum, Habakkuk, Haggai, Zephaniah, Zechariah, and Malachi). (For more information, see individual listings.) Joshua, Judges, Samuel, and Kings are traditionally referred to as the "former prophets." Isaiah, Jeremiah, Ezekiel and the 12 minor prophets are customarily referred to as the "literary prophets."

Prosbul. The Torah warned against letting the approach of the Sabbatical Year prevent one from helping a needy fellow Jew (Deut. 15:7-11). However, as the

Israelites moved from an economy based on agriculture to one also founded on business and commerce, the release of debts contracted in trading became onerous. People refrained from making loans to one another as the Sabbatical Year approached. Consequently, in the 1st century C.E., Hillel enacted the *prosbul*, in which a creditor declared before a court of law (attested by witnesses) that all debts due to him were given over to the court for collection. Since remission of loans during the seventh year applied only to individuals and not to public loans, the effect was to render the individual's loan public and therefore not nullified (and thus collectable after the Sabbatical Year).

Proselyte – see Conversion.

Prostitute (*kadesha*). This Hebrew term has been traditionally translated as "cult prostitute," a practice that was unequivocally banned because it was related to a fertility cult that was an integral element of idolatrous worship in the ancient Near East. Some modern scholars doubt that such sacred prostitution existed, and thus the word is now thought to simply mean "whore." The ancient Israelites treated prostitution as a shameful profession. The biblical injunction, "You shall not bring the fee of a whore ... into the House of the Lord in fulfillment of any vow" (Deut 23:19), forbade one from contributing money earned in an immoral way to the Sanctuary. This was designed to prevent the practice of attempting to legitimize the profits of illicit or immoral activities by contributing to charitable causes (including synagogues and other Jewish institutions). Today, the Israeli government works with women's groups and international bodies to curb the nefarious international traffic in women, which is a tragic problem not only for the Jewish State but for the international community as a whole.

Prostration. Prostrating the whole body, indicating total submission to the will of God, was closely associated with the ancient Temple service. However, the practice has been abandoned almost entirely in modern times, possibly because it is associated with other religions. Today, prostration is restricted to once during the *Aleinu* during the *Musaf Amidah* on Rosh Hashanah and three times during the *Avodah* service on Yom Kippur in the Ashkenazic ritual. At these times, it is customary for prayer leaders to actually kneel down and touch their heads to the floor. In some synagogues, all members of the congregation prostrate themselves.

Protocols of the Elders of Zion. Infamous forged document purporting to prove the existence of an international Jewish conspiracy to achieve global domination and the overthrow of Christian society. First published in Russia in the early 20th century, it has become a key staple of anti-Semitic propaganda designed to inspire fear and hatred of Jews. The Protocols were the core of a series of anti-Semitic articles that were published in the United States by Henry Ford in the 1920s and then widely disseminated by the Nazis. Today, it is found throughout the Arab world.

Proverbs (*Mishlei*). The 2nd part of the Writings section of the Bible, it is essentially a manual of instruction on how to live a moral and productive life. Traditionally ascribed to King Solomon, Proverbs is part of the "wisdom literature" of the Bible (along with Job and Ecclesiastes). Proverbs praises wisdom, but emphasizes that true wisdom is found in the love and fear of God. A famous section from Proverbs is *Eshet Chayil* (Woman of Valor).

Proverbs, Midrash to. Aggadic midrash to the Book of Proverbs, dating back to the 10th-11th century.

P'ru ur'vu (be fruitful and multiply) – see Procreation.

Psalm of the Day. Each morning in the Temple, the Levites chanted a psalm appropriate to that day of the week. As a memorial to the destroyed Temple, the Rabbis added the following psalms to the daily morning service in the synagogue: 24 (first day – Sunday), 48 (second day), 82 (third day), 94; 95:1-3 (fourth day), 81 (fifth day), 93 (sixth day), and 92 (Sabbath; see *Mizmor shir*). Sephardim recite the Psalm of the Day before *Aleinu*, which ends the service. When there is a *Musaf Amidah*, they include it after the *Amidah* of the morning service, just before the service for reading the Torah, while Askenazim always recite the Psalm of the Day following *Aleinu*.[253]

Psalms (*Tehillim*). The 1st book of the Writings section of the Bible. Its 150 religious poems, traditionally ascribed to King David, include paeans of thanksgiving and praise to a personal God who can answer human needs, songs related to festivals and historical events, hymns in honor of kings, war anthems, and songs expressing the depths of despair. Psalms appear throughout the Jewish worship services, and the prayer book contains 70 complete psalms and excerpts of others. When a Jew dies, psalms are recited constantly to accompany the body until the burial service (see *shomer*). The psalms have provided spiritual strength and succor throughout the ages.

Psalms, Midrash on. Collection of homilies and interpretations on the Book of Psalms. Although the date of composition is uncertain, it was widely known by the 11th century.

Psalms of Solomon. Pseudoepigraphical book, existing only in Greek, which contains 18 psalms attributed to King Solomon. Probably written in the Land of Israel after the death of Pompey in 48 B.C.E., it describes the desecration of Jerusalem and the Temple by the enemies of the Israelites, attacks immorality, and looks forward to the coming of the Messiah.

Pseudoepigrapha. Literally "false attribution," the collective name for a group of Jewish religious literary works written between the 2nd century B.C.E. and the

2nd century C.E. Often taking an apocalyptic perspective, they include the Psalms of Solomon, the Book of Jubilees, the Book of Enoch, the Assumption of Moses, the Ascension of Isaiah, the Testament of the Twelve Patriarchs, the Apocalypse of Baruch, and the Sibyline Oracles. The Dead Sea Scrolls have provided some significant insights into the origin of some of the Hebrew and Aramaic originals of the pseudoepigrapha.

P'tur. Certificate of divorce, issued to both husband and wife following the formal ceremony of handing over the *get*. It states that their marriage has been terminated and that each is free to marry again.

Publishing – see Printing.

Pulkes. Yiddish word for thighs, either the chubby ones of babies or the meaty ones of a chicken.

Pulpit – see *Bimah*.

Pumbedita. Site of the one of the two major talmudic academies in Babylonia during the late talmudic and geonic periods. Founded in the 3rd century C.E. after the destruction of Nehardea and rivaled only by the academy at Sura, Pumbedita remained a center of Jewish learning for almost 800 years.

Punctuation – see Masoretes.

Punishment. For civil and criminal penalties, see *corporal punishment* and *capital punishment*. For Divine punishment, see *reward and punishment* and *karet*.

Punishment, vicarious. According to traditional Jewish belief, punishment (and reward) are accorded to people according to their own actions. As the Bible explicitly declares: "Fathers shall not be put to death for their sons, and sons should not be put to death for their fathers; a person shall be put to death only for his own sin" (Deut. 24:16). However, the Second Commandment describes a "jealous God visiting the sins of the fathers upon children to the third and fourth generations" (Exod. 20:6). Faced with this apparent contradiction between the two biblical verses, the Sages explained that vicarious punishment for the sins of their fathers only applied to children who realized that what their parents did was wrong but failed to actively protest their actions, thus tacitly approving them, incorporating them into their own lives, and meriting their own individual punishment. As Ezekiel, concluded, "The person who sins, only he shall die" (18:4, 20).

Pupik. Yiddish word for "navel" (belly button).

Purification after childbirth – see Childbirth, impurity after.

Purification, ritual – see Ablution, *Mikveh*, and Red heifer.

Purim. A Hebrew word literally meaning "lots," the joyous festival on the 14th of Adar that celebrates the deliverance of the Jews from the plot of the Persian villain Haman to kill them (see Esther). The main feature of Purim is the synagogue reading of *Megillat Esther*. Popular customs are the sending of gifts to friends (see *mishlo'ach manot*) and the poor (see *mattanot le-evyonim*), the eating of hamantashen, the performance of *Purim-shpiels* and parades of costumed revelers in Israel (see *ad lo yada*). When there is a leap year, Purim is celebrated in Second Adar.

Purim Kattan (little Purim). In a leap year when there are two months of Adar, the festival of Purim is celebrated during the second, so it is always one month before Passover. The 14th day of the first Adar in a leap year is celebrated as a minor holiday known as Purim Kattan. Although there are no specific observances, fasting and funeral eulogies are prohibited and *Tachanun* is not recited. Some Jewish communities also observe a Purim Kattan on the anniversary of any day when they were saved from catastrophic danger, complete with celebrations patterned on the original Purim.

Purim-shpiel. Yiddish for "Purim play," it refers to the Ashkenazic tradition (dating back to the 16th century) of a performance given at the traditional festive family meal held on Purim afternoon. Over time, this developed from a witty monologue to a lavish production. Today, the *Purim-sphiel* often takes place in the synagogue in conjunction with the reading of the *Megillah* on Purim evening. Adults join children in the religious school in writing and producing satires directly or indirectly related to the events in the Purim story, which occurred more than 2,000 years ago.

Pursuer – see *Rodef*.

Pushke. Yiddish term for a small container, with a coin slot in the top, used to collect money for a charitable organization. It is traditional to insert coins in the *pushke* each week prior to the start of the Sabbath. Even the poor were encouraged to follow this practice so as to fulfill the commandment to give charity. The most famous *pushke* is the "Blue Box" of the Jewish National Fund.Today, the term "*tzedakah* box" is generally used.

Putz. Yiddish vulgar slang for "penis," generally used as a contemptuous term for a stupid or obnoxious person.

Q

Quail. Smallest of the pheasant family, it is featured in one of the biblical incidents in which the Israelites displayed their ingratitude for the Divine miracle of freeing them from slavery in Egypt (Num. 11). The "mixed multitude" succeeded in influencing the rest of the nation to complain about their steady diet of manna.God instructed Moses to inform the people that they would eat meat for a full month, so much that it would "come out of your nose and become loathsome to you," and they would regret their arrogant declaration that they would prefer to be back in Egypt. The story had a tragic epilogue – "the meat was still between their teeth, not yet chewed, when the anger of the Lord blazed forth against the people and the Lord struck the people with a very severe plague. God named the place *Kivrot-hatta'avah*, because the people who had the craving were buried there."

Quill. Implement used in writing a Torah scroll. The quill pen is made from the feathers of a kosher bird, usually goose or turkey. The *sofer* must painstakingly carve a point in the end of each feather, many of which are required for writing an entire Torah scroll. A metal instrument is forbidden, because iron and steel were associated with war and violence, rendering them unfit to touch a *sefer Torah*, which is an instrument of peace. The ink must be jet black and durable, but not indelible. Today, it is made by boiling a mixture of powdered gallnuts, gum arabic, and copper sulfate crystals.

Quinoa. A grain-like member of the goosefoot family, this ancient staple food of the Incas is distinguished by a curly halo when cooked. Quinoa is a naturally complete protein, which was never included in the prohibition against *kitniyot* and thus is a versatile food for Passover, permitted even for Ashkenazim.[254]

Qumran. Ancient settlement on the northwest shore of the Dead Sea that is believed to have been the home (c. 150 B.C.E.-68 C.E.) of the community that produced the Dead Sea Scrolls, which were found in nearby caves. There is an ongoing scholarly debate as to the identity of the Qumran community. One major hypothesis is that it was a settlement of Essenes.

Quorum – see *Minyan*.

R

Rabban. Variant of the title "rabbi." During the Mishnaic period, it was used as an honorary title, especially for heads of the Sanhedrin.

Rabbi (1). Literally "my master" or "my teacher" in Hebrew, this title was originally used during the 1st century C.E. to identify those Torah scholars who had been properly ordained as graduates of the talmudic academies in the Land of Israel. Because *semichah* was not granted in talmudic times outside the Land of Israel, the Babylonian sages were granted the alternative title of *rav*. Later, the title of rabbi was conferred on especially learned Jews and then applied to the appointed spiritual leaders of Jewish communities. In talmudic and early medieval times, the rabbinate was not a profession, partly because it was deemed inappropriate for someone to receive money for teaching Torah. By the 15th century, a legal fiction was instituted whereby a rabbi was paid for the time he was forced to take away from Torah study in order to fulfill his rabbinic duties. In large communities, rabbis headed *yeshivot* and served as *dayanim* in rabbinical courts. As civil courts came under government control in the modern age, rabbis have assumed more pastoral, social, and educational responsibilities. Today, congregational rabbis preach, teach, and act as the spiritual leaders of their congregations, often leading the worship services. Rabbis also counsel, officiate at life-cycle events, visit the sick, represent their congregations at Jewish and non-Jewish community events, and engage in fund-raising.

Rabbi (2). Talmudic name for Judah ha-Nasi (Judah the Prince), the 3rd-century editor of the Mishnah.

Rabbinical court – see *Beit din*.

Rabbinic ordination – see *Semichah*.

Rabbinical Assembly (RA). American organization of Conservative rabbis.

Rabbinical Council of America (RCA). Umbrella organization of Orthodox rabbis in North America.

Rabbinical seminaries. To meet community needs after the Emancipation, rabbinical seminaries developed that placed less emphasis on Talmud and related subjects and increasingly stressed a well-rounded education that included Bible, homiletics, theology, and history. In the 20th century, pastoral skills and synagogue administration also became important facets of the training program. In the United States today, all of the major movements have at least one rabbinical seminary. They include the Rabbi Isaac Elchanan Theological Seminary of Yeshiva University (Orthodox), the Jewish Theological Seminary (Conservative), the University of Judaism (Conservative), the Hebrew Union College (Reform), and the Reconstructionist Seminary. The Orthodox, Conservative, and Reform movements all have rabbinical seminaries in Los Angeles and Jerusalem.

Rabbanites. Name given by the Karaites, who rejected the Oral Law, to their rabbinic opponents, who accepted it.

Rabbis, women. The Reform and Reconstructionist movements began ordaining women in the early 1970s. The 1983 decision of the Conservative movement to ordain women provoked fierce attacks, not only from the Orthodox but also from many traditional figures in the movement (particularly among the Talmud faculty at the Jewish Theological Seminary), leading to a small group seceding from the movement. Currently, women constitute about half the graduates of the non-Orthodox rabbinical seminaries in the United States.

Rachamim. Hebrew word meaning "mercy, pity, compassion." Coming from a root meaning "mother's womb," the Rabbis taught that a Jew should have the same love and compassion toward others as a mother feels for her child. God is described as *El Rachum v'Chanun* (God of Compassion and Grace) and *Av ha-Rachamim* (Father of Compassion).

Rachel's Tomb (*Kever Rachel*). While traveling from Beit El to Efrat (now Bethlehem), Rachel died giving birth to her second son, Benjamin (Gen. 35:16-20). The heartsick Jacob buried Rachel along the road, and the ancient site of her tomb remains revered as an important religious shrine to this day. According to a midrash, Jacob buried Rachel on the road because he foresaw that the Israelites, when driven from Jerusalem into captivity in Babylonia, would need her intercession with God on their behalf. Jeremiah poignantly describes Rachel at that moment, "weeping for her children [and] refusing to be comforted" (31:15). Jacob erected a pillar on Rachel's tomb, from which arose the Jewish practice of marking the grave with some kind of monument.

Rachmones. Yiddish word meaning "pity" or "compassion." (See *rachamim*.)

Rain, prayer for. Extended plea for live-giving water that is recited on Shemini Atzeret before the open ark during the reader's repetition of the *Musaf Amidah* (in the Ashkenazic tradition) or before the *Musaf* service (among Sephardim). The prayer for rain is composed of a series of *piyyitum*, which vary among different traditions and stress the life-and-death importance of rain for the land and the people of Israel. In the Ashkenazic form, these religious hymns appeal to God to remember Abraham, Isaac, Jacob, Moses, Aaron, and the Twelve Tribes and "in their merit favor us with abundant water [rain]." The prayer for rain ends with three final pleas – "for a blessing and not for a curse, for life and not for death, for plenty and not for famine" – to each of which the congregation fervently answers "amen." From this service until the first day of Passover, when the prayer for dew is said, the sentence *mashiv ha-ru'ach u-morid ha-gashem* (Who causes the wind to blow and the rain to fall) is included in every *Amidah* prayer at the beginning of the second blessing.

Rainbow (*keshet*). Sign of the Divine covenant "between Me and the earth," in which God promised never again to send another flood to destroy all living creatures (Gen. 9:8-17). Consequently, the Rabbis decreed that, when seeing a rainbow, a Jew should say: "Praised are you, O Lord our God, King of the universe, who remembers the Covenant, is faithful to the Covenant, and keeps His promise."

Rakah. Acronym for ***R**eshiman **K**omunist **H**adashah* (New Communist list), the Israeli communist party.

Ram's horn – see *Shofar*.

Ransom of captives (*pidyon shevu'im*). An important *mitzvah* throughout Jewish history, especially during the talmudic era and in the Middle Ages. According to Jewish law, with reference to ransoming captives, women should be given precedence over men; preference should be given to a scholar; a person may ransom himself first but then must ransom his teacher and then his father; and the court has the power to compel a husband to ransom his wife. Most Jewish communities had a fund for ransoming captives, and money designated for charitable purposes or the building of a synagogue could be used for this purpose. Anyone who delays performing this *mitzvah* is considered as having spilled the captive's blood. However, the Mishnah cautions that one does not ransom captives for more than their value, lest this encourage kidnappers to seize more Jews and demand still higher ransoms.

Rasha. The wicked child, the second of the four sons mentioned at the seder. He effectively isolates himself from the Jewish people by asking, "What does this ritual mean to *you*? [i.e., not to him]." According to the Torah, the only response to the *rasha* is to "set his teeth on edge." Instead of directly answering his question, it is necessary to respond in his own terms – that we celebrate Passover because of what God did for *us* when we went out of Egypt. Had the wicked child lived at that time and similarly disassociated himself from the fate of the Jewish people, he would not have been redeemed and instead would have been condemned to disappear among the mass of slave laborers.[255]

Rashei teivot – see Abbreviations.

Rashi script. Semi-cursive form of Hebrew script used for printing the biblical and talmudic commentaries of Rashi (acronym of Rabbi Shlomo ben Yitzchak; 11th century). His clear and explicit explanations, incorporating both literal and midrashic interpretations, have become the standard guide for every Bible student. Not used by the preeminent sage himself, this script was developed by Daniel Bomberg, a 15th-century Christian printer from Venice, to distinguish Rashi's commentaries from the actual text of the Bible and Talmud. It was used in the first printed Hebrew book, a Bible with Rashi's commentary.

Ras Shamra – see Ugarit.

Rav. Literally "great" or "teacher," an alternative title in Babylonia for "rabbi."Today, some Orthodox congregations use this term to refer to their rabbi.

Reb. Yiddish term for "rabbi," generally applied to a teacher or Hasidic leader. *Reb* is also used (with the given name) as a title of respect for a man, such as when he is called up for an *aliyah* to the Torah.

Rebbe. Yiddish term for the charismatic leader and spiritual teacher of a Hasidic sect (see *tzadik*).

Rebbetzin. Yiddish term for the wife of a rabbi.

Rebellious son. The "wayward and defiant [rebellious] son, who does not heed his father or mother and does not obey them even after they discipline him" was brought to the elders of the community and, if a proper hearing determined that the son was truly incorrigible, "the men of the town shall stone him to death. Thus, you will remove evil from your midst; all Israel will hear and be afraid" (Deut. 21:18-21). This could be done only after the elders had attempted to mediate between the son and his parents. The Rabbis of the Talmud so restricted this law that it became inapplicable in practice.

Rebuke. According to the Torah, "You shall surely admonish your neighbor, and not bear a sin because of him" (Lev. 19:17). This commandment is binding on everyone, so that an inferior must reprove a man of high rank even if he is met with curses and insults. Of course, a reproof must be kindly administered with delicacy and tact. Whenever possible it should be done in private, for shaming a person in public is a mortal sin. Criticism should never be offered haughtily or lightly, but always with the deepest regard for the feelings of others and a sincere desire to help, support, and benefit the recipient. Indeed, to refrain from admonition may indicate a lack of caring or involvement. If one sees a person traveling down a self-destructive or harmful path, be it physical or spiritual, love for that individual requires action. The goal of this commandment is either to prevent the person from sinning or, if he has already committed a transgression, to inspire him to repent for his actions.

Reconstructionist Judaism. Movement that developed from the Society for the Advancement of Judaism, founded in the United States in 1922 by Mordecai Kaplan. Kaplan described Judaism as an "evolving religious civilization" emerging from the language, history, customs, laws, religion, art, and folkways of the Jewish people. This "civilization" requires the establishment of social institutions in which its basic values continue to be meaningful to those individuals who adhere to them. The movement seeks to combine social scientific scholarship and the democratic values of Western society in an effort to "reconstruct" Judaism as part of the ongoing process of adapting it to changing social and cultural circumstances. Believing that Jewish nationalism is a part of Judaism, the Reconstructionist movement stresses the ties between the State of Israel and Jewish communities in the Diaspora. However, it rejects the belief in Jews as God's chosen people, instead maintaining that all people have the ability to fulfill and express the Divine will. The movement generally favors personal autonomy (like Reform Judaism) in terms of traditional law and custom, but advocates the study of sacred texts and the practice of key rituals because they convey sacred values and insights of previous generations, as long as they are consistent with communal consensus and not imposed through rabbinic authority alone. The Reconstructionist movement was a pioneer in gender equality, holding the first bat mitzvah in 1922, extending full ritual equality to women in the 1940s, and ordaining its first female rabbi in the 1970s.

Red heifer (*parah adumah*). Unblemished young cow that had never been yoked, which was burned on a pyre and its ashes mixed with water, cedar wood, hyssop, and crimson thread. This mysterious rite resulted in the paradoxical situation in which its ashes purified people who had become ritually unclean through contact with a human corpse, yet made those who engaged in its preparation ritually impure (Num. 19:1-22). It is the quintessential example of a *chok*, a statute that defies rational explanation and the observance of which represents unconditional obedience to a Divine decree.[256] According to a midrash, King Solomon, the wisest man in the Bible, admitted that he had understood all the words of God except for the ritual of the red heifer. The Rabbis reinterpreted the ritual of the red heifer as an observance to atone for the sin of the Golden Calf. Today, the section of the Torah dealing with the red heifer is read as the *maftir* portion for Shabbat Parah, one of the four special Sabbaths before Passover.

Red Sea. Long narrow strip of water separating the Arabian Peninsula from the northeastern corner of Africa (Egypt, Sudan, Ethiopia) and forming the northwestern arm of the Indian Ocean. In the northern part of the Red Sea are the Gulf of Eilat (Aqaba) and the Gulf of Suez, which enclose the Sinai Peninsula. The opening of the Suez Canal connected the Red Sea with the Mediterranean. During the Exodus from Egypt, the Israelites crossed *Yam Suf*, often translated as "Red Sea" but more literally the "Sea of Reeds." Its precise location is a matter of scholarly debate, with the majority opinion today identifying it with one of the lagoons on the shores of the Mediterranean Sea.

Red Shield of David – see Magen David Adom.

Redemption. The Jewish concept of personal redemption is different from the Christian idea of salvation, since Jews reject the belief that humans are born condemned (see original sin) and require a messianic figure to "save" them. Rabbinic Judaism teaches that "every Jew has a share in the World to Come" (see afterlife), as do "the righteous people of other [non-Jewish] nations" who follow the elementary standards of morality embodied in the seven Noahide laws.Punishment in the next world is limited to 11 months; eternal punishment (complete loss of a share in the afterlife) is imposed for only the most serious sins, typically relating to heresy, from which atonement may still be possible. Traditional Jews also believe in a communal redemption in the Messianic Age, an era of universal peace and justice when the Temple will be rebuilt and those Jews dispersed throughout the world will be gathered to the Land of Israel. God is described as the "Redeemer of Israel" in the daily liturgy.

Redemption of the firstborn – see *Pidyon ha-ben.*

Re'ei. The 4th *parashah* in the Book of Deuteronomy (11:16-16:17), it opens with God offering the Israelites blessings for obeying the commandments and curses for disobeying them, thus emphasizing the importance of free will in Judaism and the belief that human beings have the capacity to master their instincts and desires. It includes regulations pertaining to sacrifices and the requirement that they be centralized in a single place "that the Lord your God will choose," as well as a description of the periodic tithes and the pilgrimage festivals (Passover, Shavuot, Sukkot).

Reform Judaism. Also known as Liberal or Progressive Judaism, it developed in 19th-century Germany and was rooted in the Enlightenment era and the age of political emancipation. The Reform movement rejected the authority of *halacha* and championed the idea of personal autonomy in deciding which religious observances to follow, thus maintaining the right to modify Jewish tradtions to increase their contemporary relevance. It developed the concept of "ethical monotheism" based on the moral and ethical teachings of the Hebrew prophets, emphasized *tikun olam* (repairing the world) as the dominant means of service to

God, and deemphasized the ritual aspects of Judaism. Reform dramatically shortened the worship service and introduced the use of the organ, prayers and a sermon in the vernacular, and the confirmation ceremony. It rejected the classical rabbinic teaching that the Jews were in exile, instead arguing that the dispersion of Jews to be a "light among the nations" was necessary for them to fulfill their messianic duty of spreading the teachings of ethical monotheism. Embracing modern culture in customs, dress, and common practices, Reform came to stress complete gender equality, emphasized the idea of progressive or revolving revelation, and instituted the controversial doctrine of patrilineal descent.The Reform movement in the United States was the first to organize nationwide. Rabbi Israel Mayer Wise founded the Union of American Hebrew Congregations, an organization of synagogues, the Hebrew Union College, and the Central Conference of American Rabbis.

Refu'ah (healing). The 8th blessing of the weekday *Amidah*, it asks God as "the faithful and compassionate Healer" to return to health "the sick of God's people Israel."

Refu'ah sh'leimah. Literally "complete healing," the Hebrew phrase wishing that the sick be totally cured of their illnesses.

Refuge, cities of – see Cities of refuge.

Refusenik. Term coined in the 1970s for those Jews who were denied permission to emigrate from the Soviet Union. After mass protests by concerned Jews throughout the world, many refuseniks were finally granted exit visas and a large number went to Israel. Perhaps the most famous refusenik is Natan Sharansky, who moved to Israel and became a member of the Knesset.

Rei'ach nicho'ach – see Pleasing aroma.

Reincarnation – see Afterlife.

Reishit tz'michat g'ulateinu (the dawn of our redemption). View of the establishment of the State of Israel in 1948 as the herald of the Messianic Age. This idea was accentuated after the Six Day War in 1967, when Israel captured the Old City of Jerusalem as well as Judea and Samaria (the West Bank) and Gaza. For the first time in more than 2,000 years, there was Jewish rule over all the biblically ordained homeland. Nevertheless, some extreme Orthodox sects do not recognize the political existence of the Jewish state, because the Messiah has not yet come to redeem the people (see Neturei Karta).[257]

Rejoicing in the Law – see Simchat Torah.

Release, Year of – see Sabbatical Year.

Relieving an animal of its burden. The Bible requires a person to help unload a beast that has fallen under its burden in the field, even if it belongs to an enemy (Exod. 23:5) and even on the Sabbath. Indeed, many acts otherwise forbidden on the Sabbath (such as asking a non-Jew to milk cows) are permitted when their purpose is to relieve the suffering of an animal. According to the *Shulchan Aruch*, on the Sabbath one is permitted to tend to an animal's painful wound, exercise animals as a remedy for overeating, and help them escape from a pit or body of water into which they have fallen.[258]

Religious Zionists – see Zionists, religious.

Remarriage. According to biblical law, a divorced woman who has remarried and had her second marriage also terminated (by divorce or death) is not permitted to remarry her first husband (Deut. 24:4). If this were not the case, there was fear that people would feel free to divorce one another at will to sample other mates before subsequently getting together again. Several sages suggested that this prohibition was intended to prevent the possibility of a man conspiring with his wife to leave him, marry another man, and make life so miserable for her second husband that he would agree to make a cash settlement and divorce her, thus enabling her to then return to her first husband with a financial windfall.[259]

Remez. Allegorical or veiled interpretation of the biblical text, which reached its height during the 14th-16th centuries with such commentators as Sforno and Abravanel. A classic example of this approach is the talmudic concept that the Song of Songs is not simply a secular love song, but is actually an allegory for the relationship between God and Israel. *Remez* (and *sod*) were often deemed too dangerous for those without extensive talmudic knowledge, lest such students mistakenly stumble onto a misinterpretation that could lead them into heresy.

Remnant of Israel. Prophetic concept, especially in Jeremiah, which maintains that even though Judah is doomed to captivity, some of the righteous and repentant will always endure their trials and tribulations and manage to survive so that the Jewish people will live on. The Hebrew equivalent, *She'arit Yisrael*, is a favorite name for Jewish congregations (as in the oldest synagogue in New York). Those European Jews not murdered during the Holocaust are known as "the surviving remnant."

Rending of clothes – see *Keriah*.

Rennet. Membrane lining the stomach of a calf. Most hard cheeses are made through a process that includes curdling or coagulating milk in rennet. To be strictly kosher, the rennet must come from a kosher animal that was slaughtered in a ritually correct manner and whose stomach was properly prepared and thoroughly dried. Conservative halachic interpretation permits all hard cheeses. Today, cheese can be made using vegetable enzymes.[260]

Reparations. Term in international law to denote the payments made by a state as compensation for damage or injury caused during a conflict or in the absence of a declared war. In the Jewish context, it applies to a 1951 agreement in which the Federal Republic of Germany promised to transfer funds to the State of Israel for the costs incurred in resettling and integrating into Israeli society the thousands of Jewish refugees from Eastern and Western Europe who were displaced by the actions of the Nazis during World War II. Germany also agreed to pay for the theft of, and damage to, Jewish property before and during the conflict. Recently, other European nations have paid restitution for illegally seized Jewish property and assets during the Holocaust.

Repentance – see *Teshuvah*.

Rescuers. Term applied to those who put themselves, and often their families, at risk by a concrete action to save a Jewish life during World War II, without expectation of a reward (either monetary or any other type). The exact number of rescuers (also known as the "Righteous among the Nations") is not known, though they are thought to have been in the many tens of thousands and saved countless Jewish lives. The medal that rescuers receive from Yad Vashem bears the inscription: "In gratitude from the Jewish people. Whoever saves a single life saves the entire universe."

Resh. The 20th letter of the Hebrew alphabet, with a numerical value of 200.

Resh Galuta – see Exilarch.

Resh Kallah. Literally "head of the *kallah*," the second-in-command to the Gaon in the administration of the talmudic academies in Babylonia. He played a major role in organizing the bi-annual *kallah*.

Reshut. Literally "permission," a Hebrew legal term found extensively in the rabbinic literature that can be used in three distinct contexts. Most commonly, it indicates that a certain activity is allowed but not required. Prior to the long *Musaf Amidah* on Rosh Hashanah, the cantor begs *reshut* (permission) to intercede for the congregation despite his personal unworthiness (see *Hineni*). *Reshut* can be used to mean the legitimate possession of power or authority. The word also can differentiate an area over which an individual has authority (*reshut ha-yachid*; private domain) from one in which he does not (*reshut ha-rabbim*, public domain), a distinction that is critical in the laws of carrying on the Sabbath. (See also *eruv*.)

Resident alien – see *Ger toshav*.

Resistance movement – see Partisans.

Responsa. Answers by respected rabbis to halachic questions. Each *responsum* (Hebrew, *teshuvah*) is preceded by a question (*she'eilah*) in which the inquirer describes the situation that had arisen and specifies the legal matter on which a ruling is needed. In many cases, the question includes a citation of all relevant talmudic passages, like a legal brief to a court, and the answer provides an authoritative interpretation of these texts. The accumulated body of *responsa*, through the geonic and medieval periods and extending to modern times, has provided a growing collection of both specific precedents based on concrete cases and a general interpretation of key talmudic passages. The major limitation of *responsa* is that they are randomly collected and organized, making it difficult to know whether relevant rulings exist on a given topic. This problem has diminished in recent times due to the creation of computer databases that catalog many medieval and early modern *responsa*. *Responsa* are still used today to elucidate questions of Jewish law and practice.

Resting on the Sabbath. In addition to the negative commandment to refrain from working on the Sabbath, there is a positive commandment to rest on the seventh day. Maimonides said that this was designed to remind Jews of the role of God as the Creator of the universe and the Deliverer of Israel from Egypt.[261] The phrase "[even] at plowing time and harvest time shall you rest [cease from labor]" implies that Jews must rest and not violate the Sabbath even during these critical periods of the year when they might believe that their very livelihood depends on laboring in the fields.[262] In observing the Sabbath rest, Jews traditionally "extend" the day by beginning it with the lighting of candles 18 minutes before sunset on Friday and delaying its departure until three stars appear in the night sky (about 42 minutes after sunset) on Saturday evening.

Restitution. Restoration of property wrongly taken from its owner. The term is used in relation to assets that were stolen from Jews by the Nazis in the period leading up to and during World War II.

Resurrection. The return of the dead to life has been a normative Jewish belief since late Second Temple times. The concept that the righteous would be rewarded in a future existence was one rabbinic response to the problem of theodicy – why God allows the innocent to suffer and the wicked to prosper in this life. The ideas of an afterlife and eventual Divine justice became pillars of the theology of the Pharisees and their rabbinic descendants and one of the chief points distinguishing them from the Saducees, who asserted that the soul died together with the body. To paraphrase the Talmud, if those who never lived before can live, then why cannot those who have already lived, live again? Although many rabbis envisioned a purely spiritual afterlife, most believed in the restoration of the souls into the bodies of the resurrected, who would rise from their graves fully clothed. The concept of resurrection of the body was also the source of the strong opposition in Jewish law to the practice of cremation. Traditional Judaism has maintained a consistent belief in both the future resurrection of the dead as part of the messianic redemption and in some form of immortality of the soul after death. Reform and Reconstructionist Judaism deny the idea of bodily resurrection, though many of their members retain a belief in the immortality of the soul.

Retaliation – see *Lex talionis.*

Retribution – see Reward and punishment and Punishment, vicarious.

Retzu'ot. Leather straps, about 2-3 feet in length, which are attached to the *tefillin*.Those on the *tefillin* for the head are tied in a knot and hang loose. The *retzu'ot* attached to the *tefillin* of the hand are wound seven times around the arm and three times around the middle fingers, forming the Hebrew word *Shaddai* (one of the names of God).

Revelation. An act whereby God shows the Divine Presence to human beings. According to the Torah, by far the most significant revelation was when God revealed the Ten Commandments to the Israelites as they camped at the foot of Mount Sinai. This event, which occurred seven weeks after being liberated from bondage in Egypt, is today commemorated by the festival of Shavuot. After the Revelation, Moses ascended Mount Sinai and remained there fasting for 40 days before receiving the two stone "tablets of the covenant" (see *luchot ha-brit*). These were engraved "by the finger of God" and comprised the stipulations of the Covenant between God and Israel. Jewish tradition maintains that God dictated the entire Torah, not only the Ten Commandments, to Moses on Mount Sinai (and also imparted to him the Oral Torah). The Torah was subsequently transmitted to Joshua, and then to the elders, the prophets, and the men of the Great Assembly (Avot 1:1). Thus, the Torah read and studied in later generations is believed by Orthodox Jews to be the same as the original Torah of Moses.

Revelation, continuous. Theological concept that Divine revelation continues to the present day. According to this view, Sinai and the prophets represented the major revelations, but some important revelations have occurred since then and will always occur in the future. As Rabbi Judah Loew of Prague noted, the conclusion of both Torah blessings is in the present tense (*notein ha-Torah*), implying that the act of revelation is a continuing outpouring. This idea is generally accepted by the Conservative movement, which maintains that, since the end of the prophetic age, revelation continues through the people of Israel rather than through individuals. Thus, Zechariah Frankel stated, "Judaism is the religion of the Jews." As Orthodox scholars have observed, a potential problem is that what the Jewish people accept at a given period as the will of God may be wrong. Nevertheless, those who believe in continuous revelation see it as a Divine unfolding of God's will in human history.

Revelation, progressive. According to this theological concept, not only has revelation continued to this day, but it is now of a higher quality. Thus, the greatest act of revelation was not Sinai but will be the Messianic Age at the end of time. Since we are closer to that time and "know more," we now have higher authority and thus a higher degree of revelation. This approach of the Reform movement is based on the Hegelian and Darwinian concept that there is inevitable progress as things evolve. Consequently, more has been revealed to those living today than to any past generation, and thus we now have more access to truth. This concept of revelation is the only one not found in classical Jewish sources, and it makes Jews vulnerable to claims by Christians, Muslims, and even Baha'i that later revelations have superseded those made to the Jews. After the Holocaust, the Reform movement abandoned a strict view of progressive revelation, since it was difficult to claim that history was indeed moving to a better state.

Revelation, terminal (regressive). Theological concept that Divine revelation ended with the death of Malachi, the last biblical prophet. According to this view, held by Orthodox Jews, the closer the proximity to the initial source of revelation (Sinai), the higher the authority.

Revenge (*nekamah*). According to the Torah, "You shall not take revenge or bear a grudge" (Lev. 19:18). The Rabbis offered the following illustration of these two commandments. A asks B to lend him a sickle, but B refuses. The next day, B asks to borrow A's hatchet. If A replies, "I *will not* lend it to you, just as you refused to lend me your sickle," that is taking revenge. If A replies, "I *will* lend it to you, even though yesterday you refused to lend me your sickle," that is bearing a grudge.[263]

Revisionism – see Zionists, revisionist.

Reward and punishment. As repeatedly expressed in the Torah and rabbinic literature, the traditional Jewish view is that God will reward those who observe the Divine commandments and punish those who intentionally disobey them. The contrary practical observation – that the righteous often suffer while the wicked prosper – is the basis for the problem of theodicy and the development of the concept of an afterlife. Nevertheless, as Rabbi Yannai observed, "It is not in our power to explain either the prosperity of the wicked or the sufferings of the righteous" (Avot 4:19).

Rewritten Bible. Term applied to those *midrashim* that embellish the original biblical narrative. They do not attempt to explicate the Bible in a direct or orderly manner, but instead are collections of stories and legends about individual Rabbis or biblical characters.[264]

Ribbono shel Olam (Sovereign of the universe). One of the rabbinic names for God.

Righteous among the Nations (Righteous Gentiles). Title for the approximately 20,000 men and women who have been honored by the State of Israel for risking their lives to help persecuted Jews during the Shoah. Tribute is paid to these Righteous Gentiles at Yad Vashem, the Holocaust memorial in Jerusalem. Prominent among the Righteous among the Nations are Swedish diplomat Raoul Wallenberg, who issued passports and established "safe houses" that protected thousands of Hungarian Jews, and German industrialist Oskar Schindler, who (along with his wife, Emilie) saved the lives of some 1,100 Jews working in his factory and was made famous by the film, "Schindler's List." (See also *rescuers*.)

Righteousness. A concept that includes honesty, virtue, and doing the right thing in all situations. Essentially entailing the fulfillment of all the legal and moral obligations inherent in living according to the Divine law, it is reflected in much of biblical legislation and the messages of the Hebrew prophets. According to Jewish legend, in each generation the world is sustained on account of 36 righteous people (see *lamed-vavniks*). The Hebrew root of *tzedakah*, the giving of charity, means "righteousness."

Rimonim. Literally "pomegranates," the pair of silver finials placed on the two wooden staves (see *atzei chaim*) on which the Torah scroll is rolled. The *rimonim* are often adorned with bells that tinkle during the procession, reminiscent of the robe of the High Priest that was hemmed with golden bells and blue, purple, and scarlet balls shaped like pomegranates. The use of Torah ornaments with bells enables those seated in the back of the congregation to realize that a Torah is in procession, so that they can stand up to fulfill the requirement of rising with reverential respect whenever the Torah is removed from the ark.

Rishon Le-Zion. Title of the Sephardic Chief Rabbi in Israel.

Rishonim. Earlier rabbinic authorities, as distinguished from the *acharonim* (later authorities). Among the most famous of the *rishonim* are Rashi and Maimonides. The period of the *rishonim*, "the early Sages," extends from about the 11th-15th centuries. The *rishonim* wrote commentaries on the Talmud and engaged in discussions on existing talmudic commentaries.

Ritual bath – see *Mikveh*.

Ritual impurity. In the Bible, a person who touched anything considered ritually unclean (or in certain circumstances, was only near it) was himself rendered ritually impure and subject to all the obligations relating to unclean persons. For example, he could not come into the Sanctuary, touch any holy thing, or eat any hallowed food. Among those things that could cause ritual impurity were the carcasses of animals (Lev. 11:24) and certain creeping creatures (weasel, mouse, great lizard, gecko, land-crocodile, lizard, sand-lizard, chameleon), which also were prohibited as food (Lev. 11:29-30); and food and drink in an earthen vessel into which one of these dead creatures or their droppings had fallen (Lev. 11:34). The most potent source of ritual impurity was a dead human body (Num. 19:11). It conveyed ritual uncleanness to anyone or any thing that entered or remained within the same tent or under the same roof as a corpse (including household utensils and wearing apparel), even if the person had no direct contact with it. A person who had contact with an individual who had become ritually unclean became himself ritually impure and could even transmit this state to food and drink. Another important source of ritual uncleanness was contact with a menstruating woman. During her menstrual period, anyone who touched her, her bedding, or anywhere she sat would become ritually impure. This state of ritual impurity could be removed by immersion in a *mikveh* following the completion of her menstrual cycle. Other ritual impurities could be removed by immersion in the *mikveh*, offering sacrifices, and being sprinkled with the ashes of the red heifer.

Ritual murder – see Blood libel.

Ritual purification – see Ablution, *Mikveh*, Red heifer, and Ritual impurity (above).

Ritual slaughter – see *Shechitah*.

Robbery. The taking by force and violence of the property of another, to which one has no right. The term "robbery" could also apply to misappropriation of funds entrusted to someone, or to the illegal taking of a pledge.Biblical law mandated that a robber was required to "repay the principal amount [or the actual article] and add a fifth to it" (Lev. 5:23-24). According to the literal meaning of the text, a thief who stole a wooden plank and incorporated it into his house would be required to return that identical plank, even if its removal would destroy the house. The Rabbis rejected this harsh interpretation and, in an attempt to encourage robbers to repent for their crimes, ruled that it was sufficient to pay the full monetary value of the plank. This resulted in the general rule that if the stolen object had undergone a permanent alteration (such as wool woven into a garment), the robber was to pay its equivalent value in money.[265] The Biblical term "add a fifth" was calculated in a unique way, not the 20% that it would imply today. For example, if the stolen object were worth four *shekels*, the robber would have to pay a total of five *shekels*. Thus, the additional amount would be a fifth of the *total* payment.[266] The prohibition against robbery was one of the seven Noahide laws.

Rock of Ages. The revenge motif explicit in *Maoz Tzur*, the most popular of the Chanukah songs traditionally sung after the kindling of the festival lights, troubled some segments of the Jewish community. In the 19th century, two well-known American rabbis, Marcus Jastrow and Gustav Gottheil, composed a considerably toned-down English version entitled "Rock of Ages," deeming it more palatable to contemporary sensibilities.[267] It emphasizes God's "saving power" and the strength and courage that spiritual sustenance can provide.

Rodef (pursuer). The Rabbis required that one must do whatever is necessary to save the life of one who is being pursued, even going as far as taking the life of the pursuer. However, if one can save an endangered person by merely wounding the pursuer, the rescuer must not take his life lest he be considered guilty of murder.[268] Saving the life of the pursued is the basis on which abortion is required if the life of the mother is in danger. In this situation, it is obligatory to save the life of the pregnant woman (the pursued) by destroying the fetus (the pursuer). However, if the child's head has emerged from the womb, it is regarded as alive and may not be harmed, for it is forbidden to destroy one independent life to save another.[269]

Rosh Chodesh. Literally "head of the month," the first day of the month that correlates with the sighting of the crescent of the new moon. Originally, it was the task of the Sanhedrin to determine whether a particular month had 29 or 30 days, based on the visual observation of witnesses. The members of the Sanhedrin gathered on the 30th of each month and awaited testimony. If witnesses appeared, Rosh Chodesh was celebrated and that day was counted of the first day of the month. If no witnesses came forward, the next day was celebrated as Rosh Chodesh. When Christian authorities in the Land of Israel prohibited the dissemination of information regarding the New Moon, Hillel II, the Patriarch of Jews in the Land of Israel, in about 360 C.E. published a fixed calendar based on astronomical calculations, thereby abolishing the proclamation of the New Moon based on direct observation. Work is permitted on Rosh Chodesh. However, since earliest times it has been customary for women to abstain from work; in recent years, women have formed Rosh Chodesh groups to study and worship together.[270]

Rosh Hashanah (1). Literally "head of the year," the first and second days of the month of Tishrei (September) that are celebrated as the beginning of the Jewish New Year and the anniversary of the Creation of the world. The first of the Days of Awe, Rosh Hashanah is known as the Day of Judgment and the start of the Ten Days of Repentance, a period of self-examination, atonement, and self-renewal. The *shofar* is sounded as a reminder of God's sovereignty and the need for repentance, and additions to the liturgy include *Avinu Malkeinu*, *Hineni*, and *U-netaneh Tokef*. Jews greet each other with *leshanah tovah tikateivu*, and the ceremony of Tashlich is performed.

Rosh Hashanah (RH) (2). The 8th tractate of Mo'ed (festivals) in the Mishnah, it deals with the laws concerning the sanctification of the New Moon, fixing the months and years, the blowing of the *shofar*, and the order of prayers on Rosh Hashanah.

Rosh Hashanah, day of the week of. Rosh Hashanah never falls on a Wednesday, Friday, or Sunday. If it occurred on a Wednesday, Yom Kippur would be on a Friday and thus Jews would be unable to prepare for the Sabbath. If it fell on a Friday, Yom Kippur would be on a Sunday, so that Jews who observe the Sabbath would be unable to get ready for Yom Kippur. Finally, if Rosh Hashanah were on a Sunday, Hoshana Rabbah (the last day of Sukkot; 21st of Tishrei) would be on a Saturday. This would preclude performance of the major ritual of the day – beating the willows during the synagogue services – which is forbidden on the Sabbath.[271]

Rosh yeshiva. Literally "head of the academy," the Hebrew title of the rabbi directing an institution for the study of Talmud.

Ru'ach. Literally "wind," one of the Hebrew words translated as "spirit" or "soul." According to one explanation, *nefesh* is the physical soul, which human beings share with the animal world. *Neshamah* is totally spiritual, a soul that man shares with the angels. *Ru'ach* is the transitional soul that connects the two, since it would otherwise be impossible for the physical and the spiritual to co-exist in one body.

Ru'ach ha-Kodesh – see Holy Spirit.

Rugelach. Ashkenazic cookie, this popular rolled dessert is typically filled with raisins, walnuts, and cinnamon.

Rule of the Community – see Manual of Discipline.

Ruth. The 2nd of the *megillot* and the 5th book of the Writings section of the Bible. A Moabite woman whose Israelite husband had died, Ruth demonstrated her admirable loyalty and affection by returning with her mother-in-law to the Land of Israel, where she married Boaz, a wealthy kinsman of her father-in-law.

In the synagogue, it is traditional to read the Book of Ruth on Shavuot, because the story takes place at harvest time (2:23). As a proselyte, Ruth accepted the Torah just as Israel did at Mount Sinai on that day. Ruth also was the great-grandmother of King David (4:7), whose birth and death were traditionally deemed to have occurred on Shavuot.

Ruth Rabbah. Aggadic midrash on the biblical Book of Ruth, probably written between 650-900.

S

Sabbateans. In the 17th-century, a charismatic Turkish Jew named Shabbetai Tzevi declared himself the Messiah and attracted a widespread and devoted following among Jews throughout the Diaspora. However, he was proven to be a false messiah when he converted to Islam rather than submit to the Turkish sultan's executioner. Nevertheless, Sabbatean messianism continued as an underground movement among some Jewish mystics for more than a century, though it was condemned as heretical by the mainstream Jewish community.

Sabbath. The seventh day of the week and a time of rest and spiritual renewal, the Jewish Sabbath (*Shabbat* in Hebrew) begins at sunset on Friday evening and ends on Saturday evening when three stars are visible in the sky. The importance of the Sabbath is attested to by the fact that it is the only sacred time noted in the Ten Commandments (Exod. 20:8-11). The Sabbath is linked to the idea of the Exodus, the emergence from slavery into freedom, and is a sign of the covenant between God and Israel (Exod. 31:16-19). In the home, candles are lit, *Kiddush* is recited, and a blessing is made over the *challah*. *Eshet Chayil* (Woman of Valor) is recited and *Shalom Aleichem* and special table hymns (see *zemirot*) are sung at the three meals, including one before the close of the day (see *se'udah shlishit*). In the synagogue, there are numerous changes in the prayer service, including *Kabbalat Shabbat* in the evening, and often an *Oneg Shabbat* following the prayers. Restrictions are imposed on work, carrying, and travel on the Sabbath, but all are superseded by the need to save a life (see *pikuach nefesh*). Shabbat ends with the ceremony of *Havdalah*.

Shabbat candles – see Candlelighting.

Sabbath meals. It is customary to invite guests and sing special table hymns (see *zemirot*) at the three main Sabbath meals – Friday evening, Saturday lunch, and a third meal (see *se'udah shlishit*, or *shalosh seudos*) before the close of the day. This tradition stems from the threefold repetition of the word *ha-yom* (today) in the verse: "Then Moses said: 'Eat it (the manna) *today*, for *today* is a Sabbath of the Lord, *today* you will not find it in the field" (Exod. 16:25). The Sabbath table is traditionally covered with a white tablecloth, reflecting either the white manna that covered the earth or the "pure table" (symbolized by white) on which the Showbread was laid out in the Temple. (See also *Melaveh malkah*.)

Sabbath prayers. On Friday evening, the regular *Ma'ariv* service is preceded by *Kabbalat Shabbat* (Welcoming the Sabbath), which includes the hymn *Lecha Dodi*, and a special prayer, *Ve-Shomru*.Some Reform and Conservative synagogues in the United States have instituted a late Friday evening service, which allows congregants to return home after the business day, enjoy the Sabbath meal with their families, and then attend the prayer service. The Saturday morning service includes readings from the Torah and *haftarah*, and there is an additional (see *Musaf*) service. The afternoon service (see *Mincha*) also includes a Torah reading from the portion to be read on the next Sabbath. In all Sabbath services, petitions are eliminated from the *Amidah* and replaced with special blessings in honor of the day. When the Sabbath concludes and three stars can be seen in the night sky, *Havdalah* is recited.

Sabbath restrictions. There are four major types of activities prohibited on the Sabbath – work; carrying; traveling; and starting a fire.

Sabbaths, special. Throughout the year, some Sabbaths commemorate specific events and are distinguished by variations in the liturgy and special customs. Two of these Sabbaths recur – Shabbat Machar Chodesh, when the Sabbath occurs on the day before the New Moon, and Shabbat Rosh Chodesh, when the Sabbath coincides with the New Moon. (For the others, see individual listings under "Shabbat" below.)

Sabbatical year. In Hebrew *shemitah* (lit., "release"), every seventh year in which all the land of Israel was to lie fallow (Lev. 25). During the Sabbatical Year, it was forbidden to cultivate the soil, water, and prune trees. Owner, servants, gentile laborers, the poor, the stranger, and even wild and domesticated animals had equal rights to the produce. Observance of the Sabbatical Year was a reminder to human beings that they are merely tenants with temporary rights to farm Divinely owned property, as in the verse from Psalms: "The earth is the Lord's, and all the fullness thereof " (24:1). As the need for Jews to grow food in Israel became an acute issue in modern times, the observance of the Sabbatical Year became a problem. To cope with this situation, most rabbinic authorities have permitted Jewish farmers (via a legal fiction) to sell their land to non-Jews for the *shemitah* period. In this way, they can cultivate the land as non-owners.[272] In biblical times, all debts were to be forgiven during the Sabbatical Year. Recognizing that financial concerns might lead one to refuse to give a loan to a needy fellow-Jew as the Sabbatical Year approached, the Torah warned against this practice (Deut. 15:9). To meet the needs of a more urban society, Hillel (1st century B.C.E.) developed the legal fiction of the *prosbul*.

Sabra. Prickly pear cactus, which was originally imported from Mexico in the 1600s and now grows abundantly in the Land of Israel.[273] "Sabra" has become the nickname of native-born Israelis, symbolic of being prickly and tough on the outside, but soft and sweet on the inside.

Sacrifices. The Israelites could bring five major types of offerings in homage and gratitude to God – burnt, meal, peace, sin, and guilt. The Torah provided precise regulations concerning how each of these sacrifices was to be offered, what part of them was to be burned, and what portion was to be eaten. The laws pertaining to sacrifices are primarily found in Leviticus, though some occur in the second half of Exodus and in Numbers. There were two basic classifications of offerings – voluntary and obligatory. Sacrifices could be brought on behalf of the individual or the community as a whole. The offering of sacrifices was the principal form of Jewish worship from biblical times until the destruction of the Second Temple, when prayer became the substitute for sacrifice as regular worship of the Divine.

Sacrilege (*me'ilah*). The act of profaning or violating sacred places or objects. A person who unintentionally used Temple property or ate some holy food was required to make full restitution plus pay a penalty of one fifth of its estimated value (Lev. 5:16; 22:14). Nothing related to the Sanctuary could be appropriated for common purposes. Thus, it was forbidden to make incense using the identical ingredients in the same relative weights as that used in the Sanctuary (Exod. 30:37), prepare the exact formulation of the Oil of Anointment (Exod. 30:32), or construct precise models of the Tabernacle, Temple, Menorah, or any holy vessels.

Sadducees. One of the three major sects of Judaism in the late Second Temple period. They were a predominantly aristocratic group, many of whom were priests officiating in the Temple. Moderate Hellenizers whose primary loyalty was to the religion of Israel but whose culture and practice were greatly influenced by the Greco-Roman environment in which they lived, the Sadducees derived their name from Zadok, the High Priest of the Jerusalem Temple, whose family served as heads of the priesthood throughout most of First and Second Temple times until the rise of the Hasmoneans.Unlike the Pharisees, the Sadducees rejected the Oral Law, the concept of immortality of the soul with bodily resurrection, and the idea of judgment and retribution after death. They believed in absolute free will, implying that God did not exercise direct control over the affairs of mankind. Following the destruction of the Temple in 70 C.E., the Sadducees ceased to be a factor in Jewish history.

Safed. Capital of the Upper Galilee. Along with Jerusalem, Hebron, and Tiberias, Safed came to be regarded as one of the four holy cities. In the 16th century after the expulsion of the Jews from Spain, the town of Safed became a great spiritual and educational center, attracting a large number of Jewish mystics. In Safed, Yosef Karo wrote the *Shulchan Aruch* (the major code of Jewish law) and Isaac Luria developed the Kabbalah. Much of Safed was destroyed by a powerful earthquake in the 18th century. After heavy fighting in the War of Independence, the Arab population fled. Today, its beautiful mountain setting has made Safed an art center and a popular resort.

Sages. Collective term for the *tanna'im* and *amora'im*, the Rabbis of the talmudic era cited in the Mishnah and Gemara. (See also *hazal*.)

Salt. Present in huge quantities in the area of the Dead Sea, which is known in Hebrew as *Yam ha-Melach* (Salt Sea), salt is first mentioned in the Bible in reference to Lot's wife turning into a "pillar of salt" (Gen. 19:26). With the destruction of the Temple and its sacrificial rites, the family dinner table came to symbolize the Holy Altar. Therefore, the commandment to bring salt with every offering (Lev. 2:13) is recalled by sprinkling salt over the *challah* at Sabbath and festival meals. As a prime food preservative and a symbol of permanence among ancient peoples, covenants were customarily sealed with bread and salt. To this day, bread dipped in salt is a symbol of hospitality, and these items are traditionally brought to those moving into a new home. The ability of salt to absorb blood, which Jews are forbidden to consume, is the basis for its use in the *kashering* of meat. At the Passover seder, Jews dip greens (see *karpas*) in salt water to symbolize the tears shed by their ancestors when they were slaves in Egypt.

Salt, placing in pockets and corners of the room. According to folklore, demons and other mischievous creatures could reside in new houses and cause such chaos that people were actually paid to live in them prior to their intended occupants. Because salt was generally regarded as having superb powers against evil spirits, it was often placed in the corners of a room where tiny goblins and elves could hide. By placing a few grains of salt in the pockets of clothing, its owner hoped to drive these beings away and foil their evil designs.

Salvation – see Redemption.

Samaria (*Shomron*). Capital of the North Kingdom of Israel. It reached the height of its prosperity and importance under Jeroboam II (784-748 B.C.E.). The Assyrians conquered Samaria in 722 B.C.E., and its inhabitants were exiled. Today, this term is used to describe the northern part of the area that is popularly known as the "West Bank" (of the Jordan River), which roughly corresponds to the territory of the ancient Kingdom of Israel.

Samaritans. Ancient people descended from the Israelite tribes of Ephraim and Menashe, who intermarried with non-Israelite colonists brought by the conquering Assyrians to settle in the area of the defeated Northern Kingdom. When the Israelites returned from Babylonian Exile and began to rebuild the Temple, they considered the Samaritans as non-Jews and prohibited them from assisting in the effort.

Consequently, the Samaritans built a rival temple on Mount Gerizim near Shechem, where the small remaining community still holds an annual Passover sacrifice. Although the Samaritans claim their worship is the true religion of the ancient Israelites, this assertion has been rejected by normative Judaism. There are now only a few hundred adherents of the Samaritan religion. Under the Law of Return, they are recognized as citizens of the State of Israel.

Sambatyon. Mythical river that ceased to flow on the Sabbath. According to legend, the Ten Lost Tribes of Israel were transported beyond the Sambatyon.

Samech. The 15th letter of the Hebrew alphabet, with a numerical value of 60.

Samuel. The 3rd book of the Prophets section of the Bible. (In English Bibles, the book is divided into two parts.) It relates the history of the Israelites from the end of the period of the Judges to the last days of King David and includes the biographies of Samuel (prophet and last judge of Israel), Saul (first king of Israel), and his successor, David. The Book of Samuel delineates the factors that led to the rise of the Israelite monarchy and demonstrates that the king, as well as the people, is bound by the terms of the covenant. A transitional figure, Samuel courageously guided the people from a tribal league under the judges to the era of the monarchy.

Sanctification – see *Kiddush*.

Sanctification of the Name – see *Kiddush ha-Shem.*

Sanctuary. See *Mishkan*, Temple, and Synagogue.

Sandek. The person, often a grandfather, who is given the honor of holding the newborn boy on a pillow placed on a table or on his lap during a circumcision. In many communities, the *sandek* sits on a special "Chair of Elijah;" in some traditions the chair remains unoccupied at his immediate right.

Sanhedrin (1). Supreme judicial, religious, and political body in the Land of Israel during the Roman and Byzantine periods. This assembly of 71 sages met in the Chamber of Hewn Stones in the Temple in Jerusalem. The final authority on Jewish law, the Sanhedrin was led by a president called the *nasi* (prince) and a vice president known as the *av beit din* (father of the court). The Sanhedrin proclaimed the New Moon, declared leap years, decided questions of Jewish religious law, and dealt with serious civil and criminal cases (until 30 C.E. it had the authority to inflict capital punishment). The Sanhedrin reached the peak of its power in the late Second Temple period. After the destruction of the Temple and the fall of Jerusalem, the Sanhedrin reorganized in Yavneh and then moved to different cities in the Galilee, eventually ending up in Tiberias. It existed until the abolishment of the rabbinic patriarchate in about 425 C.E.

Sanhedrin (Sanh.) (2). Fourth tractate in Nezikin (damages) in the Mishnah, it deals with courts of justice, judicial procedure, and criminal law.

Sanhedrin, French. Assembly of French Jewish notables, which was convened by Napoleon Bonaparte (July 26, 1806 to April 6, 1807) to "revive among Jews the civil morality weakened during their long debasement." In a speech to the Assembly, Napoleon attacked the Jews as "a nation within a nation" that must be reformed so that Jews would become "loyal French citizens of the Mosaic faith." Twelve questions were posed to the delegates, the responses to which emphasized the loyalty and patriotism of French Jews. To confer legitimacy on the responses, Napoleon convened a largely rabbinic French Sanhedrin of 71 members – a caricature of the supreme judicial, religious, and political body in the Land of Israel during the Roman and Byzantine periods – to translate the resolutions passed by the Assembly of Jewish Notables into Jewish religious imperatives that would cause the Jews to "look upon France as their Jerusalem." Despite the good will exhibited by the Sanhedrin, Napoleon passed descriminatory legislation against the Jews, thereby betraying the hopes of the Sanhedrin that their responses would lead to religious equality (which was only attained in 1830 under King Louis Philippe).

San Remo Conference. International meeting held in this Italian town in April 1920, which determined the allocation by the victorious powers of League of Nations mandates for the administration of the former Ottoman-ruled lands of the Middle East. Britain received the mandate for Palestine and Iraq, while France gained control of Syria (including modern Lebanon). The conference reaffirmed the 1917 Balfour Declaration, under which the British government undertook to favor the establishment of a Jewish national home in Palestine without prejudice to the civil and religious rights of existing non-Jewish communities, or the rights and political status enjoyed by Jews in any other country.

Satan. Rather than a demonic creature who is the personification of evil and the enemy of God, the biblical word "*satan*" is merely a common noun that means "adversary," "accuser," or "hinderer." The role of Satan is to make things difficult for human beings, so that they can overcome temptations and their evil inclinations and eventually succeed in accomplishing the tasks that God has prepared for them. Thus, Satan convinces God to test the faithfulness of Job. In a talmudic legend, it is Satan who challenged God to put Abraham to the test of the *Akedah* (binding of Isaac) to prove the Patriarch's allegiance. Nevertheless, throughout the Bible, Satan is clearly subordinate to God and unable to act without Divine permission. Only in the Talmud and Midrash does Satan emerge as a distinct entity (often called "Samael"), who is identified with the *yetzer ha-ra* (the inclination toward evil) and the Angel of Death.According to the Rabbis, the purpose of the sounding of the *shofar* on Rosh Hashanah is "to confuse the Accuser [Satan]"

(RH 16b), so as to prevent him from bringing any charges against the Jews before God on the Day of Judgment.

Savora'im. Literally "reasoners" and the disciples of the last *amora'im*, the *savora'im* probably completed the final editing of the Babylonian Talmud in the mid-6th century (after the work of Rav Ashi and Ravina). They were the major scholars until the rise of the *geonim* in the 8th century.

Scapegoat – see Azazel.

S'chach. Covering for the roof of the sukkah.It must be composed of plants that cannot be used for food; are in their natural state (i.e., not wooden boards); and are detached from the ground. Therefore, a grape arbor or any growing vine cannot be used. Typically consisting of cut branches or bamboo, the *s'chach* must be arranged so that there is more shade than sunshine inside the sukkah during the day, but not so dense that the stars cannot be seen through it at night.

Schnapps. Type of distilled beverage. Although often considered a generic word for hard "liquor," it specifically refers to a clear brandy distilled from fermented fruit (peach, cherry, apple, pear, plum, apricot) to which no sugar is added. The proper blessing before drinking schnapps is "*she ha-kol n'hiyeh bidvaro*."

Sciatic nerve (*gid ha-nesech*). Jews are forbidden from eating the sciatic nerve, which extends from the rear of the spinal column and runs down the inner side of the leg. This prohibition is an eternal reminder of the wrestling contest between Jacob and the mysterious "man," which took place as the Patriarch was returning to the Land of Israel after dwelling 20 years with Laban (Gen. 32:25-32). During this titanic struggle – which resulted in Jacob's name being changed to Israel – the attacker injured Jacob's thigh, resulting in a residual limp. The sciatic nerve and its surrounding fat must be removed before the hindquarters of an animal can be ritually prepared for Jewish consumption. Although some expert butchers can perform this difficult task, in general the process is so time-consuming and costly that many kosher butchers do not handle the hindquarters at all. Packinghouses usually sell the hindquarters of kosher-slaughtered animals to the general market for nonkosher cuts of meat such as sirloin or T-bone steak and filet mignon.[274]

Science of Judaism – see *Wissenschaft des Judentums*.

Scribe (1). Ancient profession that required a person who could read and write. Among the various positions scribes held in public affairs, their most important posts were as secretaries of state in preparing and issuing decrees in the name of the king. As the personal secretary of Jeremiah, Baruch "wrote from the mouth of Jeremiah all the words that the Lord had spoken to him [the prophet]" (Jer. 36:4, 32). After the exile of the Israelites to Babylonia, the scribes became experts in the law, writing numerous copies and teaching it to others. Following the return from exile, Ezra and other scribes played critical roles in the community.

Scribe (2) – see *Sofer*.

Script. The ancient Israelites adopted alphabetic script from the Canaanites in the 12th or 11th century B.C.E. The Torah is written in a square script, and the precise shape, form, and method for writing each letter is prescribed. There are two basic styles of script – the Ashkenazic, which resembles that described in the Talmud, and the Sephardic, which is identical to the printed letters of the Hebrew alphabet currently used in sacred texts. Care must be taken to ensure that each letter is clear and distinct. Although Hebrew is read from right to left, each individual letter of a word in the *sefer Torah* is written from left to right. Various forms of cursive script developed from the standard square type.

Scripture – see Bible.

Scroll – see Torah scroll and *Megillah*.

Sea of Galilee – see *Kinneret*.

Sea of Reeds – see Red Sea.

Se'ah. Biblical measurement of volume, thought to be equal to about 5 gallons.

Seal. In antiquity, seals were signs employed to identify property, as protection against theft, and to mark the clay stoppers of jars of oil and wine. With the spread of writing in the early days of the Mesopotamian dynasties, seals were used as signatures on clay-tablet inscriptions. In ancient Israel, seals were in widespread use as signatures or to mark possessions. The base of these seals was generally engraved with an inscription, which was often combined with decorative designs, mythological subjects, flora and fauna, and geometrical patterns. The name of the owner of the seal was frequently given, together with that of his father (with or without the word "son"). While most of the seals were personal, a few contained the name of a "servant" (official) and his monarch (e.g., Shema, the servant of Jeroboam). The king's ring was synonymous with his seal and symbolized royal power. In the Middle Ages, the absence of the human figure and the use of Hebrew inscriptions were unique aspects of Jewish seals.

Seal of Solomon. Designation for the hexagram, which is widely found in Arab sources regarding Jews. Legends connect this symbol with the magical signet ring used by King Solomon to control demons and spirits. The notion of a magical shield of David (see Magen David), which protected him from enemies, was originally unconnected with this sign. From 1300 to 1700, Jewish mystics (kabbalists) used the terms "Shield of David" and "Seal of Solomon" interchangeably, but slowly the former gained ascendancy.

Second Adar. Extra month added to the Jewish lunar calendar seven times in 19 years to ensure that the festivals fall during their appointed seasons in the solar year. Known in Hebrew as *Adar Sheni*, it immediately precedes the month of Nisan, the first month in the Jewish religious year. During a leap year, the festival of Purim falls in Second Adar.

Second day of festivals – see Festivals, second day of.

Second Isaiah – see Deutero-Isaiah.

Second Passover – see Passover, second.

Second Temple. After the destruction of the First Temple in 586 B.C.E. and the Babylonian Exile, the Persians conquered Babylonia and permitted the Jews to return to the Land of Israel and build a Second Temple. Construction was begun in 538 B.C.E., and it was finally completed and dedicated in 515. Desecrated by the Syrian-Greeks under Antiochus Epiphanes, it was purified and rededicated in 165 by Judah the Maccabee.Herod the Great enlarged and refurbished the building during the 1st century B.C.E., and it remained in use until destroyed by Titus and the conquering Roman army in 70 C.E. The only remnant of the Second Temple is the Western Wall, which represents a section of the outer retaining wall of the Temple Mount.

Sects. At the end of the Second Temple period, there were three major groups in Judaism – Pharisees, Sadducees, and Essenes – representing widely divergent religious and philosophical views.

Seder. Literally "order," the home celebration held on the first night of Passover (also the second in the Diaspora) that fulfills the biblical injunction that parents tell their children about the miraculous deliverance of their ancestors from Egypt. Five specific *mitzvot* must be observed during the seder. The two biblically ordained commandments are the eating of *matzah* (Exod. 12:18) and reading the Haggadah (Exod. 13:3), the recounting on the story of the Exodus from Egypt. The three practices instituted by the rabbis are the drinking of four cups of wine; eating *maror* (the bitter herb); and reciting *Hallel*. Other major aspects of the seder are recitation of the festival *Kiddush*; the four questions (*Mah nishtanah*); *Avadim hayinu*; the account of the four sons; *Dayenu; Korech*; the search for the *afikoman*; the exclamation of *le-shanah ha-ba-ah bi-Yerushalayim* (Next Year in Jerusalem); and the singing of Passover songs.

Seder plate. The major symbols of the seder are arranged on a ceremonial plate. These are *zero'ah* (roasted bone); *beitzah* (roasted egg); *karpas* (fresh green vegetable); *maror* (bitter herb); *charoset*; and *chazeret*.

Seer – see Prophet.

Sefer Chaim – see Book of Life.

Sefer ha-Bahir (Book of Brightness/Illumination). Influential kabbalistic work that first appeared in France in the 12th century, though it is traditionally attributed to Nehunia ben ha-Kaneh, a sage of the latter half of the 1st century C.E. A highly symbolic Hebrew commentary on the Bible, it related the mystical significance of the shapes and sounds of the Hebrew alphabet and introduced the concept of the transmigration of souls. One key innovative symbol in this work is the feminine characterization of the Shechinah.In its notion of a cosmic or spiritual tree that symbolizes the flow of Divine creative power, it presaged the concept of the sefirot. Much of the basic vocabulary of the Kabbalah can be found in this seminal work.

Sefer ha-Chinuch. Literally, "The Book of Education," a popular medieval work that enumerated the 613 commandments of the Torah (see *taryag mitzvot*) based on Maimonides' system of counting and explained them from a legal and moral perspective. Unlike other works, *Sefer ha-Chinuch* organized the commandments according to their order in the biblical text, making it convenient for those studying the weekly Torah portion.

Sefer Hasidim (Book of the Pious). Major text of the medieval German pietist movement, the Hasidei Ashkenaz.The most extensive Jewish ethical work written in the Middle Ages, it was authored by Judah ben Samuel of Regensburg (d. 1217).

Sefer ha-Yetzirah (Book of the Creation [of the world]). A Hebrew name for Genesis.

Sefer Torah (1) – see Torah scroll.

Sefer Torah (2). Minor tractate added to the Talmud that deals with the laws regarding the regulations for writing Torah scrolls.

Sefer Yetziat Mitzrayim (Book of the Exodus from Egypt). A Hebrew name for Exodus.

Sefer Yetzirah. Literally "Book of Creation/Formation," an influential work of science and philosophy that, because of the many kabbalistic commentaries written on it, became widely regarded as the first classic text of Kabbalah. It describes the origin and structure of the cosmos. Attributed to Abraham but dating to the early talmudic period, it offers two cosmologic systems, one based on the 10 primordial numbers (which it calls "*sefirot*") and the other based on the 22 letters of the Hebrew alphabet. Although initially a scientific work attempting to explain in rational terms the structure of reality, in the Middle Ages it began to be read as a mystical text, filled with profundity and enigmatic utterances.

Sefirat ha-Omer – see Omer, counting of the.

Sefirot. According to Kabbalah, the 10 emanations of God (see separate sections for each). They are (in descending order) – *Keter* (crown), *Chochmah* (wisdom), *Binah* (understanding), *Din* or *Gevurah* (judgment/power), *Chesed* (mercy/love), *Tiferet* (beauty), *Netzach* (eternity/victory), *Hod* (splendor), *Yesod* (foundation), and *Malchut* (kingdom). Developed by Jewish mystics in the late 12th and 13th centuries, first in southern France and then in Spain, and crystallized in the *Zohar*, "the doctrine of the *sefirot* provided future Jewish mystics with a common language, a shared set of symbols, an access code to the mysteries of existence, and a way of piercing the veil of illusions, of revealing the concealed."[275] The *sefirot* represent the unfolding of the Divine personality, the inner life of God. From the kabbalistic point of view, every religious observance, commandment, and mystical meditation is linked to a specific *sefirah*.

Segol – see Vowels.

Segulah. Hebrew term meaning "treasure," it is used to describe the Israelites as God's "cherished possession" (*am segulah*).

Seichel. Yiddish word meaning "common sense" or "good judgment."

Selah. Word of unknown meaning used about 70 times to conclude a verse in the Psalms. Because these hymns were often sung and accompanied by instrumental music, many scholars think that "*selah*" was an instruction that called for the singing to be momentarily stopped while the instruments played a brief musical interlude. This possibly was designed to allow the singers time to silently meditate upon the words they had sung. Some have translated *selah* as meaning "forever," "it is so," or "eternally, without interruption." The Septuagint translates *selah* into Greek as "*diapsalmos*," which either means a musical interlude or "play louder."

Seleucids. Hellenistic royal dynasty (312-164 B.C.E.), founded by the general Seleucus after the death of Alexander the Great. The Seleucids controlled a vast empire (including the Land of Israel) extending from the Mediterranean and encompassing much of Asia Minor. One of the last Seleucid rulers was Antiochus IV Epiphanes, whose attacks and decrees provoked the successful revolt of Judah Maccabee and the Hasmoneans that is celebrated as the festival of Chanukah.

Self-defense. Accepted principles in Jewish law are the defense of self (e.g., permitting the killing of a nighttime burglar) and the defense of others (see *rodef*).

However, lethal force must only be used as a last resort. If one can protect oneself or save someone being pursued by merely wounding rather than killing the aggressor, one must do this so as not to be considered guilty of murder. The duty of self-defense also translates to the entire community, when it is faced with an implacable enemy determined to harm it. In the modern age, Jewish self-defense organizations were organized when the governing authorities were incapable of (or uninterested in) protecting Jews, such as in response to the pogroms of czarist Russia, where the rulers often instigated the attacks, and among the Zionist settlers of Palestine, before the duty of self-defense was assumed by the new State of Israel. Duing the Holocaust, Jewish self-defense was manifested in the ghettos, among Jewish partisans in the forests of Eastern Europe, and even in several of the extermination camps, as witnessed by Jewish revolts in Treblinka, Sobibor, and Auschwitz-Birkenau.

Selichah (forgiveness). The 6th blessing of the weekday *Amidah*, in which the worshiper admits "willful sinfulness" but asks forgiveness from "the gracious One who pardons abundantly."

Selichot (1). Penitential prayers for the Divine forgiveness of sins. They originally were part of the liturgy for fast days, most of which commemorate tragic events. The *Selichot* were a way of acknowledging that all tragedies were Divine punishment for Israel's sins and that additional misfortune could be avoided with repentance. Today, Sephardic communities begin reciting *Selichot* at the beginning of the month of Elul and continue these prayers of forgiveness through Yom Kippur. Ashkenazim begin saying the penitential prayers on the Saturday night before Rosh Hashanah. However, if there are fewer than four days between this time and Rosh Hashanah, the prayers are begun the previous Saturday night, so that the number of days on which *Selichot* are recited varies from four to nine. The core of the *Selichot* prayers, which are recited after the *Amidah*, are the Thirteen Attributes of Mercy.

Selichot (2). Special midnight service on the Saturday night before Rosh Hashanah. If Rosh Hashanah falls on the next day, the service is pushed back to the preceding Saturday evening. The custom of holding *Selichot* services at midnight relates to the belief that this in when the Gates of Heaven are open the most widely, a time when God is most receptive to hearing our prayers.

Semachot. Literally meaning "joy," the euphemistic name for this late minor post-talmudic tractate that deals with the laws and customs related to death and mourning. It also details the formal laws regarding suicide, mandating that no rites be performed in honor of the dead (e.g., *keriah*, eulogy) provided that the surviving mourners are not aggrieved by such denials. However, the text makes an exception when the suicide occurred when the person was "of unsound mind," which was applied in most cases.

Semichah. Traditional ordination required before a rabbi can decide practical questions of Jewish law. Literally meaning "laying (of hands)," the practice derives from the Divine command to Moses to ordain Joshua by placing his hands on his successor, thus "investing him with some of his authority" (Num. 27:18-20; Deut. 34:9). According to tradition, Moses also ordained the 70 elders, who ordained their successors in a chain that remained unbroken until the Roman period. Although the term *semichah* is still used, rabbis are now ordained after graduating from a rabbinical seminary or *yeshiva*. This ordination certifies that the graduate is competent to serve as a rabbi.

Semites. According to the Bible, those peoples listed in the table of nations (Gen. 10) as the descendants of Shem, the son of Noah. They settled in the area around the Mediterranean, in Asia Minor, and in the Arabian Peninsula. Both Jews and Arabs are Semitic peoples, though the modern term "anti-Semitism" refers only to Jews. Therefore, it is technically a misnomer, not only because it does not refer to all Semitic peoples, but also because the term "Semite" today is not an ethnic classification but rather refers to a speaker of one of a family of related languages.

Semitic languages. Family of languages of largely Middle Eastern origin that includes Hebrew, Arabic, and Amharic, as well as such ancient tongues as Akkadian, Assyrian, Babylonian, Ugaritic, and Aramaic.

Sephardim. From the Hebrew word *Sepharad* (Spain), the inclusive term for Jews and their descendants from Spain, Portugal, the Mediterranean region, North Africa, and the Middle East. They are distinguished from Ashkenazim (Jews of Central and Eastern Europe and their descendants) in their customs, liturgy, language (Ladino vs. Yiddish), and cuisine. The Sephardic pronunciation of Hebrew has been adopted in the State of Israel and among all but ultra-Orthodox Jews in the United States. Sephardim currently constitute approximately 20% of Jews worldwide and about half of the Jewish population of the State of Israel.

Septuagint. Greek translation of the Hebrew Bible. Dating from the 4th or 3rd century B.C.E., the Septuagint had its origin in Alexandria, Egypt. This Greek translation was widely used among Hellenized Jews across the Greek-speaking world, who had lost their ability to read the Bible in Hebrew. The source of the name "Septuagint," which means "70" in Greek, derives from the 70 scholars asked to make independent translations of the original biblical text. According to the legend recounted in the Letter of Aristeas, all the translations were identical. However, important differences exist between the Hebrew and Greek versions of the Bible.

Seraphim. Supernatural beings, depicted in Isaiah's vision (6:2-3) as creatures with six wings (two covering their faces, two covering their legs, and two used for flying) that stood in attendance around the Divine Throne and called to one another: "Holy, holy, holy (*kadosh, kadosh, kadosh*)! The Lord of Hosts! The whole world is filled with His glory." (See also *Kedushah.*)

Sermon. In 19th-century Germany, the traditional *derash* was replaced by a new type of address of religious instruction or exhortation, which became a regular feature of the service and sought to express Jewish values and a Jewish message in a contemporary idiom. The early Reform preachers consciously modeled their sermons on those of the Protestant clergy, focusing on a single central theme that they developed in an orderly fashion, without the academic digressions characteristic of earlier periods. Today, especially in the United States, the sermon is generally as an integral part of Jewish worship, in which the rabbi conveys moral, ethical, and religious values to the congregation. In some liberal synagogues, however, the sermon has been replaced by a discussion session in which the rabbi briefly introduces a topic (often based on the weekly Torah portion) and members of the congregation then volunteer their views.

Serpent (snake). Since the beginning of biblical history, the snake has been considered the eternal enemy of human beings and a symbol of evil. According to legend, God originally made the serpent upright and vocal as the king of the beasts. However, the snake's intense jealousy toward human beings led to its downfall (Gen. R. 20:5).[276] After enticing Eve into disobeying the Divine prohibition against eating from the Tree of Knowledge of Good and Evil, the snake received the permanent punishment of having to "crawl on its belly and eat the dirt." The enmity between the snake and humans would be everlasting—"they shall strike at your head, and you shall strike at their heel" (Gen. 3:14-15).

Serpent, bronze/copper – see *Nechushtan.*

Se'udah shlishit (*shalosh seudos*). Literally "third meal," which is eaten on the Sabbath before the close of the day. The tradition of having three meals stems from the threefold repetition of the word *ha-yom* (today) in the verse, "And Moses said: Eat that (the manna) *today*, for *today* is a Sabbath unto the Lord, *today* you shall not find it in the field" (Exod. 16:25). The third meal at home is usually simple. When held in the synagogue, it is often sponsored by a member of the congregation in honor of a special event, such as a marriage or *yahrzeit*. Hasidim assemble around the table of the *Rebbe* for the third meal, sharing a morsel of food and listening to words of Torah wisdom.[277]

Se'udat havra'ah – see Meal of Consolation.

Se'udat mafseket. Last meal before the fasts of Yom Kippur and Tisha b'Av. The Talmud declared that, "Everyone who eats and drinks on the ninth (of Tishrei, the day before Yom Kippur) is considered by Scripture as if he had fasted on the ninth and the tenth" (Ber. 8b). Since the final meal must be eaten before sunset, it is not considered a holiday meal and no *Kiddush* is recited. Nevertheless, this *se'udah ha-mafseket* is considered a festive meal and the Grace after Meals begins with the recitation of *Shir ha-Ma'alot*. Following the meal, memorial candles are kindled for departed members of the family before the candles for Yom Kippur are lit.

Se'udat mitzvah. Festive meal eaten after religious ceremonies and celebrations, such as weddings, circumcisions, and bar/bat mitzvahs, or to mark the completion of a tractate of the Talmud (see *siyum*).

Seven (*sheva*). In the Bible, God rested on the Sabbath, the seventh day (Gen. 2:1-4). There were seven ritually clean animals in Noah's ark (Gen. 7:2), seven ancestors of Israel (three Patriarchs and four Matriarchs), seven cows and ears of corn in Pharaoh's dreams that were interpreted by Joseph (Gen. 41:1-7), seven species of foods indigenous to the Land of Israel, the Sabbatical (seventh) year when the land was to lay fallow (Lev. 25:2-7); and seven circuits around Jericho on the seventh day before the walls of the city came tumbling down (Josh. 6:15-16). The seven Noahide laws were deemed the basis of civilized society. In the Bible, Passover and Sukkot are seven-day holidays. There are seven wedding blessings (see *Sheva Brachot*), and among Ashkenazim it is customary for the bride to circle the groom seven times under the *chuppah* (see seven circuits, below). The seven-day period of intense mourning after a funeral is termed *shiva* (lit., "seven").

Seven Blessings – see *Sheva brachot*.

Seven circuits (wedding). Among Ashkenazim, it is customary for the bride to be led in seven circuits around the groom, based on the phrase, "A woman shall go around [encompass] a man" (Jer. 31:21). In medieval times, this practice was thought to produce a magic circle of protection to keep evil spirits away from the groom. Some believe that the origin of this tradition was the custom of defining and securing ownership of property by walking around it.[278] The number of circuits comes from the number of times in the Torah where it is written, "And when a man takes a wife..."[279] In some communities the bride makes only three circuits around the groom, based on the verses in Hosea (2:21-22) in which God (the groom) speaks to Israel (the bride) using the word "betroth" three times. Some liberal couples have abandoned this custom, believing it could be interpreted as the bride subordinating herself to the groom.

Seven species. Agricultural produce listed by the Torah (Deut. 8:8) as symbolizing the fertility of the Land of Israel – wheat, barley, grapes, figs, pomegranates, olive oil, and date honey. (See discussions in individual sections.)

17th of Tammuz. Minor fast day commemorating the breaching of the walls of Jerusalem by the Romans (70 C.E.), which occurred three weeks before the destruction of the Second Temple on Tisha b'Av.The Jerusalem Talmud maintains that the breaching of the walls of Jerusalem by the Babylonians (586 B.C.E.) also occurred on this date, though the Babylonian Talmud accepts the citation of Jeremiah (52:6-7) that this event took place on the 9th of the month. According to the Mishnah, other catastrophes that occurred on the 17th of Tammuz include the breaking of the First Tablets by Moses in response to the incident of the Golden Calf; the cessation of the daily sacrifices in the First Temple; and the burning of a Torah scroll and the erection of an idol in the Temple by the heathen Apostomos, about whom nothing is known.[280]

Seventh day – see Sabbath.

Seventy (*shivim*). A common round number in the Bible. Terach was 70 years old when he sired Abraham (Gen. 11:26), and there were 70 members of Jacob's family who went down to Egypt to join Joseph (Exod. 1:5). The 70 elders that Moses appointed to assist him in leading the Israelites through the wilderness (Exod. 24:9), with Moses at their head, became the prototype of the Great Sanhedrin.There are 70 holy days celebrated in the Jewish year – 52 Sabbaths (according to the solar calendar), seven days of Passover, seven days of Sukkot; and one day each of Shavuot, Rosh Hashanah, Yom Kippur, and Shemini Atzeret.[281] Seventy years is described as "the span of our life" (Ps. 90:10).

Sevivon. Literally a "spinning top," the modern Hebrew word for a dreidel.

Sexual intercourse. According to Jewish law, sexual relations should take place only within marriage. Premarital sex, adultery, and male and female homosexuality are forbidden. Unlike the Christians of the rabbinic era, who regarded celibacy as the ideal and marriage as merely a concession to humankind's weak and libidinous nature, the Rabbis championed marriage, including its sexual aspects, as the essential human relationship. They counseled that, like all aspects of human behavior, the sex drive must be expressed with moderation and self-control. The kabbalists taught that just as the masculine and feminine aspects of God achieve union on the Sabbath, so conjugal relations between husband and wife are doubly blessed on that day. Sexual desire, when properly channeled in a marital relationship, is a powerful positive force, rather than an emotion that is inherently shameful or evil. Men have a duty to procreate. A man is prohibited from having sexual relations with his wife during her menstrual period and for an additional seven days. Before sexual relations are resumed, the wife is required to bathe in the *mikveh*.Refusal of either party to engage in sexual relations is grounds for divorce.

Sha'atnez. Literally meaning "mixture," this Hebrew term refers specifically to a fabric made of a mixture of wool and linen (flax). This is explicitly forbidden in the Torah (Lev. 19:19; Deut. 22:11) as part of the biblical prohibition against various types of mixtures that were viewed as contrary to the Divinely appointed order of nature. The Rabbis ruled that the law of *sha'atnez* refers only to the weaving together of these two specific animal and vegetable fibers in the same garment. Thus, a linen tie worn with a wool suit is permitted, but a wool suit with linen-threaded buttons is prohibited. The combination of wool and linen may be mixed with cotton, silk, and other fibers in the manufacture of products other than clothing.[282] In accordance with the general principle that a positive commandment overrides a negative one, it is permitted to attach woolen *tzizit* (fringes) to a linen garment. When buying clothes, traditional Jews first check the fabric list to exclude garments with *sha'atnez*. If the label suggests that the garment may be permitted, it can be taken for testing at a special *sha'atnez* laboratory, which can be found in most cities with a substantial Orthodox community.

Shabbat (Shab.) The 1st tractate in Mo'ed (festivals) in the Mishnah, it deals with the rules governing the observance of the Sabbath, including the 39 categories of prohibited work.

Shabbat ha-Chodesh (Sabbath of the Month). The Sabbath that falls on or precedes the 1st of Nisan, the month of Passover. The additional reading from a second scroll (Exod. 12:1–20) notes that the month of Nisan "shall mark for you the beginning of the months [of the Jewish year]," describes the sacrifice of the paschal lamb on the first Passover in Egypt, and details many of the rules and preparations required for the yearly celebration of the festival.

Shabbat ha-Gadol (Great Sabbath). The Sabbath that occurs prior to the week when Passover will be observed. Its title reflects the immense historical and religious significance of the upcoming festival. Although there is no additional Torah portion, the special *haftarah* (Mal. 3:4-24) ends with the announcement that God will send Elijah the Prophet as the herald of the Messianic Age. This reference to the promise of ultimate redemption is most appropriate to the upcoming festival of Passover, which celebrates the historical redemption of the Jewish people from slavery in Egypt.

Shabbat Hazon (Sabbath of the Vision). The Sabbath that immediately precedes Tisha b'Av.The name derives from the initial word of the *haftarah* (the last of the three "*haftarot* of rebuke"), in which Isaiah prophesies the terrible afflictions that

God will visit upon the Israelites as punishment for their sins (1:1–27). Shabbat Hazon occurs during the period of mourning (see Nine Days) for the destruction of the Temples, which is commemorated on Tisha b'Av.

Shabbat Machar Chodesh. When a Sabbath occurs the day before the New Moon, a special *haftarah* (1 Sam. 20:18-42) is read that contains the phrase *machar chodesh* (tomorrow will be the New Moon). The blessing for the New Moon is also recited on that day.

Shabbat Nachamu (Sabbath of Comfort). The Sabbath that immediately follows Tisha b'Av. The name derives from the first word of the *haftarah* (Isa. 40:1), which is the first of the seven "*haftarot* of consolation" leading up to the observance of Rosh Hashanah. These selections prophesy the redemption of Israel, the ingathering of the exiles and the restoration of the Jewish people to their Land, the rebuilding of the Temple, and the coming of the Messianic Age of peace and justice.

Shabbat Parah (Sabbath of the Red Heifer). The Sabbath that immediately precedes Shabbat ha-Chodesh.The additional reading from a second scroll (Num. 19:1–22) describes the ritual purification with the ashes of the red heifer, which was required in Temple times for all those who had been defiled by contact with a corpse. Originally, this was a call for all those planning to participate in the Passover pilgrimage to Jerusalem to ritually cleanse themselves. Today, it reminds Jews to begin the extensive cleansing of *chametz* from their homes, which must be accomplished before the celebration of Passover.

Shabbat Rosh Chodesh (Sabbath of the New Month). When the New Moon falls on the Sabbath, the special *haftarah* (Isa. 66:1-24) ends with the verse, "And New Moon after New Moon, and Sabbath after Sabbath, all flesh shall come to worship Me, said the Lord" – the anticipation of the gathering of the Jewish exiles in the Land of Israel in the Messianic Age, when they and all humanity will join in worshiping the One God. The *maftir* portion (Num. 2:9-15) is read from a second Torah scroll

Shabbat shalom. Literally "[may you have a] Sabbath of peace," the Hebrew greeting among Jews on the Sabbath.

Shabbat Shekalim.(Sabbath of Shekels). The Sabbath that falls on or immediately preceding the 1st of Adar, the month of Purim.[283] The additional reading from a second scroll (Exod. 30:11–16) recounts the commandment to donate a half-*shekel* toward the upkeep of the Temple. On the 1st of Adar in ancient days, messengers were sent out to all Jewish communities to collect these donations.

Shabbat Shirah (Sabbath of Song). The Sabbath when the Torah reading includes *Shirat ha-Yam* (The Song at the Sea; Exod. 15:1-18), the prayer of thanksgiving chanted by the Israelites after safely crossing the Sea of Reeds during the Exodus from Egypt. The *haftarah* on Shabbat Shirah contains another triumphal hymn, the *Song of Deborah* (Judg. 5:1-31). The Torah portion for Shabbat Shirah also includes the story of the manna, which sustained the Israelites during their wanderings in the wilderness. According to legend, some ungrateful individuals rebelled against the authority of Moses by violating his command not to gather manna on the Sabbath. They took half of the double portion from Friday and spread it on the ground early on Saturday morning, planning to gather it and thus prove Moses a false prophet. However, the birds immediately swooped down from the skies and cleared the fields, so that not a trace of manna was left. To demonstrate our eternal appreciation for their prompt action, it is a custom among traditional Jews on Shabbat Shirah to feed the birds.[284]

Shabbat Shuvah (Sabbath of Repentance). The Sabbath that occurs during the Ten Days of Repentance between Rosh Hashanah and Yom Kippur. The name derives from the initial word of the *haftarah*, "Return (*shuvah*) [O Israel, unto the Lord your God]" (Hosea 14:2).

Shabbat Zachor (Sabbath of Remembrance). The Sabbath that immediately precedes the festival of Purim. Its name derives from the additional Torah reading from a second scroll (Deut. 25:17-19) that commands the Israelites "to remember" Amalek, the tribe that perpetrated a cowardly and unprovoked attack upon weary stragglers at the rear of the Israelite column as they wandered in the wilderness soon after the Exodus from Egypt. The recitation of the Divine commandment to "blot out the remembrance of Amalek from under heaven. Do not forget" is most appropriate at this time since, according to *Megillat Esther,* the arch-villain Haman was a direct descendant of Agag, the king of the Amalekites.

Shabbaton. Special Sabbath program for learning and socializing, usually sponsored by a synagogue or youth group.

Shabbos. Yiddish pronunciation of the Hebrew word *Shabbat*.

Shabbos goy. A non-Jew hired by an observant family to perform certain activities forbidden to Jews on the Sabbath, such as starting a fire and turning lights on and off. Today the proliferation of electronic timers has virtually eliminated the need for the *Shabbos goy*, who once played an important role, especially in the *shtetls* of Eastern Europe.

Shacharit. Literally "little morning," the term for the prayers said each morning at home or in the synagogue. It consists of the following elements (see separate entries): *Birkot ha-Shachar* (see morning blessings); *Pesukei de-Zimra* (verses of praise); *Shema* (with two blessings before and one after); *Amidah*; *Tachanun* (not on Sabbath, festivals, fast days, and other occasions); Torah reading (only on Monday, Thursday, Sabbath and festivals, and Rosh Chodesh); *haftarah* (only on Sabbath and festivals); *Musaf* (only on Sabbath, festivals, and Rosh Chodesh); *Aleinu*; *Mourner's Kaddish*; and a closing hymn. The Talmud attributes the institution of the *Shacharit* prayer to Abraham (Ber. 26b), based on the verse that he "rose up early in the morning and hurried to the place where he had stood [in the presence of the Lord]" (Gen. 19:27).

Shadchan. A professional matchmaker who, in exchange for a percentage of the dowry (typically 2-3%), would arrange marriages by taking into consideration not only the scholarship and piety of the groom and the compatibility of the couple, but also the financial status, suitability, and *yichus* (lineage) of their families. This was originally a highly esteemed profession, with Jewish tradition describing the activity as performing "God's work." However, by the end of the 16th century, the attitude toward matchmakers began to shift. No longer deemed a paragon of integrity, the *shadchan* at times became an object of derision, viewed as a miserly opportunist who misrepresented potential suitors. Indeed, some *shadchanim* became notorious for being able to glibly play down or divert attention away from any flaws, physical or otherwise, of the potential spouse. Today, numerous individuals and many Jewish organizations offer matchmaking services, some with computerized databases. In traditional circles, it is still considered completely acceptable for young people to meet their mates with the help of a third party. In ultra-Orthodox communities, marriages are often arranged.[285]

Shaddai (Almighty). One of the biblical names of God. The Hebrew word *Shaddai* – *shin, dalet, yud* – is written on the back of the parchment that is inserted into the case of a *mezuzah*, in such a way that the word can be seen through a small opening near the top of the container. According to the *Zohar*, this Divine Name is used in the *mezuzah* because its three Hebrew letters are an acronym for *Shomer d'latot Yisrael* (Guardian of the doors of Israel). The kabbalists added the practice of representing the word *Shaddai* on both *tefillin*. The first letter (*shin*) is inscribed on the head *tefillin* as well as woven with the arm straps through the fingers of the hand. This letter is written on two sides of the *tefillin* of the head – one in the usual way with three strokes, and the other with four decorative prongs. Some explanations for this practice include that the *shin* symbolizes the three Patriarchs (Abraham, Isaac, and Jacob) and the four Matriarchs (Sarah, Rebecca, Rachel, and Leah), and that the total number of prongs (seven) equals the windings of the arm strap.[286] The second letter (*dalet*) is represented by the knot at the back of the head strap and is woven on the hand; the third letter (*yud*) is indicated by the end of the head strap and the knot near the *tefillin* of the arm.[287]

Shalachmanos. Yiddish pronunciation of the Hebrew *shalach manot*, the custom of *mishlo'ach manot* (sending gifts [on Purim]).

Shaliach. Israeli citizen sent by the government for several years to live in the United States or other country to inform American Jews about Israeli life and enlist support for Israel, as well as to encourage and facilitate *aliyah*. (For the use of the term *shlichim* as emissaries of Judaism sent throughout the globe by the Chabad and Mizrachi movements, see *shaliach*.)

Shaliach l'dvar mitzvah. Literally "agent for a *mitzvah*," this Hebrew term refers to one custom designed to protect travelers. A small sum of money is given to those setting out on a journey, who become responsible for carrying out the *mitzvah* of delivering funds to a charity upon arriving at their destination. As the Talmud promises: "Those sent to perform a *mitzvah* are not harmed on their way to do a *mitzvah* nor on their return" (Pes. 8b).[288]

Shaliach tzibbur. Literally "emissary of the congregation," the Hebrew term for the person leading the communal worship. The prayer leader does not have to be a professional cantor (see *hazzan*) or an ordained rabbi; any adult male (or female, in Reform, Reconstructionist, and most Conservative congregations) may assume this role. The Talmud stresses that the *shaliach tzibbur* is not an intermediary between the congregation and God, but simply an agent who recites the prayers on behalf of the worshipers (Ber. 5:5).[289]

Shalom. One of the most beloved and recognized words in the Hebrew language, it has a multitude of meanings in addition to the well known "hello," "good-bye," and "peace." There are several variants of "shalom" in the Bible, all of which describe a positive state of affairs, such as safety, prosperity, and well-being. Indeed, the word "shalom" derives from *shalem*, which means "whole or complete" and is connected to the word for perfection (*sh'leimut*). Virtually every major blessing or prayer in the liturgy – *Amidah*, *Kaddish*, Priestly Blessing, Grace after Meals – concludes with a prayer for peace.

Shalom Aleichem (Peace be upon you). The most famous of the Sabbath table hymns (see *zemirot*), it is traditionally sung as the family gathers around the table on Friday night to welcome the "angels of peace." This hymn, sung only among Ashkenazim and believed to have been written in the 17th century, was inspired by a talmudic legend (Shab. 119b). "Two ministering angels – one good, one evil – accompany every Jew from the synagogue to his home on the Sabbath eve. If they find the candles burning, the table set, and the bed covered with a spread, the good angel exclaims, 'May it be God's will that it also be so on the next Sabbath,' and the evil angel is compelled to respond 'amen.' But if everything is disorderly and gloomy, the evil angel exclaims, 'May it be God's will that it also be so on the next Sabbath,' and the good angel is forced to say 'amen'." After extending wishes for peace to the ministering angels "of the Most Exalted, the Supreme King of kings, the Holy One, blessed be He," in the final three verses Jews successively pray: "May your coming be in peace," "Bless me with peace," and "May your departure be in peace."

Shalom bayit. Literally "peace in the home," this Hebrew term refers to the domestic harmony between husband and wife that is the cornerstone on which the Jewish home is built and necessary for it to be blessed by the Divine Presence.

Shalom zachar. Literally "peace to the male child," this Hebrew term refers to the joyous celebration on the first Friday evening after the birth of a boy. Guests visit the new baby's home to join the family in prayer, a festive meal, and a discussion of words of Torah.[290] According to the Talmud, the ceremony of *shalom zachar* developed during the Roman Empire, when Jews were forbidden to circumcise their sons. A feast was held shortly after the child's birth in an attempt to convince the Romans that no circumcision was to follow on the eighth day.

Shalosh regalim –see Pilgrimage festivals.

Shalshelet (chain). Rare cantillation mark, appearing in the form of a chain above a word, that waves up and down the musical scale. It is found three times in the Book of Genesis at critical points in the narrative, denoting a clash of deep emotions provoking anguished hesitation and anxiety. The first *shalshelet* appears when Lot hesitates to leave the sinful city of Sodom when it was about to be destroyed (19:16). The second occurs when Abraham commissions his servant Eliezer to choose a suitable wife for Isaac (24:12). The third usage is when Joseph is tempted by the enticements of the wife of Potiphar, but refuses to commit an immoral act.

Shamash (1). Literally "servant," the ninth candle on the *chanukiah* (Chanukah menorah). It is placed higher or to one side to differentiate it from the other candles. The *shamash* is not counted as one of the eight primary lights; its only role is to kindle the other candles. The light of the *shamash* can also provide illumination for reading, thus preventing any accidental use of the light of the eight primary candles that may not be used for practical purposes.

Shamash (2). Term used extensively in the Middle Ages for the caretaker or sexton of a synagogue, who summoned worshipers to prayer and served as the "community crier" for other events.

Shame. According to the Rabbis, "A person who publicly shames [lit., 'makes pale'] his neighbor is like someone who has shed blood [and has no share in the World to Come]...It would be better for a man to throw himself into a fiery furnace than publicly put his neighbor to shame!" (BM 58b-59a). When combined with bodily injury, the humiliation of the victim is considered as an additional factor in determining the extent of compensatory damages.

Shamir. A legendary worm that could split large stones by crawling on them. It replaced conventional tools in the construction of the Temple, for which no sword or iron (symbols of violence) could be used. Moses used it to engrave the names of the 12 tribes on the breastplace of the High Priest. The *shamir* was one of the 10 miraculous things fashioned at twilight on the sixth day of Creation (Avot 5:9).

Shammai. Talmudic scholar (c. 50 B.C.E.–30 C.E.) and founder of a school named after him, he was a contemporary and rival of Hillel.The School of Shammai favored a strict and conservative legal analysis, as opposed to the more lenient and liberal interpretations of the School of Hillel. Shammai served as *av beit din* (vice president) of the Sanhedrin, joining Hillel as the last of the pairs (see *zugot*) of scholars whose teachings formed the basis of the Mishnah. The rabbis considered his disputes with Hillel (and later controversies between their two schools) as arguments "for the sake of Heaven" (Avot 5:20), whose sole purpose was to determine the truth.

Shammes – see *Shamash* (above).

Shanah tovah (good year). Shortened form of *le-shanah tovah tikateivu*, the greeting for Rosh Hashanah.

Shanda. Yiddish word meaning "scandal" or "shame."

Shas (1). Abbreviation for *shisha sidrei* (six orders) of the Mishnah.The term came to designate the Talmud as a whole.

Shas (2). Ultra-Orthodox political party in Israel, also known as "Sephardic Torah Guardians," that is mainly associated with the country's Sephardic community. Since its founding in 1984, Shas has been represented in several coalition governments.

Shaving. According to biblical law, it is forbidden to shave the "corners" of the beard (Lev. 19:27), lest one imitate the practice of idolaters at that time. The Rabbis described five corners of the beard (both upper jaws, both lower jaws, and the peak of the beard), but since the precise areas were not sharply defined, the general practice was not to shave the entire beard.[291] Nevertheless, shaving the beard is halachically permitted if one uses scissors, a chemical depilatory, or an electric shaver with two cutting edges. Only instruments with a single cutting edge are forbidden. Today, some strictly observant Jews do not shave their beards as a sign of their devotion to tradition. Many more Jews do not shave or cut their beards during the *Sefirah* period of counting the Omer and for the three weeks preceding Tisha b'Av, but do trim their beards and have their hair cut before Sabbaths and the festivals.

Shavuah tov. Literally "good week" in Hebrew, the traditional greeting after the *Havdalah* ceremony at the conclusion of the Sabbath.

Shavuot. The second of the pilgrimage festivals, it occurs on the 6th of Sivan (plus the 7th in the Diaspora). Literally meaning "weeks," which reflects the seven weeks of the counting of the Omer that separate it from Passover, Shavuot is sometimes translated into English as "Pentecost" (the 50th day). Coming at the end of the barley harvest, one biblical name for Shavuot is *Chag ha-Katzir* (Harvest Festival). The festival is also known as *Yom ha-Bikurim* (Day of the First Fruits). A remarkable transformation of the festival took place in rabbinic times, when Shavuot became observed as the anniversary of the giving of the Torah on Mount Sinai and was referred to in the liturgy as *Zeman Mattan Torateinu* (the Time of the Giving of our Torah). The Ten Commandments are read in synagogue, as is the Book of Ruth; in Ashkenazic synagogues, *Akdamut* is added. Under the influence of the kabbalists, it became customary to observe an all-night vigil (*Tikun Leil Shavuot*) on the eve of the festival. Dairy foods are traditionally eaten during Shavuot because of the legend that, when the Israelites received the laws of *kashrut* at Sinai, they understood that their pots were not kosher and thus resolved to eat uncooked dairy foods until they could get new ones. A popular Shavuot dish among Ashkenazim is *blintzes*. A modern custom is the ceremony of Confirmation in many Reform and Conservative synagogues.

Shaygetz. Derogatory Yiddish term for a gentile male (masculine equivalent of *shiksa*). It derives from the Hebrew root *sheketz*, used in the Torah to refer to an unclean, non-kosher animal as an "abomination."

Shayna punim. Literally "pretty face," an endearing Yiddish expression.

Shayner Yid. Literally "beautiful Jew," a Yiddish term for a Jew of upright character and learning who is held in high esteem by fellow Jews.

Shechem. Ancient Canaanite and Israelite city situated between Mt. Ebal and Mt. Gerizim in a fertile and well-watered valley in the heart of the central hill country of the Land of Israel. Situated just east of modern Nablus, Shechem is first mentioned in connection with Abraham's arrival in Canaan as the site where the Patriarch built an altar (Gen. 12:6-7). In his wanderings, Jacob returned to Shechem where he bought land, but his sons Shimon and Levi destroyed the city following the rape of their sister Dinah (Gen. 34). Joseph was later buried there in the plot of land purchased by Jacob.

Shechinah. Translated as "Divine Presence," one of the rabbinic names for God. *Shechinah* is often depicted as the feminine aspect of God and is a name for the tenth of the *sefirot*. The Kabbalists conceived of the Sabbath as representing a wedding of the *Shechinah* and *Tiferet* (see *Malchut*), whose union brings heavenly bliss to the Jewish people. The Rabbis taught that in the World to Come, "the righteous will sit and enjoy the splendor of the *Shechinah*" (Ber. 17a).

Shechitah. Hebrew term for Kosher slaughtering, which is performed by a specially trained *shochet*. Jewish ritual slaughtering strives to prevent unnecessary suffering to the animal. It requires one continuous deep horizontal cut with a perfectly sharp blade with no nicks or unevenness. This severs the windpipe and all of the great blood vessels of the neck so that the animal instantly loses all sensation. Because an animal may not be eaten if it has not been properly slaughtered, the technical requirements must be strictly observed.

Sheep. Important domestic animals in ancient Israel, they provided meat, milk, wool, and hides for shoes and clothing. Sheep were often used as sacrifices in the Temple, giving rise to the expression "sheep [or lamb] for the slaughter." This phrase describing innocent animals being led to their deaths became metaphorically applied to the martyrdom of Jews from biblical times to the Holocaust. The curved horn of the ram, the male sheep, was the classic *shofar*. The shepherd tending his flock is a popular biblical metaphor for God caring for the Jewish people. Before the tenth plague, God commanded the Israelites to sacrifice a lamb and smear its blood on their door posts (Exod. 12:6-13) as a sign for the Angel of Death to pass over their houses when smiting the first born of Egypt. Since the destruction of the Temple, the ritual of sacrificing the paschal lamb has been symbolized by the roasted shankbone on the Passover seder plate.

Shehecheyanu. One of the best-known blessings, it thanks God for having "kept us in life, sustained us, and permitted us to reach this time." It is recited at the candle lighting and *Kiddush* ceremonies on Jewish holidays; before reading the *Megillah* on Purim; on first hearing the *shofar* on Rosh Hashanah; and when initially taking the *lulav* and *etrog* on Sukkot. The *Shehecheyanu* prayer is also said whenever one does something "new" in a given year, such as eating a fruit for the first time in the season, moving into a new house, acquiring new clothes or household effects, or having a reunion with a dear friend whom one has not seen for some time.

Sheilaism. Selective observance of religion as defined by what is acceptable to the believer, not the dictates of the authorized expositors of the faith. The term was coined by Robert Bellah and coauthors in their book *Habits of the Heart*, based on one of their interviewees named Sheila, who met her own private spiritual needs by inventing her own religion with a participant of one - herself.

Sheimot. Literally "names," this Hebrew term refers to sacred books containing the Divine Name that can no longer be used. They are stored in the synagogue (see *genizah*) and then removed periodically and reverently buried in the cemetery. The term "*sheimot*" is also used for pages or portions of books containing the Name of God that cannot be discarded and must be buried.

Sheitel. Yiddish word for a wig, which is often worn by Orthodox women after marriage. This custom among Eastern European Ashkenazim, dating back to the 18th century, is in keeping with the Jewish tradition forbidding a woman from leaving her hair uncovered in the sight of a man who is not her husband. Some Orthodox women choose to cover their hair with a hat or scarf.

Shekalim (Shek.). The 4th tractate in Mo'ed (festivals) in the Mishnah, it deals with the half-*shekel* tax that was used to maintain the worship services during the Second Temple period. The symbolic "ceremony of the half-*shekel*" takes place in traditional synagogues before the reading of the *Megillah* (scroll of Esther) on the eve of Purim.

Shekel. Biblical unit of weight for measuring silver. It derived from an ancient Babylonian unit of weight equal to about 2/3 of an ounce. The idea of the *shekel* was revived by the modern Zionist movement, which gave the term to the annual contribution allowing participation in elections. The *shekel* is now the basic unit of currency in Israel.

Sheket. Literally "be quiet," this Hebrew word is often used in the phrase *sheket b'vakashah* (Quiet, please!)

Shelach Lecha. The 4th *parashah* in the Book of Numbers (13:1-15:41), it narrates the episode of the 12 Israelite chieftains send to spy out the Land of Canaan. Ten brought back an "evil report" that led to the Israelites being condemned to wander 40 years in the wilderness, where everyone over age 20 (other than Joshua and Caleb) would die. The new generation would be free of the slave mentality of their parents and be ready to summon the strength and courage to fight for the Promised Land. This *parashah* includes the case of the man who gathered wood in violation of the Sabbath and was executed by stoning, and the commandment to wear *tzitzit*.

Sheloshim. Literally "30," the period of mourning after the death of close relatives (parents, child, brother, sister, husband, wife), counted from the time of the burial. This period may reflect the 30 days of mourning observed by the Israelites in the wilderness after the deaths of Aaron (Num. 20:29) and Moses (Deut. 34:8). During this time of modified mourning, the bereaved begins to return to normal life and may resume work. Mourners may sit on regular chairs; mirrors are uncovered; and the prohibitions against wearing leather shoes, studying Torah, and engaging in sexual intercourse are lifted. Services are no longer held in the home, and mourners go to the regular synagogue *minyan* to say *Kaddish*.[292] For all but parents – who are mourned for 11 months – *sheloshim* constitutes the entire period of mourning.

Shema. Declaration of faith of the Jewish people in the Unity and Oneness of God and their acceptance of the yoke of the Kingdom of Heaven (*Shema Yisrael, Adonai Eloheinu, Adonai Echad*; Hear, O Israel: the Lord is our God, the Lord is One; Deut. 6:4). When this first verse of the *Shema* is recited in the synagogue, it has been customary from rabbinic times to silently recite the Temple response: "Praised is the Name ..." (see *baruch shem k'vod*). The term *Shema* also refers to the prayer composed of three biblical passages – *Ve-ahavta* (Deut. 6:5-9); a second paragraph (Deut. 11:13-21) emphasizing the study of Torah and the observance of the *mitzvot*, indicating some of the rewards for following the teachings of the Torah and the punishments for disobedience; and a third paragraph (Num. 15:37-41) that is primarily concerned with the commandment of wearing *tzitzit* (fringes). The *Shema* is recited twice daily, in the morning and evening, and it is also said when the Torah scroll(s) is removed from the ark, as part of the *Musaf Kedushah*, and at the closing service on Yom Kippur (see *Ne'ilah*). It is said as a bedtime prayer and before death.

Shemini. The 3rd *parashah* in the Book of Leviticus (9:1-11:47), it describes the first formal sacrifice in the Tabernacle, the deaths of Nadab and Abihu (two of the sons of Aaron) for offering "alien fire" before the Lord, and issues of ritual impurity. Much of this section (chapter 11) details the laws of *kashrut*.

Shemini Atzeret. Literally "Eighth Day of Assembly," it is often considered as the eighth day of Sukkot but is actually an independent festival in certain respects. Shemini Atzeret marks the conclusion of the festivities and observances of Sukkot – though none of the Sukkot ceremonies apply to it – and as such it was selected as the day for the recitation of *Yizkor*, the memorial service that is said by Ashkenazim on the final day of all three pilgrimage festivals. The Book of Ecclesiastes is read before the Torah reading, and the prayer for rain is recited. In Israel, the observances of Shemini Atzeret and Simchat Torah are combined, as they are in Reform synagogues.

Shemitah – see Sabbatical Year.

Shemoneh Esrei – see *Amidah*.

Shemot (1) – see Exodus.

Shemot (2). 1st *parashah* in the Book of Exodus (1:1-6:1), it opens with the Israelites enslaved under a new king "who did not know Joseph" and proceeds to describe the bravery of the midwives in subverting Pharaoh's plot to drown all the male Hebrew infants in the Nile; the birth and youth of Moses and his slaying the Egyptian taskmaster beating an Israelite; and the flight of Moses to the land of Midian, where he marries Zipporah, the daughter of Jethro (a local priest), encounters God at the Burning Bush, hears the holy Name of God, and receives the Divine command to be the agent to lead the people out of bondage into a "land flowing with milk and honey."

She'ol. The dwelling place of the dead according to the Bible. In this gloomy Hades-like world, an abode of worms and decay (Job 17:13-16), the dead live an ethereal, shadowy existence (Num. 16:33; Ps. 6:6; Isa. 38:18). When Jacob heard that his favorite son Joseph had been torn to pieces by a wild beast, he moaned that he "would go down in grief to his son in *She'ol*" (Gen. 37:35).

Shep nachas. Yiddish for taking pride in the accomplishments of loved ones.

Sheva Brachot. Literally "seven blessings," the seven benedictions recited at the wedding ceremony under the *chuppah* after the bridegroom places the ring on the finger of his bride. The first is said over a second cup of wine, from which the bride and groom drink. The shared cup of wine is symbolic of holiness, joy, and union. The other blessings praise God for Creation (particularly of human beings), invite Jerusalem (Zion) to rejoice as her children marry, and speak of the joy and happiness of the groom and bride.[293] In traditional communities, the wedding celebrations continue for an entire week. The *Sheva Brachot* are recited as part of the *Birkat ha-Mazon* after each meal where there is a *minyan* and a new guest present, as a way of extending the joyous festivities associated with the wedding.

Shevach. Literally "praise of God," the collective term for the three introductory blessings in the *Amidah* – *avot* (forefathers); *gevurot* (powers); and *kedushat ha-Shem* (holiness of the Name [of God]). During the reader's repetition of the *Amidah*, the short third blessing is replaced by the *Kedushah*.

Shevarim. One of the three sounds of the *shofar*, it is a series of three short broken notes that resemble a sobbing sound, in recognition of the sins we have committed.

Shevat. The 11th month of the Hebrew calendar (January/February). The holiday of Tu b'Shevat occurs on the 15th day of the month.

Shevat, 15th of – see Tu b'Shevat.

Shevi'it. The 5th tractate in Zera'im (seeds) in the Mishnah, it deals with the laws of the Sabbatical Year, including the release from debts and the rabbinic institution of the *prosbul*.

Shevu'at bittui. The prohibited uttering of a vain oath by which one swears to do or not do something that Judaism neither requires nor prohibits. Thus, it is forbidden to take an oath declaring that one will eat or not eat a specific food, or that one will go or not go to a given place.

Shevu'at shav. Two types of vain oaths prohibited by the third of the Ten Commandments (Exod. 20:7; Deut. 5:11). These are swearing to an obvious, self-evident fact, such as that a stone object is stone; and swearing that an existing object is what it obviously is not, such as that "a pillar of stone is of gold" or "a man is a woman." Other examples include swearing that something impossible exists (a camel that flies) and swearing to violate a Torah commandment, such as not to read the *Shema*, build a sukkah, or wear *tefillin*.

Shevu'ot (Shev.). The 6th tractate of Nezikin (damages) in the Mishnah, it deals with different types of oaths.

Shibboleth (test word). After mutual recriminations with the Ephraimites, Jephthah the judge used this word as a test to determine the nationality of every fugitive attempting to cross the Jordan River. Those 42,000 who betrayed their Ephraimite origin by saying "*sibboleth*"(thus omitting the "h") were put to death (Judg. 12).

Shidduch. Hebrew word that originally referred to an arranged marriage, traditionally by a *shadchan*.It now is a more general term for a good match.

Shield of David – see Magen David.

Shikker. Yiddish term for a drunk. The one time that being *shikker* is permitted is on Purim, when a rabbinic sage maintained that a person should get so tipsy that he "cannot tell the difference between 'Blessed is Mordecai' and 'Cursed is Haman'" (Meg. 7b). (See *ad lo yada*.)

Shiksa. Often-derogatory Yiddish word for a gentile female (the feminine equivalent of *shaygetz*).

Shikun. From a biblical root meaning "to dwell" and related to the *Mishkan* (Tabernacle) in which God "dwelled" among the Israelites, in modern Hebrew the word refers to a housing project (historically one that was quickly constructed) or residence in Israel. The related word *shechunah* means "neighborhood."

Shiloh. Capital of Israel during the time of the judges, situated north of Beit El in the mountains of the territory of Ephraim. After the conquest of Canaan under Joshua, the Tabernacle was erected at Shiloh (Josh. 18:1), which became the major religious center of the Israelites prior to the conquest of Jerusalem. Here Joshua distributed territorial allotments to the tribes who had not previously received them (Josh. 18:2-10), and Israel assembled in Shiloh to settle its dispute with the tribes beyond the Jordan (Josh. 22:9, 12). As the center of Israelite worship, it was in Shiloh that Hannah vowed that her child Samuel would serve the Lord in the Sanctuary (1 Sam. 1-2).

Shin. The 21st letter of the Hebrew alphabet, with a numerical value of 300.

Shir ha-Kavod (Song of Glory) – see *An'im Zemirot*.

Shir ha-Ma'alo*t* (Song of Ascents). The 15 psalms (120-134) that were chanted by pilgrims as they went up to Jerusalem for the festival celebrations in the Temple. They were also chanted by the Levites in the Temple on Sukkot, during the joyous water-drawing ceremony.[294] During the 16th century, the custom developed of chanting Psalm 126, popularly known as *Shir ha-Ma'alot*, in the home before the Grace after Meals on Sabbaths and festivals. It prophetically describes the return to Zion from Babylonian Exile and contains the famous line, "those who sow with tears will reap with joy." When sung on the Sabbath, it relates to the tradition that on this day one experiences a foretaste of the redemption and the World to Come.

Shir ha-Shirim – see Song of Songs.

Shirat ha-Yam (Song at the Sea). Victory hymn using powerful poetic metaphors and celebrating the mighty acts of God, which Moses and the Israelites sang after crossing the Sea of Reeds to escape the pursuing Egyptians (Exod. 15:1-18). Along with the *Song of Deborah*, *Shirat ha-Yam* is one of the oldest extended poems in the Hebrew Bible. It is also known as *Az Yashir* (Then sang [Moses]), the first two words of the song. During Temple days, *Shirat ha-Yam* was sung by the Levites on Sabbath afternoon, in conjunction with the *Mincha* offering. After the destruction of the Temple, when communities in the Land of Israel wanted to perpetuate as much of the Temple worship as possible, the recitation of the song was incorporated into the daily *Pesukei de-Zimra*. This practice later spread throughout the Jewish world, and *Shirat ha-Yam* is now said immediately after the six basic psalms and just before the concluding blessing, *Yishtabach*.[295]

Shisha sidrei mishnah. Hebrew term for the six orders of the Mishnah, abbreviated *shas*.

Shi'ur Komah. Literally, "measurement of height," this early kabbalistic text describes in anthropomorphic terms the immense dimensions of the "body" of God. It was written as a commentary to a chapter in the Song of Songs, which R.

Akiva argued was a metaphor for the love between God and Israel. Just as the woman in the biblical book describes the body of her beloved, the depiction in *Shi'ur Komah* must be viewed as a description of the body of God with precise measurements (given in Persian parsangs) of each Divine limb. Denounced by some as heretical, the defenders of *Shi'ur Komah* argued that it was a metaphor for God's greatness and should not be taken literally.

Shiva. Literally "seven," the most intense period of mourning that is observed for father, mother, wife, husband, son, daughter, brother, and sister (including half-brother and half-sister). In computing the seven days, the day of burial is considered the first day and the seventh day is considered a full day after the morning service. *Shiva* is suspended for the duration of the Sabbath, though that day is counted as one of the seven days of mourning, because the Sabbath is a day of joy and delight in which not even death may intrude. The bereaved family gathers to "sit *shiva*" in the home of the deceased. Mourners sit on low stools or benches. It is considered an obligation for relatives and friends to visit mourners during the *shiva* period, comforting them and providing them with food and other needs. The activity of mourners is strictly limited while they are sitting *shiva*. Mourners do not bathe (except to wash for basic cleanliness), anoint the body, or engage in sexual intercourse. As a sign of their withdrawal from society, they do not use cosmetics, shave, cut the hair, or wear new clothes. Slippers of cloth, felt, or rubber are worn instead of comfortable leather footwear because the mourners remain indoors. Mourners do not leave the house, perform manual labor, or conduct business transactions (unless it would prevent irreversible financial loss), and they refrain from such plesureable activities as attending parties, including wedding and bar or bat mitzvah receptions, listening to music, and watching television. In the house of mourning, it is customary to cover mirrors or turn them to the wall. A memorial candle is kept burning in a house of mourning throughout the seven-day *shiva* period.

Shiva Asar be-Tammuz – see 17th of Tammuz.

Shiviti. Ornamental plaque, often containing a biblical or talmudic passage, placed on the eastern wall of some synagogues beginning in the 18th century. The term derived from the verse, *Shiviti Adonai le-neged tamid* ("I have set the Lord always before me;" Ps. 16:8).[296] Traditionally, the eastern wall was the site where seats were reserved for the rabbi and other dignitaries. (See also *mizrach*.)

Sh'lamim – see Peace offering.

Shlemiel. Yiddish term for a fool or bungler, an unfortunate person or born loser for whom nothing ever turns out right (similar to *nebbish*). It may derive from the name Shlumiel, a general and son of a leader of the tribe of Shimon, who "always seemed to lose his military battles."[297]

Shlep. Yiddish term meaning to carry or lug.

Shleper. Yiddish term for an untidy or unkempt person, or someone who carries heavy baggage.

Shlimazel. Literally someone born "under an unlucky star," a Yiddish term for a habitual failure.

Shlock. Yiddish term describing shoddy merchandise, especially clothing, which is cheaply made and of inferior quality.

Shlub. Yiddish term for a clumsy, stupid, coarse, or bad-mannered person.

Shlump. Yiddish term for a dull, colorless person (a "drip" or "wet blanket").

Shmaltz. Yiddish term for rendered chicken fat, traditionally used instead as a shortening and for frying and flavoring food.

Shmaltzy. Yiddish term used to describe music or literature that is excessively sentimental, overly romantic, or gushingly sweet.

Shmatte. Literally "rag," a Yiddish term denoting an old, worn piece of clothing. It can also denote a person unworthy of respect.

Shmeer. Yiddish term meaning a spread, typically cream cheese on a bagel. In slang, the word also can denote a bribe, figuratively "spreading" money over the palms of the recipient. Among salesmen, *shmeer* means to flatter a customer. The term "whole *shmeer*" refers to the entire amount or the full deal.

Shmegegge. Yiddish term for a stupid or incompetent person.

Shmendrick. Yiddish term for a person of no importance, usually weak and of small stature. It comes from a popular Yiddish operetta, by the Romanian-Jewish composer Abraham Goldfaden, whose title character was an idiotic and clueless mama's boy and a hopelessly incompetent student at religious school.[298]

Shmo. A shorter and nicer synonym for *shmuck*, a hapless fool or jerk.

Shmooze. Yiddish term for conversing in a friendly, casual manner.

Shmuck. Literally "penis," a vulgar Yiddish term for a clumsy or stupid person. It often may be used to apply to an obnoxious or detestable individual. (Calling someone a *shmuck* is similar to terming him a "prick" in American English.)

Shmuel – see Samuel.

Shmurah matzah – see *Matzah, shmurah.*

Shmutz. Yiddish term for dirt or filth.

Shnook. Yiddish term for an incompetent or easily victimized person, the fall guy or patsy who gets the blame. It often denotes a passive and gullible simpleton who is likeable and deserving of pity.

Shnorrer. Derived from a German word for a beggar, this Yiddish term refers to a panhandler, cheapskate, or bum. It can denote a person who habitually takes advantage of the generosity of others, a chronic borrower who has no intention of ever repaying.

Shnoz. Yiddish term for nose, especially one that is extremely prominent, like the late comic Jimmy Durante.

Shoah. Hebrew term meaning "catastrophic destruction," referring to the deliberate intentional murder of two thirds of European Jews by the Nazis and their collaborators during World War II. Shoah is used by many who believe that the more common word, "Holocaust," has become cheapened by being frequently misapplied to other situations. Leaders of the Zionist movement and intellectuals in Palestine used the term "Shoah" when the destruction of European Jewry was occurring.

Shochet. Ritual slaughterer who is carefully trained in the complex and minute regulations of *shechitah*.A *shochet* must be an observant Jew and pass a rigorous examination in Jewish law and animal anatomy. In addition to slaughtering the animal, the *shochet* must also carry out a detailed examination of the carcass (see *bedikah*).

Shofar (ram's horn). Ancient musical instrument that is the most recognizable symbol of Rosh Hashanah. It can be made from the horn of any kosher animal except a cow, because our advocate on Rosh Hashanah should not be a reminder of the Golden Calf. The *shofar* is also blown throughout the preceding month of Elul and at the end of Yom Kippur. (The three sounds of the *shofar* – *tekiah, shevarim, teruah* – are discussed in separate sections.) According to tradition, there are precisely 100 blasts of the *shofar* on Rosh Hashanah (but it is not sounded if Rosh Hashanah falls on the Sabbath). Today, 40 sounds are blown after the Torah reading and 30 during the reader's repetition of the *Musaf Amidah* – 10 at the conclusion of each of its three major sections (*Malchuyot, Zichronot, Shofarot*; see separate sections). The final 30 sounds of the *shofar* are blown either during the silent *Musaf Amidah* (Sephardic tradition) or during the full *Kaddish* at the end of the *Musaf* service (Ashkenazic ritual). Both the morning and *Musaf* sets of *shofar* blasts end with a *tekiah gedolah*.[299]

Shofarot. Third of the three long intermediate sections in the *Musaf Amidah* on Rosh Hashanah, it recounts some of the symbolical meanings of the *shofar*. The three Torah verses (Exod. 19:16, 19; 20:15) describe the awesome experience of the Revelation at Mount Sinai, which culminated with the mighty sound of the *shofar*. The four verses from the Psalms (47:6; 98:6; 81:4-5; 150:1-6) depict the joyous sounding of the *shofar* in praise of God. The prophetic verses (Isa. 18:3; 27:13; Zech. 9:14-15) speak of the future sounding of the great *shofar*, which will signal the ingathering of the Jewish people and usher in the Messianic Age.

Shoftim (1) – see Judges.

Shoftim (2). The 5th *parashah* in the Book of Deuteronomy (16:18-21:9), it describes the powers and limitations of the judges, kings, priests, and prophets.This Torah portion also includes the cities of refuge, laws of warfare, and the case of the unwitnessed murder (see *eglah arufah*). Its most famous verse is, "Justice, justice shall you pursue" (16:20).

Shomer. Literally "watcher," the Hebrew term for a person who remains at the side of a dead person from the moment of death until burial so that the body of the deceased is never left alone. The *shomer*, preferably a member of the family or a personal friend, recites psalms throughout the night. While engaged in this *mitzvah*, the *shomer* is exempt from the performance of other positive commandments. As a mark of respect for the dead, eating, drinking, smoking, and unnecessary or derogatory conversation are forbidden in the room that contains the body.[300]

Shomer d'latot Yisrael – see *Shaddai*.

Shomer Shabbas. Literally "Sabbath guardian," this Yiddish term refers to a Jew who strictly observes the Sabbath according to *halacha*.

Shomron – see Samaria.

Shoresh (root). Three- (or rarely four-) letter consonant root of Hebrew verbs, which is modified by prefixes and suffixes to indicate the case, tense, and gender.

Showbread. Twelve large flat, oblong loaves of wheat flour (corresponding to the number of the tribes of Israel and a representative gift from each) that were placed in two equal rows on the Table in the Sanctuary each Sabbath. They were left there until the next Sabbath, when they were removed (miraculously still fresh) and eaten by the *kohanim* (Lev. 24:5-9). The Hebrew term is *lechem panim*, literally the "bread of the Presence."

Shpiel. Yiddish term denoting either a long involved story or a sales pitch. (See also *Purim-shpiel*.)

Shpilkis. Yiddish term meaning an inability to sit still or remain seated ("on pins and needles").

Shroud (*tachrichim*). Simple garment made of inexpensive muslin, cotton, or linen in which a Jew is traditionally buried. It indicates that rich and poor are equal before God. Since the 16th century, the accepted color for a shroud has been white, which symbolizes purity. Shrouds are made without seams, knots, or buttons and have no pockets, signifying that it is a person's soul, not wealth, which will be judged in the World to Come. Traditionally, a man's shroud consists of seven parts – headpiece, pants, shirt, belt, *kitel* (robe), *tallit*, and sheet. The *kitel* is stripped of its snaps or buttons, and the *tallit* of its ornaments. One of the *tzitzit* (fringes) is cut and placed in a corner of the *tallit*, indicating that this Jew is no longer required to perform the *mitzvot* and symbolizing the severing of the bond of life.[301]

Shtadlan. From an Aramaic word meaning "persuader," the title given to a representative of the Jewish community who was a skilled negotiator and advocate with access to high dignitaries and legislative bodies (see Court Jew). Although many *shtadlanim* throughout the centuries acted with great courage and effectiveness, the term "*shtadlan*" began to acquire a negative connation in the late 19th century when applied to Jewish notables who showed an excessive eagerness to compromise with the authorities.

Shtetl. Yiddish term for one of the small towns or villages throughout Eastern Europe where Ashkenazic Jews lived before either moving to escape severe economic and political pressure in the years after World War or being destroyed during the Shoah. The *shtetl* embodied a unique social, cultural, and communal pattern in which the secular and the holy were integrated into a way of life built on the Jewish ideals of piety, learning, scholarship, and communal justice and charity. Life in the *shtetl* could be parochial and constricting, but also warm and intimate.

Shtibel. Literally meaning a "small room," this Yiddish term refers to a side room in a synagogue used for public prayer. Used in Eastern Europe to denote a Hasidic synagogue, the term also was applied to one of the many small synagogues founded by Eastern European immigrants to the United States.

Shtick. Yiddish term for a characteristic or contrived gesture, talent, or gimmick that is helpful in securing recognition or attention, especially in an entertainment routine. Comedian examples are Jack Benny being perpetually 39 years old and acting as notoriously stingy and a bad violinist (though in real life he was an expert violinist and philanthropist), and Groucho Marx with his trademark stooped walk, lascivious eyebrow raising, and cigar.

Shtreimel. Yiddish term for a broad-brimmed black hat, usually trimmed with velvet or edged in fur, worn by Hasidic and other ultra-Orthodox men, especially for the Sabbath and festivals.

Shtunk. Literally "stinker," a Yiddish term for a nasty, offensive, or ungrateful person. At times, it may be used as a term of endearment for a child, meaning "a little stinker."

Shtup. A Yiddish vulgar slang term for sexual intercourse, it may be used to mean filling someone up with food.

Shuckling. Literally meaning "shaking," the Yiddish term for the ritual swaying that is a characteristic of worshipers in traditional synagogues. Although many erroneously believe that these bodily movements originated with the Hasidim in the 17th century, they merely accentuated a practice dating back to geonic and even talmudic times to produce deeper concentration and more intense devotion in prayer. The medieval poet Judah Halevy believed *shuckling* was a remnant of the trembling and shaking with fear that the Israelites experienced as they stood in awe at the foot of Mount Sinai to receive the Torah.

Shul. From a root meaning "school," the Yiddish term for a synagogue. It reflects the fact that Jewish worship and learning most often take place in the same building. In Eastern Europe, the opponents of the Hasidim (see *mitnagdim*) referred to their synagogue as a "*shul*," whereas the Hasidim termed theirs a "*shtibel*"

Shulchan Aruch (Set Table). Compiled by Yosef Karo in the 16th century, the most influential code of law in modern Jewish life and the last comprehensive one to be written. Like the earlier *Arba'ah Turim* (Four Rows) of Jacob ben Asher, the *Shulchan Aruch* is divided into four major sections – *Orach Hayyim* (OH), concerning prayers, Sabbaths, and festivals; *Yoreh De'ah* (YD), dealing with various subjects such as dietary laws, interest, purity, and mourning; *Even ha-Ezer* (EH), on marriage, divorce, and related topics; and *Hoshen Misphat* (HM), dealing with civil and criminal law. In his decisions, Karo relied on three major authorities: Isaac Alfasi (11th century, known as the "Rif"), Maimonides (12th century, known as the "Rambam"), and Asher ben Jehiel (late 13th to early 14th century, known as the "Rosh"). When they disagreed, Karo generally followed the majority. (See also *Mappah*.)

Shuruk – see Vowels.

Shushan Purim. The Jews of Shushan, the Persian capital, continued to battle against their enemies for an extra day and did not rest until the 15th of Adar, when they celebrated their deliverance (Esth. 9:18). Because Shushan was a walled city, the Rabbis ruled that Jews living in all cities that had a fortified outer wall around them at the time of Joshua would observe Purim on the 15th of the month. Therefore, in modern Israel Purim is celebrated on the 15th of Adar in Jerusalem, a walled city in ancient times, whereas in Tel Aviv and elsewhere the festival is observed on the 14th of the month.

Sh'va – see Vowels.

Shvartze Shabbos. Literally "Black Sabbath," the Yiddish term for the Sabbath immediately preceding Tisha b'Av, the saddest day in the Jewish calendar. This Sabbath is more commonly known as Shabbat Hazon.

Shvartze yohr. Literally "a black year," this Yiddish phrase is often used as a curse equivalent to "may you fall on hard times."

Shvartzer. Literally "black," an often-derogatory Yiddish term used in the United States for an African-American.

Shviger. Yiddish word for "mother-in-law."

Shvirat ha-keilim – see Breaking of the vessels.

Shvitz. Yiddish term meaning to "sweat," it is also the word for a steam bath. Going to the *shvitz* used to be a popular activity for Jewish men, possibly serving as a reminder of the *mikveh*.[302] One who sweats profusely is called a "*shvitzer*."

Shylock. Derogatory term used by gentiles to refer to a Jewish moneylender. It is based on the central character in Shakespeare's *The Merchant of Venice*, who literally demands his "pound of flesh." In the play, Shylock also has a sympathetic side, giving the audience some understanding of his motivations.

Sicarii. Literally "dagger-men," a name applied in the decades prior to the fall of Jerusalem in 70 C.E. to Jewish Zealots attempting to expel the Romans from Judea and to silence their Jewish collaborators. They concealed small daggers (*sicae* in Latin) under their cloaks to stab their enemies and then escape detection.

Sick, prayer for the. The Rabbis included a prayer for the healing of the sick as the eighth blessing in the daily *Amidah*.It praises God as the "faithful, merciful

Physician...Who heals the sick of His people Israel." The custom of invoking a get-well blessing for the sick (see *Mi she-Berach*; May He who blessed) in conjunction with the reading of the Torah developed during the Middle Ages. On the Sabbath, the prayer concludes: "It is the Sabbath, when one must not cry out, and recovery will come soon." When reciting the prayer for the sick, one mentions the person who is ill using their first name (and middle name) followed by *ben* (son of) or *bat* (daughter of) and then the first (and middle) name of the *mother* – instead of the father, which is generally used on other occasions, especially in traditional circles.

Sick, visiting the – see *Bikur holim.*

Siddur. Also known as *seder tefillot* (order of prayers), the collection of all the prayers designated for public and private worship for weekdays, Sabbaths, festivals, and fast days. For centuries, the liturgy remained a purely oral tradition. The person who led the congregation needed to know the prayers by heart; the worshipers either knew the prayers by memory or repeated them after the reader. This practice explains why the *Amidah* is recited twice during both the morning and afternoon services. Those who knew the prayers by heart recited them silently, while the reader repeated the *Amidah* for those who could only respond with the traditional "amen." The earliest *siddurim* were compiled in the geonic period, starting about 850 C.E. As the number of prayers increased steadily during the Middle Ages, in the early 16th century the *siddur* was first published in two volumes – one containing the daily and Sabbath services, which retained the original name, and a second consisting of the prayers for the festivals, which among Ashkenazim was called the *machzor*. There is no uniformly accepted version of the *siddur*, and each Jewish denomination has its own variant. With the development of desktop publishing, individual congregations now can produce custom-made *siddurim.*

Sidelocks – see *Payot.*

Sidrah (order). Sephardic term for the weekly Torah portion read in the synagogue (see *parashah*).

Sifra. Halachic midrash on the Book of Leviticus, probably written in the 2nd or 3rd century.

Sifrei. Halachic midrash on the Books of Numbers and Deuteronomy (3rd century).

Sifrei Torah – see Torah scrolls.

Silent prayer. Alternative term for the *Amidah.* It relates to the custom that developed during the rabbinic period of members of the congregation reciting the

Amidah silently, in order to individualize the worship experience, before it was repeated by the prayer leader.

Siloam Pool. Collection of overflow water from an open channel, constructed during the reign of Solomon or earlier, that carried water from the Gihon spring along the eastern slope of the City of David to irrigate the gardens of the Kings of Judah. It later was enhanced by the overflow of water in Hezekiah's tunnel, built in 701 B.C.E. This remarkable underground structure led from the Gihon spring into Jerusalem, providing a hidden water supply that allowed the inhabitants of the city to withstand the Assyrian siege.

Siman tov. Literally meaning "good omen," a Hebrew expression of congratulations used by Sephardim. Today, it is often combined with the Ashkenazic equivalent (*mazel tov*) in the song "*Siman Tov u-Mazel Tov*," which is sung at *simchas* (happy occasions) such as at a wedding and after a bar/bat mitzvah concludes the chanting of the *haftarah*.

Simcha. Literally "joy" or "happiness," the generic Hebrew term for a celebration such as a wedding ceremony, circumcision, or bar/bat mitzvah, as well as any joyous occasion.

Simchat Bat (Rejoicing for a Daughter). Custom that has developed in response to the demand of modern feminists to celebrate the birth of a girl. In the absence of established ritual, the parents often design a ceremony that may include passages from Song of Songs and Psalms, as well as biblical selections featuring such famous women as the four Matriarchs and the seven prophetesses, followed by a special blessing over wine and a festive meal.[303]

Simchat beit ha-sho'evah – see Water-drawing ceremony.

Simchat Torah (Rejoicing in the Law). Day on which the annual cycle of reading the Torah scroll is completed and immediately begun again. Simchat Torah developed during the Middle Ages, but became so popular that it became a major celebration. At the evening service, all the Torah scrolls are removed from the ark and carried around the synagogue in seven processions (see *hakafot*), followed by children who traditionally carry flags reminiscent of those under which the Israelites marched in the wilderness. Prescribed alphabetical verses are recited initially, but as these finish there is an opportunity for singing Hebrew songs as well as dancing with the Torahs. When the seven circuits have been completed, all but one of the Torah scrolls are returned to the ark. Traditionally, the last section of Deuteronomy is chanted from the remaining scroll (the only time during the year when the Torah is read at night). An innovation is to read three Torah portions on the evening of Simchat Torah. All the men are called up for the first *aliyah*; all the women for the second (the end of Deuteronomy); and all the children, covered by a *tallit* over their heads, for the third (the first few verses of Genesis). On the following morning, the *hakafot* are repeated. From the first scroll, the reader repeatedly chants a series of verses (from Deut. 33:1-26) until all the adult Jews (only the males in Orthodox synagogues) have a chance to recite the blessings over the Torah. The final two *aliyot* are the end of Deuteronomy (see *Hatan Torah*) and the beginning of Genesis (see *Hatan Bereshit*).

Sin (1). Transgression of the Divine commandments. Sins were divided into three basic categories – *chet*, *avon*, and *pesha*.Because no human being is without sin, Judaism offers the possibility of repentance (see *teshuvah*). The Day of Atonement (Yom Kippur) secures Divine forgiveness for transgressions between human beings and God. However, for sins against another person, it is first necessary to seek forgiveness from that individual and redress any wrong. This is the source of the custom in many communities, immediately preceding the recitation of *Kol Nidrei*, of worshipers walking around the synagogue and asking forgiveness from one another for offenses committed during the past year.

Sin (2). Alternative pronunciation of *shin*, depending on the position of the dot at the top of the letter.

Sin offering. Know in Hebrew as *chatat*, meaning "to miss the mark," it was brought by one who sinned in error as a result of carelessness (*bish'gagah*) (Lev. 4:1-5:13). The purpose of the sin offering was not to bribe God to overlook the sin or to balance it with an act of generosity. Rather, its goal was to make the donor aware of his more generous side, so that he would not see himself as merely weak and rebellious. It was an opportunity to clear one's conscience, not a penalty for having done wrong. A special sin offering had to be brought by members of a Great Sanhedrin that erred by making a mistaken halachic ruling that resulted in the entire nation inadvertently sinning. The specific animal brought for any sin offering depended entirely on the personal status of the violator. The High Priest or Sanhedrin brought a bull, the *nasi* (political leader) a male goat, and a commoner a female goat or sheep.

Sinai – see Mount Sinai.

Sinai Campaign. Military operation launched by Israel in the fall of 1956 (October 29-November 7) in the wake of mounting aggression by Egyptian *fedayeen* (terrorist) squads. The Sinai Campaign coincided with an Anglo-French assault launched to counteract Egyptian seizure of the Suez Canal. In response to the rapid arming of Egyptian forces, the establishment of a joint Arab military command including Egypt, Jordan, and Syria, and fortification of the Straits of Tiran to block the Red Sea route to Eilat, the Sinai Campaign was a preemptive offensive to catch the Egyptians off balance before their hostile preparations were completed. The goals of the Sinai Campaign, all of which were achieved, included: destruction of the *fedayeen* bases in the Gaza Strip and on the Sinai border; prevention of an Egyptian attack on Israel by destroying Egypt's command and control centers and the airfields in Sinai; and opening the Gulf of Eilat to undisturbed Israeli shipping. Following the campaign, Israel was compelled by the United States and the Soviet Union to evacuate the Sinai Peninsula. United Nations troops were posted on the Egyptian side of the border as well as at Sharm el-Sheik, where they served to guarantee Israeli shipping through the Straits of Tiran.

Sinai Peninsula. Situated between the two continents of Africa and Asia, this triangular land lies between the Mediterranean Sea and the twin arms of the Red Sea. The Sinai Peninsula is mainly desert, sparsely settled by wandering Bedouins. After the Exodus from Egypt, the Israelites traveled through the Sinai Peninsula on their circuitous route to the Promised Land.

Sinat chinam. Literally "causeless hatred," which the Rabbis maintained was as serious a sin as idolatry, immorality, and murder, it was considered the underlying cause of the destruction of the Second Temple.[304]

Sitra Atra. Aramaic for "other side," the talmudic term for the folk belief in an evil or demonic realm, an invisible malevolent "counter world" to the Divinely created world.

Sivan. The 3rd month of the Jewish calendar (May/June). Shavuot falls on the 6th of the month (6th and 7th in the Diaspora).

Sivivon – see Dreidel.

Six (*sheish*). In the Bible, there are six days of Creation (Gen. 2:2) and hence six working days of the week (Exod. 20:9). There were six cities of refuge, where those who had committed accidental homicide could flee to escape the blood avenger (Num. 35:6), and a maximum of six years that a Hebrew slave could serve (Exod. 21:2). There also are six orders of the Mishnah, and a major symbol of Judaism is the Magen David, a six-pointed star.

Six Day War. Brilliantly conceived preemptive attack in which Israeli forces crushed the armies of Egypt, Syria, Jordan, and Iraq in 1967 (June 5-10). By the end of the war, Israel controlled Judea and Samaria (the West Bank), the Gaza Strip, the Sinai Peninsula, the Golan Heights, and all of Jerusalem. Israel was prepared to discuss the return of almost all captured territory in exchange for some form of peace or mutual coexistence with the Arabs. However, at the Khartoum Conference in August, the Arabs affirmed a policy of the "three noes" – no recognition of Israel, no negotiations with Israel, and no peace with Israel."

613 Commandments – see *Taryag mitzvot.*

614th Commandment. Concept popularized by Emil Fackenheim of an additional *mitzvah,* issued in the wake of the Holocaust, that forbids Jews from "giving Hitler a posthumous victory" and orders the Jewish people to survive as Jews. For Fackenheim, the establishment of the State of Israel was a collective fulfillment of this commandment revealed during Jewry's darkest hour, the ultimate revenge against the Nazis.

Six million. Estimated number of Jews murdered during the Holocaust, representing about two thirds of the Jews of Europe.

Siyum. Literally "termination" or "completion," a celebratory meal (see *se'udat mitzvah*) held upon completing the study of a tractate of the Talmud, usually accompanied by a halachic discourse. The *siyum* also includes a special *Kaddish* and a prayer expressing the hope for ongoing Talmud study.

Skullcap – see *Kippah.*

Slander – see *Lashon ha-ra.*

Slaughter, ritual – see *Shechitah.*

Slave, fugitive. The Bible expressly prohibited the Israelites from handing over or wronging a fugitive slave (Deut. 23:16-17). Unlike the Babylonian Code of Hammurabi, in which aiding and abetting the escape of a runaway slave was a crime punishable by death, the Torah teaches that the Jew should always be merciful in protecting and assisting those who are in need of help.[305] Slaves and prisoners escaping from a besieged enemy city must be given their freedom and allowed to settle wherever they wish in the Land of Israel. Sending a man seeking his freedom back to a life of idolatry would be inconsistent with the ideal of sanctity permeating the Israelite camp. Indeed, Nachmanides noted that asylum seekers often provided information that was valuable in permitting the conquest of the territory of the slave's former master.[306] The biblical fugitive slave law is in stark contrast to laws existing in the United States before the Civil War, which mandated the return of runaway slaves to their masters.

Slavery. There were two ways in which a Jew could be sold into slavery. A free man could choose to sell himself to escape from extreme poverty (Lev. 25:39), becoming a member of the household of another and earning his food and shelter through his labor; or a thief might be sold by the court to raise funds to pay his victims (Exod. 21:2). He would serve for a maximum of six years, and in the seventh year would be set free (Deut. 15:12). Until a girl reached puberty, an impoverished father had the right to "sell" her to a wealthy family as a bondwoman. However, this practice was designed to be for *her* benefit, because the Torah commanded that the purchaser or his son was to marry her (Exod. 21:7-11). Failure of either of them to marry her was considered a "betrayal." The master was commanded to give generous gifts to Hebrew bondmen or bondwomen when they gained their freedom (Deut. 15:13-14), thus helping them make a fresh start in life. At times, an indentured servant might be so afraid of regaining his freedom and fending for himself that he would prefer to remain a slave for life. If that were the case, "He shall be brought to the door or the doorpost, and his master shall pierce his ear with an awl, and he shall serve him forever" (Exod. 21:5-6).

Sleep. The Talmud states that "sleep is a sixtieth part of death" (Ber. 57b). According to Jewish tradition, God takes each person's soul and judges it during the night. When He returns it in the morning, we say "*Modeh Ani*" to thank God for mercifully restoring our souls. Because it may be that our soul does not deserve to be returned, the prayer ends by thanking God for His "great faith" that we will be better in the future.

Sneezing on the truth. Rather than a mere irritation of the nasal passages, a sneeze in ancient times was deemed a grave omen of impending death. Indeed, this may be the underlying reason for the development of the custom of saying "long life" and "good health" to one who has sneezed. A traditional belief is that when a person sneezes during a conversation, whatever has just been said will occur, based on the concept of "sneezing on the truth." While not as foolproof as direct prophecy, it is said to indicate that events that are rational and plausible will actually come to pass, or that an event that has already occurred really happened just as the story related.

Sneezing, pulling one's ears after. Especially common among Jews from Galicia and Lithuania, this superstitious practice has engendered heated arguments as to whether one ear or both should be pulled and whether it should be up or down. The reason for this custom is unclear. Originally, it was performed if the sneeze occurred when speaking about one who was dead. However, ear pulling has long been extended to all sneezes and is usually accompanied by reciting the Yiddish phrase *tzu langeh mazaldikker yohrn* (to long, lucky years).

Sobibor. One of six death camps situated in the Lublin district of Nazi-occupied Poland near the village of the same name. It functioned from May 1942 until October 1943, when the Jewish camp laborers revolted. About 300 inmates escaped and 50 survived to the end of the war. During its time of operation, Sobibor claimed some 250,000 victims.

Society for the Advancement of Judaism. American Jewish congregation founded by Mordecai Kaplan to further his new movement of Reconstructionism.

Sod. The secret, esoteric, mystical interpretation of the Bible that was emphasized by the kabbalists. *Sod* posits that truth is beyond human sensory perception and cognition and thus cannot be expressed solely in words. Therefore, the true meaning of the Divinely inspired language of the Bible cannot be understood by merely analyzing the connotations and denotations of the text itself. Instead, it requires an entirely different approach because, as the mystics observed, "many lights shine forth from each letter." Among the numerous techniques used to reveal the hidden meanings of the words of the biblical text are *gematria* and notarikon.

Sodom and Gomorrah. Two cities in the Jordan Valley, which God resolved to utterly destroy because of the wickedness and depravity of their inhabitants. When Abraham bargained with God to spare the cities, not even 10 righteous men could be found within them (Gen. 18:16-32). Lot, his wife, and two daughters escaped Sodom before fire and brimstone rained down upon it. Although warned not to look back while they were fleeing to the mountains, Lot's wife disobeyed and was turned into a pillar of salt (Gen. 19:26).

Sofer. A scribe who is specially trained to write a Torah scroll with pious care. The term is a shortened form of the title *sofer stam*; the last word is an acronym for "*sefer Torah, tefillin* and *mezuzot*" – the three items containing texts that the *sofer stam* writes. Literally meaning "one who counts," the name *sofer* probably relates to the practice of some early scribes who counted all the letters, words, and verses of the Torah to make certain that none were inadvertently added or omitted. Working full time, a skilled *sofer* requires about nine months to complete the 5,888 verses and 79,976 words in the Torah.[307]

Soferim (Sof.). Minor tractate added to the Talmud that deals with the laws regulating the activities of scribes.

Song at the Sea – see *Shirat ha-Yam*.

Song of Deborah. Glorious hymn of triumph to the Lord (Judg. 5). Deborah sang this paean of thanksgiving for God's deliverance of her people in their victorious campaign against Jabin, Canaanite King of Hatzor, who had oppressed Israel for 20 years. Following the Israelite victory, the Canaanite general (Sisera) fled the scene, only to be killed by the courageous Jael.

Song of Glory – see *An'im Zemirot*.

Song of Miriam. After the chariots and horsemen of Pharaoh were drowned in the Sea of Reeds, Miriam "took a timbrel in her hand, and all the women went out after her to dance with timbrels." Celebrating the Divine deliverance of the Israelites, Miriam chanted: "Sing to the Lord, for He has triumphed gloriously; horse and driver He has hurled into the sea" (Exod. 15:20-21).

Song of Songs (*Shir ha-Shirim*). The 4th book of the Writings section of the Bible and first of the five *megillot*, it is read in the synagogue on Passover. A cycle of vivid poems, largely in the form of a dialogue between two lovers, Song of Songs is traditionally attributed to King Solomon (10th century B.C.E.). Because of its erotic thematic material, and the fact that God is never mentioned by name, many Rabbis argued against including the Song of Songs in the biblical canon. Championed by R.Akiva, who stated that "all the Writings are holy, but the Song of Songs is the Holy of Holies," the book has been interpreted by Jewish tradition as an allegory for God's love of the Israelites and the love of the soul for the Divine.

Song of Songs Rabbah (Song R.). Aggadic midrash to the Song of Songs, probably written between 650-900.

Songs of Ascent – see *Shir ha-Ma'alot.*

Son of man – see *Ben adam.*

Sons of God (*B'nai ha-Elohim*). According to the Torah, "When mankind began to multiply on the earth and daughters were born to them, the *b'nei ha-elohim* [lit., 'sons of God'] saw how beautiful were the daughters of men and took wives from among them. The Lord said, 'My spirit shall not abide in man forever, since he is flesh. Let the days allowed him be 120 years' " (Gen. 6:1-3). All traditional commentators rejected the mythological implications of a semi-divine race arising from the sexual union between divine beings and mortals, though relationships between gods and mortals resulting in demigods were popular themes in pagan mythology. In the Israelite concept, the offspring of such unnatural unions were flesh and blood like all humans, and their life span was severely limited compared to those individuals cited in the immediately preceding list of genealogies (Gen. 5).

Sons of Light. Term used in the Dead Sea Scrolls to describe the forces of good – the community at Qumran where the scrolls originated – who would be victorious over the Sons of Darkness (the forces of evil).

Sorcery. The Bible explicitly prohibits the pagan practices of divination.and sorcery (Deut. 18:10). Unlike the diviner, who predicted the future, the sorcerer attempted to alter the future by pronouncing blessings and curses and employing other magical techniques to manipulate unseen powerful forces. The classic biblical example of a sorcerer was Balaam, who was hired by the Moabite ruler Balak to curse the Israelites but blessed the people instead (Num. 22-25).

Sotah (suspected adulteress) **(1)**. If a man and a married woman had been alone for enough time that they could have engaged in sexual relations, the suspicions of a jealous husband were proved or disproved by the complicated ordeal of her drinking the "water of bitterness." The wife could not be forced to undergo this test; however, if she refused, she was divorced from her husband and did not receive the financial settlement stipulated in the *ketubah*. In this ordeal, the woman was taken to the Sanctuary in Jerusalem, where a *kohen* would mix "sacred water" with earth in an earthenware vessel. Into this was dipped a parchment scroll containing a curse and the Name of God, the letters of which were dissolved in the water. Before drinking the mixture, the woman was forced to take an oath that she was not guilty of any improper acts. If she were indeed innocent of the charge, no injuries would result (commentators said that she would bear a child to compensate for her ordeal). If she were guilty, however, the combination of the ordeal and the accompanying oath would produce terrible physical effects. According to the Rabbis, this ordeal was not effective if the husband himself was guilty of immorality. The ordeal of jealousy (the only trial by ordeal mentioned in the Bible) was intended to remove the very suspicion of marital unfaithfulness from the midst of the Israelite community. At the same time, this procedure provided protection for the innocent wife against the unreasonable jealousy of her husband.

Sotah (Sot.) (2). The 5th tractate in Nashim (women) in the Mishnah, it deals with the woman suspected of adultery (see above).

Soul. In biblical times, the idea of the soul as an independent entity had not yet emerged. After death, the deceased was thought to lead a shadowy existence in the underworld (see *She'ol*). It was only in the late Second Temple period, under the influence of Greek thought, that the concept arose in Judaism of the soul as distinct from the body. As the part of a human being that is most like God, the soul was considered the seat of the intellect, spirituality, creativity, and the Divine spark implanted within. (See also *nefesh*, *neshamah*, *ru'ach*, and *transmigration of the soul*.)

Soul, immortality of the. Concept in which the incorporeal soul survives bodily death and is transported to a spiritual realm beyond the dimensions of time and space, where after the final Divine judgment it enjoys eternal repose (see soul, above).

Soul, transmigration of the – see Transmigration of the soul.

Southern Kingdom – see Judah, Kingdom of.

Sovereign Self. As described by sociologists Stephen Cohen and Arnold Eisen, a term denoting the modern shift in religious practice from being rooted in a sense of community to one founded upon personal autonomy. Based on Kant's idea of "individual moral autonomy," the concept developed of Jews having the right to decide what in Judaism to accept and reject, which logically extended to each person effectively defining a personal Judaism. When combined with the American ideal of "rugged individualism," the Sovereign Self has become the paradigmatic approach to Judaism in certain segments of the Jewish community. For some Jews, the new arbiter of Jewish involvement is personal meaning – an individual approach focused on the self and its fulfillment rather than community responsibility. With each person interacting with Judaism in a unique way, no one is capable of determining for others what constitutes a Jew. However, Judaism based on such individual choice may not be really Judaism, but rather a recipe for communal anarchy. In the Book of Judges, whenever society was in an anarchic and morally chaotic state, the text describes the situation as "everyone did what was right in his own eyes."

Sparing the mother bird. The Bible requires that, if one chances upon a mother bird sitting over fledglings or eggs in her nest, it is necessary to let her go and take only her young (Deut. 22:6-7). It is also forbidden to slaughter an animal and its young on the same day (Lev. 22:28). For Maimonides, the rationale for these commandments was that animal mothers, just like humans, experience severe pain when seeing their young slain. According to Nachmanides, the purpose of this commandment was directed not toward the animal but toward humans, to purge them of callousness, cruelty, and savagery. The reward for sparing the mother bird is, "so that it will be good for you and prolong your days," strikingly similar to the promise for observing the Fifth Commandment to honor parents ("that your days may be long upon the land that the Lord your God gives you"; Exod. 20:11), implying that God will treat human beings in accordance with how well they care for animals.

Speech, evil – see *Lashon ha-ra*.

Spice box. Container for the fragrant spices used in the *Havdalah* ceremony at the conclusion of the Sabbath. Over the centuries, the spice box has been constructed in imaginative designs and remains a favorite creation of ceremonial artists. Because spices came from the Orient and were extremely expensive, Europeans guarded them as treasures, often in spice-towers. Therefore, Ashkenazic spice boxes were sometimes made in the shape of a tower topped with a pennant and having a clock face to indicate when the Sabbath ended that week. Other spice boxes took the form of fruit, animals, windmills, and trains. During the Inquisition, *Conversos* disguised spice boxes as ornamental pieces or children's toys to hide their Jewish symbolism from the authorities.

Spices. The blessing over aromatic spices (*borei minei besamim*) is one of the rituals of *Havdalah*. During the Middle Ages, perhaps in memory of the incense used in the Temple service, it was customary to smell fragrant spices to refresh the spirit and dispel the sadness accompanying the end of the Sabbath day. A more mystical reason is that the spices provide spiritual compensation for the additional soul (see *neshamah yeterah*) that each Jew figuratively possesses on the Sabbath.[308] According to an ancient legend, the fires of *Gehinnom* (netherworld) that are rekindled at the end of the Sabbath produce such a noxious odor that the *Havdalah* spices are needed to guard against it.[309]

Spies. Chiefs of the twelve tribes of Israel sent by Moses to "scout the land of Canaan" (Num. 13). Ten spies described the richness of the land that "flowed with milk and honey," but argued that it would be impossible to conquer it because of the size and strength of its inhabitants. Only Joshua and Caleb urged the people to rely on the Divine promise that the Israelites would gain possession of the land. However, the Israelites were petrified by the majority report and determined to return to Egypt. Caleb and Joshua, along with Moses, argued with them but to no avail. Disgusted with the people's lack of faith and courage, God decreed that all those who were aged 20 or older (except for Caleb and Joshua) would be prohibited from entering the Promised Land. The Israelites were condemned to wander 40 years in the wilderness, one year for each day the spies scouted the land, while the 10 who "spread calumny about the land died of plague" (Num. 14:26-38).

Spitting three times. Whether done literally or figuratively (by saying "pooh, pooh, pooh"), spitting three times (a mystical number) is a classic response to something exceptionally evil or good. For centuries, Jews have performed this ritual after witnessing a bad sight, hearing a terrible tale, or learning something similarly tragic, unfortunate or distasteful, as a prophylactic measure to prevent such an evil from happening or recurring. Ironically, it is traditional to perform the same in response to something wonderful – such as good news or the birth of a beautiful and healthy child – to ward off the Evil Eye.Because spitting eventually became viewed as a crude and unsanitary practice, it was replaced by the more refined ritual of simply saying "pooh, pooh, pooh."

SS. Abbreviation for the German phrase for "Protective Squadron," the SS was established in the 1920s as a personal guard unit for Nazi leader Adolph Hitler. Under the leadership of Heinrich Himmler, the SS grew from a small paramilitary unit to become one of the most elite and powerful organizations in Germany, with its members selected on the basis of racial purity and absolute loyalty to the Führer and the Nazi party. Indoctrinated with a virulently racist anti-Semitic ideology, SS members became the instrument of Nazi genocide.

Stamps. The first postage stamps issued by the State of Israel – pictures of ancient Jewish coins – appeared on May 16, 1948, two days after its statehood was proclaimed by David Ben Gurion formally reading its Declaration of Independence. Since that time, nearly 2,000 stamps have appeared depicting all aspects of Jewish history and culture. Each year, special stamps are issued for Memorial Day, Independence Day, and the Jewish New Year. Moreover, thousands of stamps throughout the world have featured famous Jews, scenes of Israel, and Judaic content.

Star of David – see Magen David.

Stars. A biblical symbol of limitlessness, God promised Abraham that his descendants would be "as numerous as the stars of Heaven and the sand on the seashore" (Gen. 22:17). This verse is sung at the *Havdalah* ceremony, when the presence of three stars in the sky on Saturday night indicates the conclusion of the Sabbath. Stars are also forecasters of future events. A midrash relates that a bright star appeared in the eastern sky marking the birth of Abraham, which is strikingly similar to the Christian description of the astral activity accompanying the birth of Jesus. When forced to bless Israel against his will, Balaam predicted that "a star rises from Jacob, a scepter [leader] comes forth from Israel; it smashes the brow of Moab" (Num. 24:17). When the Jews revolted against Roman rule in 135 C.E., the rebel leader, Bar Koziba, was nicknamed "Bar Kochba" (son of a star) because of the general belief that he was the Messiah of Balaam's prophecy. (See also *astrology*.)

State of Israel – see Israel, State of.

Stealing – see Theft.

Stele. Stone slab, painted or inscribed with a religious text, legal code, or record of military victories, which was commonly used in the ancient Near East. Upon their entry into the Promised Land, Joshua and the Israelites were commanded to "set up large stones, coat them with plaster, and inscribe upon them all the words of this Torah...and set up these stones...on Mount Ebal" (Deut. 27:2-4). According to tradition, this referred to most of the Book of Deuteronomy.

Sterilization – see Castration.

Stern Gang – see Lehi.

Stockade and watchtower. Plan utilized for the rapid establishment of small Jewish settlements in the Land of Israel between 1936-1947. In the late 1930s, the Jewish National Fund had acquired large tracts of land in areas far from Jewish population centers, but *de facto* possession was in jeopardy unless the land was settled. Due to Arab antagonism, ordinary methods of construction could not be used. Convoys carrying hundreds of helpers, prefabricated huts, and fortifications set out at daybreak, protected by Jewish Settlement Police. By nightfall they completed the erection of the settlement, surrounded by a double wall of planks with a filling of earth and stones, which was dominated by a central tower equipped with an electric generator and searchlight and to detect signs of hostility. Over a 10-year period, 118 settlements were established in this way.

Straits of Tiran Two small bays on the southeastern coast of the Sinai Peninsula that open out to the Red Sea. After the War of Independence (1948), the Egyptians built fortifications along its shores to block Israeli shipping from the port of Eilat. This blockade was broken in the Sinai Campaign (1956), but Israel eventually evacuated all of Sinai when the United Nations agreed to place a force along the Straits of Tiran to guarantee free shipping through them. However, in May 1967, Egypt demanded the withdrawal of the UN troops and once again declared the Straits of Tiran closed to Israeli shipping. This was a major factor precipitating the Six Day War, which ended with the waterway and the entire Sinai under Israeli control. The region was returned by Israel to Egypt as part of the Camp David Accords in 1979, and the Straits of Tiran have remained open.

Stranger – see Love of the stranger.

Struma. Old cattle boat that, in defiance of British restrictions on Jewish immigration, carried Jewish refugees fleeing the massacres in Romania to Palestine in 1941. It managed to limp into Istanbul harbor before its woefully inadequate engine finally ceased working. For the next 70 days, the British refused to grant permission for the refugees to enter Palestine, and the Turks would not let them repair the engine, disembark, or remain in that country. With only the food and water supplied by the local Jewish community and no sanitary facilities, conditions on the unbearably cramped ship rapidly deteriorated. On the evening of February 23, 1942, Turkish police seized control of the Struma and towed it out into the Black Sea. With no engine, the ship drifted overnight, and at dawn a Russian submarine sank her (apparently in error) with a single torpedo. Only a single passenger was saved. In the wake of the Struma tragedy, the British made only a minor revision in their harsh refugee policy, which condemned countless Jews to destruction.

Stumbling block. The biblical prohibition against putting a "stumbling block before the blind" (Lev. 19:14) was interpreted as forbidding one from giving misleading advice to an unsuspecting or uninformed person, especially if the advisor may benefit from his error. This commandment was extended to include causing someone to sin, especially the young and innocent and the morally weak. An example would be selling a knife or other lethal weapon to a person of dubious or dangerous character. The overall import of this commandment is to stress that each person is responsible for the welfare of others and may not do anything to endanger it.[310] As *Sefer ha-Chinuch* noted, the three pillars on which the world is established are truth, shared confidence, and mutual trust.[311]

Suffering – see Theodicy.

Sufganiyot. Small jelly doughnuts, fried in oil, a traditional Israeli treat served during Chanukah (see olive oil). They are a reminder of the sweetness of the Maccabee's victory and the oil used in the menorah during the rededication of the Temple.

Suicide. Because the duty to preserve life (*pikuach nefesh*), including one's own, is a paramount injunction in Judaism, suicide is prohibited. (For an exception see *martyrdom*.) This is ultimately based on the belief that God created and thus owns the entire universe, which includes the bodies of all human beings. Therefore, the individual does not have the right to destroy Divine property. Traditionally, a suicide was denied normal burial and mourning. It was, and in some places still is, the custom to bury suicides in a special section of the cemetery, near its outer limits and at least six feet from other Jewish dead. In recent years, however, there is a growing tendency to remove this stigma from those who take their own life, due in part to a recognition of the effects of mental illness.

Suicide, assisted. Since suicide is forbidden in Jewish law, so is assisting people in ending their lives. This applies even if one hands an overdose of pills to an individual or sets up a machine so that a person can administer a lethal substance intravenously (i.e., so that once supplied the means to commit suicide, the person acts independently). While free of liability in human courts, the assistant would be culpable in the judgment of Heaven. An assistant who knowingly administers a lethal dose of medication or poison with the intent to bring about the person's death has committed murder, even if the ultimate motive was benign.[312]

Sukkah (1). Name for the hastily constructed, insubstantial structure that Jews erect as part of the observance of the fall festival of Sukkot. This is in accordance with the Biblical commandment: "You shall dwell in booths (*sukkot*) for seven days" (Lev. 23:42), a remembrance of the temporary dwellings of the Israelites during their sojourn in the wilderness. The sukkah must be a temporary structure, only strong enough to withstand normal gusts of wind. It must have a minimum of three walls (31 inches or higher), at least two of which must be complete. The sukkah may be constructed of any material, though it is often of wood or canvas suspended on a metal frame. It must be built under the open sky, not under a tree or inside a house. The roof of the sukkah is covered with *s'chach*, and it is customary to decorate the sukkah with colorful fruit, which must remain in place and not be eaten during the festival, and with signs quoting verses from the Bible or depicting beautiful scenes from Israel. The Talmud indicates that during this festival Jews should regard the sukkah as their principal dwelling place, eating and sleeping within it. However, modern rabbinic authorities, cognizant of the cold and rainy climates to which Jews have wandered during their long exile, have permitted sleeping inside the house during this holiday, as well as eating inside when the weather is bad.[313]

Sukkah (Suk.) (2). The 6th tractate of Mo'ed (festivals) in the Mishnah, it deals with the laws concerning the festival of Sukkot and the four species.

Sukkot. Last of the three agricultural pilgrimage festivals. Also known as Tabernacles, this seven-day festival (eight in the Diaspora) begins on the 15th of Tishrei (the full moon five days after Yom Kippur). It is a festival of thanksgiving, celebrating the joy of the harvest, and commemorates the temporary shelters (*sukkot*) in which the Israelites dwelled as they wandered through the wilderness. In biblical times, Sukkot was the most important holiday of the Jewish calendar. It was known as *Zeman Simchateinu* (the Season of our Joy) or simply *he-Chag* (The Holiday) as the main feast of the year. In Temple times, a highlight was the water-drawing ceremony.Today, the four species are carried in *hoshanot* around the synagogue and the book of Ecclesiastes (Kohelet) is read. Honored guests (see *ushpizin*) are invited into the sukkah.

Sumer. Ancient civilization located in the southern part of Mesopotamia (modern day southeastern Iraq) from the time of the earliest historical records in the mid-4th millennium B.C.E. until the rise of Babylonia in the late 3rd millennium. Considered the first urban society in the world, the Sumerians invented picture-hieroglyphs that later developed into cuneiform and represent the oldest known written language that evolved into an effective form of communication. A non-Semitic people, the Sumerians are credited with inventing the wheel, ushering in the era of intensive agriculture and irrigation, developing mathematics using an alternating system of base 10 and 6, and originating the first codified legal and administrative systems and the first city-state. Some Sumerian words and laws, as well as literary motifs and genres, are found in the Bible.

Sumptuary laws. Regulations enacted in the Middle Ages by some Jewish communities (and some non-Jewish local rulers) that limited excess in dress, food, and festivities (including the number of guests invited to weddings and circumcisions). They were designed to reduce competitive conspicuous consumption among Jews as well as to decrease anti-Jewish feelings engendered by accusations of ostentatious living.

Sun (*shemesh*). Although worshiped as a deity by its pagan neighbors, for Israel the sun was merely "the greater light to rule the day," which was formed on the fourth day of Creation (Gen. 1:16). In Joseph's dream, the sun and the moon personified his parents (Gen. 37:9–10). The sun was said to have stood still to give Joshua and the Israelites time to defeat the Amorites (Josh. 10:12-14). The Bible expressly forbade sun worship (Deut. 4:19, 17:3), and one who violated this prohibition was to be stoned at the gates of the city (Deut. 17:2-5). Nevertheless, sun worship was introduced into Judah by the evil King Manasseh. King Josiah then abolished the cult, destroying his grandfather's altars as well as chariots that had been dedicated to sun worship at the entrance of the Temple (2 Kings 23:5). Hellenized Jews renewed worship of the sun and even wore amulets blasphemously referring to Helios (the Greek sun god) as "God in the Heavens." Mosaic floors in some ancient synagogues, especially Beit Alpha in the Galilee, depicted Helios as a handsome youth riding in a chariot drawn by the four horses of the sun (placed in the center of the signs of the zodiac).[314]

Sun, blessing of the (*Birkat ha-Chamah*). Once every 28 years, at the vernal equinox early on the first Tuesday of the month of Nisan, the sun begins a new cycle and, according to tradition, stands at the same position as at its creation. After the morning service on Wednesday, Jews traditionally recite the Blessing of the Sun, which thanks God for the sun and its continued beneficence. At the conclusion of the ritual, worshipers express the hope that they will be privileged to live until the coming of the Messiah, to witness the fulfillment of the prophecy of Isaiah (30:26): "and the light of the sun shall be sevenfold, as the light of the seven days." The next occasion for the *Birkat ha-Chamah* service will be on April 1, 2009.

Supersessionist doctrine. Also called "replacement theology," the Christian claim that Israel is no longer the chosen or covenantal people.This concept is based on the assumption that the covenant between God and the Jewish people was conditional, rather than the traditional Jewish belief of it being unconditional. According to this view, by rejecting Divine law and perpetually sinning (especially idolatry), the Jews forfeited their favored position and consequently were superseded by a new covenant ("New Testament") forged between God and the Christians. As evidence for their contention, Christians point to the desperate straits of the Jews in their midst as proof that the Church had inherited the role of the "true Israel," God's Chosen People.

Superstition. Although the Bible forbids divination and magic, the Talmud refers to a variety of amulets and belief in demons, the Evil Eye, and the significance of dreams.As with all cultures, Jews have developed numerous superstitious practices applicable to a variety of occasions. Some of the most popular are spitting three times, chewing on thread, pulling one's ears after sneezing; sneezing on the truth; closing books that have been left open; and placing salt in pockets and corners of the room.

Sura. Ancient city in southern Babylonian and the site of one of the two major talmudic academies, which was founded in the early 3rd century C.E. by Rav. In the 4th and 5th centuries, the Talmud was edited by Ashi and Ravina in Sura, which remained a center of Jewish learning for 700 years.

Susannah and the Elders. Apocryphal book added at the end of the canonical Book of Daniel in ancient versions. The virtuous and beautiful wife of a prosperous Jew of Babylon, Susanna (whose name means "lily") was unjustly accused by two Jewish elders of having committed adultery and was condemned to death. However, she was proved innocent when the elders, interrogated by Daniel, disagreed about the tree under which the adultery allegedly took place. In accordance with biblical law, which visits false witnesses with the punishment that the accused would have received, the elders were executed.

Sykes-Picot Agreement. Secret agreement between Britain and France, concluded in 1916, that defined their respective spheres of influence and control in the Middle East following their presumed victory in World War I and the dismantling of the Ottoman Empire. Britain was allocated control of areas roughly comprising what is now Jordan and Iraq and a small area around Haifa. France was allocated control of what is now Southeastern Turkey, Northern Iraq, Syria, Lebanon, and Upper Galilee. The controlling powers were permitted to determine the precise boundaries of states to be established within these areas. The land that subsequently came to be called Palestine was slated for international administration, pending consultations with Russia and other powers. The Arabs denounced the Sykes-Picot Agreement because it contradicted other pledges made to them. The Jews viewed it unfavorably because it did not explicitly establish a Jewish national home. The Sykes-Picot Agreement was officially abrogated in 1920 when Britain assumed the Mandate for Palestine.

Synagogue. From a Greek word meaning "house of assembly," the synagogue is considered by many Jews to be the most important institution in Judaism. The three Hebrew designations for the synagogue indicate its major functions – *beit knesset* (house of assembly); *beit tefillah* (house of prayer); and *beit midrash* (house of study). The Yiddish term for a synagogue is *shul* (school), reflecting the fact that Jewish worship and learning most often take place in the same building. Early Reform Jews chose the term "temple" for their synagogues. This indicated that in the post-Enlightenment age they no longer yearned for a return to the Land of Israel and the rebuilding of the Temple in Jerusalem, instead considering the country of their citizenship to be their everlasting homeland.[315] Historically, the synagogue represents the site of the first communal worship divorced from sacrifice. Unlike the Temple, which could only be in Jerusalem and was run by a specifically sanctified clergy born to the task (*kohanim* assisted by Levites), the synagogue could be housed anywhere, not necessarily in a spot with some sacred connotation. It did not have to adhere to a rigid architectural pattern and had prayer leaders and teachers whose roles were not determined by birth, ancestry, or socioeconomic level.[316] Probably originating during the Babylonian Exile, by the end of the Second Temple period (first century C.E.) the synagogue as a house of prayer and study was a firmly established institution both in Israel and in the Diaspora.[317] After the destruction of the Second Temple in 70 C.E., the synagogue became the center of Jewish communal and spiritual life. (For further information, see rabbi, cantor, ark, *bimah*, *parochet*, *mechitza*, *ner tamid*, and individual Jewish denominations.)

Syncretism. The attempt to unify or reconcile different, even opposing, beliefs, principles, and schools of thoughts. In the religious context, the term can refer to the introduction into Judaism of certain aspects of the beliefs, thought, and practices of the religions of the cultures with whom Jews repeatedly came in contact throughout their history.

T

Ta'am. Yiddish word meaning "taste, good taste, flavor."

Ta'amei ha-mitzvot (reasons for observing the *mitzvot*). Throughout the centuries, sages have debated why Jews should observe the commandments. Are they to be obeyed merely because they represent the will of God, or because they possess some intrinsic meaning designed to spiritually improve the person who performs them, or for both reasons? Some have argued that we should not search for reasons for the *mitzvot* since they transcend our understanding, while others have maintained that every effort should be made to discover their underlying meanings. For the Jewish mystics and practitioners of Kabbalah, fulfilling the commandments restores union and harmony in the spiritual realm of the *sefirot*, which ultimately channels positive Divine energy into our material world.

Ta'anit (Taan.). The 9th tractate in Mo'ed (festivals) in the Mishnah, it deals with the fast days other than Yom Kippur.

Ta'anit Esther – see Fast of Esther.

Tabernacle – see *Mishkan*.

Tabernacles – see Sukkot.

Table hymns – see *Zemirot*.

Tablets of the Law – see Ten Commandments.

Tachanun (supplication). Prayers containing confessions of sins and petitions for God's grace and mercy, which are is recited immediately after the reader's repetition of the *Amidah* in the morning and afternoon services on weekdays. A major feature of *Tachanun* is the act of *nefilat apayim* (lit., "falling on the face"). *Tachanun* is not said on festive occasions and other joyous days when expressions of tragedy and grief would detract from the celebration. Therefore, *Tachanun* is not recited on Sabbaths, festivals (Passover, Shavuot, Sukkot, Rosh Chodesh, Purim, Chanukah, Tu b'Shevat, Yom ha-Atzmaut, Lag ba-Omer, Yom Yerushalayim), between Yom Kippur and Sukkot, and the entire month of Nisan. It is also not said on Tisha b'Av, which according to tradition will be transformed from a day of sorrow to one of rejoicing in the Messianic Age.

Tachlis. Yiddish term for the heart of a matter, getting down to business, or the bottom line.

Tachrichim – see Shroud.

Tagin. Aramaic for "daggers," the decorative flourishes that embellish seven letters (*shin, ayin, tet, nun, zayin, gimel, tzadi*) whenever they occur in the Torah scroll. According to the Talmud, God affixed the *tagin* to the letters of the Torah before Moses ascended Mount Sinai to receive it. Some modern scholars believe that early scribes introduced these calligraphic flourishes to enhance the beauty of the Torah lettering. Kabbalah places great stress on the mystical meaning of the *tagin*, viewing every additional stroke or sign as a symbol revealing extraordinary secrets of the universe and Creation.

Tahara (cleansing or purification). Ceremony of washing the dead before burial, which is performed by members of the *chevra kadisha* (burial society). The basis for this ritual cleansing of the body is the verse, "As one came [into the world], so shall one leave" (Ecclesiastes 5:15). This means that just as a baby is washed immediately after birth, so must the body be washed prior to burial. The essential part of the ritual purification of the *tahara* ceremony is the pouring of warm water over the entire body, while it is held in an upright position, as certain prayers and biblical passages are recited. The body is then thoroughly dried and dressed in a shroud. In addition to washing the body, the hair is combed and the fingernails and toenails are cut.

Taharat ha-mishpachah (purity of the family). Although the Bible only forbids intercourse during a woman's menstrual period (see *niddah*), subsequent rabbinic rulings have also precluded any physical contact that could conceivably be sexually stimulating. This includes kissing, hugging, or otherwise touching one's spouse during the forbidden days, during which husband and wife sleep in separate beds. The rule forbidding touching a *niddah* has led many Orthodox men to protect the privacy and modesty of their wives by never touching them in public, so no one knows whether or not they are in a state of *niddah* at the time. Similarly, they do not shake hands with any woman, not knowing whether or not she is a *niddah*. After seven days counted following the final day of menstrual flow, the woman immerses herself in the *mikveh* as an act of symbolic ritual purification. Only then can marital relations be resumed. According to R. Meir, the reason for the seven-day waiting period is so that the wife "will be as beloved by her husband as at the time of her first entry into the bridal chamber" (Nid. 31b).

Tahini (tahina). Sesame seed paste, which most commonly is mixed with humus or used as a sauce on a falafel sandwich.

Tahor – see Ritual purity.

Takanah. A rabbinic regulation, not derived from any biblical commandment, instituted to cope with a new socioeconomic or historical situation or to improve compliance with existing *halacha*. The term comes from the Hebrew word *tikun* (meaning "repair" or "improve"), implying that there are "flaws" in the Torah that occasionally need to be "repaired." Examples include the *mitzvah* of lighting candles on Chanukah, a post-biblical holiday, and the practice of public readings of the Torah every Monday and Thursday, which was instituted by Ezra. Some *takanot* vary from community to community or from region to region. An example is the *takanah* issued by Rabbenu Gershom about 1000 C.E. prohibiting polygamy, a practice that is clearly permitted by the Torah and the Talmud. This ruling was accepted by Ashkenazic Jews living in Christian countries where polygamy was forbidden, but was not adopted by Sephardim residing in Islamic countries where men were permitted up to four wives.

TALI. A Hebrew acronym for ***T**igbur **L**imudei **Y**ahadut* (enhanced Jewish studies), the goal of this organization is to introduce, in cooperation with parents, teachers, and pupils, a pluralistic, liberal version of Judaism and prayer into the secular state school system in Israel. The TALI network of schools was originally established in 1976 by the foundation for Masorti (Conservative) Judaism in Israel, though it has tried to separate the schools from the Conservative Movement to allow each school maximum freedom to create a hand-tailored educational program without the restraints of denominational practice and ideology.

Tallit. Traditional prayer shawl worn during daily morning prayers and all services on Yom Kippur. (On Tisha b'Av, it is only worn during the afternoon service.) A *tallit* is also worn by the prayer leader at the afternoon service; in some congregations, the prayer leader also wears a *tallit* for the evening service on Sabbaths and festivals. Ritual fringes (see *tzitzit*) are attached to each of the four corners of the *tallit* in accordance with biblical law (Num. 15:38). Because the explicit purpose of the *tzitzit* is "that you may *see* them [and recall all the commandments of the Lord and obey them, so that you do not go astray after your own heart and eyes]" (Num. 15:39), the *tallit* is only worn during the day. The sole exception is Yom Kippur, when the *Kol Nidrei* service actually starts just before evening and the *tallit* adds sanctity to the occasion. Wearing a *tallit* is obligatory for Jewish males 13 or older, though some Orthodox synagogues follow the Eastern European tradition of having a *tallit* worn only by married men. However, all men wear a *tallit* whenever they are leading the congregation in prayer or are called up for an *aliyah* to the Torah. In liberal synagogues, some women wear a *tallit* during worship services.

Tallit kattan (little *tallit*). Light undergarment that is fitted over the neck and shoulders so that the *tzitzit* hang down and are visible throughout the daylight hours. Use of the *tallit kattan*, also called *arba kanfot* (four corners), developed when it became awkward and inconvenient to wear an outer garment with fringes throughout the day, especially when changes in fashion dictated that clothes no longer always had four distinct corners.[318] Furthermore, wearing fringes on an inner garment shielded from view (i.e., not hanging down far enough to be seen) was a safer alternative in those communities where exposed *tzitzit* identifying the wearer as a Jew might single him out for persecution.[319]

Talmid Hacham. A learned scholar or a disciple of the wise. This Hebrew term refers to a person who is an expert in Jewish studies, especially the Talmud.

Talmud. In general use, the term "Talmud" refers to the Babylonian Talmud, though there is also a much smaller Jerusalem Talmud.The Babylonian Talmud is a compendium of the extensive discussions and interpretations of the Mishnah in the great academies of learning by scholars known as *amora'im* from the first half of the 3rd century C.E. (Rav and Samuel) to the editing by Rav Ashi and Ravina around 500. It makes no attempt to transform the vast amount of material into a concise or systematic form. On every page of the Talmud, the Mishnah and Gemara are situated in the center and set in larger type. Surrounding the text are the two most famous medieval commentaries – toward the binding is that of Rashi (11th century), while in the outside column are the subsequent discussions of the Tosafot (12th-14th centuries). Beyond these commentaries, at the margins of the page, are a potpourri of cross-references to other talmudic sources; a key to quotations from the Bible and the great codes of Jewish law; and additional, shorter commentaries from the Middle Ages and even recent centuries. In the upper outer corner is the Hebrew letter(s) indicating the number of the page (*daf*), which applies to both sides of the sheet. Thus, references to a source in the Talmud always indicate whether they fall on the "a" or "b" side of the page. Both the Babylonian and Jerusalem Talmuds provide knowledge of the Jewish world of late antiquity and of classical Jewish doctrine and law. The Babylonian Talmud, in particular, has exerted a profound influence on Jewish life and thought.

Talmud, Babylonian – see Babylonian Talmud.

Talmud, burning of the. Throughout the ages, there have been periodic attempts to suppress Judaism in various countries. Some of these resulted in the destruction of copies of the Talmud and other Jewish texts. In the Middle Ages, false charges by the convert Nicholas Donin that the Talmud blasphemed Jesus led to the first public disputation between Jews and Christians in 1240 and the first burning of copies of the work in Paris two years later. Burnings of the Talmud continued in later centuries, with the last public burning taking place in Poland in 1757, when 1000 copies were thrown into a pit and burned by a hangman).

Talmud, Jerusalem – see Jerusalem Talmud.

Talmud, Sea of. Post-talmudic expression indicating the immensity and scope of the Talmud. Although the phrase is not found in the Talmud itself, the Bible compares the vastness of knowledge to the sea: "The earth shall be full of the knowledge of the Lord, as the waters cover the sea" (Isa. 11:9), and "Can you find out the deep things of God?... its measure is longer than the earth and broader than the sea" (Job 11:9).

Talmud Torah. Literally "study [of the] Law," the intermediate Jewish school between *cheder* and *yeshiva* where Torah, Talmud, and other religious subjects are studied. The term also can be used generically to mean the study of Torah.

Talmudic academies. Centers of rabbinic scholarship. The first was established in the Land of Israel by R. Yochanan ben Zakkai at Yavneh after the fall of Jerusalem in 70 C.E. In Babylonia, the major academies were in Nehardea, Sura, and Pumbedita.

Tam. Used to describe the third child at the seder, this Hebrew word is usually translated as "simple." It is meant as a praiseworthy characteristic, as in the verse commanding the Jew to be *tam* (wholehearted) with the Lord your God (Deut. 18:13). The mystics considered this the highest level of religious consciousness, representing unquestioning faith and unsophisticated surrender to the Divine will ("religiously naïve").[320]

Tamei – see Ritual impurity.

Tamid (1). Literally meaning "perpetual," the Hebrew name for the burnt offering that was sacrificed twice daily (in the morning and the evening) in the Tabernacle and later in the Temple (Num. 28:3-8).

Tamid (Tam.) (2). The 9th tractate in Kodashim (holy things) in the Mishnah, it deals with the regulations for the daily burnt offerings in the Temple as well as the general organization of that institution.

Tammuz. The 4th month of the Jewish calendar (June/July). The 17th of the month is a fast day.

Tanach. Hebrew term for the Bible, the acronym *Ta-Na-Kh* (or *Tanach*) is derived from the initial letters of the names of its three major divisions – Torah; *Nevi'im* (see Prophets); and *Ketuvim* (see Writings).

Tanhuma. Aggadic midrash on each *parashah* of the Torah. It is attributed to Tanhuma bar Abba, 4th-century Palestinian *amora* and prolific aggadist, because of his repeated appearances throughout the text. Each section is introduced by the phrase "Our teacher taught...," followed by a legal question leading to a long and complex answer, which ends with a proof text that is the beginning of the biblical verse according to the triennial Palestinian cycle.

Tanna. Literally "repeater" in Aramaic, the initial teachers of the Mishnah in the 1st and 2nd centuries C.E. Because of the prohibition against writing down the Oral Law, the *tanna'im* acted as "living books" in transmitting the teachings of the Mishnah to their disciples. The classical period of the *tanna'im* began with the deaths of Hillel and Shammai and ended with the generation after Judah ha-Nasi, the editor of the Mishnah. The *tanna'im* were followed by the *amora'im*, whose discussions of the Mishnah are contained within the *Gemara.*

Tanninim. Hebrew term for the "great sea monsters," which the Bible relates were created by God on the fifth day. Unequivocally stating that these sea monsters were a Divinely designed part of God's plan for Creation, the Bible polemicizes against the prevailing pagan concept of a conflict between independent water deities to achieve supremacy in the pantheon, which was a core belief in ancient Near Eastern mythology.

Tanya. Masterwork of Jewish mysticism written in the late 18th century by Shneur Zalman of Liadi, the founder of the Lubavitch (see Chabad) movement. For Chabad, the *Tanya* is the basic work of Hasidic spirituality.

Targum. Generic term for any Aramaic translation of the Bible or an individual book within it. (For the need for such translations, see *meturgeman.*)

Targum Onkelos. Official Aramaic translation of the Bible (2nd century), which is printed next to the Torah text in most rabbinic Bibles. A convert to Judaism and student of R. Akiva, Onkelos apparently developed a close relationship with Rabban Gamaliel II and arranged for a lavish funeral for the *nasi*.

Targum Sheni. Literally "Second Translation," an Aramaic paraphrase of the book of Esther.

Taryag mitzvot. Hebrew term for the 613 biblical commandments, since the numerical value of these letters (*tav*, *resh*, *yud*, *gimel*) equals 613. Although the Torah is the source of all the commandments, it does not specifically enumerate them. The first mention of a precise number of commandments appears in a talmudic statement by R. Simlai, a 4th-century sage in the Land of Israel, who observed that "613 commandments were communicated to Moses; 365 negative commandments [*mitzvot lo ta'aseh*], corresponding to the number of days in the solar year, and 248 positive commandments [*mitzvot aseh*], corresponding to the number of parts of the human body." During the talmudic period, there was no attempt to precisely enumerate the individual commandments. The major monumental work listing and elucidating the meaning of the commandments was the *Sefer ha-Mitzvot* (Book of the Commandments) of Maimonides, the major Jewish philosopher of the Middle Ages. Later works describing the *mitzvot* include *Sefer ha-Chinuch* (Book of Education) and *Sefer ha-Mitzvot ha-Katzar*.

Tas. Silver plaque inscribed with the name of a specific festival or Sabbath, which is placed within the window of the breastplate that adorns the Torah scroll. It indicates that the scroll has been rolled to the proper place for that service.

Tashlich (You will cast). From the verse in Micah (7:19), "You will cast (*v'tashlich*) all our sins into the depths of the sea," the ceremony on the afternoon of the first day of Rosh Hashanah in which Jews recite special penitential prayers and psalms and throw crumbs or small pieces of bread into a body of water (river, lake, or ocean) to symbolically cast away their sins. It is postponed to the second day of Rosh Hashanah if the first day falls on the Sabbath, because of the proscription against carrying on that day. *Tashlich* was not a ritual devised by the Rabbis, but rather a popular practice of uncertain origin that was eventually accepted by rabbinic authorities after they had fought against it as a superstitious custom of pagan origin designed to propitiate the spirits of the rivers on critical days of the year.[321] The Rabbis feared that Jews would consider this ceremony sufficient to absolve them of their sins, rather than appreciating the need to change their conduct and return to God's path.

Tattoo. The Bible (Lev. 19:28) prohibits making incisions into the skin and inserting colors of indelible dyes or inks to create a tattoo on one's body. This is in keeping with the concept of reverence for the human body as the work of God. Both the person who wore the tattoo and the one who produced it were guilty of violating this commandment.[322] According to Maimonides,[323] this heathen custom indicated "that the tattooed person was a slave sold to the idol and marked for its service."

Tav. The 22nd and final letter of the Hebrew alphabet, with a numerical value of 400.

Tazria. The 4th *parashah* in the Book of Leviticus (12:1-13:59), it opens with the purification rites for a new mother (see childbirth, impurity after) before embarking on a detailed description of symptoms and purification rites for persons afflicted with *tzara'at* and other skin diseases.

Tchotchke. Literally a "toy," this Yiddish word is used to denote any attractive but insignificant trinket or inexpensive souvenir.

Teacher of Righteousness. The title given in the Dead Sea Scrolls to the organizer of the community at Qumran.

Techeilet. Thread of blue to be put with the seven white ones on each corner of the *tallit*, according to the last half of the Torah verse commanding the wearing of *tzitzit*. This blue was made from a rare dye that was extracted from a sea snail (*chilazon*) by a few families on the Mediterranean coast. After the destruction of the Second Temple, the secret of obtaining this exact shade of blue was lost, and the use of the blue thread in the fringes was discontinued. Recently, a close relative of the snail has been discovered, and *tallitot* with blue fringes are now available. The blue stripes often woven in *tallitot* symbolize this ancient *techeilet*.

Tefillah – see Prayer.

Tefillah. The 16th blessing of the weekday *Amidah*, which asks God to "hear our voice…pity and be compassionate to us…and accept our prayers with compassion and favor."

Tefillat Geshem – see Rain, prayer for.

Tefillat ha-Derech. The recitation of this "Prayer for a Journey" or "Wayfarer's Prayer" is based on the talmudic dictum that a person who "passes through a place infested with beasts or bands of robbers" must say a short prayer to travel through it safely. It is recited at the start of each day's travels and is always said in the first person plural (Sephardim use the first person singular), both as a reflection of the talmudic statement that "a man should always associate himself with the congregation" and since it applies not only to the Jewish traveler who recites it but to all those who are making the trip. The *Tefillat ha-Derech* is still widely used in modern travel, especially by airplane, where appropriate additions have been made to the text. One custom designed to protect travelers is to give a small sum of money to any person setting out on a journey (see *shaliach l'dvar mitzvah*).

Tefillat Tal – see Dew, prayer for.

Tefillin (1). Two small black leather boxes that are bound by black leather straps (see *retzu'ot*) to the forehead and arm. Also known as phylacteries, they contain parchments on which are written the four sets of biblical verses that mention the commandment to wear them as "a sign [*ot*] upon your hand and as frontlets [*totafot*] between your eyes" (Exod 13:1-10, 11-16; Deut. 6:4-9, 11:13-21). The Kabbalists interpreted this commandment as a reminder to bind one's thoughts and actions to the will of God. Originally worn all day and removed at night, *tefillin* now are worn only during each weekday morning service. *Tefillin* are put on after the *tallit* and are not worn on the Sabbath or on festivals. Although an obligation only for men, some women also don *tefillin* and a *tallit* for morning prayers.

Tefillin (2). Minor tractate added to the Talmud that deals with the laws regarding *tefillin*.

Tehillim – see Psalms.

Teiku. Meaning "let it stand," a talmudic designation for any cryptic, enigmatic, or mysterious text that must remain unresolved until the coming of Elijah, who will clarify the situation. *Teiku* is a Hebrew acronym for "*Tishbi Yitaretz Kushiyat V'abayot*" (lit, "the Tishbite [Elijah] will resolve difficulties and problems [when he comes]").

Teivah. Literally "box," the Sephardic term for the *bimah* where the prayer leader conducts much of the service and the Torah is read. *Teivah* is also the biblical word for both Noah's ark (Gen. 6:14) and Moses' basket (Exod. 2:5), as well as the talmudic word denoting the Ark of the Covenant.

Tekiah. One of the three sounds of the *shofar*, a long sustained blast. A biblical verse relating to the commandment of blowing the *shofar* (Num 10:6) uses the phrases *u-tikatem teruah* (you should blow a *teruah*) and *teruah yitku* (and the *teruah* will be blown). From the two placements of the word "blow" (varying forms of the Hebrew word *tekiah*) in relation to the word *teruah*, the Rabbis deduced that there should be a long *tekiah* sound both before and after the *teruah*. Thus evolved the pattern of blowing the *shofar* that persists today: *tekiah—shevarim teruah—tekiah*; *tekiah—shevarim— tekiah*; and *tekiah—teruah—tekiah*. The *tekiah* has been symbolically interpreted as a wake up call to examine one's ways and spur repentance.

Tekiah gedolah. Literally "great blast," the final note that ends the two sets of *shofar* blasts in the Rosh Hashanah service and concludes the Yom Kippur service. The *tekiah gedolah* is sustained as long as the *shofar* blower can manage.

Tel. Archeological term for a mound representing the site of habitation of multiple cultures devastated by some major natural catastrophe that caused it to be abandoned forever.

Tel Amarna letters. Archive of correspondence, mostly diplomatic, between the Egyptian administration and its representatives in Canaan and Amurru dating to the reign of Pharaoh Amenhotep IV, better known as Akhenaten (14th century B.C.E.). Written in Akkadian cuneiform on clay tablets, they contain the first mention of a Near Eastern group known as the Habiru, which some scholars have identifed as the ancient Hebrews.

Tel Aviv. Economic and cultural center of Israel. Founded in 1909 as the first all-Jewish modern city, Tel Aviv (lit., "Hill of Spring") was initially developed by a group of Jewish residents from Jaffa (immediately to the south), who bought two stretches of sand dunes to build a garden suburb. In subsequent years, Tel Aviv developed into a major urban center, which contained almost 40% of the Jewish population of Palestine by the outbreak of World War II. With Jerusalem under siege in 1948, Ben-Gurion proclaimed the independence of Israel in Tel Aviv. The city is home to the Israel Philharmonic Orchestra, the Habimah Theater and New Israel Opera, and the campus of Tel Aviv University, which houses the Diaspora Museum. Since 2003, Tel Aviv has been a world heritage site due to its unique Bauhaus architecture.

Temple (1). Central site of Jewish worship and sacrifice in ancient Israel. The First Temple was built by King Solomon (10th century B.C.E.) and destroyed by the Babylonians in 586 B.C.E. The Second Temple, constructed on its ruins by those who returned from the Babylonian Exile, was dedicated 515 B.C.E and destroyed by Titus and the conquering Roman army in 70 C.E. At the entrance to the Temple were the two columns of Jachin and Boaz; within its confines were the *Ezrat Nashim*, *Ezrat Yisrael*, the Menorah, and the Showbread. Separated from the rest of the Temple by the *parochet* was the Holy of Holies, which contained the Ark of the Covenant.

Temple (2) – see Synagogue.

Temple Mount. Site of the First and Second Temples in Jerusalem. According to Jewish tradition, this will also be the place where a Third Temple will be erected at the time of the Messiah. In the late 7th and early 8th centuries, two major Muslim religious shrines were built on the Temple Mount – the Dome of the Rock, popularly known as the Mosque of Omar (over the foundation stone, the site where legend maintains that Abraham was prepared to sacrifice Isaac [*Akedah*] and Mohammed ascended to heaven), and the Al-Aksa Mosque. The Western Wall, part of the Herodian retaining wall surrounding and supporting the Temple Mount, became a site of Jewish worship in the Middle Ages.

Temple Scroll. Longest of the Dead Sea Scrolls, measuring over 28 feet and originally with 66 columns of text. Written in Hebrew, it contains regulations concerning buildings and rituals of the Jerusalem Temple, mostly adapted from biblical sources, as well as rules dealing with cleanness and uncleanness and laws related to the king.

Temple tax. Annual levy of a half-*shekel* toward the upkeep of the Sanctuary and later the Temple.The qualification that "the rich shall not pay more and the poor shall not pay less" indicated that the Tabernacle belonged to the entire community, without regard to wealth or social status, since all were are equal in the eyes of God. The half-*shekel* tax also taught the moral lesson that one Jew alone is only half a Jew; one must establish community to becomes a complete individual.[324] The Mishnah reported that Jews of the Second Temple period, whether they lived in the Land of Israel or in the remotest corners of the Diaspora, cherished this commandment as a sacred privilege and a means of participating in the public offerings brought daily in the House of God in Jerusalem.[325]

Temurah (Tem.). The 6th tractate of Kodashim in the Mishnah, it deals with substituting one sacrificial animal offering for another.

Ten (*eser*). In addition to the Ten Commandments, there were 10 plagues and 10 miraculous things that were created at twilight as the sixth day of Creation drew to a close. Ten men constitute a *minyan*, and there are Ten Days of Repentance.Historically, the conquest of the Northern Kingdom of Israel in 721 B.C.E. led to the Jews of this region being scattered throughout the Assyrian empire and disappearing – the Ten Lost Tribes. In Kabbalah, there are 10 *sefirot* representing the emanations of God.

Ten Commandments. Core moral principles that have become the essential code of human behavior in the Western tradition (Exod. 20:2-14; Deut. 5:6-18).[326] Also known as *Aseret ha-Dibrot* (lit., "Ten Words/Utterances") in Hebrew and by the Greek word Decalogue, the Torah relates that God revealed the Ten Commandments to the Israelites as they encamped at the foot of Mount Sinai, seven weeks after being liberated from bondage in Egypt. After the Revelation, Moses ascended Mount Sinai and remained there fasting for 40 days before receiving the two stone "tablets of the covenant" (see *luchot ha-brit*), which were engraved "by the finger of God" and included the conditions of the covenant between God and Israel (Deut. 4:13). Outraged over the blasphemy of the Golden Calf, Moses broke the first pair of tablets (Exod. 32:19; Deut. 9:17) and again ascended the mountain, remaining another 40 days pleading on behalf of the people. After God forgave the Israelites, Moses was ordered to write a second pair of stone tablets identical to the first. God commanded that these be placed inside the Ark of the Covenant, which was housed first in the *Mishkan* (Tabernacle) and ultimately in the Temple in Jerusalem. The Ten Commandments are: "(1) I am *YHWH* your God; (2) You shall have no other gods before me (or make any graven image); (3) You shall not take the name of *YHWH* in vain; (4) Remember/observe the Sabbath day; (5) Honor your father and mother; (6) You shall not murder; (7) You shall not commit adultery; (8) You shall not steal; (9) You shall not bear false witness; and (10) You shall not covet." Representations of the two tablets containing the Ten Commandments are a popular decorative motif in synagogues.

Ten Commandments, use in liturgy of the. Although said daily as part of the Temple service, Israelites outside the Temple were forbidden to recite them, so as to disprove insinuations by heretical sects that only the Ten Commandments and not the entire Torah were Divinely revealed at Mount Sinai. Therefore, the Ten Commandments were excluded from the liturgy. The only emphasis given to the Decalogue is that the congregation rises when it is read in synagogue twice each year as part of the designated weekly Torah portions and on the festival of Shavuot, the anniversary of the Revelation at Sinai. Two sets of cantillations (see *trope*) are indicated in the text. The so-called "upper" set, which represents the traditional manner in which Israel heard the Ten Commandments at Sinai, is used for public reading of the Decalogue in the synagogue. The "lower set" is used on all other occasions, such as when reading the commandments in private.

Ten Days of Repentance (*Aseret Y'mei Teshuvah*). Inclusive period from Rosh Hashanah through Yom Kippur. According to Jewish tradition, Rosh Hashanah is the day when God decides the fate of every individual for the upcoming year. However, since the final judgment is not "sealed" until Yom Kippur, the Ten Days of Repentance (lit., "return") provide an opportunity for intensive soul searching and reconciliation (see *U-netaneh Tokef*). Changes in the regular liturgy during this period reflect its penitential character. On the intermediate Sabbath between Rosh Hashanah and Yom Kippur (see Shabbat Shuvah), it was traditional for rabbis in Europe to deliver a sermon on the theme of repentance (one of only two sermons they gave each year, the other being on Shabbat ha-Gadol before Passover).

Ten Lost Tribes of Israel. The tribes of the North Kingdom of Israel that, after the Assyrian conquest in 721 B.C.E., were scattered throughout the empire, assimilated, and lost to history. Over the centuries, various groups have claimed that they are the descendants of these lost tribes.

Ten Martyrs. Renowned sages executed by the Romans following the unsuccessful Bar Kochba revolt (132-135) for defying Emperor Hadrian's prohibition, under penalty of death, against the observance and study of Jewish law. According to several late *midrashim*, the Roman emperor decided to execute ten great Jewish sages to correspond to the ten sons of Jacob who had sold Joseph into slavery. Although their identity is uncertain, they probably were among these 11 rabbis: Akiva ben Joseph, Ishmael ben Elisha, Elazar ben Dama, Hanina ben Teradyon, Judah ben Bava, Hutzpit the Interpreter, Yeshevav the Scribe, Eleazar ben Shammua, Hanina ben Hakhinai, Shimon ben Gamaliel I, and Ishmael the High Priest. The theme of the Ten Martyrs was a popular subject for medieval *piyyutim*, such as *Eileh Ezkerah*.

Ten men of leisure – see *Batlanim*.

Ten miraculous things (created at twilight on the sixth day of creation). According to *Pirkei Avot* (5:9), these were: (1) mouth of the earth that swallowed up Korach and his fellow conspirators (Num. 16:32); (2) mouth of the well that supplied water for the Israelites in the wilderness; (3) mouth of the donkey that spoke to Balaam (Num. 22:28); (4) rainbow that was shown to Noah after the Flood; (5) manna that came from heaven to feed the Israelites for 40 years in the wilderness; (6) staff on which was engraved the four-letter Name of God, with which Moses performed the signs in Egypt (Exod. 4:17); (7) *shamir*; (8) forms of the letters (Hebrew alphabet) engraved on the tablets of the Ten Commandments; (9) instrument used to engrave the tablets of the Decalogue; and (10) first set of stone tablets of the Ten Commandments, which were miraculously written "on both sides" (Exod. 32:15), unlike the second set that was carved by Moses himself.

Ten Plagues. Afflictions suffered by the Egyptians because of Pharaoh's refusal to allow the enslaved Israelites to leave Egypt (Exod. 7:24-12:34). As agents of God, Moses and Aaron announced, signaled, and removed the plagues in the Divine Name. The ten plagues were: (1) blood; (2) frogs; (3) vermin (lice); (4) wild beasts; (5) pestilence (disease of the flocks); (6) boils; (7) hail; (8) locusts; (9) darkness; and (10) slaying of the firstborn. Over the centuries, the plagues have been interpreted as attacks on the principal divinities that were worshipped since time immemorial in the Nile Valley. Some have suggested that the plagues represented miraculous intensification of natural local or seasonal phenomena that occurred by Divine power in a single year. According to tradition, when each of the plagues is recited at the Passover seder, participants dip their little fingers into the wine and spill a drop of it (or pour some wine out of the cup) to symbolize their grief at the loss of any human life, even that of their bitter enemies.

Tena'im. Set of conditions agreed to during medieval times by the parents of the bride and groom. These prenuptial arrangements included "the date and place of the wedding, the dowry, the gift for the groom, the parents' financial commitment to the couple, delineation and separation of the bride's estate, and inheritance rights." Although initially agreed to orally, these terms eventually were committed to writing in a formal document and signed at the *kiddushin* ceremony.[327]

Tent of Meeting (*ohel mo'ed*). – see *Mishkan*.

10th of Tevet. Minor fast day that comes shortly after Chanukah and marks the beginning of the siege of Jerusalem by Nebuchadnezzar, which eventually resulted in the Babylonians destroying the First Temple.

Teraphim (household gods). Although denounced by the Israelite religion, *teraphim* were apparently in common use both in Israel and among the neighboring Canaanites. The Bible relates that Rachel stole the *teraphim* of her father Laban (Gen. 31:19) and then hid them by placing them under her camel cushion and sitting on them (Gen. 31:34). When Michal learned that her father Saul had sent agents to kill her husband, David, she urged him to flee to save his life. "Michal then took a *teraph*, laid it down on the bed, and covered it with a cloth; and at its head she put a net of goat hair." By making it appear as if her husband was still asleep and reporting that he was sick in bed, Michal allowed David time to escape (1 Sam. 19:11-17).

Terezin – see Theresienstadt.

Teruah. One of the three sounds of the *shofar*, a blast of at least nine staccato notes that has been interpreted as symbolic of wailing.

Terumah (heave offering) **(1)**. From a Hebrew root meaning "life up from," a generic term for the various offerings given to the *kohanim*. In addition to the great heave offering (Deut. 18:4), they also included the heave-offering of the tithe (Num. 18:26-29), the first fruits (Exod. 23:19), and the dough-offering (*challah*; Num. 15:20). The *terumah* could be eaten only by a ritually clean *kohen* and members of his household, including his Israelite wife and gentile slaves.

Terumah (2). The 7th *parashah* in the Book of Exodus (25:1-27:29), it presents detailed instructions for the construction of the objects in the Tabernacle (Ark, *Kaporet* and *Cherubim*, Table, Menorah, sacrificial Altar) as well as its wooden structure and outer coverings.

Terumot (**Ter**.). The 6th tractate in Zera'im (seeds) in the Mishnah, it deals with the offerings to the *kohanim* from the Israelites and Levites.

Teshuvah (repentance) **(1)**. Prerequisite for Divine forgiveness. It requires a combination of genuine remorse for the wrong committed plus evidence of changed behavior. From the Hebrew root *shuv* (return), it encompasses both a turning away from evil and a turning toward the good. A central biblical concept, *teshuvah* is the theme of the Ten Days of Repentance and the central focus of the prayers on Yom Kippur. The talmudic dictum, "Repent one day before your death," means it is necessary to spend every day in repentance, for none know which will be their last. This concept was championed by the 19th-century Musar movement.For the kabbalists, who were concerned with how human deeds influence God, the goal of *teshuvah* was to repair the torn fabric and inner balance of the Divine.

Teshuvah (2). The 5th blessing of the weekday *Amidah*, it asks God to "influence us to return in perfect repentance before You."

Teshuvot – see *Responsa*.

Testaments of the 12 Patriarchs. Pseudoepigraphical work dating from the Second Temple period, which claims to be the testaments of the sons of Jacob to their descendants. Using a format modeled on Jacob's deathbed blessings to his sons (Gen. 49), each of these sons recounts the sins and merits of his own life and exhorts his children to follow the path of righteous living.

Tet. The 9th letter of the Hebrew alphabet, with a numerical value of 9.

Tetragrammaton. Greek for "four-letter word," the holiest name of God and the one that is most distinctly Jewish. Written in the Hebrew Bible with the four consonants *YHVH*, it occurs 6,823 times in the Bible[328] and probably reflects a form of the verb "to be." It may have derived from *Eh'yeh Asher Eh'yeh* ("I am Who I am" or "I will be Who I will be"), the name by which God was revealed to Moses at the Burning Bush (Exod. 3:14). In the Bible, *YHVH* is used when describing the relationship between God and human beings or when stressing the Divine qualities of lovingkindness and mercy. The first two letters (*YH*) are often added at the beginning or end of a Hebrew name – as in Yehoshua (Joshua, meaning "the Lord is my salvation) and Eliyahu (Elijah, meaning "My God is the Lord"). Once pronounced with its proper vowels by all Israelites, *YHVH* eventually became the "ineffable" name of God (see *Adonai* and *ha-Shem*).

Tetrarch (lit., "ruler of one-fourth" in Greek). After the death of Herod the Great, Judea was divided into four parts, each ruled by one of Herod's sons. Archelaus, who was granted the territories of Samaria, Judea, and Idumea, was removed and exiled to Rome. His territories were placed under the authority of the Roman governor (procurator). One of the other territories was the Galilee, where the tetrarch Herod Antipas ruled from 4 B.C.E. to 39 C.E. The tetrarch was appointed by the Roman Emperor and subject to his control.

Tetzaveh. The 8th *parashah* in the Book of Exodus (27:20-30:10), it continues the detailed instructions for the construction of the Tabernacle begun in *Terumah*. It focuses on the incense altar, the vestments of the *kohanim* and the *Kohen Gadol*, and the procedures for the installation of priests into the Divine service. The first section of the *parashah* deals with the lighting of the Menorah, which is reflected in the *ner tamid*, the only commanded practice of the Tabernacle that persists to this day.

Tevel. Agricultural produce that may not be eaten because it has not been tithed (i.e., the portions of *terumah* and *ma'aser* have not been separated). Today, packaged items from Israel under reliable supervision have these tithes separated before being exported to the United States.

Tevet. The 10th month of the Jewish calendar (December/January). The 10th of Tevet is a minor fast day.

Tevilah. The act of immersing oneself in the *mikveh* for ritual or spiritual purification.

Tevul Yom (TY). The 10th tractate in Tohorot (purity) in the Mishnah, it deals with those forms of minor uncleanness that remain until sunset even after ritual bathing (Lev. 15:7-18).

Thanksgiving blessing – see *Gomel.*

Thanksgiving offering – see Peace offering.

Theft. Unlike a robber, a thief steals the property of another secretly. The general rule is that a thief, who of his own free will admits his theft, must return what was stolen and is not subject to further punishment. In contrast, a convicted thief must pay double the value of the stolen property (i.e., pay a fine equal to the value of what he took). Special rules pertained to the theft of a sheep or an ox, for which a thief was required to make fourfold or fivefold restitution, respectively. A thief who was unable to pay restitution could be sold as a bondman to raise the funds to compensate his victim (see slavery).

Theism. Traditional Jewish belief that God is both transcendent and immanent.According to this theological concept, God is in the universe and involved in all its processes (unlike Deism), but also is beyond the universe (i.e., if there were no universe there would still be God, but without God there could be no universe).

Theocracy. Greek term meaning the government of a state by immediate divine guidance or by priestly officials who are regarded as divinely guided. In a Jewish context, it refers to the period from Moses to the time of the monarchy. During the Persian and Hellenistic eras, the High Priest was regarded as the supreme Jewish authority by the non-Jewish government. During the Middle Ages, Jewish communal life was a type of theocracy, with the rabbis exercising legislative authority based on Divinely revealed *halacha*. Ultra-Orthodox Jews look forward to a Messianic Age when God will directly govern the world.

Theodicy. From the Greek *theos* (god) and *dikç* (justice), an attempt to "justify the ways of God to man" and explain the meaning of human suffering, especially the seemingly unjustified suffering of the righteous who faithfully fulfill the commandments of a good and just God. The goal is to show that there is no contradiction between the biblical principle that each person is rewarded or punished during life for his good or evil deeds and the observable fact that this is often contradicted by ordinary experience. The theodicy problem of why the innocent suffer and the wicked prosper in this life, especially as presented in the Book of

Job, appeared to be a Divine mystery. A rabbinic solution to this conundrum was the concept of the resurrection of the dead, with the righteous rewarded in the World to Come. The concepts of an afterlife and eventual Divine justice became pillars of the Pharisees and their rabbinic descendants and one of the chief points of difference between them and the Sadducees, who asserted that the soul died together with the body. Today, the problem of theodicy remains one of the most fundamental challenges to traditional Jewish theology, especially in the wake of the Holocaust.

Theology. The study of the existence and nature of the Divine. It is an attempt to coherently understand a religious faith that already exists as a historical phenomenon, with a set of sacred texts, and to discover its relevance for adherents today. Although Judaism has traditionally been more concerned with religious practice than beliefs, theological speculation has existed throughout its history. In the Middle Ages, systematic expositions of theology were developed by such Jewish philosophers as Saadia Gaon, Judah Ha-Levi, and Maimonides. Famous Jewish theologians since the Enlightenment include Moses Mendelssohn (1729-1786), Leo Baeck (1873-1956), Franz Rosenzweig (1886-1929), and Abraham Joshua Heschel (1907-1972).

Theresienstadt. Nazi concentration camp in Czechoslovakia, established as a "model settlement" to conceal from the free world the fact that European Jewry was being exterminated. From October 1942 on, it was in reality a gateway to Auschwitz. The deportees to Theresienstadt included many artists, writers, and scholars, who organized an intensive cultural life including several orchestras, an opera and theater troupe, lecture series, and satirical entertainment. In late 1943, when information on the extermination camps began to filter through to the free world, the German authorities decided to show off Theresienstadt to an investigating committee of the International Red Cross. To improve the appearance of the ghetto, a bank, false shops, a café, kindergartens, and schools were set up and the town was adorned with flower gardens. Overcrowding was lessened by additional deportations to Auschwitz. The June 1944 visit of the committee, all of whose meetings with inmates were carefully prepared in advance, was followed by the filming of a Nazi propaganda film on the "new life of the Jews under the protection of the Third Reich." When the filming was finished, most of the actors, including almost all the members of the autonomous administration and most of the children, were sent to the gas chambers at Auschwitz-Birkenau. More than 33,000 Jews perished in Theresienstadt, and over 88,000 were deported to their deaths.

Thirteen (*shalosh-esrei*). Although an unlucky number in many cultures (as in Friday the 13th), it has many positive connotations in Judaism. Thirteen is the age of bar mitzvah.After the disastrous episode with the Golden Calf, God revealed to

Moses the Thirteen Attributes of Mercy. In the talmudic period, Rabbi Ishmael developed 13 hermeneutical principles with which to explain the Torah. The Thirteen Principles of Faith were compiled by Maimonides. The fringes (*tzitzit*) of the *tallit* contain five knots binding eight threads for a total of 13, which is also the numerical value of the Hebrew letters in the word *echad* (one) that is used in the *Shema* to indicate the Unity of God.

Thirteen Attributes of Mercy. The core of the *Selichot* prayers, these are traditionally the exact words that God taught Moses for the people to use whenever they needed to beg for Divine compassion. In the Bible, they are found after the incident of the Golden Calf, when God threatened to destroy the people of Israel rather than forgive them (Exod. 32:10). The Thirteen Attributes of Mercy are based on two verses in Exodus (34:6-7) – "The Lord! The Lord! God, Compassionate and Gracious, Slow to anger and Abundant in kindness and truth, Preserver of kindness for thousands of generations, Forgiver of iniquity, willful sin, and error, and Who Cleanses [– but does not cleanse completely, recalling the iniquity of parents upon children and grandchildren, to the third and fourth generations]."[329] The Rabbis ingeniously cut off the end of this verse, thus changing the meaning to indicate that God does forgive all sins! This remarkable midrashic transformation has become the standard format whenever this Torah verse is used in a synagogue service. The kabbalists introduced the current custom of reciting the Thirteen Attributes of Mercy before taking the Torah from the ark during the three pilgrimage festivals of Passover, Shavuot, and Sukkot (unless they occur on the Sabbath).

Thirteen Principles of Faith. Statement of the basic doctrines of the Jewish faith, as set down by Maimonides in his commentary to the Mishnah (12th century). They are: (1) God the Creator exists; (2) God is one; (3) God is incorporeal; (4) God is eternal; (5) God alone is to be worshipped and obeyed; (6) the prophets are true; (7) Moses is above all other prophets; (8) the entire Torah was given to Moses by God; (9) the Torah is unchangeable; (10) God is omniscient; (11) reward and punishment; (12) the Messiah will come; and (13) the resurrection of the dead. Although never formally adopted as the Jewish creed, the Thirteen Principles of Faith were incorporated into the prayer book as *Ani Ma'amin* and are the basis for *Yigdal*.

Thirty days of mourning – see *Sheloshim*.

32 Paths of Wisdom. Mystical concept, originating in the *Sefer Yetzirah*, that the 22 letters of the Hebrew alphabet and the numbers one through ten were the building blocks of Creation. According to the kabbalists, the 10 *sefirot*, the emanations of Divine reality, energized the creative process and defined its parameters. The 32 Paths of Wisdom are the channels through which the Divine Presence flows through the *sefirot* and into the world.

Three (*shalosh*). According to *Pirkei Avot* (1:2), the continued existence of the world depends on three things – Torah (study), *avodah* (initially the Temple service, later prayer), and *gemilut chasadim* (deeds of lovingkindness). There are three Patriarchs (Abraham, Isaac, and Jacob), three pilgrimage festivals (Passover, Shavuot, Sukkot), and three major divisions of the Bible (Torah, *Nevi'im* [see Prophets], and *Kituvim* [see Writings]). There are three major prayer services on weekdays – *Shacharit* (morning), *Mincha* (afternoon), and *Ma'ariv* (evening). At the Passover seder, the three *matzahs* represent the basic divisions of the Jewish people (*kohen*, *levi*, Israel), which are also recognized during the traditional Torah service. There were three so-called "women's" commandments – taking *challah*, going to the *mikveh*, and lighting Shabbat candles.

Three Weeks. Period of mourning that extends from the 17th of Tammuz through the 9th of Av (Tisha b'Av). Also known in Hebrew as *bein ha-meitzarim* ("between the straits," i.e., the two fasts), it commemorates the destruction of the First and Second Temples in Jerusalem. The traditional mourning rituals during the Three Weeks include abstention from weddings and other joyous celebrations, as well as musical and other public entertainment; and the prohibition against the purchase or wearing of new clothing or the eating of new fruit, for which the *Shehecheyanu* blessing (an expression of joy) must be recited.[330] (See also *Nine Days*.)

Throne of God – see Divine Chariot and *Merkava* mysticism.

Tiberias. City on the western shore of the Sea of Galilee and the largest settlement in the Jordan Valley. Tiberias was built by King Herod in honor of the reigning Roman emperor, Tiberius Caesar, and declared the capital of the Galilee. With its hot springs and mild climate, Tiberias became one of the most elegant winter resorts in this part of the ancient world. After the failure of the Bar Kochba revolt, Tiberias became a major Jewish center and the home of the Sanhedrin. In this city, R. Judah ha-Nasi completed the Mishnah (c. 200 C.E.), the Jerusalem Talmud was compiled (c. 400 C.E.), and scholars introduced vowels and punctuation into Hebrew grammar and developed a standard masoretic text of Scripture. Pilgrims have flocked to Tiberias to pray at the tombs of Maimonides, R. Yochanan ben Zakkai, and R. Meir Ba'al ha-Nes. Today, Tiberias is the economic center and metropolis of Lower Galilee.

Tiferet (glory/beauty). The 6th of the *sefirot* and the offspring of *Chochma* and *Binah*.In Kabbalah, it is the point where God's judgment and mercy flow together in the ideal balance needed for the proper running of the universe. In the diagram of the *sefirot*, *Tiferet* (also known as "peace") is usually placed at the center of the torso, indicating its central role of bringing harmony between justice and mercy, limitation and freedom. According to the *Zohar*, *Tiferet* was originally a hermaphrodite, a bisexual entity having two sides like Siamese twins. When separated, the male side became *Tiferet* and the female side became the 10th *sefirah*, *Malchut*.

Tigris. River in Western Asia, one of the four that watered the Garden of Eden (Gen. 2:14). The talmudic academy at Machoza was located on the banks of the Tigris, which at the time formed the eastern boundary of Babylonia.

Tik. Cylindrical or octagonal case, divided into two pieces and hinged in the back, which encloses the Torah scroll in the Middle Eastern and Sephardic traditions. The tik originated in 10th-century Iraq and is usually elaborately decorated and inscribed. It opens like a book to reveal the scroll, which is not removed and is read in an upright position. The term "tik" is also used to designate the square black box on the *tefillin* or the bag in which the boxes are held.

Tikun. Book used by a *baal korei* to prepare for the Torah reading in the synagogue. The unadorned script of the Torah appears on one column of the page, while on the facing column is the parallel text with vowel markings, punctuation, and symbols indicating the *trope*.

Tikun Leil Shavuot. Literally "the Prepared [Texts] of the Night of Shavuot," an all-night vigil devoted to the study of passages from the Bible, Talmud, and *Zohar*. Inspired by the kabbalists, this custom was designed to prepare Jews spiritually for the holiday commemorating the giving of the Torah at Mount Sinai. The popular explanation is that staying up all night on the eve of Shavuot atones for the behavior of the Israelites at Sinai, who according to tradition slept late that morning and had to be awakened by Moses. In some communities, the Shavuot eve study session is climaxed with the only sunrise service of the Jewish year, a symbol either of the light of the Torah or of Jews as a "light unto the nations" (Isa. 49:6).[331]

Tikun olam. Literally "repair of the world," a powerful mystical concept attesting to the central role of human beings, who are crucial in maintaining both the natural world and the upper world of the *sefirot* This idea reached its climax in the kabbalistic system of Isaac Luria in 16th-century Safed, which posits that through good deeds and repentance human beings are capable of assisting God by elevating the holy sparks entrapped in the *klipot* (husks) in this material world and restoring them to their original Divine source. This would mend the world, overcome evil, restore cosmic harmony, and ultimately usher in the Messianic Age, thus completing and perfecting the work of Creation. Liberal streams of Judaism have extended the classic concept of *tikun olam* to the pursuit of social justice and care for the environment, which for some congregations has become the essence of Judaism.

Tisch. Literally "table" in Yiddish, in Hasidic tradition it refers to the celebratory Shabbat eve or afternoon meal led by the *Rebbe* and attended by his disciples. At this meal, the *Rebbe* leads the singing of *nigunim* (wordless melodies) and offers teachings on the weekly Torah portion.

Tisha b'Av. Ninth day of the month of Av (July/August), the saddest day in the Jewish calendar. This major fast day marks the anniversary of the destruction of the First Temple by the Babylonians in 586 B.C.E. and the Second Temple by the Romans in 70 C.E. Tisha b'Av eventually became a symbol for all the catastrophes that have befallen the Jewish people throughout its history. According to the Mishnah, on Tisha b'Av: (a) the 10 spies delivered their negative report about the Land of Canaan to Moses, condemning the Israelites to spend 40 years wandering in the wilderness until they were permitted to enter the Promised Land; and (b) the Bar Kochba revolt was finally crushed when Betar, the last stronghold, was captured by the Romans in 135 C.E. According to tradition, Tisha b'Av was also the date of the expulsions of the Jews from England (1290) and Spain (1492). Like Yom Kippur, in addition to fasting, Tisha b'Av is observed by refraining from wearing leather shoes, anointing with perfume, bathing, and sexual intercourse. If the 9th of Av day falls on the Sabbath, on which no mourning is permitted, the entire Tisha b'Av observance is moved to the next day. In synagogue, the congregation sits on the floor, footstools, or low benches, reading the Book of Lamentations and reciting *kinot* (lamentations) by the light of candles or dim lights as a symbol of the darkness that has befallen Israel on that day. There is a tradition that the Messiah will be born on Tisha b'Av, reversing the centuries of travail and suffering that have been the lot of the Jewish people.

Tishrei. The 7th month of the Jewish religious year and 1st month of the civil calendar. The first day of Rosh Hashanah falls on the 1st of Tishrei, Tzom Gedaliah on the 3rd, Yom Kippur on the 10th, the first day of Sukkot on the 15th, Shemini Atzeret on the 22nd, and (in the Diaspora) Simchat Torah on the 23rd.

Tithe (*ma'aser*). Tenth part of the yield of the fields and flock, which was set aside as a religious offering. A *first tithe* of one-tenth of the crops was given to the Levites (after separation of the *terumah* for the *kohanim*) as a reward for their dedication to the service of God. After the *kohen's* portion and the Levite's first tithe had been removed from a harvested crop, the owner was required to separate a *second tithe* (*ma'aser sheni*). During the first, second, fourth, and fifth years of the seven-year Sabbatical Year cycle, this second tithe had to be brought to Jerusalem, where it was to be eaten by the owner and members of his family (Deut. 14:22). If this were impossible due to the distance or the weight of the produce, the owner was to redeem the tithe and bring its monetary value (plus one-fifth extra) to the Temple, where he was required to spend it exclusively on food and drink. The *poor man's tithe* was due in the third and sixth years of every

Sabbatical cycle (Deut. 14:28). In these years, what would have been the second tithe (to be eaten in Jerusalem) was kept at home for the poor to eat. During the Middle Ages, the Roman Catholic Church forcibly imposed an ecclesiastical tithe on Jews in various parts of Europe.

Tobit. Apocryphal book of unknown authorship, written about the 3rd century B.C.E., in which Tobias (Tobit's son) traveled to claim money lent by his father to a relative named Raguel. Raguel had an only daughter, Sarah, who had already been married several times; however, on each occasion, the bridegroom had died on the wedding night. According to the biblical law of levirate marriage, Sarah was obligated to marry her young kinsman Tobias rather than a stranger. After magically driving away Ashmedai, the demon who slew the grooms, Tobias married Sarah. When his father-in-law saw that Tobias had survived, he doubled the duration of the wedding banquets from seven to 14 days. In the concluding portion of the work, Tobit speaks to his son about the ingathering of the exiles and the restoration of Jerusalem.

Tochachah. Literally "admonition," the two chilling prophecies detailing an extensive list of dire consequences that will befall the Israelites if they spurn God and the *mitzvot* in the Torah (Lev. 26:3-39; Deut. 28:1-68). They follow a recital of a shorter list of the blessings that the nation will receive for fulfilling the commandments. Together, these elaborate lists of blessings and curses represent the quintessential descriptions of reward and punishment in the Bible.

To'evah – see Abomination.

Tohorah – see *Tumah* and *Tohorah.*

Tohorot (1). Literally "purifications," the Hebrew word for the laws of ritual cleanness. This term also was used in Temple times for foods that could be eaten only by those in a state of ritual purity.

Tohorot (2). The 6th order of the Mishnah, its 12 tractates are Kelim, Oholot, Nega'im, Parah, Tohorot, Mikva'ot, Niddah, Machshirim, Zavim, Tevul Yom, Yadayim, and Ukzin. Dealing with the laws concerning ritual purity and impurity, Tohorot is the largest order, an indication of how important the Rabbis considered these issues.

Tohorot (Toh.) (3). The 5th tractate in Tohorot (purity) in the Mishnah, it deals with purification from those minor degrees of ritual uncleanness that last only until sunset.

Toledot. The 6th *parashah* in the Book of Genesis (25:19-28:9), it recounts the narrative of Jacob and Esau, the sale of the birthright by Esau and the ruse of

Jacob (and Rebecca, his mother) to secure his father Isaac's blessing, and Jacob fleeing to escape the wrath of his brother. In the *parashah*, Esau appears to be the innocent victim of a duplicitous scheme, though the Rabbis generally regarded Esau as the villainous spiritual ancestor of Imperial Rome and other persecutors of the Jewish people.

Tolerance, religious. Peaceful existence between adherents of different religions or religious denominations. In the fullest sense of the term, it requires sincere mutual respect and understanding.

Tomb. In biblical times, members of a family were buried together in a natural cave or chamber cut into soft rock. Instead of the bodies being buried in the ground, they were laid on the floor or on rock shelves specially constructed on three sides of the chamber. As the tomb filled with the deceased from generations of the same family, it was necessary to pile up the skeletons or to extend the tomb into a side chamber to make room for new burials. In the rabbinic period, bones were collected after a year and placed in an ossuary.

Tombstone – see Headstone.

Torah (1). The first five books of the Bible (see *Chumash*). Also known as the Pentateuch, the Torah begins with Creation and ends with the death of Moses, as the Israelites are poised to cross the Jordan River into the Promised Land. Interspersed with the ancient narrative of the Jewish people are the 613 Divine commandments (see *taryag mitzvot*). In the Torah, the Jewish people develop from a single family into a covenantal people, committed to carrying out these commandments to fulfill the will of God.

Torah (2). Inclusive term used for all of Jewish law and learning – both the Written Law and the Oral Law, as well as all the commentaries and *responsa* produced during the subsequent centuries to the present day.

Torah blessings. Originally, only two blessings were recited by those called to the Torah – one by the first person called before he began to read, and the second by the last person called after he had completed his reading. Those in between read their Torah portions without reciting any blessings at all. The current practice, in which each person called to the reading of the Torah recites both blessings (and the preliminary *Barchu*) is a later rabbinic innovation. Each Torah blessing contains 20 words, and the total of 40 symbolizes the number of days that Moses spent on Mount Sinai to receive the Written Law. The first blessing emphasizes that God chose Israel to receive the Torah; the second blessing thanks God for giving us *Torat emet* (Torah of truth). Each person called up for an *aliyah* traditionally touches the fringes (*tzitzit*) of the *tallit* to the scroll at the place where the reading is to begin and then kisses them before reciting the first blessing.

After each portion is completed, the person called touches the fringes of the *tallit* to the scroll where the reading ended and then kisses them before reciting the second Torah blessing.

Torah, fence around the. To avoid the performance of actions forbidden by the Torah, the Rabbis decreed that one also must not do anything that: (1) resembles a prohibited act or could be confused with it; (2) reinforces a habit linked with a prohibited act; or (3) usually leads to performing a prohibited act. The rabbinic enactment of measures to prevent these possibilities was termed "putting a fence around the Torah" (Avot 1:1). For example, on the Sabbath, ripping up a piece of paper was forbidden since it resembles "cutting to shape" (prohibited by the restrictions against work) or could be confused with it. Similarly, agreeing to buy something was prohibited since one is in the habit of confirming agreements in "writing;" and climbing a tree is forbidden since it may lead to breaking twigs or tearing leaves, which could be construed as "reaping" (i.e., separating part of a growing plant from its source).[332]

Torah mi-Sinai. Literally "Torah from Sinai," the traditional Jewish belief that the Torah is the direct word of God, given to Moses on Mount Sinai, and thus its commandments must be observed exactly as they were transmitted (Deut. 13:1). The Torah is complete and perfect as is ("The Torah [law] of the Lord is perfect, restoring the soul;" Ps. 19:8), and any attempt to "improve" it by using human intelligence to add or subtract commandments may only detract from the original Divine meaning of the text and thus be abhorrent to God.[333] As Rashi observed, Israel was not to invent new additions to the laws, nor arbitrarily diminish them, such as by using five species instead of four in the commandment of the *lulav* on Sukkot or leaving out one of the three Priestly Blessings.

Torah ornaments. The beginning and end of the parchment scroll are attached to two carved wooden rollers, called *atzei chaim* (trees of life). Atop the *atzei chaim* is either a crown (see *keter*) or a pair of silver finials called *rimonim* (lit. "pomegranates"). In the Middle Eastern and Sephardic traditions, the Torah is enclosed in a cylindrical or octagonal case (see *tik*). Among Ashkenazim, the Torah scroll is covered by a cloth mantle, over which is placed a silver breastplate or shield.The scroll is bound by a long, wide ribbon (see *wimpel*, or *gartel*). Rather than touch the parchment of the scroll with bare hands, the Torah reader follows the text with a hand-shaped pointer (see *yad*).

Torah reading. Originally, each person called to the Torah read his own portion. However, as learning among the lay people declined and few were able to read from the scroll, an official Torah reader (see *baal korei*) would read for everyone. The *baal korei* chants the Torah reading using a special series of musical notations (see *trope*), which must be memorized since they are not marked in the scroll.

Although it is customary to stand up when the Torah is removed from or returned to the ark, members of the congregation are seated while the Torah is read. A practical reason for this tradition is that it would be difficult for many worshipers to remain standing for the entire Torah reading. However, congregants do stand during especially significant passages – the Ten Commandments (Exod. 20:1-14; Deut. 5:6-18), *Shirat ha-Yam* (Exod. 15:1-19), and the last verse of each of the Five Books of Moses. Certain Torah verses that depict disastrous scenarios are traditionally read softly and rapidly, based on the superstitious belief that their mere mention may cause them to occur or recur. These sections include the curses (see *Tochachah*) that will befall the Israelites if they do not follow the Divine commandments (Lev. 26:14-39; Deut. 28:15-68) and the blasphemy of the Golden Calf (Exod. 32).

Torah scroll. The text of the Five Books of Moses that is inscribed on parchment by a scribe using a quill pen. (See also *Torah ornaments*.)

Torah scroll, obligation to write a. The last of the 613 commandments in the Torah is the obligation to write a Torah scroll (Deut. 31:19). This assures continuity of the tradition and enables future generations to have access to all the *mitzvot* so that they can study and fulfill them. Even if given a Torah scroll by one's parents, each individual is still obliged to write one. Realizing the tremendous challenge and difficulty involved in actually writing one's own Torah scroll, Maimonides stated that "if he cannot write it himself, he is obliged to purchase one, or to hire a scribe to write it for him." Based on the talmudic statement, "Even if he corrected but one letter [in a *sefer Torah*] he is regarded as if he had written it [the entire Torah]," in recent centuries the custom has developed for the scribe who completes the writing of a Torah scroll to merely trace the outline of the letters of the first verses in Genesis and the last verses in Deuteronomy. At a festive celebration (*siyum*), various members of the congregation, often selected by auction, fill in each letter and thus symbolically participate in the writing of a Torah scroll.

Torah, separate scrolls for reading the. It is traditional to use a different scroll for every extra Torah reading that is required on special occasions (such as when Rosh Chodesh or a festival falls on the Sabbath and a description of the appropriate sacrifices (from Parshat Pinchas) is read as the *maftir* portion from the second scroll. Occasionally, readings are made from three separate scrolls, as when the Sabbath of Chanukah coincides with the New Moon of the month of Tevet. When this occurs, the ordinary weekly portion is read from the first scroll, the special portion for Rosh Chodesh from the second, and the section for Chanukah from the third. Employing a separate scroll for each special reading, rather than using a single scroll and simply rolling it to the next passage to be read, is based on the principle of *kavod ha-tzibbur* (regard for the honor of the congregation) and the principle of not imposing an unnecessary time burden on the community (*tircha* *de-tzibbura*).[334] For similar reasons, the Torah scroll is always prepared in advance and rolled to the proper place before the service begins.

Torah she b'al peh – see Oral Law.

Torah she bichtav – see Written Law.

Torah study and teaching. The command to teach and study the Torah (*Talmud Torah*) is derived from the verse, "And you shall teach them diligently to your children" (Deut. 6:7). The rabbis elevated the study and teaching of the Torah to the highest degree of religious devotion and experience, declaring that when a group of Jews engages in Torah study, the Divine Presence dwells among them. Traditionally, women were not considered bound by the commandment to study Torah because the verse was translated as, "And you shall teach them to your *sons*." Instead, they were taught the various laws pertaining to women, which include almost all the negative commandments and many positive ones. However, most modern translations use the word "*children*" (rather than sons), so that the commandment to study Torah applies equally to both men and women.

Torah Umesorah. American organization of Orthodox Jewish day schools. Founded in 1944 by Rabbi Shraga Feivel Mendlowitz, it provided an alternative model of education that was not based on the previous accepted practice of having children attend government non-sectarian public schools during the day and Hebrew schools in the afternoons or on Sundays. This system was viewed as failing to transmit Judaism properly to students who arrived tired in the afternoons and also were being subjected to the secularizing forces in American society. The Torah Umesorah solution was a dual-curriculum Jewish day school that would offer both excellent Judaic and secular education under one roof.

Torah v'Avodah (Torah [study] and Labor). Slogan of the religious Zionist pioneers. It remains the motto of the Bnei Akiva youth wing of the Mizrachi movement.

Torat Kohanim – see Leviticus.

Tosafot. Critical and explanatory notes on the Talmud, composed by some 300 French and German scholars (tosafists; lit., "men of additions") from the 12th-14th centuries. With Rashi's commentary serving as their point of departure, the most illustrious of the Tosafists were his sons-in-law and grandsons. The Tosafists sought to answer their questions by pointing to differences and distinctions between talmudic cases and sources to produce new *halachic* deductions and conclusions. Their extensive writings were effectively records of the animated oral discussions of *halacha* between the heads of *yeshivot* and their pupils on selected talmudic passages, mainly when they disagreed in principle or detail from the ideas of Rashi. Their view of the Talmud and methods of argumentation influenced subsequent generations of talmudic scholars.

Tosefta. In Hebrew *tosafah*, a collection of *beraitot* arranged according to the order of the Mishnah. About four times larger than the Mishnah itself, the Tosefta (meaning "supplement") is an independent work that contains versions of *halachot* that supplement but sometimes contradict the Mishnah, and at other times appear to be completely unrelated to it so as to operate as an independent work.

Tower of Babel – see Babel, Tower of.

Tractate (*masechet*). Individual volumes into which each order of the Mishnah is divided. Generally arranged according to their length, in the Babylonian Talmud there are a total of 63 tractates – 11 in Zera'im (seeds), 12 in Mo'ed (festivals), 7 in Nashim (women), 10 in Nezikin, 11 in Kodashin (holy things), and 12 in Tohorot (purity). (See also entries for individual tractates.)

Tradition – see *Mesorah*.

Transcendence. A condition or state of being that surpasses and is independent of physical existence. Although the diametric opposite of immanence, the concepts are not mutually exclusive and can be seen as complementary aspects of the relationship of the Divine to the physical world. In Judaism, the transcendence of the Deity is reflected in God's oneness, omnipotence, and omniscience, in God's creation of a world distinct from the Divine Essence. Nevertheless, the transcendent Deity then entered into a covenantal relationship with the Jewish people, through whom God became immanent and involved in the progressive unfolding of human history.

Translation. See Bible translations, *Targum*, Targum Onkelos, and *meturgeman*.

Transliteration. The process of changing words from one language into similar-sounding letters of another language. Many prayer books include transliterations of Hebrew words into English letters, so that those who do not read Hebrew can participate in the service.

Transmigration of souls (*gilgul*). Mystical view, prominent in Eastern religions, which became normative in Judaism between the 16th-18th centuries and has had even longer influence in the Hasidic community. It may have developed as a response to the problem of theodicy.Since some individuals are born disadvantaged, either physically or mentally, it would seem unjust to expect the same achievement of everyone. In effect, this concept maintains that each soul deserves more than one opportunity at life, and thus it is placed in a variety of bodies in order to realize its potential. The body to which the soul is assigned in any given life reflects the moral quality of its former life. When fully developed (i.e., when it has truly embraced the moral and spiritual world), the soul breaks out of the wheel of transmigration and finds final repose with God. According to the mystics, the soul does not necessarily go into a new human body after death. The soul is assigned to a new life form according to the sins committed. Indeed, the mystics made detailed lists indicating which sins led to one coming back as which animal. They also analyzed which heroes of the Bible and later Jewish history, including the great rabbis, were transmigrations of earlier figures. Furthermore, the mystics claimed that they could read the lines of a person's face to determine the state of that individual's soul in this life and in all past lives.

Transplantation – see Organ donation.

Travel, prayer for – see *Tefillat ha-Derech.*

Traveling. The Rabbis did not restrict movement within one's town on the Sabbath, but prohibited walking more than 2,000 cubits (approximately a half-mile) beyond the town boundaries "because traveling interrupts the rest of both man and beast."[335] Orthodox rabbis forbid driving an automobile on the Sabbath, based on the fact that it involves turning on the ignition, which in turn ignites sparks – an act that violates the Torah law against making a fire on the Sabbath (Exod. 35:3). Conservative rabbis permit congregants to drive to synagogue on the Sabbath – a ruling made in response to the migration of Jews to the suburbs, where most no longer live within walking distance of a synagogue. Continuing to forbid driving on the Sabbath would have forced many congregants to remain at home. Fearing an erosion of Jewish identity if synagogue attendance dropped precipitously, these rabbis permitted driving as the "lesser of two evils." In Israel, public transport does not operate on the Sabbath in Jerusalem and Tel Aviv, but it does run in Haifa. (For the traveler's prayer invoking Divine protection, see *Tefillat ha-Derech.*)

Treblinka. Town in central Poland northeast of Warsaw that was the site of a Nazi death camp. Opened on July 1942, Treblinka was second only to Auschwitz in the number of Jews murdered in its gas chambers (about 750,000). Miraculously, 50 survived, some escapees and others who participated in the heroic revolt of Jewish prisoners in August, 1943.

Tree of Knowledge of Good and Evil. The first command given by God to Adam in the Garden of Eden was to not eat of the Tree of Knowledge of Good and Evil (Gen. 2:17). Legends variously identify this as the fig, apple, pomegranate, *etrog*, carob, palm, or nut tree.[336] Induced by the serpent to eat the forbidden fruit of the tree, Eve in turn gave some to her husband to eat (Gen. 3:6). Ibn Ezra and many modern scholars have argued that the "knowledge" imparted by eating of the fruit of the tree was carnal knowledge: "The eyes of both of them were opened and they perceived that they were naked; and they sewed together fig leaves and made themselves loincloths" (Gen. 3:7). The shame that this engendered was so intense that Adam and Eve "hid from the Lord God among the trees of the Garden" (Gen. 3:8). Their punishment was expulsion from the Garden of Eden.

Tree of Life. Planted in the middle of the Garden of Eden (Gen. 2:9), the Tree of Life has long been associated with the Torah. When the Torah scroll is returned to the ark, the congregation proclaims that "it is a tree of life (*etz chaim*) to all who hold fast to it, and all who uphold it are *me-ushar* [variously translated as 'praiseworthy, happy, content, or safe']" (Prov 3:18). The blessing recited after each *aliyah* states that the Torah represents "eternal life planted within us." The wooden rods around which the Torah parchment is rolled are called *atzei chaim* (trees of life). Consequently, the image of the Tree of Life as a symbol of the Torah is a frequent synagogue decoration.

Trees. An important source of food and shelter in ancient Israel. Their wood provided for the construction of houses, boats, the Tabernacle in the wilderness, and the Temple in Jerusalem. The shade of trees was especially valuable in the hot landscape of the Land of Israel, and their fruit was a valuable commodity for nutrition and export. For more information, see sections relating to specific trees as well as Tree of Knowledge of Good and Evil and Tree of Life (above), *atzei chaim*, the proscriptions against destroying fruit trees during war (see *bal taschit*) and eating fruit from a tree before its fifth year (see *orlah*), and Tu b'Shevat, the "New Year of the Trees."

Trees, New Year of the – see Tu b'Shevat.

Treif. Non-kosher food forbidden under Jewish law. In addition to slaughtering an animal, a *shochet* (ritual slaughterer) must also carry out a detailed examination (see *bedikah*) of the carcass to detect any defect of major organs that would render it *treif.* Initially referring to the flesh of an animal torn by a wild beast or wild bird, the word *treif* was later applied to the flesh of any injured or diseased animal that would not have lived for more than a year. Eventually, *treif* became the generic term for any nonkosher product unfit for Jewish consumption.

Tribes of Israel – see Twelve Tribes of Israel.

Triennial cycle. Ancient tradition in the Land of Israel, in which the text of the Torah was divided into 155 portions that were read on each Sabbath in the synagogue so as to cover the entire Torah in three years. In effect, what now is considered the weekly Torah portion (termed *parashah* by Ashkenazim and *sidrah* by Sephardim) was read over three successive weeks. This practice probably originated because of the necessity of accommodating an Aramaic translation and exposition of the biblical verses during the reading so that they could be understood. The large and influential Jewish community in Babylonia developed the custom of completing the entire Torah in a single year, and this rule eventually became the generally accepted practice throughout the world. Some American Conservative synagogues have reintroduced a triennial cycle, reading only one third of each *parashah* every year. They begin with the initial third of a given portion read in the first year, the middle third in the second year, and the final third in the third year – resulting in the entire Torah being read every three years. Although this practice has become increasingly popular, it has the distinct disadvantage that the Torah is no longer read consecutively, so that there are interruptions in the narratives and bodies of biblical legislation.

Trito-Isaiah. Scholarly name for chapters 56-66 of Isaiah, which some believe are the work of a third prophet who, unlike Deutero-Isaiah, wrote in a Judean setting.

Trope. Series of musical notations used for the chanting of the Torah and *haftarah*, as well as the *megillot* on festivals. (The word derives from a Greek root meaning "turn" or "figure of speech.") Although dating back to talmudic times, the *trope* system was not perfected until the work of the Masoretes, primarily members of the ben Asher family of Tiberias in the 9th and 10th centuries. They devised universally accepted symbols that over the years were developed into distinctive melodic phrases by various Jewish communities. The Torah reader must memorize the cantillation, since there are no *trope* markings in the scroll. In some congregations, an official standing next to the *baal korei* uses hand signals to cue the reader regarding vocal modulations, the length of specific notes, and the word that ends each verse.[337] Though the symbols are the same, there are distinct *tropes* for reading the *haftarah*, the five *megillot*, and the Torah readings on Rosh Hashanah and the morning of Yom Kippur.

Tsedreyt. Yiddish term meaning "crazy."

Tsetummelt. Yiddish word meaning "confused" or "bewildered" by a chaotic situation.

Tsuris. Yiddish word meaning "troubles, problems, suffering, or aggravation."

Tu b'Av. The 15th day (full moon) of the month of Av (July/August), a minor holiday that in Second Temple times celebrated the beginning of the grape harvest in ancient Israel. According to the Mishnah, on this day (as well as on Yom Kippur afternoon) the daughters of Jerusalem used to dress in white garments and go out dancing in the vineyards, with the young men following them. Eventually, this led to Tu b'Av becoming a day when women could actively search for an eligible husband. On Tu b'Av, the Romans finally permitted the burial of the remains of the Jewish soldiers who had fallen three years earlier in the defense of Betar, the last stronghold of Bar Kochba. This event was considered so momentous for the Jews of that time that it led to the composition of a fourth blessing in the Grace after Meals (*ha-tov v'ha-meitiv*; "Who is good and does good"), which thanks God both for not permitting these corpses to decay and spread disease and for making the Romans finally allow the Jews to bury them.[338]

Tu b'Shevat. Occurring on the 15th day (full moon) of the month of Shevat (January/February), this "New Year of the Trees" is traditionally thought to be the day on which God decides how bountiful the fruit of each tree will be in the coming year. From a naturalistic point of view, it is the time the sap begins to rise in the trees in the Land of Israel. The name "Tu" derives from the Hebrew alphabetical form for the number "15" – *tet* (9) plus *vav* (6) – rather than *yud* (10) plus *hei* (5), which would be more logical mathematically but would spell out one of the holy names of God.[339] Long a minor festival, Tu b'Shevat became substantially more important among Sephardic Jews under the influence of the 16th-century kabbalists of Safed, who devised a Tu b'Shevat seder. In modern Israel, Tu b'Shevat has acquired increased importance as a symbol of the revival and redemption of the land by the planting of trees and growth of forests. It has assumed the character of an Arbor Day, on which children engage in tree-planting ceremonies.

Tu B'Shevat seder. Attempting to stimulate the flow of positive Divine energy into the world, the kabbalists of Safed created a Tu b'Shevat seder that was loosely modeled after the Passover seder. It involved eating multiple kinds of fruit and nuts, especially those native to the Land of Israel, and drinking four cups of wine, accompanied by appropriate readings.[340] (For the four worlds or levels of creation symbolized by fruits and nuts in the Tu b'Shevat seder, see *asiyah*, *yetzirah*, *beri'ah*, and *atzilut*.) Each of the four cups of wine also has symbolic value. Beginning with a cup of white wine, participants at the Tu b'Shevat seder add increasing amounts of red wine so that the next three cups are pink, deep rose, and almost completely red. This sequence symbolizes the gradual transition of the land "from the cold whiteness of winter through the pale buds of spring into the full-blooming flowers of summer and the striking colors of the leaves before they fall from the trees in autumn." The four cups also represent the four letters of the Tetragrammaton (*YHVH*), the most holy Name of God.[341]

Tuchis. From the Hebrew word *tachat* meaning "underneath," the Yiddish term for the rear end. (It is also abbreviated as *tush*.)

Tumah and **Tohorah**. Hebrew words for ritual impurity and purity, respectively (the adjectives are *tamei* and *tahor*). *Tumah* can be contracted by contact with earthenware, wooden vessels, and water, but not by vessels made of skin, bone, or feathers.

Tummel. Yiddish word meaning "noise" or "commotion."

Tummler. Yiddish word that usually denotes a clown or prankster who is the "life or the party." When the Borsht Belt was thriving, *tummler* was the term for the social director at one of the Jewish Catskills resorts, who was responsible for providing the guests with entertainment day and night so there would "never be a dull moment."

Twelve (*shteim-esrei*). In addition to the 12 tribes of ancient Israel, there were 12 "minor" prophets and 12 loaves of Showbread used in the Tabernacle (Exod. 25:30; Lev. 24:5-9). Traditionally, 12 is also the age at which a Jewish girl first becomes obligated to fulfill the *mitzvot*.

Twelve Tribes of Israel. Founders of the Jewish people, listed in two ways in the Bible. Jacob had twelve sons with his wives Leah and Rachel and his concubines, Bilhah and Zilpah – Reuben, Shimon, Levi, Judah, Dan, Naphtali, Gad, Asher, Issachar, Zebulun, Joseph, and Benjamin. However, for purposes of settling the Promised Land, Joseph received a double share that was passed on to his sons, Ephraim and Menashe. The post-settlement listing of the Twelve Tribes of Israel excludes Levi, because this tribe inherited the priesthood rather than any of the tribal lands and was scattered among the people. Jews today are the descendants of the two southern tribes (Judah and Benjamin) plus the Levites, since the 10 northern tribes were lost after the Assyrian conquest (see Ten Lost Tribes of Israel).

Twilight. The period of evening just after sunset but before night. Twilight persists as long as only two stars of medium size are visible in the sky. The appearance of three stars means that night has fallen.

Two (*sh'tayim*). The Ten Commandments were inscribed on two tablets of stone; the Israelites collected a double portion of manna on Friday to last them through the Sabbath, when all work was forbidden (Exod. 16:22); and the unclean animals entered Noah's ark two by two (Gen. 6:19). Furthermore, pairs of contrasting siblings play major roles among the ancestors of the Jewish people – Isaac and Ishmael, Jacob and Esau, Rachel and Leah, Moses and Aaron. There are two parts of the *tefillin*, and the testimony of two witnesses is required in capital and other criminal cases under Jewish law (Deut. 8:6).

Tza'ar ba'alei chaim. Literally "pain of living things," a fundamental Jewish value prohibiting cruelty to animals. It is based on the concept that human beings are responsible for all God's creatures. Not only is cruelty to animals forbidden, it is a positive commandment for human beings to show compassion and mercy to them. The antipathy toward cruelty to animals is strikingly illustrated in the rabbinic prohibition against reciting the festive blessing *Shehecheyanu* before the act of ritual slaughter or before putting on new leather shoes. As explicitly stated in the Ten Commandments, animals as well as human beings must be allowed to rest on the Sabbath (Exod. 20:10; Deut. 5:14). The Rabbis understood several commandments as explicitly related to the prohibition against cruelty to animals – *shechitah* (kosher slaughtering); not working with two animals of unequal strength; not muzzling an animal as it threshes; sparing the mother bird; and relieving an animal of its burden. One of the universally binding seven Noahide laws is the prohibition of eating flesh cut from a living animal.

Tzadi. The 18th letter of the Hebrew alphabet, with a numerical value of 90.

Tzadik. A righteous and honorable man who is pious and God-fearing. Among Hasidim, it is a term for the *Rebbe*, a holy man of surpassing virtue who was often believed to wield supernatural powers. In the mystic tradition, the *tzadik* is a person who is venerated for his ability to draw down Divine grace from the inner realm of God and to channel its power to improve the spiritual and material lives of his community. Unlike most rabbinic leaders, the power and authority of the *tzadik* derive not from mastery of Jewish law or prominent lineage (though many *tzadikim* have founded influential Hasidic dynasties), but rather from an innate ability to relate with God, which must be maintained through constant study of the Torah and cultivation of the moral virtues, especially humility.[342]

Tzadikim. The 13th blessing of the weekday *Amidah*, it asks for Divine compassion on "the devout, on the elders of Your people the family of Israel, on the remnant of their scholars, on the righteous converts and on ourselves." It calls upon God to "give goodly reward to all who sincerely believe in Your Name [and] put our lot with them forever, and we will not feel ashamed."

Tzahal. Acronym of the *Tzeva Haganah le-Israel*, the Hebrew words for the Israel Defense Forces.

Tzara'at. Although often translated as "leprosy," the signs described in the Torah and the reversibility of this skin condition make it doubtful that it refers to that incurable disease. The Rabbis regarded *tzara'at* as a Divine punishment for slander or tale-bearing (see *lashon ha-ra*), indicating that such a person is a "moral leper" who must be excluded from the camp of Israel. The prime biblical example was when Miriam developed *tzara'at* after she "spoke against Moses because of the

Cushite woman whom he had married" (Num. 12:1). *Tzara'at* could also contaminate garments through contact with an afflicted individual or his sores (Lev. 13:47-59) or affect a house, which might require its partial or even complete demolition (Lev. 14:33-53). This condition was most likely due to a fungus similar to that which causes dry rot, though some have suggested that it represented parasitic insects or a collection of nitrous material that had formed in the walls.[343]

Tzav. The 2nd *parashah* in the Book of Leviticus (6:1-6:36), it describes the grain offering (see *mincha*), sin offering (see *chatat*), and peace offering. Most of the *parashah* focuses on instructions to the priests about how to carry out their part of the sacrificial service.

Tzedakah. Literally "righteousness" but often translated as "charity," in Jewish law this is not simply a generous or magnanimous act but rather the performance of a religiously mandated duty to provide something to which the poor have a right. Unlike the Christian concept of "charity," which comes from the Latin *caritas* (love), or the Greek term *philanthrophy*, which literally means "love of human beings," *tzedakah* is given because it is right – a person with resources is obligated to help one in need. Ideally, however, *tzedakah* should also be motivated by compassionate feelings toward others. The Jewish concepts of love or philanthropy are *gemilut chasadim*, acts of lovingkindness, and *lifnim mishurat hadin* actions that go beyond the simple requirements of the law. According to Jewish law, every person has a duty to give charity; even one who is dependent on charity should give to those less fortunate. Although a Jew should do everything possible to avoid having to take alms – accepting any work that is available, even if he thinks it is beneath his dignity – he should not feel embarrassed to accept charity when unable to obtain money and support in any other way.

Tzedakah box – see *Kuppah*.

Tzeirei – see Vowels.

Tzeniut (modesty). Fundamental Jewish principle dealing with dress and behavior. This Jewish value fosters physical and personal modesty, and in traditional Judaism includes keeping one's body clothed in unrevealing attire; not wearing the clothing of a member of the opposite sex; avoiding touching a person of the opposite sex publically in a sexual manner; not dwelling on lascivious or immoral thoughts; averting one's eyes from staring at members of the opposite sex; and avoiding the company of unrefined individuals and situations in which there is an atmosphere of lustfulness. The reserved dignity of *tzeniut* has been defined as "discrete habits, quiet speech, and affections privately expressed ... intended to preserve the sanctity of the inner human being from assault by the coarseness of daily life."[344]

Tzimmes. Stew dating back to the medieval German practice of combining meats and vegetables with fruits and honey or sugar. Over the centuries, *tzimmes* emerged as a popular dish for Sabbaths and festivals in the Ashkenazic community. *Tzimmes* may contain meat or be vegetarian, and be sweetened with fresh or, more frequently, dried fruits (especially prunes). Recipes include at least one root vegetable, primarily carrots or sweet potatoes. On Rosh Hashanah, Jews in Eastern Europe traditionally prepared *tzimmes* with carrots, based on that vegetable's Yiddish name *mehren* (more), expressing the hope for a productive year with many blessings. Initially coming from the two Yiddish words "*zum*" and "*essen*," meaning "to eat," the word *tzimmes* has entered the English language as denoting making a fuss over something or a big deal over nothing –reflecting the chopping, stirring, and stewing required to prepare the dish.

Tzimtzum. Literally "contraction," the self-limitation of God to allow space for the creation of a finite independent world. According to this essential concept in Lurianic Kabbalah, the primeval act of creation by God was the contraction, concealment, and withdrawal of the Infinite Divinity in order to allow for a "conceptual space" in which a finite, seemingly independent world could exist. Only after this act of contraction did God turn outwards, sending a thread of the light of Divine Essence into the primeval void created by *tzimtzum*, from which emanated the *sefirot*.

Tzitzit (1). Ritual fringes that are attached to each of the four corners of the *tallit* in accordance with biblical law (Num. 15:38). The Rabbis noted that the numerical value of the Hebrew word *tzitzit* (fringes) is 600. When combined with the eight threads and five knots on each fringe, this adds up to 613 – the precise number of *mitzvot* in the Torah. Thus, by looking at the fringes we are to "remember all the Lord's commands and obey them" (Num. 15:39).[345]

Tzitzit (2). Minor tractate added to the Talmud that deals with the laws regarding *tzitzit*.

Tzom (fast) – see Fast days.

Tzom Gedaliah (Fast of Gedaliah). Occurring on the day after Rosh Hashanah (3rd of Tishrei), this minor fast day commemorates the assassination of the last governor of Judea, who in 586 B.C.E. was named to the post by the conquering Babylonians. The murder of Gedaliah was apparently instigated with the hope of overthrowing Babylonian rule and restoring Jewish self-government, but instead his death was the final blow to any immediate hope of restoring Jewish sovereignty and independence and led to further dispersal of the Jewish people.[346]

Tzu langeh (mazeldikker) yohrn. Yiddish phrase expressing the wish that the recipient be blessed literally with "long [lucky] years."

Tzur Mishelo. Literally "Rock from whose store [we have eaten]," this anonymous hymn introduces the Grace after Meals on the Sabbath. The refrain recalls the invitation to the *Birkat ha-Mazon* (see *zimun*), while the four stanzas summarize the contents of its first three blessings – praising God for providing food; giving thanks for the "good land" bequeathed to Israel; and asking God to have mercy on the Jewish people and restore the Kingdom of David and the Temple in Jerusalem.

Tzuris. Yiddish word meaning "troubles."

U

Uganda Proposal. Offer by the British government in 1903, in response to pogroms against Jews in Russia, to give the Zionist Organization about 5,000 square miles in what is today Kenya for an autonomous Jewish settlement where Jews could be saved from persecution. The proposal created controversy within the Zionist movement when Herzl proposed the British Uganda Program as a temporary refuge for Jews in immediate danger, even though he stressed that it would not affect the ultimate aim of establishing a Jewish entity in the Land of Israel. The Uganda Proposal was rejected in 1905 by the majority of Zionists, who considered Palestine as the only valid choice for Jewish national aspirations.

Ugarit. Ancient Canaanite city, now the modern town of Ras Shamra, on the northern coast of Syria. Extensive archeological excavations at Ugarit have unearthed an archive of writings dating from the 15th–13th centuries B.C.E. in a language closely related to Hebrew. These provide a better understanding of Canaanite culture and religion, as well as the impact they may have had on Israelite civilization and the cultural and literary background of the Hebrew Bible.

Uktzin. The 12th tractate in Tohorot (purity) in the Mishnah, it deals with the transfer of ritual impurity to a harvested plant when its roots, stalks (*utzkin*), or pods come into contact with an unclean person or thing.

Ulpan. Intensive Hebrew language course. In Israel, *ulpanim* are available to new immigrants, college students, tourists, and others who need to acquire language skills quickly. An *ulpan* course includes immersion in Jewish culture, as well as practical tips for adjusting to life in Israel.

Ultra-Orthodox. Generic term for the most traditional members of the Orthodox movement, who separate themselves more from secular society and interpret *halacha* more strictly than the modern Orthodox.A prominent group among the ultra-Orthodox are the Hasidim.

U-netaneh Tokef (We shall ascribe holiness [to this day]). Beloved *piyyut* (liturgical poem) recited before the *Kedushah* of the *Musaf Amidah* on Rosh Hashanah and Yom Kippur. It epitomizes the traditional significance of the High Holy Days by describing the Day of Judgment on which all creatures pass before God, one by one, like a flock before the Shepherd who decrees their fate. Composed in the 11th century by the martyred Rabbi Amnon, *U-netaneh Tokef* emphasizes the precarious nature of humanity and details the many possible destinies that may befall us. It stresses that all is Divinely determined, for God decides the general fate of entire populations ("how many will pass away and how many will be born") and individuals ("who will live and who will die"). For those who are condemned to die, the mechanism is decided by Divine decree ("who by fire and who by water ..."); similarly, for those who are to live, God determines "who will be serene and who will be disturbed ... who will be impoverished and who enriched, who will be humbled and who will be exalted." *U-netaneh Tokef* unequivocally asserts that the Divine judgment of being inscribed in the Book of Life or the Book of Death is based on an assessment of each individual's actions. This litany of deterministic fates is, however, followed by the stirringly optimistic phrase – "but repentance (*teshuvah*), prayer (*tefillah*), and charity (*tzedakah*) avert the severity of the decree."

Union of American Hebrew Congregations (UAHC). Now known as the Union of Reform Judaism, the association of Reform congregations in the United States, founded by Isaac Mayer Wise in 1873.

Union of Orthodox Jewish Congregations of America. Association of Orthodox synagogues, *yeshivot*, and day schools throughout the United States, founded in 1898. The "OU" symbol of this organization is a popular designation that a product is kosher.

Union of Sephardic Congregations. Umbrella organization, founded in 1929, that furthers the general interests of Sephardic Jews in the United States. It assists the Sephardic community as a network for providing Sephardic-trained rabbis, cantors, and scholars.

United Jewish Appeal (UJA). Founded in 1939, for years it was the major means for providing American financial support for Jews in Israel and other overseas areas. The UJA contributed significantly to the rescue and resettlement of immigrants brought to Israel. The annual fund-raising campaigns also supported local programs such as Jewish day schools, day-care centers, Y's and community centers, vocational workshops, medical care, family counseling, youth guidance, home and institutional care for the elderly, aid to the indigent, and a full range of resettlement services for Jewish immigrants to the United States.

United Jewish Communities (UJC). Central fund-raising organization for Jewish communities in North America. It was incorporated in 1999 by the merger of the United Jewish Appeal, the Council of Jewish Federations, and the United Israel Appeal, taking over the various functions of these organizations.

United States Holocaust Memorial Museum. National institution, opened in 1993, which is dedicated to documenting, studying, and interpreting the history of the Shoah. It also serves as the official American memorial to the 6 million European Jews (and other victims of Nazism) who were murdered during the Holocaust. The Museum is located on The Mall in Washington, D.C., on a street named for Raoul Wallenberg (1912-?), the Swedish diplomat who saved thousands of Hungarian Jews from the hands of the Nazis during World War II. Since its opening, the museum has been visited by millions and has performed a valuable service in training Holocaust educators and raising public awareness regarding other genocides.

United Synagogue of America. Association of Conservative congregations in the United States, founded by Solomon Schechter in 1913. It works closely with the Jewish Theological Seminary of America and strives to promote lay participation in Conservative Jewish religious and educational life.

Universalism. Jews believe that the Jewish people was chosen to be in a unique covenantal relationship with God (see Chosen People). As such, the Torah imposes particular obligations and responsibilities upon them (see *taryag mitzvot*). However, this does not preclude God having a relationship with other peoples, who are only required to conform to the seven Noahide laws. Isaiah spoke of the Jews being "a light unto the nations" (42:6; 49:6). The *Aleinu* prayer ends with words of Zechariah, who prophesied the coming of the Messianic Age when all the nations will recognize the universal kingdom of God in Jerusalem – "And the Lord shall be King over all the earth; in that day the Lord shall be one and His Name one" (14:9).

University of Judaism (UJ). Initially founded in Los Angeles in 1947 as the West Coast branch of the Jewish Theological Seminary of the Conservative movement, the University of Judaism is now a separate institution with academic programs for undergraduates, graduates, and rabbinical students. In 2007, the University of Judaism merged with the Brandeis Bardin Institute to form the American Jewish University.

Unleavened bread – see *Matzah*.

Unveiling. In Western Europe and especially in the United States at the beginning of the 20th century, it became the norm to formally "consecrate" the headstone at the cemetery with a ceremony, though there is no religious obligation to do so. Since in the United States the tombstone is covered with a cloth, the ritual has been termed the "unveiling." Recitation of psalms, a brief eulogy, the chanting of *El Malei Rachamim*, and the *Mourner's Kaddish* (said aloud only if there is a *minyan*) are often part of the custom.[347]

Urechatz. Washing the hands (without blessing) before eating the *karpas* at the beginning of the Passover seder. This reflects the ancient practice of ritual purification before partaking of anything dipped in liquid.

Urim and Thummim. Typically translated as "lights and perfections" or "revelation and truth" (Exod 28:30; Num. 27:21), an oracular device sanctioned by the Bible for determining the will of God on specific issues that were beyond human ability to decide. They may have been two sacred stones or lots drawn out of the breastplate (*hoshen mishpat*) worn by the High Priest in the process of consulting God, especially when there was a choice between two alternatives (i.e., a question requiring a yes or no answer). Thus, the *Urim* and *Thummim* could determine a person's guilt or innocence, be used in special elections, or be employed on behalf of the leader of the people in matters of vital importance. The *Urim* and *Thummim* are not specifically mentioned after the time of King Solomon (10th century B.C.E.). The words *Urim* and *Thummim* in Hebrew, emblazoned on an open book, are pictured on the shield of Yale University.

Ushpizin. An Aramaic word meaning "guests," it refers to the mystical seven biblical personalities whom, according to the Lurianic kabbalistic tradition, Jews invite to visit the sukkah during the seven days of Sukkot. Each of these "guests" is symbolic of one of the *sefirot* (Divine Emanations) – Abraham (*Chesed*, lovingkindness); Isaac (*Gevurah*, strength); Jacob (*Tiferet*, beauty); Moses (*Netzach*, victory); Aaron (*Hod*, splendor); Joseph (*Yesod*, foundation); and David (*Malchut*, sovereignty). All seven are welcomed in the sukkah throughout the seven days of the festival, but on each day one of them is the special guest of honor. After reciting an appropriate blessing, it is customary to tell stories, sing, or study traditional texts about that night's personality.[348] A popular practice is to decorate the wall of the sukkah with a plaque or ornamental chart bearing an inscription that includes the names of these seven *ushpizin*. Some liberal Jews also "invite" female *ushpizin* to the sukkah. Based on medieval sources, these include the seven prophetesses: Sarah, Miriam, Deborah, Hannah, Abigail, Hulda, and Esther.

U-va le-Zion Go'el (And a redeemer shall come to Zion). The first words (Isa. 59:20) of verses of comfort (not recited in the Sabbath or festival morning service) in which God promises to send a Messiah to redeem Jerusalem and the people of Israel. Salvation will be granted not only to the righteous living through the tribulations of exile, but even "to those of Jacob who repent from willful sins."[349] During a period of harsh oppression when it was forbidden to recite the *Kedushah* during the reader's repetition of the *Amidah*, the rabbis inserted its three major biblical verses into *U-va le-Zion Go'el*, because it was recited after the government censors had already left the synagogue.[350] *U-va le-Zion Go'el* is also recited at the afternoon service on the Sabbath and on Saturday night at the end of the evening service.

U-v'nucho yomar (When it rested, he [Moses] said). Opening words of the biblical verse (Num. 10:36) that was said by the Israelites in the wilderness when the Ark of the Covenant rested. Today, it is now recited when the Torah scroll is returned to the ark after being read (see *va-yehi binso'a ha-aron*).

V

Va'ad ha-Kashrut. Local organization of rabbis and *mashgichim* that oversees standards of *kashrut* in the community and provides stores and restaurants with certification.

Va'ad ha-Lashon Ivrit (Hebrew Language Council). Co-founded in 1889 in Jerusalem by Eliezer ben Yehuda, the "father" of modern Hebrew, this organization determined correct and grammatical Hebrew usage. Working through various committees, each specializing in a particular linguistic field, it established the proper Hebrew words for tens of thousands of technical terms. In 1954, the Knesset established the Academy of the Hebrew Language to succeed the *Va'ad ha-Lashon Ivrit*.

Va'ad Le'um*i* (National Committee). The National Council of the Jews of Palestine, the *Va'ad Le'umi* functioned as the executive organ of the *yishuv* from 1920 until the establishment of the Provisional Government of the State of Israel in May 1948. It cooperated closely with the Zionist and Jewish Agency Executive, which was responsible for major policy on immigration, settlement, economic development, and legal defense. The *Va'ad Le'umi* represented the *yishuv* in its relations with the British Mandatory government and Arab leaders. It served as the main organ of the Jews of Palestine before the League of Nations and the numerous inquiry commissions into the "Palestine problem" until the United Nations proposed partition in 1947.

Vach Nacht – see *Leil Shimurim.*

Va'eira. The 2nd *parashah* in the Book of Exodus (6:2-9:35), it describes the first seven of the ten plagues that God inflicted upon Egypt and the Divine promise of ultimate redemption of the Israelites from bondage (four separate statements that are commemorated on Passover by the four cups of wine).

Va'etchanan. The 2nd *parashah* in the Book of Deuteronomy (3:23-7:11), it contains the repetition of the Ten Commandments, the *Shema*, and *Ve-ahavta*, as well as an appeal by Moses to the Israelites that they obey God's law and thus receive Divine favor. The *parashah* reflects a reciprocal covenantal love and commitment between God and the Jewish people.

Valuations. Voluntary contributions (monetary and physical property) for the upkeep of the Sanctuary, which were considered a true expression of devotion to the House of God. In addition to vowing to donate a specific amount of money to the Sanctuary, Israelites also could obligate themselves to contribute their own "value" (or that of another person or thing) to the Temple treasury for any necessary expenditures. Rather than determined on the commercial value of the individual person (relating to health, strength, and earning capacity if sold as a slave), the biblical approach to the "valuation" of a person was based solely on age and sex (Lev. 27:2-8).[351] Valuations could also be made for animals (Lev. 27:9-13), houses (Lev. 29:14-15), or fields (determined not according to their actual value and quality, but rather on the basis of their size and the number of crops remaining until the Jubilee Year (Lev. 26:16-25).

Vants. Literally "bedbug," this Yiddish term generally denotes a despicable person.

Vav. The 6th letter of the Hebrew alphabet, with a numerical value of 6.

Vayacheil. The 9th *parashah* in the Book of Exodus (35:1-38:20), it describes the construction of the Tabernacle under master craftsman Bezalel. It opens with the admonition that work on this vital project could only be performed on six days of the week and not on the Sabbath.

Vayechi. The 12th and final *parashah* in the Book of Genesis (47:28-50:26), it describes Jacob's adoption of Ephraim and Menashe (the sons of Joseph) to the status of full Israelite tribes, Jacob's deathbed blessings of his sons, and the deaths of Jacob and Joseph, which conclude the narrative of the Patriarchs. Jacob was immediately buried with his grandparents, parents, and wife Leah in the Cave of Machpelah in the Land of Israel. Joseph's body remained in Egypt during the period of slavery and was carried with the Israelites during their 40 years of wandering, eventually being buried in Shechem when the Jews returned to the Promised Land.

Vayechulu (And they were completed). Opening word (and name) of the introductory paragraph describing the seventh day of Creation (Gen. 2:1-3), which is recited in synagogue after the *Amidah* on Friday evening. At home, these verses begin the *Kiddush* for the Sabbath eve. *Vayechulu* is preceded by the words *yom ha-shishi* (the sixth day), the last two words of the preceding verse (Gen. 1:31), so that the first four letters spell out *YHVH* (the Tetragrammaton).

Va-yehi binso'a ha-aron. Opening Hebrew words of the biblical verse (Num. 10:35), "When the Ark would journey [Moses said, 'Arise, God, and let Your foes be scattered, let those who hate You flee from before You']." It describes the Ark of the Covenant going forward at the head of the tribes of Israel as a symbol of

God protecting the people and leading them to final victory. Today, it is recited when the Torah scroll is taken out of the ark to be read. In the scroll, this verse and *u-v'nucho yomar* are set off from the rest of the text by inverted *nuns*. This indicates either that they are not here in their original place, or that they are taken from another source – such as the *Book of the Wars of the Lord*, which apparently contained an anthology of poems describing the Divine victories over the enemies of Israel – and form a distinct section, scroll, or even "book" of the Torah.

Vayeilech. The 9th *parashah* in the Book of Deuteronomy (31:1-31:30), it describes the appointment of Joshua as the new leader to replace Moses, the command to periodically read the Law to the people every seven years on Sukkot, and the Divine order to Moses to "write down this poem and teach it to the people." It was placed next to the Ark of the Covenant, so that when the Israelites inevitably went astray it would serve as a "witness" against them. (The "poem" refers to the next *parashah, Ha'Azinu.*)

Vayeira. The 4th *parashah* in the Book of Genesis (18:1-22:24), it narrates the announcement by the Divine visitors that the aged Sarah would bear a son. It includes the devastation of Sodom and Gomorrah (after Abraham bargained with God but was unable to find 10 righteous men within these wicked cities to prevent their destruction),[352] the birth of Isaac, the expulsion of Hagar and Ishmael, and the famous story of the *Akedah* (binding of Isaac).

Vayeishev. The 9th *parashah* in the Book of Genesis (37:1-40:23), it focuses on Joseph – his dreams and their interpretations that anger his brothers, their selling him to a caravan of traders heading toward Egypt, and the false accusation by Potiphar's wife that resulted in his being sent to prison, where he successfully interprets the dreams of Pharaoh's baker and cupbearer. It also recounts the narrative of Judah and Tamar and the birth of Peretz, the ancestor of King David. The story of Joseph, which extends for the following three *parshiyot*, is the longest single narrative in Genesis.

Vayeitzei. The 7th *parashah* in the Book of Genesis (28:10-32:3), it narrates Jacob's dream of a ladder connecting earth and heaven with angels ascending and descending, his marriages to Leah and Rachel,[353] the birth of his children (including the four sons by the handmaidens, Bilhah and Zilpah), and the return of the family to the Land of Israel.

Vayigash. The 11th *parashah* in the Book of Genesis (44:18-47:7), it describes Judah's impassioned speech to save his brother Benjamin, the reconciliation between Joseph and his brothers, and Jacob's journey to Egypt to be reunited with his son Joseph.

Vayikra (1) – see Leviticus.

Vayikra (2). The 1st *parashah* in the Book of Leviticus (1:1-5:26), it details such sacrifices as the burnt offering, grain offering (see *mincha*), peace offering, sin offering, and guilt offering.[354]

Vayishlach. The 8th *parashah* in the Book of Genesis (32:4-36:43), it opens with the wrestling match between Jacob and the "mysterious stranger." It then recounts the meeting between Jacob and his estranged brother Esau, the rape of Dinah followed by the revenge of Shimon and Levi on the men of Shechem, the birth of Benjamin, and the deaths of Rachel and Isaac. In this *parashah*, Jacob is renamed Israel, meaning one who has "striven with God and man and has prevailed" (Gen. 32:29). Similarly, the Jewish people, known as *B'nai Yisrael* ("Children of Israel"), have struggled throughout their history and overcome great odds.

Ve-ahavta (You shall love [the Lord Your God]). The first paragraph of the *Shema*, it stresses that one should not observe the commandments due to fear of punishment or as an attempt to gain Divine favor, but rather out of pure love, which represents the highest level of a human relationship with God.[355] The Mishnah explains that a person should serve God with passionate love ("with all your heart"), even if this means giving up your life ("with all your soul") and wealth ("with all your resources").[356] This paragraph also contains the commandments to teach Torah to your children; learn Torah on every possible occasion; put *tefillin* on one's arms and head; and place a *mezuzah* on the doorposts of the house.

Vegetarianism. According to the dietary laws, all fruits and vegetables are permitted, based on the verse: "See, I give you every seed-bearing plant that is upon all the earth, and every tree that has seed-bearing fruit; they shall be yours for food" (Gen. 1:29). Indeed, this verse and the subsequent one, giving "all the green plants for food," indicate that the earliest biblical ideal was that human beings be vegetarian. Only in the time of Noah did God allow a carnivorous diet, with the proviso that "You must not…eat flesh with its lifeblood in it" (Gen. 9:3).

Veil, bridal – see *Bedeken di kallah*.

Vengeance – see Revenge.

Ve-Shamru ([the Children of Israel] shall keep [the Sabbath]). Opening word of the passage from Exodus (31:16-17) that stresses the obligation of the Jewish people to observe the Sabbath as an eternal covenant between themselves and God, the Creator of heaven and earth. It is recited before the *Amidah* on Friday evening, during the *Amidah* on Saturday morning, and before the blessing over wine at the *Kiddush* following the service.

Vessels, sacred (*k'lei kodesh*). Collective Hebrew term for the furnishings in the Tabernacle in the wilderness and later in the Temple. These included the Ark, Menorah, *parochet*, table, laver, altars, coal shovels, and large shovel. Surrounding the First Temple were chambers containing gold and silver objects that were taken to Babylon when the Jews were exiled and brought back to Jerusalem when the Jews were permitted to return. When the Second Temple was destroyed, the sacred vessels were taken to Rome.

Vichy. Collaborationist *de facto* government of France, led by Marshal Pétain, during the German occupation of the country during World War II (1940-1944). The name derived from the city southeast of Paris in central France that became the capital of the government. While officially neutral in the war, Vichy was essentially a Nazi puppet state. Beginning in November 1942, the area of France nominally controlled by the Vichy government was directly occupied by Germany. The claim of the Vichy government to *de jure* status was challenged by the Free French Forces under Charles de Gaulle, based first in London and later in Algiers, who accused it of being an illegal regime ruled by traitors. The Vichy government was involved in the persecution and deportation of some 77,000 French Jews, who were either murdered in the death camps in Poland or died while in detention.

Vidui – see Confessions.

Vine – see Grapes and Wine.

Virginity. As in other ancient cultures, virginity was prized in Israelite society. According to the Bible, a man who raped an unbetrothed virgin *must* marry her (if she and her father gave their consent) and could never divorce her (Deut. 22:29). A man who seduced an unbetrothed virgin *should* marry her if she and her father agreed (Exod. 22:15-16), but was not required to do so. If any of the three parties disagreed, the seducer was obliged to pay a fine to the girl's father (or directly to her, if she had no father), as well as monetary damage for "indignity and blemish" (i.e., the humiliation he caused her). A man who falsely accused his new bride of not being a virgin (i.e., accusing her of committing adultery between the time of their betrothal and the marriage ceremony) was beaten by the elders of the city, required to pay a fine to her father, and forbidden from ever divorcing her (Deut. 22:19).

Virtues. Physical practices and states of mind that are conducive to the good life. For Maimonides, the ideal of perfection of the soul required dispelling vice and inculcating the moral virtues (see *midot*). The Hebrew prophets attained the highest state of moral and intellectual perfection because their minds were illuminated by Divine "active intellect."

Vision. Mystical or religious experience that, in Jewish tradition, is especially associated with revelation of the Divine Will to a prophet. The *Zohar* and subsequent kabbalistic literature report visions in great detail, as do many tales relating to the Baal Shem Tov, the founder of the Hasidic movement.

Visiting the sick – see *Bikur holim.*

Vocalization – see Vowels and Masoretes.

Voluntary offerings (*nedavah*). These consisted of the burnt (*olah*), meal (*mincha*), and peace (*sh'lamim*) offerings that individuals *could* bring should they so desire. The voluntary offerings reflected the wish of individuals to *improve* their relationships with God, and the sections of the Torah describing them virtually always end with the phrase "an offering of fire, a pleasing odor to the Lord." (See also *obligatory offerings.*)

Vows – see *Nedarim.*

Vows, annulment of. The general rule was that anything a person has promised to God must be fulfilled (see *nedarim*). From the traditional standpoint, however, there were three situations in which the vow of a woman "under authority" could be annulled. A father could annul the vow of a young unmarried woman while she was under his guardianship. Halachically, this was restricted to the six-month period following her puberty; after that time, she was considered sufficiently mature to be responsible for her own vows. When a woman had completed the first step in marriage (see *kiddushin*), but not the second phase (see *nesuin*) that permitted the couple to live together, both her father and her prospective husband shared authority over her vows. Following the completion of the marriage ceremony, a husband was empowered to annul a vow of his wife when he first learned about it. The vow of a widow or divorcée could not be annulled by anyone. (See also *Kol Nidrei.*)

Vowels. Rather than letters as in English, Hebrew vowels (*nikudot*) are denoted as symbols written below, above, or between the letters of a word. Originally, Hebrew was written only with consonants, which were later "vocalized" by the Masoretes.Indeed, the Torah scroll has no vowels (or punctuation), and the reader must know from memory, experience, and context how to pronounce the words. The major vowels are: *patach* (line under the letter, like the "a" in "father"); *kametz* ("T" under the letter, having the same sound as *patach* in Sephardic pronunciation, but given the sound "aw" in Ashkenazic pronunciation); *cholam* (dot over the letter, like the "o" in "blow"); *segol* (triangle of dots below the letter, like the "e" in "get"); *tzeirei* (two horizontal dot below the letter, like the long "a" in "day"); *sh'va* (two vertical dots under the letter, either silent or a short "i" as in "sip"); *shuruk* (dot in the middle of the letter *vav*, like the "oo" in "food"); *kubutz* (three dots in an oblique line under the letter, like the "oo" in "food"); and *chirik* (one dot under the letter, like the long "e" in "feel").

Vulgate. Major Latin translation of the Bible. Made by the Church father Jerome in the Land of Israel in the late 4th-early 5th century, it became the official Latin version of the Bible for the Roman Catholic Church.

V'zot ha-Bracha. The 11th and final *parashah* in the Book of Deuteronomy (33:1-34:12) and the entire Torah, it contains the farewell blessings of Moses to the Twelve Tribes of Israel.It concludes with his death at age 120 with "his eyes undimmed and his vigor unabated." Moses led the Israelites out bondage in Egypt and was the only prophet with whom the Lord spoke "face to face." Although Moses died before the Israelites entered the Promised Land, he was permitted to view it from afar as he stood on Mount Nebo.

Wages. Parallel verses in the Bible – "You must give him his wages on the same day, before the sun sets" (Deut. 24:15) and "You shall not withhold a worker's wage with you all night until morning" (Lev. 19:13) – require that the wages of a day laborer be promptly paid on the day they are earned and not delayed. The reason offered is that the laborer is poor, living from hand to mouth, and needs to buy food for his family in the evening. The Rabbis taught that withholding an employee's wages was like taking his life. Maimonides extended this commandment to require that workers be treated mercifully and not denied any of their rights. A worker hired on a weekly basis must be paid at the end of the week, not a portion each day. As part of the prohibition against abusing a needy or destitute laborer, the payment of substandard wages was forbidden (Deut. 24:14).

Wailing Wall – see *Kotel*.

Walking in God's ways. The duty of human beings is to pattern their actions after those of God, to be like God as much as possible given the limitations of our mortal state. As the Talmud observed, this means clothing the naked just as God clothed Adam and Eve (Gen. 3:21), visiting the sick as God visited Abraham after his circumcision (Gen. 18:3), comforting the mourners as God did for Isaac (Gen. 25:11), and burying the dead as God buried Moses (Deut. 34:6). This duty of imitating God is a fundamental teaching of Judaism, which finds its classic expression in the verse: "You shall be holy, for I, the Lord your God, am holy" (Lev. 19:2). Whereas paganism depicted its gods in the physical image of man, Judaism portrays man as being made in the image of God (Gen. 1:27).

Wandering Jew. A figure in medieval Christian folklore, represented as a Jewish shoemaker or other tradesman who refused Jesus a moment of rest against the wall of his house on the road to the Crucifixion and was then condemned to walk the earth until the Second Coming. This figure has been interpreted as a metaphoric personification of Jewish responsibility for the Crucifixion, which was punished by the destruction of Jerusalem. The Wandering Jew became an anti-Semitic symbol for the Jewish people.

War. Although Jews pray for peace every day (see shalom), they realized that the ideal of true universal peace must await the Messianic Age, when "nation shall not lift up sword against nation, neither shall they learn war any more" (Isa. 2:4). Until this utopian era, war may sometimes be justified and may even be obligatory. However, Jews are warned never to lose their humanity during wartime. There is a biblical proscription against destroying fruit trees during a military campaign so as not to cause distress and suffering to the inhabitants of a besieged city (Deut. 21:19-20). Even during times of war, Jews must remain conscious of the need to maintain their concern for the general welfare, including that of their enemies. This led the Rabbis to develop the general principle of *bal tash'chit*, the prohibition against the wanton destruction of anything valuable to human existence. The Israelites were required to give their enemy an opportunity to make peace (Deut. 20:10). If these peace overtures were accepted, no person or property would be harmed, and the city would become a tributary (paying a fixed yearly sum in taxes, performing national service, and obeying the order of the Israelite king "in fear and humility, as befitted subjects"). In the State of Israel, religious obligations of soldiers are found in halachic directives issued by the military rabbinate.

War criminals. Name for those Germans and other nationals convicted following World War II for crimes against humanity related to the Holocaust and other atrocities perpetrated by the Nazis. The most famous war crimes trial was held at Nuremburg. Beginning in October 1945 and lasting for almost a year, 22 German defendants stood trial on four counts: crimes against the peace, war crimes, crimes against humanity, and conspiracy to commit such crimes. Twelve were sentenced to death and seven to long prison terms; three were acquitted. The Nazi Party leadership, the SS, and the Gestapo were condemned as criminal organizations.

War of Independence (Israel) – See Israel, State of.

War Scroll. One of the Dead Sea Scrolls, it describes the apocalyptic struggle between the Sons of Light and the Sons of Darkness, in which the forces of righteousness are victorious and destroy evil forever.

Warsaw Ghetto. Largest of the Nazi ghettos of Eastern Europe, which at its height housed more than 450,000 Jews living in intolerable conditions. It was the site of the most famous example of armed resistance during the Holocaust, a revolt that began on the first night of Passover (April 19, 1943) in response to the German order to completely evacuate ("liquidate") the ghetto. For 28 days, a small band of Jews with smuggled and homemade weapons put up a gallant struggle against the heavily armed Germans sent to destroy them. Led by young commander-in-chief Mordecai Anielewicz, the Jewish resistance battled heroically. A handful of fighters managed to escape the ghetto through the sewers, and several survived the war. The bulk of the ghetto population resisted passively by barricading themselves in underground bunkers until forced out by German troops.

Washing hands – see *Netilat yadayim.*

Water-drawing ceremony. A special ceremony of "water-libation" was celebrated during the Sukkot festival at the Temple in Jerusalem. Known as *Simchat Beit ha-Sho'evah* (rejoicing of the house of water drawing), the major symbolic act was the bringing of water in a golden flask from the Pool of Siloam to the Temple, where it was poured on the Altar as a supplication for an abundant rainy season. The Talmud reports that renowned Rabbis performed remarkable feats of dexterity, and that one who had not seen the ceremony of the water drawing had never witnessed real joy (Suk. 5:1).

Wayfarer's Prayer – see *Tefillat ha-Derech.*

Wealth. In Judaism, riches are seen as both a blessing and as a responsibility. The wealthy are expected to share their blessings with others and to be personal role models of social and communal responsibility. Yet true wealth derives from inner peace and contentment. As *Pirkei Avot* concludes, "Who is wealthy? He who is happy with his lot" (4:1). (See also *business ethics.*)

Wedding – see Marriage.

Wedding ring. The custom of the groom giving a ring to the bride reflects the ancient understanding of marriage as essentially a business transaction, in which the groom "acquired" his bride and sealed the deal by the payment of a silver or gold coin that had a value of not less than one *perutah.*The ring must belong to the groom and be a simple solid band, without jewels or ornaments. The groom places the wedding ring on the forefinger of the bride's right hand and then recites the marriage formula: "Behold, you are consecrated to me with this ring, according to the law of Moses and Israel." After the ceremony, the ring is transferred to the traditional fourth finger of the left hand. In many congregations in the United States, a "double ring" ceremony is performed in which the bride also places a ring on the groom's finger, saying "*Ani l'dodi v'dodi li*" (I am my beloved's, and my beloved is mine; Song of Songs 6:3).

Weeks, Feast of – see Shavuot.

Weights and measures. In biblical times, the major units of measure were the cubit, *ephah, hin, homer, kav, log, omer, se'ah,* and *shekel* (see individual entries).The olive was a common standard of measurement, even though the fruit of different varieties comes in different sizes. Indeed, the phrase *ke-zayit* ([as large] as an olive) is often used to indicate the minimum amount required to fulfill a ritual obligation. The egg was also an important standard of measurement. (See *false weights and measures.*)

Weizmann Institute of Science. Major Israeli scientific center in Rehovot. Numbering some 2,500 scientists in 18 research departments, it developed from the Daniel Sieff Research Institute, founded in 1934 by Chaim Weizmann and subsequently named for this distinguished scientist, Zionist leader, and first President of Israel. Institute scientists were the first to introduce cancer research in Israel, designed and built the first computer in the country, and established Israel's first research accelerators for studying atomic nuclei as well as its first nuclear physics department and first advanced solar research facility.

West Bank – see Judea and Samaria.

Western Wall – see *Kotel*.

Wheat. One of the seven species symbolizing the fertility of the land (Deut. 8:8), wheat was a central crop in Israel since ancient times and considered the "staff of life." Like barley, in Israel wheat was sown at the beginning of the winter, but it develops more slowly and ripens about two months later. Therefore, the first barley crop (see *omer*) is brought on Passover, but the "first fruits of the wheat harvest" are offered seven weeks later on Shavuot. The choicest wheat was used in meal offerings, and this grain was considered superior to barley. Although wheat was initially the food of the rich, as agriculture improved during mishnaic and talmudic times it became a common food.

White Paper (1) (Churchill, 1922). The first important official statement of British government policy after the Balfour Declaration, it reaffirmed the call for a Jewish national homeland in Palestine with the development of the existing Jewish community, but not "the disappearance or the subordination of the Arabic population, language or culture in Palestine" or the imposition of Jewish nationality "upon the inhabitants of Palestine as a whole." Immigration of Jews was to be limited by "the economic capacity of the country at the time to absorb new arrivals." This White Paper was reluctantly accepted by the Zionist authorities but not by the Arabs, because it called for the establishment of a Jewish national home in Palestine.

White Paper (2) (Passfield, 1930). Issued following the Arab riots of 1929, it argued that land purchase, settlement, and agricultural labor by Jews were creating unemployment among landless Arabs. Its solution was to restrict Jewish immigration and land acquisition. Accusing the document of damaging the aspirations of the Jews for a national home, Chaim Weizmann resigned from the Presidency of the Jewish Agency in protest. A subsequent British letter of interpretation of the Passfield White Paper abrogated much of its anti-Zionist implications.

White Paper (3) (MacDonald, 1939). Regarded by the Zionist movement and many outside it as a final betrayal of Britain's obligations to the Jewish people under the Balfour Declaration and the Mandate, it restricted Jewish immigration to only 75,000 over 5 years at a time when hundreds of thousands of Jews were attempting to flee from the Nazis throughout Europe. After 1944, Jewish immigration would only be allowed with Arab acquiescence. Land sales from Arabs to Jews were limited in some areas and completed banned in others. The White Paper envisioned the establishment in 10 years of an independent Palestinian state in which both Jews and Arabs would participate in the government. The blatantly anti-Jewish tone of this White Paper was the catalyst for the active struggle of the *yishuv* against the Mandatory regime in the Land of Israel.

Who is a Jew. A vexing controversy in Israel, where the Orthodox Chief Rabbinate has consistently refused to recognize as Jews those who have converted under the auspices of non-Orthodox rabbis. According to the Law of Return as interpreted by the Supreme Court of Israel, all converts must be registered as Jews on their identity cards and in the population registry. The underlying problem is that various denominations within Judaism, especially Reform, have substantially different requirements for conversion.

Wicked Priest. The opponent of the Teacher of Righteousness in the Dead Sea Scrolls. Also known as "The Man of Lies," he originally followed the truth. However, once in office and ruling Israel, he betrayed God for the sake of wealth and even persecuted the Teacher of Righteousness. As punishment for his sins, God condemned the Wicked Priest to destruction, and his historical identity remains in dispute.

Widow. After the death of her husband, a widow is entitled to receive the sum stipulated in the marriage contract (*ketubah*). Although according to Jewish law a widow does not inherit her husband's estate and she is to be supported by his heirs, the prevailing halachic opinion is that the widow can decide between this and the sum stipulated in her *ketubah*. (See also *orphan*.)

Wig – see *Sheitel*.

Wilderness. Generic term for the area in the Sinai Peninsula and the east bank of the Gulf of Aqaba, Dead Sea, and Jordan River through which the Israelites wandered during the 40 years between their Exodus from slavery in Egypt and their crossing the Jordan River to reach the Promised Land.

Will. Formal document indicating how property is to distributed after one's death. Assets normally pass to the next of kin, after any debts incurred by the estate have been paid. However, it is possible for a person (of sound mind and "testatory capacity") to choose to dispose of property in a manner different from the legal order of succession. At times, a critically ill person "in contemplation of death" may make an oral declaration before witnesses about how to dispose of property. If the individual recovers, however, these verbal instructions are considered void. Until modern times, wills disposing of property were uncommon among Jews since traditional law dictated inheritance. As *halacha* lost its binding nature for many Jews, individual wills have become much more common.

Will, Divine. Theological issue of the extent of the relationship between God and human beings. Difficulty arises in trying to reconcile human free will with the omnipotence and omniscience of God and the doctrine of predestination. Normative Jewish thinking attempts to resolve the problem by affirming that Divine will does not abrogate the free will of the individual.

Will, ethical – see Ethical will.

Will, free – see Free will.

Willow (*aravah*). Described in the Bible as a tree that grows rapidly near water (Isa. 44:4), the willow is one of the four species used on Sukkot. It is characterized as having "neither taste nor fragrance," symbolizing those among the people of Israel "who are neither learned nor possessed of good deeds" (Lev. R. 30:12). On Hoshana Rabbah, the seventh day of Sukkot, worshipers beat willow branches on the ground or against the seats of the synagogue until the leaves fall, a reenactment of the major ritual in the Temple on that day. It symbolizes a final casting away of sins during the High Holy Day period and the last time that unfavorable judgments can be averted before the final seal is placed on the Books of Life and Death.

Wimpel. German term for the long, wide band of material that encircles and tightly binds the two rolls of a Torah scroll. Known as a *gartel* in Yiddish, it dates back to talmudic times. In some congregations, especially in southern Germany, it was customary to cut the linen cloth on which a boy was circumcised and sew it into an elaborately embroidered or painted work of art, which was presented to the congregation on the child's first visit to the synagogue. Used to secure the Torah from which the boy read when he became bar mitzvah and before he married, the wimpel symbolized his "binding" himself to the Torah and to the Jewish community.[357]

Windows. There is a halachic requirement that a synagogue must have windows. This derives from the description of Daniel having "had windows made [in his upper chamber where he prayed] facing Jerusalem" (Dan. 6:10). According to Rashi, windows are required because they allow the worshiper to see the sky, which inspires reverence and devotion during prayer. Some have recommended that there be 12 windows in a synagogue, corresponding to the Twelve Tribes of Israel. Each has a special angel who carries its prayers (reflecting the distinct spirit and soul of the tribe) through a particular "window in heaven" directly to the Throne of God.[358]

Wine. The drinking of wine is an essential element of Jewish ceremonial celebrations. The Sabbath and festivals are greeted and conclude with blessings over a cup of wine (see *Kiddush* and *Havdalah*), and four cups of wine are drunk at the seders on Passover and Tu b'Shevat. Wine is also included at circumcisions and weddings.Jewish tradition appreciates the positive qualities of wine and its capacity to "gladden the heart of man" (Ps. 104:15), however it permits drinking only in moderation and in the context of holiness and community.

Wine, Kosher. To be considered kosher, wine must be produced under rabbinic supervision. Only Sabbath-observant Jews are permitted to handle the wine or operate the wine-making equipment from grape crushing to consumption. (For a partial exception, see *mevushal.*) This prohibition against Jews drinking wine prepared by gentiles was initially instituted lest some of it may have been used as a libation in a pagan ceremony connected with idol worship. In rabbinic times, this decree remained in effect to prevent Jews from fraternizing with gentiles in social situations, which could lead to assimilation or intermarriage. Conservative and Reform Jews reject the prohibition against drinking wine touched by a gentile.

Wisdom. Multifaceted term that the Bible uses to refer to the technical skill of the artisan, the aptitude for government leadership, and the practical ability to cope with life. The Book of Proverbs stresses that wisdom entails the pursuit of a lifestyle of proper ethical conduct, and that "the fear of the Lord is the beginning of wisdom" (9:10). The ideal of Jewish education is to develop a *talmid hacham*, a wise scholar.

Wisdom literature. Collective term for biblical books (Proverbs, Job, and Ecclesiastes) and apocryphal literature (e.g., Wisdom of Ben Sira, Wisdom of Solomon) in which the essence of wisdom is defined as the fear of God and observance of the commandments. Proverbs and Ecclesiastes are traditionally attributed to King Solomon, who was famous for his wisdom.

Wisdom of Ben Sira. Book of the Apocrypha dating back to the 2nd century B.C.E. Written in Hebrew by Ben Sira of Jerusalem and translated into Greek by his grandson, it is a collection of ethical teachings, moral maxims, and various pieces of advice to love wisdom and pursue moderation (resembling the Book of Proverbs) that are applicable to a broad spectrum of practical situations. It also contains some liturgical poems and psalms.

Wisdom of Solomon. Book of the Apocrypha written in the 1st century B.C.E. A glorification of wisdom, especially that of King Solomon, the book stresses the important role of wisdom in history, the superiority of the wise over the wicked, and the evils of idolatry.

Wissenschaft des Judentums. German phrase literally meaning "Science of Judaism," it was applied to a movement that emerged in early 19th-century Germany and championed the scientific study of Jewish history, literature, and sacred texts using modern critical methods and scholarly tools that were not influenced by Christian scholars or traditionalist rabbis. The underlying impetus for this activity was to provide objective evidence to non-Jews that Jews deserved the same civil rights and privileges, as well as freedom from discrimination, and to demonstrate that Judaism could be viable in the modern age. Some Orthodox Jews criticized the scientific study of Judaism for reducing all of Judaism to historical phenomena, whereas it is essentially religious and theological. They also attacked the claim that it was "scientific," arguing that it was not being used to discover objective truth but only as a tool to enhance the Jewish communal agenda. As the 19th century progressed, centers of Jewish scholarship developed in other countries that produced significant historical, philosophical, and philological works.

Witnesses. Judges are required by Jewish law to diligently inquire into the testimony of witnesses and to interrogate them rigorously in the greatest possible detail before giving a verdict or inflicting punishment (Deut. 13:15). Meticulous care is required to prevent a judge from rendering an ill-considered and hasty decision that would harm an innocent person. According to the Rabbis, there were seven inquiries by which witnesses were tested: "In what sabbatical cycle [did the matter under consideration take place] ? In what year? In what month? On which day of the month? On what day? At what hour? In what place?" (Sanh. 40a). Failure to provide a reasonable response led to the person's evidence being deemed inadmissible. Under cross-examination, however, the witness could be asked a limitless number of questions. Indeed, the Talmud states that "the more exhaustive the cross-examination, the more praiseworthy the judge." Traditional Jewish law prohibits individuals from testifying against themselves.

Witnesses, disqualified. Under rabbinic law, 10 types of witnesses were disqualified from testifying in court. They included: (1) women (who were thought to be too emotional to render a reasoned judgment); (2) slaves; (3) minors; (4) the mentally retarded; (5) deaf-mutes (who could not hear questions nor speak in response to them); (6) the blind (who could not be "eyewitnesses"); (7) relatives of the parties involved in the case; (8) those personally involved in the case; (9) a "shameless" person; and (10) a wicked person (such as a compulsive gambler, thief, or userer).

WIZO. Acronym for "**W**omen's **I**nternational **Z**ionist **O**rganization," which was founded in 1920 to provide professional and vocational training for women, with special emphasis on preparation for agricultural pioneering in the Land of Israel and the care and education of children and youth. WIZO has expanded its activities to defending the rights and status of women in Israel and achieving gender equality in all fields, as well as combating domestic violence, contributing to family and community welfare, and providing absorption services to immigrants.

Woman of Valor – see *Eshet Chayil*.

Women's commandments. Collective term for three *mitzvot* – the lighting of Sabbath candles, observing the laws of family purity (see *taharat ha-mishpachah*) through immersion in a ritual bath (see *mikveh*), and separating out a portion of dough (see *challah*) when baking bread.

Women's Zionist Organization of America – see Hadassah.

Work. Despite the explicit biblical proscription against working on the Sabbath (Exod. 20:10), the Bible does not list those specific labors that are prohibited. In the Mishnah (Shab. 7:2), the Rabbis enumerated 39 major categories (with hundreds of subcategories) of labor that were forbidden, based on those types of work that were related to the construction of the Tabernacle in the wilderness, which ceased on the Sabbath. Activities that cannot be performed on the Sabbath are basic tasks connected with preparing the showbread (sowing, plowing, reaping, binding, threshing, winnowing, selecting, grinding, sifting, kneading, baking); work related to making the coverings in the Tabernacle and the vestments used by the *kohanim* (shearing [sheep], bleaching, carding [changing tangled or compressed material into separate fibers], dyeing, spinning, stretching [material], making two loops [meshes], threading needles, weaving, separating, tying [a knot], untying [a knot], sewing, tearing); activities concerned with writing, including the preparation of parchment from animal skin (trapping or hunting, slaughtering, flaying [skinning], treating skins [curing hides], scraping pelts, marking out [to make ready for cutting], cutting [to shape], writing, erasing); construction (building, demolishing); kindling a flame (lighting, extinguishing); carrying (from private to public domain, and vice versa), and putting the finishing touches to a piece of work already begun before the Sabbath.[359]

Working with two different kinds of animals. The Bible explicitly states, "You shall not plow with an ox and a donkey together" (Deut. 22:10). According to Rashi, this prohibition applied to the coupling of any two different species and to any activity (not only plowing). The ox and donkey differ greatly in temperament, size, and strength, and it would be cruel to the weaker animal to yoke them together.[360]

Workmen's Circle. American Jewish fraternal and cultural organization with initial socialist leanings. Founded in New York in 1892 by Jewish immigrant workers, in 1916 the Workmen's Circle entered the field of Jewish education and went on to establish the largest network of Jewish secular schools in North America. Eventually, the Workmen's Circle abandoned its socialist orientation for a leftist-liberal political stance. Now a fully English-speaking organization, it focuses on offering public programs on Yiddish and general Jewish culture, education, and social action.

World Jewish Congress (WJC). International Jewish organization that was founded in Geneva in 1936 to protect the interests and rights of individual Jews and Jewish communities throughout the world as the Nazi menace became ever more threatening. The World Jewish Congress acts as a representative body on behalf of Jewish communities before governmental, intergovernmental, and other international authorities on matters concerning the Jewish people, especially the protection of Jewish rights and status, the encouragement of the development of Jewish social and cultural life, and the defense of Israel.

World to Come – see *Olam ha-ba*.

World Zionist Organization. Since 1960, the new name of the Zionist Organization.

Worship – see Prayer.

Writings (*Ketuvim*). Third of the three major divisions of the Bible. Also known as the Hagiographa, it is composed of Psalms, Proverbs, Job, The Song of Songs, Ruth, Lamentations, Ecclesiastes, Esther, Daniel, Ezra, Nehemiah, and Chronicles. (For more information, see listings for individual books.)

Written Law. The Five Books of Moses (see *Chumash*).

Y

Ya'aleh (May it arise). Opening word and title of a hymn sung in Ashkenazic synagogues immediately after the *Amidah* during the evening service on Yom Kippur. Based on the prayer *Ya'aleh v'Yavo*, it is divided into three-line stanzas whose final words can be translated as "at nightfall," "in the morning," and "at dusk."

Ya'aleh v'Yavo ([Our God and God of our forefathers, may our remembrance] rise up and come ... [before You]). Prayer requesting that on this day God "remember us for good [well-being], be mindful of us for a blessing, and save us for life." After each of these supplications, the congregation responds "amen." *Ya'aleh v'Yavo* is added to the *Amidah* on Rosh Chodesh and on the pilgrimage festivals of Passover, Shavuot, and Sukkot (and is part of the Grace after Meals on these holidays). The prayer is incorporated into the blessing that asks for a return to the Temple service and makes allusion to the special offerings that were brought on these days. Since the destruction of the Temple, Jews can no longer bring tangible gifts to offer God on the festivals. Nevertheless, just as they remember the historical events relating to each of these occasions and perform the prescribed rituals, Jews pray that God will remember the people of Israel and grant them both material benefits and ultimate redemption.[361]

Yachatz. Literally "division," the Hebrew term used at the Passover seder for the breaking of the middle matzah, half of which is hidden for the *afikoman*.

Yachne. Yiddish term for a troublemaking woman.

Yad. Literally "hand," the Hebrew term for a pointer with a hand-shaped tip that is used by the *baal korei* to indicate the words being read in the Torah. Because it is forbidden to touch the parchment of the scroll with bare hands, Torah readers initially merely pointed with their index fingers to the words being read. However, this often made it difficult for the person who was called up for an *aliyah* to see the script and follow the reading. The *yad* is often a fine work of art, made of wood, silver, or gold.[362]

Yad Hazakah. Literally "strong hand," this Hebrew term is used anthropomorphically in the Torah to refer to God's redeeming the Israelites from slavery in Egypt "with a strong hand and an outstretched arm." *Yad Hazakah* is also a popular name for the Mishneh Torah of Maimonides, since the numerical value of the Hebrew letters *yud* (10) and *dalet* (4) equal 14 – the number of volumes in this massive legal code.

Yad Sarah. Leading volunteer agency in Israel, which provides home care support, medical equipment, and numerous other services to those in need. Founded in 1976 by Uri Lupolianski, later a mayor of Jerusalem, the activities of this non-profit agency have expanded to assist Diaspora Jewish communities and developing countries.

Yad Vashem. Literally "Monument and Memorial," the Holocaust memorial institution of Israel and the Jewish people. Yad Vashem is dedicated to perpetuating the memories of the Jewish communities and individuals who perished in the Shoah. Located on a ridge called Mount of Remembrance, Yad Vashem is reached by the Avenue of the Righteous Among the Nations, which is lined with trees planted in tribute to individual gentiles known to have helped save Jewish lives during the Nazi era. The Hall of Remembrance is a huge stone, crypt-like room in which an eternal flame sheds an eerie light over plaques on the floor listing the major concentration camps. Other memorials include a 20-foot high monument dedicated to the 1.5 million Jewish soldiers among the allied armies, partisans, and ghetto fighters; the Valley of the Destroyed Communities that commemorates the 5,000 Jewish communities that disappeared during World War II; and the memorial to the Children of the Holocaust, in honor of the more than 1.5 million murdered youth. Yad Vashem also contains an extensive library with the most comprehensive collection of works on the Holocaust in the world, and a new Holocaust history museum. At the end of the museum's historical narrative is the Hall of Names, which contains more than 3 million pages of testimony as well as the names, photographs, and personal details of as many as possible of those who perished in the Holocaust. The Yad Vashem archives is the most important repository of information about the Holocaust in the world. Yad Vashem also has an International School for Holocaust Studies, which attracts thousands of educators from Israel and throughout the world, and an International Institute for Holocaust Research.

Yadayim. The 11th tractate of Tohorot (purity) in the Mishnah, it deals with the laws of ritual impurity of the hands and how to cleanse them.

Yah Ribbon Olam (God, Master of the universe). Opening words and title of a popular Sabbath table hymn, though it does not mention the Sabbath at all. Written in Aramaic by Israel Najara, a major liturgical poet belonging to the Safed circle of mystics, the opening letters of the verses are an acrostic for the first name of the author. The song praises the glorious and mighty "King who reigns over kings," whose "powerful and wonderful deeds it is beautiful to declare." It continues by extolling God as the Creator of all life and a Worker of wonders. Finally, it concludes with a request that God redeem the Jewish people from exile and permit them to rebuild the Temple in Jerusalem, "the city of beauty."

Yahrzeit. Literally "year time," this Yiddish term is used by Ashkenazic Jews to refer to the yearly commemoration of the anniversary of the death of one's parents according to the Jewish calendar. Many extend it to the other five close relatives for whom mourning is required – brother and sister, son and daughter, and spouse. Hasidic communities observe the *yahrzeits* of the leaders of their specific dynasties as festive occasions celebrating the day that these *tzadikim* ascended to the spiritual realm. In modern times, annual commemorations have been instituted in Israel to mark the death of such prominent figures as Theodore Herzl, Vladimir Jabotinsky, Chaim Nachman Bialik, Rav Kook, and Yitzhak Rabin. A person observing *yahrzeit* recites the *Mourner's Kaddish* at each of the three daily services, often leading them if able to do so. If the Torah is read on that day, the mourners are given *aliyot*; otherwise, they are called to the Torah on the preceding Sabbath. A 24-hour memorial candle is lit at home in accordance with the biblical verse, "the soul [spirit] of man is the lamp of God" (Prov. 20:27).

Yakir Yerushalayim. Literally "Honored/Treasured Citizen of Jerusalem," an award given by the municipal government each year to one or more city residents for "contribution to the cultural and educational life of Jerusalem and the Diaspora." Winners of the award are often scholars who have promoted education and knowledge of the history of Jerusalem.

Yalkut. Literally "compilation," the title of several midrashic anthologies including Yalkut Shimoni, Yalkut ha-Meiri, and Yalkut Reuveni.

Yam ha-Melach – see Dead Sea.

Yam Suf (lit., "Sea of Reeds") – see Red Sea.

Yamim Nora'im (Days of Awe) – see High Holy Days.

Yarkon. Second largest source of water in Israel. The Yarkon River arises about 8 miles inland in the vicinity of Tel Aphek and flows for about 16 miles in a northward arc before descending into the Mediterranean Sea at Tel Aviv. It divides the coastal plain into the Shephela (lowland) to the south and the Plain of Sharon to the north. The name Yarkon is derived from the Hebrew word *yarok* (green), which refers either to the color of its waters or to the abundant vegetation on its banks. In the 19th century, the Yarkon basin became a major center for Jewish settlement, beginning with Petah Tikvah and then Bnai Brak, Ramat Gan, and Tel

Aviv. The crossing of the Yarkon by Allenby's army in 1917 marked the culmination of the first British campaign in Palestine. In recent years, half of its waters have been diverted to irrigate the Negev.

Yarmulke – see *Kippah*.

Yasher ko-ach ("may you grow in strength" or "may your strength be directed in the right path"). In Ashkenazic synagogues, the greeting from fellow congregants when one returns from having an *aliyah* to the Torah. This custom may reflect the belief in talmudic times that intense study of the Torah, symbolized by the Torah reading, "weakens the strength of man." Thus, the greeting expresses the hope that the recipient of the *aliyah* will be revitalized as a result of the honor just bestowed on him.

Yavneh. Site of the Sanhedrin and capital of Jewish learning after the destruction of Jerusalem in 70 C.E. An ancient city on the coastal plain between Jaffa and Ashdod, Yavneh was well populated and fortified by the time of the Second Temple. During the Roman siege of Jerusalem, R. Yochanan ben Zakkai escaped from the city and made his way to the camp of the Roman general Vespasian, predicting that he soon would become Emperor of Rome. When this transpired, Vespasian granted Ben Zakkai's request for permission to gather a small community of sages and organize an academy of learning at Yavneh. The Sanhedrin was reestablished, with Ben Zakkai as its head, and Yavneh remained the seat of Jewish scholarship and culture, helping to define Judaism in the absence of the Temple until the Bar Kochba revolt (132-135), when the Sanhedrin was disbanded and many of the inhabitants of the city fled.

Yayin nesech. Literally "wine of libation" (Deut. 32:38), the Hebrew term refers to wine that had been used in connection with idol worship and was forbidden to the Israelites. (See *wine, kosher*.)

Year, calculation of current. The numbering of years in the Jewish calendar is based on the time since the "Creation of the world" on Rosh Hashanah. To calculate this, the Rabbis combined the life spans of the early generations listed in the Bible – starting with Adam – with the time that had elapsed since then. To determine the current Jewish year, add 3760 to the year in the civil calendar from January to Rosh Hashanah and 3761 from Rosh Hashanah until the end of December. Thus, the first part of the year 2008 in the civil calendar would equal 5768 in the Jewish calendar; after Rosh Hashanah it would be the year 5769.

Year of Release – see Sabbatical Year.

Yedid Nefesh (Beloved of the soul). Popular Sabbath hymn that often opens the Friday evening service. Composed by Eleazar Azikri, a 16th-century kabbalist of

Safed, the first letters of its four stanzas spell out *YHVH* (Tetragrammaton). *Yedid Nefesh* extols the love between God the Creator and human beings, who humbly yearn for Divine mercy and favor.[363, 364]

Yediot Aharonot. Literally "last information," the title of the Hebrew daily afternoon newspaper founded in 1939. It adopted a tabloid layout in the early 1950's, an approach that constituted an innovation in Israeli journalism. Nevertheless, *Yediot Aharanot* was filled with news and editorial content of interest to Israeli professionals and went on to achieve a very high circulation rate.

Yehi Ratzon (May it be Your will). Introductory prayer for the announcement of the New Moon.It asks that the new month be "for goodness and for blessing" and that God will give us "long life" – of peace, goodness, blessing, sustenance, and physical health, in which there is no shame or humiliation; a life of wealth and honor in which we will have love of Torah and fear of heaven, and in which out heartfelt requests will be fulfilled for the good.

Yekke. Colloquial Yiddish term for a German Jew. Derived from the formal attire that German Jews used to wear (i.e., suits with well-fitting "jackets"), *yekke* is a perjorative term that refers to the stereotype of compulsive, authoritarian, rigid, and pedantic German behavior.

Yekum purkan (May salvation arise). Collective name for a set of three prayers that immediately follow the reading of the *haftarah* on the Sabbath in the Ashkenazic ritual. They ask Divine favor for those who uphold the Torah – by teaching, study, and support of scholars, and especially by undertaking the difficult responsibilities of communal leadership. The first two of these prayers open with the words *Yekum purkan* and were composed in Babylonia in the 10th or 11th century, when the famed academies were in decline and in need of funds. In addition to pleading for God's mercy, they were designed to inform the people of the immense value and critical financial needs of the academies so that they would generously support them. Since the prayers were directed to the worshipers as much as to God, they were composed in the Aramaic vernacular and recited at every Sabbath morning service.[365] The second *Yekum purkan*, also written in Aramaic but in post-geonic times, is similar and requests God's blessings for the members of the congregation and their families.[366] (For the third prayer, see *Mi she-Berach*.) The first *Yekum purkan* prayer is not found in the Conservative *siddur*, and the first and second prayers have been removed from the prayer book of the Reform movement.

Yemach shemo (May his name be blotted out). Hebrew phrase said after mentioning the name of an enemy of the Jewish people. To fulfill the commandment to "blot out the name of Amalek" (Deut. 25:19), some people write the name

Haman (a descendant of Amalek) on the soles of their shoes so as to literally blot out the name as they stomp their feet during the reading of the *Megillah* on Purim.

Yenta. Yiddish term for a gossip.

Yerushalayim (1). Hebrew word for Jerusalem. Examples of its use include Yom Yerushalayim (Jerusalem Day) and Naomi Shemer's classic song, *Yerushalayim shel Zahav* (Jerusalem of Gold).

Yerushalayim (2). The 14th blessing of the weekday *Amidah*, it calls for the rebuilding of the Holy City in all its former grandeur and the "speedy establishment of the throne of David within it."

Yeshiva. From a Hebrew root meaning "to sit" and literally an "academy," the term refers to a Jewish school or seminary of higher learning where students intensively study Torah, Talmud, and rabbinic literature. The *yeshiva* is a continuation of the academies in Babylonia and the Land of Israel during the talmudic and geonic periods. The great European *yeshivot* were all destroyed in the Holocaust, though survivors were able to reconstitute some of them in the United States and Israel. Some modern *yeshivot* combine a secular college education with training in religious studies (see Yeshiva University, below).

Yeshiva bocher. Yiddish term for a young man studying in a *yeshiva*. It sometimes is used to denote any young boy who is a good student of Talmud and Jewish texts.

Yeshiva shel ma'alah. Literally, "Torah academy on high," the rabbinic and later liturgical concept of the afterlife as a heavenly house of study reflected the highest values of the Jewish people. In traditional Jewish thinking, admission to this *yeshiva* was reserved for the souls of Torah scholars and teachers and those who supported them financially. The medieval comment, "in *prayer* we speak to God; in *study* God speaks to us," indicated the belief that the Torah represents both the link of the Jew to God and the pathway to eternity. Before reciting *Kol Nidrei* on Yom Kippur eve, the *hazzan* declares in solemn legalistic terminology: "By the authority of the Heavenly Court (*yeshiva shel ma'alah*) and by the authority of this earthly court, with Divine consent and the consent of this congregation, we hereby declare it permissible to pray with those who have transgressed." Thus, this preliminary to *Kol Nidrei* dispels arrogance, for each of us may be the transgressor in the congregation, and on this day the barriers between the righteous and the sinners are broken down

Yeshiva University. Flagship institution of higher learning of the modern Orthodox community in the United States. Founded in 1897 as the first advanced *yeshiva* in the country, students at the separate undergraduate schools for men (Yeshiva College) and women (Stern College) pursue a dual program of Jewish and secular studies in order to achieve "synthesis – a mastery of two intellectual worlds. Yeshiva University includes the Rabbi Isaac Elchanan Theological Seminary for the training of Orthodox rabbis and such secular, non-sectarian divisions as the Albert Einstein College of Medicine and the Benjamin Cardozo School of Law.

Yesod. The 9th of the *sefirot*.Portrayed as the phallus of *Adam Kadmon*, it appears along the middle axis of the Divine Flow directly below *Tiferet*. It is the channel through which *Tiferet* strives to unite with the *Shechinah* and pass on the creative and benevolent Divine forces to our world.

Yetzer ha-ra and **Yetzer ha-tov**. Literally the "inclination toward evil" and the "inclination toward good," these Hebrew terms reflect the rabbinic concept that within each person there are opposing natural drives continually in conflict. The *yetzer ha-ra* rarely conducts a frontal attack on one's spirituality. Rather, the individual is lured into an apparently innocent pastime, while the *yetzer ha-ra* imperceptibly tempts progressively greater indulgence, until one becomes totally devoid of morality and enslaved to biological drives.[367] Some commentators related this to the insidious entrapment of the Israelites by the Egyptians. Initially they took a soft approach, hiring them as highly paid workers; but then they hardened their grasp on them as they gradually converted the Israelites into slaves. At times, the *yetzer ha-ra* can be a powerful positive force if channeled correctly. As the Midrash observed, "Were it not for the *yetzer ha-ra* [referring here to the sexual urge], no man would build a house, marry a wife, or beget children." The Rabbis view the Torah as a powerful means to master the *yetzer ha-ra*, which, in the Kabbalah, was identified with demonic forces.

Yetzi'at Mitzrayim – see Exodus.

Yevamot (Yev.). The 1st tractate in Nashim (women) in the Mishnah, it deals with levirate marriage and *chalitzah*, as well as prohibited marriages.

YHVH – see Tetragrammaton.

Yibbum. See Levirate marriage.

Yichud (joining, union). Short period during which the bride and groom remain alone following the wedding ceremony, breaking their fast and spending a few quiet moments together. This private act, which in ancient times included sexual consummation, validates the marriage. The couple then rejoins their families and friends for the wedding feast and celebration.

Yichus. Family lineage and prestige. The *yichus* of the prospective bride and groom was an important factor considered by a *shadchan* in arranging a traditional Jewish marriage.

Yid. Yiddish term for a Jew.

Yiddish. From the German word *judisch* meaning "Jewish," the daily language of Ashkenazic Jews for the past 1,000 years. Dating back to the Middle Ages in the Rhine and Danube basins and written with Hebrew characters, Yiddish derives primarily from German dialects with a significant Hebrew component along with some Slavic elements. Among the famous authors of modern Yiddish literature were Shalom Aleichem, Isaac Bashevis Singer, Mendele Mocher Sforim, Isaac Leib Peretz, Sholem Asch, and the playwright S. Anski. In the late 19th and early 20th centuries, there was also a thriving Yiddish press, theater, and educational system. With the destruction of Jewish communities in Eastern Europe in the Holocaust, and the adoption of Hebrew as the official language of the State of Israel, it appeared that Yiddish was a "dying" language. However, Yiddish continues to be spoken by many in the ultra-Orthodox community, and in recent years has had a revival among less traditional Jews, aided in part by the 1997 opening of the National Yiddish Book Center on the campus of Hampshire College in Amherst, MA., and by the introduction of Yiddish language study into some university curricula.

Yiddish theatre. Dramas, comedies, revues, and operettas that were written and performed by Jews in Yiddish from the late 19th century until just before World War II. Professional Yiddish theatres were wildly popular in Jewish areas of Eastern and Central Europe, as well as in New York and other major American cities where large numbers of immigants congregated upon arriving in the United States.

Yiddishkeit. Literally "Jewishness," this all-inclusive Yiddish word refers both to Orthodox religious belief and practice and to an emotional attachment and identification with the Jewish people, including its traditions and culture.

Yigdal (Exalted [be the living God]). Hymn ascribed to Daniel ben Judah, a judge in the rabbinical court in Rome during the first half of the 14th century. It is based on the Thirteen Principles of Faith of Maimonides. In the Ashkenazic prayer book, *Yigdal* can be found at the start of the daily morning service. However, it is usually recited at the conclusion of the Friday and festival evening services, as in the Sephardic and Middle Eastern traditions. The Ashkenazic version is composed of 13 lines, one for each principle of faith. The Sephardic prayer contains 14 lines, the last of which is "These are the Thirteen Principles of Faith; these are the foundation of the Divine faith and of God's law."[368]

Yirat ha-Shem – see Fear of God.

Yirat Shamayim – see Fear of God.

Yishtabach (Praised). Final prayer of *Pesukei de-Zimra.*The number "15" is fundamental in the structure of the *Yishtabach* prayer. The first half contains 15 expressions of praise, and there are 15 words after the phrase *Baruch ata Adonai.* The number alludes to the 15 Songs of Ascents (Psalms 120-134; see *Shir ha-Ma'alot*) and the numerical value of the Divine Name *yah* (*yud* = 10; *hei* = 5), which God used to create heaven and earth. The initial letters of the second through fifth Hebrew words spell *Shlomo* (Solomon), giving rise to speculation that this was the name of the unknown author or that the prayer was written in honor of King Solomon.

Yishuv. The Hebrew name for the Jewish community in the Land of Israel before the formal establishment of the State in 1948.

Yisrael. Hebrew word for Israel.

Yitro. The 5th *parashah* in the Book of Exodus (18:1-20:23), it is named for the father-in-law of Moses, who helped his son-in-law organize the judiciary. This section contains the awesome Revelation at Mount Sinai and the giving of the Ten Commandments, the most significant event in the history of the Jewish people.

YIVO. Founded in 1925 in Vilna, the YIVO Institute for Jewish Research is dedicated to researching and studying the history and culture of Ashkenazic Jewry in a scholarly and empiral manner. Headquartered in New York City since 1940, today YIVO is the world's preeminent resource center for Eastern European Jewish Studies; Yiddish language, literature and folklore; and the American Jewish immigrant experience. YIVO's library and archives contain the world's largest collection of materials documenting Yiddish culture and the history and contributions of Eastern European Jewry and their offspring in various parts of the globe.

Yizkor (May [God] remember). Commonly used Hebrew term for *Hazkarat Neshamot* (remembrance of the souls), the memorial service for the departed. In the Ashkenazic ritual, *Yizkor* is recited after the reading of the Torah during the morning service on the last days of each of the three pilgrimage festivals (Passover, Shavuot, and Sukkot) and on Yom Kippur. Sephardim also recite the memorial service (*Hashkavah*) during the evening service immediately preceding the Day of Atonement. Rather than congregational memorial prayers after the holiday Torah service, Sephardim personally recite a memorial prayer for their relatives when called to the Torah. Today, the traditional memorial service consists of three prayers that are recited standing and with the Torah scrolls taken out from the ark. The first prayer, *Yizkor Elohim* (May God remember [the soul of] ...) expresses the mourner's hope that the departed souls will enjoy eternal life in the presence of

God. The second prayer in the memorial service is *El Malei Rachamim*. A special prayer is frequently added for the victims of the Holocaust and for Jewish soldiers who have died in war, particularly in Israel. The traditional memorial service concludes with the recital of *Av ha-Rachamim.* It is customary for those individuals whose parents are living to actually leave the sanctuary until the *Yizkor* service has concluded. Both Conservative and Reform congregations end the memorial prayer with a communal recitation of the *Mourner's Kaddish.*

Yom ha-Atzmaut (Independence Day). Israeli national holiday celebrated on the 5th of Iyar (immediately following Yom ha-Zikaron), the Hebrew date of Israel's Declaration of Independence and the establishment of the State of Israel on May 14, 1948. It is a day of rejoicing with fireworks, dancing in the streets, and a variety of official ceremonies and public entertainment. At the conclusion of the day, the Israel Prize is granted to individuals who have made special contributions to Israeli culture, intellectual life, and science. Other events include the International Bible Contest for Jewish Youth and the Hebrew Song Festival. In the Diaspora, Yom ha-Atzmaut is celebrated with a variety of parades, cultural events, fairs, and public ceremonies designed to foster solidarity with Jews in the State of Israel.

Yom ha-Bikurim (Day of the First Fruits). Biblical name for the festival of Shavuot, when pilgrims would march joyously to the Temple in Jerusalem, offering up baskets of their first ripe fruits and bread baked from the newly harvested wheat in thanksgiving to God.

Yom ha-Din – see Day of Judgment.

Yom ha-Shoah (Holocaust Remembrance Day). Day to commemorate the Holocaust and its victims, which the government of the State of Israel established as the 27th of Nisan. After much debate, this date was chosen because it occurs between the Warsaw Ghetto uprising (which began on the first day of Passover, the 15th of Nisan, in 1943) and Yom ha-Zikaron and also falls during the traditional mourning period of the Counting of the Omer. In Israel, theaters and places of entertainment, schools, and most businesses are closed. Wreath-laying ceremonies are held at Yad Vashem, Israel's national memorial to the victims of the Holocaust. In the United States, Holocaust Remembrance Day is often celebrated on April 19 (or the nearest appropriate Sunday), the day on which the Warsaw Ghetto uprising broke out according to the civil calendar.

Yom ha-Zikaron (Remembrance Day). Memorial day for those who died defending the State of Israel. It is observed on the 4th of Iyar, the day before Israel Independence Day (see Yom ha-Atzmaut). At 11 A.M., sirens are sounded throughout Israel, signaling two minutes of silence and the virtual cessation of all activity in the country.[369] In addition, a memorial ceremony is held at the Mount Herzl military cemetery, flags are flown at half-mast, and places of entertainment are closed.

Yom Huledet Same'ach. Hebrew for "Happy Birthday."

Yom Kippur (Day of Atonement). Major fast day on the 10th of Tishrei that is devoted to individual and communal repentance (see *teshuvah*). It is the most solemn day in the Jewish calendar and the climax of the 40-day period of self-examination that begins with a month of spiritual preparation during Elul and intensifies on Rosh Hashanah and the remainder of the Ten Days of Repentance. The Torah (Lev. 16:31) describes Yom Kippur as a *Shabbat Shabbaton* (a Sabbath of solemn rest), on which all manner of work is forbidden and Jews are to practice self-denial (lit, "afflict your souls"; Lev. 16:29). According to the sages, the duty of afflicting the soul requires the prohibition of (1) eating and drinking; (2) bathing for pleasure; (3) anointing of the body with oil; (4) wearing leather shoes; and (5) engaging in sexual relations. In Temple times, Yom Kippur was a day of elaborate rituals to effect the atonement of the people (see Azazel and Holy of Holies). In traditional households, the *kaporos* rite is performed. Today, there are five synagogue services on Yom Kippur, one more than is usual for a Sabbath or festival – *Kol Nidrei;* (b) *Shacharit*; (c) *Musaf*; *Avodah*; and *Ne'ilah*. The *Yizkor* memorial prayer is recited, as well as numerous additions to the liturgy including the two confessions of sin, *Al Chet* and *Ashamnu*; *Ki anu amecha*; *Ki hinei ka-chomer*; and *Avinu malkeinu*. At the conclusion of the day, a *tekiah gedolah* is sounded on the *shofar* followed by the prayer, *Le-shanah ha-ba'ah bi-Yerushalayim* (Next year in Jerusalem!). The traditional Yom Kippur greeting is *g'mar chatimah tovah*, which literally means "may the final sealing [of the Divine judgment] be good."

Yom Kippur Kattan. Literally "little Day of Atonement," a partial or complete fast observed on the day before each New Moon. The custom was introduced by Rabbi Moses Cordovero, a 16th-century Kabbalist in Safed. He and his mystical colleagues believed that each New Moon was a time of forgiveness from sins. Therefore, by repenting fully on the preceding day, one can enter the new month in a spirit of sin-free renewal. On Yom Kippur Kattan, special penitential psalms are added to the usual prayers. While popular in past centuries in Europe, Yom Kippur Kattan is infrequently observed today and is not even mentioned in the *Shulchan Aruch*, the authoritative Code of Jewish Law.

Yom Kippur War. After Israel Intelligence dismissed a military buildup on both the Egyptian and Syrian fronts, convinced that the Arab armies were not yet ready for a major all-out war, on October 6, 1973 (Yom Kippur) these two countries launched a concerted attack that caught Israel off guard. Initially, the Arab armies made substantial inroads and the very existence of the Jewish State was in doubt. Once the reserves were fully mobilized, and aided by a crucial infusion of American military supplies, Israeli forces eventually succeeded in capturing all the territories taken by the invading armies and surged to within 20 miles of Damascus before the Syrians agreed to a ceasefire. The Yom Kippur War resulted in heavy loss of life on both sides and helped to undermine confidence in the Labor Party-dominated government, which in 1977 gave way to a right-wing coalition under the Likud.

Yom Teruah. Literally "day of blowing the horn," a biblical name for Rosh Hashanah that reflects the *mitzvah* of hearing the sounding of the *shofar*, which is the primary commandment of the day.

Yom tov. Literally "good day," the generic Hebrew word for a holiday or festival.

Yom Yerushalayim (Jerusalem Day). Celebration on the 28th of Iyar that commemorates the unification of the city of Jerusalem on June 7, 1967, when the Israeli army swept to victory over Arab forces during the Six Day War. For the first time since the Second Temple fell to the Romans in 70 C.E., the Temple Mount and the Western Wall were under Jewish control. On Yom Yerushalayim, a thanksgiving service is held at the Western Wall, torches are lit in memory of those Israeli soldiers who died in the battle for Jerusalem, and there is a parade through the streets of Jerusalem followed by a fireworks display.

Yom Zeh l'Yisrael (This day is for Israel). A table hymn for the Sabbath, composed by master-kabbalist Isaac Luria, which describes a mixture of spiritual and physical pleasure and concludes with a vision of the messianic days when life will become one great Sabbath. The second verse refers to the additional soul (see *neshamah yeterah*) that is given to each Jew on Friday evening and then taken away when the Sabbath ends.[370]

Yom Zeh Mechubad (This day is honored). Sabbath table hymn describing how God will provide those who observe this holy day with everything they need – the ceremonial wine for *Kiddush*; two loaves of *challah*; meat and fish; rich foods, sweet drinks, and all delights, including special clothes to wear – based on the talmudic statement promising that all Sabbath expenses would be restored. The refrain to the six stanzas is a reminder that "This day is honored among all other days, because on it the Eternal rested."[371]

Yoma. The 5th tractate in Mo'ed (festivals) in the Mishnah, it deals with the Temple service on the Day of Atonement as well as the regulations concerning the Yom Kippur fast and the significance of atonement and repentance.

Yoma arichta (one long day). The rabbinic concept that both days of Rosh Hashanah, observed even in Israel, constitute a single 48-hour day. This raised the question of whether on the second day one should say *Shehecheyanu*, the blessing expressing gratitude for special occasions. To avoid this problem, the custom arose of eating a new fruit or wearing a new garment on the second night of Rosh Hashanah, acts that would themselves require a *Shehecheyanu* blessing.[372]

Yontif. Yiddish equivalent of the Hebrew "*yom tov*," meaning a holiday or festival.

Yored (pl., *yordim*). From a root meaning "to descend," the Hebrew term for an Israeli who leaves the Land of Israel to live elsewhere. The opposite of *aliyah* (meaning to "go up"), the act of emigrating from the country (*veridah*) is considered a negative move by many.

Yoreh De'ah – see *Shulchan Aruch*.

Yotzer. Initial word and name of the first blessing preceding the *Shema*. In the morning, the first blessing focuses on the concept of light. Since the morning service was usually held at sunrise, it was natural to start with *Yotzer or* (He who creates light), a blessing thanking God for the sunrise as well as for the other miracles of Creation. Based on the verse from Isaiah (45:7), "I form light and create darkness, I make peace and create woe," the blessing was put in the third person and the last word changed to "everything." Not only did the Rabbis deem this a euphemism or "more appropriate language," but the new wording also emphasized that God is the sole source of Creation. This served as a polemic against the once-prevailing dualistic doctrine that day and night, and good and evil, were created and ruled by different deities. The first blessing before the evening *Shema* is similar, but praises God as the Creator of the night.[373]

Young Israel. Short for the National Council of Young Israel (NCYI), an organization founded in 1912 to combat assimilation by providing a positive user-friendly Orthodox synagogue experience for newly arrived immigrants in the United States and Canada. Now an umbrella organization for a number of congregations in North America, Young Israel is dedicated to fostering Orthodoxy and the study of Torah through a variety of educational, religious, social, spiritual, and communal programming.

Young Judea. Oldest Zionist youth movement in the United States, it was founded in 1919 and is now sponsored by Hadassah. A non-denominational organization, Young Judea is dedicated to instilling Jewish values, pride, identity, and a lifelong commitment to Israel through summer camps, Israel programs, and university campus events.

Youth Aliyah. Branch of the Zionist movement founded in 1933 for the purpose of rescuing Jewish children and teenagers from hardship and persecution and giving them care and education in the Land of Israel. The work was largely financed by Hadassah and organized by its leader, Henrietta Szold. Youth Aliyah started its activities in Germany on the eve of the Nazis' rise to power and saved many children who had to leave their families or were orphaned by the Holocaust. Since the establishment of the State of Israel, Youth Aliyah has cared for those children entrusted to its educational and social care by new immigrant parents, or by Israeli families in distress, in its own centers and children's villages such as Neurim and Meir Shfeya.

Yovel – see Jubilee Year.

Yud. The 10th letter of the Hebrew alphabet, with a numerical value of 10.

Z

Zachur la-tov. Hebrew phrase meaning "may he [one who has died] be remembered for good." Today, this has generally been replaced by the expression *Zichrono livracha* ("May his memory be for a blessing").

Zadokites. When King David was dying, the priests Zadok and Abiathar supported different claimants for the throne – Abiathar favored Absalom, while Zadok championed the cause of Solomon (1 Kings 1:7-8). After Zadok anointed Solomon as the new king (1 Kings 1:39), he was rewarded for his loyalty by being named High Priest (1 Kings 2:35). This position remained in the family of Zadok until the rise of the Maccabees.

Zaftig. Literally "juicy," a Yiddish word meaning plump, full-bodied, or voluptuous.

Zahal – see Israel Defense Forces.

Zavim (Zav.). The 9th tractate in Tohorot (purity) in the Mishnah, it deals mainly with genital discharges rendering a person unclean.

Zayde. Yiddish for "grandfather," the word may be used to denote any grandfatherly older man.

Zayin. The 7th letter in the Hebrew alphabet, with a numerical value of 7.

Zealots. Jewish political faction during the late Second Temple period. Founded by Judah the Galilean and Zadok the priest, it resisted the idolatrous practices of Herod the Great and rose in revolt when the Roman governor of Syria attempted to take a census, which they considered a plot to subjugate the Jews. Fervently religious with a deep belief in messianic salvation, the Zealots were at the forefront of Jewish resistance fighters in the unsuccessful war against Rome, which ended in the destruction of the Temple in 70 C.E. The final Zealot garrison perished at Masada.

Zechariah. The 11th of the minor prophets. Zechariah lived in Jerusalem after the return from Babylonian Exile (c. 520 B.C.E.) His writing is filled with mystic visions replete with symbolic figures. Zechariah called for rebuilding the Temple and prophesied the coming of the Messianic Age, when all nations will recognize the universal kingdom of God in Jerusalem – "And the Lord shall be King over all the earth; in that day the Lord shall be one and His Name one" (14:9) – which is also the concluding verse of the *Aleinu*.

Zecher tzadik livracha (*zt"l*). Literally "[May] the memory of the righteous [be] for a blessing," a phrase often added after the mention of the name of a deceased rabbi or saintly person.

Zechut Avot. Literally "merit of the Fathers," the traditional concept that the pious deeds of the ancestors of the Jewish people (primarily the Patriarchs) invoke Divine protection and favor for their descendants.[374]

Zeman Mattan Torateinu (Time of the Giving of our Torah). Liturgical term for the festival of Shavuot.

Zeman Simchateinu (Season of our Joy) – see Sukkot.

Zemirot. Hebrew term used by Ashkenazim for the table hymns sung during or immediately after Sabbath meals. These medieval songs represent a unique blend of the holy and the secular, the serious and the playful, and allow family and friends to heighten the Sabbath experience. Some well-known *zemirot* were composed by the kabbalists, who considered it proper to chant table hymns in honor of the spiritual guests visiting the Jewish home on the Sabbath eve. Among these are *Shalom Aleichem* (Peace be upon you), *Tzur Mishelo* (Rock from whose store [we have eaten]), *Yah Ribon Olam* (God, Master of the Universe), *Yom Zeh l'Yisrael* (This day is for Israel), and *Yom Zeh Mechubad* (This day is honored).

Zephaniah (Zeph.). The 9th of the minor prophets. Living in Jerusalem during the reign of King Josiah (640-609 B.C.E.) and a strong supporter of his religious reforms and national restoration, Zephaniah prophesied the downfall of Nineveh and the Assyrian empire. He warned the people of a cataclysmic "Day of the Lord" (1:12-18), when they would be punished for their evil deeds. Eventually, however, salvation would come to Israel and the entire world. His statement that God "will search Jerusalem with candles" (1:12) is reflected in the ceremony of searching for leaven (*bedikat chametz*) by candlelight on the night before the Passover seder.

Zera'im (seeds). The 1st order of the Mishnah, its 11 tractates are Berachot, Pe'ah, Demai, Kilayim, Shevi'it, Terumot, Ma'aserot, Ma'aser Sheni, Challah, Orlah, and Bikurim. Zera'im deals primarily with agricultural regulations; the first tractate, Berachot, is concerned with blessings and prayers.

Zero'ah. Roasted bone, usually a shankbone, which is placed on the seder plate as a reminder of the paschal lamb (Exod. 12:2-3, 5-6). Some vegetarians substitute a roasted beet.

Zevachim (Zev.). The 1st tractate in Kodashim (holy things) in the Mishnah, it deals with the sacrificial system in the Temple and emphasizes the proper intent that must accompany sacrifices.

Zichrono livracha. Literally "of blessed memory," a phrase often added after the mention of a deceased person. When the name of the person appears in print, the phrase is abbreviated as *z"l* or with the Hebrew letters *zayin* and *lamed*. The feminine form of the phrase is *zichrona livracha*.

Zichronot (Remembrances), Second of the three long intermediate blessings in the *Musaf Amidah* on Rosh Hashanah. It describes God's role in remembering the deeds of nations and individuals, determining their destinies in justice and mercy by punishing the wicked and rewarding the good. It affirms that God eventually will remember the covenant and redeem Israel from exile and suffering.[375]

Zimun (invitation). Formula used whenever three or more have eaten bread together, with one of them summoning the others to say the Grace after Meals. It asks permission "of the distinguished people present" to "praise Him of whose food we have eaten."

Zion. Prophetic and poetic biblical name for the city of Jerusalem, which included the walled city and the Temple Mount. Deemed the capital of this world and the future messianic city of God, the term Zion became a symbol for the ingathering of the Jewish people to their ancient homeland and the restoration of Jewish sovereignty in the Land of Israel.

Zionism. Modern political movement for the return of the Jewish people to Zion, the old prophetic name for the Land of Israel. Ever since the destruction of Jerusalem by the Romans in 70 C. E. and the exile of the Jewish people from their ancient homeland, Jews clung passionately to the hope for a return to Zion. Despite extreme poverty and physical dangers that threatened their very survival, Jews turned in prayer toward Zion three times each day. With the rise of nationalism in Europe during the 19th century, Jews slowly became convinced that the time was ripe for them to develop an independent state in their own land. The Zionist political movement they developed had largely secular leadership, but deep religious and historical roots. A major political victory was achieved with the 1917 issuance of the Balfour Declaration, but the Jews living in the Land of Israel faced serious obstacles such as incessant Arab violence, British White Papers limiting immigration, and the Second World War. Prior to the Holocaust, there was opposition to Zionism among a number of Orthodox and Reform Jews, as well as by Jews who were adherents of socialism and communism. However, following this cataclysm much of the opposition diminished. Eventually, the United Nations approved the compromise solution of dividing Palestine into separate Jewish and

Arab states. After the British withdrew, the Declaration of Independence proclaimed the State of Israel as the fulfillment of the Zionist dream. Zionism still has a role to play in Jewish history by nourishing a vibrant Jewish culture in Israel, which can serve as a positive national beacon to world Jewry and the international community.

Zionism, post-. As defined by Yoram Hazony,[376] post-Zionism is a set of beliefs held by some left-wing Israelis who attack Zionism as an inherently immoral project, one that throughout the 20th century led to unjust acts especially toward the Arab inhabitants of today's Israel. A particular form of post-Zionism, advanced by some Israelis, which Hazony calls post-Judaism, portrays Judaism as a teaching of universal humanism that can only be sullied through a particular national and political expression. Hazony attributes the rise of post-Zionism in Israel to "an exhausted people, confused and without direction," who are now actively engaged in the destruction of their own national spirit. He adds that the spread of post-Zionism poses a real danger that could lead to Israel no longer being the "Jewish state" or possibly even ceasing to exist.

Zionist Congress. Highest authority in the Zionist Organization. The first Zionist Congress, called by Theodor Herzl as a symbolic Parliament for those in sympathy with Zionist goals, began on August 29, 1897, in the Swiss city of Basel. After holding 22 Zionist Congresses in a variety of European venues, all the meetings since 1951 have taken place in Jerusalem.

Zionist Mule Corps. Company of ammunition carriers in the British army during World War I. "The first specifically Jewish fighting force since Roman times,"[377] it was primarily composed of Jews who had been expelled from the Land of Israel by the Turkish authorities because of their nationalist aspirations. When Vladimir Jabotinsky proposed the formation of a Jewish legion to join the British in liberating the Land of Israel from the Turks, the British rejected the idea of Jewish volunteers fighting on the Palestinian front. Instead, they suggested that the Jews serve as a detachment assisting with mule transport on the Gallipoli front, under the leadership of Joseph Trumpeldor. Jews served with distinction, and elements of the Zionist Mule Corps formed the nucleus of what became the Palestinian Jewish Legion, which helped establish a modern Jewish military tradition.

Zionist Organization. Founded by Theodor Herzl at the first Zionist Congress in Basel as the umbrella agency of the Zionist movement, it has established programs and institutions to carry out its policies. In 1960, the name was changed to the World Zionist Organization.

Zionist Organization of America (ZOA). Founded in 1897, this oldest and largest pro-Israel body in the United States was critical in building support for the creation of the State of Israel. Among its many activities designed to solidify ties between the two countries are educational, cultural, and public affairs programs, encouraging Israel tourism and investment, supporting pro-Israel legislation, and attacking anti-Israel bias in the media.

Zionists, cultural (spiritual). Championed by Ahad Ha-Am, they advocated the restoration of Palestine as a cultural and spiritual center, imbued with the ideals of the Hebrew prophets, that would serve and inspire the entire Jewish people both in the national homeland and throughout the Diaspora.

Zionists, labor. For many Jews, neither political Zionism nor cultural Zionism seemed to be a realistic alternative. Moreover, neither of these movements addressed the urgent need to appeal to the increasing number of young Jews who were joining the growing socialist and communist movements in Eastern Europe. To meet this challenge, Labor Zionism emerged as the dominant activist force in the Zionist world and in Palestine. A host of settlements were set up on a communal basis, with thousands of workers tilling the land and building a national infrastructure. Almost exclusively secular, Labor Zionism saw itself as a revolutionary movement that would not only change the situation of the land, but also transform the traditional Jewish social and economic structure and the character of the entire Jewish people. The Labor Zionists took the traditional belief in a coming of the Messianic Age and secularized it into the concept that a utopia based on social justice and human dignity could be created by the efforts of the people themselves. Almost all of the major political and military leaders of the *yishuv* and the State of Israel for its first 30 years were members of the Labor Zionist movement.

Zionists, political. Led by Theodor Herzl, those who wanted to concentrate all efforts on securing a charter to establish a Jewish state in Palestine. They were convinced that the practical work of mass settlement would come once legal guarantees had been achieved though the support of a major world power.

Zionists, practical. The view of the Lovers of Zion stressing settlement in Palestine. They were convinced that the presence of a large number of Jews in the land would give greater weight to the political efforts of the Zionist movement.

Zionists, religious. Religious pioneering and labor movement in the Land of Israel. Beginning with members of the Third Aliyah in the early 1920s, they founded Ha-Po'el ha-Mizrachi, whose program stated that it "aspires to build the land according to the Torah and tradition and on the basis of labor, to create a material and spiritual basis for its members, strengthen religious feeling among the workers, and enable them to live as religious workers." They opposed the predominant view of the labor pioneers, who regarded religion as obsolete and adherence to the *mitzvot* as an obstacle to building the land according to socialist principles.

The spiritual leader of the Religious Zionist movement was Abraham Isaac Kook, the first Ashkenazic Chief Rabbi of Palestine. Rav Kook was among the few religious leaders of his time who believed that the return to the Land of Israel marked the beginning of Divine redemption, which would result in the return of the Jewish people to Zion. Terming the existing Zionist movement incomplete, since it had only addressed the revival of the secular and material needs of the Jewish people, Kook called for an emphasis on the spiritual aspects of the national revival. With the establishment of the State of Israel, the religious Zionists formed the National Religious Party.

Zionists, revisionist. Zionist political movement founded in 1925 by Vladimir Jabotinsky, which was both anti-socialist and militantly nationalistic. It criticized the official Zionist policy as too conciliatory toward Britain and advocated the speedy creation of a Jewish state on both sides of the Jordan River. After Hitler's rise to power in 1933, the Revisionists espoused the total boycott of Nazi Germany by the Jewish people and opposed the Jewish Agency's agreement with the Berlin regime. Intent on thwarting the harsh British regulations limiting immigration to Palestine, the Revisionist movement resorted to "illegal" immigration (see *Aliyah Bet*).

Zisse. Yiddish word for "sweet."

Zocher ha-Brit. Literally "remembering the covenant," another name for the ceremony of *Shalom Zachar* (peace to the male child).

Zodiac. Greek for "little animals," the 12 symbols representing the constellations of astrology that many ancient peoples believed governed the character traits and ultimate fate of a person. The 12 signs and their relation to the months of the Hebrew year are as follows: Aries (Nisan), Taurus (Iyar), Gemini (Sivan), Cancer (Tammuz), Leo (Av), Virgo (Elul), Libra (Tishrei), Scorpio (Cheshvan), Sagittarius (Kislev), Capricorn (Tevet), Aquarius (Shevat), and Pisces (Adar). These symbols were frequently incorporated in early Jewish art, especially on the mosaic floors of ancient synagogues (such as Beit Alpha) and later in *ketubot* (marriage contracts).

Zohar. Known as the "Book of Splendor," the principal kabbalistic book that is the basis for all subsequent Jewish mystical works. Its central tenet is that human actions such as good deeds, prayer, and mystical meditation can impact the Divine world, thus promoting a harmonious union between the "upper" and "lower" spheres that increases the flow of Divine energy to the human world. Conversely, sinful and unrighteous behavior impedes this life-giving flow. According to tradition, this immense mystical commentary on the Pentateuch and parts of the Writings, written in both Hebrew and Aramaic and consisting of some 20 separate treatises, is attributed to the 2nd-century C.E. rabbinic authority Shimon bar Yochai and his colleagues and disciples. However, scholars now attribute the *Zohar* to the late 13th-century Moses de Leon.

Zugot. Literally "pairs," the Hebrew term for the pairs of sages in the Land of Israel who for five generations (2nd century B.C.E. to 1st century C.E.) were the leaders of rabbinic Judaism. In each pair, one was the *nasi* (president of the Sanhedrin) and the other was designated as the *av beit din* (head of the religious court). The *zugot* were: Jose ben Yo'ezer and Jose ben Yochanan; Joshua ben Perachyah and Nittai of Arbela; Judah ben Tabbai and Shimon ben Shetach; Shemaiah and Avtalyon; and Hillel and Shammai.

Bibliography

ArtScroll Haggadah Treasury. Brooklyn. Mesorah Publications, 1985.
ArtScroll Kaddish. Brooklyn: Mesorah Publications, 1991.
ArtScroll Machzor. Brooklyn: Mesorah Publications, 1994.
ArtScroll Shemoneh Esrei. Brooklyn: Mesorah Publications, 2001.
ArtScroll Siddur. Brooklyn: Mesorah Publications, 1986.
Biale, Rachel. *Women and Jewish Law*. New York: Schocken, 1984.
Blech, Benjamin. *More Secrets of Jewish Words*. Northvale, N.J.: Aronson, 1993.
Bluestein, Gene. *Anglish-Yinglish: Yiddish in American Life and Literature*. Athens: University of Georgia Press, 1989.
Chavel, Charles B., *Commandments: The 613 Mitzvot*. New York: Judaica Press, 2000.
Chill, Abraham. *The Mitzvot*. New York: Bloch, 1974.
Cohen, Jeffrey. *Blessed Are You: A Comprehensive Guide to Jewish Prayer*. Northvale N.J.: Aronson, 1993.
Donin, Hayim. *To Be a Jew: A Guide to Jewish Observance in Contemporary Life*. New York: Basic Books, 1972.
Donin, Hayim. *To Pray As a Jew: A Guide to the Prayer Book and the Synagogue Service*. New York: Basic Books, 1980.
Dorff, Elliott N. *Matters of Life and Death: A Jewish Approach to Modern Medical Ethics*. Philadelphia: Jewish Publication Society, 1998.
Dosick, Wayne. *Living Judaism: The Complete Guide to Jewish Belief, Tradition, and Practice*. San Francisco: Harper San Francisco, 1995.
Etz Hayim. Senior editor David Lieber. Philadelphia: Jewish Publication Society, 2001.
Frankel, Ellen, and Betsy Platkin Teutsch. *The Encyclopedia of Jewish Symbols*. Northvale N.J.: Aronson, 1992.
Gilbert, Martin. *The Illustrated Atlas of Jewish Civilization: 4000 Years of History*. New York: Macmillan, 1990.
Ginzberg, Louis. *Legends of the Jews*. 7 vols. Philadelphia: Jewish Publication Society, 1909–1938.
Greenberg, Blu. *How to Run a Traditional Jewish Household*. New York: Simon & Shuster, 1983.
Hammer, Reuven. *Entering the High Holy Days*. Philadelphia: Jewish Publication Society, 1998.
Hammer, Reuven. *Entering Jewish Prayer: A Guide to Personal Devotion and the Worship Service*. New York: Schocken, 1994.
Harvard Hillel Songbook. Boston: Godine, 1992.
Haut, Irwin H. *Divorce in Jewish Law and Life*. New York: Sepher-Hermon, 1983.
Hazony, Yoram. *The Jewish State: The Struggle for Israel's Soul*: New York: Basic/New Republic Books, 2000.
Hertz, J. J. *The Pentateuch and Haftorahs*. London: Soncino, 1978.
Heschel, Abraham Joshua. *Man's Quest for God*. Santa Fe: Aurora Press, 1998.
Holtz, Barry. *Back to the Sources*. New York: Summit Books, 1984.

Idelsohn, A.Z. *Jewish Liturgy and Its Development*. New York: Dover, 1995.
Kadden, Barbara Binder, and Bruce Kadden. *Teaching Jewish Life Cycle*. Denver: A. R. E. Publishing, 1997.
Kadushin, Max. *Worship and Ethics. A Study in Rabbinic Judaism*. Westport (CT): Greenwood Publishing Group, 1978.
Klein, Earl. *Jewish Prayer: Concepts and Customs*. Columbus, Ohio: Alpha, 1986.
Klein, Isaac. *A Guide to Jewish Religious Practice*. New York: Jewish Theological Seminary of America, 1979.
Kolatch, Alfred J. *The Jewish Book of Why*. Middle Village, NY: Jonathan David, 1981.
Kolatch, Alfred J. *The Second Jewish Book of Why*. Middle Village. NY: Jonathan David, 1985.
Kolatch, Alfred J. *This Is the Torah*. Middle Village, NY: Jonathan David, 1988.
Lamm, Maurice. *The Jewish Way in Death and Mourning*. New York: Jonathan David, 1972.
Lamm, Maurice. *The Jewish Way in Love and Marriage*. New York: Harper & Row, 1980.
Lau, Israel Meir. *Practical Judaism*. Jerusalem, Feldheim, 1997.
Lewittes, Mendell. *Jewish Marriage: Rabbinic Law, Legend, and Custom*. Northvale N.J.: Aronson, 1994.
Lutske, Harvey. *The Book of Jewish Customs*. Northvale N.J.: Aronson, 1986.
Maimonides, Moses. *The Commandments*. Trans. Charles Chavel. London: Soncino, 1967.
Maimonides, Moses. *Guide of the Perplexed*. Trans. Shlomo Pines. Chicago: University of Chicago Press, 1963.
Maimonides, Moses. *Mishneh Torah*. Trans. Philip Birnbaum. New York: Hebrew Publishing, 1974.
Marks, Gil. *The World of Jewish Cooking*. New York: Simon & Schuster, 1996.
Millgram, Abraham. *Jewish Worship*. Philadelphia: Jewish Publication Society, 1971.
Millgram, Abraham. *Sabbath, the Day of Delight*. Philadelphia: Jewish Publication Society, 1959.
Moldenke, Harold, and Alma Moldenke. *Plants of the Bible*. New York: Dover, 1986.
Rabinowicz, Rachel Anne, Ed. *Passover Haggadah: The Feast of Freedom*. New York: Rabbinical Assembly, 1982.
Rabinowicz, Tzvi. *A Guide to Life: Jewish Laws and Customs of Mourning*. Northvale, N.J.: Aronson, 1989.
Reider, Freda. *The Hallah Book: Recipes, History, and Traditions*. Hoboken, N.J.: Ktav, 1987.
Riskin, Shlomo. *The Passover Haggadah*. New York: Ktav, 1983.
Roden, Claudia. *The Book of Jewish Food*. New York: Knopf, 1997.
Schauss, Hayyim. *The Lifetime of a Jew*. Cincinnati, Ohio: Union of American Hebrew Congregations, 1950.
Sherwin, Byron. Kabbalah: *An Introduction to Jewish Mysticism*. New York: Rowman & Littlefield, 2006.
Sherwin, Byron. *Jewish Ethics for the Twenty-First Century: Living in the Image of God*. Syracuse (NY): Syracuse University Press, 2000.
Shostek, Patti. *A Lexicon of Jewish Cooking*. Chicago, Contemporary Books, 1979.

Sperling, Abraham Isaac. *Reasons for Jewish Customs and Traditions*. Trans. Abraham Matts. New York: Bloch, 1968.

Steinsaltz, Adin. *A Guide to Jewish Prayer*. New York: Schocken, 2000.

Stone Chumash. Brooklyn: Mesorah Publications, 1994.

Strassfeld, Michael. *The Jewish Holidays: A Guide and Commentary*. New York: Harper & Row, 1985.

Strassfeld, Sharon and Strassfeld, Michael. *The Second Jewish Catalogue*. Philadelphia: Jewish Publication Society, 1976.

Telushkin, Joseph. *Jewish Literacy*. New York: William Morrow, 1991.

Toperoff, Shlomo Pesach. *The Animal Kingdom in Jewish Thought*. Northvale N.J.: Aronson, 1995.

Trepp, Leo. *The Complete Book of Jewish Observance*. New York: Summit Books, 1980.

Twerski, Abraham J. *From Freedom to Bondage*. Brooklyn: Shaar Press, 1995.

Waskow, Arthur. *Seasons of Our Joy*. New York: Bantam Books, 1982.

Wentworth, Harold and Flexner, Stuart Berg. *Dictionary of American Slang*. New York, Crowell, 1960.

Werblowsky, R.J. Zwi, and Geoffrey Wigoder, eds. *Oxford Dictionary of the Jewish Religion*. Oxford: Oxford University Press, 1997.

Witty, Abraham B., and Rachel Witty. *Exploring Jewish Tradition*. New York: Doubleday, 2001.

Zohar. Trans. Harry Sperling. London: Soncino Press, 1949.

NOTES

[1] The name of the *parashah* means "after the death" and refers to the untimely demise of Nadab and Abihu, two of the sons of Aaron, who took their fire pans and incense and offered "alien fire" before the Lord. This unauthorized service, an action "that He [God] had not enjoined upon them," resulted in Nabab and Abihu being consumed by a fire that "came forth from the Lord" (Lev. 10:1-2).

[2] Hammer. *Entering Jewish Prayer*, 144.

[3] Reform, Reconstructionist, and some liberal Conservative synagogues have abolished this distinction (see *aliyah* [1]).

[4] Donin. *To Pray as a Jew*, 350.

[5] Frankel and Teutsch, *The Encyclopedia of Jewish Symbols,* 6.

[6] Strassfeld, *The Jewish Holidays: A Guide and Commentary,* 93.

[7] Prohibiting sculptured images, swearing falsely, murder, adultery, stealing, bearing false witness, and coveting.

[8] According to the Talmud (Ber. 4b), this is because that letter may suggest the Hebrew word *naflah* (fallen) and thus imply a reference to a verse from the Prophets that speaks of the destruction of Israel (Amos 5:2). However, one of the Dead Sea Scrolls has a verse beginning with *nun—ne'eman Elohim bid'varav ve-chasid be-chol ma'asav* (God is faithful in His words, and gracious in all His works).

[9] *ArtScroll Siddur*, 456.

[10] Hammer. *Entering the High Holy Days*, 67.

[11] Witty and Witty, *Exploring Jewish Tradition,* 266.

[12] Strassfeld, 74.

[13] Millgram. *Jewish Worship*, 183-184.

[14] Marks, *The World of Jewish Cooking,* 284-285; Shostek, 17-18.

[15] *ArtScroll Siddur*, 321-322.

[16] Hammer. *Entering Jewish Prayer*, 113.

[17] Donin. *To Pray as a Jew*, 249.

[18] Kadden and Kadden, *Teaching Jewish Life Cycle,* 61.

[19] Dosick, *Living Judaism: The Complete Guide to Jewish Belief, Tradition, and Practice,* 294.

[20] This type of celebration is observed in some modern Orthodox communities today (Kadden and Kadden, 28).

[21] Steinsaltz, *A Guide to Jewish Prayer,* 312.

[22] *ArtScroll Siddur*, 292.

[23] Donin. *To Pray as a Jew*, 331.

[24] Millgram. *Jewish Worship*, 300.

[25] Millgram. *Sabbath*, 21.

[26] *Etz Hayim*, 691.

[27] Chill, *The Mitzvot,* 263.

[28] Marks, 224.

[29] Earlier in the biblical text (Gen. 9:4), Noah and his descendants were forbidden from consuming the blood of animal flesh.

[30] Kadden and Kadden, 65.

[31] Sefer ha-Chinuch, cited in Chill, 97.

[32] *Stone Chumash*, 545.

[33] As the Talmud states, "a Sanhedrin [Great Court] that executes one man to death is seven years is branded a 'destructive' tribunal. R Eleazar ben Azariah says 'one in 70 years'. R. Tarfon and R. Akiva say, 'Were we members of a Sanhedrin, no person would ever be put to death' " (Mak. 1:10, 7a), implying that their cross-examination of the witnesses would have been so exhaustive that some flaw would have appeared in their testimony. However, Rabban Shimon ben Gamaliel retorted, "[Yes] and they would also multiply shedders of blood in Israel!", believing that the attitude of his colleagues would have diminished respect for the law and the fear of punishment, thus increasing the number of murderers. All members of a court that pronounced a capital sentence were obliged to abstain from eating on the day of execution (Sanh. 63a).

[34] Telushkin, *Jewish Literacy,* 600.

[35] Chill, 465.

[36] *Stone Chumash*, 674.

[37] Chavel, *Commandments: The 613 Mitzvot,* 150.

[38] Reider, *The Hallah Book,* 13-16.

[39] Frankel and Teutsch, 68; Roden, *The Book of Jewish Food,* 98.

[40] Frankel and Teutsch, 69.

[41] See www.lisaekus.com/food_media_resources/hadassahjewishholidaycookbook recipes.html

[42] Greenberg, *How to Run a Traditional Jewish Household,* 303.

[43] Marks, 185.

[44] *Etz Hayim*, 650.

[45] *Hertz, The Pentateuch and Haftorahs,* 519.

[46] Frankel and Teutsch, 77.

[47] Mishneh Torah, Avodat Kochavim 5:6

[48] Maimonides. *The Commandments*, 199.

[49] *Etz Hayim*, 1026.

[50] Kadden and Kadden, 46-47.

[51] *Stone Chumash*, 1063.

[52] Chill, 54.

[53] M. Lamm. *The Jewish Way in Death and Mourning,* 84.

[54] Kadden and Kadden, 102.

[55] Torah study is praiseworthy when combined with *derech eretz* (Avot 2:2).

[56] Many modern scholars attribute chapters 56-66 to a third Isaiah (see Trito-Isaiah).

[57] Haut, *Divorce in Jewish Law and Life,* 43.

[58] *Stone Chumash*, 861.

[59] Witty and Witty, 491-492.

[60] *Zera'im* (Seeds), *Mo'ed* (Festivals), *Nashim* (Women), *Nezikin* (Damages), *Kodashim* (Holy Things), and *Tohorot* (Purities).

[61] *Bereshit* (Genesis), *Shemot* (Exodus), *Vayikra* (Leviticus), *Bamidbar* (Numbers), *Devarim* (Deuteronomy).

[62] Sarah, Rebecca, Rachel, Leah.

[63] Abraham, Isaac, Jacob.

[64] Chill 445.

[65] Donin. *To Pray as a Jew*, 214-215.

[66] Sherwin. *Kabbalah*, 56-57.

[67] *ArtScroll Siddur*, 90.

[68] Maimonides. *The Commandments*, 225-226.

[69] Donin. *To Pray as a Jew*, 187

[70] Kadden and Kadden, 106.

[71] Maimonides. *The Commandments*, 300

[72] Telushkin, 621.

[73] Biale, *Women and Jewish Law,* 78.

[74] Witty and Witty, 167.

[75] Sherwin. *The Nature of Ethics*, 50.

[76] Greenberg, 400-401.

[77] Chill, 252.

[78] Maimonides. *The Commandments*, 257.

[79] Strassfeld, 16.

[80] Donin. *To be a Jew*, 208.

[81] Donin, *To be a Jew*, 210-211

[82] Steinsaltz, 148-149.

[83] *Etz Hayim*, 1115.

[84] Chill, 452.

[85] Mishory, Alec. "The Flag and the Emblem." Available at: www.israel-mfa.gov.il/mfa/go.asp?MFAHeph

[86] I will *bring you out* [from under the burdens of the Egyptians]," "I will *deliver you* [from their bondage]," "I will *redeem you* [with an outstretched arm and with great

judgments]," and "I will *take you* [to Me for a people]." However, the next verse contains a fifth expression, "And I will *bring you* [into the land that I vowed to Abraham, to Isaac, and to Jacob]," but this was not considered as warranting an extra cup (see Cup of Elijah).

[87] *Art Scroll Haggadah Treasury*, 55.

[88] Donin. *To Pray as a Jew*, 248.

[89] Adam, Seth, Enosh, Kenan, Mechalalel, Jared, Enoch, Methusaleh, Lamech, Noah.

[90] Shem, Arpachshad, Shelach, Eber, Peleg, Reu, Serug, Hachor, Terach, Abraham.

[91] Telushkin, 622.

[92] Biale, 98-100.

[93] Haut, 28-29.

[94] Lewittes, *Jewish Marriage,* 200.

[95] Dosick, 264.

[96] Maimonides, *Guide of the Perplexed* 3:33.

[97] *Stone Chumash*, 1048.

[98] *ArtScroll Siddur*, 143.

[99] Donin. *To Pray as a Jew*, 253-254.

[100] Kadden and Kadden, 105.

[101] Lamm, M. *The Jewish Way in Death and Mourning*, 65.

[102] Steinsaltz, 392.

[103] *ArtScroll Haggadah Treasury*, 55.

[104] Rabinowicz, Rachel, 39.

[105] Telushkin, 243-245.

[106] Frankel and Teutsch, 66.

[107] Rabinowicz, Rachel, 30.

[108] Millgram. *Jewish Worship*, 210-211.

[109] Frankel and Teutsch, 70.

[110] Donin. *To Pray as a Jew*, 163-164.

[111] Strassfeld, 98.

[112] Mishneh Torah, De'ot 6:6, 9.

[113] Donin. *To Pray as a Jew*, 333.

[114] Frankel and Teutsch, 29.

[115] Cohen, 248-249.

[116] Rabinowicz, Tzvi, 101-102; Kadden and Kadden, 107.

[117] Schauss, *The Lifetime of a Jew,* 254.

[118] Adapted from lectures by Dr. Byron Sherwin at Spertus Institute in Chicago.

[119] Strassfeld and Strassfeld, *The Second Jewish Catalogue,* 117-118.

[120] Used in the translation of the phrase, "a burnt offering to God" (1 Sam. 7:9).

[121] *Stone Chumash*, 653.

[122] Cohen, *Blessed Are You: A Comprehensive Guide to Jewish Prayer,* 186-187.

[123] Donin. *To Pray as a Jew*, 50.

[124] Strassfeld, 136-137.

[125] http://www.shj.org - accessed January 2007.

[126] Mishneh Torah, Ishut 21:1-4.

[127] Dosick, 270.

[128] Maimonides. *The Commandments*, 256.

[129] *Stone Chumash*, 703.

[130] Chill, 87.

[131] As an example, one of the boundaries of the Ammonite territory is described as "the wadi Jabbok" (Deut. 3:16).

[132] Professor Byron Sherwin, Spertus Institute, Chicago, IL. Dr. Sherwin agrees with Maimonides' notion that even if one is born a Jew, he must do something to actualize it, such as by learning and acting like a Jew.

[133] http://www.jewishpub.org - accessed January 2007

[134] http://www.aleph.org/renewal.html - accessed March 2007

[135] The Hebrew word *Shofetim*, usually translated as "judges," actually comes from an Akkadian root (*Shafatu*) meaning a "military leader." This explains why the major figures in the biblical Book of Judges were called by that name, though none (except Deborah) judged and all were military leaders.

[136] Sherwin. *Kabbalah*, 5-6.

[137] *Kabbalah*, 2.

[138] Hammer. *Entering the High Holy Days*, 104.

[139] Cohen, 46-48.

[140] Lau, *Practical Judaism,* 117-119.

[141] Cohen, 173-176.

[142] Hammer. *Entering the High Holy Days*, 134.

[143] Hammer. *Entering the High Holy Days*, 132.

[144] Millgram. *Jewish Worship*, 299.

[145] *Stone Chumash*, 412.

[146] Trepp, *The Complete Book of Jewish Observance,* 283.

[147] Donin. *To be a Jew*, 180.

[148] Frankel and Teutsch, 91.

[149] Witty and Witty, 248.

[150] Chill, 438.

[151] Maimonides. *The Commandments*, 235.

[152] *Etz Hayim*, 1100.

[153] Trepp, 16.

[154] It also applied the provisions of the Law of Return to "a child or grandchild of a Jew, the spouse of a Jew, the spouse of a child of a Jew, and the spouse of a grandchild of a Jew, except for a person who has been a Jew and voluntarily changed his religion."

[155] Cohen, 196-197.

[156] *Stone Chumash*, 1 973.

[157] Donin. *To Pray as a Jew*, 150.

[158] Dosick, 173.

[159] Mishneh Torah, Shoftim, Hilchoth Ohel 14:1.

[160] Frankel and Teutsch, 174-175.

[161] Donin, *To Pray as a Jew*, 12-14.

[162] Millgram, 389-390.

[163] Shlomo Riskin. *From curse to blessing* (International Jerusalem Post, July 6, 2001), 39.

[164] Chill, 106.

[165] Hammer. *Entering the High Holy Days*, 80.

[166] Holtz, *Back to the Sources,* 161-162.

[167] Frankel and Teutsch, 102.

[168] Frankel and Teutsch, 188.

[169] Lamm. *The Jewish Way in Love and Marriage*, 40.

[170] Kolatch. *This is the Torah*, 216-219.

[171] Strassfeld, 191.

[172] From a symbolic viewpoint, *matzah* is regarded as a token of purity while leaven is seen as a sign of impurity.

[173] Frankel and Teutsch, 103.

[174] Kadden and Kadden, 106.

[175] Millgram. *Jewish Worship*, 340.

[176] Strassfeld, 188.

[177] Millgram. *Sabbath*, 21-22.

[178] Millgram. *Jewish Worship*, 113-114.

[179] Cohen, 190.

[180] *ArtScroll Siddur*, 451.

[181] Millgram. *Jewish Worship*, 188.

[182] Midrashic tradition has identified Shiphrah and Puah as Jochebed and Miriam, respectively the mother and sister of Moses (Sot. 11b).

[183] Dosick, 270.

[184] Telushkin, 619.

[185] Millgram. *Jewish Worship*, 105-106.

[186] *ArtScroll Siddur*, 107.

[187] Millgram. *Jewish Worship*, 343.

[188] Sefer ha-Chinuch, cited in Chill, 118.

[189] Maimonides *The Commandments*, 281-288.

[190] *The Commandments*, 266.

[191] Fish is not considered meat in this context, and thus it can be eaten with dairy products.

[192] Donin. *To Pray as a Jew*, 260.

[193] *ArtScroll Siddur*, 320.

[194] *Stone Chumash*, 683.

[195] Millgram. *Jewish Worship*, 138.

[196] Maimonides. *The Commandments*, 8-9.

[197] Millgram. *Jewish Worship*, 144.

[198] Hammer. *Entering Jewish Prayer*, 109. It also reformulated the first blessing to read, "enabling us to distinguish day from night."

[199] Witty and Witty, 193.

[200] Dosick, 289.

[201] Frankel and Teutsch, 118.

[202] Trepp, 323.

[203] Hertz, 592.

[204] *Etz Hayim*, 800.
[205] *Stone Chumash*, 851.

[206] Frankel and Teutsch, 149.

[207] Based on the biblical verse, "For the blood is the life" (Deut. 12:23).

[208] *ArtScroll Siddur*, 132.

[209] Millgram. *Jewish Worship*, 260.

[210] "The commandment is a lamp and the Torah is a light" (Prov. 6:23).

[211] Roden, 634.

[212] Donin. *To Pray as a Jew*, 331.

[213] Millgram. *Jewish Worship*, 300.

[214] Lutske, 279-280.

[215] Biale, 147.

[216] Hammer, *Entering Jewish Prayer*, 18-19.

[217] Donin. *To Pray as a Jew*, 22.

[218] Kadushin, *Worship and Ethics*, 159-185.

[219] Maimonides. *The Commandments*, 121.

[220] Kolatch. *The Jewish Book of Why*, 76.

[221] Blech, 202.

[222] Maimonides. *The Commandments*, 165

[223] Holtz, 129-130.

[224] Trepp, 23.

[225] *Stone Chumash*, 663.

[226] Mishneh Torah, De'ot 6:10.

[227] Klein, Earl. *Jewish Prayer: Concepts and Customs*, 87-88.

[228] *ArtScroll Kaddish*, 46.

[229] Mishneh Torah, Retzichah U'Shimirath Nefesh 11:8.

[230] Kolatch. *This is the Torah*, 68-70.

[231] Frankel and Teutsch, 13.

[232] Werblowsky and Wigoder.

[233] *Etz Hayim*, 593.

[234] *Stone Chumash*, 553.

[235] Cohen, 181-182.

[236] Adapted from lectures given by Byron Sherwin at Spertus Institute in Chicago.

[237] Toperoff, 195.

[238] Maimonides. *The Commandments*, 122.

[239] Frankel and Teutsch, 128.

[240] Cohen, 46-48.

[241] Hertz, 353.

[242] Heschel, *Man's Quest for God,* 13.

[243] Lutske, 261.

[244] Earl Klein, 95-98.

[245] This custom appears to derive from a commentary on the verse, "My beloved [Israel] is like a gazelle or a young deer who stands behind a wall and looks in through the windows; he peers through the lattice-work" (Song 2:9).

[246] *Etz Hayim*, 10.

[247] Maimonides, *The Commandments*, 228.

[248] Lamm, *The Jewish Way in Love and Marriage*, 31.

[249] 2 Kings 9:11; Jer. 29:26; Hos. 9:7.

[250] Even the major prophets of Israel acted strangely. Elijah raced in front of the chariot of Ahab, Isaiah "went naked and barefoot for three years" (Isa. 20:3), and Jeremiah made "thongs and bars of a yoke and put them on his neck" (Jer. 27:2).

[251] Concerning the 70 elders, "And when the spirit rested upon them, they spoke in ecstasy, but [once it left them] did not continue" (Num. 11:25). Prophetic ecstasy was not limited to the early prophets and is clearly found in the Book of Ezekiel.

[252] Mishneh Torah, Yesodei Ha-Torah 10:4.

[253] Donin. *To Pray as a Jew*, 214.

[254] Aish ha-Torah, *Exploring Judaism*, 2002.

[255] Riskin, *The Passover Haggadah,* 56.

[256] Hertz, 652.

[257] Frankel and Teutsch, 108.

[258] *Stone Chumash*, 1057.

[259] Chill, 478.

[260] Dosick, 264.

[261] Maimonides. *Guide of the Perplexed*, 2:31.

[262] Hertz, 367.

[263] Chill, 232.

[264] Holtz, 186-189, 198.

[265] Maimonides. *The Commandments*, 208.

[266] *Stone Chumash*, 565.

[267] Jonathan Groner. Northern California Jewish Bulletin, December 2000.

[268] Chill, 227-228.

[269] Chill, 228.

[270] Frankel and Teutsch, 141.

[271] Kolatch. *The Jewish Book of Why*, 227-228.

[272] Kolatch. *Second Book of Why*, 321.

[273] Moldenke, *Plants of the Bible,* 5.

[274] Kolatch. *The Jewish Book of Why*, 94.

[275] Sherwin. *Kabbalah*, 49.

[276] Frankel and Teutsch, 149.

[277] Trepp, 77.

[279] Greenberg, 226.

[280] Steinsaltz, 234.

[281] Ginzberg. *Legends of the Jews,* 3:165-166.

[282] Kolatch. *The Second Jewish Book of Why*, 286.

[283] In a leap year, this special Shabbat occurs on the Sabbath that falls on or immediately preceding the 1st of the extra month of Second Adar.

[284] Toperoff, *The Animal Kingdom in Jewish Thought.*, 30.

[285] Witty and Witty, 399.

[286] Lutske, 121.

[287] Frankel and Teutsch, 171.

[288] Witty and Witty, 489.

[289] Donin. *To Pray as a Jew*, 14-16.

[290] Klein, 205.

[291] *Stone Chumash*, 664.

[292] Kadden and Kadden, 106.

[293] Kadden and Kadden, 68.

[294] Millgram. *Jewish Worship*, 196.

[295] Donin. *To Pray as a Jew*, 173-174.

[296] Gross, 589.

[297] Wentworth, Harold and Flexner, Stuart Berg. *Dictionary of American Slang*, 224.

[298] Bluestein. *Anglish-Yinglish: Yiddish in American Life and Literature,* 88.

[299] Maimonides stated that the act of blowing the shofar is the equivalent of an alarm clock, rousing us from our spiritual slumber with a call to examine our deeds, return in repentance, and remember God our Creator (Donin, *To Pray as a Jew*, 279-280).

[300] M. Lamm. *The Jewish Way in Death and Mourning*, 5.

[301] Frankel and Teutsch, 157.

[302] Bluestein, 94.

[303] Strassfeld and Strassfeld, 30-37.

[304] Hertz, 501.

[305] Maimonides. *The Commandments*, 243.

[306] *Stone Chumash*, 1056.

[307] Cohen, 170.

[308] Donin. *To Pray as a Jew*, 331.

[309] Frankel and Teutsch, 160..

[310] *Stone Chumash*, 660.

[311] Chill, 225.

[312] Dorff, 183-184.

[313] Frankel and Teutsch, 164.

[314] Frankel and Teutsch, 166.

[315] Trepp, 15.

[316] Hammer. *Entering Jewish Prayer*, 62.

[317] Millgram. *Jewish Worship*, 64.

[318] Kolatch, *The Book of Why*, 105.

[319] *Etz Hayim*, 1469.

[320] Riskin, 59.

[321] Hammer. *Entering the High Holy Days*, 92.

[322] Chill, 246.

[323] Mishneh Torah, Avodat Kochavim 12:11.

[324] Sperling, *Reasons for Jewish Customs and Traditions*, 265.

[325] Hertz, 353.

[326] These two versions differ in several stylistic particulars but not in substance.

[327] Kadden and Kadden, 63.

[328] Lutske, 181.

[329] There is no unanimity among scholars as to the precise correlation of the Thirteen Attributes with the biblical text.

[330] Strassfeld, 87.

[331] Frankel and Teutsch, 153.

[332] Witty and Witty, 187.

[333] *Stone Chumash*, 1007.

[334] Cohen, 192.

[335] Hertz, 277.

[336] Ginzberg, 5:97-98.

[337] Kolatch. *This is the Torah*, 137, 144-145.

[338] Strassfeld, 89-90.

[339] Frankel and Teutsch, 182.

[340] Strassfeld, 180.

[341] Waskow, 108.

[342] Sherwin. *Kabbalah*, 21-22.

[343] Waskow, 473.

[344] Lamm. *The Jewish Way in Love and Marriage*, 98-101.

[345] Maimonides. *The Commandments*, 22.

[346] Strassfeld, 103.

[347] Kadden and Kadden, 107.

[348] Frankel and Teutsch, 185.

[349] *ArtScroll Siddur*, 154.

[350] Millgram. *Jewish Worship*, 152-153.

[351] *Stone Chumash*, 719.

[352] In this context is the famous question of Abraham, "Shall not the Judge of all the earth deal justly?" (Gen. 18:25), indicating that God is subject to the same moral standard that is Divinely decreed for human beings.

[353] Just as Jacob had deceived his blind father in the previous *parashah*, in this section he is deceived by Laban into marrying Leah instead of Rachel.

[354] The Torah views sacrifices as a means to express devotion to God and seek communion with the Divine.

[355] Donin. *To Pray as a Jew*, 150.

[356] *ArtScroll Siddur*, 92.

[357] Frankel and Teutsch, 179-180.

[358] Sperling, 83.

[359] Lau, 194.

[360] Hertz, 844.

[361] Millgram. *Jewish Worship*, 209-210; Donin. *To Pray As a Jew*, 131-132.

[362] Steinsaltz, 276.

[363] *Pray and Tell*, 117.

[364] *Harvard Hillel Songbook* , 94, 97.

[365] Millgram. *Jewish Worship*, 187.

[366] *ArtScroll Siddur*, 451.

[367] Twerski, 140.

[368] Idelsohn, 74

[369] Idelsohn, 62.

[370] *Harvard Hillel Songbook*, 48.

[371] Witty and Witty, 183.

[372] Strassfeld, 102-103.

[373] Ibid., 135-138.

[374] This is an example of Judaism's emphasis on "original merit" rather than on original sin.

[375] Millgram. *Jewish Worship*, 242.

[376] Hazony.

[377] Gilbert, 192.